CW00922474

Nothing to Do with Dionysos?

Nothing to Do with Dionysos?

Athenian Drama in Its Social Context

JOHN J. WINKLER AND FROMA I. ZEITLIN, EDITORS

PRINCETON UNIVERSITY PRESS   PRINCETON, NEW JERSEY

Library of Congress Cataloging-in-Publication Data

Nothing to do with Dionysos? : Athenian drama in its social context /
    edited by John J. Winkler and Froma I. Zeitlin.
      p.   cm.
    Includes index.
    ISBN 0-691-06814-3
    ISBN 0-691-01525-2 (pbk.)
    1. Greek drama—Social aspects—Greece—Athens.   2. Literature and
society—Greece—Athens.   3. Greek drama—History and criticism.
4. Athens (Greece)—Social conditions.   5. Theater—Greece—Athens—
History.   6. Athens (Greece) in literature.   7. Social problems in
literature.   8. Dionysus (Greek deity)   9. Dionysia.   I. Winkler,
John J.   II. Zeitlin, Froma I.
PA3136.N68   1989
813'.08709—dc20   89-34974

First Princeton Paperback printing, 1992

Publication of this book has been aided by the Magie Publication Fund
of the Classics Department of Princeton University

This book has been composed in Linotron Bembo and Helvetica Lite

*Frontispiece: Cover of a sarcophagus dating from probably the sec-
ond or early third century A.D., discovered in the excavations of the Roman amphitheater in Arles. Photograph by Michel Lacanaud, Musées d'Arles.*

CONTENTS

List of Illustrations   vii

Abbreviations   ix

Introduction   3

The Theater of the *Polis*
ODDONE LONGO   12

The Ephebes' Song: *Tragōidia* and *Polis*
JOHN J. WINKLER   20

Playing the Other: Theater, Theatricality, and the
Feminine in Greek Drama
FROMA I. ZEITLIN   63

The Great Dionysia and Civic Ideology
SIMON GOLDHILL   97

Thebes: Theater of Self and Society in Athenian Drama
FROMA I. ZEITLIN   130

Kreousa the Autochthon: A Study of Euripides' *Ion*
NICOLE LORAUX   168

An Anthropology of Euripides' *Kyklōps*
DAVID KONSTAN   207

Why Satyrs Are Good to Represent
FRANÇOIS LISSARRAGUE   228

Drama, Political Rhetoric, and the Discourse of
Athenian Democracy
JOSIAH OBER AND BARRY STRAUSS   237

The *Dēmos* and the Comic Competition
JEFFREY HENDERSON   271

Drama and Community: Aristophanes and Some
of His Rivals
  JAMES REDFIELD   314

Making Space Speak
  RUTH PADEL   336

The "Interior" Voice: On the Invention of
Silent Reading
  JESPER SVENBRO   366

The Idea of the Actor
  NIALL W. SLATER   385

Notes on Contributors   397

Index of Passages Discussed   401

General Index   403

ILLUSTRATIONS

FIGURES   *page* 353

Figure 1. Rough sketch of possible *skēnographia* of fifth-century tragedy.

Figure 2. Rough sketch of *skēnē* wall with real door.

PLATES   *following page* 405

Plate 1. Pronomos Vase, red-figure volute-krater, later fifth or early fourth century B.C.E. Naples, Museo Nazionale Archeologico, 3240; drawing from Margarete Bieber, *The History of the Greek and Roman Theater*, 2d ed. (Princeton, 1961).

Plate 2. Polychrome fragment showing actor and mask, around 340 B.C.E. Würzburg 832.

Plate 3. Attic red-figure pelike by the Phiale Painter. Chorusmen dressing. Boston, Museum of Fine Arts, H. L. Pierce Fund; 98.883. Museum photograph.

Plate 4. Apulian bell-krater by the Tarporley Painter, ca. 400–380 B.C.E. Three tragic/satyric choristers. Sydney 47.05.

Plate 5. Peiraieus actors' relief. Athens, National Museum, NM 1500.

Plate 6. Red-figure column-krater in the Mannerist style, ca. 500–490 B.C.E. Six choristers and muffled figure at tomb. Basel, Antikenmuseum, inv. BS 415.

Plate 7. Tondo of a red-figure cup by Makron, ca. 480 B.C.E. A figure dressed in the characteristic short garment of a satyr. Munich 2657. Museum photograph.

Plate 8. Attic red-figure bell-krater, ca. 420 B.C.E. attributed to Polion. Three men dressed as hairy satyrs prance along with lyres toward a flute-player. The Metropolitan Museum of Art, Fletcher Fund, 1925; 25.78.66. Museum photograph.

Plate 9. Red-figure cup, early fourth century B.C.E. by Painter Q. A woman dances before Dionysos in a satyr's short garb. Korinth (unnumbered). From a museum photograph.

Plate 10. Red-figure hydria, ca. 470 B.C.E. by the Leningrad Painter. Five satyrs in short garments with postiche advance toward a flute-player, each carrying a part of a piece of furniture. Boston 03.788. After a photograph in L. D. Caskey and J. D. Beazley, *Attic Vase Paintings in the Museum of Fine Arts, Boston* (London, 1931–1963).

Plate 11. Red-figure lekythos, red-figure oinochoe, ca. 470 B.C.E., class CL. A satyr advances with a curved sickle in his right hand and with his left hand extended. Paris, Louvre CA 1728. Photograph by Chuzeville.

Plate 12. Red-figure oinochoe, ca. 470–460 B.C.E., by a painter of the Berlin Group. A satyr, armed like Herakles with club and animal skin, attacks a tree defended by a serpent. Bologna 190; after F. Brommer, *Satyrspiele: Bilder Griechischer Vasen*, 2d ed. (Berlin, 1959).

Plate 13. Red-figure column-krater, ca. 470 B.C.E., by the Orchard Painter. Men participate in the pressing of grapes. Ferrara T 254c. Photograph by Held.

Plate 14. Red-figure column-krater, ca. 470 B.C.E. Same scene (and painter) as that shown in plate 13, but with satyrs instead of men. Bologna 241. Photograph by Held.

Plate 15. Red-figure column-krater, ca. 470–460 B.C.E., by the Orchard Painter. Jason approaches the Golden Fleece under the protection of Athena. The Metropolitan Museum of Art, Harris Brisbane Dick Fund, 1934. Museum photograph.

Plate 16. Red-figure krater. Same scene (and painter) as plate 15, but with a satyr for Jason and Dionysos for Athena. Bologna 190. After a museum photograph.

Plate 17. Fragment of a kalyx-krater showing a temple in three-quarter view, with a statue of Athena in the foreground. Würzburg, Martin von Wagner Museum, H 4695. Museum photograph.

Plate 18. Athenian krater from Orvieto, 475–440 B.C.E., showing figures (Argonauts?), one of whose spear protrudes above the picture's upper frame. Paris, Louvre, 65EN5579. Cliché des Musées Nationaux.

Plate 19. "Würzburg fragment," showing a portico with a half-open door and a woman behind it. From Taranto, ca. 350 B.C.E. Würzberg, Martin von Wagner Museum, H 4696. Museum photograph.

Plate 20. Pyxis, ca. 425 B.C.E., showing preparations for a wedding (Alkestis?). London, British Museum, 1920; 12–21.

Plate 21. Black-figure oinochoe, bird chorus. British Museum B509. Museum photograph.

Plate 22. Red-figure bell-krater; bird choristers and flute-player. J. Paul Getty Museum, 82 AE.83. Museum photograph.

Plate 23. Red-figure fragments; boy holding mask. American School of Classical Studies at Athens, Agora excavations, Agora P11810.

ABV	Beazley, John D. *Attic Black-Figure Vase-Painters*. Oxford, 1956.
ARV²	Beazley, John D., ed. *Attic Red-Figure Vases*. 2d ed. Oxford, 1968.
Ath. Pol.	[Aristotle], *Athenaion Politeia (Constitution of the Athenians)*.
DFA	Pickard-Cambridge, Arthur W. *The Dramatic Festivals of Athens*. Rev. John Gould and D. M. Lewis, 2d ed. Oxford, 1968.
DTC	Pickard-Cambridge, Arthur W. *Dithyramb, Tragedy, and Comedy*. Rev. Thomas B. L. Webster, 2d ed. Oxford, 1962.
FGrHist	Jacoby, F., ed. *Die Fragmente der griechischen Historiker*. Leiden, 1926–1958.
FVS	Diels, H., and W. Kranz, eds. *Die Fragmente der Vorsokratiker*. 3 vols. 6th ed. Berlin, 1951.
HCT	Gomme, A. W. *A Historical Commentary on Thucydides*. 3 vols. Oxford, 1945–1956.
IG	*Inscriptiones Graecae*. 2d ed. Berlin, 1913–1929.
IGD	Trendall, A. D., and Thomas B. L. Webster. *Illustrations of Greek Drama*. London, 1971.
LSJ	Liddell, H. G., R. Scott, and H. S. Jones, eds. *A Greek-English Lexicon*. Oxford, 1968.
Nauck²	Nauck, A., ed. *Tragicorum Graecorum Fragmenta*. 2d ed. Hildesheim, Germany, 1964.
PA	Kirchner, J., ed. *Prosopographia Attica*. 2 vols. Berlin 1901–1903.
PCG	Kassel, Rudolf, and Colin Austin, eds. *Poetae Comici Graeci*. Berlin and New York, 1983–.
PMG	Page, Denys L., ed. *Poetae Melici Graeci*. Oxford, 1962.
RE	Wissowa, Georg, ed. *Paulys Real-Encyclopaedie*. Stuttgart, 1894–1963.
SEG	Hondius, J.J.E., ed. *Supplementum Epigraphicum Graecum*. Leiden, 1923–.
SIG	Dittenberger, W., ed. *Sylloge Inscriptionum Graecarum*. 3d ed. Leipzig, 1915–1924.

TDA	Pickard-Cambridge, Arthur W. *The Theatre of Dionysus in Athens*. Oxford, 1946.
AA	*Archäologischer Anzeiger*
AAntHung	*Acta Antiqua Academiae Scientiarum Hungaricae*
AC	*L' Antiquité Classique*
AFLN	*Annali della Facoltà di Lettere e Filosofia della Università di Napoli*
AJA	*American Journal of Archaeology*
AJP	*American Journal of Philology*
AK	*Antike Kunst*
ArchEph	*Archaiologike Ephemeris*
BCH	*Bulletin de Correspondance Hellénique*
BICS	*Bulletin of the Institute of Classical Studies*
BSA	*Annual of the British School at Athens*
CJ	*Classical Journal*
ClAnt	*Classical Antiquity*
C&M	*Classica et Medievalia*
CP	*Classical Philology*
CQ	*Classical Quarterly*
CR	*Classical Review*
CSCA	*California Studies in Classical Antiquity*
DArch	*Dialoghi di Archeologia*
EMC	*Echos du Monde classique*
G&R	*Greece & Rome*
GRBS	*Greek, Roman, and Byzantine Studies*
HSCP	*Harvard Studies in Classical Philology*
ICS	*Illinois Classical Studies*
JHS	*Journal of Hellenic Studies*
MDAI(A)	*Mitteilungen des Deutschen Archäologischen Instituts (Athenische Abteilung)*
MH	*Museum Helveticum*
PCPS	*Proceedings of the Cambridge Philological Society*

QS	*Quaderni di Storia*
QUCC	*Quaderni Urbinati di Cultura classica*
REA	*Revue des Etudes Anciennes*
REG	*Revue des Etudes Grecques*
RhM	*Rheinisches Museum*
StudClas	*Studii Clasice*
TAPA	*Transactions of the American Philological Association*
WJA	*Würzburger Jahrbücher für die Altertumswissenschaft*
YCIS	*Yale Classical Studies*
ZPE	*Zeitschrift für Papyrologie und Epigraphik*

Nothing to Do with Dionysos?

EVEN AT the first mention of the old Athenian proverb, "nothing to do with Dionysos," its meaning was already being debated.[1] It referred in some fashion to the musical performances (dithyramb, tragedy, and comedy) staged at the Athenian festivals of Dionysos, and ancient commentators explained it in various ways as an audience protest, a comic quip against the growing complexity and innovation of those performances, as if they had strayed far from the myths of the god Dionysos himself. We can come no closer than they to solving this riddle, which presumes an anterior, even utopian, moment in the development of theater when what was performed in honor of the god would most logically have focused only on him. For although the "hard" historical and archeological facts about those festivals, especially the Great (or City) Dionysia, have been authoritatively assembled,[2] these studies are woefully incomplete and often contestable. They must often depend upon interpretation: of this proverb, of the *Poetics* of Aristotle (himself an interpreter), of the fragmentary physical remains. Whatever the contrast may have been between an "original" time and what later transpired, "nothing to do with Dionysos" takes only the most literal view of the god's significance. But if we turn to consider the circumstances of the festivals that centered on the god brought into the midst of the *polis* and the citizens, then we might propose the contrary—"everything to do with Dionysos"—or (as we have done in the title) repunctuate the negative statement with a skeptical question mark.

In thus broadening the outlook of what is meant by theater to include the entire social context of the festivals, we signal our difference from those studies of Attic drama that still tend to concentrate more narrowly on just one type of script, tragic or comic, or even on a single play. Such studies regularly ignore the multiple stylistic and generic interactions among types of plays, but even when these are noticed they more generally close out the entire social context in which the plays took place. But this methodological *sparagmos* (rending limb from limb) performed on the body of the Dionysian festival crucially alters our basic perception of how those musical scores and scripts had meaning, since it obscures both the telling similarities between theatrical enactments and other

---

[1] Max Pohlenz, "Das Satyrspiel und Pratinas von Phleius," *Nachrichten der Gesellschaft der Wissenschaften zu Göttingen, Philologisch-Historische Klasse* (Göttingen, 1927), 298–321, esp. 299–304, reprinted in Pohlenz, *Kleine Schriften* 2:473–96; *DTC*, 124–26.

[2] *DFA*.

types of public performance (military, political, forensic), and the experi-
mentally significant differences of theater from such nonfictional (but not
undramatic) social scenes.

We, the editors and our contributors, are particularly interested in the
extratextual aspects of tragedy (along with its satyr-plays, of course) and
of comedy, thus violating one of the familiar premises of formalist criticism, that "the text is the thing!" and the only thing. Instead, we will
look behind the masks and under the costumes and peer out into the audience, and investigate the various elements that went into a finished performance. We will consider what happened before and after the plays and
take notice of other locations in ancient Athens, such as the Assembly
and the courts of law, where para-dramatic social events took place. We
will consider how individual plays or groups of dramas directly or indirectly pertained to the concerns of the body politic, which were reflected
or deflected in the complex conventions of the stage. The worth of this
enterprise, of course, will lie in the detail of its execution and its power to
reorganize and illuminate our understanding of performances in the Attic
theater.

The more we learn about the original production of tragedies and
comedies in Athens, the more it seems wrong even to call them plays in
the modern sense of the word. For us a play is something we can see on
any night when tickets are available for it, providing we can afford the
price; usually it will be performed by people we do not know, of various
ages and both sexes. The rest of the audience members are likely to be
strangers too, unless it is an opening night when celebrities and VIPs are
there to honor the event. In classical Athens, by contrast, the price of a
ticket was distributed by each local town council (deme) to the citizens in
good standing on their records; theater attendance was thus closely
linked to citizenship. What is more, the audience sat in the open-air theater below the Akropolis in wedge-shaped sections designated for each of
the ten political tribes, just as they did for other city meetings. The audience was overwhelmingly male and, except for tourists and visiting
dignitaries, was composed of the same few thousands of active citizens to
be seen at any important public meeting, plus those who had traveled
from their farms to the city for the five-day holiday known as the Great
(or City) Dionysia.

Then there is the question of stamina—both for the performers and for
the audience. The audience watched three tragedies and a satyr-play each
day for three successive days. On other days of the same festival they
watched five comedies and twenty choral hymns (dithyrambs) to Dionysos.[3] The same two or three actors performed all the speaking parts of a

---

[3] The probable order of events was: contest of ten boys' dithyrambs (one from each

tragedy, with appropriate changes of mask and costume, so that the actors were almost continuously speaking and moving through four elaborate performances (three tragedies and one satyr-play), starting early in the morning and lasting much of the day. This grueling exhibition of physical endurance and prodigious memory was made somewhat easier for the actors when the officials in charge of the festival began assigning them to work for all three of the competing tragedians in turn, so that each actor appeared in one tragedy per day. But the chorus members never received that relief: the same twelve or (by Sophokles' time) fifteen chorus members performed the singing and dancing of all four plays on the same day.

These daylong marathons were also political events, in the sense that they were part of the *polis*' official celebration of itself and the god Dionysos. Because the Dionysia was a city festival for an important god, it had social aspects to it—of ceremony and ritual, processions and sacrifices—that are lacking in the production of modern plays. Even to come close to the authentic experience, and hence in some part the meaning, of attending a "play" in ancient Athens, we would have to imagine that Arthur Miller, Tennessee Williams, and Sam Shepard had each written three serious plays and a farce for a one-time performance on a national holiday—say, the Fourth of July—in honor of an ancient hero-god, perhaps a cross between George Washington and Johnny Appleseed, and that these were preceded by a parade of congressional representatives and cabinet secretaries and federal judges and governors and mayors, that the plays were performed after ceremonies honoring the war dead and our national allies, that bishops and generals and mothers superior had prominent places in the front rows, and that the choruses who sang and danced were composed (so Winkler argues) of West Point cadets, dressed sometimes as old veterans, sometimes as servants or refugees or prisoners of war, occasionally (but only rarely) as young men.

We begin with a brief but powerful broadside by Oddone Longo, calling for a more wide-angle view of the actual social dynamics that shaped the selection and content of Athenian plays. Traditional criticism focuses on the "closed circle of author/work—where the author is taken to be re-

---

tribe) and contest of ten men's dithyrambs (one from each tribe) on the first day; contest of five comedies on the second day; contest of the three tragic ensembles (each with three tragedies and a satyr-play) on the next three days. The law of Euēgoros quoted by Demosthenes (21.10) and the victors' list (*IG* II/III² 2318) support the order boys' dithyramb, men's dithyramb, comedy, tragedy. The older theory that one comedy was presented on each day of the festival (based on Aristophanes, *Birds* 785–96) has been refuted by Wolfgang Luppe in "Die Zahl der Konkurrenten an den komischen Agonen zur Zeit des Peloponnesischen Krieges," *Philologus* 116 (1972): 53–75.

flected in the work . . . and the work in turn furnishes the almost exhaustive testimony to the identity and significance of the author." Thus
we have innumerable books and articles on "Sophoklean tragedy" and
the like, where the methodological premises construct a mirroring pair
of self-sufficient entities, the writer and his writing, each of which is
"read" exclusively in terms of the other. Rather than exploring this
closed circle, "which repeats the same short journey an infinite number
of times, doomed from the first step to unprogressive repetition," Longo
reminds us that the audience was a political community, the assembled
citizenry of the *polis* of Athens, and that its delegates in charge of all the
festival arrangements—from preparing the shared sacrificial meals to
judging the qualifications of choral competitors, from making seating arrangements in the theater to awarding prizes and overseeing the erection
of public monuments by the victors—conducted themselves as conscious
agents of social consolidation. Such language, to be sure, is very modern,
but the reality it describes is authentic and ancient.

The festival arrangements to which Longo alludes are set out in greater
detail in two essays, by Winkler and by Goldhill, each of which is paired
with an essay by Zeitlin. The pairing in each case gives a more rounded
view of the subjects: the role of gender and of civic ideology in the total
dramatic communication. Thus, where Winkler, according to his hypothesis of the chorus' age group, focuses on the athletic and paramilitary features of tragic choral dancing as a display of masculine
qualities in the youngest generation of citizen-warriors, Zeitlin brings
out the features of tragic performance that are culturally marked as feminine—elaborate costume, emotional display, subjection to physical
weakness, reliance on plotting—to argue that though performers (exclusively) and audience (at least predominantly) are male, "theater uses the
feminine for the purposes of imagining a fuller model for the masculine
self, and 'playing the other' opens that self to those often banned emotions of fear and pity." Goldhill stresses the contrast between the opening
ceremonies of the festival, which display the proper political hierarchy of
the city-state and celebrate its power, and the serious questioning of that
very authority in the course of many plays, using the *Aias* as his principal
example. Zeitlin, on the other hand, while not questioning the fundamental relevance of tragedy's debates to the Athenian audience that com-
missions and watches them, observes that Athens itself occupies a rather
privileged position in tragedy's portrayal of the imagined world of
mythic-heroic times. Thebes, just across the mountains in neighboring
Boiotia, is the typical scene of social and familial relations gone awry,
whereas Athens typically comes onto the stage to clean up the mess made
by Thebes and to function as a place of welcome for outcasts, a sort of
refuge from tragedy. The "wide-angle lens" she uses is meant both to

"extend our conceptions of what constitute formal conventions in the theater" and to "illuminate the ideological uses of the theater in Athens as it portrays a city onstage that is meant to be dramatically 'other' than itself."

Loraux adds a third term to each of these pairings. Her focus on the central role of the feminine figure in a political play dealing explicitly with the city of Athens joins up with the first set in its concern with the cultural and political definitions of gender, and with the second in its demonstration of how Athens "invents" itself on the tragic stage. Zeitlin's piece on Thebes, which surveys the entire extant corpus of relevant plays, closes with an examination of *Oidipous at Kolonos*, where Thebes and Athens directly confront one another through the person of Oidipous. Loraux, on the other hand, takes up Euripides' *Ion*, where the protagonist, though a foundling like Oidipous, is of Athenian rather than Theban descent. The potentially tragic issues involved with Athenian identity and citizenship are played out away from the *polis*, on the sacred terrain of Delphi. Loraux charts what she calls the "tragic interference" between the mythic and the political discourses that thicken the texture of the play and take it out of the realm of bourgeois comedy or of heroic myth.

Clearly in both these pairings (and their pivotal third) we have several views of the same social reality. So too with our next pair, dealing with satyr-play. In the hierarchy of modern generic eminence, satyr-play obviously ranks a distant third after tragedy and comedy, but in the scheme of the Attic festival the satyr-play was not a separate "genre" but an element of the tragic competition, another performance by the same ensemble; therefore we place it with tragedy, not after comedy, in our scheme of things. Konstan uses the one completely surviving satyr-play, Euripides' *Kyklōps*, to delineate an implied anthropology of human (that is, Greek, and specifically democratic Athenian) society in terms of three groups—human, satyric (wild human), and kyklopean (monstrous human). In Konstan's analysis, *Kyklōps* does not merely reenact an exciting tale from Homer's *Odyssey*. It represents to the audience (and for the audience) a series of proper and deviant social relationships: the manners in which food is eaten or goods are exchanged set up a pair of significant boundary lines, one separating proper human society from the undisciplined chorus of always-erect wild men who behave in (merely) unconventional ways, another separating those two forms of humanity from their monstrous, sacrilegious, and antisocial enemy. In this structuralist perspective, the use of polar oppositions to organize conceptions of otherness and difference has the important effect of clarifying (and endorsing) the approved social norms in a context of parodic exuberance which is at the other extreme from tragedy.

Lissarrague also develops elements of an anthropology by looking at the Attic vases which portray satyrs and satyr-plays. It is often difficult to tell whether the highly playful and imitative satyrs of red-figure painting are imagined as being from a specific play, or simply seen as iconography's universal parodists, indulging in the play of signs (taking pseudoheroic postures, aping the professions, reinventing the lyre) that the theatrical satyrs also loved.

The next three essays consider Athenian drama as a form of (and a forum for) political speech. Ober and Strauss set out the general principle: "Like legal trials and Assembly speeches, Athenian theatrical performances and dramatic texts were closely bound up in the mediation of conflicting social values." Further, both the literally political and the dramatically political discourses were fashioned, the authors propose, by an elite for presentation to a democratic mass, and both types of discourse can be seen to share (in their different ways) in the political process of framing a social consensus on issues that are divisive for a nominally democratic but still highly stratified society. Ober and Strauss bring their general analysis to bear on four test cases—the orators' use of poetry and myth, the "tragic" color which Andokides gives to the portrayal of his dilemma in *On the Mysteries*, the uses of political rhetoric in Sophokles' *Antigone*, and the fantasy Assembly which institutes a new constitutional order for Athens in Aristophanes' *Assemblywomen*.

Henderson argues that the claims of comic speakers to be giving serious advice to the *polis* are to be taken seriously as well as facetiously. The comic poets "were the constituent intellectuals of the *dēmos* during the period of full popular sovereignty that began with the reforms of Ephialtes in 462–461, and in their institutionalized competitions they influenced the formulation of its ideology." This analysis accords with the ancient views of Athenian comedy as well as with the consistent pattern of statements about itself inside comedy, and stands in opposition to the carnivalesque view that would see Attic comic discourse as a merely playful, "anything goes" inversion of contemporary social reality. Redfield, approaching the same material from a slightly different angle, compares and contrasts four types of social performance—debate, ritual, games, and theater—in order to situate comedy's distinctive manner of reenacting the *polis'* class structure: "In the Assembly men explored the possibilities before them in this world; in the theater they examined another world, isomorphic to our own, but simplified and made lucid." The comic poet, competing like an athlete in a contest for a victory, deliberately and amusingly strives to convince the audience to vote for his point of view: "His play is a kind of campaign to be adopted as their representative—not in life, but in art"; but to maintain his special right to heckle authorities, "the poet must abandon any claim to rule, to take an actual part in debate."

Our last three pieces look at some issues pertaining to the stage itself, its performers and texts. Padel is interested first of all in establishing the "otherness" of the Athenian theater in comparison to ours. She stresses the shared experience of actors and audience and the continuing interchange between the "theater's fictive world" and its "real context," which includes both its physical and its psychological dimensions. Investigating the archeological details of theatrical spaces and the uses to which the spaces were put, Padel draws upon different kinds of evidence, such as the iconography of the vase paintings of the period, to argue for a syntax of space, a symbolic topography, that is organized especially around the suggestive relations of inside and outside. "Through the hieroglyphics of Athenian tragedy, movements in space, both seen and unseen, convey the culture's understanding of movements into and out of mind and self."

The role played by writing in fifth-century cultural history is little-known and very controversial. Svenbro, in a highly experimental piece, suggests that the relation of writing to dramatic performance is complex, and should be seen in terms of both the unquestioned dominance of sonority over letter shapes (actual speaking over the merely potentially spoken) and the development of what he calls a "theatrical passivity" in the spectator "who is not supposed to participate in" (or interfere with) "the acting." The actors take the place of the written text which they "transpose into a kind of 'vocal writing' " to which the audience *listens* as it *watches* what goes on. Ultimately Svenbro's thesis on dramatic spectatorship as a propaedeutic to silent reading may not stand (much evidence suggests that Athenian audiences were rather intrusive and noisy)[4], but it is an original and stimulating approach which may inspire new insights. Although in the concerns it addresses and the evidence it musters, Svenbro's contribution differs broadly from Padel's mapping of stage syntax, they share the perception that the theatrical experience is highly conducive to developing the sense of an interior dimension—whether of house or of mind. Slater, on the other hand, looks at the actor in a more sociological context than does Svenbro, as an individual who develops from a performer through whom the poet speaks to one whose talents are praised on their own. Slater takes up the question of reperformance and carefully marshals the evidence for the emergence in the fifth century of the category "actor" as a distinct element in the dramatic ensemble. Un-

---

[4] *DFA*, 272–75; V. Bers, "Dikastic *Thorubos*," in *Crux: Essays Presented to G.E.M. de Ste. Croix on His 75th Birthday*, ed. P. A. Cartledge and F. D. Harvey (= *History of Political Thought*, vol. 6, issue 1/2 [Exeter, Eng., 1985], 1–15).

til the mid-fifth century, a single prize was awarded to the best (group
of) plays; after that two prizes were awarded, one to the best (group of)
plays and one to the best actor. By the fourth century, actors were celebrities and in great demand, traveling from city to city, and plays themselves were beginning to be reperformed. The end result of these
developments was not only to classicize certain scripts, making them
monuments generally available to widely separated (Greek) audiences,
but also to convert them from being specific interventions in the network
of social self-representations in Athens to being "plays." And so the
story which we have set out to tell is told.

This collection, of course, is only a beginning, not a final statement. A
fuller treatment would ideally include essays on the other festivals of
Dionysos and on the other Athenian musical competitions. One would
like to know more about the flourishing theater of Magna Graecia, where
comedy seems to have achieved important status sooner than it did in
Athens, and where the proliferation of so-called *phlyax* vases in the
fourth century shows that raucous comedy was still booming. Much further information may remain to be gleaned from the competitive
records[5] and from analyses of the elite who would meet to compete—
that is, the wealthy sponsors of democracy's various public projects
ranging from tragedies to triremes. And of course there are the fragments, the plot summaries, and the extant scripts, which we mention last
because they have been so often studied as if they existed not in the living
force-field of a specific social context but in a hermit's isolation, which is
to make of them precisely monsters like Polyphemos. All this and much
more remains to be done, and we invite our readers whose appetites are
whetted by these essays to take up the task.

   Yet, as we make our exit, we must also take cognizance of what cannot be done. One confronts the daunting reality again and again that
what remains is only a tiny fraction of what once existed and was performed. It is easier to *proclaim* dutifully that, of course, there was a vast
theatrical enterprise which produced hundreds of plays by poets of all
kinds that we will never know, than actually to *imagine* the magnitude of
the loss, especially in the context of an anthropology of theater. About
the dithyrambs, twenty of which were performed at each City Dionysia,
we know practically nothing. The satyr-play is only slightly better
understood. For a grasp of the realities of ancient drama such as, for example, we have of the Elizabethan stage, we would need more than all
those lost dramas of the leading poets, the quality of which may have

5 Hans Joachim Mette, *Urkunden dramatischer Aufführungen in Griechenland*, Texte und
Kommentare 8 (Berlin and New York, 1977).

varied widely. We would need the work of those minor playwrights who proliferated during this period and whose (presumably?) less impressive work would provide the indispensable backdrop against which the poets and works that were canonized might better be judged. The list of desiderata could go on and on. In sum, we, like the audience watching a play unfold on the stage and in the orchestra, may have to content ourselves with the knowledge that we have only an illusory depth of field.

ODDONE LONGO

The Theater of the *Polis*

UNTIL quite recently a wider, more than merely literary, consideration of the ancient theater has been blocked by the resistance displayed in more traditionalist sectors of classical philology to the methods of modern social studies. (That resistance is felt even against those social studies that come in a politically neutral format, such as functionalist sociology, which is perfectly integrated into the current social system.) What a broader analysis would seek is a careful assessment of the multidimensional social relationships that informed the dramatic events—between author and work on one side and producers and public on the other. The current, prevailing understanding of ancient drama privileges the author in his individual autonomy, taking him as the principal agent of dramatic production and leaving to one side the context of the work, minimizing the impact of social institutions as a whole on the genesis and destination of the drama. As Escarpit put it, "Through the ages, literary history has been occupied, and is still all too occupied, with the study only of authors and works—spiritual biographies and commentaries on the text; it considers the collective context as a sort of backdrop or choral accompaniment that may be left to the curiosity of political historians." Thus in practice it absolutizes the author, positing him or her as a subject entirely unbound by concrete social relations, the artificer of a literary exercise utterly self-enclosed and fulfilling itself within the limits of the text. An analogous process of isolation is applied to the work, which is understood essentially as a piece of writing, a thing destined for individual consumption by private readers, and which is imperiously assigned an absolute autonomy, evading any possible connection with the actual corporate audience at which it was originally aimed. All too often this is just the way ancient drama is "read" and explained, as if it had not been designed and destined for a precise public—the public composed of the Athenian citizen body—but rather the modern reader, if not immediately the modern professor of classics.

This closed circle of author/work—where the author is reflected in the work (so that our discussion of it is a discourse about the author, who is constructed entirely and only in terms of his work), and the work in turn furnishes the almost exhaustive testimony to the identity and significance

Note: This essay was originally published in *Dioniso* 49 (1978): 5–13, and is used with permission; translated by John J. Winkler.

of the author—not only repeats the same short journey an infinite number of times, doomed from the first step to unprogressive repetition; it
effectively immobilizes investigation of the ancient theater, for it sets up
a sort of ideological roadblock that prevents the field from being invaded
by "methodologies," which it is determined to exclude from the privileged area of immortal and ever-resplendent "classics."[1]

To discuss the wider context of ancient theater, which includes the
problem of the connections among patron, author, and public, in the
first place means to abandon the use of any concept that gives unwar-
ranted privilege to the "autonomy" of text or author. It would be more
correct to say that the dramatic author can only be located as a moment
of mediation, a nexus or transfer point between the patron or sponsor
(the institution which organizes and controls the Dionysian contests) and
the public (the community at which the theatrical communication is
aimed).[2] It may not be amiss to insist from the beginning on the collective or communitarian character of the Athenian theater public in the
classical period: a public which is quite unparalleled in the history of
drama in that it coincided—in principle and to a great extent in fact—
with the civic community, that is, the community of *citizens*.[3] This communitarian character of the Athenian scene is tangibly displayed in the
spatial relationship between the factitious community (the assembled audience) and the arena of the dramatic action—a relationship which reproduces that between a real community and a forum for political action.[4]
The convention that governed theatrical staging and the relationship between scene and public required "that the audience were the citizens, sitting round the marketplace to watch the royal family conducting its
affairs."[5]

This "communitarian" public seems also to be invested, though in a

[1] Interesting perspectives concerning a sociopolitical consideration of Greek theater are
now put forward in an essay by Heinrich Kuch, "Voraussetzungen und Sujet in der tra-
gischen Dichtung der Griechen," in *Die griechische Tragödie in ihrer gesellschaftlichen Funk-
tion*, ed. H. Kuch (Berlin, 1983), 11–39, 61–83.

[2] On the specific relations between theatrical spectacle and the social structures of the
polis, see Diego Lanza, "Lo spettacolo," in *Oralità scrittura spettacolo*, ed. Mario Vegetti
(Turin, 1983), 107–26.

[3] I have tried to outline this "collective" character of Greek drama, in specific reference
to the forms of social communication, in my article "Tecniche della communicazione e
ideologie sociali nella Grecia antica," *QUCC* 27 (1978): 63–92, which is mainly concerned
with Aiskhylos' *Seven against Thebes*. An excellent analysis of this piece from a semiotic
point of view is found in Froma I. Zeitlin, *Under the Sign of the Shield: Semiotics and Aeschylus' Seven against Thebes* (Rome, 1982).

[4] On this topic see F. Kolb, "Polis und Theater," in *Das griechische Drama*, ed. Gustaf
A. Seeck (Darmstadt, 1979), 504–45; this important paper focuses on understanding the relation between the Athenian public and the structures of the theater building.

[5] Thomas B. L. Webster, *Greek Theater Production* (London, 1972), 2.

mediated form, with a function of patronage, even if this is then transferred precisely to the institutional structure in charge of the dramatic
contests, which actually selects the works and then resolves their execution. The two terms—patron and public—in any case are not mutually
exclusive; they constitute rather an extended area of interaction. There is
no public which is not also, in some measure, a patron; in our case, the
patron or sponsor (the institution) is distinguished from the public insofar as it supplies a separate service in the process of production. On the
other hand, in contrast to the public, it also performs the action of ori-
enting and controlling representations, to which the dramatic text is pre-
liminarily submitted. The patron (let us call it more generally the *polis*,
understood as a social institution) operates toward the public with an end
in view that might be roughly formulated as "consolidating the social
identity, maintaining the cohesion of the community." But this end is
not something extraneous to the public itself, not something simply proposed to, or imposed on, the unsuspecting public. The reinforcement of
community cohesion, in a context of social rituals and spectacles that
clinch the axioms of the community's own ideology, is not just the
"goal" pursued by the patron; it is also the "request," the "expectation"
of the public itself. In a system such as the one we are describing, the
sponsor's "goal" and the community's "expectation" tend to converge,
in a constant process of reciprocal adjustment.

    We have thus outlined in very sketchy strokes the "frame" of social in-
stitutions within which the dramatic poet finds himself operating. This
summary sketch in itself would be enough to topple any claims one
might make to consider the dramatic work under a privileged principle
of autonomy. In the total machine of this "*polis* theater," the author is
but one of the mechanisms of dramatic production, located between two
acts of selection: the preliminary selection (we would perhaps hesitate to
call it preventive censorship) administered to his text-outline, on which
depends the possibility that his text, when perfected in a script, will see
the light (be realized on the stage), and the subsequent selection made by
the public (or more precisely by the jury, chosen from the public according to procedures strictly analogous to those used for political proceedings).[6]

    On the other hand it would be a mistake to view the dramatic author
in such a context as a discrete individual, one who comes to the theatrical
institution as a singular person. His access to the theatrical arena does not
come about as a matter of personal right but in the context of a collective
trial, within the bounds of a group (namely, that of competing poets), a

---

[6] Valuable information on this matter can be found in Harold C. Baldry, *The Greek
Tragic Theatre* (London, 1971). The French translation (Paris, 1975) has an important intro-
ductory essay by Pierre Vidal-Naquet.

group which acquires some degree of de facto homogeneity in virtue of its members' mutual conditioning or the positive constraints of the context itself (one only reached the stage through a competition, and in observance of the rules of the genre).

In other words: the concepts of artistic autonomy, of creative spontaneity, of the author's personality, so dear to bourgeois esthetics, must be radically reframed, when speaking of Greek theater, by considerations of the complex institutional and social conditions within which the processes of literary production in fact took place. These conditions predetermine the possible "creative" area of the individual poet, and they offer a preliminary framework to the coordinates within which admissible poetic trajectories will be plotted. Literary history and traditional esthetics have tended to downplay these conditions, restricting them to the complex of rules imposed by the literary genre. But it is the very concept of literary genre which has to be fundamentally redesigned, since a literary genre cannot be understood as an abstract definition of formal or structural rules operating merely on the work, but rather should be understood in terms of the ensemble of *institutions*, with their many interlocking levels and connections; the consideration of mechanisms such as those described above should be introduced in more than an accessory role or as an afterthought. If someone then were to object, stressing the contribution of the individual poet, via his unique personality, to the very process of constituting a genre and to the definition and establishment of theater's contents and rules, it would be easy to respond by simply recalling the well-known collective matrix of institutionalized drama in ancient Athens, inseparable from the vast conglomerate of ritual-festive activities, of which the dramatic contest was but a single element.

This collective character of ancient drama and its pertinence to the citizen community allows us to deepen our discussion, providing it with a component more than simply general and abstract. The theatrical event in ancient Athens was a public event par excellence. The Athenians' dramatic performances were not conceivable as autonomous productions, in some indifferent point in time or space, but were firmly located within the framework of a civic festival, at a time specified according to the community calendar, and in a special place expressly reserved for this function. This place, which was the scene of the collective festival, provided a proper home not only for the dramatic contest but also for other celebrations, which were no less strictly tied to the civic system: at the City Dionysia, honors voted to citizens and to foreigners were proclaimed in the theater; the tribute from Athens' allies was exhibited in the theater; the orphans of war who had been raised at the city's expense were paraded in the theater in full panoply in the year when they reached

their majority. These rituals were understood to be celebrations of the
polis and of its ideology, and they constituted the immediate framework
of the plays. The community of the plays' *spectators*, arranged in the auditorium according to tribal order (no different from what happened on
the field of battle or in the burial of the war dead), was not distinct from
the community of *citizens*. The dramatic spectacle was one of the rituals
that deliberately aimed at maintaining social identity and reinforcing the
cohesion of the group.

Inside the structure of the spectacle, the communitarian aspect of dramatic performance had its most distinctive and obvious realization in the
chorus. The original matrix for tragedy (and for comedy) is to be sought
in a choral action. But this carries us back to a stage in which there was as
yet no clear separation into two groups—the community of actors (the
chorus) and the community of spectators (the public). In the earliest performances there was no split or distinction between the stage area and the
auditorium (this was before the construction of stage or auditorium), nor
between the actors and the public.[7] The public—that is, the community—was also the collective which acted the "drama." Then, as dramatic performances emerged from that early limited context and
gradually came to involve an ever-larger and more diversified community, they demanded a more diversified structure, one better suited to
their changed circumstances. Collective participation was replaced by a
delegation of the chorus (which is exactly what created its difference
from the whole community). The community that was involved in the
dramatic performance no longer took a direct part in the action, and thus
it came to be a true and proper public—a public still profoundly implicated and involved in the action itself, but now in a mediated form. We
do not know, and surely never will, the details of this history, which is
substantially unrecorded. But it is highly probable that a primary role in
the process of establishing the Attic drama was played by the rural community, in its interactions and confrontations with the urban community. We have every reason to suppose that the history of Athenian
theater is also the history of a progressive urbanization of dramatic rites;
the community originally invested with these rites must have been the
rural community, the village.[8]

Given this scheme of the genesis of drama—hypothetical, of course, as

[7] In the archaic period, until the end of the sixth century, tragic performances took
place in Athens on an *orkhēstra* in the Agora; it was only at about the beginning of the fifth
century that a theatrical space, with provisional (wooden) structures, was arranged on the
south slope of the Akropolis (the theater of Dionysos Eleuthereus); see Frank Kolb, *Agora
und Theater* (Berlin, 1981).

[8] On this topic there is a very good book by Francisco Rodriguez Adrados: *Festival,
Comedy, and Tragedy* (Leiden, 1975).

are all discussions of origins—it remains secure that the essence of the chorus, the essential and distinctive feature of Attic drama, must be recognized in its role as "representatives of the collective citizen body." But if the chorus is something like the staged metaphor for the community involved in the dramatic performance, this does not mean that it later took on a distinct detachment from the scene and the public, not even in the "classical" period when tragedy and comedy, in their mechanics of spectacle, had reached the most "mature" form involving an opposition between auditorium and stage, between public and actors. The dramatic contest remained an involving performance, functioning solely in the presence of and by virtue of the civic corporation, and unthinkable outside that place and that time. Certainly, this original "chorality" of drama also underwent a process of reduction in the course of that brief century, which saw the emergence at last of some recorded dramatic history from a dim past. That process resulted, as we know, in the demotion of the chorus to a mere lyric intermezzo (in the late works of Euripides) or in the complete suppression of any choral speaking (in the late works of Aristophanes, and then in New Comedy, where the chorus is no more than an intermezzo danced or mimed between acts). This choral diminishment has usually been understood, and historically interpreted, as an evolution of the literary genre (even if this evolution is considered to be implicated in some fashion in the decline of the *polis*). In reality the phenomenon is much more complex, and an inquiry into the subject ought to proceed in less simplistic terms; in any case, it should not be reconstructed as an evolutionary line in a single direction. Consider the uncompromising and peremptory nature of the collective voice in Aiskhylos' choruses, a voice that expresses the opinion of the group and so exercises a vigilant control over the individual, subjecting each member to the community and appealing to the collective's inherited store of opinions, consolidated and crystallized at the religious level. It would be difficult to avoid the impression that this imperative corporate wisdom, not subject to discussion, goes back to a specific social situation where such an attitude was at home, namely to a rural community and specifically to the social organization of a village. If this suggestion can be maintained, we then have a new coordinate along which to trace one of drama's possible lines of development in the contradiction between city and countryside. In that case, the reduction of the choral element in favor of the actors' debates might be seen as the product of a progressive integration of the drama into the more pluralistic system of the *polis*, where division of labor, social stratification, and class struggle reduce precisely the area of unanimity in the community. As a result, dialectical distinction increases, and along with it the opposition of roles and parts.

One might object, then, to a too simplistic interpretation of tragedy as

a directly communitarian ritual, or to a reading of Attic drama as somehow expressive of a completely collective situation. We have spoken thus
far of the civic community (that is, the public that makes the chorus its
delegate) as a solid group or as an undifferentiated unity; we are thus in
danger of adopting the ideological premises of functionalist sociology,
which takes group unity and social concord as primary data. In actuality
there certainly never existed in Athens any solid collectivity free from
contradictions and class conflict; such a form of strict solidarity would
rather be sought at the level of the village community. What we meet in
the fifth century is a highly differentiated society, structured by antagonistic classes, although it could still maintain (beyond any sense of interior dichotomy and in specific contexts) a corporate identity in a model
acceptable to all, within an ideological system supported by a general
consensus. Tragedy and comedy, emerging from and formed by the
context of village society in the countryside, were successively adopted
and incorporated in the civic institutions. If that is what happened, it was
precisely insofar as tragedy and comedy were able to take on the function
of being a place of consensus, which underscores what we have already
specified as the "goal" pursued by the sponsoring institution that organized the dramatic events: the maintenance and reinforcement of community cohesion, the creation of an area of consensus, in the context of
an enlarged community which more or less coincided with the citizen
body, divided as it was by contradictions which the original rural community had not known.[9] The stage took charge of these contradictions in
its attempts to surmount them, within the circumscribed limits of the
festival's time and place. It accomplished this, fundamentally, by em-
ploying the institutional format of the theater itself, in particular the chorus. For it is not so much in the specific content of the dramatic
representations, or in the consolidated system of opinions that are repeatedly proposed and clinched in the text, in such a way that they become
the connective tissue of theatrical discourse—it is not here that the process occurs of framing a consensus which can involve diverse social
classes. The level at which this social process occurs is more deeply involving; it looks to the very situation of the spectator as a participant in
the dramatic event. The fact of spectatorship sets in motion the mechanisms of identification with the dramatic characters and with the theatrical space; here, in the specific form of *choral* tragedy, what is elicited from

---

[9] A very important feature of ideological compactness, which strongly held together
the political community, was the mythical tradition, a social heritage that supplied the very
matter of tragic subjects. Important works on this topic have been published by the French
school: see, most recently, Jean-Pierre Vernant and Pierre Vidal-Naquet, *Mythe et tragédie
deux* (Paris, 1986); Nicole Loraux, *Tragic Ways of Killing a Woman* (Cambridge, Mass.,
1987); and in the U.S., Charles P. Segal, *La musique du sphinx* (Paris, 1987).

the spectator is a collective identification, insofar as the mass of spectators is brought to identify itself with the "delegated" group that makes
up the chorus. We have therefore a mechanism which is complex, and
yet quite simple in the directness with which it pursues the goal of the
"spectacular" institution. Through this establishment of the theater as a
socially conglomerating enterprise and through the mechanisms of collective identification, the dramatic enactment brings into being a "theatrical community," which in a certain sense is the passing hypostasis of
the actual *polis*, but without its inevitable conflicts and cleavages.[10]

This does not mean that tragedy (or comedy) dispelled the contradictions from the heart of the *polis* or assuaged its conflicts; simply recall that
the fundamental situation of the tragic "hero" is that of a bearer of contradictions. What we mean rather is that those contradictions are examined and unfolded only within the boundaries of the work, in the
dialectic of the drama, without thereby compromising the unity of the
social institution of theater. We have in fact two levels of identification.
The first is that of the spectator as an individual person who assumes the
contradictions of the tragic character via a process of identification of the
real individual with the fictitious individual (and it is on this level that
any "katharsis" would operate, with any psychological effects of resig-
nation or consolation). The other level of identification is that which is
imposed precisely, even if invisibly, through the theater as a collective
institution, as a heightening of the audience's consciousness of its social
integration, its determinate membership in a group, a corrective and a
check on the escape into individuality that is prompted by identifying
closely with the dramatic hero's personal destiny. This "consolidated"
identification accompanies, and is inseparable from, the audience's following along with the "author's perspective": after identifying completely with the character, at the end of the spectacle the individual
member of the "collective of spectators" finds himself brought to the
ideological positions of the author (positions which are explicitly displayed in the chorus but which are already contained in the structure and
unfolding of the drama).

Thus it is that one closes the circle of author/public, in a harmony that
precisely answers the audience's "expectation"; the patron in turn is assigned the office of supporting the complex structure of the theatrical institution, the secular arm of the governance of the *polis*.

---

[10] On the mechanisms of identification between public and tragic hero, see again, although from a somewhat different perspective, Lanza, "Lo spettacolo." Lanza published a
very good book on the dramatic figure of the tyrant, *Il tiranno e il suo pubblico* (Turin, 1977).

JOHN J. WINKLER

The Ephebes' Song: *Tragōidia* and *Polis*

THE QUESTION of tragedy's early days has for quite some time been
stuck at an impasse, with the same few bits of ancient information being
constantly and inconclusively recycled. Comedy seems, if anything, in
worse condition: with less anecdotal evidence and scripts later by half a
century, its early days and development are even more of a mystery and
equally the object (or victim) of speculation about ritual, myth, and the
seasons. The average skeptic (and I count myself one) might rightly
doubt that anything new—much less true—could be said on such subjects. Nevertheless, the present essay does try to offer an original approach to the old questions of where tragic choruses came from, or as I
prefer to put it, what they were doing in the life of the city. Part of this
essay's difference is the feature exemplified by this entire collection: that
it considers Athenian drama in terms of the social context of its original
performance at the festivals of Dionysos (the Rural Dionysia, the Lenaia,
and the City Dionysia) and tries to notice the untranslatable cultural differences between the Athenian theater and ours.

The present essay suggests that, in a large sense, those festivals were
the occasion for elaborate symbolic play on themes of proper and improper civic behavior, in which the principal component of proper male
citizenship was military. Such play at festivals, just as at private symposiums, occurred in both serious and facetious formats, for both tragedy
and comedy were built on representations of behavior (and physique) in
terms of the taut and the slack. (The application of this idea to comedy
must await another occasion.) A central reference point for these repre-

sentations—the notional learners of its lessons (*paideia*) about the trials of manhood (*andreia*)—were the young men of the city, and they were also the choral performers at least of tragedy, and perhaps also of comedy.

If I may be allowed just one small attempt to elicit the skeptical reader's benevolence: I hereby acknowledge that each of the items here assembled could, taken separately, be construed in another way than I have construed it. Some are late, some are incomplete, most are relatively small and either ambiguous or inconclusive; most have to do with performance and social context rather than with the dramas themselves. Indeed, it is because of these very features in the evidence, especially our fetishizing of the "dramas themselves" and the Text, that no one has noticed the coherence that I am about to trace. To reach the fuller cultural understanding of Athenian drama mentioned above requires as thick a description as possible, and (to speak frankly) the overall persuasiveness of the present argument rests not on any one irresistible fact but on the ensemble of many details. My ideal reader, therefore, will be of two minds: on one level, he or she will check the weight and accuracy of each fact or interpretation to see how far it contributes to a reasonable and believable version of what was once a living practice, and on this level the final judgment may have to be "Not Proven"; but on another level, I expect the serious reader not to be content with a merely skeptical attitude but to take responsibility for explaining what the aggregate of evidence here assembled does mean. To make these readerly activities possible I have laid out some of the significant evidence about Athenian fighting, dance training, and citizenship, topics usually slighted in accounts of Athenian drama.

The subject here treated would traditionally be labelled "the origin of Greek tragedy," but the word "origin" seems to me to claim too much, suggesting as it does something primal—whether seminal or oval—before which there was nothing. Founding events do, of course, occur, but the more usual social operation is not to create but to adapt whatever is at hand. In the hope of avoiding the mystification that often attends discussions of origins, I would rather say that the hypothesis advanced here is about the early character of Attic tragedy (and comedy) rather than about their absolute beginning.

Since the evidence that follows is arranged in ascending and then descending order of importance, circling from the merely suggestive at the periphery of the subject (sections I, II, IV) to the relatively solid in the center (section III), it might be well to indicate at the outset what I take to be the hard outline of the data. Like the individual poles which form a tepee, no one of these data can stand alone, but their coincidence forms a structure which is far stronger than its simple components. The essential framework of my tepee consists of three crucial facts about performances in the theater of Dionysos.

1. The chorus members for tragedy are represented on the Pronomos Vase (plate 1) as young men with fully grown bodies and curls of sideburn creeping down their cheeks, but no beards. They are, iconographically speaking, ephebes—young adult (or late adolescent) males represented in their athletic prime. Their portrayal is in systematic opposition to that of the three actors on the same vase who are represented as older men with beards.

2. The distinctive and regular formation of the chorus for tragic dancing was rectangular, by rank and file. This stands in systematic contrast to the circular dancing of dithyrambs at the same festival (performed by the age groups above and below the ephebes—men and boys).

3. The eighteen- to twenty-year-old male citizens, who underwent military and civic training in the ephebate, as the institution is known from the fourth century B.C.E., displayed at the beginning of their second year their hoplite military maneuvers and close-order drill in front of the assembled citizen body. They did so not on exercise fields outside the city but in the orchestra of the theater of Dionysos ([Aristotle], *Ath. Pol.* 42.4).

Together these three facts suggest that one might perceive the role and movement of the tragic chorus as an esthetically elevated version of close-order drill. The very persons (or rather a representative selection of them)[1] who marched in rectangular rank and file in the orchestra as second-year cadets, performing for the assembled citizenry, also marched and danced in rectangular formation at the City Dionysia, but did so wearing masks and costumes.

Supporting this perception, but in second rank (section II), is the audience's character as a civic assembly—not a fortuitous gathering of "theatergoers" but a quasi-official gathering of citizens. They were seated in tribal order, one tribe per wedge, which was evidently the seating arrangement for the Athenian Assembly (Ekklēsia) when it met in the Pnyx. The more prominent citizens sat toward the front, with a special section for the Council (Boulē). The layout of the auditorium thus dis-

---

[1] The average year-class of ephebes recorded on inscriptions (334 to 327/6 B.C.E.) was about 450 to 500 strong, based on individual tribes having a recorded complement between 37? and 62. O. W. Reinmuth, *The Ephebic Inscriptions of the Fourth Century B.C.* (*Mnemosyne*, supp. 14, 1971). The entire two years therefore contained upward of a thousand. The number of tragic dancers annually at the Dionysia was 36 (3 × 12) or, after the chorus was enlarged, 45 (3 × 15).

played the organization of the body politic in terms both of tribal equality and of social hierarchy. Further, the entire festival had a civic-military aura, suggesting that *polis* and *tragōidia* in Athens were not so distant from each other as the modern understandings of "politics" and "tragedy" would imply.

The least "hard" items of evidence, though in some ways the most suggestive, are those with which the following essay actually begins and ends, namely, the etymology of *tragōidoi*, "billy goat singers" (section IV), and the symbolism of the black-caped Dionysos and the relation of the Apatouria and the Dionysia (section I). Section I serves simply as an occasion to inform the general reader about some basic facts of the military and festive aspects of Athenian citizenship.

Absent from this dossier of evidence are the scripts. From the early days of tragedy to its later and more fully represented period, the character of its scripts changed in marked ways. That is an esthetic history which has been told on its own terms, but such a history, if it is to avoid being a Rorschach fantasy of the modern interpreter, needs to be founded on a concrete knowledge of the performance—particularly on the shared and usually unspoken presuppositions of the composers, performers, and audience. This essay, therefore, does not aim at a general interpretation of tragedy *based on* the surviving scripts, but rather tries to reconstruct from the facts of festival performance the framework of understanding which the audience originally brought to its viewing of the plays. What we may learn from such a study is, as it were, how to light and hang the tragic pictures so that we are viewing them from the right angle and thus can better estimate what the original audience was intended to notice.

I. A DUEL ON THE BORDER: THE TRICK OF THE BLACK GOATSKIN

A story will focus the issue. In the old days of the kings, a dispute arose between Attika and Boiotia over the control of a village in the hill country which forms the natural boundary between them. Border squabbles, of course, were endemic in a culture which is aptly described as not only face-to-face but scowling, and it is not surprising to find disagreement too over the name of the hamlet, which is variously given as Melainai, Oinoē, Panakton, or Eleutherai.[2] An agreement was reached to settle the issue by single combat between Xanthos, king of Boiotia, and Melan-

[2] Melainai and Oinoē are demes, Panakton a fort, Eleutherai a village; L. Chandler, "The North-West Frontier of Attica," *JHS* 46 (1926): 1–21. The history of actual fighting over these settlements on both sides of Mount Kithairon is surveyed by Angelo Brelich, *Guerre, Agoni e Culti nella Grecia Arcaica*, Antiquitas, ser. 1 (Bonn, 1961), 7:53–59. On border-fighting in general, Aristotle, *Politics* 7.10:1330a14–25.

thos, who had been promised the kingship of Attika if he won the fight. As Melanthos strode forward, he either saw or claimed to see behind Xanthos an apparition of a beardless man wearing a black goatskin over his shoulders. He shouted out to Xanthos that it was unfair for him to bring a helper to fight what was agreed to be a single combat; as Xanthos turned to look behind him, Melanthos struck with his spear and killed Xanthos.[3]

There is a curious fact about the use of this story, which will set up the parameters of my hypothesis. In the cycle of Athenian festivals, the tale of Melanthos' trick or deception (*apatē*) served as the etiology for the Apatouria, a very old kinship celebration in the fourth month of the Attic year (called Pyanopsiōn, roughly September–October).[4] On the three days of this festival, the phratries (clans) recognized boys and girls born in the preceding year with sacrifices to Zeus Phratrios and Athena Phratria, and also acknowledged the coming manhood (*hēbē*) of sixteen-year-old boys with a sacrifice called the *koureion* (on the day Koureōtis). The latter words were etymologized either by reference to *kouros*, youth/young man, or to *kourā*, cutting the hair, which was then dedicated to Artemis,[5] who was one of the several goddesses known as Kourotrophos because she watched over the nurturance and successful growth (*troph-*) of youngsters to adulthood.

The Apatouria was thus a clan festival at which birth and adolescence were acknowledged, but it seems also to have been overlaid with themes pertaining to slightly older males, *kouroi* in a different sense. *Kouroi* in Homer are young warriors, not sixteen-year-olds. The later word for *kouroi*, young men in the prime of life on the threshold of adulthood, was "ephebes" (*ephēboi*), literally those at (*ep'*) their youthful prime (*hēbē*). In

---

[3] A similar Butch Cassidy trick in a territory dispute between two kings is recorded by Plutarch, *Quaestiones Graecae* 13 (294b–c). Hyperokhos, king of the Inakhians, advancing to the field, was accompanied by his dog; his opponent Phemios, king of the Ainianians, objected to the dog as a second combatant; while Hyperokhos was shooing his dog away and had his back turned, Phemios hit him with a stone and killed him, thus winning for his people possession of the country. A less violent trick solved another border dispute between Athens and Boiotia over the region called Sida. Epaminōndas during the debate reached out and plucked a pomegranate, a plant growing profusely in that area, and asked the Athenians what they called it. "*Rhoa*," they said. "But we call this a *sida*," he replied, thus winning the day (Agatharakhides, *Eurōpiaka* = Athenaios, 650f–651a = *FGrHist* 86F8).

[4] Ludwig Deubner, *Attische Feste* (Berlin, 1932), 232–34; Herbert W. Parke, *Festivals of the Athenians* (Ithaca, 1977), 88–92.

[5] Scholiast to Aristophanes, *Akharnians* 146; Hesykhios, s.v. "Koureōtis." The young men having their locks cut also honored Herakles (whose divine consort was Hēbē) by a special libation and shared cup; Hesykhios, s.v. "Oinistēria"; Pamphilos quoted in Athenaios, *Deipnosophists* 11.494f. Eustathios (582.20) accepted the derivation of *kouros* from *keirō*; in such a discussion, into which I will not enter, perhaps it should be emphasized that *keir-* is not simply "cut a lock" or "trim" but "crop closely."

addition to denoting the ideal youth at the first flowering of his adult vigor (a flexible usage not bound to birthdays), "ephebe" also came to be the specific designation in the fourth century for the eighteen- to twenty-year-old citizens in training to be heavily armed soldiers (hoplites), learning to fight in a phalanx against the hoplites of other cities.[6] This training began, after their enrollment as eighteen-year-olds in the register of tribe and deme, in the third month of the Attic year (Boēdromiōn), the month before Pyanopsiōn.

The Apatourian phratry induction at sixteen had natural analogies to the *polis* induction at eighteen, at which civic-military duties were paramount.[7] The sixteen-year-old is registered with and celebrated by his clan as one able to succeed his father, to maintain the line of the *oikos* (household) by begetting his own children; the eighteen-year-old is registered with and acknowledged by the *polis* as one able to start taking his place in the closed ranks of adult male citizens, who collectively administer the commonwealth and defend its territory and its *oikoi* by force of arms. The slide between the two may be illustrated by the mythic-historic figure who is represented as a young warrior cutting his hair—that is, both as a *kouros/ephēbos* ready for battle and as one who cuts his hair like a sixteen-year-old at the Apatouria. He is Parthenopaios, one of the seven against Thebes, portrayed on seven Attic vases (all dated to about 500–470 B.C.E.). On some he is a beardless warrior, on others bearded.[8] Aiskhylos chooses to describe him in terms of age- and beard-class as an ephebe: "a man-boy man [*andropais anēr*], the down is just now creeping along his cheeks as his youthful beauty grows and the hair there thickens" (*Seven against Thebes*, 533–35). A reason for the association of the tale of Melanthos with the Apatouria has been discerned by Pierre Vidal-Naquet, using the young warrior as its focus.

But before looking at what he has dubbed the "black hunter," we must briefly dip our toes in the swirling waters of controversy. Concern for the registry and training of young citizen-soldiers must have been as old as the quasi-democratic city and the hoplite phalanx. The seventh-century B.C.E. revolution in military tactics in which the older heroic soloists and horsemen were replaced by shield-to-shield masses of heavily armed infantry is connected by most analysts as cause, effect, or both, of the social revolution in which citizen rights in the *polis* were extended to

[6] P. Krentz, "The Nature of Hoplite Battle," *ClAnt* 4 (1985): 50–62.

[7] On the relation of the phratry's enrollment at age sixteen (*hēbē* proper) to the deme's enrollment at age eighteen (technically described as *epi dietes hēbēsai*, "having reached one's *hēbē* for two years"), see Jacques Labarbe, "L'âge correspondant au sacrifice du *koureion* et les données historiques du sixième discours d'Isée," *Bulletin de la Classe des Lettres de l'Académie Royale de Belgique*, 5th ser., no. 39 (1953): 358–94; Chrysis Pélékidis, *Histoire de l'éphébie attique* (Paris, 1962), 52–70; Mark Golden, "Demosthenes and the Age of Majority at Athens," *Phoenix* 33 (1979): 25–38.

[8] Norbert Kunisch, "Parthenopaios," *AK* 17 (1974): 39–41, pl. 8.

a larger landowning but not aristocratic class.[9] Not all eligible citizens
need have been so trained, just enough to man the ranks, but membership in the interdependent fighting team must have been regulated with
regard both to eligibility and to capability. One cannot send untrained
and unknown men to fight in the close array of a hoplite phalanx: one
would not trust one's own battle safety to men in the same line who
might be untrained fools or Thebans.

Yet plentiful and solid testimony to the existence of military training
in Athens which is both city-wide and compulsory does not exist before
the 330s B.C.E. The inscriptions which begin to appear from that time are
usually related to a *nomos peri tōn ephēbōn* said to have been proposed by
one Epikrates.[10] Since the earliest certainly dated inscription concerning
an ephebic class is from the year 334/3,[11] Epikrates' proposal must
have been passed in 335/4 at the latest. The move can be plausibly related to the Athenian defeat at Khaironeia (338 B.C.E.) as an attempt to
bolster the city's military strength and confidence, as well as to the wider
Lykourgan program of renewing the physical and cultural institutions of
Athens. How plausible is it, therefore, to relate the training of young
citizen-soldiers, as known mainly from chapter 42 of [Aristotle]'s *Constitution of the Athenians* (*Ath. Pol.*), to the performance of tragedy in the
sixth and fifth centuries? Three positions have been taken, spanning the
field of possibilities: the Lykourgan ephebate was a wholly new creation,[12] a codification of existing practices,[13] or (as Pélékidis maintains)

9 Marcel Detienne, "La phalange: Problèmes et controverses," in *Problèmes de la guerre en
Grèce ancienne*, ed. Jean-Pierre Vernant (Paris, 1968), 119–42; Anthony Snodgrass, "The
Hoplite Reform and History," *JHS* 85 (1965): 110–22; P.A.L. Greenhalgh, *Early Greek
Warfare: Horsemen and Chariots in the Homeric and Archaic Ages* (Cambridge, Eng., 1973),
esp. chaps. 4 and 7; Paul Cartledge, "Hoplites and Heresies: Sparta's Contribution to the
Technique of Ancient Warfare," *JHS* 97 (1977): 11–27, esp. 21–24; J. Salmon, "Political
Hoplites?" *JHS* 97 (1977): 84–101. Joachim Latacz, *Kampfparänese, Kampfdarstellung und
Kampfwirklichkeit in der Ilias, bei Kallinos und Tyrtaios, Zetemata* no. 66 (Munich, 1977), gives
an excellent analysis of the phalanx formation in Homer, which sometimes assumed a close
and quasi-hoplitic order for defensive purposes (esp. 55–65).

10 "There is another Epikrates whom Lykourgos mentions in his speech *On the Financial
Administration*, saying that a bronze statue of him was erected on account of his enactment
concerning the ephebes; they say he possessed an estate of six hundred talents." Harpokration, s.v. *Epikratēs*; John K. Davies, *Athenian Propertied Families* (Oxford, 1971), 4909; see n.
13 of S. C. Humphries, "Lycurgus of Butadae: An Athenian Aristocrat," in *The Craft of the
Ancient Historian: Essays in Honor of Chester G. Starr*, ed. John W. Eadie and Josiah Ober
(Latham, Md., 1985), 199–252.

11 Reinmuth, *Ephebic Inscriptions*, claimed to have found an earlier inscription, but its dating has been challenged by D. M. Lewis in his review of Reinmuth (*CR*, n.s. 23 [1973]:
254–55), and by F. W. Mitchel ("The So-called Earliest Ephebic Inscription," *ZPE* 19
[1975]: 233–43).

12 The existence of an earlier ephebate was denied briefly but with his customary authority by U. von Wilamowitz-Moellendorff, *Aristoteles und Athen*, 1:193–94. His objection is answered by Nicole Loraux, *The Invention of Athens*, trans. A. Sheridan (Cambridge,

nothing new at all, having existed virtually unchanged since before the fifth century.[14]

Let us introduce some distinctions to sort out this issue. First, we should distinguish the linguistic development of such age-designating words as *kouros* and *hēbē* from the institutional development leading from archaic warrior training to the fourth-century ephebate. Just as the noun *ephēbos* is a later coinage[15] than *kouros*, so the organization of the Athenian ephebate as known in the fourth century was undoubtedly different from whatever earlier measures were taken to train future hoplite-citizens. Both of these fields show changes, more recoverable for the words than for the practices, and those changes may be interrelated. Second, we should mark off, apart from the shifts either of vocabulary or of social organization, the cluster of themes and propositions that underlies both of them. These themes show much less variation over the years and should be regarded as the framework of social concern within which the developments of language and practice took place. Principal among those themes are the son's ability to defend himself and his father's *oikos* against challenges, his ability to continue the line by begetting his own children, and (symbolic of both those things) the growth of his beard.

Mass., 1986); also by Arthur A. Bryant, "Boyhood and Youth in the Days of Aristophanes," *HSCP* 18 (1907): 73–122. (On the authority of Wilamowitz, see S. Nimis, "Fussnoten: Das Fundament der Wissenschaft," *Arethusa* 17 [1984]: 105–34.)

[13] F. W. Mitchel, "Derkylos of Hagnous and the Date of *IG* II² 1187," *Hesperia* 33 (1964): 337–51, esp. n. 34: "Aristotle's description contains many elements which were already ancient. . . . In fact the ephebeia, as it is known from Aristotle and the contemporary inscriptions, is but a temporary phase in an institution which had ancient precedents and one which later, beginning with the oligarchic revolution of 322/1, underwent many further changes." Mitchel suggests that it was organized by tribes, as were most things military. Other defenders of an earlier ephebate in some form are John O. Lofberg, "The Date of the Athenian *Ephebeia*," *CP* 20 (1925): 330–35; H. W. Pleket, *Mnemosyne*, ser. 4, vol. 18 (1965): 441–46; Philippe Gauthier, *Un commentaire historique des "Poroi" de Xénophon* (Geneva, 1976), 190–95. H. Y. McCulloch and H. D. Cameron see a reference to soldiers of ephebic age in the prologue of Aiskhylos' *Seven against Thebes*: "Septem 12–13 and the Athenian Ephēbia," *ICS* 5 (1980): 1–14.

[14] "If the ephebate is attested before 336–335, one has no right to suppose that it is a different ephebate from the one we know." "The ephebate before the fifth century—a period in which it must have had a form more or less close to that which we know for the fourth century" (Pélékidis, *Histoire*, 9, 52).

[15] First in Xenophon, *Kyropaidia*. 1.2.4, describing the Persian disposition of soldier-citizens into four distinct groups: boys, ephebes, grown men, and those beyond the years of campaigning. The ephebes alone sleep away from their homes in common quarters (except for those who are married) and are commanded by twelve leaders since the citizen body is divided into twelve tribes. The Persian ephebate begins at the age of sixteen or seventeen and lasts ten years. During that time the ephebes often serve as the King's guard when he goes hunting, "which they consider the truest practice of skills needed for warfare" (1.2.10), and also for manning the guard posts (*phrourēsai*), pursuing wrongdoers, and intercepting bandits.

Already in the fifth century, the verb *ephēbaō* was one of the vocables in use to articulate those concerns. "Argos was bereft of men to such an extent that their slaves ruled and managed all affairs, until the children [*paides*] of the slain men reached manhood [*epēbēsan*]" (Herodotos, 6.83.1). Eteokles of Polyneikes: "Justice has never watched over him or deemed him worthy, not when he first fled the darkness of his mother's womb nor in his nurtured years [*en trophaisin*] nor when he reached his prime [*ephēbēsanta*] nor in the dense collection of his chin's hair" (Aiskhylos, *Seven* 664–67). But the issues or themes are as old as Telemakhos, the first "ephebe" *avant la lettre* in Greek literature, whose just-appearing beard precipitates not only his own tentatively bold moves to confront the despoilers of his father's stores but his mother's readiness to consider taking a new husband, as Odysseus had advised her years before: "When you see our son's beard growing, then marry whom you will."[16]

Greek culture generally displays a strong sense of age-classes[17] and a particular fascination with the downy advent of manhood on the cheek.[18] But these and the undeniable need for some measure of hoplite training do not establish the existence of the Aristotelian ephebate. My argument about *tragōidoi* depends on there having been some recognizable training of some young warriors in Athens in the sixth and fifth centuries, but it need not have been (and I do not believe it was) citywide or compulsory. The evidence suggests rather that hoplite or cavalry service was not so much a duty as an arena for voluntary excellence, an opportunity to acquire and display honor (*timē*), motivated by personal ambition (*philotimia*), within a controlling matrix of patriotic necessity. As Xenophon says, pointedly I think, of cities without the Persian system of public training, "Most *poleis* leave it to individual fathers to educate their children as they wish" (*Kyropaidia*. 1.2.2).[19] Xenophon, as Philippe Gau-

---

[16] Homer, *Odyssey* 18.269–70; "now that he is big and has reached the measure of *hēbē*" (19.532); "for now your son has reached that age: you always prayed the gods to see him grow his beard" (18.175–76); "for he is already a man [*ēdē gar anēr*]" (19.160).

[17] Pierre Roussel, *Etude sur le principe de l'ancienneté dans le monde hellénique*, Académie des inscriptions et belles-lettres, Extrait des Mémoires de l'Académie, vol. 43, pt. 2 (Paris, 1942), a book very difficult to obtain; H. J. Mette, "Von der Jugend," *Hermes* 110 (1982): 257–68.

[18] "Like to a princely youth with his first under-beard, whose *hēbē* is the most gratifying," Homer, *Iliad* 4.347f.; Solon, frag. 27 West on the ten heptads of a man's life (the child up to seven without *hēbē*, the boy up to fourteen who starts to show the signs of *hēbē*, the growing youth whose chin gets downy, and so on), seconded by Aristotle, *Politics* 1336b37; Plato, *Protagoras* 309a–b; Xenophon, *Symposion* 4.23, *Anabasis* 2.6.28; *passim* in Greek culture. I do not know why, in a representation of the Dioskouroi reported by Pausanias (5.19.2, the chest of Kypselos in the Heraion at Olympia), one is bearded, the other not. Are they two sides of the same ephebic figure, one a boy, the other a man?

[19] In the discussion of training for warfare in Plato's *Lakhes*, it is up to the individual fathers to ensure their sons' skill and readiness by sending them to specialist instructors.

thier has discerned, had specific recommendations to make about the state organization and financing of the fourth-century practices that were equivalent to the Aristotelian ephebate.

Those practices, known as early as Eupolis and Thoukydides, segregated the youngest soldiers into a distinct group (the *neōtatoi*) and assigned to them guard duty on the frontier fortresses, in which capacity they were known as *peripoloi*.[20] Aiskhines twice mentions his service in that corps at that age and refers to himself and his fellow-*peripoloi* as *synephēboi* (co-ephebes): "When I left the ranks of childhood I became a *peripolos* of this territory for two years, and as witnesses of this I shall offer you my *synephēboi* and our commanders" (2.167); "Misgolas in fact is my age-mate [*hēlikiōtēs*] and *synephēbos* and this is our forty-fifth year" (1.49). From the latter passage it is clear that Aiskhines (born in 390) served as *peripolos* in 372. Even if his use of the term *synephēbos* were anachronistic (and it does not seem so), it still antedates Epikrates' legislation by some ten years (the speech against Timarkhos was delivered in 346–345) and presents us with a picture of a two-year service on the frontier organized in 372 under commanders and manned by those who have just "left the boys."[21]

Further, Demosthenes specifically refers to Aiskhines' taking the ephebic oath (*ton en tōi tēs Aglaurou tōn ephēbōn horkon*, 19.303, delivered in 343 B.C.E.), an apparently ancient formula which applies to the duties of hoplite warriors in their phalanx: "I will not disgrace these sacred weapons [*hopla*] and I will not desert the comrade beside me [*parastatēn*] wherever I shall be stationed in a battle line."[22] The language of the ephebic oath not only has the patina of antiquity but also seems to resonate, at least faintly, in fifth-century literature. Moreau found a reference to the oath in Aristophanes' *Hōrai* (produced ca. 420): "You have corrupted our oath."[23] Pélékidis[24] detects it twice more in Aristophanes. "But I will

[20] Pélékidis, *Histoire*, 35–41.

[21] If Aiskhines' birth is placed as early as 399/8 (a possibility set out by D. M. Lewis, *CR*, n.s. 8 [1958]: 108), his "ephebate" will have been in 381.

[22] G. Daux, "Le serment des éphèbes athéniens," *REG* 84 (1971): 370–83. The reliance of a hoplite on his comrades is emphasized at Euripides' *Herakles* 190–94: "A hoplite is the slave of his weaponry; when he breaks his spear he has no way to defend his body from death, it is his one defense; and if those stationed in line with him are not good men he dies through the cowardice of his neighbors."

[23] Frag. 579 *PCG* (= frag. 568 Kock); Jacques Moreau, "Sur les *Saisons* d'Aristophane," *La Nouvelle Clio* 6 (1954): 327–44 (341).

[24] P. 76, n. 2. He rightly remarks (72) that later authors such as Plutarch (*Alkibiades* 15.4) cannot be taken as decisive when they assume the existence of the oath in the fifth century, though the fact that they can do so is of some weight. Similar references to the ephebate occur in the *Letters of Themistokles* 8 (ed. Rudolph Hercher, *Epistolographi Graeci* [Paris, 1873], 747) and the Athenian decree honoring Hippokrates (Hercher, *Epistolographi Graeci*, 311; Hippokrates, *Opera Omnia* 9:402, ed. Littré; Pélékidis *Histoire*, 187).

never ever disgrace the fatherland," says the First Creditor at *Clouds* 1220, meaning "but I must do my duty." Since it intrudes oddly into his speech it could well be intended to be recognized as a fixed phrase known to the audience. His second instance is slightly less compelling: "I will not disgrace my clan," says the Sykophant at *Birds* 1451, "my grampa was a sykophant and so am I." This again could be a reference to a known phrase, given a twisted application.[25] Siewert and Loraux find further echoes of the oath in fifth-century texts.[26]

The text which comes nearest to being decisive on the issue of a pre-Lykourgan ephebic training is Xenophon's *Poroi* 4.52, which is his specific recommendation concerning the corps to which Aiskhines belonged: "If my advice concerning revenues is enacted I claim not only that the city will be wealthier but also more obedient, more disciplined and better for battle, for those who are assigned to exercise would do so much more attentively if they received an allowance in the gymnasiums greater than those being trained for the torch-races; similarly those assigned to guard-duty in the guard-posts and those assigned to light-armed duty and to patrolling [*peripolein*] the countryside—they would do all these duties better if an allowance is granted to each of these jobs." Though the passage had been briefly noticed by others,[27] it was Gauthier who first drew the conclusion that Xenophon is essentially recommending (in 355/4) that the several forms of young men's military training should be funded by the state.[28] This implies both that the state-funded ephebate did not yet exist and also that several "ephebic" duties—training in the gymnasiums, frontier duty, and country patrol—were at least informally recognized, just waiting (as it were) to be organized. Gauthier makes the further interesting suggestion that Xenophon's rather clumsy circumlocutions ("those who are assigned to . . . ") are due to his sense that "ephebe" is still too ambiguous a term, mainly referring to an age-class but not to everyone in that class. It is the functions performed by certain of those young men which need to be organized and paid for from the public purse.[29]

---

[25] The skeptical side of us, however, might wonder whether what was later called the ephebic oath was in the fifth century taken by ephebes. The answer must be that it is a hoplite soldier's oath and would certainly be taken by all citizen-soldiers from the first time they served, ordinarily in their youthful prime. The open question is whether training for phalanx warfare was conducted as a corporate two-year exercise for all eligible eighteen-year-olds in the fifth century.

[26] Peter Siewert, "The Ephebic Oath in Fifth-century Athens," *JHS* 97 (1977): 102–11 (citing Aiskhylos, *Persai* 956–62, Sophokles, *Antigone* 663–71, and Thoukydides, 1.144.4, 2.37.3); Loraux, *Invention*, 305 (citing Aristophanes, *Peace* 596–98; cf. *Akharnians* 995–99).

[27] Lofberg, "Date"; O. W. Reinmuth, "The Genesis of the Athenian Ephebeia," *TAPA* 83 (1952): 34–50 (37).

[28] Gauthier, *Commentaire*, 190–95.

This range of evidence supports the moderate or centrist position of the three possibilities: that young men's military training before 335/4 existed in a form similar to but not identical with that described in *Ath. Pol.* 42. We do not know whether these young men displayed their close-order drill to the citizen body, or to the Boulē, and if so where the performance took place. If it was in the orchestra of Dionysos, the analogy between tragic choral dancing and phalanx movement would have been visibly confirmed each year, as it certainly was after 335/4. It is also possible that the ephebic display in the theater was an innovation, but if so it was one that seemed appropriate to its devisers because it mirrored the significance expressed by the rectangular formation of masked young *tragōidoi*.

In what follows I will continue to use the term "ephebe," meaning thereby young citizen-warriors in their years of military training, older than boys but not yet men, and probably well-off rather than poor. Readers who cannot dissociate the term "ephebe" from the controversy over *Ath. Pol.* 42 might simply substitute the phrase "young warrior" for it (as I sometimes do). For my hypothesis about tragic performance to work, the minimum requirement is that some visible segment of the young male population of Athens underwent hoplite training of some sort on some days of the year—no more. (It is even possible that the *tragōidoi* were actually recent graduates of such training, rather than eighteen- to twenty-year-olds proper.)

If pre-Lykourgan ephebic training was not publicly financed, then it was, like other forms of education in Athens,[30] privately undertaken— not a universal requirement for *polis* membership but an ambition of those families who could afford it. This corresponds to the picture of the Persian *ephēboi* described (or invented?) by Xenophon in his *Kyropaidia*. They do not comprise all Persian youth of the right age (though all are eligible), but only those whose fathers can afford to support them. Sons who must work are not enrolled (*Kyr.* 1.2.15). In Athens, class and wealth seem similarly to have interfered with the universality of conscription and service. It certainly does not offend our common sense about ancient life to imagine that corporate and individual exercises may

[29] Plato also experiments with an organizational plan for the military training of young men (25–30) as border guards, *Laws* 760b–763c; Pélékidis, *Histoire*, 25–31.

[30] K. J. Dover, in his edition of Aristophanes' *Clouds*, lx–lxi, cites [Lysias], 20.11; Demosthenes, 18.265; Xenophon, *Memorabilia* 2.2.6; and Plato, *Protagoras* 326c on education as a private endeavor, heavily dependent on wealth. Cf. also Plato, *Protagoras* 327d on the competitive pressure to strive for excellence. Loraux (*Invention*, 150–53) has signally clarified the ideological slant which shapes the self-image of Athenian "nonprofessionalism"; it casts a filtered and flattering light on citizen-soldiers so that they look like aristocratic warriors, whose nature alone (not any training) is a sufficient explanation of their valor.

have been more pursued by the wealthier and more ambitious families
than by those in straitened circumstances. Oarsmen presumably did not
need hoplite training; unarmored fighters (*psiloi*) were the poor.[31] "The
hoplites" is sometimes virtually a synonym for those citizens who are
noble, rich, and good ([Xenophon], *Ath. Pol.* 1.2: *gennaioi, plousioi,
khrēstoi*). Of course in all these matters we should not underestimate the
messiness of actual arrangements—one citizen volunteers to put up the
mess-money for two fellow-demesmen who find themselves short of
cash (Lysias, 16.14); sailors are conscripted from the deme catalogues for
service on a trireme but "only a few showed up and those were feeble, so
I sent them all away" and hired the best available sailors (Demasthenes,
50.6–7).

Not only was ephebic and hoplite status the prerogative of Athens'
better citizens before Lykourgos, but even the apparent universality of
ephebic training in *Ath. Pol.* 42 has been seriously doubted.[32] This is a
text, after all, whose editorial opinion is that Athens was best organized
when citizenship rights were invested exclusively in a hoplite property-
class of five thousand (33.2; cf. 23.2). That view was shared by others
who put their opinions on record, such as Thoukydides (8.97.2), and
corresponds to a general tendency to see the best men as the truest representatives of the community: "the hoplites and cavalry, who are evidently preeminent among the citizens in fine human qualities
[*kalokagathia*]" (Xenophon, *Memorabilia* 3.5.19). How curious it would
be if ephebic training passed from being the informal province of relatively well-to-do citizens before ca. 335/4 to universal conscription in
the brief period from ca. 335/4 to 323/2 and thereafter to an elite school
under the aristocratic constitutions of Antipatros and subsequent leaders.[33]

The issue of class ranking in military organization also suggests important issues (which cannot be entered into here) about the class structure of
Athenian drama, whose early history, more clearly for comedy than for
tragedy, seems to have been one of privately sponsored performances incorporated into the system of publicly financed festivals. The Dionysian
dances were socially and economically structured as a gift from the
wealthy few to the self-sustaining many—a gift that expressed and me-

[31] Thoukydides, 4.94.1; Plutarch, *Phokion* 12.3; Arrian, *Tactics* 2.1; A. W. Gomme, *A Historical Commentary on Thucydides* (Oxford, 1945–1946), 1:15.

[32] Peter J. Rhodes, *A Commentary on the Aristotelian "Athenaion Politeia"* (Oxford, 1981), 503; "Ephebi, Bouleutae, and the Population of Athens," *ZPE* 38 (1980): 191–97, arguing on population figures against Ruschenbusch "Epheben, Buleuten, und die Bürgerzahl von Athen im 330 v. Chr.," *ZPE* 35 (1979): 173–76, who replied in *ZPE* 41 (1981): 103–5.

[33] Pélékidis, *Histoire*, 155ff. Mitchel, "Derkylos," shows that in the oligarchy of Phokion (322 to 319–318) the ephebate was either seriously diminished or abolished altogether.

diated the privileged position of nobler families, putative descendants of tragedy's old heroes, within the democratic city.

Now back to the so-called black hunter.[34] In developing this theme we must allow for (and watch out for) not only a certain play between the looser and stricter senses of "ephebe" and between the older phratry organization and the newer deme-and-tribe organization of the *polis*, but also the even more important ambiguity inherent in the institution of the ephebate itself. Ephebic training is not only a practical induction into the techniques of infantry fighting; it is also a passage between two distinct social identities.[35] "The Spartiates call ephebes 'sideuneis'; they separate them at *hēbē*, that is when they are about fifteen or sixteen years old, from the younger boys and in isolation they practice becoming men [*kath' heautous ēskoun androusthai*]" (Photios, s.v. *sunephēbos*). The ephebate therefore contains not only training in military discipline and in civic responsibility, but also rites and fictions which dramatize the difference between what the ephebes were (boys) and what they will be (men). The myth of Melanthos told at the Apatouria expresses the character and status of the new soldiers as in-betweeners, mixing the categories, specifically by an implied contrast between that disciplined and honorable phalanx-fighting on the plains which was the duty of every citizen-soldier, and Melanthos' tricky, deceitful, solo fighting in the mountains.

To appreciate how shocking was Melanthos' trick, one must read chapters 7 to 9 of W. K. Pritchett's *The Greek State at War: Part 2*:[36] warfare between Greek *poleis* was governed by rules of honor comparable to those for dueling.[37] Enemy armies might camp quite close to each other without fear of surprise attack; battles took place in response to a formal challenge, which might be declined for several days in succession; ambuscades and night attacks were serious violations of honor, at least between Greeks.[38]

There is some indication that the exercises of the Athenian ephebate

[34] Pierre Vidal-Naquet, "The Black Hunter and the Origin of the Athenian Ephebeia," in *Myth, Religion, and Society*, ed. Raymond L. Gordon (Cambridge, Eng., 1981), 147–62, and in his collection *The Black Hunter: Forms of Thought and Forms of Society in the Greek World*, trans. A. Szegedy-Maszak (Baltimore, 1986), 106–28. In "The Black Hunter Revisited," *PCPS*, n.s. 32 (1986): 126–44, Vidal-Naquet raises some objections to my argument about tragedy.

[35] Thus Artemidoros (*Oneirokritika* 1.54) sees a dream of being an ephebe as symbolic of transitions—for the unmarried, marriage; for an old man, death.

[36] W. K. Pritchett, *The Greek State at War: Part 2* (Berkeley, Los Angeles, London, 1974).

[37] "No one who is a man and courageous [*anēr eupsykhos*] thinks it right to kill his enemy secretly, but advances to meet him face to face" (Euripides, *Rhesos* 510–11).

[38] Zeus exiled Herakles for killing Iphitos *doloi*, by a trick, when Iphitos' eye was one way and his mind another, looking for his strayed mares: Sophokles, *Trakhiniai* 270–80.

contained a literal acting-out of Melanthos' role, though it may have
been symbolic and conventional, rather than the literal program described by Vidal-Naquet. Like all things military and most things archaic, the discipline of the young is best attested for Sparta, where the
sons of citizens were segregated in "herds" (*agelai*) according to a carefully regulated system of age-classes. The training of Spartan youth is
known to have included distinctly non-hoplitic exercises—unarmed forays in the hills, feeding off the wild land instead of in a company mess,
stealthy night-fighting. Such exercises do contain a component of the
practical, insofar as they promote ruggedness and self-reliance, but on
the whole they are quite useless for Greek intercity fighting since they do
not develop that corporate discipline and well-drilled obedience which
was the essence of infantry maneuvers.[39]

   The Attic evidence is much more sparse but contains some significant
parallels. Specifically, the ephebes in Aristotle's account of military training were sundered from all citizen duties or claims at law and were taken
out of the city to the series of forts on the perimeter of Attika.[40] It is not
necessarily the case that the youngest Athenian soldiers in this period
were much exercised in mountain foraging and ambuscades, as Vidal-
Naquet concludes from the Spartan parallel.[41] The discussion of border
patrol (*phylakē*) at Xenophon, *Memorabilia* 3.6.9–11, is quite straightforward and practical, implying that the point of the young soldiers' duty
there (Glaukon is not yet twenty, 3.6.1) is mainly to prevent raiding parties of Boiotians from stealing Attic sheep and such.[42] Insofar as the goal
of the ephebate is to produce hoplites who would not break ranks, lone

[39] Henri Jeanmaire, "La cryptie Lacédémonienne," *REG* 26 (1913): 121–50. However,
one must be more reserved than Jeanmaire and Vidal-Naquet about the simple identification of the Spartan *krypteia* as an *ephēbeia*.

[40] [Aristotle], *Ath. Pol.* 42.3–4; *peripolousi tēn khōrān*, "they patrol the countryside." Such
guard duty was typical service for young warriors in other cities too: "[For watching prisoners,] use should be made, where the system of ephebes or guards exists, of the young
men" (Aristotle, *Politics* 6.8:1322a27–28). A specific instance was Sikyon, where a fourth-
century historian (perhaps Ephoros) described the career of the seventh-century tyrant Or-
thagoras as follows: "When he moved out of the age-class of boys and became one of the
peripoloi guarding the countryside. . . . " (*Oxyrhynchus Papyri* 1365.22–28 = *FGrHist*
105.2).

[41] A more cautious formulation is found in his "Recipes for Greek Adolescence": "What
was true of the Athenian ephebe *at the level of myth* is true of the Spartan *kryptos in practice*:
the *kryptos* appears in every respect to be an anti-hoplite" (Vidal-Naquet, *Black Hunter*,
147).

[42] The passes are steep and narrow and therefore do not require, indeed hardly allow, full
hoplite armor and tactics to defend them: Xenophon, *Memorabilia* 3.5.25–28. On modern
sheep-stealing, see M. Herzfeld, *The Poetics of Manhood: Contest and Identity in a Cretan
Mountain Village* (Oxford, 1986).

wolf training must form only a very limited and subordinate part of the program; the point that such training serves is more symbolic than practical.

We should rather say that in the ephebes' time of novitiate, when they were segregated from the regular community and waiting for entry into the ranks of full citizen-soldiers, the Melanthos tale becomes theirs for its border setting, its patriotism, its unproven hero, and above all because Melanthos is one who has not yet learned the honorable conventions of phalanx battle. Because the ephebate is a period of practical military training and contains rituals of passage by segregation and inversion, a tale of a fighting trick set on the border captures the very character of the ephebic ideal (or anti-ideal). This is strikingly confirmed when we observe that the mysterious apparition is both beardless (the iconographic sign for ephebes) and black-caped, for Athenian ephebes wore a distinctive black cape.[43]

But, granting all that, there remains a problem. The black-caped apparition is Dionysos, explicitly named in some versions of the story, and well-known by that title (Melanaigis) elsewhere.[44] Dionysos, as far as we know, has no particular connection with the Apatouria;[45] in fact the association is distinctly odd.[46] The place-names Oinoē and Eleutherai fall

[43] Pollux, 10.164: "The ephebes' uniform is a *petasos* [broad-brimmed felt hat] and a *khlamys* [cloak]," citing Philēmōn's *Door-keeper* (frag. 34 Kock). Artemidoros (*Oneirokritika* 1.54) knows three colors of ephebic cloak—white, black, and crimson (later second century C.E.). The substitution of white for black cloaks at the Eleusinian procession was a beneficence of Herodes Attikos about 176 C.E., known both from Philostratos' *Lives of the Sophists* 2.550 and a contemporary inscription (*IG* II,² 3606). Pierre Roussel, "Les chlamydes noires des éphèbes athèniens," *REA* 43 (1941): 163–65; P. G. Maxwell-Stuart, "Remarks on the Black Coats of the Ephebes," *PCPS* 196, n.s. 16 (1970): 113–16. The inscription relates the change from white to black with Theseus' failure to change his black sails to white when he returned from Krete. It is just possible, therefore, that Simonides' reference to the fatal sails not as black but as crimson has some bearing on the color of ephebic cloaks (*PMG*, 550). Aristotle, *Rhetoric* 3.2.9, speaking of appropriateness, says that the *phoinikis* (a bright red or purplish military cloak) is right for a young man but not for an old man. The cloaks worn by pyrrhic dancers on a black-figure vase in Australia have been painted red, but the significance of this is perhaps diminished by the fact that the artist has also painted each figure's hair, the borders of other cloaks, and alternate palmette leaves red: illustration in J. R. Green, *Antiquities: A Description of the Classics Department Museum in the Australian National University, Canberra* (Canberra, 1981), 31.

[44] For instance at Hermion, where there were annual contests in music, swimming, and boat racing in his honor (Pausanias, *Description of Greece* 2.35.1).

[45] None, that is, except this story, whence the rare report that the Apatouria was celebrated in honor of Dionysos—*Etymologicum Magnum* 118.55.

[46] Dionysos does not figure in the list of gods in the ephebic oath; neither does Apollo Lykeios, a principal patron of their accomplished initiation; Michael H. Jameson, "Apollo Lykeios in Athens," *Archaiognosia* 1 (1980): 213–35. In addition to the gods mentioned above, Hephaistos was honored at the Apatouria by men dressed in fine robes who lit torches from the hearth and sang a hymn to him; Harpokration, s.v. "Lampas."

36   *John J. Winkler*

within his sphere of influence, the former suggesting *oinos* (wine), the latter the title Eleuthereus under which he was worshipped at the City Dionysia, the five-day dramatic festival each spring. The title Melanaigis is explained in the Souda by the story that the daughters of Eleuthēr (eponymous hero of Eleutherai) saw an apparition of Dionysos wearing a black goatskin and, because they mocked it, went mad; to cure their insanity their father followed the advice of an oracle to institute the cult of Dionysos Melanaigis. This type of tale is fairly common. Its most significant instance for our investigation is the foundation myth of the City Dionysia: a certain Pegasos *of Eleutherai* brought the statue of Dionysos to Attika but the Athenians did not receive it with honor. The angry god then sent an incurable affliction on the genitals of the men, which could only be cured (said an oracle) by paying every honor to the god, which they proceeded to do by fashioning phalluses for use in his worship as a memorial to their suffering.[47]

Most telling for present purposes is the fact that the entry of Dionysos into Athens was reenacted each year by the ephebes. They inaugurated the festival by bringing the cult statue in procession from the Academy (just outside the city boundaries on the road to Eleutherai) back to its temple and theater precinct on the southeast slope of the Akropolis. This reenactment of the origin of Dionysos Melanaigis by the ephebes for the city seems to mirror (with the normal cloudiness and unevenness of ancient metal mirrors, rather than with the sharpness of our silvered glass ones) those ceremonies of induction and that myth of apprenticeship located at the opposite end of the year.

One might, of course, try either to expunge Dionysos from the tale of the warrior's trick or to sever the tale from the Apatouria.[48] An older style of analysis, well exemplified by W. R. Halliday, excelled in the use of text-editorial methods to detect inconsistencies and to delete intrusive elements in the myth.[49] Like restorers of old paintings, such scholars

---

[47] Scholiast on Aristophanes, *Akharnians* 243. Athenian colonies were evidently required to send a phallus to the mother city for the Dionysia; we have a record of one such from Brea: *IG* I³ 47.12. On the practice of sending offerings from colony to father-city, see Thoukydides 1.25.4, and A. J. Graham, *Colony and Mother City in Ancient Greece* (Manchester, 1964), chap. 8. See also *IG* II² 673, and the proliferation of phallic *veneranda* associated with Dionysos on Delos: Ernst Buschor, "Ein choregisches Denkmal," *MDAI(A)* 53 (1928): 96–108; Gregory M. Sifakis, *Studies in the History of Hellenistic Drama* (London, 1967), 7–10. (A fragment of a Megarian bowl found in a Dionysian context on Delos shows a phallus with goat legs: *BCH* 31 [1907]: 500–501.)

[48] At least one ancient scholar understood that *Apatouria* was not derived from *apatē*, "trick," but referred rather to the old community of clans: Scholiast to Aristophanes, *Akharnians* 146. O. Szemerényi derives the word from *ha-patro-woroi*, "watchers, worshippers of the same father"; *Gnomon* 43 (1971): 656.

[49] "The proximity to Eleutherai, the name Oinoē and the name Melanthos may all have played a part in bringing Dionysos Melanaigis into the story"; R. Halliday, "Xanthos and

aimed to uncover the authentic original from centuries of grime and inexpert retouching. The current understanding of such myths, however, recognizes that logical gaps and overlay are sometimes not the unfortunate accretions of time but signs of a social process, of an ongoing negotiation among various groups or points of view. Our story seems caught in some sort of force-field between the Apatouria and the City Dionysia: I propose that a specific feature of these two festivals make it seem to belong to both, and that the city's youngest warriors are the link.

There are in fact numerous indications—all of them a matter of record but not hitherto assembled in this way—that the City Dionysia was a social event focused on those young warriors. By "focused" I mean that in the complex and ever-changing organization of the City Dionysia, the newest generation of male citizens was both physically and analytically a center of attention—often (as we will see) a still center. This conclusion is based not on a reading of the extant scripts of Attic tragedy (though they are rich enough in ephebic themes), but rather on a study of the conditions of performance: namely, the political nature of the assembled audience (section II) and, even more, the identity and movement of the chorus (section III). That investigation, which forms the bulk of this essay, leads to the possibility of a new etymology for *tragōidoi*[50] (section IV).

II. AUDIENCE

The opening event of the City Dionysia was the ephebes' reenactment of the advent of Dionysos, which included a sacrifice at a hearth-altar (*eskharā*) near the Academy, a torchlight procession with the cult statue, and (perhaps on the next day, as part of the general barbecue) their sacrifice of a bull on behalf of the entire city.[51] The daylight parade was a lavish spectacle—red-robed metics (resident aliens), phalluses and other precious religious objects carried by priests and honored citizens, twenty dithyrambic choruses (ten of fifty boys each and ten of fifty men each) in

---

Melanthos and the Origin of Tragedy," *CR* 40 (1926): 179–81 (179). Halliday argues against the theory that the combat of Melanthos/Xanthos, understood as Black Man/Fair Man and Winter/Spring, served as a ritual background for the development of classical tragedy. *DTC*, 120–21.

[50] *Tragōidia*, "tragedy," is a secondary formation, derived from *tragōidoi*, plural and naming the group of *tragos*-singers themselves. *Tragōidoi* rather than *tragōidia* is the term used in inscriptions and in ordinary speech in the fifth and fourth centuries; *DFA*, 127–32; W. Burkert, "Greek Tragedy and Sacrificial Ritual," *GRBS* 7 (1966): 92.

[51] Many cattle were killed on this occasion. William S. Ferguson uses inscriptional evidence for an estimate of 240 slaughtered animals in 333 B.C.E.; "Demetrius Poliorcetes and the Hellenic League," *Hesperia* 17 (1948): 134.

their elaborate and expensive costumes. In the center of all this, the ephebes stood as the god's immediate acolytes.[52]

They also had a special block of seats in the theater. Aristophanes refers explicitly to the *bouleutikon*, the section of the auditorium where the members of the Boulē sat—fifty councillors from each of the ten tribes.[53] The scholiast thereon, seconded by Pollux and Hesykhios, informs us that the ephebes too were so honored.[54] The parallelism between the dithyrambic choruses (ten groups of fifty in competition) and the Boulē (fifty councillors from each of the ten tribes) is not accidental.[55] The City Dionysia, like the Panathenaia, was an occasion for marking the structure as well as the magnificence of democratic Athens, that is, the specific structure given to the democracy by the constitutional reforms of Kleisthenes (509/8 B.C.E.).[56] At the Great Panathenaia the money paid out to citizens to attend the festival was distributed by deme and was tied to registration on the deme census lists (Demosthenes, 44.37); the same was presumably true of the Dionysia. The prominent elements of the Kleisthenic structure were carefully displayed in the arrangement of the audience—the ten tribes; the governing Council; and the newest generation of citizens, the ephebes. The layout of the auditorium formed (at least

[52] *DFA*, 59–67. "The dates of the ephebic inscriptions which are the authority for these statements all fall between 127 and 106 B.C., and the *eisagōgē* [advent procession] disappears from later texts; but the re-enactment of the god's advent does not look like an afterthought and probably goes back to the earliest days of the festival, when, after his first cold welcome, it was desired to make amends by doing him special honor" (60).

[53] One inscribed stone from the late-fifth-century theater, "subsequently built upside down into the outer western wall of the auditorium (where it may now be seen) bears the inscription *bolēs ypēreton* [servants of the Council]." *TDA*, 20, where the stone is illustrated.

[54] Aristophanes, *Birds* 794 and scholion (= Souda, s.v. "Bouleutikos"); Pollux, *Lexicon* 4.122; Hesykhios, s.v. "Bouleutikon"; Trugaios at Aristophanes, *Peace* 887 addresses the Boulē and *prytaneis* directly as audience members; the scholiast on *Peace* 882 confirms the seating arrangement.

[55] Note too that the number of ephebes per year seems, at least in the later fourth century, to have been in the neighborhood of five hundred (see n. 1).

[56] E. Capps argues that the new Kleisthenic organization of ten-tribe competitions did not begin until 502/1. B.C.E.; "The Introduction of Comedy into the City Dionysia," *The Decennial Publications of the University of Chicago*, 1st ser., vol. 6 (1904): 261–88; "A New Fragment of the List of Victors at the City Dionysia," *Hesperia* 12 (1943): 1–11. See *DFA*, 71–72, 102–3; Rhodes, *Commentary*, 263, on 22.*ii*. Capps assumes, in reconstructing *IG* II² 2318, that the boys' dithyramb was present from the beginning, requiring eight lines for each year-entry (one for the *arkhōn*, two for the boys' dithyramb, two for the men's dithyramb, three for tragedy). But if the boys' dithyramb was, like comedy, a later addition, there would be room on the stone for more year-entries, perhaps allowing the record to go back as far as the first men's dithyrambic victory reported by the Marmor Parium for the year 510/9 or 509/8.

ideally) a kind of map of the civic corporation, with all its tensions and balances.

The fundamental contrast was that between the internal competition of tribe against tribe (mirrored on other levels of Athenian society by the always-vigorous competition of individuals and households) and the equally strong determination to honor and obey legitimate authority, so that the *polis* as a whole would display a united front against its enemies. These two vectors of civic manliness cross at a balance point which is a locus of no little anxiety, particularly since the unit of intra-Athenian competition, the tribe, is also the unit of military organization.[57] In describing the concerns that were written into the physical organization of the audience we will at the same time be characterizing the expectations of that audience, its readiness to perceive certain messages eliciting its sympathy and anxiety (in the language of Aristotle's *Poetics*, *eleos* and *phobos*). This in turn will explain why the city's youngest warriors were placed precisely at the cross hairs of those powerful forces.

Consider first the seating of the ten tribes. Three statue bases found at the foot of the thirteen seating sections (*kerkides*, wedges) correspond to the traditional order of the ten tribes, assuming that the central wedge was that of the Boulē and ephebes and the two outermost wedges were assigned to noncitizens, perhaps to citizen-wives.[58] The statue bases are of Hadrianic date and are located at the foot of the first, sixth, and eighth wedges (as one looks from the orchestra to the audience). Of course, the number of tribes did not remain constant over the years, and this fact too may be read in the light of theater and assembly seating. The traditional order of Kleisthenes' ten tribes is Erekhtheis, Aigeis, Pandionis, Leontis,

[57] R. T. Ridley, "The Hoplite as Citizen: Athenian Military Institutions in Their Social Context," *AC* 48 (1979): 508–48.

[58] Seating: *DFA*, 270. Tribal seating in the theater was first suggested by Pickard-Cambridge in his revision of A. E. Haigh, *The Attic Theater*, 3d ed. (Oxford, 1907), 337 and n. 5. Of the two theaters at Peiraieus the one still visible, at Zea, also has thirteen wedges: P. E. Arias, "Alcune osservazioni sul teatro del Pireo in Attica e su quello di Tera," *Dioniso* 4 (1934): 93–99. On citizen-wives in general, see C. Patterson, "*Hai Attikai*: The Other Athenians," in *Rescuing Creusa: New Methodological Approaches to Women in Antiquity*, ed. Marilyn Skinner (special issue of *Helios*, n.s. 13/2 [1987]): 49–67. The most interesting feature of the question, "Did women attend the dramatic festivals?" is that it is so hard to answer. I believe they did, on the basis of Aristophanes' *Skēnas Katalambanousai* (if it means *Women Occupying the Stage*, a thoroughly Aristophanic conception), because a fragment of that play represents a woman speaking of her *syntheatria*, fellow-spectatrix. The audience is always addressed, by Aristophanes and Menander, as composed of men in various age-classes, which means that the notional or proper audience is one of men. I imagine that women, aside from the priestesses in the front row of thrones, may have sat in the outer two wedges and even more likely in the higher regions, where there were fewer than thirteen seating wedges. (It is only in the lower auditorium that the seating sections numbered a full thirteen; hence only in that portion was the political structure of the city mapped.)

Akamantis, Oineis, Kekropis, Hippothontis, Aiantis, and Antiokhis.
Changes were made in 307/6 B.C.E. (addition of two tribes, Antigonas
and Demetrias), 224 B.C.E. (addition of one tribe, Ptolemais), 201/200
B.C.E. (omission of Antigonas and Demetrias, addition of Attalis), and
126/7 C.E. (addition of Hadrianis). An interesting feature of these rear-
rangements is that the added tribes are placed sometimes at the beginning
of the list (Antigonas and Demetrias), sometimes at the end (Attalis), and
twice in the very center (Ptolemais, Hadrianis).

One can understand the conservatism lying behind additions to the beginning or end, which keeps the previous order internally untouched,
but why on two occasions did the Athenian body politic rearrange itself
with a new unit in the center? On both occasions it was an increase from
twelve tribes to thirteen, and the additional tribe is located at number
seven on the list. It is worth proposing that the rationale for placing the
new tribe in this position was that though it was a greater disturbance of
the operations governed by tribal order, it was the minimal disturbance
to the seating plan in a thirteen-wedge theater, assuming that the central
wedge in the ten- or twelve-tribe system had been occupied by the Boulē
and perhaps the ephebes. (I do not want to insist that everyone always sat
where he was supposed to, only that provisions existed for each tribe to
have its wedge.) A similar seating arrangement into ten wedges for the
ten tribes may have existed for the Pnyx, in which the full citizen Assembly met four times a month.[59] (Some Assembly meetings were also held
in the theater.)[60]

Much earlier evidence pertinent to seating exists in the form of lead
theater tickets, whose spelling conventions and letter forms put them at
least in the early part of the fourth century B.C.E., if not earlier. These
tickets are marked with tribal names.[61] If the citizens were seated (at least
grosso modo) by tribal affiliation, these ten tribal blocks would inevitably

[59] W. A. McDonald, *The Political Meeting Places of the Greeks* (Baltimore, 1943), 71–75;
E. S. Stavely, *Greek and Roman Voting and Elections* (London, 1972), 81–82; F. Kolb, *Agora
und Theater, Volks- und Festversammlung* (Berlin, 1981), 93. *Contra*, M. H. Hansen, "How
Did the Athenian *Ecclesia* Vote?" *GRBS* 18 (1977): 135–36 (but citing Aiskhines, 2.64–68,
where two members of tribes contiguous in the official order are seated adjacent to each
other) and "The Athenian *Ecclesia* and the Pnyx," *GRBS* 23 (1982): 244–49. My argument
does not require that all citizens always sat in the wedge assigned to their tribe, either in the
Pnyx or in the theater; only that the number of wedges in both cases was notionally related
to the configuration of the citizen body into ten tribes. The argument for tribal (and *trittys*)
seating has recently been extended to include Pnyx I and II by G. R. Stanton and P. J. Bick-
nell, "Voting in Tribal Groups in the Athenian Assembly," *GRBS* 28 (1987): 51–92, who
notice other tribally seated theaters at 86–87.

[60] The second of two theaters at Peiraieus (see n. 58), that at Mounikhia, now entirely
covered by modern buildings, could be used for Assemblies: Thoukydides, 8.93.1, 3; Lysias, 13.32, 55; cf. Xenophon, *Hellenika* 2.4.32.

[61] On tickets, see *DFA*, 270–72.

have taken on the character of cheering sections during the dithyrambic competition, which, unlike comedy and tragedy, was a competition among the tribes. The panel of ten judges for all events was composed of one selected from each tribe, and as a matter of course the judges were carefully sworn not to show favoritism. Of the ten ballots, five were selected randomly to count for the voting while five were discarded. The recorded instances of bribery and cheating show that the oath and other such safeguards were necessary.

The lateral spread of the auditorium thus formed an axis of competition among the ten citizen groups, with the Boulē as its representatives and mediators at the center. The vertical axes up and down the blocks displayed relative prestige. *Prohedria*, front-row seating, was one of the highest honors that could be paid to benefactors and special friends of the city, attested to in numerous decrees and in one funny story about Demosthenes.[62] Since this festival took place just when the winter storms had ceased and travel became tolerable,[63] its splendor attracted a large audience of sightseers, guests, and other noncitizens. Athens used the opportunity to score propaganda points. Before the musical events, ceremonies were held in the orchestra: golden crowns were bestowed on favored friends of the city, the tribute paid by the allies was carried in and displayed (fifth century), and boys whose fathers had died in war and who had been supported by the city until they reached *hēbē* were paraded in suits of hoplite armor supplied to them by the city, now that they were ready to enter the ranks of the ephebes.[64]

If the tribute and the presence of the city's friends represent its active military alliances, the war orphans who are ready to become soldiers in their fathers' places inevitably bring to mind the city's battles, both past and future.[65] This description may sound like an account of a West Point

[62] The inscriptional evidence is surveyed in chap. 4 of Michael Maass, *Die Prohedrie des Dionysostheaters in Athen* (Munich, 1972). See also E. Pöhlmann, "Die Proedrie des Dionysostheaters im 5. Jahrhundert und das Bühnenspiel der Klassik," *MH* 38 (1981): 129–46. The Demosthenes anecdote can be found in Aiskhines, *Against Ktesiphon* 76. When the Athenians took over control of Delos in the mid-second century B.C.E., they transferred the announcement of civic honors from the Apollonia to the Dionysia; Sifakis, *Studies*, 14.

[63] Aristophanes, *Akharnians* 502–8; Theophrastos, *Characters* 3: the chatterer mentions a string of banal items, including that the sea is sailable from the time of the Dionysia.

[64] Ronald S. Stroud, "Greek Inscriptions: Theozotides and the Athenian Orphans," *Hesperia* 40 (1971): 280–301, esp. 288–89.

[65] The city's military preparedness was also advertised by the ten generals (one per tribe) who offered a ceremonial libation at the beginning of the performances. Plutarch attests this for an early date (468 B.C.E.) in a story about competition so fierce that the *arkhōn* refused to select judges by the usual lot but instead persuaded the generals, who were present for their customary libation, to act as the panel; *Life of Kimon* 8.7–9. On the generals' *prohedriā* in the theater, see Aristophanes, *Knights* 573–77, 702–4; Aristophanes, *Thesmophoriazousai* 832–35; Theophrastos, *Characters* 5.7; *IG* 2 500.32–35.

graduation ceremony, but it is important to underscore the fact that the *toto caelo* difference we experience between the military realm and the theatrical, between marching to war and going to a play, did not apply to the City Dionysia. To cite a caricature whose degree of truth will later become apparent, Aristophanes presents Aiskhylos in the *Frogs* defending his tragedies as a form of martial art: his *Seven against Thebes* made every man in the audience lust for battle (1022).

On the map of the body politic formed by the theater seating, the lateral axis of intracity competition among tribes is crossed in the center by a vertical axis containing the Boulē and ephebes. Like the Boulē, the ephebes are organized by tribe. That central axis thus contains two kinds of tribal representative—citizen-governors and citizens-in-training—whose competition is muted by their function as administrators and defenders of the *polis* as a whole. Since the vertical axes in all the wedges are used to symbolize rank (*prohedria*), the presence of councillors and ephebes on the central axis highlights the relationship between the citizens most fully identified with the *polis*' interests and the citizen-initiates. (My conjecture that the ephebes were seated in the central wedge is not the only conceivable arrangement. They might, for instance, have sat according to tribe but in the same row or rows of each wedge. Putting them in the center simply accords well with the social map of the auditorium, making them separate, central, and subordinate to the Boulē.)

In sum, then, the entire audience is organized in a way which demonstrates its corporate manliness as a *polis* to be reckoned with, comprising individuals who are both vigilant to assert excellence against other members of the city (tribe versus tribe) and ready to follow legitimate authority against external threats (cadet soldiers and Council).

III. Performance

The habits of modern play-reading and play-going make it all too easy for us to scant the chorus when reading Greek tragedy. Note for instance that we always refer to such a performance as a "tragedy," whereas the fifth-century designation was not *tragōidia* but *tragōidoi*, "tragic choristers" or, literally, "billy goat singers."[66] As a convention, not only is the chorus foreign to our dramatic sense, but there is even evidence that in the fifth century it was already coming to seem an archaic institution. When we do try to give full weight to the role of the chorus our attention is usually drawn to the beauty and power of some of the choral odes. But few will declare themselves partisans of the chorus' (actually the chorus

---

[66] See n. 50. Athenaios, relying perhaps on Aristokles' monograph *On Choruses* (630b), asserts that "in ancient times satyric poetry consisted entirely of choruses, just like the tragedy of that time, so it had no actors" (630c).

leader's) standard trimeter comments of praise and warning. My account, however, emphasizes that the events and characters portrayed in
tragedy are meant to be contemplated as lessons by young citizens (or
better, by the entire *polis* from the vantage point of the young citizen),
and therefore it makes the watchful scrutiny of the chorus structurally
important as a still center from which the tragic turbulence is surveyed
and evaluated.

Consider now the relation of role to performer, first for actors and
then for chorus members. While the actors portray those (young men
and maidens, older men and women) who carry or support the responsibility of correct social action, the chorus usually performs in the guise
of persons who do not bear such responsibility—slave women, prisoners
of war, old men—who will certainly be implicated in the effects of unwise, headstrong, or ignorant action on the part of their principals. On
the level of roles, then, there is a vector of attention from the watchful
(though not personally responsible) chorus to the actors. This seems to
be balanced by an inversion on the level of performers, for several kinds
of evidence conspire to suggest that the three actors for each tragedy
were *men*, but the twelve (or, after Sophokles, fifteen)[67] chorus members
were *ephebes*.

There are many vase paintings based on tragic plays from which we
can cautiously deduce information about plots, scenery, and costumes,[68]
but there is only one unbroken representation of the complete (or nearly
complete) cast for a tragic competition. It is a late fifth- or early fourth-
century Attic volute-krater now in the Naples Museum[69] (plate 1),
whose obverse depicts the three actors, each dressed for one of the parts
of a play (Herakles, Pappasilenos, and probably Laomedon) and holding
the mask for that role; eleven chorus members in costume and holding
their masks (one has donned his mask and is practicing a kick step); the
poet-trainer Demetrios watching to ensure that a chorus member gets his

---

[67] Anonymous, *Life of Sophokles* 4, in A. C. Pearson, *Sophoclis Fabulae* (Oxford, 1961),
xix.

[68] Listed in Thomas B. L. Webster, *Monuments Illustrating Tragedy and Satyr Play*, London University, Institute of Classical Studies Bulletin, supp. 14 (London, 1962). There is a
fine collection of photos in *IGD*, mainly on play subjects rather than on theatrical equipment; see also *DFA*, chap. 4.

[69] Museo Nazionale Archeologico, 3240; Paolo E. Arias, *A History of Greek Vase Painting*, trans. and rev. Brian B. Shefton (London, 1962), 377–80, with bibliography, pl. 218–
19; F. Brommer, "Zum Deutung der Pronomosvase," *AA* (1964): 109–14; E. Simon, "The
'Omphale' of Demetrios," *AA* (1971): 199–206. The names, invisible on most photographs, are included in the drawing of the vase in Margarete Bieber, *The History of the Greek
and Roman Theater*, 2d ed. (Princeton, 1961), fig. 32 (reproduced, in plate 1), and much
more visibly in the huge reproductions of Adolf Furtwängler and Karl Reichhold, *Griechische Vasenmalerei* (Munich, 1904–1932).

pose right; the aulos-player Pronomos (from whose prominence in the composition the krater is nicknamed the Pronomos Vase) in full costume and playing his double aulos; an auxiliary lyre-player; the god Dionysos and his consort (perhaps Ariadne); and another figure seated on the divine couch whose sex, identity, and function in this context are debated. It appears to be the victory dedication of a successful ensemble, who have chosen to be portrayed in the equipment of their final and more hilarious satyr-play rather than in that of one of their three tragedies. (The personnel is of course identical for all four plays.)

I take it to be significant that the three actors are represented as full-grown men with beards, while the chorus members have full-grown bodies but are beardless; they are, iconographically speaking, ephebes. (In what sense they are ephebes—merely in terms of age or also with reference to their role as the city's young warriors—remains to be seen.) The number of persons involved is obviously too large for the distinction to be due to coincidence, and if it is not coincidence it must represent some sort of rule or principle, at least for this group of actors and *tragōidoi*. Now if it is a rule for this particular group of competitive performers, given the careful regulation of who was allowed to perform in various contests, it is virtually certain that it was a rule for other performing groups in the same competition of the same year. We cannot with quite the same confidence assert that the rule (however we may formulate it) must have been operative for tragic competitions in some or all years previous to this one; but, since innovations in festival procedures were well-deliberated and far from casual, there would seem to be every likelihood that such was the case. Thus, although sufficient ingenuity could of course devise other explanations of this visible rule distinguishing actors from chorus members on the Pronomos Vase, the prima facie interpretation is that in the late fifth century and for some time prior to that, Attic tragedy was performed by choruses of young men.[70]

Though the chorus' contribution to the whole performance was probably being overshadowed more and more in the course of the fifth century by that of the actors, the Pronomos Vase is witness both to the continued importance of chorus membership and to the segregation of actors from chorus. Note that the honor of the upper register is given to

[70] Unfortunately the krater fragments from Taranto, now in Würzburg, which evidently showed a complete tragic cast with a chorus in female dress, very close in style and date to the Pronomos Vase, are severely broken. Not a single face of an actor or chorister survives (*DFA*, 187–88 with pl. 50a, b, c; *ARV²* 1338). Vidal-Naquet, "Black Hunter Revisited" (137), opines that the Pronomos Vase is too exceptional to support the weight of my argument, but aside from the fact that the Taranto fragments show it not to have been unique, surely its scale and detail do not compromise its information. On the contrary, the inscribed names of its chorus members anchor it more firmly in social reality than any other partial representation of chorus or actors.

the divine figures and the heroic roles, but it is the musical and dancing performers who are dignified with their personal names: the two musicians, the poet-trainer, and nine of the eleven members represented from the chorus have their names inscribed; the actors do not (though the role played by one is labeled Herakles).[71] The names are all attested as those of Athenian citizens, many of them found in the wealthiest families (as recorded in J. K. Davies' *Athenian Propertied Families*). Several details on this vase are of uncertain interpretation,[72] but the matters of controversy do not touch on the distinction between the two groups of performers—fully mature, bearded men (actors) and young men who have yet to grow beards (chorus members).[73]

[71] *IGD*, 29, aptly cites Plato, *Symposium* 173a: the symposium took place on the day after Agathon, and his chorus members celebrated their victory sacrifice—no mention is made of actors. An inscription published by M. Mitsos, *Archaiologikē Ephēmeris* (1965), 163, lists Sokrates as producer (*khorēgos*, probably Sokrates [II] of Anagyrous, the ancient deme located at Varikasa where the stone was found); Davies, *Athenian Propertied Families*, 13103), lists Euripides as poet-trainer (*didaskalos*), and fourteen *tragōidoi*—no actors; Paulette Ghiron-Bistagne, *Recherches sur les acteurs dans la Grèce antique* (Paris, 1976), 119–21; see n. 72 on the number of performers.

[72] The feminine-looking couch-sitter seems to be holding the mask and wearing the costume of a fourth *role* in the play. Since one of the three actors already pictured in other roles would have acted this part, he is not drawn a second time. Some have tried to identify the figure—as Paideia (Bulle) or Tragedy (Curtius) or Paidia (Fröning). Why eleven chorus members? The poet-trainer Demetrios himself could have performed as the twelfth person in the chorus, presumably the chorus leader, a practice attested for the earliest days of tragedy; but all other evidence points to fifteen as the expected number for this time (see n. 71). Since even inscriptional lists of Boulē members sometimes record only forty-nine names, we should not be too surprised at a vase painter's inexactitude. It is also possible that the vase could be taken as evidence for a reduction of the chorus during the Peloponnesian War from fifteen members to twelve, by analogy with the reduction of comedies in that period from five to three (*DFA*, 83). The wartime reduction of comedies, however, has been challenged by W. Luppe, "Die Zahl der Konkurrenten an den komischen Agonen zur Zeit des Peloponnesischen Krieges," *Philologus* 116 (1972): 53–75. One might speculate that satyr-plays retained the older convention of a twelve-man chorus even when that of tragedy increased to fifteen; that is, only twelve of the fifteen performed in all four plays. But that would leave other questions: if the vase is a victory dedication for the entire chorus, would the three who performed only in the tragedies be omitted? And why are only nine personal names inscribed? Another possibility is that the tragic choruses were reduced *after* the Peloponnesian War as a small retribution against the pro-oligarchic elite. The variation in costume is of some interest. Could the chorus member in fancy dress already have changed his clothes for the victory celebration? Why does one chorus member alone wear star-embroidered pants (found on other vases showing satyr-chorusmen or female athletes) rather than the shaggy drawers of the rest? Did they serve as the undercostume for the hairy pelt?

[73] Even on Ernst Buschor's hypothesis that the roles are taken not by human actors but by the heroes themselves, the contrast is still evident; see Buschor in Furtwängler and Reichhold, *Griechische Vasenmalerei*, 3:132–50. Pickard-Cambridge (*DFA*, 187) sees a certain "melting" between the faces of the actors and their masks; I should say rather that the actors look very like each other and not particularly like their masks. At some point Pron-

The other monuments known to me are consistent with this distinction. Among them I would single out the lovely polychrome fragment in Würzburg (plate 2) showing an actor with a commoner's face holding the mask of a noble-visaged king; the man has salt-and-pepper hair, which is thinning and receding, and a three-days' growth of stubble on his cheeks and chin.[74] Several vases show two or three chorus members in different stages of dress: a "maenad" holds the costume for a young man who is hurriedly pulling on his *kothornoi*[75] (plate 3); a "maenad," whose face is clearly a mask, does a dance step while a beardless youth wearing the same loose-sleeved dress and holding a woman's (?) mask looks on;[76] two ephebes in furry drawers hold satyr masks while a third has donned his mask and is practicing a hip thrust[77] (plate 4). There are some other fragments which might, if they had remained whole, have been informative on this subject.[78]

The sharp rule formulated above may have to be qualified in one respect. A famous dedicatory relief found in Peiraieus (Athens *NM* 1500, plate 5) shows Dionysos on a couch approached by three persons in costume, two of whom are holding their masks. They are often taken to be the three actors of a successful production, though the similarity of their costumes might suggest that they are chorus members. The differentiation of the masks would be decisive, but unfortunately, of the two masks still somewhat visible, that held by the right-hand figure is very worn. The left-hand figure was evidently wearing his mask, and his entire head has been obliterated. Though the whole surface is in poor condition,

---

omos' own beard or beardlessness became an issue. "Agyrrhios was an effeminate general who held a command in Lesbos; he reduced the payment of the poets. . . . Pronomos was an aulos-player who had a big beard, Agyrrhios was sexually submissive to men: so he borrowed Pronomos' beard and no one noticed that he was a woman" (Scholiast on Aristophanes, *Ekklesiazousai* 102). This sounds like a joke from Old or Middle Comedy: either in later life Pronomos was famous for having a big beard or for having a false one which could be lent out to other effeminate men.

[74] Würzburg 832, from Taranto, around 340 B.C.E.; color reproduction in Ghiron-Bistagne, *Recherches*, frontispiece, and also in Paolino Mingazzini, *Greek Pottery Painting* (London, 1969), fig. 57; see also Bieber, *History*, fig. 306a–b, and *DFA*, fig. 54a. Erika Simon interprets the role as Tereus: "Tereus," *Festschrift des Kronberg-Gymnasiums* (Aschaffenburg, 1968), 155ff.

[75] On a red-figured Attic pelike by the Phiale Painter (Boston 98.883), see *ARV²* 1017; Thomas B. L. Webster, *The Greek Chorus* (London, 1970), pl. 8; *DFA*, fig. 34; Bieber, *History*, fig. 90.

[76] Red-figure bell-krater, about 460–450 B.C.E. (Ferrara T 173C); *DFA*, fig. 33, where the mask is said to be certainly that of a young man—it seems to me too poorly drawn to be certain.

[77] Apulian bell-krater by the Tarporley Painter, 400–380 B.C.E. (Sydney 47.05); *IGD* II.2; Frank Brommer, *Satyrspiele*, 2d ed. (Berlin, 1959), fig. 7.

[78] See n. 70.

there is no real doubt that the two surviving faces of the three standing figures are those of young men.

Though the Peiraieus relief *may* show chorus members, consistent with the strong distinction on the Pronomos Vase, they may also be actors, and this leads to an important qualification. On the Pronomos Vase not only the chorus but the poet, lyre-player, and aulos-player (and the god) are young. Though some poets such as Aiskhylos, Sophokles, and Euripides lived to be senior citizens and were portrayed by tradition with the dignity of their mature look, dramatic performances were clearly an arena where young men could excel. Tradition puts Aiskhylos and Sophokles somewhere in their mid-twenties when they first exhibited their own plays, Euripides closer to thirty. Aristophanes claims to have been a shy young man at the time of his first production, Menander was only twenty, and Ameinias was officially an ephebe when his comedy *The Fainting Woman* (*Apoleipousa*) took third prize in 312–311 (*IG* II^2 2323a46–47). *Mousikē* (poetry, dance, music) is not learned overnight, and we must assume that all these dramatists were active in stagecraft for some years before they took responsibility for mounting a full production of their own. It should not be surprising, therefore, that Demetrios, the poet on the Pronomos Vase, is a young man and that his company of musical personnel is so youthful. Nor would it be surprising if younger men sometimes served in the less musical and less athletic function of *hupokritēs*, which may be the sense of the Peiraieus relief. What would be of interest, and does not seem to exist, would be evidence of mature, bearded men as chorus members of tragedy.

The Pronomos Vase is the principal *positive* evidence for the hypothesis that tragic-satyric choruses were composed of young men who were just reaching their *hēbē*. Other literary evidence is consistent with that hypothesis. Direct testimony about the constitution of choruses is extremely meager. Aristotle (*Politics* 3.3 [1276b4–6]) remarks that the same persons (*anthrōpoi*, not *andres*) may perform in a comic and in a tragic chorus.[79] A scholiast on Aristophanes (*Ploutos* 953) says that noncitizens could not perform in the choruses of the City Dionysia, though they could perform (and metics could produce) at the Lenaia, a Dionysian festival held two months before the City Dionysia.[80] To which choruses

[79] Cf. the bell-krater, 390–370 B.C.E. (Heidelberg B 134), showing two comic chorus members impersonating women, one with his mask thrown back to reveal a beardless young face; Thomas B. L. Webster, *Greek Theater Production* (London, 1956), pl. 15a; Bieber, *History*, fig. 208.

[80] The rule is stated by the scholiast on Aristophanes, *Ploutos* 953: "it was not allowed for a noncitizen [*xenos*] to dance in a City chorus . . . but in the Lēnaia it was allowed, since metics too sponsored choruses." A recently discovered example is found in Colin N. Edmondson, "Onesippos' Herm," *Hesperia*, supp. 19, *Studies in Attic Epigraphy, History, and Topography Presented to Eugene Vanderpool* (1982): 48–50.

did that law apply? [Andokides] 4.20 recounts a fistfight between two *khorēgoi*, Alkibiades and Taureas, over the disputed citizenship of a boy dithyrambist; Plutarch (*Phokion* 30.6) gives an example of a *khorēgos* who allowed some noncitizens to perform in his dithyramb. For tragedy and comedy we cannot claim to be so sure, though the entire tendency of my argument would suggest that it was properly an affair of citizens.

One occasionally encounters a statement in modern writers to the effect that chorus members had a special exemption from military service, which would imply that they were men rather than ephebes, but this half-truth merely serves to reveal our own collective (I do not exempt myself) insensitivity to age-classes and festivals. There was a military exemption during their year of office for members of the Boulē (Lykourgos, *Leōkrates* 37) and for customs officers ([Demosthenes], 59.27). Twice Demosthenes mentions such an exemption for choral performers, but we must then ask in what kind of chorus—comedy, tragedy, men's dithyramb (boys' dithyramb is obviously out of the question)—and at what festival? One of them certainly refers to a men's dithyrambic chorus at the City Dionysia (21.15 and scholion); the other is apparently also at the City Dionysia, but what chorus is not clear (39.16).[81]

On the surface this meager evidence about military exemption does not tell against the ephebic-choral hypothesis; on a deeper level it speaks for it. The question to ask is: why should there have been an exemption from marching and fighting for the five hundred men each year who danced the dithyramb in honor of Dionysos? Part of the answer may be sheerly practical—a feeling that in the winter and early spring a busy citizen could be expected to spend about the same amount of time either practicing drill with his (tribal) company and getting in shape for the coming summer's battles or rehearsing the (tribal) dance, but not both. Was there in addition any deeper, symbolic equivalence between these two civic duties which made sense of the exemption? In what framework does a dance for Dionysos equal a season of campaigning?[82] The relation is one of contrast and of similarity. Aristophanes, for instance, shows us

[81] At 21.58–61, Demosthenes refers to two persons who had been convicted of *astrateia* and yet had later directed or performed in choruses. The point is that they were such exceptionally skilled individuals that no citizen who observed them wanted to take the responsibility of enforcing the legal ban on their participation. Presumably the year in which they had been convicted of *astrateia* was not a year in which they had been dancing for Dionysos.

[82] Note that in the second case cited from Demosthenes, the speaker contrasts military service not only with choral dancing at the City Dionysia but with the celebration of the Dionysian Anthesteria a month earlier. (At the back of my mind in this argument is the role of army musicians today—"privates on parade"; behind the ideology of the citizen-soldier must lie the practical recognition that not all men are suited to that role.) It must be admitted that it is unclear whether the exemption covered the entire year or only the period of training for the festival.

the opposition in a diptych contrasting the general Lamakhos called up to service against midwinter bandits in Boiotia while Dikaiopolis, the man who refuses to fight, celebrates the Anthesteria with the priest of Dionysos (*Akharnians* 1071–end).[83] The similarity, on the other hand, can be seen in the military tone of some dithyrambs and other choral performances,[84] and in the fact that they were performed, at least for a time, in the region of the agora that was also the location of war monuments.[85] But such mimeto-militarism is actually best seen not in the dithyrambs but in the oldest component of the City Dionysia, the dances of the *tragōidoi*. It is this component of the performance that will justify my reading of the young men on the Pronomos Vase as ephebes in the stricter sense of the word—young citizen-soldiers in training.

One must recall that the history of performances at the City Dionysia is marked by three stages: *tragōidoi* first perform for city-sponsored prizes under the direction of Thespis in about 534 B.C.E. during the long tyranny of Peisistratos (*Marmor Parium*, *FGrHist* 239A43); prizes for men's (and boys'?) dithyrambs are added at the time of the constitutional reforms of Kleisthenes, 509/8 B.C.E.[86] (or perhaps 502/1; see note 56); *kōmōidoi* are introduced as a prize category in 486 B.C.E.[87] (Of course, at least dithyrambic and comic choruses are much older than these particular festival arrangements, which simply give a new financial and competitive structure to old traditions.) There are two contrasts in the structure of this set of performances which are "ephebically" significant. The first is that the dithyrambs are designated as belonging to two age-classes, men and boys. "Men's chorus" and "boys' chorus" are the

[83] Conversely, Eupolis' *Taxiarkhoi* portrayed Dionysos living the hard life of a soldier and learning about military life from the famous general Phormion (frag. 274 *PCG*).

[84] Especially the mysterious piece Bakkhylides 18, which is a fully dramatized encounter between King Aigeus of Athens and a chorus of young citizen-warriors (13–14) about the advance of an apparent enemy toward the city: he is the ephebe (*paida . . . prōthēbon*, 56–57) Theseus, wearing the young warrior's cloak (*khlamyd'*, 54). Merkelbach goes too far in reconstructing the details of its ephebic ceremonial referents ("Der Theseus des Bakkhilides," *ZPE* 12 [1973]: 56–62), but the general relevance of the poem both to choral drama and to mythic-military subjects is undoubtable. Without arguing that this piece was a dithyramb, much less that it was necessarily performed at the City Dionysia, I would observe that early fifth-century dithyrambs were, like this piece, antistrophic ([Aristotle], *Problems* 19.15:918b19–20. See also A. P. Burnett, *The Art of Bacchylides* (Cambridge, Mass., 1985), 117–23.

[85] Peter Siewert, *Die Trittyen Attikas und die Heeresreform des Kleisthenes*, Vestigia, no. 33 (Munich, 1982), 150–53. N.G.L. Hammond stresses that early tragic performances were also in the agora: "The Conditions of Dramatic Production to the Death of Aeschylus," *GRBS* 13 (1972): 387–450.

[86] Hammond, "Conditions," 62–67. The Marmor Parium records the first men's dithyrambic victory at the City Dionysia in that year; the winning composer was Hypodikos of Khalkis (*FGrHist* 239A46).

[87] *Souda*, s.v. Chiōnidēs; Capps, "Introduction"; *DFA*, 82.

terms, both official and popular, for these dances at all times for which
we have records. This is at least consistent with the hypothesis that *tragōidoi* specifically designated ephebes. When the dithyrambs officially became a competitive event in the City Dionysia, they were composed of
and named for the two nonephebic age groups—men and boys.

The second contrast is that men's and boys' dithyrambic dances were
circular dances, while *tragōidoi* moved in a rectangular formation. Reasonably detailed information survives about this "square" dancing.[88]
The chorus members processed in three files and four or five ranks (depending on whether there were twelve or, from sometime in the second
quarter of the fifth century, fifteen persons marching). Since they entered
the orchestra three abreast and the left-hand file was nearest the spectators, the best performers were stationed in the leftmost file. When that
file contained five members, the *koryphaios* occupied the central position.
The orchestra in later times was a circular space, but there is no evidence
that tragic choruses ever took up a circular formation;[89] on the contrary,
the name *kyklios khoros*, which is used as a general term for all dithyrambs, seems to guarantee that *tragōidoi* characteristically performed in
rank and file.[90]

We often and quite casually use the term "marching" when the chorus'
entrance song is in anapestic meter without really thinking about its implications. Rectangular formation above all requires that the dancers
move with precision, since they are ordered along two sight lines. Circular dancing, by comparison, especially in masses of fifty, can be impressive while admitting a certain degree of, not sloppiness, but
looseness. The usual reconstruction of tragic choral movement imagines
that the dancers sometimes occupied the center of the orchestra, sometimes split into two groups, at times facing the actors and at other times
facing the audience. The performance of such maneuvers would have exercised the same precision skills that were required for hoplite marching,[91] and though I do not imagine that the *koryphaios* actually barked

---

[88] *DFA*, 239–54; L. B. Lawler, *The Dance of the Ancient Greek Theatre* (Iowa City, 1964).
Timaios speaks of "the so-called Lakōnistai who sang in tetragonal choruses" (Athenaios,
181c = *FGrHist* 566F140), but the context and referent are wholly unknown. The rectangular formation of tragic dancing is ignored by H.D.F. Kitto, "The Dance in Greek Tragedy," *JHS* 75 (1955): 36–41.

[89] *DFA*, 239 n. 2.

[90] Lysias, *Oration* 21.3; *DFA*, 239; "Alkman referred to the maidens dancing in order [*en
taksei*] as 'in the same file' [*homostoikhous*]," *PMG*, 33. (*Zygon* and *stoikhos* are the technical
terms for rank and file in tragic dancing: *DFA*, 239.)

[91] "There is an enormous difference between an ordered army and a disordered one,"
Xenophon, *Memorabilia* 3.1.7; Aristotle too notes that the essence of hoplite fighting is coordination (*syntaxis*). Before men discovered *taxis* and so made heavily armored infantry
useful, cavalry was supreme; *Politics* 4.13:1297b18–22.

sotto voce "Right face," "Company halt," and so forth to his squadron
of ephebes, such commands were implicit in its well-regulated motion.[92]
Members of any chorus must focus their attention very carefully on the
leader, as Xenophon implies when describing the similar attention rowers give to their boatswain (*Mem.* 3.5.6).

Not only our phrase "rank and file" but a number of traditional Greek
choral terms point to a homology between the movement of *tragōidoi* and
of hoplites: *parastatēs* and other compounds of -*statēs*, *psileis* ("unpro-
tected") of the persons with an exposed side in the formation, *hēgemōn* of
the chorus leader.[93] Sometimes the comparison is explicit, as in this very
significant fragment of Khamaileon:

> [The older dances were dignified and manly;] therefore Aristo-
> phanes or Plato in his *Gear*, as Chamaileon writes, spoke as follows:
> "So that when anyone danced well it was a real spectacle, but now
> they do nothing; they just stand in one place as if paralyzed by a
> stroke and they howl." For the form of dancing in choruses then
> was well-ordered [*euskhēmon*] and impressive and as it were imita-
> tive of movements in full armor [*kinēseis en tois hoplois*]; whence
> Sokrates says in his poems that the finest choral dancers are best in
> war; I quote, "Those who most beautifully honor the gods in cho-
> ruses are best in war." For choral dancing was practically like a
> troop review [or maneuver in arms, *exhoplisia*] and a display not
> only of precision marching [*eutaxia*] in general but more particularly
> of physical preparedness.[94]

Teachers of each discipline are even found giving the same advice to
put the best soldiers or dancers in the front and rear ranks, the less good
ones in the middle.[95] At other times a contrast between the two activities

[92] Command words are listed by Asklepiodotos, *Tactics*, chap. 12; chaps. 10–11 describe
the various troop formations for marching and turning; text and translation in the Loeb
Classical Library along with military texts by Aeneas Tacticus and Onasander (London,
1923). For the sixth and fifth centuries our positive knowledge of military training is almost
zero; Pritchett, *Greek State*, chaps. 11–12; John K. Anderson, *Military Theory and Practice in
the Age of Xenophon* (Berkeley, 1970), chaps. 5–6.

[93] DFA, 241.

[94] Khamaileon, frag. 42 (ed. Fritz Wehrli) = Athenaios *Deipnosophists* 14.268e–f. (This
may be two quotations, one from Khamaileon, one from Sokrates.) It is important to note
that Khamaileon gets his information, and his authority, principally from Old Comedy,
which he cites not only in this instance but to back up many of his surviving opinions about
early tragedy (frags. 40–42 Wehrli). This relocation of their authority at once makes such
pronouncements both earlier and more oblique: they remain important evidence even if
they were originally the grouchy exaggerations of a curmudgeon on the comic stage.

[95] "In battle the best soldiers should be placed first and last, the worst in the middle, so
that they may be led by the ones in front and pushed by the ones in back," Xenophon,
Memorabilia 3.1.8, cf. *Kyropaidia* 7.5.5; "The three middle files not visible in some pas-

reveals that they are assumed to be comparable in ways that would not spring readily to our minds. "The best in the chorus are stationed on the left . . . since in choruses the left side is more honorable, in battles the right."[96] Mention *eutaxia* and the conversation will turn as readily to precision movement in a dancing corps as to gymnastics or the timed stroke of oars (Xenophon, *Mem.* 3.5.18), even implying that dancing is more disciplined than generalship since war maneuvers are often improvised (Xenophon, *Mem.* 3.5.21). The grandest such comparison is surely the elaborate comparison of polyphonic choral singing, where all the various voices await the leader's signal, and the coordinated responses of soldiers to a general's command ([Aristotle], *De mundo* 399a15–b10).

The homology extends to the accompanying music (Dorian in large part) and the instrument (aulos).[97] The presence of an aulos-player is one way of identifying the earliest representations of hoplite fighters on seventh-century vases.[98] The Spartans took this so seriously that they employed numerous aulos players in unison (*pollōn homou*, Thoukydides 5.70, who does not, *pace* Lorimer and others, say that the Spartans *alone* marched to the flute; they may have invented the technique or may have been best known for it, as Aristotle [quoted by Aulus Gellius, *Attic Nights* 1.11.17–19] alleged, but they did not patent it). Thoukydides also makes clear that the point of the music is not to raise spirits but to ensure rhythmic stepping and so to maintain *taxis*. The aulos-player who served on Athenian triremes evidently had the same function (*IG* II² 1951.100).

We may have a depiction of such precision dancing on a red-figure column-krater in the Mannerist style, ca. 500–490 B.C.E. (plate 6).[99] Six performers arranged in three pairs move with identical steps and upraised arms toward or past a tomb, behind which a cloaked figure stands. His open mouth indicates that he is not the trainer or the *khorēgos* or the god

---

sages are called *laurostatai*; the worse performers are stationed in the middle, the principal ones are placed first and last," Hesykhios, s.v. *Laurostatai*; "the underlap of the chorus: the valueless positions of the choral station," Hesykhios, s.v. *Hyokolpion tou chorou*, cited at *DFA*, 241 n. 1.

96 Scholiast on Aristeides (3.535, ed. Dindorf), cited in *DFA*, 241 n. 1.

97 On the Dorian mode and the occasional use of other modes for special effect in tragedy, see *DFA*, 258–60.

98 Hilda L. Lorimer, "The Hoplite Phalanx," *BSA* 42 (1947): 76–138. "It must be conceded, however, that experiments in the handling of massed infantry had been undertaken before [the mid-seventh century]: an observant critic has recently drawn attention to the presence, in a battle-scene on a Corinthian vase of about 675, of a piper [i.e., *aulētēs*]—an indispensable participant in the later Spartan phalanx where his music kept the men in step, and therefore perhaps a sign of incipient phalanx tactics, although the morale-boosting effect of military pipers, as modern parallels show, is not confined to those operating in close formation."

99 Antikenmuseum Basel, Inv. BS 415: Margot Schmidt, "Dionysien," *AK* 19 (1967): 70–81.

Dionysos but a performer, most likely a ghost emerging from the tomb. Invisible on the photograph, letters at the dancers' open mouths indicate their choral song, though no aulos-player is shown. At that period the tragic chorus consisted of twelve persons, so this group is half a chorus; perhaps we are to imagine the other half approaching the tomb from the other side.

M. Schmidt, who first published this vase, was inclined to believe that they were dancing a dithyramb, but their rectangular formation and their costumes argue for tragedy rather than dithyramb.[100] Dithyrambists could perform in splendid array,[101] but not in mask or character costume. The attempt to see a satyr chorus on a red-figure krater by Polion of about 425 B.C.E. as dithyrambic performers in costume misreads that vase entirely.[102] The label *OIDOI PANATHENAIA*, "Singers at the Panathenaia," above three aged Pappasilenoi does not mean that actual dithyrambic choruses at the Panathenaia did or could dress up as satyrs (nor even that there were comic turns at the Panathenaia.)[103] The aulos-player facing them holds his pipes down at his sides, in consternation not only at these singers' lyres[104] but at their identity.[105] These are not regulation contestants but wild men who, monkeylike, imitate forms of civilized behavior.[106]

It seems likely from the chin line that the six choristers are indeed wearing masks, in which case they would be, in my interpretation, ephebes dressed as a chorus of ephebes, as in Aiskhylos' *Neaniskoi* or

---

[100] Heide Fröning, *Dithyrambos und Vasenmalerei in Athen*, Beiträge zur Archäologie 2 (Wärzburg, 1971), 23–24; Erika Simon, *The Ancient Theatre*, trans. C. E. Vafopoulou-Richardson (London, 1982), 8–9.

[101] Demosthenes sponsored a men's dithyrambic chorus in 351–350 which wore gold crowns (21.16).

[102] New York 25.78.66; Bieber, *History*, fig. 17; *DTC*, 20, 34, pl. 1.

[103] J. D. Beazley, "Hydria-Fragments in Corinth," *Hesperia* 24 (1955): 305–19 (314–15). Bieber, *History*, 6 (fig. 17) relates it to a comedy, Kratinos' *Satyroi* (424 B.C.E.), without commenting on the label *PANATHENAIA*.

[104] "It would be very remarkable for participants in a dithyrambic chorus each to play his own instrumental accompaniment." Fröning, *Dithyrambos*, 25.

[105] "The aulos-player stands there thunderstruck like a tavern-keeper who one day sees three of his best customers, now converted soldiers in the Salvation Army, march into his saloon with Bible and hymnbook in hand rather than their usual bottle and drinking-mug." Ervin Roos, *Die tragische Orchestik im Zerrbild der altattischen Komödie* (Lund, 1951), 228. Roos sees the scene as a comic takeoff on Perikles' reorganization of musical contests at the Panathenaia and suggests a relationship with three lyre-playing satyrs on a black-figure amphora of the late sixth century (227–30, figs. 32–33). Fröning, *Dithyrambos*, 25–26 suggests that it represents a satyr-play on the subject of the founding of the Panathenaia, comparable to Aiskhylos' *Isthmiastai*.

[106] Elsewhere satyrs pretend to be honest citizens by wearing cloaks (*ARV²* 175, no. 16) and carrying staffs instead of *thyrsoi* (*ARV²* 785, no. 11).

Thespis' *Ēitheoi*. More importantly for the correct interpretation of this vase, dithyrambists formed a circle, not a rectangle. For contrast consider the dithyrambic men's chorus represented on an Attic red-figure bell-krater in Copenhagen, ca. 425 B.C.E.[107] Five bearded (not masked) men in single file, the central one facing forward, are dressed in fancy chitons and wraparound cloaks (not as characters), and they are singing to the accompaniment of an aulos-player. While five unmasked and uncostumed men in a ring may represent fifty dithyrambists, six masked and costumed performers in rectangular formation cannot be dithyrambists but must represent a semichorus of early fifth century tragedy—or something very like it.

In presenting the Pronomos Vase, I left it open whether its chorus members are to be thought of as ephebes in the loose sense of boys-who-are-almost-men or in the stricter sense of young Athenian citizens in military training. The evidence of choral dancing in tragedy seems to me an irresistible argument for the relevance of the specifically military aspect of their young manhood, however their training in those skills may have been organized by and for the *polis*.

At Athens our information converges from two directions and just misses meeting at a description of ephebic military dancing in the theater of Dionysos. On the one hand, we know of athletic-esthetic training for young males which both prepared them for war and led to the Theater of Dionysos (Aristoxenos, middle or later fourth century B.C.E. (Athenaios, 631c). On the other hand, the late fourth-century ephebes performed—not in disguise but as themselves—in the same theater. These two lines of information, which I will now trace, approach each other asymptotically; the ephebic hypothesis closes the gap.

Several forms of young men's proto-military training are known which resembled the martial arts in their combination of graceful, rhythmic movement with the physical and spiritual training of a warrior. Recommending an esthetics of restraint, Athenaios praises classical, specifically pre-Hellenistic, culture as a period when the postures of statues and the styles of dancing were equally dignified (14.629b–c). "They transferred the poses [of sculpted figures] to the choruses." Images of effete pseudo-classical dancing may spring to the mind's eye at this point, but he goes on: "and from the choruses to the wrestling mats" (629b). The governing idea behind this language of dignity in posture and movement is the athletic body, disciplined to a state of tough grace. "In their music and in the care of their bodies they aimed at masculinity [*andreia*,

---

[107] *ARV²* 1145; *DTC*, pl. 1b; K. Friis Johansen, "Eine Dithyrambosaufführung," *Arkaeologisk-kunsthistoriske Meddelelser udgivet af Det Kongelige Danske Videnshabernes Selskab*, Bind 4, no. 2 (Copenhagen, 1959).

down-translated as 'courage'], and to be able to move in heavy armor they prepared themselves with song: that is the origin of the so-called pyrrhics and all such styles of dancing" (629c).

The two most prominent versions of this martial art for male adolescents, both always described as dances, are *gymnopaidikē* and *pyrrhikhē*. The former was a gentler exercise which imitated wrestling and *pankration*: "The *gymnopaidikē* is similar to the dance called *anapalē* in the old days. All the boys dance it naked, performing various rhythmic movements and various figures with their arms in a gentle manner, and thus depict scenes from the wrestling school and the *pankration*, moving their feet in rhythm."[108] Two etymologies of the older term *anapalē* seem to be contained in Athenaios' (or his source's) description of the *gymnopaidikē*, one from "gentle" (*hapalos*) and another from "wrestling" (*palē*). The latter seems considerably more likely,[109] but both designate the dance as a preparatory stage for the less gentle, partly weaponed *pyrrhikhē*, a fast, warlike dance performed by *enhoploi paides*, older boys in partial armor.[110]

Both *gymnopaidikē* and *pyrrhikhē* are simply the Athenian versions of what must have been a universal practice in all Greek cities. In other cities, besides the dances described by Xenophon for the Thracians, Thessalians (Ainianians, Magnesians), Mysians, and Arkadians (*Anabasis* 6.1.5–13), we hear of dances in armor with the names *telesias*, *orsitēs*, and *epikrēdios*.[111] Ephoros (fourth century B.C.E.) described the training of

[108] Athenaios, 631b–c (trans. Andrew Barker, *Greek Musical Writings*, [Cambridge, Eng., 1984] 1:290–91). Note also "the *gymnopaidikē* is comparable to the tragic dance called *emmeleia*: weightiness and solemnity may be observed in each." Athenaios, 630e (trans. Barker, 289).

[109] "A transference of a technique, and the description of it, from wrestling to hoplite fighting is scarcely surprising when one remembers how firmly the Greeks believed that the former was an important and essential training for the latter, so that one might become *brithus hoplitopalas, daios antipaloisi* (Aiskhylos, fr. 700 Mette) ['a weighty hoplite-wrestler, ferocious to one's antagonists,' in which Aiskhylos underlines the faded metaphor of wrestling implied in *antipalos*]." E. K. Borthwick, "Two Scenes of Combat in Euripides," *JHS* 90 (1970): 15–21 (18).

[110] "The pyrrhic is like the satyric, since both are speedy; it seems to be warlike since boys in armor dance it; speed is necessary in battle both for pursuit and for the losers to flee" (Athenaios, 630d). W.E.D. Downes, "The Offensive Weapon in the Pyrrhic," *CR* 18 (1904): 101–6; J.-C. Poursat, "Les représentations de danse armée dans la céramique attique," *BCH* 92 (1968): 550–615; Paolo Scarpi, "La pyrrichē o le armi della persuasione," *DArch*, n.s. 1 (1979): 78–97. That the pyrrhicists were somewhat older than the gymnopaidicists is indicated not only by the fact that they needed greater strength to carry the metal equipment but by such phrases as "beardless pyrrhicists" (Lysias, 21.4), indicating that the dancers were man-size boys.

[111] "That is the origin of the so-called pyrrhics and all such styles of [proto-military] dancing; numerous in fact are their names, e.g., the Kretans' *orsitēs* and *epikrēdios*" (629c); "There is also the dance called the *telesias*—a military dance taking its name from a certain

Kretan boys, who from an early age were trained to use army gear (*hopla*), to harden themselves to blows in the gymnasium and in battle formation, and specifically to dance in armor. "In order that courage [*andreia*], not cowardice, might prevail, the lawgiver commanded that from boyhood they should be raised with armor [*hopla*] and hard labor, so as to scorn heat, cold, rugged and steep roads, and blows received in gymnasiums or phalanx [*kata suntagma*] battles; and that they should practice both archery and armored dancing [*enhoplioi orkhēsei*], which was first displayed by the Kourētes and later by him who organized [*suntaksanta*] the pyrrhic, named after himself, so that not even their boyish play should be without something useful for warfare . . . and that armor [*hopla*] should be the most valued gift given to them" (Strabo, 10.4.16).

The younger boys' dances were evidently meant to develop their poise, strength, and stamina as future citizen-soldiers. The dancing of the *tragōidoi* was a still harder exercise in the same qualities: just think of the sheer physical endurance required to perform all the singing and dancing of three tragedies and one satyr-play consecutively. Performing in a tragic chorus must have been an athletic feat as exacting and grueling as any of the Olympic competitions. Indeed, this is a strong reason for accepting the youth of such choruses as an across-the-board rule, not just a peculiarity of the chorus depicted on the Pronomos Vase. Certainly, the older the man, the less all-around vigor he usually has, especially for sustained, energetic dancing, as Teiresias and Kadmos agree in Euripides' *Bakkhai* 175–209.

Aristoxenos connects the two boys' dances as phases of a regular sequence: "Aristoxenos says that the ancients first practiced *gymnopaidikē*, then progressed to *pyrrhikhē* before they entered into the theater" (Athenaios, 631c). From this we know that, in the view of this prominent fourth-century music historian, himself the author of *On Choruses* and *On Tragic Dancing*, Dionysos' theater was and had been since archaic times the final stage where boys well-trained in military dancing would perform. To what might this refer? The boys' dithyramb is a possibility, though nothing suggests that it had the quasi-military features of tragic choral dancing. Did the rectangular pyrrhic choruses perform in the theater? I propose that the athletic-cultural *cursus* described by Aristoxenos moves from the younger boys' unarmed wrestling dance to the older boys' armed solo dance and culminates "in the theater" with the ephebes' tragic marching, a small corps display of virtuoso dancing that was, in coordination and in refinement, one grade higher than the vigorous, paramilitary dancing of boy soloists.

---

man Telesias who first danced it in full armor [*meth' hoplōn*]" (630a = Hippagoras, *FGrHist* 743F1).

From the other side we have one secure witness to the institutionalized ephebes actually performing in a body in the presence of Dionysos and the people, though what they perform is a regular drill of the whole class rather than a virtuoso display by three top squads of fifteen each: "In their second year, before an Assembly convened *in the theater*, the ephebes made a display to the populace of all that pertained to *taxeis* [orderly formations]" ([Aristotle], *Ath. Pol.* 42.4). Though some translators have fudged the word *taxeis* with vague renderings such "their military skill" (Fritz and Kapp) or "their knowledge of warfare" (Moore), "the reference here should be to their skill at maneuvering in formation."[112]

The early fifth-century vase showing six young men doing a precision dance in three pairs fits neatly here as an image of that toward which both wings of our evidence converge.[113] Altogether, the evidence is richly suggestive of the cultural framework within which my hypothesis operates, though it falls short of converting that hypothesis into an ironclad surety.

In sum, then, our evidence about tragic performance contains reasonably strong indications that the chorus members were young men in (or viewed in relation to) military training. If true, this would allow us to sense a complex and finely controlled tension between role and role-player, for the ephebes are cast in the most "disciplined" part of the tragedy—disciplined in the exacting demands of unison movement, subordinated to the more prominent actors, and characterized as social dependents (women, slaves, old men)—while the actors, who are no longer ephebes, perform a tale showing the risks, the misfortunes, and sometimes the glory of ephebic experience. Occasionally in performance there may be a tentative allusion to the reality under the costume, as when the senior citizens of Aiskhylos' *Agamemnon*, too old to serve in the expedition to Troy ("our strength is like a boy's . . . there's no War in us," 72–78), declare that old men are "ephebic" in their willingness to learn (*hēbāi tois gerousin*, 584) and at the climax make an attempt to resist Aigisthos' takeover as if they were an armed squadron (*lokhitai*, 1650).[114]

What most makes the tension come alive is the scrutiny of the watchful audience, the body politic of Athens arranged in seating which confirms both their individual competitive spirit and their precarious, hard-won civic unity. These social tensions in the audience are focused on the cru-

---

[112] Rhodes, *Commentary*, 508, aptly citing Plato, *Lakhes* 182a7–b7 and Xenophon, *Kyropaidia* 2.2.6–7. "In later centuries the *apodeixis* was made not to the assembly but to the boule (first in *Hesp.* vii 20, 17–18, of 258/7)," Rhodes, *Commentary*, 508.

[113] Antikenmuseum Basel, Inv. BS 415: Schmidt, "Dionysien."

[114] E. Fraenkel follows Stanley in assigning *Agamemnon* 1650 to Aigisthos, holding that the *philoi lokhitai* are his bodyguards.

cial and central transition-figures of the youngest warriors, who are (as it were) the growth point, the bud and flower of the city. Tragedy is the city's nurturance of that precious youth by a public ritual of discipline, enacting tales (more often than not) of its blight.

IV. A CONJECTURE

Tragōidoi seems obviously to mean "billy goat-singers"—not just "goat-singers." Connections between Dionysos and generic goats, such as the famous antipathy between the goat and the grapevine,[115] should not be relevant to the specifically masculine term *tragōidoi*.[116] The etymology is as patent as its significance is obscure.[117] Given the habits of sophistic playfulness,[118] and the reluctance of ancient scholars ever to doubt that the path of least resistance to an explanation was correct, it would be amazing if someone had not conjectured that a billy goat was the prize for the winning tragic chorus. This conjecture is indeed found in a document of the third century B.C.E.—a chronology of famous events in Greek history with a special emphasis on data of literary interest.[119] The notion became dogma and was repeated numerous times by later ancient writers, though other possibilities long continued to be entertained. It may even be true, but it can hardly be anything else than a good guess. The exhaustive inquiry of W. Burkert[120] finds goats from earliest times in the pictorial and literary entourage of Dionysos but no explicit evidence of a goat-prize or (what would be in this context the same thing) a goat-sacrifice. Burkert nevertheless believes that a goat was sacrificed to Dionysos and that *tragōidoi* were named from this.[121]

---

[115] Pausanias, 2.13.6.

[116] The paradoxical term *tragaina*, "female billy goat," is used by Aristotle of a hermaphrodite goat, *Generation of Animals* 770b35.

[117] For fun one may cite J. E. Harrison, "Is Tragedy the Goat-Song?" *CR* 16 (1902): 331–32, who proposes, by emending Stephanos, s.v. *tragos*, that tragedy is a beer-song.

[118] Plato, *Kratylos* 408c–d is the earliest association of tragedy with goats—because of their rough (*trakh-*) hides.

[119] A long marble inscription found on the island of Paros, hence known as the Marmor Parium; *FGrHist* 239.

[120] Burkert, "Greek Tragedy."

[121] My reservations about Burkert's magisterial treatment have to do not with the existence of a goat prize but with the elaboration of a cultural performance on sacrificial themes (his interpretation of tragedy) at the one festival for which a sacrificial prize is least attested. If tragedy as such is viewed as mainly and originally about issues of sacrifice, it might as well have developed at any of the numerous animal slaughters of ancient Greece. Further, that it should have grown from the sacrifice of a goat rather than, say, a bull seems to me faintly ludicrous: can we imagine Aiskhylos saying of great Agamemnon that he was cut down like a goat at the manger? In reply, however, it might be possible to hold that it was precisely because there was *not* a literal enactment of an animal sacrifice (or only a slightly

As it happens, there is a hitherto-unnoticed billy goat sacrifice on Ela-
phebolion 10, the first day of the City Dionysia, not in Athens proper
but in the Marathonian Tetrapolis—*IG* II² 1358b17–18. Surely this could
be regarded as the smoking gun to confirm Burkert's theory. But no
sooner does the evidence for it once appear propitious than it confounds
us with its generosity, for on that sacred calendar the billy goat victim is
specified as one that is all black (*pammelas*). This is just as surely a confirmation of the ephebic symbolism of the Dionysian black goatskin seen
by Vidal-Naquet. Were *tragōidoi* so called because they sang at the sacrifice of a billy goat, or was an all-black billy goat sacrificed in a northern
region of Attika in solidarity with the ephebic celebration going on in
Athens at the Dionysia? The ephebic hypothesis makes another interpretation of the name itself possible, one which does not entail the denial of
a goat-prize/sacrifice, but may stand independently beside it.

It goes like this. In dealing with the social institution of the Athenian
ephebate we should try to give equal weight to the practical discipline
which exercises young men in doing what men are to do (march in file
and be honorable and prudent) and to the symbolic inversions that variously informed that liminal period. Such inversions also have their practical side. For instance, just as it still happens in modern military training,
the young men are degraded in order to be upgraded: that is, they are insulted as sissies, girls, and crybabies in order to promote their decisive rejection of all boyishness. The army, as we say, turns boys into men: "and
they were not allowed to return to the city until they had become
men."[122] Here we must briefly allude to the well-known distinction between physical puberty and social puberty.[123] A rite of passage to manhood is symbolically a puberty rite which may take place years after a
boy's body has begun to undergo the physical changes of adolescence.

With this in mind I will simply mention that, among the meanings of
tragos, only one has any prima facie connection to the human voice or to
singing (*-ōidos*). Aristotle, once in a discussion of puberty and again in a
discussion of voice-pitch,[124] uses the word *tragizein* to mean the breaking
or changing in voice which adolescent boys experience. Aristotle attaches "what they call" (*ho kalousi*) to *tragizein*, indicating that adolescent

---

ludicrous one) that a choral meditation on sacrifice developed at the Dionysia. A billy goat
is sacrificed for a city foundation in Aristophanes, *Birds* (902, 959, 1056–57), but that, of
course, may be some sort of joke.

[122] Justin, 3.3 on the Spartan *krypteia*.

[123] Arnold van Gennep, *The Rites of Passage*, trans. M. B. Vizedom and G. L. Caffee
(Chicago, 1960), chap. 6.

[124] Aristotle, *History of Animals* 7.1; *Generation of Animals* 5.7.787b32–788a2. The words
continue in use; see Porphyry on Ptolemy's *Harmony* 253a; Alexander of Aphrodisias *Problemata* 1.125.

voice-change is not the primary referent of the root *trag-* but one that is in use in some special circumstance which his reader might need reminding of. An analogy would be our use of "frog" in the phrase "a frog in one's throat": the word "frog" alone does not make one think of a person with a hoarse voice. The usage also occurs in [Aristotle], *De audibilibus* 804a17, and in later writers.[125] The term at Hippokrates, *Epidemics* 6.3.14 may refer to voice-breaking or it may be a general expression for those undergoing puberty: *epēn aphrodisiazein arxōntai ē tragizein*, "whenever they begin to be sexually active or to *tragizein*."

I propose that *tragōidoi* began as a slightly jocular designation of ephebic singers, not because their voices were breaking (that was long past, and anyway no one can sing well whose voice is breaking) but because they were identified as those undergoing social puberty.[126] More accurately, they were *representative* of those undergoing social puberty: only a select group of the best ephebic singer-dancers could actually perform.[127] Given the low repute of goats, not to mention goatherds, the name must be regarded—perhaps paradoxically to us—as a somewhat comic formation.[128]

Other derived senses of the *tragos* word-family can be related to the actual being of goats—rank smell, indiscriminate lust; like ephebes, goats are noticeably wayward and must be controlled.[129] On one level, *tragi-*

---

[125] Porphyry on Ptolemy's *Harmony*, 253a; Alexander of Aphrodisias, *Problemata* 1.125; Hesykhios, s.v. *tragizein*.

[126] There may be a more literal aspect which reinforced this metaphorical designation of their singing. David S. Margoliouth, *The Poetics of Aristotle* (London, 1911), 61–62, brought adolescent voice-breaking into connection with tragedy on the basis of the mournful and *uneven* nature of the singing, as described by [Aristotle], *Problems* 19.6: "for in great misfortune or grief the uneven [*anōmales*] is expressive [*pathētikon*], while the even is less mournful." The same language is found in Aristotle's discussion of voice-change during puberty, *History of Animals* 7.1 (*anōmalesteron, homalē*, 581a18–19) and *Generation of Animals* 5.7 (*anōmalos*, 788a1). The goat's voice is also related to the thin, bleating voices of epileptics; Plutarch, *Quaestiones Romanae* 111 (290a), Hippokrates, *Sacred Disease* 4.21.

[127] Because of this, I have not stressed what will seem to many the most obvious connection between *rites de passage* and the ephebes' tragic chorus—their sometimes dressing as women. The ephebes as a group have just as important a role to play in the festival by being in the audience as their representative best dancers and singers do by being in the orchestra. Further, the key ephebic issues are family and political authority, responsibility to the gods and the dead, and a young man's maximizing of personal *timē* without insulting his peers or betters. Gender is a key item in the system, but it is a dependent rather than an independent variable. Finally, they did not always dress as women; sometimes they even dressed as ephebes.

[128] As was held by the ancient scholar reported in the *Etymologicum Magnum*, who said that tragedy is so called "because the choruses were mainly composed of satyrs, whom they jokingly [*skōptontes*] called billy goats."

[129] Plutarch remarks that dogs and billy goats exemplify lack of self-control and proneness to pleasure; *Conjugalia Praecepta* 139b, cf. *Quaestiones Romanae* 111 (290a); Ailianos, *De*

zein used of the boy's voice may simply mean "bleat," but the implications are probably wider. It may in the Greek folk-system also be a way of saying that a boy's change of voice is a warning sign of the onset of other goatlike qualities. *Tragizein* (and *tragān*) might best be translated "to go through puberty," "to show the signs of adolescence," of which voice-change is only one. The noun *tragos* indicates another such change in its occurrence in a cryptic Hippokratic saying at *Epidemics* 6.4.21 about the swelling of a boy's testicles at puberty: *tragos, hokoteros an phanēi exō orkhis, dexios, arsen, euōnumos, thēlu*, "billy goat, whichever testicle appears outside, right-side male, left-side female,"[130] on which Galen commented.[131] Martial, 3.24, associates the billy goat's foul smell specifically with its testicles, which are cut off at the moment of sacrifice. Burkert deduces from this that "the procedure was the same at every he-goat sacrifice."[132] Aristotle's explanation of the connection between testicular and vocal change is in terms of mechanics: the increased tension caused by heavier testes on the channels that lead from the scrotum through the heart to the vocal chords causes the voice to drop lower; he compares the effect to that of loom weights.[133] Two activities affect this natural process—sexual activity accelerates it; the voice exercises of boys who take frequent part in choruses retards it.[134] We seem to have in the *tragos* word-group a coherent and rather interesting view of puberty as a complex of new smells, attitudes, and bodily changes summed up in the emblem of the goat.[135]

---

natura animalium 7.19; Adamantios Judaeus, *Physiognomika* 2.2.14; on the malodor of billy goats, Herodotos, 3.112 (*dusodmatatoï*); Horace, *Satires* 1.2.27; Seneca, *Epistulae* 86.13; *tragion* is the name of a plant which stinks like a billy goat in the fall; Dioskorides, 4.50. E. Eyben, "Antiquity's View of Puberty," *Latomus* 31 (1972): 678–97, esp. 688–91 on the voice and smell of teenage boys.

[130] Cf. *Epidemics* 2.5.1. Latin has an analogous usage of *hirquitallus* from *hircus*, "goat," for boys becoming men: *hirquitalli pueri primum ad uirilitatem accedentes: a libidine [sc. hircorum] dicti*; Paulus, *Festus* 101M; 105M. Censorinus brings this Latin expression into conjunction with the Greek and mentions the connection with voice rather than lust: *in secunda hebdomade, uel incipiente tertia, uocem crassiorem et inaequabilem fieri quod appellat [tragizein], antiqui nostri hirquitallire*; Censorinus, *De die natali* 5.

[131] *De usu partium* 14.7 (4.172–74. Kühn) and Galen's commentary on *Epidemics* 6 (17b211ff. Kühn). See also *De semine* 2.5 (4.633 Kühn).

[132] *Homo Necans: The Anthropology of Ancient Greek Sacrificial Ritual and Myth* (Berkeley, 1983), 68.

[133] *Generation of Animals* 787b20–788a7.

[134] *History of Animals* 581a21–27.

[135] Professor Evelyn B. Harrison drew my attention to Plutarch's account that Theseus, just before he set sail to Krete (the last and greatest of his ephebic exploits), was sacrificing a she-goat by the seaside and it suddenly turned into a he-goat; *Theseus* 18. This story illustrates not only the dramatic change of state that ephebes were thought to go through but the complex involvement of several divinities and social classes: Theseus' sacrifice is di-

This last line of argument about boys' breaking voices is very speculative indeed. Even without it, the hypothesis I have offered remains, I think, a stable construction, one whose interest lies in its suggestive recentering of the field of Attic tragedy as a very specific form of social and religious ritual, a hypothesis whose power is drawn from its new integration of discrete realms of information. The surviving scripts, of course, are highly elaborated compositions, built on this framework of social concerns as some clay statues are built on a wire core: the core supports and is concealed by the visible exterior of the statue. The complete picture is bound to be more complex and detailed than I have sketched, but I propose that, as a ground-plan for the City Dionysia, these features of the original presentation and social occasion show us that the audience's experience of tragedy was built on a profoundly political core, and that Athens' youngest citizen-soldiers occupied a central (though in various ways masked) role in this festival of self-representation.

---

rected to Aphrodite, and the story is tied to a procession of Athenian maidens to the temple of Apollo Delphinios on Mounykhion.

FROMA I. ZEITLIN

Playing the Other: Theater, Theatricality, and the Feminine in Greek Drama

FOR A SPECIMEN of sheer theatrical power, it would be difficult to match the climactic scene of Euripides' *Bakkhai* (788–861) where Pentheus at last comes under the spell of his adversary, the god Dionysos, and acknowledges his secret desire to spy on the women of Thebes who have left the city to go as maenads to the mountain. His violent antagonism toward the women who, in abandoning their homes, children, and domestic tasks, have challenged the civic, masculine authority of the king, gives way to a sudden softening of will—a yielding to the cunning wiles of the god disguised onstage as the Asiatic stranger, the leader of his own troops of maenads. This first surrender is followed by another. In giving up his original intention to marshal his forces for an open combat of men against women, Pentheus gives up his stubborn claim to an unequivocal masculine identity. To see what the women are doing without himself being seen, Pentheus must trade his hoplite military tactics for an undercover operation, which involves adopting a devious stratagem and assuming a remarkable disguise. He must let the god take him inside the palace and dress him as a woman in a flowing wig and headdress, a long pleated robe and belt, to which he adds the typical insignia of the maenads—the dappled fawnskin and ritual thyrsus. When the god completes this elaborate toilette, Pentheus will also resemble Dionysos himself, whose effeminate appearance the king had earlier mocked.[1] But as much

Note: This essay was originally published (with some small differences) in *Representations* 11 (1985): 63–94, and is reprinted here through their kind permission. An earlier, reduced version of this paper was presented at a conference, "After the Second Sex," held at the University of Pennsylvania, and at a symposium honoring Professor Helen Bacon at Barnard College in New York, both in April 1984. I wish to thank the commentators on these two occasions, Carolyn Heilbrun and Marylin Arthur, respectively, as well as others who participated in the discussion. Thanks also to the members of the Women's Studies Colloquium at Princeton University, who offered acute and thoughtful comments at the presentation of this paper; in particular, Natalie Davis, Suzanne Keller, and Elaine Showalter. Jean Rudhardt and Philippe Borgeaud also made useful remarks at the University of Geneva, as did Claude Calame at the University of Lausanne. I am especially grateful to Jack Winkler, Simon Goldhill, and Jean-Pierre Vernant, who read the manuscript and from whose incisive and valuable criticism I have, as always, greatly profited. Finally, I gratefully acknowledge the assistance of a fellowship from the Guggenheim Foundation in 1984–1985, under whose auspices this work was completed.

[1] E.g., *Bakkhai* 451–59; Dionysos is called *thēlymorphos*, 351 (cf. Pentheus' description as *gynaikomorphos* [his costume as imitating a woman's, *gynaikomimoi*; 981]).

as they might seem doubles of one another, the power relations between them have been decisively reversed. Now Dionysos will turn Pentheus from the one who acts to the one who is acted upon, from the one who would inflict pain and suffering, even death, on the other, to the one who will undergo those experiences himself. For now, however, the preliminary sign of Pentheus' total defeat, first at the hands of Dionysos and then at the hands of the women, is given to us onstage in the visual feminization of Pentheus when he is induced against all inhibitions of shame to adopt the costume and gestures of a woman.

But if feminization is the emblem of Pentheus' defeat, Dionysos' effeminacy is a sign of his hidden power. Here are two males, cousins in fact through their genealogical ties, both engaged in a masculine contest for supremacy. One, however, gains mastery by manipulating a feminized identity, and the other is vanquished when he finally succumbs to it. What we might perceive in their ensemble at the moment when the two males appear together onstage in similar dress is an instructive spectacle of the inclusive functions of the feminine in the drama—one on the side of femininity as power and the other on the side of femininity as weakness.

Pentheus, first ashamed of wearing women's clothing, and terrified that he will make a ridiculous spectacle of himself for all the city to see, now has a fleeting intimation of the new force he has acquired; he exults in the surge of unnatural physical strength that suffuses him, and dreams of uprooting mountains with his bare hands. But under the god's gentle prodding, he just as eagerly abandons his desire for violence to acquiesce with pleasure in the contrary tactics of hiding and deception by which he will confront the women on their own terms (953–56). The moment of triumph and confidence, however, is brief. We know in advance what the fate of Pentheus will be once the feminized god Dionysos, who plays his role to perfection, delivers his disguised victim, his man clumsily concealed in woman's dress, to the "real" women who will tear the imposter apart in a terrible ritual *sparagmos*, while the god reverts to his function of divine spectator at the drama he has arranged onstage.

I have chosen to begin with the robing of Pentheus, for beyond its dramatic impact within the context of the play, the mechanics of this scene also suggest a wider and more emblematic set of significations. These refer both to the conditions of Dionysiac ritual itself as a deadly version of initiation into the mysteries of the god's worship, and to the conditions of the theater of Dionysos and the accepted terms of its artistic representations.[2] For the first, Pentheus must be dressed as a woman for conse-

---

[2] For the fullest account of this hypothesis, see Richard Seaford, "Dionysiac Drama and Dionysiac Mysteries," CQ 31 (1981): 252–75.

cration to the god as the surrogate beast-victim he will become in the ritual on the mountain; for the second, the costuming of Pentheus reminds us that the theater requires mimetic disguise by which it creates and maintains its status as dramatic festival.[3] Through this scene we arrive at the dynamic basis of Greek drama, catching a glimpse of the secrets of its ritual prehistory as it merges with and is imitated by the techniques of the theater. In particular, the fact that Pentheus dons a feminine costume and rehearses in it before our eyes exposes perhaps one of the most marked features of Greek theatrical mimesis: that men are the only actors in this civic theater; in order to represent women onstage, men must always put on a feminine costume and mask.[4] What this means is that it is not a woman who speaks or acts for herself and in herself onstage; it is always a man who impersonates her.[5]

If we consider that in order to direct the proceedings of the drama, to manipulate its theatrical effects, contrive its plots, set its stage, and control its mimetic play of illusion and reality, Dionysos, the god of the theater, must also take on womanish traits, then perhaps we may venture yet further: can there be some intrinsic connections linking the phenomenon of Athenian tragedy, invented and developed in a historical context as a civic art form, and what the society culturally defined as feminine in its sex/gender system?[6]

There is nothing new in stressing the associations of Dionysos and the feminine for the Greek theater. After all, madness, the irrational, and the emotional aspects of life are associated in the culture more with women than with men. The boundaries of women's bodies are perceived as more fluid, more permeable, more open to affect and entry from the outside,

[3] For the metatheatrical aspects of this scene in particular (and the play as a whole), see Helene Foley, "The Masque of Dionysus," *TAPA* 110 (1981): 107–33; and Charles Segal, *Dionysiac Poetics and Euripides' Bacchae* (Princeton, 1982), 215–71.

[4] See further Froma I. Zeitlin, "Travesties of Gender and Genre in Aristophanes' *Thesmophoriazousae*," in *Reflections of Women in Antiquity*, ed. Helene P. Foley (New York and London, 1981), 169–217 (a shorter version appears in *Critical Inquiry* 8 [1981]: 301–28, and is collected in *Writing and Difference*, ed. E. Abel [Chicago, 1982], 131–58).

[5] It should be noted that, unlike other public Dionysiac festivals in Attika (and elsewhere) where both men and women participate, the City Dionysia seems to belong to men only (with the sole exception of a girl assigned to carry the ritual basket in the preliminary procession).

[6] The question I raise here about the development of drama in Athens and its political and social motivations is obviously too complex for this limited discussion. I would suggest merely that the historical conditions of drama, interestingly enough, coincide with a period that sharply polarizes definitions and distinctions of masculine and feminine roles. Drama, like the woman, we might say, is useful for its society, and at the same time potentially subversive and destructive. It is also worth remarking that as theater reaches its full flowering in the fifth century, the iconography of Dionysos undergoes a shift in the vase paintings from a masculine, bearded figure to one, more youthful, who displays effeminate and more androgynous features.

less easily controlled by intellectual and rational means. This perceived physical and cultural instability renders women weaker than men; it is also all the more a source of disturbing power over them, as reflected in the fact that in the divine world it is, for the most part, feminine agents who, in addition to Dionysos, inflict men with madness—whether Hera, Aphrodite, the Erinyes, or even Athena, as in Sophokles' *Ajax*.

On the other hand, we might want to view the androgyny of Dionysos, already in Aiskhylos called a *gunnis* (womanish man) and *pseudanor* (counterfeit man, frag. 61 Nauck²), as a true mixture of masculine and feminine. This mixture, it can be argued, is one of the emblems of his paradoxical role as disrupter of the normal social categories; in his own person he attests to the *coincidentia oppositorum* that challenges the hierarchies and rules of the public masculine world, reintroducing into it confusions, conflicts, tensions, and ambiguities, insisting always on the more complex nature of life than masculine aspirations would allow.[7] Such a view would stress male and female aspects alike; it would regard the god as embodying a dynamic process or as configuring in his person an alternate mode of reality. Convincing as this view may be, it runs the risk of underrating the fact that it is precisely Dionysos' identification with the feminine that gives him and his theater their power.

Along the same lines, in the quest for equivalence of the genders, one could remark, not without justice, that although all the actors in tragedy are men, within the plays feminized males are countered by masculinized women: for example, Aiskhylos' Klytemnestra of the "man-counseling mind" (*Agamemnon*), Euripides' Medea, and, of course, the maenadic Agave herself, who in the *Bakkhai* boasts of her warrior prowess over the body of Pentheus, her yet unrecognized son whom she has killed. This notion of a balanced, symmetrical inversion finds support in Greek festivals outside Athens where men and women change their costumes for a day, each imitating the appearance and behavior of the other.[8] Better yet, there is evidence that in initiation rites at puberty, and sometimes in nuptial arrangements, young men and women in their own spheres temporarily adopt the dress and behavior of the other sex.[9] Such

[7] For the bisexual consciousness of Dionysos, see esp. James Hillman, *The Myth of Analysis* (Evanston, Ill., 1972), 258–66. For the more general paradoxes of Dionysos' role, see the synthesis of Segal, *Dionysiac Poetics*, 10–19.

[8] These festivals are occasions for riotous carnival (e.g., the Kretan Ekdysia, the Argive Hybristika). Dionysiac merriment also lends itself to such behavior, at least as Philostratos, a late source, describes a painting of a Dionysiac revel: "Dionysos is accompanied by a numerous train in which girls mingle with men, for the revel [*kōmos*] allows women to act the part of men, and men to put on women's clothing and play the woman" (*Imagines* 1.2).

[9] On the various forms of transvestism in Greek rite and myth, see Marie Delcourt, *Hermaphrodite: Myths and Rites of the Bisexual Figure in Classical Antiquity*, trans. J. Nicholson (London, 1956), 1–16; Clara Gallini, "Il travestismo rituale di Penteo," *Studi e materiali per*

reversals are usually explained according to a ritual logic that insists that each gender must, for the last time, as it were, act the part of the other before assuming the unequivocal masculine and feminine identities that cultural ideology requires.[10]

As a theoretical concept, this proposition makes eminent sense. On the level of practice, however, these symmetries are often more apparent than real; the notion conforms better with our habits of binary thinking than with recorded evidence, as these rites are far better and more numerously attested for men than for women, not least because their performance, aimed at creating men for the city, is of greater concern to the culture at large.

Second, and more to the point, critics treat inversion of roles as a sufficient explanation in itself—that is, a temporary reversal before its decisive correction. They do not extend their analysis to consider what the various aspects of the actual experience might imply for achieving male identity. What more specifically might these actions and attitudes teach a man? How might the processes of imitating the feminine prepare him for access to adult status, other than to teach him the behaviors he must later scrupulously avoid? Unless there were something to learn and something necessary to repeat, we would not need the genre of tragedy at all to call these different roles into question and, most of all, to challenge the male's civic and rational view of the universe.

Finally, the pairing of feminized men and masculinized women, a useful notion in many respects, runs the risk of assuming mutually inverted categories without looking to the internal dynamics of tragic conventions that shape and predict the conditions of this exchange. Even more, such a concept tends to reduce the scope of the feminine in the drama. It is too limited to encompass the woman's double dimensions— she is a model of both weakness and strength, endowed with traits and capacities that have negative and positive implications for self and society.

Thus my emphasis falls not upon the equal interchange or reversal of male and female roles but upon the predominance of the feminine in the

---

la storia delle religioni 34 (1968): 211–18, esp. 215 n.6; and Walter Burkert, *Structure and History in Greek Mythology and Ritual* (Berkeley, 1979), 29–30.

[10] "For both sexes the initiation through which a young man or woman is confirmed in his or her specific nature may entail, through a ritual exchange of clothing, temporary participation in the nature of the opposite sex whose complement he or she will become by being separated from it." (Jean-Pierre Vernant, "City-State Warfare," in *Myth and Society in Ancient Greece*, trans. J. Lloyd [Sussex, 1980], 24). Cf. also Henri Jeanmaire, *Couroi et Courètes* (Lille, 1939), 153, 321. See further, Pierre Vidal-Naquet, "The Black Hunter and the Origin of the Athenian Ephebeia" and "Recipes for Greek Adolescence," in *Myth, Religion, and Society*, ed. R. L. Gordon (Cambridge, 1981), 147–85. I borrow his term "law of symmetrical inversion."

theater, a phenomenon that used to (and may still) puzzle some commentators, who have perceived a serious discrepancy between the mutedness
of women in Athenian social and political life and their expressive claims
to be heard and seen onstage.[11] And my focus on imbalances rather than
on equivalences between the genders is aimed here not so much at the
content and themes of the various dramas in their political and social dimensions, but on the implications of theater and theatricality as these are
integrally related to and reflective of the thematic preoccupations of
drama. If tragedy can be viewed as a kind of recurrent masculine initiation, for adults as well as for the young,[12] and if drama, more broadly, is
designed as an education for its male citizens in the democratic city, then
the aspects of the play world I wish to bring into sharper relief may well
merit the speculations I am about to offer on theater, representation, plot
and action, experience and identity—all linked in some radical way with
the feminine.

     From the outset, it is essential to understand that in Greek theater, as in
fact in Shakespearean theater, the self that is really at stake is to be identified with the male, while the woman is assigned the role of the radical
other.[13]

[11] The best recent discussion of the question is Helene P. Foley, "The Conception of
Women in Athenian Drama," in *Reflections of Women*, 127–68. This is a judicious and nuanced analysis although it perhaps leans too far in proposing a match between masculine
and feminine roles.

[12] On tragedy as initiation, related both to the mysteries and to puberty rites, see the discussion in Seaford, "Dionysiac Drama" (drawing on the early pioneering work of George
Thomson, *Aeschylus and Athens*, 2d ed. [London, 1946]). For aspects of puberty ritual re-
flected imaginatively in the various dramas see, for Aiskhylos' *Oresteia*, Pierre Vidal-Na-
quet, "Hunting and Sacrifice in Aiskhylos' *Oresteia*," in Jean-Pierre Vernant and Pierre
Vidal-Naquet, *Tragedy and Myth in Ancient Greece*, trans. J. Lloyd (Sussex, 1981), 150, and
Froma I. Zeitlin, "The Dynamics of Misogyny: Myth and Mythmaking in the *Oresteia*,"
Arethusa 11 (1978): 149–84 (now in *Women and the Ancient World: The Arethusa Papers*, ed.
John Peradotto and J. P. Sullivan [Albany, 1984]); for Sophokles' *Philoktetes*, Pierre Vidal-
Naquet, "Sophocles' *Philoctetes* and the Ephebeia," in *Tragedy and Myth*, 175–79; for Euri-
pides' *Hippolytos*, see esp. Charles Segal, "Pentheus and Hippolytus on the Couch and on
the Grid: Psychoanalytic and Structuralist Readings of Greek Tragedy," *CW* 72 (1978–
1979): 129–48 (now in Segal, *Interpreting Greek Tragedy: Myth, Poetry, Text* [Ithaca, N. Y.,
1986], 268–93), and Froma I. Zeitlin, "The Power of Aphrodite: Eros and the Boundaries
of the Self in Euripides' *Hippolytus*," in *Directions in Euripidean Criticism*, ed. Peter Burian
(Durham, N. C., 1985): 52–111, 187–206. For the *Bakkhai*, in addition to Seaford,
"Dionysiac Drama," see Segal, *Dionysiac Poetics*, chap. 6, "Arms and the Man: Sex Roles
and Rites of Passage," 158–214. See also the essay by Winkler in this volume. Also relevant
to these speculations is Louis Montrose, "The Purpose of Playing: Reflections on a Shakespearean Anthropology," *Helios*, n.s. 7.2 (1980): 51–74, who discusses the public functions
of Shakespearean theater as a secularized means of confronting the transitions of life which
had earlier been framed in the milieu of Catholic ritual.

[13] I am indebted here to the stimulating discussion by Linda Bamber, *Comic Women,
Tragic Men: A Study of Gender and Genre in Shakespeare* (Stanford, 1982), as much for its

It perhaps seems unfair that, given the number and importance of female protagonists in Greek tragedy (in contrast, it should be said, to the case of Shakespeare),[14] theoretical critics from Aristotle on never consider anyone but the male hero as the central feature of the genre; they devote their attention to outlining *his* traits, configurations, and dilemmas. Yet despite Klytemnestra, Antigone, Phaidra, Medeia, and many others, it must be acknowledged that this critical blindness is also insight. Even when female characters struggle with the conflicts generated by the particularities of their subordinate social position, their demands for identity and self-esteem are nevertheless designed primarily for exploring the male project of selfhood in the larger world; these demands impinge on men's claims to knowledge, power, freedom, and self-sufficiency—not for greater entitlement or privilege, as some have thought, that the female might gain for herself; not even for revising notions of what femininity might be or mean. Women as individuals or chorus may give their names as titles to plays; female characters may occupy center stage and leave a far more indelible emotional impression on their spectators than do their male counterparts (as does Antigone, for example, over Kreon). But *functionally* women are never an end in themselves, and nothing changes for them once they have lived out their drama onstage. Rather, they play the roles of catalysts, agents, instruments, blockers, spoilers, destroyers, and sometimes helpers or saviors for the male characters. When elaborately represented, they may serve as antimodels as well as hidden models for that masculine self, as we will see, and, concomitantly, their experience of suffering or their acts that lead them to disaster regularly occur before and precipitate those of men.[15]

An excellent case in point is Sophokles' *Trakhiniai*, a play that will serve us well throughout this essay. The distress and despair of Dei-

provocative arguments as for its use in confronting some fundamental differences between the feminine in Greek and in Elizabethan tragedy. There are other "others," to be sure, on the Athenian stage (e.g., barbarians, servants, enemy antagonists, and even gods), but the dialectic of self and other is consistently and insistently predicated on the distinctions between masculine and feminine, far more even than in Shakespeare. Even the plays with more strictly military and political themes (excepting only Sophokles' *Philoktetes*) arrange their plots around critical confrontations between masculine and feminine.

[14] No Shakespearean tragedy has a woman as its main character, although sometimes she shares double billing—Juliet, Cleopatra. By contrast, in extant Greek drama women often lend their individual names or collective functions to the titles (Antigone, Elektra, Medeia; Khoephoroi, Trakhiniai, Bakkhai). Moreover, women play far more extensive roles in Greek tragedy, roles which increase in subtlety and variety as the genre develops.

[15] The functional argument is even more obviously true in the case of those plays, which I will not discuss in this essay, in which the plot revolves around the demand made upon an army for a virgin sacrifice (such as of Iphigeneia and Polyxena) and where female heroic nobility in dying is used most often to offer an ironic counterpoint to masculine *Realpolitik*.

aneira, the innocent, virtuous wife, commands our attention for most of the play. She loses none of our sympathy when unwittingly destroying her husband Herakles for love of him. Yet we come to realize that her entire experience, her actions and reactions, are in truth a route to achieving another goal, the real telos or end of the drama. She is the agent designated to fulfill the deceptive, riddling oracles, which predict, as it turns out, not the well-earned respite from his labors here on earth, but the tragic destiny of Herakles. Deianeira kills herself offstage in remorse, but his are the sufferings we witness publicly onstage, and it is he who, in his first and last appearance before us, provides the climax and resolution of the drama.

Moreover, if we consider more generally that the tragic universe is one that the specifically male self (actor, spectator, or both) must discover for himself as other than he originally imagined it to be, then the example of Deianeira is particularly instructive for articulating the complex position occupied by that feminine other. For in the course of the action, Deianeira indeed does come to that discovery for herself, realizing too late that she has been duped. The love charm the centaur had bequeathed to her was in fact a deadly poison, whose fiery potential had been concealed within the recesses of the house until exposed to the warming heat of the sun. But her education into the treacherous opacity of the tragic world holds no interest for Herakles, preoccupied as he is with unraveling the riddle of his own story. The ensemble of her life and death seems to have nothing to teach Herakles that he can acknowledge openly on his deathbed, and, even more telling, neither will he allow it to have meaning for their son Hyllos when Herakles makes plans for the boy's future in terms that define him only as his father's son.

Medeia in Euripides' play comes closest to demanding an equivalence of the feminine self to the male, preferring, as she says, to stand three times in the van of battle than to bear one child (*Medeia* 250–51). Yet although she has a defined geographical destination to which she will go once she leaves Korinth in exile, having obtained in advance from its king the promise of sanctuary in Athens, her spectacular departure from the city on the dragon chariot of her immortal ancestor, the Sun, suggests that there can be no place for her in the social structure down here on earth. A woman who insists on the binding nature of the compact she made on her own with a man, a woman who defends her right to honor and self-esteem in terms suspiciously resembling those of the male heroic code, and finally a woman who would reverse the cultural flow in founding a new genre of poetry which celebrates now the exploits of women rather than those of men (as the chorus sings, 410–45), is meant not for human but superhuman status.[16] Accordingly, it is only logical that she disappear once the drama is over—upward and out of sight. Yet even in

[16] See especially B. M. W. Knox, "The *Medea* of Euripides," *YClS* 25 (1977): 198–225, for the discussion of Medeia's "imitation" of male heroic traits.

this revolutionary play the typology still holds. Medeia's formal function in the plot is to punish Jason for breaking his sacred oath to her, through an exacting retribution of tragic justice, and she is the typical and appropriate agent, even if embodied in exotic form, for accomplishing that crucial end.

Let us return now to the central topic—to identify those features that are most particular to drama, serving to differentiate it from all other art forms that precede it: narrative (epic), choral lyric and dance, solo songs, and perhaps even stylized exchanges of dialogue. Though profoundly indebted, to be sure, to ritual representations and reenactments, to ritual costumes and masks, drama develops along the deeper lines of character and plot, and establishes its own conventions and entitlements in the more secular sphere.[17]

At the risk of drastic (I repeat, drastic) oversimplification, I propose four principal elements as indispensable traits of the theatrical experience, all linked in various ways to one another and to the sum total of the tragic spectacle. And I will assume another, more dangerous risk by boldly proposing in advance that each of these traits can find not its only, to be sure, but its more radical cultural referent in the traits and aspects the society most associates with the feminine domain.

First, the representation of the body itself onstage as such—its somatic dimensions and the sense of its physical reality. Second, the arrangement of architectural space onstage, which continually suggests a relational tension between inside and outside. Third, the plot itself; that is, the strategies by which theater best represents a tragic story onstage and contrives to bring that story through often surprising means to the conclusion that the terms of its myth demand. In this sense, plot as the shape of the story often coincides in fact, as we shall see, with the other connotation of plot as intrigue and deception. And finally, the most extensive category—the condition of theatrical mimesis itself, limited in this discussion to the question of role-playing and disguise—or more generally, the representation of a self as other than it seems or knows itself to be, a self with inner and outer dimensions.

THE BODY

The emphasis in theater must inevitably fall upon the body—the performing body of the actor as it embodies its role, figures its actions, and

---

[17] It should be stressed that I equate drama here with serious drama rather than with comic types such as satyr-play and comedy itself, whose primitive elements may well have preceded the growth of the strange mutant that is tragedy. For even if we renounce any hope of reconstructing a plausible story of origins, there seems no doubt that the tragic play is the first to achieve the status of art and that the other forms only follow subsequently in its wake and under its influence. To speak of theater, then, is to speak first of tragedy.

is shown to us in stylized poses, gestures, and attitudes. We see this body before us in the *theatron*, the viewing place, in rest and in movement. We observe how it occupies different areas at different times onstage, how it makes its entrances and exits, how it is situated at times alone or, more often, in relation to others. This performing body engages at every moment its sensory faculties—it hears, sees, touches, and moves; above all, it is the actor as body or body as actor who projects the human voice in all its inflections.

Theater has been defined as the "adventure of the human body,"[18] but for Greek tragedy it would be more accurate to call it the "misadventure of the human body." What interests the audience most in the somatics of the stage is the body in an unnatural state of *pathos* (suffering)—when it falls farthest from its ideal of strength and integrity. We notice it most when the body is reduced to a helpless or passive condition—seated, bound, or constrained in some other way; when it is in the grip of madness or disease, undergoing intermittent and spasmodic pain, alternating between spells of dangerous calm before the stormy symptoms assail the body again. Tragedy insists most often on exhibiting this body, even typically bringing corpses back onstage so as to expose them to public view. When characters are still alive, some of them demand that we witness the spectacle of their suffering so we may pity them. Others call for a covering to hide their shame, or wish to be hidden inside the house—or in some supernatural way to vanish from the eyes of the beholders. More to the point, at those moments when the male finds himself in a condition of weakness, he too becomes acutely aware that he has a body—and then perceives himself, at the limits of pain, to be most like a woman.

Herakles, at the end of Sophokles' *Trakhiniai*, when his flesh is being devoured by the poison of the fateful robe, appeals to his son:

> Pity me
> For I seem pitiful to many others, crying
> and sobbing like a girl, and no one could ever say
> that he had seen this man act like that before.
> Always without a groan I followed a painful course.
> Now in my misery I am discovered a woman.
> (*Trakhiniai* 1070–75; cf. Euripides, *Hercules Furens* 1353–56)

Sophokles' Ajax, in despair after the madness that the goddess Athena had sent upon him has abated, and determined now to die a manly death that will restore his heroic image to himself, considers the temptation to yield through pity to his wife's entreaties. If he tempers his will, his

---

[18] Y. Belaval, "Ouverture sur le spectacle," in *Histoire des spectacles*, ed. R. Queneau (Paris, 1965), 3–16, esp. 8.

tongue which is hard and firm like a sword, he has blunted its sharp edge; he has in effect feminized it, as he says (*ethēlunthēn*), for the sake of a woman (*Ajax* 650–52). A warrior man often likens himself to a sword; his mind is obdurate, his will and words are whetted like iron (cf. Aiskhylos, *Seven against Thebes*, 529–30, 715). His is the instrument of power that wounds others, while his body remains impenetrable to outside forces. Ajax will harden his will; he will have his heroic death by the sword of iron. But how? By burying that sword in the earth and falling upon it, breaking through the flesh of his side (*pleuran diarrexanta*, 534). As he violates the boundaries of his body, he also violates tragic convention by staging his death as a public act. Yet paradoxically, there is yet another anomaly in the method he chooses. Suicide is a solution in tragedy normally reserved only for women—and what we are given to witness is this convention borrowed for a man's version of it. He dies a heroic death, then, in the woman's way, a whetted will penetrated by a whetted weapon, befitting (as we will discuss further in another context) the curious ambiguities of this most masculine hero.[19]

My last example here is Hippolytos in Euripides' play. Refusing eros, refusing the touch, even the sight, of a woman, he is brought back onstage in mortal agony after his horses have stampeded in fright before the apparition of the bull from the sea. Then he cries out that pains dart through his head and spasms leap up in his brain, while his desire is now all for a sword to cleave himself in two and "put his life at last to bed" (*Hippolytos* 1351–52, 1371–77). His symptoms are those of a woman, racked with the pain of childbirth or the torment of sexual desire.[20] We remember then Phaidra's last words, which prophesied that he would "share in her disease" (*Hipp.* 730–31)—the deadly pangs of unrequited eros, which earlier had reduced her to a sick and suffering body. Yet in that first scene, when no one onstage yet knows the cause of her malady, the chorus speaks in generic terms about the body of a woman. They call

[19] Nicole Loraux, *Tragic Ways of Killing a Woman* (Cambridge, Mass., 1987) views Ajax's suicide unequivocally as a warrior's death. "Even suicide in tragedy obeys this firm rule that a man must die at a man's hands by the sword and with blood spilled. . . . Ajax kills himself by the sword, faithful to the end to his status as a hero who lives and dies in war where wounds are given and received" (12). It is true, of course, that the sword is a man's weapon and that if women resort to it, it is they who are violating the rules of gender. Yet it is also true that Ajax's death, by whatever means and in whatever mood, is still a suicide, an act the culture regards as inherently shameful in itself and therefore imagines as a more feminine solution.

[20] On the general question of the female body as the model of male suffering, see the superb study by Nicole Loraux, "Le lit, la guerre," in *L'homme* 21 (1981): 36–67. For these symptoms in *Hippolytos*, see respectively Loraux, "Le lit," 58–59, and Charles Segal, "The Tragedy of the *Hippolytus*: The Waters of Ocean and the Untouched Meadow," *HSCP* 70 (1965): 117–69, esp. 122 (now in Segal, *Interpreting Greek Tragedy*).

it a *dustropos harmonia*, an ill-tuned harmony; it suffers the misery of help-lessness (*amēkhania*), and is open to the breeze that darts through the womb in pregnancy, as well as to the torments of eros.[21] This body is permanently at odds with itself, subject to a congenital dissonance be-tween inside and outside. Woman can never forget her body, since she experiences its inward pain, nor is she permitted to ignore the fact of its outward appearance in that finely tuned consciousness she acquires with respect to how she might seem in the eyes of others. Bodiliness is what most defines her in the cultural system that associates her with the physi-cal processes of birth and death and stresses the material dimensions of her existence, as exemplified, above all, in Hesiod's canonical myth of how the first woman, Pandora, was created.[22] Men have bodies, to be sure, but in the gender system the role of representing the corporeal side of life in its helplessness and submission to constraints is primarily as-signed to women.

Thus, it is women who most often tend the bodies of others, washing the surface of the body or laying it out for its funeral. Theirs is the task of supplying the clothing that covers the body, and they have a storehouse of robes which may encircle the male victim in textured folds. When men suffer or die in the theatrical space, it is the female who most typi-cally is the cause. She seems to know, whether consciously or not, how vulnerable, how open—how mortal, in fact—is the human body. These figures may be goddesses like Aphrodite and Hera or, above all, the Eri-nyes, avenging ministers of retributive justice. But these are also women like Klytemnestra, Deianeira, Hekuba, and, of course, Agave, the mother of Pentheus.[23]

On the other hand, dressed as a woman, Pentheus makes the first dis-covery of his corporeal self. Before this he has defended himself mili-tantly against any touch of the other. But now he allows Dionysos to make contact with his body and, in a grotesque parody of female coque-try, is eager for the god to adjust the fine details of his costume and to ar-range the stray locks of hair peeping out from beneath its snood (*Bakkhai* 925–38). With this laying on of hands, Dionysos breaches the physical

[21] See the discussion of this remarkable passage and its key function in the play in Zeitlin, "Power of Aphrodite," 68–74.

[22] On Pandora in the Hesiodic text, see especially the fine analyses by Jean-Pierre Ver-nant, "The Myth of Prometheus in Hesiod," in his *Myth and Society*, 168–85, and Nicole Loraux, "Sur la race des femmes et quelques-unes de ses tribus," *Arethusa* 11 (1978): 43–88 (collected in her *Les enfants d'Athéna: Idées athéniennes sur la citoyenneté et la division des sexes* [Paris, 1981], 75–117).

[23] It is worth noting too that the details of the sacrifice of the virgin's body are described with particular fascination in the messenger speeches of the relevant tragedies.

integrity so dear to the male and prepares Pentheus for the terrible sequel, when the voyeur, coming to see as a spectator what he imagines are
the women's illicit physical contacts with others, is himself exposed to
view, his body becoming instead the focus of their ministering hands.
Then they indeed touch his body, and in the strength induced by their
maenadic state they easily tear it apart in the literal act of *sparagmos*.

In this primitive regression, women undo the body; its structures cannot hold, its limbs are unbound, and the masculine self, originally so intent on opposing himself to anything feminine, is fragmented and flies
apart. Female violence may be viewed through the lens of role reversal,
but in the Greek imagination the maenadic woman is regularly endowed
with this power, especially over the masculine body, and is the model
herself for the male who, when he too is seized like Euripides' Herakles
in the grip of this madness, can only be described as "playing the Bacchant" and imitating the part of the woman.[24]

THEATRICAL SPACE

The second indispensable element of the theatrical experience is the space
itself onstage in the Greek theater, where the human actors situate themselves and the theatrical action takes place before the spectator. By convention this space is constructed as an outside in front of a facade of a
building, most often a house or palace, and there is a door that leads to an
inside, which is hidden from view. What happens inside must always in
some way be brought outside—for example, through use of the wheeled
platform called the *ekkuklēma*, most often used to display the corpses of
those who have met their doom within the house—visual proof of the
violence that must also by convention take place offstage.[25] But the very
business of entrances and exits, of comings and goings through the door
of the house, continually establishes a symbolic dialectic between public
and private, seen and unseen, open and secret, even known and unknown.[26]

---

[24] See further, Ruth Padel, "Women: Model for Possession by Greek Daemons," in *Images of Women in Antiquity*, ed. Averil Cameron and Amelie Kuhrt (London, 1983), 3–19. It
is remarkable that in Euripides' *Herakles*, where the great Herakles goes mad and kills his
wife and children, the chorus in response compares him only with women: the Danaids
(who slew their husbands on their wedding night) and Prokne (who slew her child in revenge for her husband's rape and mutilation of her sister, Philomela; *Hercules Furens* 1016–
27).

[25] For a discussion of this device (and the controversies over its use), see the essay by Padel in this volume.

[26] On the uses of these stage conventions and the relations of the inside to the outside, see

In this simple mapping of spatial relations, the stage conventions not only chart the bounded areas of social relations between the genders, which assign men to the outside and women to the inside; they also suggest an analogy to the tragic world itself, which in the course of its plot and actions inevitably reveals its hidden and unknown dimensions.[27]

Earlier I defined the tragic universe as one that is other than the self originally imagined it to be. Going one step further, we may add that tragedy is the epistemological form par excellence. What it does best through the resources of the theater is to chart a path from ignorance to knowledge, deception to revelation, misunderstanding to recognition. The characters act out and live through the consequences of having clung to a partial, single view of the world and themselves.[28] In the process, in the conflicts and tensions that mark the relations between the opposing characters, all come in some way to experience the complexities of the world—its multiple dimensions, its deceptions and illusions. Inside and outside organize the dramatic action of the drama, and they refer not only to the shifting planes of reality (the known and the unknown) but to the tragic self—both mind and body—and find their material referent in the house and the facade it presents to the outside world.

The house, let us now observe, is the property of the male and his family line. The *oikos* is the visual symbol of paternal heredity which entitles sons to succeed their fathers as proprietors of its wealth and movable goods and as rulers over its inhabitants. As the male in tragedy is often conflated with the king, the house is extended further as a locus of masculine power to include the sign of sovereignty over the city as a whole, and the solidity of its architectural structure symbolically guarantees the enduring stability of the social order. Yet the house, as we know, is primarily the proper domain of the woman, to which the social rules of the culture assign her, while its men go forth into the outside world to pursue manly accomplishments in war and politics.

Thus, in the conflicts between house and city or between domestic and political concerns that are the recurrent preoccupations of tragic plots, the woman, whether wife or daughter, is shown as best representing the

---

especially A. M. Dale, "Seen and Unseen on the Greek Stage," in Dale, *Collected Papers* (Cambridge, Eng., 1969), 119–29; Padel, "Women"; and Zeitlin, "Power of Aphrodite," 74–79.

[27] The locus classicus is Xenophon's *Oikonomikos*. The best discussion is found in Jean-Pierre Vernant, "Hestia-Hermes: Sur l'expression religieuse de l'espace et du mouvement chez les Grecs," in Vernant, *Mythe et pensée chez les Grecs* (Paris, 1965), 97–143.

[28] See, for example, the incisive remarks of Jean-Pierre Vernant, "Tensions and Ambiguities in Greek Tragedy," in Vernant and Vidal-Naquet, *Tragedy and Myth*, 6–27. This epistemological emphasis therefore both exploits and is conditioned by the special capacity of theater to represent and embody the interactions among other points of view, attitudes, gestures, and language.

positive values and structures of the house, and she typically defends its interests in response to some masculine violation of its integrity. As a result, however, of the stand she takes, the woman also represents a subversive threat to male authority as an adversary in a power struggle for control which resonates throughout the entire social and political system, raising the terrifying specter of rule by women. Here we might note how strongly alien is the presence of this feminine other who, in asserting the legitimate values most associated with her social role, is also perceived as illegitimately asserting the rights reserved for the masculine project of self. She never achieves these in any permanent way. But in the contest over rights to control domestic space that the stage conventions exploit, it is the woman and not the man who, by reason of her close identification with the house as her intimate scene, consistently rules the relations between inside and outside and shows herself as standing on the threshold betwixt and between.

Men find out in tragedy that they are likely to enter that interior domain mostly at their peril; consider Agamemnon as he walks on the crimson carpets his wife has spread to lead him to his death at her hands within the house, or Hippolytos confronted inside with the nurse's revelation to him of Phaidra's guilty secret, which is the beginning of his doom, or Polymestor, the Thracian king in Euripides' *Hekuba*, whom the Trojan queen lures into the tent in order to take a woman's revenge on him for killing her child, who was entrusted to him for safekeeping.

As a general principle, the absent hero returns to his house never to enter through its doors again, as in the extreme case of Herakles in the *Trakhiniai*, or to meet with his own destruction within, as in the cases cited above, or finally, like the Herakles in Euripides' play, to go mad once inside the house, slaying his wife and children and literally ensuring the fall of the house by toppling its columns. On the other hand, if the male would successfully penetrate the interior of the house and reclaim it for his own, he typically requires feminine assistance, best exemplified by the fact that, as we will discuss further in a different context, all the extant versions of Orestes' story insist on pairing him with his sister, Elektra.

Men imagine they can control that interior space by attempting to control the women within it. The men object, often violently as Pentheus does in the *Bakkhai*, when in the most dramatic reversal the women leave the stifling environment of the house to venture forth to the open (although equally uncivic) world of forest and mountains. But the king's authority lapses on all fronts. He is unable to bring back his Theban women from the mountains to put them in their rightful place, and ultimately goes out to meet them on their new terrain, with results we already know. He fails too on domestic territory when he wants to lock up the other maenads (and their leader Dionysos) and imprison them in the house. Binding them with fetters, he discovers all too soon the futility of applying coercive force as they easily—magically—loosen themselves from his restraints. His larger demands for mastery over the house literally collapse when Dionysos sends the earthquake to shake the *oikos* to its very foundations.

The situation of Pentheus leads to a further point. The king erects barriers around himself (and his psyche) against the invasion of Dionysos even as he struggles to maintain the integrity of the house and the walled city of Thebes.[29] If tragedy, as I have suggested, is the epistemological genre par excellence, which continually calls into question what we know and how we think we know it, it often does so by confronting the assumptions of rational thought with those psychological necessities that may not be denied.

The master example of Pentheus therefore gives another turn to the dialectic of inside and outside that focuses on the woman and the house as containers for the emotional energies of the self and the society. The house has its many kinds of secrets that men do not know, and the challenge to male authority over it therefore takes place on several levels—social, cognitive, and psychological. If men enter this domain, assuming their legitimate rights to its custody, only to meet with a welcome they had not foreseen, at the same time they inevitably fail to repress those powerful forces hidden in the recesses of the house. Quite the contrary; the tragic process, for the most part conveyed through the catalyzing person and actions of the feminine, puts insistent pressure on the facade of the masculine self in order to bring outside that which resides unacknowledged and unrecognized within. Here in the *Bakkhai*, where the inversion of roles is expressly posed in spatial terms that send the women outside and situate the man within, the stage conventions are used to their best effect as Pentheus leaves the interior space now for the last time—for his liberation and for his destruction—dressed, as we might now expect, like a woman.

THE PLOT

Third, we come to the plot itself, that which brings about the recognition, the *anagnōrisis*; the plot whose process Aristotle describes as a combination of *desis*, binding, and *lusis*, unbinding, denouement, and which in its complex form he calls by the corresponding Greek term, a *sum-*

---

[29] On the symbolic value of the house, see J. Wohlberg, "The Palace-Hero Equation in Euripides," *AAntHung* 16 (1968): 149–55; and the much fuller discussion in Segal, *Dionysiac Poetics*, 86–94 and *passim*.

plokē, an interweaving, which describes the fabric, the texture of the play (*Poetics* 1455b).

At a higher level, these terms are even more suggestive, reminding us how the tragic world works its ruinous effects through modes of entrapment and entanglement which cause characters first to stumble through ignorance and error and then to fall. In the elaborate tragic game, the metaphoric patterns of binding and unbinding continually exhibit reciprocal tension; signs of constraint and necessity, on the one hand, and of dissolution and death, on the other, define the parameters between which characters are caught in the "double bind."[30]

In the cognitive psychology of tragic man, inner choice and external necessity (or *ethos*, character, and *daimōn*, divine power) finally converge to sanction whatever form of tragic justice the plot demands for its satisfying fulfillment. Thus the "nature of tragic action appears to be defined by the simultaneous presence of a 'self' and something greater at work that is divine."[31] In this sense, the gods finally may be said to direct the energy of the action and to be understood retrospectively as supporting and advancing the outcome of the myth.

Gods sometimes appear onstage (and I have already remarked how frequently these figures are goddesses), although most often they operate from afar as inhabiting that other unknown dimension of existence which mortals may only grasp dimly and, of course, too late. But it is remarkable how often that energy is channeled through the feminine other, who serves as the instrument of the gods even when she acts or seems to act on her own terrain and for her own reasons, and even when she acts out of ignorance or only partial knowledge of the tragic world she inhabits. Women frequently control the plot and the activity of plotting, and manipulate the duplicities and illusions of the tragic world.

On the one hand, women's exclusion from the central area of masculine public life seems to be matched by their special access to those powers beyond men's control, to those outside forces that make sudden forays into human lives, unsettling typical assumptions. On the other hand, that same exclusion which relegates women to the inside as mistresses of the interior space equips them for deviousness and duplicity, and gives them a talent, or at least a reputation, for weaving wiles and fabricating plots, marks of their double consciousness with regard to the world of men.

Tragedy is the art form, above all, that makes the most of what is

---

[30] For a fuller discussion of these terms and their relation to the structures and structuring capacities of plots, see Zeitlin, "Power of Aphrodite," 58–64.

[31] Jean-Pierre Vernant, "Intimations of the Will in Greek Tragedy," in Vernant, *Myth and Society*, 51. His is the most nuanced discussion of the psychology of the double determination that is often misperceived as a conflict between fate and free will.

called discrepant awareness—what one character knows and the other doesn't, or what none of the characters knows but the audience does. Thus it is that irony is tragedy's characteristic trope; several levels of meaning operate at the same time. Characters speak without knowing what they say, and misreading is the typical and predictable response to the various cues that others give.

This pervasive irony may manifest itself in many ways, and it owes its effectiveness to a strong conviction about the ambiguous, even opaque nature of verbal communication that is reflected in the belief in oracles. These riddling, divine utterances invite their hearers to feats of interpretation or evasion and, at the same time, suggest, when the outcome proves disastrous, how misguided and ignorant these human attempts may be. Apollo and his oracle often serve as a primary source, as Oidipous, his most famous client, confirms. But other factors make for dramatic irony, particularly in connection with the deceptive powers of the feminine and the special verbal skills that accompany these.

Klytemnestra in Aiskhylos' *Agamemnon* is the most powerful paradigm of the woman who plots, who through the riddling doubleness of the language to which she resorts builds the play to its climax in the murder of her husband within the house where she entangles him in the nets of the robe, and only Kassandra, another woman with second sight, perceives, but cannot convey, what lies behind the guileful persuasion. The case of Phaidra, the virtuous wife in Euripides' *Hippolytos*, is also instructive. Caught in the conflict between desire and honor and determined to preserve her integrity at any cost, Theseus' queen, despite herself, or rather in defense of that apparently indefensible feminine self, fabricates the lying message that will implicate Hippolytos as the cause of her death and lead to his entanglement in the reins of his own chariot.

The pattern holds even at the other end of the dramatic spectrum, in the late romantic plays of Euripides, which shift to exotic locales, where the feminine other takes on a different configuration as the remote object of a mythic quest. Now men are sent forth, albeit unknowing, in search of the absent, forgotten woman who longs to return to the home and loved ones she has lost; in the process of rescuing the feminine, the men find out they have redeemed and refound a version of male heroic identity. But still it is the woman who plots and now openly devises a plan onstage before us, this time for the best of reasons—her own rescue and that of her menfolk, as does Iphigeneia in *Iphigeneia in Tauris* or Helen in the play of the same name. The men here are only adjuncts of the women; they offer prior schemes of their own but inevitably yield to and cooperate in the women's superior plans, which all involve elaborate dramas of deception.

If we take a rapid inventory of the plot as intrigue in the extant plays of the tragic corpus, some interesting principles emerge.[32] First, it is the women whose plots are more generally successful.[33] If men succeed, however, it is precisely because they have allied themselves with women—for example, in the Euripidean plays just cited, and more broadly in the various treatments of the Orestes story where Orestes succeeds in avenging his father through the murder of his mother because he has joined forces with his sister, Elektra. Thus the recognition between them must necessarily precede the *praxis* of vengeance. In the *Khoephoroi* of Aiskhylos (the second play of the *Oresteia*), for example, it is only after the long interchange among Oresles, Elektra, and the female chorus of libation-bearers that Orestes is able at last to interpret the dream of Klytemnestra, and thus, psychologically equipped, is ready to assume the stranger's disguise that will allow him his successful entry into the feminine domain of the house.[34]

Second, whereas deceit and intrigue are condemned in woman, they are also seen as natural to her sphere of operations and the dictates of her nature.[35] For the male, however, resort to *dolos*, trickery, is what most undermines masculine integrity and puts him under the gravest of suspicions. These are best mitigated when the one to be deceived is a cruel, barbarian king of another land (as in the late Euripidean plays), a king whose adversary status comes closer to the role of melodramatic villain.[36] The case of Orestes at home in Argos is even more informative in this regard. His success, it is true, depends on reunion with his sister, but his resort to trickery and disguise (*dolos, mēkhanē*) entails a further risk to his masculine stature, no matter how urgent and obligatory his task of

[32] For discussions of intrigue plots in general, see especially Friedrich Solmsen, "Zur Gestaltung des Intriguenmotivs in den Tragödien des Sophokles und Euripides," *Philologus* 84 (1932): 1–17, and Hans Strohm, "Trug und Taüschung in der euripideischen Dramatik," *WJA* 4 (1949–1950): 140–56, collected in *Euripides*, ed. E. Schwinge, *Wege der Forschung*, 89 (Darmstadt, 1968) as 326–44 and 345–72, respectively. See also the wider-ranging discussion by Frances Muecke, " 'I Know You—By Your Rags': Costume and Disguise in Fifth-Century Drama," *Antichthon* 16 (1982): 17–34.

[33] The *Ion* of Euripides, a play in many ways a precursor of New Comedy, foils the woman's plot against her unrecognized son (not without some fancy help from the gods) so as to bring about the joyful reunion. The play, I might add, is careful not to credit the woman Kreousa as the one who initiates the intrigue.

[34] Euripides' *Elektra* is still more complex, as the play separates the two acts of vengeance against Klytemnestra and her lover, Aigisthos. The old servant suggests the plot against Aigisthos (to take place outside far away from the house), while Elektra contrives the elaborate and doubly deceitful intrigue against Klytemnestra.

[35] This is a commonplace in tragic texts (as elsewhere): e.g., *Iphigeneia among the Taurians* 1032; *Medeia* 834–35; *Andromakhe* 85; *Hippolytos* 480–81; *Ion* 483.

[36] Even in these plays, masculine honor is protected, as it were, in that each man (Orestes, Menelaos) first proposes force before he accedes to the woman's practical, clever schemes (Iphigeneia, Helen), and each, just before the end, is permitted a display of manly strength against the forces of the barbarian king in question.

vengeance. Appeal to the authority of Apollo the god is therefore needed
to justify this mode of action. The god (in both Aiskhylos and Sophokles) must explicitly decree a retribution that exactly matches the original
crime: as she (Klytemnestra) killed, so must she be killed in turn—by
guile (Aiskhylos, *Khoephoroi* 556–59; Sophokles, *Elektra* 32–37).

Sophokles' *Trakhiniai*, that schematic model of gender relations, again
supplies an excellent version of the norm. Herakles too practices deception, first to conquer the girl Iole, the current object of his erotic desire
and the immediate cause of all his woe, and then to introduce her secretly
into the house. But in his case, deception returns quite literally (and most
dramatically) against him. His deception, revealed by others to his wife,
activates the Centaur's ruse, plotted long ago as the deadly poison entrusted as a secret love charm to Deianeira's safekeeping inside the house.
The point is that, innocent as Deianeira may be of conscious intent to
harm her husband, she still easily proves a better and more successful
plotter than he. Masculine guile is repaid in full—even when retaliation
does not openly bear the name of revenge.

If this Herakles conforms so well to the normative pattern, Ajax, that
other great hero, does not. His is a curious case, but one whose anomaly
might just prove the point. At the crucial moment of Sophokles' play,
having determined to die an honorable death, he delivers a deceptive
speech which suggests he has changed his mind and has learned to bend
with the vicissitudes of time and change. With this speech he puts off
those who would guard him and leaves himself alone to stage the elaborate suicide to which I have earlier referred. Critics have energetically
contested the status of this speech as truth or lie. While the outcome of
the plot tells us that Ajax has not undergone any fundamental conversion
of spirit, he also seems to have arrived at the kind of tragic knowledge we
recognize as intrinsically true to the genre.

How then can we read the enigma of this speech? Better still, how can
we read Ajax, the traditional epic hero, who would resort to a deceptive
plot which goes against the grain of strict masculine values in which Ajax
puts too much store? This is the man, after all, we might note with respect to spatial relations, who could not endure, as the oracle riddlingly
suggests for his salvation, to remain *inside* the tent even for the space of
one single day. But it is precisely the ambiguities of this hero who in his
madness has not acted the part of the hero, and precisely the question of
dishonor converted finally to honor, that account for the interesting ambiguities of his subsequent actions, which rewrite the theatrical conventions associated with gender. Thus the deceptive speech makes sense as a
feminine strategy enlisted in the service of restoring an unequivocal manliness he can only achieve, as I suggested before, by dying the manly
death—heroically and publicly onstage—yet in the woman's way.

When other male characters, those not designated as tragic figures in the dramatic action, seek to deceive, their devices flounder, and such men as these are dismissed out of hand.[37] Agamemnon, so easily duped by his wife in Aiskhylos' play, miserably fails, for his part, when in Euripides' *Iphigeneia in Aulis* he and Menelaos plot to bring Iphigeneia as a sacrifice for the expedition to Troy under the pretext of a marriage with Akhilleus. Klytemnestra finds them out—by a fortuitous accident—and the sacrifice only takes place through Iphigeneia's voluntary and open choice of the role assigned to her by her father and the myth. Most telling of all perhaps, Odysseus, the master plotter on his own epic territory (and a familiar trickster figure in the plots of mischievous satyr-plays), only sees his plans go awry on the tragic stage—for example, in Sophokles' *Philoktetes* when Neoptolemos, son of Akhilleus, rejects finally the man and his plans, he of whom his father had said in the *Iliad*, "I hate like the gates of Hades a man who hides one thing in his heart and speaks another" (9.312–13).

The *Bakkhai*, as we might expect, furnishes the most remarkable example of the uses of plotting and exposes the conventions of its theatrical deployment as the pivotal point around which the entire play revolves and the peripeteia depends. All the operative terms come into play—secrecy, guile, entrapment, and femininity—as Dionysos and Pentheus engage in their power struggle for control over one another, the city, the women, and ultimately, over the outcome of the plot itself. Pentheus aligns himself, of course, with physical force as the masculine means to victory, trying and failing to bind his adversary (and his followers), and ready to dress as a soldier and deploy an army for a military battle against the women. Dionysos retaliates against threats of force at this critical moment with a devious plot—to entice Pentheus to go alone to the mountains in secrecy.

What this means is that he persuades Pentheus to trade his ready reliance on physical combat for that other, diametrically opposite mode of action—resort to a cunning plot of self-concealment. In other words, Dionysos' strategy for victory over his opponent is first to lure him into embracing the same kind of strategy. They are coconspirators now, plotting together but for ultimately divergent results; for one the intrigue will succeed in every respect and for the other it will disastrously fail.

But the first conquest of Pentheus already lies in the fact that he agrees to shift his tactics from open force to the secret deception of hiding; the second, which follows directly on the first, is the change in dress from male to female, which, as Dionysos argues, is essential for the success of

[37] The one exception that comes to mind is Euripides' strange play, *Andromakhe*, where Orestes, not a major character, successfully plots to have Neoptolemos killed at Delphi so as to reclaim the latter's wife, Hermione, for his own.

the project. These two steps, however, imply one another—the woman has recourse to devious plotting, the very charge Pentheus has laid against both Dionysos and the maenads (e.g., 475, 487, 805–6), and the costume Pentheus dons therefore matches and visually represents the feminine nature of the strategy he has already chosen. But in the ways of women Pentheus is only an imposter, easily betrayed by the other, superior plotter, and hence the scheme he contrives and carries out can only recoil against him for his own doom.

Mimesis

I come now very briefly to my fourth and most inclusive element—that of mimesis itself, the art of imitation through which characters are rendered lifelike, and plot and action offer an adequate representation of reality. Yet mimesis also focuses attention on the status of theater as illusion, disguise, double-dealing, and pretense. There is a serious and wonderful paradox here. For while theater resorts continually to artifice, as it must, to techniques of make-believe that can only resemble the real, it can also better represent the larger world outside as it more nearly is, subject to the deceptions, the gaps in knowledge, the tangled necessities, and all the tensions and conflicts of a complex existence.

Role-playing is what actors must literally do in the theater as they don their costumes and masks to impersonate an other—whether king or servant, mortal or god, Greek or barbarian, man or woman. But the reverse side of the coin is to be dubbed an actor, a *hupokritēs*, who is only playing a role, offering only a persona (a *prosōpon*) to the other that does not match what lies behind the mask.

Recognition, *anagnōrisis* of persons whose identities were unknown or mistaken is, of course, a typical and even focal device of tragic action. But this kind of recognition is the overtly theatrical event that condenses the epistemological bias of the entire phenomenon of drama. Thus recognition extends along a far wider spectrum, embracing the world, the other, and the self. The problem of accurately reading the other is a continuing, obsessive concern in Greek tragedy which increases in urgency as the genre displays a greater self-consciousness with regard to its own theatrical resources. But recognition of the unknown self, as for Oidipous, or of the hidden self, as for Pentheus or even for Deianeira, is perhaps the most elusive but also the most psychologically significant result on the tragic stage, suggesting what the invention of theater for and in the city might imply about an emerging image of the private individual and the growing pains of masculine identity.[38]

---

[38] "The covert theme of all drama," Michael Goldman suggests, "is identification, the

This double dimension of role-playing is a feature that Greek society would perceive as not exclusively but yet fundamentally feminine.[39] Woman is the mimetic creature par excellence, ever since Hesiod's Zeus created her as an imitation with the aid of the other artisan gods and adorned her with a deceptive allure.[40] Woman is perennially under suspicion as the one who acts a part—that of the virtuous wife—but hides other thoughts and feelings, dangerous to men, within herself and the house. "Counterfeit evil" is the charge that Hippolytos is not alone in bringing against the *genos*, the race of women, for she has the best capacity, by her nature and origin, to say one thing and hide another in her heart, to sow doubt in her husband's mind, to cite perhaps the radical cause, that the child she bears may be his but again may not be.[41]

Woman speaks on the tragic stage, transgressing the social rules if she speaks on her own behalf. In this role, her speech and action involve her in the ensemble of tragic experience and thereby earn her the right to tragic suffering. But by virtue of the conflicts generated by her social position, the woman is ambiguously defined between inside and outside, interior self and exterior identity; she is already more of a "character" than the man, who is far more limited as an actor to his public (social and political) roles. Woman comes equipped with a "natural" awareness of the very complexities men would resist, if they could. Situated in her more restrictive and sedentary position in the world, she is permitted— she is asked, we might say—to reflect more deeply, like Phaidra, on the paradoxes of herself. Through these she can better arrive at the paradoxes of the world that she seems to know are subject to irreconcilable conflict, and are subject as well to time, flux, and change (the very themes, I might add, of Ajax's great deceptive speech). Hence the final paradox may be that theater uses the feminine for the purpose of imagining a fuller model for the masculine self, and "playing the other" opens that self to those often banned emotions of fear and pity.

---

establishment of a self that in some way transcends the confusions of self"; *The Actor's Freedom: Toward a Theory of Drama* (New York, 1975), 123. I have learned much from this stimulating study of the workings of theater.

[39] Odysseus is the exemplar in the masculine sphere, but he does not generically represent "the race of men;" nor, let me repeat, is this adaptable survivor (with strong affinities, in fact, to the feminine) a candidate for tragedy in the dramatic milieu. On the contrary, he is a favorite character in satyr-plays.

[40] Earlier I alluded to the creation of Pandora as exemplifying the physical, "creaturely" side of life. I emphasize now the other aspect of woman's creation as an object cunningly wrought; she is a deceptive gift in return for Prometheus' deception of Zeus, herself endowed with a crafty intelligence. Woman therefore embodies both extremes of nature and culture which together conspire to waste a man's substance and dry him up before his time.

[41] For a similar idea, see Ann Bergren, "Language and the Female in Early Greek Thought," *Arethusa* 16 (1983): 74, 77.

Woman may be thought to speak double, and sometimes she does. But she also sees double; the culture has taught her that too, and it is perhaps not an accident that only when Pentheus dresses as a woman does he see double for the first time—two suns, two Thebes. This is a symptom of madness, to be sure, attributed by the ancient commentators to inebriation, but madness is the emblem of the feminine, and seeing double is also the emblem of a double consciousness which a man acquires by dressing like a woman and entering into the theatrical illusion. The very fact of that dressing up already demonstrates the premise in unequivocal and theatrical terms.

The feminine figure onstage is tragic; she is also the mistress of mimesis, the heart and soul of the theater. The female instructs the other through her own example—that is, in her own name and under her own experience—but also through her ability to teach the other, whether Pentheus or Dionysos, to impersonate her.

This brief discussion can suggest only in outline how closely the tragic genre in its theatrical form, representation, and content is linked to Greek notions of gender, and how for the most part man is undone (or at times redeemed) by feminine forces or himself undergoes some species of "feminine" experience. On the simplest level, this experience involves a shift at the crucial moment of the peripeteia from active to passive, from mastery over the self and others to surrender and grief. Sometimes there is madness, always suffering and pathos, which lead in turn to expressions of lamentation and pity from the chorus or the characters. In a more complex view, tragedy, understood as the worship of Dionysos, expands an awareness of the world and the self through the drama of "playing the other" whose mythic and cultic affinities with the god logically connect the god of women to the lord of the theater.

If drama, however, tests masculine values only to find that these alone are inadequate to the complexity of the new situation, it also, as Linda Bamber remarks, "does not dismiss them" but rather most often shows that manliness and self-assertion need no longer compete with pity and even forgiveness.[42] Moreover, the male characters whose sufferings are the most stringent and reductive of self are also allowed to discover the internal strength for transcending them.[43] In the end, tragedy arrives at closures that generally reassert male, often paternal, structures of au-

[42] This is a combined quote and paraphrase (with one small alteration) of Bamber, *Comic Women,* 15.

[43] In this respect, there are strong continuities with the earlier epic tradition. See the interesting conclusions of Hélène Monsacré's fine study, *Les larmes d'Achille: Le héros, la femme et la souffrance dans la poésie d'Homère* (Paris, 1984), 199–204.

thority, but before that the work of the drama is to open up the masculine view of the universe. It typically does so, as we have seen, through
energizing the theatrical resources of the female and concomitantly ener-
vating the male as the price of initiating actor and spectator into new and
unsettling modes of feeling, seeing, and knowing.

We can trace the persistence of this "initiatory" process from the work
of the first tragic poet to the third.[44] History has cunningly arranged that
Euripides' last play, the *Bakkhai*, should also refer back to the archaic
scenario that underlies the ritual conditions of the theater.[45] Yet viewed
in its metatheatrical aspects, the *Bakkhai* also makes claims to be considered in a diachronic perspective as a belated exemplar of the genre that by
now has developed a keen awareness of its own properties and conventions. As a result, the play is in a position to exemplify and reflect what
was always implicit in the theater, and at the same time, by the very admission of that theatrical awareness, to transform its object of reflection
and reorient it in new and different directions.

If my basic hypothesis is valid, then the distinctive features of Euripidean theater (which are more obvious, in fact, in plays other than the
Bakkhai) may well lend support to what I have been suggesting about the
intimate relations between the feminine and the theater. I see all the following traits of Euripidean drama as various and interlocking functions
of one another, starting with Euripides' greater interest in and skill at
subtly portraying the psychology of female characters, and continuing to
his general emphasis on interior states of mind and on the private emotional life of the individual, most often located in the feminine situation.
We may add to these his particular fondness for plots of complex intrigue
(usually suggested by women) that use *dolos*, *apatē*, *tekhnē*, and *mēkhanē*,
which with their resort to disguise and role-playing are an explicit sign of
an enhanced theatricality. Finally, we may include more generally Euripides' thematic concern with metaphysical questions of reality and illusion in the world.

The *Helen* is the most splendid example, as it is a drama that allows itself the fullest play with the resources of theater and uses these to direct
the most elaborate inquiry into the complexities of being and seeming
and the paradoxical crossings of illusion and reality.[46] The source of the

---

[44] We might note that initiation into the "real" Eleusinian mysteries involved some
forms of imitating the specifically feminine experiences of Demeter and Kore.

[45] More accurately, it is one of the very last, produced posthumously in Athens, as was
Iphigeneia in Aulis.

[46] For the interplay of illusion and reality, see Friedrich Solmsen, "Onoma and Pragma
in Euripides' *Helen*," *CR* 48 (1934): 119–21; Ann Pippin [Burnett], "Euripides' *Helen*: A
Comedy of Ideas," *CP* 55 (1960): 151–63; Charles Segal, "The Two Worlds of Euripides'

confusion is the ontological status of the feminine itself. There are two Helens: the real, chaste version who was left in Egypt and never went to Troy, and the more traditional adulterous wife whom Menelaos thinks he has recovered at Troy but who is really a phantom, an *eidōlon*, impersonating Helen's true self. I alluded earlier to the symbolic implications we might infer from Pentheus dressing as a woman and seeing double for the first time. Here in the *Helen*, where double vision rules the play in every respect, the woman is a character who to her irremediable sorrow learns firsthand about the most fundamental problems of the self's identity and, at the same time, serves as an objective referent through which the man must question all his previous perceptions of the world. What is more, the essential strategy for ensuring the success of the intrigue she invents for their rescue requires that he too adopt a disguise and pretend to be other than himself, allowing her to recount the most dangerous fiction that the real Menelaos has died.

The uses of the play, to be sure, have their deadly serious side for all concerned, and the unhappy residue of spoiled lives persists behind the successful outcome of the play. But for love of this woman, whether in her imagined or real persona, the man willingly enters into the theatrical game and shows a capacity now to act a part and enter into a stage illusion. The *Helen* is a rare play; it pushes its original improbable (and theatrical) premises as far as they can go, but the uxorious Menelaos is also a novelty, and the erotic element already diverts the play from the more typical tragic mode to that of romance. In this new kind of play-world Euripides invents, the uses to which he puts the feminine and the theater may be seen as the logical result of the premises of tragedy. On the other hand, by disclosing those premises too well, he also alters them and subverts the genre that was so firmly bound up with the context of the masculine civic world.

In this sense, Euripides may be said to have "feminized" tragedy and, like his Dionysos in the *Bakkhai*, to have laid himself open to the scorn that accrues to those men who consort with women. Aristophanic comedy, which loves to lampoon Euripides and all his newfangled ideas, continually presses the scandal of his erotic dramas, especially those that let women speak more boldly (and hence more shamefully) on the stage, until Aristophanes, in his own late play, the *Frogs*, evaluates on a full-fledged scale the development of the tragic genre by staging an open contest between the old poet, Aiskhylos, and the new, Euripides (755–1853).

Helen," *TAPA* 102 (1971): 553–614 (now in Segal, *Interpreting Greek Tragedy*, 222–67); and see too George Walsh, *The Varieties of Enchantment: Early Greek Views on the Nature and Function of Poetry* (Chapel Hill, N. C., 1984), 96–106. On the connections with theater and femininity in the context of comic parody, see Zeitlin, "Travesties," 186–89.

At stake is the choice of which poet Dionysos should bring back from the underworld to the city and theater of Athens. Who is more worthy to save the city, which seems to link its loss of political potency to the absence of a fertile, potent poet in the tragic theater? Broadly stated, the contest develops into one between masculine and feminine sides, with Aiskhylos espousing a manly, virile art which exhorts its citizens to military valor, and Euripides representing a feminine, slender muse who is weaker and more insubstantial, leaning toward the sensual and the pathetic. Not surprisingly, when these two are tested in the scales, Aiskhylean tragedy outweighs the Euripidean by its superior mass and weight. Dionysos therefore abandons his original desire for Euripides, to whose seductive allure he had earlier succumbed, in favor of resurrecting the heroic warrior energies of the earlier poet and, by extension, of the past.[47] Aristophanes not untypically assumes that when things go badly for men and masculine interests, the cause lies in a decay of moral and esthetic values, from which he slides easily into hints of effeminacy and all that that implies.

In any case, the solution of the *Frogs* in bringing back the archaic spirit of Aiskhylos as a solution to the city's problems is also a formal, generic one. It is predicated on the controlling convention of Old Comedy that fulfills its festive function of social renewal by consistently choosing the idealized past over the distressing, chaotic present, even as it prefers to rejuvenate the old (father) rather than, as in New Comedy, to promote the young (son). Moreover, the comic poet paints with a broad, satirical brush, and whatever the justice or truth of the cause he thinks he is advancing (and *his* play, of course, is what he imagines will save the city), he has the generic right to misrepresent, and how he does it here affects Aiskhylos even more perhaps than it does Euripides.

Leaving aside the fact that Euripides too has his military and patriotic plays, Aristophanes would have us believe that the essence of the *Seven against Thebes*, that drama "full of Ares" invoked to support Aiskhylos' case, was some conventional treatment of military prowess. It was rather a tragedy concerning the sons of Oidipous and the dangers they posed to the safety of the city by their resort to armed combat in the style of the old heroic duel, while the function of the avenging Erinys returning to fulfill the father's curse conforms precisely, even schematically, to the rules of the feminine in the theater as I have earlier outlined them.

Nevertheless, Aristophanes is a witness we cannot afford to ignore. He speaks about the theater from within the theater. Skewed as his caricature of Euripides (and his drama) may be, his strategy of clustering the poet's

---

[47] I simplify here the terms of the debate. Both sides are thoroughly satirized in this brilliant parody. For an excellent discussion, see Walsh, *Varieties of Enchantment*, 80–97.

theatrical, psychological, and noetic innovations around a particular affinity for the feminine is valuable testimony to a popular contemporary perception of Euripidean theater, even if it is bought at the price of suppressing the continuities with earlier drama.

Along the same lines, we may even be able to swallow Aristophanes' parting shot, which implies that Euripides' loss of the tragic art is due to "sitting at the feet of Sokrates" (1491–95), another favorite target for comic misrepresentation. Yet however justified Aristophanic comedy may be to single out both Euripides and Sokrates as spokesmen for the new intellectual trends that confuse and unsettle the older, simpler (hence more manly) values of the city, philosophy would never consort with tragedy, which it comes to see as its implacable rival in laying claim to teach the truth, impart knowledge, improve its fellow citizens, and—without doubt—save the city.

Sokrates, as Plato in the next generation has him argue, makes no distinctions whatsoever among any of the tragic poets when he comes to discuss the theatrical arts. Indeed, he founds his critique of drama on Homer, whom he characterizes as the first teacher and guide of tragedy.[48] That same Aiskhylean play is invoked again when Sokrates' interlocutor in the *Republic* first quotes a famous verse from it in a proper context, only at the next moment to turn around the meaning of the lines that follow it so as to apply it to the unjust man rather than to the just.[49] The argument in Plato between tragedy and philosophy is well known, and it is not my intention to air all the old questions or to solve the old dilemmas. But I want to suggest that Plato, standing outside the drama, can be called in as a last witness to support my claims about the intrinsic links between femininity and theater, viewed now from a wholly negative perspective. Plato's insistence on banishing tragedy from his ideal state and his consistent distaste throughout his career for the tragic poets, whom he sometimes associates quite closely with sophists and rhetoricians, are based, to be sure, on a number of complex and disparate factors. But in addition to the explicitly philosophical issues, I want to argue that Plato's position on theater can also be illuminated by considering its relation to his notions of gender and his attitudes toward the feminine.[50]

Strange as it may seem, Plato's aim is not very remote from what Aristophanes wants in the *Frogs*. The project is more far-reaching, to be sure, in every respect, and the means are those which will forever change the shape of Western thought. But, like Aristophanes, Plato is concerned

[48] See especally *Republic* 595c, 598d, 605c–d, 607a, 602b.

[49] *Republic* 2.366a–b; cf. 361b–c. Strictly speaking, the Aiskhylean quotes precede the discussion of the mimetic arts in book 3, but their misuse may not be fortuitous.

[50] I include in the discussion the relevant portions of *Republic*, *Gorgias*, and *Laws*, to be followed by the *Symposium*.

with restoring men and their morals in the city, and, like the comic poet, he insists on the relevance of esthetic style and form. Briefly put, for the purposes of this discussion, Plato's larger concerns may also be translated into his general desire to remake man in a masculine society and through philosophical training to purify and enhance the traditional heroic notion of manliness (*andreia*) in a new, revised version in which courage, vigilance, and strength may be better used for the improvement of self and society.

Certainly, Plato comes closest to codifying under the name of philosophy the dream of the Greek male for a world that is constituted as his alone, where he might give birth to himself and achieve finally the immortality he has always craved. In tragedy, this desire leads to disaster, most often, as we have seen, through the resistance of the gods—and of the women. Philosophy, on the other hand, offers the promise of success in this endeavor, provided one follows the blueprints that are carefully designed to retrain the masculine self.

It may be objected that Plato breaks with the old stereotypes of gender when he insists that women may be just like men with the exception of a natural inferiority in physical strength, which does not disqualify them from participating as guardians (and even warriors) in his vision of the ideal city in the *Republic*. This is a revolutionary proposal whose significance we ought not minimize.[51]

But we should note that this reevaluation of women does not really upgrade the feminine in its differences from the masculine. Quite the contrary—Plato defuses the power and specificity of the feminine when he would abolish the family and the domestic sphere in which that influence operated. If he includes the participation of certain women who may prove to possess masculine abilities, it is precisely because in the *Republic* he believes that they may be successfully taught to imitate the masculine model. Even here, the principle of equality falters when Plato would reward with special breeding privileges men who have distinguished themselves in battle, but does not suggest granting the same opportunities to their female counterparts. This may or may not be a trivial slip. What is striking, however, is that elsewhere femininity plays for Plato throughout his work its usual role of negative foil to the masculine as it heads the long list of undesirable models for men which descends to the servile, the buffoonish, the bestial, and the nonhuman (*Republic* 3.395d–396b).

Plato's attack on tragedy and its traditional repertory operates on several fronts: he objects to the deceptiveness of theatricality as a misleading and deficient imitation of reality, deplores the often unworthy quality of

---

[51] This issue deserves far more attention than space permits here.

what or who is being imitated, and insists on the damaging effects such imitations are liable to produce on the actors and spectators in the theater.[52]

For the first case, I would not go so far as to claim that Plato explicitly refers the art of making illusions to the feminine per se, even if women, like children, are most susceptible to its charms (e.g., *Laws* 658d, 817c) and most likely, in fact, to tell those lying stories about the gods to their young (*Rep.* 377c). But Plato's interest never focuses for long on women as such but rather on the inferior type of man, who deceptively passes off appearances for truth and who appeals to the inferior parts of the self (and the citizenry) that will yield to the emotions and pleasures (not lessons) of make-believe. Thus, although he confirms the conventional dictum that woman is inclined by nature to be secretive (*lathraiōteron*) and crafty (*epiklopōteron*) because of her intrinsic weakness (*to asthenes*)—and concomitantly, that her natural potential for virtue is inferior to a man's (*Laws* 781a–b)—Plato hardly sees her (or her representation) as a powerful, active force in the world of men.[53]

But by a whole series of innuendos and juxtapositions, poets (and artists) are enrolled in the ranks of male trickster figures who fall furthest from the ideal of manliness and seek only to cajole, seduce, and pander to the tastes of their audience. Imitators (artists and musicians) and poets and their entourage of actors, dancers, and producers join the multitude of callings that are signs of the luxury that corrupts the primitive city, and these directly precede those "makers of all sorts of goods, especially those that have to do with women's adornment"; the sequence then continues with those servants like "beauty-shop ladies, barbers, cooks, and confectioners" (*Rep.* 373b–c).

Once assimilated into the larger category of sophists, dramatic art, reduced finally to prose rhetoric on a par with oratory, shares in the same field of reference that likens their false imitations of justice to those activities practiced by and for women: cookery (especially confectionery), which "puts on the mask of medicine and pretends to know what foods are best for the body" (*Gorgias* 464c–d), and beauty-culture, "the counterfeit to physical training . . . a mischievous, swindling, base, servile trade, which creates an illusion by the use of artificial adjuncts and make-up and depilatories and costume" (*Gorg.* 465b–c). All these arts

---

[52] Tragedy is the real target, despite the remarks about epic poetry and comedy. See especially *Laws* 816d–e, and 935d–936b for comedy, and 817a–d for tragedy, where Plato expressly sets up the legislators as authors of their own true tragedies as "rivals . . . artists and actors of the fairest drama."

[53] One single exception is the woman (wife and mother) who instigates in her son the slide toward timocratic behavior by her nagging and greed (*Republic* 549c–e). We will take up the function in the *Symposium* of the priestess, Diotima, in the appropriate context.

traffic in deceptive appearances, and their effect on others is to pander to appetites and pleasurable gratification.

The *Gorgias* stresses a certain sensual, effeminate pleasure. But the *Republic*, in which Plato specifically addresses the emotional power of the tragic, emphasizes the experience of pain and suffering, and evaluates its effects on those who act in and attend the tragic spectacles. Here the association with the feminine is clear and explicit, reiterated each time Plato returns to the topic: when heroes are shown to weep and lament their misfortunes, they are not only endorsing a false theology about the justice of the gods but are weakening themselves and others by their indulgence in womanish grief (*Rep.* 387e–388a, 605d–e). Such a man does not remain steadfast to himself, exercising self-control and rationally pondering the events that have happened to him. Rather he gives way to cowardice, terror, and a host of conflicting, changeful emotions which ill suit the model of brave and noble manliness that the state (and the soul) requires. Worst of all, he entices the spectators into the pleasures of vicariously identifying with his pitiable state, and ends by setting them the example they unfortunately will learn to imitate.[54]

For Plato, who so often strives to efface or remove all mixture, confusion, and changeability, his theory of drama is simple because, stripped down to essences, his categories are also simple. The mobility of temporary reversals and dialectical play with opposites already introduces a cognitive complexity that is the sign itself of a dangerous indeterminacy; it undermines the principle of like to like which regulates his thought and is designed, by its literalness, to reinforce a simple stability. At the most inclusive level is the dictum that no man can play more than one part, in life or in the theater (e.g., *Rep.* 3.394e–395b).

The other is always weaker and inferior to the self, whose idealization requires that, once perfectly established, it cannot change and still be itself. That lack of strength (attributable to the lack of mastery by the rational faculty and hence equal finally to a lack of wisdom) can be most

[54] The ostensible motive for banning poets in book 3 is the education of the young guardians to protect the city. Courage in battle is the model for control over warring forces within the self, as is emphasized in the second discussion of imitation in book 10. Cowardice is the radically feminine trait, despite Plato's willingness to train selected women as guardians. (The locus classicus is *Timaios* 90e–91a, in which Plato describes the first creation of women as due to "creatures generated as men who proved themselves cowardly and spent their lives in wrongdoing and were transformed at their second incarnation into women.") I simplify Plato's intricate argument, as he further sees this lack of control over the emotions, engendered by tragedy, as leading to an unruliness and violence he does not specify as feminine. Yet the tyrannical man, the most "theatrical" in Plato's view, whose exterior pomp and costume does not at all match his inner self (*Rep.* 577b), is seen ultimately as a slave to his passions who becomes so fearful that he "lives for the most part cowering in the house like a woman" (*Republic* 579b–c).

easily codified according to the conventional terms of the society under the name of the feminine other, to include the cognate negative traits of cowardice, fearfulness, and emotional lability. Hence, in Plato's reductive view of drama and of gender, playing the other is a species of wrongful imitation which threatens to infect reality and degrade the aspiring, virile self. It is therefore forbidden, above all, "for a man, being a man—in training, in fact to become a good/brave man," to imitate a woman in any way whatsoever: "whether old or young, whether railing against her husband, or boasting of a happiness which she imagines can rival the gods, or overwhelmed with grief and misfortune; much less a woman in love, or sick, or in labor" (*Republic* 3.395d–e). Men are neither permitted to impersonate a woman nor to show themselves in a male persona as undergoing the experiences of a woman, precisely the routes I have proposed as leading to masculine initiation into the lessons (and benefits) of the tragic world.

Limited as his discussion of theater may be, Plato, as a spectator who fails to come under the spell of tragic mimesis (or who perhaps once did and was cured), nonetheless darkly confirms the inextricable relationship between theater and the feminine. Tragedy cannot control the ambiguities of role-playing, most particularly when the male actor is called upon to represent the woman who is not under control either because she is actively unruly or because she succumbs to the pressures of her body. More generally, tragedy by its very nature and intention can make no solid provision for controlling the ambiguities of a worldview that theater is expressly designed to represent. Thus Plato, from his point of view, is entitled to deny to "the solemn and marvelous poiesis of tragedy" the very task we might agree it is well-equipped to accomplish, namely that of imparting "beneficial if unpleasing truths," and to claim instead that it gives its uncritical and vulgar audience what it desires to see and hear (*Gorgias* 502b).

Plato goes still further into the matter of gender and drama in the playful contest he stages between theater and philosophy in the *Symposium*, where the party to celebrate the recent victory of the tragic poet, Agathon, at the City Dionysia ends with the crowning of Sokrates instead of Agathon. In mounting his own rival drama to explore the subject of *erōs*, Plato excludes the presence of the feminine at the banquet but subtly and significantly uses the categories of effeminacy and femininity to enhance the philosophical position that is meant to include and supersede the appeal of the theater.

The *Symposium* is one of Plato's most artful and complex dialogues and deserves, of course, much fuller discussion.[55] It is established early on

---

[55] In particular, the discussion would benefit from including the important contribution

that love of women is an inferior sort of *erōs* (181a–d). This is not the crucial point. But we may note in our context the persuasive if unfair value of using Agathon as the representative of all tragic art. Agathon speaks second to last, just before Sokrates, and in his flowery speech on *erōs*, which parodies perhaps the very play that earned him the tragic victory (*Anthos* [or *Antheus*] = flower), he demonstrates the soft and effeminate nature for which he was known and which Aristophanes wickedly lampoons in his comedies (e.g., *Thesmophoriazousai*).[56] Although Aristophanes in the *Symposium* is made at the end to fall asleep before Agathon, thus establishing his rank in the hierarchy that leads from comedy to tragedy and then to philosophy, the comic poet is represented as a far more robust character than the tragic poet, and his contribution to the theme of *erōs* is more memorable and more substantial.[57] The contrast, to be sure, is even more striking between the lovelorn Agathon and Sokrates, whose physical endurance and resistance to pederastic temptation attest to the remarkable self-control of this soldier/philosopher/lover/hero.

On the other side, however, philosophy appropriates for its own use the one kind of feminine authority the culture acknowledges as legitimate when Sokrates names the prophetic priestess, Diotima, as the source of his initiation long ago into the sacred mysteries of Eros and as the original author of the inspiring discourse on *erōs* he now is about to deliver. The feminine retains here her more "instinctive" alliance with the erotic as well as her mysterious connection with that other world and its secrets whose power we have come to recognize when manifested in the theater. And the woman, armed with the prestige of her sacred vocation, is called upon to instruct men in how they might transcend feminine influence and, through the sublimations of pederastic love, even give birth to themselves.[58]

---

made by Alkibiades, the disruptive latecomer and party crasher, but it would not in any case substantially alter my argument.

[56] In this comedy, which satirizes Euripidean tragedy through the women's indignation at the poet for his unflattering (and oversexed) portraits of them, Agathon comes off as the truly effeminate male, in contrast to the trickster (but more manly figure), Euripides. Agathon appears in feminine accessories, claiming that to write female parts for the theater one must dress as a woman. He refuses to infiltrate the women's festival on the grounds that he would provide unfair competition for the "real" women, and finally supplies the feminine costume for Euripides' kinsman, who has been persuaded to go instead.

[57] Aristophanes presents the famous myth of the spherical human beings who, separated by Zeus for their hybris toward the gods, are forever searching for reunion with their other halves. These may be of the same or opposite sex, depending on the original composition of each.

[58] See now David Halperin, "Why Is Diotima a Woman?" in *Before Sexuality: The Construction of Erotic Experience in the Ancient Greek World*, ed. D. M. Halperin, J. J. Winkler, and F. I. Zeitlin (Princeton, 1989).

In Plato's counter-drama, the female as benevolent priestess has no cause of her own to protect and no conflictual interests to distract her. She is then free to lend wholehearted support to the cause of men and to transmit to them a wisdom without tragic pain that may become entirely theirs. She imparts a myth about the genealogy of Eros that makes the erotic principle a male child and explains his nature by assigning potency and presence to his father, *poros* (ways and means), and a famished emptiness to his mother, *penia* (poverty), who deceitfully (and characteristically) tricks the one who is endowed into consorting with the one who is not.

In suborning theater as well as the feminine, Plato's drama puts the former to sleep in the presence of the wakeful philosopher and transfers feminine oracular power to Sokrates—the midwife—who also incorporates the Dionysiac into his satyr-like image of Silenos. In the process Plato obviates the tragic necessity that requires the feminine presence upon the stage and whose complicated and essential functions in the theater of Dionysos we have followed throughout the course of this essay.

SIMON GOLDHILL

The Great Dionysia and Civic Ideology

THERE HAVE BEEN numerous attempts to understand the role and importance of the Great Dionysia in Athens, and it is a festival that has been made crucial to varied and important characterizations of Greek culture as well as to the history of drama or literature.[1] Recent scholarship, however, has greatly extended our understanding of the formation of fifth-century Athenian ideology—in the sense of the structure of attitudes and norms of behavior[2]—and this developing interest in what might be called a "civic discourse" requires a reconsideration of the Great Dionysia as a city festival. For while there have been several fascinating readings of particular plays with regard to the *polis* and its ideology,[3] there is still a considerable need to place the festival itself in terms of the ideology of the *polis*. Indeed, recent critics, in a justifiable reaction away from writers such as Gilbert Murray, have tended to emphasize on the one hand that the festival is a place of entertainment rather than religious ritual, and on the other hand that the plays should be approached primarily

Note: Two earlier versions of this article have appeared: "The Great Dionysia and Civic Ideology," *JHS* 107 (1987): 58–76; and "Anthropologie, idéologie, et Grandes Dionysies," in *Anthropologie et théâtre antique*, ed. P. Ghiron-Bistagne (Montpelier, France, 1987). This article is based on the *JHS* version, but includes new material and bibliography. This paper has been greatly helped by discussions, questions and comments from many friends and colleagues, especially O. Taplin, A. Bowie, E. Bowie, C. Sourvinou-Inwood, P. Easterling, R. Osborne, J. Henderson, G.E.R. Lloyd, and P. Cartledge.

[1] Particularly since Nietzsche's *The Birth of Tragedy* (on which see M. S. Silk and J. P. Stern, *Nietzsche on Tragedy* [Cambridge, Eng., 1981], especially 90–131). Many histories of Greek culture, or elements in Greek culture, have extended discussions of tragedy, e.g., E. R. Dodds, *The Greeks and the Irrational* (Berkeley, 1951), or B. Snell, *The Discovery of the Mind*, trans. T. Rosenmeyer (Oxford 1953). I have found especially interesting J.-P. Vernant and P. Vidal-Naquet, *Myth and Tragedy in Ancient Greece*, trans. J. Lloyd (Brighton, 1981), esp. chaps. 1–3.

[2] I am thinking especially of the studies of Vernant, Vidal-Naquet, Detienne, Loraux, and their followers. For the extensive influence of Vernant in particular, see *Arethusa* 16 (1983).

[3] See for example Nicole Loraux, *Les enfants d'Athéna* (Paris, 1981), particularly 157–253. F. Zeitlin, *Under the Sign of the Shield: Semiotics and Aeschylus' Seven against Thebes* (Rome, 1981), particularly 15–51. H. Foley, *Ritual Irony: Poetry and Sacrifice in Euripides* (Ithaca, 1985). See also S. D. Goldhill, *Reading Greek Tragedy* (Cambridge, Eng., 1986), esp. chap. 3.

as *dramatic* performances. This results in the following type of description:

> For the Athenians the Great Dionysia was an occasion to stop work,
> drink a lot of wine, eat some meat, and witness or participate in the
> various ceremonials, processions and priestly doings which are part
> of such holidays the world over. It was also the occasion for tragedy
> and comedy; but I do not see any way in which the Dionysiac occa-
> sion invades or affects the entertainment. . . . To put it another
> way, there is nothing intrinsically Dionysiac about Greek tragedy.[4]

I hope to show in this article how such a characterization of the Great
Dionysia provides a fundamentally mistaken view of the festival and its
historical context. While there are certain similarities between the Great
Dionysia and religious festivals the world over, I shall demonstrate that
there are specific ceremonies, processions, and priestly doings that form
an essential and unique context for the production of Greek drama and
which do indeed importantly affect the entertainment.

There are two further arguments which often have been linked to the
sort of description of the festival that Taplin offers. The first is that dramatic criticism should concentrate on the plays as pieces for performance
—"in action." I shall attempt to demonstrate how the understanding of a
play in performance requires an understanding of the complexities of a
context for performance which involves more than the technical details
of the instantiation of a script in the fifth-century theater. The second argument that has been thought to follow from the nature of the Dionysia
as described in the more generally read studies is that the requirements of
performance before a mass audience preclude, or at any rate severely
limit, the possibilities of complex, problematic, or obscure expression in
the tragic texts. I shall argue that scholars' appeals in their dramatic criticism to criteria of a *necessary* clarity, simplicity, or directness distort not
only the readings of particular passages or plays, but also the fundamentally questioning or agonistic nature of Greek tragedy. This article is not,
of course, meant to resuscitate the theories of Gilbert Murray and his followers, but rather to aid the understanding of Greek tragedy as a social,
political, and theatrical phenomenon.

What happened on the days immediately before the days on which
plays were performed is the part of the festival least well known to us,
and it is also the part that interests me least for my present purposes. I
will, however, briefly summarize (with some added comments) Pickard-
Cambridge's account as emended by Gould and Lewis[5] in order to provide a sense of the background of the main days of the Dionysia. The

---

[4] O. Taplin, *Greek Tragedy in Action* (London, 1978), 162.
[5] *DFA*, 58ff.

first part of the festival may not even be regarded as part of the festival—
the *eisagōgē apo tēs eskharās*, "the leading in from the sacred hearth."[6] This
was a reenactment of the original advent of Dionysos from Eleutherai.
The statue of Dionysos Eleuthereus was taken to a temple on the road to
Eleutherai, a sacrifice was offered there, and then the statue was escorted
back to the temple. It is interesting to note that second-century inscriptions indicate that the leading part in this procession was taken by the
ephebes.[7] There is, however, no fifth- or fourth-century evidence for
this—or indeed for the whole rite—and it is perhaps incautious, if attractive, to assume that the ephebes played the same major role in fifth-
century ceremonies (as Pickard-Cambridge assumes).

The *eisagōgē apo tēs eskharās* was followed by the *pompē*,[8] which was a
great procession leading up to the sacrifice in the sacred precinct of
Dionysos. In the second century, the sacrifice was conducted by the
ephebes, as Richard Seaford has recently discussed.[9] There is mention
also of a *kanēphoros*, a bearer of a basket of offerings, and Pickard-Cambridge suggests that color and show were particularly important in making this a glorious occasion. The *pompē* was perhaps followed by a *kōmos*,
a "celebratory revel," of which next to nothing is clearly known, even if,
indeed, the *kōmos* should be taken as separate from the *pompē*[10] and the
singing of choruses, the dithyrambic competitions that also took place at
the Great Dionysia.[11] For example, the famous inscription sometimes
called "Fasti" (*IG* II² 2318), with its list of victors, appears to refer to the
festival in general as "the *kōmoi* for Dionysos."[12] The combination of
procession, sacrifice, and celebration was itself a structure typical of fifth-
century Athenian religious practice (and Greek practice in general).

There was also a preparatory day for the festival on which a Proagon
was held. After 444 B.C.E. it was held in the Odeion, but it is not known
where or if it was held before that date.[13] Numerous documents hint at
what happened in the Proagon, and an interesting account of the Proagon for the Lenaia is to be found in Plato's *Symposium* (1194aff.). It
would appear that each poet mounted a temporary platform with his actors and chorus, and announced the subject of the plays he was about to
present in the competition. It would also appear from Plato that this

---

6 See *DFA*, 59–61, with bibliography (esp. 61 n. 1).

7 *IG* II² 1028, *IG* II² 1008. The earliest reference to this is 127/6 B.C.E. (*SEG* 15, 104).

8 See *DFA*, 61–63. A second-century inscription (*IG* II² 1006) separates the *eisagōgē* and
the *pompē*.

9 R. Seaford, "Dionysiac Drama and the Dionysiac Mysteries," *CQ* 31 (1981): 252–75.

10 As G. Thomson, *Aeschylus and Athens*, 2d ed. (London, 1946), 165–74, assumes in his
description of the festival.

11 It is suggested plausibly (*DFA*, 74–79) that the Dithyrambic competition took place in
the two days before the dramas.

12 See *DFA*, 71–73, 101–4.

13 See (contra Müller) *DFA*, 68.

might be thought of as something of an ordeal, and a nice, if thoroughly unreliable, anecdote in the *Life of Euripides* relates that shortly after the death of Euripides, Sophokles appeared for the Proagon in mourning and his performers were without their customary garlands. The people observing burst into tears. The question of the relative dates of these various ceremonials is extremely vexed and I have nothing to add to Gould's and Lewis' necessary corrections to Pickard-Cambridge (augmented by Pélékidis[14] and by Allen,[15] who sets out clearly the evidence, particularly with regard to the comedies).

It is what happened in the theater itself before the plays, however, that is my main concern, and I want to look in particular at four specific moments of ceremony that are rarely discussed or even mentioned in the context of tragedy.[16] The evidence for the first comes from Plutarch's life of Kimon (*Kim.* 8.7–9):

> When Sophokles, still a young man, entered the lists with his first plays, Apsephion the Arkhōn, seeing that the spirit of rivalry ran high among the spectators, did not appoint judges of the contest as usual by lot, but when Kimon and his fellow-generals advanced into the theater and made the customary libation to the god, he would not allow them to depart, but forced them to take the oath and sit as judges, being ten in all, one from each tribe. So, then, the contest, because of the unusual dignity of the judges, was more animated than ever before.

Plutarch describes how in 468 the *arkhōn*, by a bold stroke, set aside the regular procedure in the theater by appointing the generals as judges. Pickard-Cambridge notes that the probable point in the proceedings was just before the performances of the tragedies, when the judges were

[14] C. Pélékidis, *Histoire de l'éphébie attique* (Paris, 1962), esp. appendix 3, 301–6.

[15] J. T. Allen, *On the Program of the City Dionysia during the Peloponnesian War*, U.Cal. Publ. in Class. Phil. 12.3 (1938): 35–42.

[16] There is no mention of these ceremonies in Taplin, *Greek Tragedy*, J.-P. Vernant, *Myth and Society in Ancient Greece*, trans. J. Lloyd (Brighton, 1980), and P. Vidal-Naquet, *Le chasseur noir: Formes de pensée et formes de société dans le mond grec* (Paris, 1981), trans. A. Szegedy-Maszak under the title *The Black Hunter: Forms of Thought and Forms of Society in the Greek World* (Baltimore, 1986), nor, for example, in P. Arnott, *An Introduction to the Greek Theatre* (London, 1959), A. Lesky, *Greek Tragedy*, trans. H. A. Frankfort (London, 1965), and, most recently, M. J. Walton, *The Greek Sense of Theatre* (London, 1984). They are mentioned briefly without any analysis by H. L. Baldry, *The Greek Tragic Theatre* (London, 1981), 27, and N. Loraux, *L'invention d'Athènes* (Paris, 1981), trans. A. Sheridan under the title *The Invention of Athens* (Cambridge, Mass., 1986), 26–31, discusses the orphans briefly in terms of the ephebate but not in terms of the theater. P. Cartledge, in *Greek Religion and Society*, ed. P. E. Easterling and J. V. Muir (Cambridge, 1985), briefly mentions the possible political significance of three of the ceremonies, but does not consider the plays, or the overall effects of the festival.

about to be chosen.[17] What the passage indicates is that the libations before the tragedies were poured by the ten generals. The nature of the offerings is unclear—*nenomismenās*, "customary," is the only description
we have—but it is interesting that for the beginning of the tragic festival's days of drama it was the ten most powerful military and political
leaders, the *stratēgoi*, who were actively involved before the whole city.
A fourth-century inscription (*IG* II² 1496) confirms that the generals
were involved religiously in the dramatic festivals, but also suggests that
the number of occasions in the calendar on which all the generals acted
together in such a way were very few—no more than four occasions are
attested for any one year—and usually it was for some occasion more obviously linked to their civic functions. The inscription mentions, for example, offerings to *dēmokratia*, "Democracy," to *eirēnē*, "peace," and to
agathē tukhē, "good fortune."[18] On the major state occasion of the Great
Dionysia it was, then, the most influential and important representatives
of the state who were involved in the opening religious ceremony.

The second element of ceremony can be seen directly in a scholion to
Aristophanes' *Akharnians* (on 504):

It had been ordained that the cities bring their tribute to Athens at
the Great Dionysia, as Eupolis says in *The Cities*.

In the Great Dionysia, the tribute of the cities of the Athenian empire
was brought into the theater. This ceremony is outlined in more detail by
Isokrates (*De pace* 82, Loeb ed., trans. G. Norlin):

For so exactly did they gauge the actions by which human beings in-
cur the worst odium that they passed a decree to divide the funds derived from the tributes of the allies into talents and to bring it onto
the stage, when the theater was full, at the festival of Dionysos; and
not only was this done but at the same time they led in upon the
stage the sons of those who had lost their lives in the war, seeking
thus to display to our allies, on the one hand, the value of their own
property which was brought in by hirelings, and to the rest of the
Hellenes, on the other, the multitude of the fatherless and the mis-

---

[17] *DFA*, 95–96.

[18] The fragmentary state of the inscription makes certainty here finally impossible. There
is, for example, a surprising reference in one year (333 B.C.E.) to a sacrifice by the generals
at the temple of Ammon. It is not known when or why Ammon became part of the state
religion in Athens, but Foucart, noting this inscription and the name Ammonias given to a
sacred galley as mentioned in [Aristotle], *Ath. Pol.* 61, suggests that 333 was the year of the
inauguration of the temple of Ammon in Athens, and hence the sacrifice by the generals: P.
Foucart, "Décret athénien de l'an 333," *REG* 6 (1893): 1–7, in particular 6–7, and see *SIG*,
281.

fortunes which result from this policy of aggression. And in so doing they counted the city happy.

Here, following Raubitschek's generally accepted analysis,[19] it is evident from the opening sentence that the tribute was divided into talents and displayed in the orchestra.[20] Isokrates' rhetorical use of this event is interesting, however. As Pearson comments, "Isokrates deplores the *aselgeia* [outrageousness, insolence] of their ancestors in having the tribute publicly presented at the Dionysia."[21] Such a ceremony, Isokrates claims, was a precise way to become hated by other people. This presumably was not the actual aim of such an event. Rogers comments in his edition of the *Akharnians*, "the tribute brought by the allies was spread out talent by talent over the theatrical orchestra in the sight of the assembled Hellenes";[22] that is, the display was not just a piece of pomp and splendor, nor, as Isokrates rhetorically supposes, to show how the Athenians valued the property of the allies. Rather, it was a demonstration before the city and its many international visitors of the power of the *polis* of Athens, its role as a force in the Greek world. It was a public display of the success in military and political terms of the city. It used the state festival to glorify the state.

That this ceremony involved such a projection of self-image, such a projection of power, may be hinted at in Aristophanes' *Akharnians* 496–509 (Sommerstein, adapted by Goldhill): "Be not indignant with me, gentlemen of the audience, if, though a beggar, I speak before the Athenians about public affairs in a comedy. Comedy too knows about Justice; and what I will say will be shocking but it will be right." Dikaiopolis is preparing to speak to the city as city, to *didaskein tēn polin*, "teach the city." He goes on, "For now at any rate Kleon won't slander me, that I foul-mouth the city when there are *xenoi* present. For we're just ourselves and it is the Lenaian contest, and there are no strangers here yet. For the tribute hasn't arrived, and the allies are away from the city." Unlike the Great Dionysia, the Lenaia was a more private affair. Unlike the Great Dionysia, the Lenaia involved no tribute, no allies, no problem about speaking home truths to the city.[23]

---

[19] A. Raubitschek, "Two Notes on Isocrates," *TAPA* 72 (1941): 356–62.

[20] Raubitschek, "Two Notes," 358–59 (referring to B. D. Meritt, *Documents on Athenian Tribute* [Cambridge, Eng., 1937], 50 n. 3) goes so far as to suggest that each talent was carried in a terra-cotta vessel of the sort known to have been used to store and transport money, or perhaps in leather bags, similar to those seen in an extant fragment of a relief which surmounted a decree concerning the collection of Athenian tribute.

[21] L. Pearson, "Historical Allusions in the Attic Orators," *CP* 36 (1941): 228.

[22] B. B. Rogers, *The Acharnians of Aristophanes* (London, 1910), 76.

[23] This speech has been much commented on. For the didactic role that comedy is claiming here see O. Taplin, "Tragedy and Trugedy," *CQ* 33 (1983): 331–33; and for the poles

A further passage from the *Akharnians* makes this example seem less straightforward. The chorus—also speaking to the city as city—remarks in the parabasis (641–51, Sommerstein):

> For doing that our poet deserves a rich reward at your hands, and also for showing what democracy meant for people of the allied states. That is why they will come now from those states bringing you their tribute, eager to see that superb poet who took the risk of talking justice before the Athenians. So far has the fame of his bold-ness already spread that even the King, when he questioned the Spartan embassy, first asked them which side was more powerful in ships, and then which side received plenty of abuse from this poet; "for those people," he said, "have been made much better men, and will win the war decisively with him for an adviser."

Again the subject of the speech is the opportunity and license to speak out freely in the democracy. The allies bringing the tribute are said to come because they want to see the best poet—the one who is prepared to speak out *ta dikaia*, "what is just, right," among the Athenians. The Per-sian King, indeed, in order to test the Spartan embassy, would want to know who had the best navy and against which city the poet had spoken *kaka polla*, which means "many bad things of the city" ("plenty of abuse," as Sommerstein translates), with perhaps also a hint of "many bad things to the city," that is, many foul tales. "That's what gives strength for fighting." It is always difficult to evaluate the balance of joke and serious comment even in the parabasis of an Aristophanic play,[24] but it is interesting that once more Aristophanes, or at least his chorus, seems to be defending the right to free and scurrilous speech, and once more the context for this defense is the occasion of the Great Dionysia when all the *xenoi* are there. Many passages from Aristophanes and elsewhere could be used to show the commonplace that poets are the educators of the citizens—"les maîtres de verité," as Detienne puts it—but these two pas-sages suggest a more specific awareness of the connection of the Great

---

of the discussion on this speech overall (with further bibliography), W. Forrest, "Aristo-phanes' *Acharnians*," *Phoenix* 17 (1963): 1–12; D. MacDowell, "The Nature of Aristo-phanes' *Akharnians*," *G&R* 30 (1983): 143–62.

[24] Against the commonly adopted position that in the parabasis the chorus speaks simply "for the poet," see the sensible remarks of R. Harriott, *Aristophanes, Poet and Dramatist* (London and Sydney, 1986), 25: "The reader of parabases studies works of fiction," and C. Whitman, *Aristophanes and the Comic Hero* (Cambridge, Mass., 1964), 22: "It would be un-safe . . . to accept as sober truth some of the hair raising assertions which occur in many a parabasis"; also the more general statements of G. M. Sifakis, *Parabasis and Animal Choruses* (London, 1971) especially 7–22, J. Carrière, *Le carnaval et la politique* (Paris, 1979), 17–143, and especially, A. Bowie, "The Parabasis in Aristophanes: Prolegomena, *Acharnians*," *CQ* 32 (1982): 27–40.

Dionysia, the ceremony of bringing in tribute in the presence of the *xenoi*, with the city on display, the city aware of its role and image as an international power.

This ceremony moreover can have been introduced only at a relatively late date—after the transfer of the treasury from Delos—and it shows how, with the development of Athenian democracy, the power of the *polis* as such became increasingly emphasized in public ritual and display. (The ceremonies I am discussing were not merely organizational relics from an earlier era.) The public funeral of the war dead and the establishment of the casualty list *stēlai* which I will discuss below, also appear to have been introduced no earlier than the 470s.[25] In both cases, the development of civic ideology is seen in the development of ritual.

The third moment of ceremony I want to discuss is also clearly linked to the authority of the *polis*. Before the tragedies the names of those men who had greatly benefited Athens in some way were read out in front of the whole city, and the honors that had been bestowed on them in the form of a crown or garland were specified. It was a great honor to be singled out in this way before the city, but a passage from Demosthenes, where such crown-giving is discussed, suggests a different kind of reasoning behind such a ceremony (*De corona* 120, Loeb ed., trans. C. Vince):

> But, really now, are you so unintelligent and blind, Aiskhines, that you are incapable of reflecting that a crown is equally gratifying to the person crowned wheresoever it is proclaimed, but that the proclamation is made in the Theater merely for the sake of those by whom it is conferred? For the whole vast audience is stimulated to do service to the city, and applauds the exhibition of gratitude rather than the recipient; and that is the reason why the state has enacted this statute.

The whole audience was stimulated by such a ceremony to do service to the *polis*. The ceremony was "pour encourager les autres." Indeed, Demosthenes suggests further that the audience was actually applauding the exhibition of thanks rather than the person being crowned: *kai tous apodidontas tēn kharin māllon epainousi tou stephanōmenou*. Demosthenes' rhetoric appeals here to a fundamental and well-known tenet of democratic ideology, namely, that a man acts and should act to benefit the city; so

[25] On the date of the funeral speech and public grave *stēlai*, see C. W. Clairmont, *Patrios Nomos: Public Burial in Athens During the Fifth and Fourth Centuries B.C.* (London, 1983), 16–45; Loraux, *L'invention*, 28ff. F. Jacoby, "*Patrios Nomos*: State Burial in Athens and the Public Cemetery in the Kerameikos," *JHS* 64 (1944): 37–66 has been tellingly questioned by O. W. Bradeen, "The Athenian Casualty Lists," *CQ* 19 (1969): 145–59. In general, see also R. Stupperich, *Staatsbegräbnis und Privatesgrabmal im klassischen Athen* (Diss. Westfälische Wilhelms-Universität zu Münster 1977).

the individual himself and his success were not what was important; it was the city recognizing and being thankful for a contribution to the city that was enacted in such a ceremony. For Demosthenes, this ceremony of announcing the names of civic benefactors was fundamentally connected to the projection and promotion of civic duties and civic self-image.

If Demosthenes' rhetoric appeals to the fervor of democratic ideology, a long argument in Aiskhines (*Against Ktesiphon* 41–56) hints at ways in which this ceremony was sometimes less straightforward, and that vying for this honor, as for others, was something that the Athenians competed in vigorously.[26] Aiskhines argues at length both on the technicalities of the laws of giving a crown in the theater and on the possible justification for the specific case of Demosthenes receiving a crown; nonetheless, like Demosthenes, he takes it for granted that the announcement of the crown before the people in the theater was closely connected with the authority and status of the *dēmos*, and moreover, that the presentation was "before all the Hellenes" (43.8; cf. 49.3). Even with allowance for the rhetorical overkill in Aiskhines' speech (against Demosthenes as much as against Ktesiphon, of course) and the specific technicalities of his argument, it is clear that this ceremony was perceived as an important public occasion. The proclamation of the names of those who had benefited the city was another way of asserting the ties, connections, and duties between individuals and the city. Above all it stressed the moral and social imperative of doing good for the city as a key way of defining behavior in the democratic *polis*.

The fourth ceremonial aspect of the tragic festival is also closely tied to the civic ideology of the Athenian democratic *polis*. Again, the orators provide an important insight into the occasion. The first piece of evidence is Isokrates, *De pace* 82, the passage quoted earlier. Isokrates says that the children of those who died in war were brought onstage. This, he says, was to show the other Greeks how many orphans and what disasters resulted from a policy of aggression. The *De pace* is, as its title suggests, something of an anti-imperialist, anti-war tract, and there can be few better examples of a misrepresentative use of a past historical event to further a rhetorical argument. For as we will see, the ideology of this event may imply an attitude quite different from that of Isokrates.[27]

<hr />

[26] The evidence for the presentation of crowns to Athenian citizens in the fifth century, however, is much less secure than for the fourth century.

[27] See for discussion and bibliography, e.g., P. Harding, "The Purpose of Isocrates, *Archidamos* and *On the Peace*," *CSCA* 6 (1973): 137–49. Isokrates' treatment of the ceremony is particularly important in emphasizing that while one may talk of the expected norms of an ideology (even in the complex, developing world of the fifth-century *polis*), the construction of the meaning of the ceremonies depends also on the viewer. The relations of indi-

I wrote "past historical event" because, as is clear from a fascinating passage of Aiskhines (330 B.C.E.), this ceremony was already no longer performed by the time of the speech *Against Ktesiphon* (Loeb ed., trans. C. D. Adams):

> For what Greek nurtured in freedom would not mourn as he sat in the theater and recalled this, if nothing more, that once on this day, when as now the tragedies were about to be performed, in a time when the city had better customs and followed better leaders, the herald would come forward and place before you the orphans whose fathers had died in battle, young men clad in the panoply of war; and he would utter that proclamation so honorable and such an incentive to valor: "These young men, whose fathers showed themselves brave men and died in war, have been supported by the state until they have come of age; and now clad thus in full armor by their fellow citizens, they are sent out with the prayers of the city, to go each his way; and they are invited to seats of honor in the theater." Such was the proclamation then, but not today. (154)

This passage of Aiskhines—as rhetorical as Isokrates—gives us, however, a much clearer view of what happened and of its relation to the expected norms of a civic discourse. The young men whose fathers were recognized as heroes of the city because they had died in battle[28] were brought up and educated at the expense of and by the city. When they reached the end of maintained childhood, they were paraded in full military uniform, again provided by the *dēmos*, and they were sent forth to whatever good fortune they might find, and were honored with special places in the theater. The herald proclaimed what the city had done for the boys and what as men they would do for the city.

Each of the four ceremonies which opened the days of the tragedies in the Great Dionysia, then, is closely linked to a sense of the authority and dignity of the *polis*. But before I turn to consider the relations between these ceremonies and the tragedies, I want to focus briefly on the parade of orphans, a ritual which seems to have flourished with democracy and to have disappeared at the time when certain evidence for the institution of the ephebate itself starts to appear. For it is certainly possible to specify in considerably more detail the way in which this ceremony relates to civic ideology, and such an analysis will be important for our understanding of the festival and its plays.

I begin with the well-known statement of Vernant, recently quoted by

---

viduals in and to an ideology cannot be considered as *necessarily* determined or univocal, least of all in a period of rapid social change.

[28] On *andres agathoi genomenoi*, see Loraux, *L'invention*, s.v. "agathoi," especially 99–101.

Lloyd-Jones in his discussion of Artemis and the transition from girlhood to womanhood: "Marriage is to a girl what war is to a boy."[29] Marriage and childbirth provide the *telos* of a woman's life when she is clearly and completely separated from the male sphere and she adopts the role by which she is essentially defined.[30] In the word *gunē* it is difficult to separate the senses of "woman" and "wife." For the man, the *telos* is to stand in the hoplite rank as a fully accepted citizen.[31] It is a moment by which his role in society is essentially defined. The parallels in achievement between childbirth and fighting give a peculiar force to Medeia's famous remark that she would rather stand in the battle-line three times than give birth once.[32]

The parallels between war and marriage as states defining male and female roles in society have been discussed at length by Vernant, Vidal-Naquet, Loraux, and others.[33] I want in particular to look here at the notion of war and fighting as the role into which a man is initiated. Now, cross-cultural parallels for initiations connected with fighting and manhood are numerous.[34] The notions of first blood, first kill, and taking up

[29] Vernant, *Myth and Society*, 23, quoted by H. Lloyd-Jones, "Artemis and Iphigeneia," *JHS* 103 (1983): 99.

[30] See Vernant, *Myth and Society*, 19–70. See also, e.g., F. Zeitlin, "Cultic Models of the Female: Rites of Dionysus and Demeter," *Arethusa* 15 (1982): 129–57. For interesting collections of essays on this and related topics, see *Reflections of Women in Antiquity*, ed. H. Foley (London, Paris, New York, 1982); *Arethusa* 6 (1973) and 11 (1978), now published under the editorship of J. Peradotto and J. P. Sullivan as *Women in the Ancient World: The Arethusa Papers*; *Images of Women in Antiquity*, ed. A. Cameron and A. Kuhrt (London and Melbourne, 1983); *Sexual Assymetry: Studies in Ancient Society*, ed. J. Blok and P. Mason (Amsterdam, 1987). A good general introduction is J. P. Gould, "Law, Custom, and Myth: Aspects of the Social Position of Women in Classical Athens," *JHS* 100 (1980): 38–59. I have discussed this material with regard to tragedy in Goldhill, *Reading*, chap. 5.

[31] See Vernant, *Myth and Society*, 19–70; see also *Problèmes de la guerre en grèce ancienne*, ed. J.-P. Vernant (Paris, 1968), and the sensible comments of J. K. Davies, *Democracy and Classical Greece* (Hassocks, Eng., 1978) 31ff.

[32] *Medeia* 250–1. See the excellent study of N. Loraux, "Le lit, la guerre," *L'Homme* 21.1 (1981): 37–67.

[33] See, e.g., Bradeen, "Athenian Casualty Lists"; Clairmont, *Patrios Nomos*; M. Detienne, *Les maîtres de vérité dans la grèce archaique* (Paris, 1967); Goldhill, *Reading*; Loraux, *L'Invention* and *Les enfants*; C. P. Segal, *Tragedy and Civilization: An Interpretation of Sophocles* (Cambridge, Mass., 1981); Taplin, *Greek Tragedy*; Vernant, *Myth and Society*; Vernant and Vidal-Naquet, *Myth and Tragedy*; Vidal-Naquet, *Le chasseur noir*; R. I. Winnington-Ingram, *Sophocles: An Interpretation* (Cambridge, Eng., 1980); Zeitlin, "Cultic Models"; Foley, *Reflections*; Cameron and Kuhrt, *Images*; Blok and Mason, *Sexual Assymetry*; and Gould, "Law, Custom, and Myth."

[34] A vast bibliography could be given. A. van Gennep, *Les rites de passage* (Paris, 1908) remains standard. For a standard case study (and further bibliography on cross-cultural parallels), see V. W. Turner, *The Forest of Symbols* (Ithaca, N.Y., 1967) and *The Ritual Process* (Rochester, 1969). For the classical material, see H. Jeanmaire, *Couroi et Courètes* (Lille,

a role with a specifically male group of hunters or fighters occur again and again. But the culture of fifth-century Athens offers a particularly interesting view of a changing attitude to warfare. The Homeric warrior is a man who fights primarily as an individual, for his *kleos*, "renown," "fame." When he meets or challenges another warrior, the exchanging of names and boasts, the named catalogues of victims, point to the connections of individual military prowess and the perpetuation of an individual's *kleos*. The hero is supreme. The narrative of the *Iliad* revolves around Akhilleus' need for *timē*, "honor," which is the external, visible sign of *kleos* and *kudos*, "glory," the loss of which makes him withdraw from the battle. It is an essential dynamic of the *Iliad*'s tragic force that Akhilleus, the best of the Akhaians, is also the one who takes the logic of a heroic ethos to an extreme in that he is prepared knowingly to go to his death, to choose an early death, in part at least in order to perpetuate an everlasting *kleos*. The notions of single combat, a hierarchy of warriors, and the search for the perpetuation of a *name* are essential structurings of the heroic ethos of the Homeric poems.[35]

The Homeric poems remained throughout the fifth century in a position of considerable authority. Despite the attacks of Xenophanes, say, or from a different viewpoint, those of Stesikhoros, Plato's judgment of Homer as the best and most divine of the poets remained the most common esthetic and moral evaluation.[36] Indeed, Plato's hostility to the poets is to a large degree due to the status of authority held by poets as teachers or controllers of knowledge—the role which Plato wishes to appropriate for philosophy alone. But one of the most striking points of tension between the poetry of Homer and its use in the fifth century is in the sphere of military values. Of course, certain standards were retained: appeals to bravery, strength, courage, *aretē*, "excellence," as military values were as common in fifth- and fourth-century generals' mouths as they are in Homeric leaders' speeches. But the invention and dominance of the hoplite phalanx on land and the growing importance of naval power at sea introduced a new series of values. The nature of the phalanx required not individual expression of prowess but the values of group cooperation. The phalanx was only as strong as its weakest member—a phalanx broken was easily routed and destroyed. Unlike the Homeric view of the Trojan War, where so much of the fate of both sides depended on the behavior of its strongest individuals, Akhilleus and Hektor, in warfare dominated by the hoplite phalanx, it was as a group that

---

1939); A. Brelich, *Paides e parthenoi* (Rome, 1969); C. Calame, *Les choeurs de jeunes filles en Grèce archaique* (Rome, 1977).

[35] I have discussed these ideas at further length with bibliography in a forthcoming book, *The Poet's Voice.*

[36] Plato, *Ion* 530b9–10. See Detienne, *Les maîtres*, and Goldhill, *Reading*, esp. chap. 6.

the phalanx fought and won and lost. So too a ship succeeded or failed as a unit.[37] It would be a banal view of cultural change—indeed, it would simply be false—to suggest that there are no signs of cooperative or group ethics in Homer. Similarly, it is quite incorrect to suppose that desire for individual honor disappeared in the fifth and fourth century.[38] But it is also the case that the qualities required of a fighting man were channelled in a different direction in fifth-century Athens and were given a different emphasis.[39] What is more, these different requirements of military involvement were closely linked to the idea of the democratic *polis* as well as to its history. For in the fifth century the army was truly a citizen army. To be a citizen one had to play one's role in the hoplite rank or take one's place in a warship, and to take one's place in the hoplite rank or warship one—in general[40]—had to be a citizen. When Vernant says that war is an essential determinant of a man's role in society, in part he is referring to the way in which citizenship and military values were inherently intertwined in fifth-century Athens. Moreover, as Finley writes, there were very few years and almost no years in succession without some military engagements for Athens in particular.[41] When war was debated by the citizens in the Assembly, it was debated by the men who would follow the decision into battle. The involvement of Athenians in war and military values was not only deeply embedded in the myths and stories told as examples, but in the actual running of the city.

One of the most interesting recent works on this connection of Athenian military values and the democratic *polis* is Loraux, *L'invention d'Athènes*. In this exhaustive study of funeral orations, Loraux has superbly illuminated both a major state event and the way the Greeks conceptualized the city and a person's involvement in it. I want briefly to use some of Loraux's findings to outline some further aspects of Athenian

[37] The more the Athenians depend on naval power, the more the constant appeals to the values of the hoplite seem tinged with an ideological import, even a nostalgia for days when military and political success was more easily assimilable to earlier ideals. Nor did being a member of the Athenian navy involve the expense that being a hoplite always required (with all the possible implications of a financially determined class).

[38] See the comments of K. Dover, *Greek Popular Morality in the Time of Plato and Aristotle* (Oxford, 1974), 229–34.

[39] Recent attacks on the notion of the hoplite reform by scholars who claim to detect evidence of organized group fighting in Homer have tended to undervalue the importance of this shift in values and representation; see, e.g., the fundamental study of J. Latacz, *Kampfparänase, Kampfdarstellung und Kampfwirklichkeit in der Ilias, bei Kallinos und Tyrtaios* (Munich, 1977), and, most recently (with further bibliography), I. Morris, *Burial and Ancient Society* (Cambridge, Eng., 1987), 196–205.

[40] See the qualification of Loraux, *L'invention*, quoted below, n. 49. These exceptions, like the use of slaves (later given the same rights as Plataean allies) at the battle of Arginusae, are seen as specific exceptions to the general rule by ancient and modern sources.

[41] M. I. Finley, *Politics in the Ancient World* (Cambridge, 1983), 60.

ideas of military service, because the funeral speech as an institution offers a fascinating comparison with the tragic festival.[42] The funeral
speech for those who had died in war was delivered yearly by a man ap-
pointed by the state and, of course, for the first year of the Peloponnesian
war the speaker was Perikles. The speech was delivered specifically for
those who had died fighting for the city. The ceremony involved a
procession, and then the speech at the burial site. What is particularly interesting is the content of the speech itself, and the restrictions apparently
surrounding the event. Individual rites and offerings were allowed on the
two days before the speech, but on the day of burial, everyone, citizens
and foreigners, men and women together, followed a line of wagons in
which the bones of the dead were arranged tribe by tribe. At the cemetery the speaker addressed the crowd, but he did not deliver what one
might at first expect from a funeral speech. The subject of the speech was
not exactly the glories and valor of the men who died, but rather the glories of the city itself. Indeed, the names of those who had fallen were not
even mentioned. The speech glorified the city and, as I earlier quoted Demosthenes saying, it was a way of applauding the act of giving thanks
rather than of applauding the individuals. The most famous example of a
funeral speech is Perikles' in Thoukydides, and this speech has certainly
been used again and again to explain, prove, or determine Athenians' attitudes to their city. Perikles' speech concentrated on the glories of the
city of Athens—in the first year of the war which would destroy the
city's power. Thoukydides' placing of that particular speech in that particular place in the narrative of Athens' rise and fall is certainly a composition of rhetorical artfulness by the historian, but it also helps us
formulate a sense of the important change of attitude with regard to
fighting. For now men were said to fight not for individual *kleos*, nor for
the perpetuation of their names through the retelling of acts of individual
prowess. Now fighting was for the city. One might fight to free a land,
to protect homes, women, and children, as in Homer, but success was
measured in terms of the city's fortunes, and each individual's success
was subsumed in the *kleos* of the city. So in the funeral speech it was the
city, and a citizen's role in democracy, that were discussed. Perikles' soldiers were a class, a group, not individuated. Military values were separated from individuals and individualism. No names were given in a
funeral speech—the reverse of Homeric name-filled battle narratives,
where there are no anonymous heroes.

Closely linked with the development of the funeral speech and the

---

[42] I am aware that in the available space I will not be able to do justice to the subtlety of
Loraux's argument or the wealth of her material. Since Loraux, a further long study in English has been published—Clairmont—which sets out the evidence usefully but lacks Loraux's grasp of the issues. For a good correction of Clairmont on Herms, see R. Osborne,
"The Erection and Mutilation of the Hermai," *PCPS* 31 (1985): 47–73.

public burial of the war dead, however, is the establishment of the Athenian casualty list *stēlai*, which certainly must qualify the sense of the
anonymity of the democratic war dead.[43] Although it is at present impossible to discover the precise chronological connection between the institution of the public funeral address and the erection of the casualty lists
(except that the address is probably a later innovation),[44] scholars are
generally agreed that, as with the funeral oration, "erecting of casualty
lists . . . is contemporary with the rise of Athenian democracy."[45] These
lists certainly recorded the names of those who died for the city, but here
too in a fascinating way we can see the influence of civic ideology. For
the individual names were given in lists according to the Kleisthenic
tribal divisions, without patronymic, without demotic—without, in
other words, the normal markers of a Greek male's position in society.[46]
Loraux writes: "The official list proclaims the equality of all Athenian
citizens . . . the dead citizens have no other status but Athenian."[47]
There are, it must be added, certain titles which appear very occasionally
in these lists, but even these are only military, civic roles, such as *stratēgos*, *trierarkhos*, and *taxiarkhos* ("general," and "trierarch," "taxiarch").[48]
The casualty lists show how the democratic egalitarian ethos attempted
to "intégrer les valeurs aristocratiques de la gloire,"[49] ("assimilate the
aristocratic values of glory"), in that each man was offered a degree of

[43] For descriptions of these *stēlai*, see in particular Bradeen, "Athenian Casualty Lists";
Clairmont, *Patrios Nomos*, 46–59; also D. W. Bradeen, "Athenian Casualty Lists," *Hesperia*
33 (1964): 16–62; "The Athenian Casualty Lists of 464 B.C.," *Hesperia* 36 (1967): 321–28;
and "New Fragments of Casualty Lists," *Hesperia* 37 (1968): 237–40. Loraux, *L'Invention*,
31ff. has an interesting discussion.

[44] See Thuk. 2.35. For bibliography on the question, see Clairmont, *Patrios Nomos*, 250
n. 17. For the important role of the Marathon victors and their memorial, see Clairmont,
Patrios Nomos, 10–11, and particularly Loraux, *L'Invention*, s.v. "Marathon," especially
157–73. For contrasting views on the reference to Marathon in Thuk. 2.35, see H. Konishi,
"The Composition of Thucydides' *History*," *AJP* 101 (1980): 35–41, esp. n. 19; and M.
Ostwald, *Nomos and the Beginnings of Athenian Democracy* (Oxford, 1969), 175.

[45] Clairmont, *Patrios Nomos*, 20.

[46] See N. Loraux, "Mourir devant Troie, tomber pour Athènes: De la gloire du héros à
l'idée de la cité," in *La mort, les morts dans les anciennes sociétés*, ed. G. Gnoli and J.-P. Vernant
(Cambridge, Eng., and Paris, 1982), 28.

[47] Loraux, *L'Invention*, 22–23.

[48] Conveniently listed in Bradeen, "Athenian Casualty Lists," 147, with references.
There are also *xenoi* mentioned on some lists. For the evidence, see Bradeen, "Athenian
Casualty Lists," 149–51; for discussion, see Loraux, *L'Invention*, 33–35, who concludes
(35): "pour les *astoi* comme pour les étrangers les regles d'inscription ont probablement
varié au cours de l'histoire athénienne: oscillant entre l'exclusivisme et l'ouverture, entre
une conception large et une conception étroite du statut d'Athénien" ("For the *astoi* [free-
born male and female inhabitants of the *polis* of Athens] as for foreigners the rules of enfran-
chisement probably varied through Athenian history, varying between exclusivity and
openness, between a broad and a narrow conception of the status of Athenian").

[49] Loraux, "Mourir," 28.

immortal *kleos*, but at the same time the values of democratic collectivity and the primacy of the city were stressed in a new form of memorial. As Thoukydides says, "We do not need the praises of a Homer" (2.441); the city provided its own honors. The institution of the public funeral speech, the collective memorial of those who died for the city, marked most clearly the shift in military ideology from Homer to the fifth-century democratic *polis*.

The importance of the duties, obligations, and affiliations between individuals and the state was one of the strongest tenets of the developing democratic ideology, despite—or perhaps because of—the fact of the continuing strength of affiliation to the *oikos*, "household." For regardless of the evident changes in ideology in fifth-century democracy, one of the most marked continuities of ethical norms was the belief in the need for the continuity of the *oikos* through both economic stability and the generational continuity of children.[50] But even in the sphere of the family, an area of great tradition and conservatism, the city made inroads. Important tensions between the requirements of civic duties and the requirements of the *oikos* have been outlined by, for example, Humphreys and Finley—both of whom see tensions between the norms of public and private life.[51] Fighting, jury duty, *leitourgia* (public expenses such as the cost of a trireme or a festival, to be borne by a private citizen), and the other appurtenances of direct democracy can all be seen as a possible challenge to the economic and generational continuity of the *oikos*. But I want here to focus rather on the way in which the city increasingly appropriated the vocabulary of the family. For the city "nourished"; the citizens were the "children" of the laws; the city became a "father," a "mother." The term "father-land" was extended in its connotations. To attack one's city was like patricide; to reject the laws was to reject that which gave one life and upbringing.[52] The emotionally and morally charged terminology of the family was appropriated in civic ideology to express the citizen's relations to the city and its laws, and this appropriation may be viewed as a product of the tensions between public and private felt in the (sometimes) competing claims of the democratic city and the more traditional *oikos*.

This attitude to civic involvement influenced, then, the attitude to childhood, and in particular the attitude to the moment of transition

---

[50] See, e.g., W. K. Lacey, *The Family in Classical Greece* (London, 1968); G. Glotz, *La solidarité de la famille dans le droit criminal en Grèce* (Paris, 1904).

[51] S. Humphreys, *The Family, Women, and Death* (London, 1983), especially 1–32; M. I. Finley, *Economy and Society in Ancient Greece* (London, 1981), 77–94; see also Dover, *Greek Popular Morality*, 301–6.

[52] A good example of this shift in vocabulary is to be found in Plato's *Krito*, especially 503c ff.

from childhood to adulthood. The most important moment of this transition is almost certainly the *dokimasia* in which the child was recognized by the deme as a citizen and fit to be enrolled (*eggraphesthai*) as a citizen.[53] The common phrases to express this enrollment—*dokimazesthai eis tous andras*, "to be registered among the men," or *andra gignesthai*, "to become a man," or *andra einai dokimazesthai*, "to be registered to be a man," or *exelthein ek paidōn*, "to pass from the boys," or *apallattesthai ek paidōn*, "to make the transition from the boys"—emphasize that this was not just a question of citizenship but also of being an *anēr*, "adult male," "man." The notion of being a *politēs*, "citizen," or *dēmotēs*, "demesman," implies becoming an *anēr* and stopping being a *pais*, "child," "boy." To stop being a *pais* and start being an *anēr* in fifth-century Athens meant a radical change in role and responsibility, in that the immediate requirements and obligations of a citizen in a direct democracy devolved on a person when he changed *ek paidōn*, "from the boys" and became an *anēr*. The status of ephebe provided the notional and ritual separation between the two classes.

In the light of this necessarily somewhat impressionistic view of the sense of a self in fifth-century democratic Athens, it is interesting to look back to the ceremony which was part of the opening of the tragic festival, the parade of young men in full military uniform, and to investigate how it relates to the norms of the civic discourse that I have been discussing. It is quite clearly a moment in which the full weight of civic ideology is felt. Here are the children of men who have died fighting for the city, now preparing to take *their* place in the hoplite-citizen body as men. The city has educated them, the city has taken the place of parents or family, the city has provided the armor in which they stand. Before the whole city in the theater, the young men are paraded and the ties and obligations of city and individuals are proclaimed. Not only do the boys at the point of becoming men reaffirm their ties to the city, but also these ties are constructed markedly in a military sense. The young men appear in full military dress, and the reason for their state education and upbringing is that their fathers died in war for the city. Moreover, in pointing out that the city has brought them up and paid for and directed their education, the involvement of the city in a traditional area of private concern is strongly marked. (Education is often thought of as a community matter, but not in terms of the effacement of the family's interests here enacted.) The fact that the festival of the Great Dionysia, a major civic occasion, is chosen for the moment of this expression of the city's relation to its young men endows it with considerable force. Childhood, the

[53] See, on the *dokimasia*, D. Whitehead, *The Demes of Attica* (Princeton, 1986), 97–109, and on the importance of the institution of the deme, R. Osborne, *Dēmos: The Discovery of Classical Attika* (Cambridge, Eng., 1985).

moment of leaving childhood and becoming a man, what it means to be a man, are all influenced by democratic *polis* ideology. The city's claim on the citizen as man affects the status of the child.

What I hope to have shown so far is this: the four moments of ceremony preceding the dramatic festival were all deeply involved with the city's sense of itself. The libations of the ten generals, the display of tribute, the announcement of the city's benefactors, the parade of state-educated boys, now men, in full military uniform, all stressed the power of the *polis*, the duties of an individual to the *polis*. The festival of the Great Dionysia is in the full sense of the expression a civic occasion, a city festival. And it is an occasion to say something about the city, not only in the plays themselves. The Great Dionysia is a public occasion endowed with a special force of belief. This is fundamentally and essentially a festival of the democratic *polis*.

After such preplay ceremonies, the performances of tragedy and comedy that follow could scarcely seem—at first sight—a more surprising institution (at least if one judges from modern examples of state occasions with a particularly strong nationalistic or patriotic ideology). For both tragedy and comedy, in their transgressive force, in their particular depictions and uses of myth and language, time after time implicate the dominant ideology put forward in the preplay ceremonies in a far from straightforward manner; indeed, the tragic texts seem to question, examine, and often subvert the language of the city's order.

Before I turn to justify these generalizations with more detailed examples, I want to make clear certain things I am not claiming and certain ways in which I do not think that tragedy questions the city. First, I do not think that the *polis* is seriously questioned as the necessary basis of civilization. To be *apolis*, "without a city," is regarded as a state beyond civilization, and Aristotle's expressions that the city is logically prior to individuals and family, or that man as an animal is essentially *polis*-based, are enshrined in tragedy as well as in the prose writing of the fifth and fourth centuries.[54] Second, I do not think Athens is seriously challenged as the home of that civilization of the *polis*. Not only is Athens the subject of several well-known passages of eulogistic writing—and the patriotism of plays such as the *Persai* has rarely been questioned by critics[55]—but recent research, particularly by Vidal-Naquet and Zeitlin, has begun to outline a sense of the differences in conceptualization of the cities of Ar-

[54] See the remarks of Finley, *Politics*, 122ff., e.g., 125, "Not all Athenians held the same views and not all Greeks were Athenians, but the evidence is decisive that nearly all of them would have accepted as premises, one might say as axioms, that the good life was possible only in a *polis*."

[55] I have discussed the *Persai* in light of the claims of this present article in "Battle Narrative and Politics in Aeschylus' *Persai*," *JHS* 108 (1988) (forthcoming).

gos and Thebes and Athens in the tragic texts—a system of differences in which Athens seems positively constituted in opposition particularly to the negative aspects of the tragic city of Thebes.[56] It is important that the tragic narratives are most often set in cities other than Athens, in times other than the present. Third, I am not seeking to make any contribution to the always vexed question of reading specific allusions to contemporary political debates in the tragic drama. When I write of questioning a dominant political ideology, I do not mean to imply a topic such as whether the *Oresteia* was written to comment on the zeugite admission to the arkhonship.[57] Fourth, I do not want it thought that I am claiming to explicate the way all audience members responded at all times to the tragedies and comedies of the Great Dionysia. We cannot expect to know how an Athenian audience would react to any tragedy, and, more importantly, it is an intolerably naive idea to suppose that an audience for a drama has only a uniform, homogeneous collective identity or response, or that such a supposed collective response (however determined) should be the sole proper object of criticism. I am not suggesting that every member of an audience left the theater deeply perplexed and reflecting on the nature of civic ideology—but the picture of an audience uniformly and solely interested in "pleasure," "entertainment," is equally banal. What I hope to describe here is a tension between the festival of drama as a civic institution and a reading of the texts of that institution. How different Athenians reconciled or conceived that tension is simply not known.

With these provisos, I want now to investigate the sense of tension between the texts of tragedy and the ideology of the city—which I shall approach first through a general example and second through two more specific cases.

In the last twenty-five years much excellent work has been done on the nature of the Sophoklean hero. Knox's well-known description of this Sophoklean type has been taken up by Winnington-Ingram, who has carefully attempted to see how a figure like Ajax extends and perverts a Homeric model.[58] It is not difficult to see that the Sophoklean hero, with

[56] P. Vidal-Naquet, "Oedipe entre deux cités," in *Mythe et tragedie deux* (Paris, 1986); see the second essay by Zeitlin in this volume, who suggests that "We look at Thebes as a *topos* in both senses of the word: as a designated place, a geographical locale, and figuratively, as a recurrent concept or formula, or what we call a 'commonplace.' . . . This . . . can also illuminate the ideological uses of Athenian theater as it portrays a city onstage that is meant to be dramatically 'other' than itself."

[57] See S. Goldhill, *Language, Sexuality, Narrative: The Oresteia* (Cambridge, Eng., 1984), 208–83.

[58] B.M.W. Knox, *The Heroic Temper* (Berkeley, 1964); Winnington-Ingram, *Sophocles*, esp. 11–72 and 304–29. And on Ajax specifically, see now P. E. Easterling, "The Tragic Homer," *BICS* 31 (1984): 1–8.

fierce demands for his or her individualism, his or her commitment to his or her own needs and demands in the face of society or social pressure, is scarcely a figure who would sit easily in democratic ideology, and it is indeed relevant that figures like Ajax and Antigone are set in conflict with figures who use standard arguments with a contemporary ideological slant. Antigone is faced by a man who attempts—at least at one level—to enforce the notion of the city having supreme claim on an individual's allegiance. Ajax, or rather the dead body of Ajax, is faced by trite arguments of Menelaos and Agamemnon who require *sōphrosunē*, "right thinking," as a political virtue in the form of obedience to the rulers of the state. It is also significant that both Kreon and the Atreids descend to lower forms of argument and appeal under the pressure of their oppositions' disobedience. The point is this: at one level, it might be neat and convenient to think of the Sophoklean depiction of heroes like Antigone or Ajax as moral tales which demonstrate the dangers of individualism. After all, both Ajax and Antigone die in less than glorious ways, and the actions of both lead to social upheaval and the disastrous violence of tragedy. This would imply that the tragedies offer a sort of reversal, common in the "sacred time"[59] of festivals: as, for example, men about to become warriors may be dressed as women; and ephebes are often described as reversing the values of the hoplite rank they are to join.[60] But it is clearly not so simple as that. The problem of evaluating Ajax, particularly in comparison with the men who follow him, and the difficulty of evaluating Antigone and her actions have resulted in some of the most polarized and aggressively debated judgments in the criticism of tragedy. Sophokles himself was actively involved in the cult worship of the heroes—a religious phenomenon of growing importance in the fifth century. The question of the evaluation of Ajax both in his qualities as a warrior and in his behavior as a man is problematic in Sophokles' play because the negative example of Ajax is touched with a certain glory. It is an essential dynamic of Sophokles' tragedy that Ajax should seem both an outstanding hero and also unacceptable in society. The hero does not simply *reverse* the norms of what it means to fit into society but *makes a problem of* such integration.

But this problem of the evaluation of Ajax is particularly interesting in terms of the tragic festival itself. For after the pre-play ceremonials of civic display which express the role of man as warrior in civic terms, and the city's claims of allegiance and obligation on the individual, a tragedy

---

[59] A common notion in anthropology developed from van Gennep, *Rites*. See, e.g., E. R. Leach, "On Time and False Noses," in Leach, *Rethinking Anthropology* (London, 1966).

[60] See, e.g., Vidal-Naquet, *Le chasseur noire*, Jeanmaire, *Couroi*; Brelich, *Paides*; Calame, "Choeurs."

like *Ajax* depicts a man who transgresses those qualities and those obligations, and achieves his greatness, his superhuman status, precisely by such transgression. Ajax acts in a manner which goes against all the tenets of contemporary democratic civic ideology, but this going-too-far leads him to a sort of awesomeness. Few today think of Sophokles as "turning away in disgust from a degenerate world to enjoy the congenial company of heroes";[61] in their tensions and paradoxes, his plays are marked by their genesis in the fifth-century Athenian *polis*. In particular, it is the way that Sophokles' plays echo against the developing civic ideology, so forcibly represented in the preplay ceremonies, which makes his dramas considerably more radical and questioning than the image of "pious Sophokles" sometimes allows. Indeed, the Sophoklean hero is the paradoxical figure so well described by Knox and Winnington-Ingram particularly because of the interplay of such a figure with the dominant ideology of the city. It is the way in which the hero can find only an uneasy place in the city's order that makes problematic both the hero's status and the security of the civic discourse.

This difficult status of the Sophoklean hero can be seen more precisely through an analysis of a key passage in Sophokles' *Ajax* where the hero speaks for the final time to Eurysakes, his son (545–82). In this speech which echoes the famous Homeric scene of Hektor, Andromakhe, and their son at the Skaian gates, Ajax turns to his child and expresses the values he expects his son to follow, and how he should use his father as a model. He asserts that if his son is truly of his father's blood (*eiper dikaios est' emos ta patrothen*) he will not fear the sight of the slaughtered sheep (545–47). It is necessary (548–49) that Eurysakes learns to form his nature (*phusis*) in the wild, savage ways of his father (*ōmois . . . en nomois patros*). Indeed, the child should use his father as a model in everything but his fortune: "My child, may you prove luckier [*genoio eutukhesteros*] than your father, but in other respects the same [*ta d' all' homoios*]" (550–51). When his time comes, the child will have to show his birth and breeding (556–60). Ajax further claims that he will ask Teukros to be the boy's guardian (561–64) and asks the chorus too to look out for him (565–66) and make sure Teukros gets the message to have the boy sent to Telamon and Eriboia, his grandparents (507–9). As for weapons, Ajax leaves his son his shield, but announces that he will himself be buried with the rest of his armor (574–76). This scene raises the problem of Ajax as role model, the question of how to evaluate the hero. What sort of example does he provide for his son? The question is set up in this scene in terms of the passing on from father to son of a material and spiritual inheritance, and, in particular, in terms of military values. The echoes of

---

[61] Winnington-Ingram, *Sophocles*, 307.

the Homeric scene of Hektor and Andromakhe do not merely mark the difference between Hektor and Ajax, but also stress the values and attitudes of the world of epic in which tragedy is rooted but from which it is being permanently sundered.[62] But these important elements in the construction of this scene must also be viewed in terms of the discourse of fifth-century Athens in which the play finds its genesis. And the difference between Ajax's attitudes and the fifth-century democracy could hardly be better expressed than by the juxtaposition of Ajax's admonitions to his child, Ajax's sense of military and social behavior, Ajax's heroic extremism, and that preplay ceremony of the orphans, state-educated and armed, professing their allegiance to the *polis* and taking their proper place in the hoplite rank. The inheritance Ajax hopes to leave and leaves stands in significant contrast to the fifth-century city's representation of his action and attitudes.

Such a juxtaposition is not, of course, a dramatic juxtaposition in the normal sense of a grammar of theatrical practice: it is a juxtaposition of values that would be in play without any ceremony preceding the drama. But the specific events in the theater which mark so strongly the festival as a *polis* occasion bring into vivid highlight the contemporary world and values against which Ajax's depiction and, indeed, the whole tragedy resound. The scene of Ajax with his child, juxtaposed with the preplay ceremony of the orphans in military uniform, significantly alters the way we look both at Sophokles' tragedy and at the notion of a child, at offering advice and a role model to a child. The context for understanding this scene goes beyond its instantiation in a performance in the theater, beyond its interrelations with Homer. This scene cannot fully be appreciated or understood without realizing the complex interplay of its writing with the ideology of the fifth-century *polis* of Athens.

A similar analysis could be applied to several Sophoklean heroes,[63] but I wish to consider briefly here another example which further demonstrates the range and complexity of relations between the tragic texts and the civic ideology of the preplay ceremonies. In *Philoktetes*, the question of the integration of the hero into society is certainly raised; indeed it is essential to the play—in which Sophokles has made Lemnos deserted,[64] Philoktetes bereft of all human contact, and Odysseus' plan a temptation for Philoktetes precisely to return to the civilized world. Critics have concentrated extensively on Philoktetes as a hero, on the tension between

[62] See Goldhill, *Reading*, chap. 6, for discussion and bibliography.

[63] I have discussed in particular *Oid. Tyr.* and *Antigone* in such terms in Goldhill, *Reading*, chaps. 4, 6, 8.

[64] The scholia suggest it is only part of the island that is deserted—presumably to reconcile Sophokles' description with Homeric and indeed contemporary Lemnos. Both Aiskhylos and Euripides in their plays on Philoktetes seem to have used choruses of Lemnians.

culture and wilderness in the play, and on the complex plotting which revolves around luring Philoktetes and his bow to Troy.[65] But for my
present purposes, it is on the figure of Neoptolemos that I wish to focus.
For Neoptolemos is the orphaned son of a great military hero who had
died nobly in war.[66] He is also at the point of committing himself to the
Trojan expedition—a young man about to take his place in the male
military group. Moreover, from the beginning of the play Neoptolemos'
attitudes and behavior are being put to the test (50–51):

'Αχιλλέως παῖ, δεῖ σ' ἐφ' οἷς ἐλήλυθας
γενναῖον εἶναι, μὴ μόνον τῷ σώματι . . .

Child of Akhilleus, you must be noble for the task
For which you have come, not only with your body . . .

In the dialogue which follows Odysseus' instructions, Neoptolemos
questions whether he can adopt a policy of deceit and be "noble."[67] He
would prefer, he claims, to fail acting in a right way than to succeed by
wrongdoing (βούλομαι δ', ἄναξ, καλῶς/δρῶν ἐξαμαρτανεῖν μᾶλλον ἢ
νικᾶν κακῶς, "I wish, my lord, to fail by acting rightly, rather than to
achieve victory in an evil manner" [94–95]). Surely, he asks (105), it is
disgraceful (aiskhron) to lie? Even when the young man accepts Odysseus' instructions, it is with the recognition that he is about to compromise his values (120):

ἴτω ποιήσω, πᾶσαν αἰσχύνην ἀφείς

Let happen what will! I will give up all sense of shame and do it.

When Philoktetes realizes that Neoptolemos has deceived him—at the
same time as Neoptolemos hesitantly confesses his part in the deception
(895ff.)—both Philoktetes and Neoptolemos himself refer to his "true
nature" (phusis [902]; en sautōi genou, "be yourself" [950]; cf. 971) as mili-
tating against the deceit. Nonetheless, at first Neoptolemos rejects the
possibility of returning the bow with an appeal to his duty (925–26):

ἀλλ' οὐκ οἷόν τε · τῶν γὰρ ἐν τέλει κλύειν
τό τ' ἔνδικόν με καὶ τὸ σύμφερον ποιεῖ.

[65] For a good critical survey, see P. E. Easterling, "Philoctetes and Modern Criticism,"
ICS 3 (1978): 27–39. Since that article, two important studies have appeared, Winnington-
Ingram, Sophocles, and Segal, Tragedy and Civilization.
[66] Emphasized often—e.g., 336, "Well, noble [eugenēs] was the killer and the slain." See
P. W. Rose, "Sophocles' Philoctetes and the Teachings of the Sophists," HSCP 80 (1976):
50–105, especially 97, n. 97.
[67] On the changing sense of gennaios in this play, see H. C. Avery, "Heracles, Philoctetes, Neoptolemus," Hermes 93 (1965): 289.

But it is not possible. What is right and what is expedient
Make me listen to those in authority.

What is right (to endikon) and what is expedient (to sumpheron) constrain
Neoptolemos to listen to those in command (which is both a general
point about obedience and a specific indication of whose instructions he
is still following here). Obedience toward "the authorities" (hoi en telei) is
a standard requirement, of course, for the maintenance of the bonds of a
democratic as well as a more hierarchical society. This value, however,
along with the more pragmatic values espoused by Odysseus, is put at
stake first by Neoptolemos' confession of pity (965–66) and his anguished question οἴμοι τί δράσω, "alas, what am I to do?" (968), and
then by the act of returning the bow. As he had previously claimed to be
willing to fail (ἐξαμαρτανεῖν, 94) nobly rather than to succeed basely,
now he rejects his deception precisely as failure (ἐξήμαρτον, "I have
failed," 1224; τὴν ἁμαρτίαν/αἰσχρὰν ἁμαρτών, "I have failed and my
failure is disgraceful [aiskhros]" (1248–49); as he had previously feared
being disgraceful (aiskhros), and claimed to do to endikon, "what is right,"
now he claims his actions have been both disgraceful and without right
(1234):

αἰσχρῶς γὰρ αὐτὰ κοὐ δίκῃ λαβὼν ἔχω

Yes I have it [the bow], but I took it disgracefully and contrary to
what is right.

At the moment of handing over the bow, however, Neoptolemos is
forcibly reminded of what he had previously called his duty, as once
again Odysseus enters at the decisive moment (1293–94):[68]

ἐγὼ δ' ἀπαυδῶ γ', ὡς θεοὶ συνίστορες
ὑπέρ τ' Ἀτρειδῶν τοῦ τε σύμπαντος στρατοῦ.

But I forbid it, as the gods are my witnesses,
On behalf of the Atreids and the whole army.

It is precisely his obligations to the Atreids, to the army at Troy, and indeed even to divine oracles on his part in the fall of Troy that Neoptolemos is rejecting in favor of a different set of values. Indeed, the young

---

[68] Compare 974, where Odysseus enters to echo Neoptolemos' question ti drōmen, andres
("What are we to do, men?") with O kakist' andrōn, ti drās ("O most evil of men, what are
you doing?").

man is essentially prepared to desert from the army[69] and return home with Philoktetes (despite some misgivings, 1403–4). His newfound relation with the hero seems to outweigh what had before seemed to be his duty. Neoptolemos is turning his back on his part in the Trojan War as he prepares to leave the stage at 1407. "Neoptolemos cannot . . . both maintain his standard of honor and win martial glory."[70]

The appearance of the *deus ex machina* (or perhaps rather the *heros ex machina*), who redirects Philoktetes and Neoptolemos back toward Troy, has given rise to one of the most controversial debates in Sophoklean criticism. Herakles certainly resolves the tension between Neoptolemos' decision and the standard version of the fall of Troy. It is certainly a *coup de théâtre*, a "second ending," as it is often called, which must be read in the light of the "first ending." But what is implied by the reestablishment of the expected pattern of myth? Does it mean that Neoptolemos' adherence to a sense of honor and pity and his observation of the duties of his relation of *philia* with Philoktetes are to be rejected or transcended? If this is the gods reordering the passage of events, how does it relate to the human values implicated in the drama? Is Sophokles in a Euripidean manner cynically showing how his characters must sacrifice their true nature and best feelings to live out the myths, or divine commands, that they inherit? Is this Sophokles questioning whether Philoktetes and Neoptolemos are right to have rejected the Trojan expedition? Perhaps one can conclude only that in the tension between the "first" and "second" ending one can specify the constituent factors in the critical problem without necessarily ever being sure of its resolution?[71] As Winnington-Ingram concludes, "It is unlikely that interpreters will ever agree about the precise tone of the play's close."[72]

But what of Neoptolemos in this? The play has raised questions about his education (in a general sense),[73] about how he should act in a specific difficult situation. But above all, it has set in tension, on the one hand, the possibility of his simply taking part in the Trojan expedition, simply obeying his leaders, simply adopting the course that will lead to military success, and, on the other hand, his conception of what is right, what is

[69] The threat of desertion recalls his father at Troy, as well as, say, Agamemnon's different plight in Aiskhylos' *Oresteia*, where he asks *pōs liponaus genōmai* ("How could I prove a deserter?"), *Ag.* 212–13.

[70] Winnington-Ingram, *Sophocles*, 298.

[71] Each of the positions has been adopted. For a survey see Easterling, "Philoctetes."

[72] Winnington-Ingram, *Sophocles*, 301. C. Gill, "Bow, Oracle and Epiphany," *G&R* 27 (1980): 137–45, and K. Mathiessen, "Philoktet oder die Resozialisierung," *WJA* 7 (1981): 11–26, both have interesting comments, particularly on the sense of reintegration of Philoktetes as hero and man, but both underestimate the problematic nature of Neoptolemos' dilemma for the ending of the play.

[73] See Rose, "Sophocles' *Philoctetes*."

noble, what is the correct way to behave. It is the tension between these
aspects that leads to the archetypical tragic question *oimoi ti drāsō*, "Alas,
what am I to do?" Vidal-Naquet has described Neoptolemos' decision as
a rejection of collective civic values in favor of the values of the household: "He chooses the values of the family as opposed to the city."[74] This
decision, followed by its eventual reversal in favor of the expedition to
Troy, is to be seen, argues Vidal-Naquet, as part of Neoptolemos' transition from the status of ephebe to the status of hoplite. While it is clear
that the material Vidal-Naquet has collected on the conceptualization of
the ephebe is extremely important and provides an interesting range of
ideas against which to view this play in particular, it seems difficult to see
Neoptolemos as conforming absolutely and completely to the pattern of
initiation Vidal-Naquet has so well delineated. The values with which
Neoptolemos is concerned are not merely the values of the family—one
must also consider conflicting aspects of *heroic* duty with regard to fifth-
century changing attitudes—and, as other critics have pointed out, the
imagery of wildness and culture in the play does not conform simply to
the clear pattern Vidal-Naquet requires.[75] Perhaps most importantly, the
use of the anthropological model can be thought to lead to an underesti-
mation of the *uncertainty* of the double ending of the play, particularly
with regard to Neoptolemos. This uncertainty can be clearly seen in the
light of the preplay ceremonies. The herald at the parade of orphans proclaims the city's education and support of the boys, and the boys' future
support of the city as hoplites and citizens. The requirement of commitment to the collective ethos of a fifth-century democratic military ideology is firmly established. The individual's involvement in such an
ethos is unquestioningly asserted in the ritual. Yet Neoptolemos' involvement in the *Philoktetes* dramatizes a conflict between moral and social values and a commitment to the collective need of the Trojan
expedition. Neoptolemos is put in the position of refusing his military
role in order to maintain his notions of what is right. Neoptolemos' *uncertainty* and awareness of a conflict in his system of beliefs contrast strikingly with the opening ritual's assuredness. In the ephebic oath, the
young Athenian promised to stand by his colleague wherever in the line
he was stationed;[76] Neoptolemos shows that it is not always clear what

[74] Vernant and Vidal-Naquet, *Myth and Tragedy*, 185–86. See also Vidal-Naquet, *Le chasseur noir*, 125–207.

[75] See Segal, *Tragedy and Civilization*, 292–361; Winnington-Ingram, *Sophocles*, 301 and
"Sophoclea," *BICS* 26 (1979): 10–11; Easterling, "Philoctetes," 36–39; and the highly po-
lemical V. di Benedetto, "Il Filottete e l'efebia secondo Pierre Vidal-Naquet," *Belfagor* 33
(1978): 191–207.

[76] οὐδὲ λείψω τὸν παραστάτην ὅπου ἂν στοχήσω. On the date of the ephebate and the
ephebic oath, see text and references at n. 81.

this might involve. One cannot see Neoptolemos, then, as offering either a straightforwardly positive example in his nobility, or a straightforwardly negative example in his willingness to desert the army and in his role in the fall of Troy. Herakles' commands to Philoktetes at the close of the drama may be thought to reconcile the development of Sophokles' plot with the expectations of myth, but do not resolve the tension that led to Neoptolemos' anguished question as to what he should do. Both the basis and the evaluation of Neoptolemos' decision remain problematic (even if the *deus ex machina* removes the need for Neoptolemos to follow through the implications of his choice). The text of *Philoktetes* seems to question, then, and set at risk the direct assertion of ideology that the preplay ceremonies seem to proclaim. As with *Ajax*, the relation between the ritual of the festival and the drama is complex. Rather than the negative example, a reversal of the norm, we see the far more unsettling process of an investigation of a possible *conflict* in the system of belief that is instantiated in the preplay ceremonies. Neoptolemos does not merely represent or reflect a fifth-century Athenian notion of the ephebe, but raises questions about it.

I have focused here on two plays that can be directly related to the fourth of the ceremonies I discussed earlier. There are, of course, numerous other examples of varying complexity that could be investigated. For as much as the parade of orphans before the city is part of a system of belief, so numerous other scenes or themes or conflicts of the tragic texts can be properly appreciated only in terms of the pervasive power of this civic discourse (so much in evidence in the preplay ceremonies). Again and again, for example, as has been discussed by critics from Hegel onward, tragedy dramatizes conflicting obligations of household and state—especially emphasized, for example, in the *Septem*, the *Antigone*, or the *Oidipous Tyrannos*.[77] The hierarchical order of family and state is depicted in tragedy as a locus of tension and conflict—tension and conflict between members of the same family and between the duties of civic and familial roles. Again and again, as has been the subject of numerous important studies, tragedy investigates and undercuts the secure meanings of key words in the discourse of social order—*dikē*, "justice," *kratos*, "power," *sōphrosunē*, "right thinking"—and depicts tensions and ambiguities in their sense and usage.[78] Again and again, tragedy portrays the

[77] A vast bibliography could be given: see, e.g., on *Septem*, Zeitlin, *Under the Sign*; on *Antigone*, see Segal, *Tragedy and Civilization*, 152–206; V. Rosivach, "The Two Worlds of the *Antigone*," *ICS* 4 (1979): 16–36; J. Hogan, "The Protagonists of the *Antigone*," *Arethusa* 5 (1972): 93–100; on the *Oidipous Tyrannos*, see Segal, *Tragedy and Civilization*, 207–48; also Goldhill, *Reading*, chaps. 3, 4, 7, 8.

[78] In general, see Vernant and Vidal-Naquet, *Myth and Tragedy*, chaps. 1–3; on Aiskhylos, see Goldhill, *Language*; Zeitlin, *Under the Sign*; on Sophokles, see Segal, *Tragedy and*

dissolution and collapse of the social order, portrays man reaching beyond the bounds and norms of social behavior, portrays a universe of
conflict, aggression, impasse. In part, it must be in the relation between
the proclamation of civic ties, duties, and obligations in the civic festival
of the Great Dionysia and the questioning, challenging plays produced in
the festival that an understanding of the tragic moment will lie.[79]

Rather than simply reflecting the cultural values of a fifth-century audience, then, rather than offering simple didactic messages from the
city's poets to the citizens, tragedy seems deliberately to make difficult
the assumption of the values of the civic discourse. And it is precisely this
unsettling force of the tragic texts that makes certain critics' assertions of
the necessarily simple, clear, and straightforward nature of texts for performance quite so insufficient. Indeed, it would seem more appropriate
to claim that it is exactly the refusal to accept the simple, clear, and
straightforward that constitutes the extraordinary force of the tragic dramas of Athens.

This discussion of the nature of the questioning of civic language and
ideals in the tragic theater could certainly be extended and treated in
greater detail but I wish to conclude this article by looking briefly at the
question of the ephebate which I have mentioned with regard to *Philoktetes*. I want here merely to make some general observations. The first is
this: it is clear that a great many of our extant plays are explicitly concerned with young men at the key times of taking up a role as a man in
society—all the Orestes plays, *Philoktetes*, *Bakkhai*, and *Hippolytos* immediately spring to mind. Vidal-Naquet, Zeitlin, and Segal have each
written studies in which the connections between those dramas and the
institution of the ephebate are drawn out—particularly the significance
of the imagery of hunting and warfare, and also the elements of ritual reversal in the ephebate that are paralleled in many initiation rituals around
the world.[80] One of the most common criticisms brought against this
work is the lack of evidence for the institution of the ephebate in the fifth
century, although it may be assumed that the oath of the ephebes goes
back to the fifth century.[81] It may be worth pointing out that the existence of the oath at an early stage, the treatment of the orphan ephebes in

---

Civilization, 52–59, and s.v. "Language"; on Euripides, see Goldhill, *Reading*, chap. 5, on
Hippolytos, with bibliography.

[79] "Tragic moment" is Vernant's phrase; see Vernant and Vidal-Naquet, *Myth and
Tragedy*, chaps. 1–3.

[80] Vidal-Naquet, *Le chasseur noir*, F. Zeitlin, "Dynamics of Misogyny: Myth and Mythmaking in the *Oresteia*," *Arethusa* 11 (1978): 149–84; C. Segal, *Dionysiac Poetics and Euripides' Bacchae* (Princeton, 1982), 158–214. See also Goldhill, *Language*, 193–95.

[81] See P. Siewart, "The Ephebic Oath in Fifth-century Athens," *JHS* 97 (1977): 102–11;
H. Y. McCulloch and H. D. Cameron, "*Septem* 12–13 and the Athenian *Ephebeia*," *ICS* 5
(1980): 1–14.

the theater in the fifth century, and the key role played by ephebes in the tragic festival at a later date, may indicate a certain connection between tragedy and males at the age of manhood (in terms of adoption and definition of a social role), even if there is no formal institution of the ephebate at the time of fifth-century tragedy—a fact in itself neither finally proven or disproven yet.[82] I do not wish to revive Mathieu's thesis that the ceremony of the orphans at the Great Dionysia is actually the institutional origin of the ephebate,[83] but I do stress the connection between tragedy as a didactic and a questioning medium and the affirmation of the duties and obligations of a citizen. As Mathieu comments, the ephebic oath is a civic oath, concerned fundamentally with expressing and upholding the tenets of *dēmokratia*[84]—and, as Reinmuth comments on the ephebate at a later date: "Every opportunity was taken to foster their [the ephebes'] civic consciousness."[85] In other words, any suggested relations between the institution of tragedy and the institution of the ephebate itself must be too delimited a tool to outline the complex relations among tragedy, its attitude to past and present values, and the transgressions enacted onstage, but it is important to keep in mind the connections among times of transition, particularly transition into adulthood, and the educative role of poetry, the complex, often paradoxical examples offered by the staging of myth in the tragic festival.[86] The juxtaposition of the young men affirming their civic duties and affiliations in the theater and the young Orestes, forced to lie, deceive, and kill his mother, and yet to be vindicated, seems to me to be of some importance to the way we think of the Athenians conceptualizing the move from childhood to adulthood and the role of the moral example of myth.

[82] See O. Reinmuth, *The Ephebic Inscriptions of the Fourth Century B.C.* (Leiden, 1971); Pélékidis, *Histoire*, especially 7–17.

[83] G. Mathieu, "Remarques sur l'éphébie attique," in Mathieu, *Mélanges Desrousseux* (Paris, 1937), 311–18. Mathieu had been anticipated by A. A. Bryant, "Boyhood and Youth in the Days of Aristophanes," *HSCP* 18 (1907): 87 and n. 4. It is important that this ceremony constitutes for the orphans the *conclusion* of ephebic status, as they now take their place in the hoplite rank. Their assumption of full armor, therefore, is a significant gesture in marking this conclusion, since the ephebe is conceived of as lightly armed specifically in contrast with the panoply of the hoplite. In the theater, they appear as *andres polītai*, "adult male citizens," for the first time (in full armor).

[84] Mathieu, "Remarques," 313. Wilamowitz, who admittedly did not have the inscriptional evidence now available, is nonetheless importantly mistaken particularly when he argues that the ephebate could not be a fifth-century phenomenon because of its "antidemocratic" nature (*Aristoteles und Athen*, vol. 1 [Berlin, 1893], 191, 193–94). Wilamowitz is criticized by Pélékidis, *Histoire*, 8–14.

[85] O. Reinmuth, *The Foreigners in the Athenian Ephebeia* (Lincoln, Neb., 1929), 6.

[86] For an attempt to show how closely linked tragedy and ephebes may be, see now the essay by Winkler in this volume. Winkler is criticized in P. Vidal-Naquet, "The Black Hunter Revisited," *PCPS* 32 (1986): 137–38.

To conclude: I outlined first some moments of ceremony from the days of the drama festival. These I showed were indicative of the festival's production in the democratic *polis*. In particular, these ceremonies were concerned with the relations of an individual to the city, his ties and obligations, and how these were expressed in terms of military involvement and the recognition of the man's duty as soldier in the city, which affects the view of youth as youth—his place in society. But the tragedies and comedies which follow—both tragedy and comedy may be described as "genres of transgression"—constitute in some important senses a questioning of the terms of that civic discourse. Tragedy again and again is concerned with *competing* obligations of household and state. Tragedy again and again focuses on young men whose behavior in society puts society at risk. Tragedy again and again takes key terms of the normative and evaluative vocabulary of civic discourse, and depicts conflicts and ambiguities in their meanings and use.

How does this relate to Dionysos, the god in whose name the festival takes place? The Athenians had an expression, "nothing to do with Dionysos." Were they right to apply it to the City Dionysia? Dionysos is the divine figure of the ancient world most studied in the modern age.[87] Henrichs, in his recent sober study of the god and his interpreters, begins by outlining four main areas of influence for the god, namely, wine and vitality, ritual madness, the mask and theater, and a happy afterlife.[88] But he quickly begins to qualify and redefine these areas ("god of wine and vitality" [205] becomes "god of wine and escape from everyday reality" [209]), and he finally writes "Virtually everybody who has an informed opinion on the subject seems to concede that a balanced and unified view of Dionysos and his place in history is not only difficult to achieve but is essentially incompatible with the complexity of the god and with his disparate manifestations. . . . Dionysos defies definition" (209). Henrichs goes on to suggest, however, that perhaps the most profitable way for analysis is opened by Otto, who "summed up Dionysos as a god of paradox" (234). This view finds an echo in Daraki's recent study. She writes: "All these joinings of opposites repeat on various levels what is already announced in the contradictory identity of the mortal god"; and "'Dionysos' est *une autre façon de penser*,"[89] "'Dionysos' is *an other way of thought*." So, too, Segal writes that "Dionysos operates as the

---

[87] For an interesting survey and bibliography, see A. Henrichs, "Loss of Self, Suffering, Violence: The Modern View of Dionysus from Nietzsche to Girard," *HSCP* 88 (1984): 205–40.

[88] Henrichs, "Loss of Self." See also J. N. Bremmer, "Greek Maenadism from Olympias to Messalina," *ZPE* 55 (1984): 267–86; A. Henrichs, "Greek Maenadism Reconsidered," *HSCP* 82 (1978): 14–65; and most recently M. Daraki, *Dionysos* (Paris, 1985).

[89] Daraki, *Dionysis*, 28 (my translation); 232.

principle that destroys differences,"[90] and he has attempted at length to describe "the multiple inversions and contradictions of Dionysos"[91] in the *Bakkhai* in particular. Along with the illusions and transgressions of the theatrical experience, along with the release of maenadic ecstasy or wine, Dionysos' sphere would seem to encompass precisely the sense of paradox and reversal I have been describing in the relations between the preplay ceremonies and the plays in the City Dionysia. It is the *interplay between norm and transgression* enacted in the tragic festival that makes it a Dionysiac occasion.

Anthropologists regularly analyze the "sacred time" of a festival as a period of inversion—men dressed as women, slaves becoming masters, the carnival. The social order is reversed.[92] Fifth-century Athenian tragedy's depictions of society collapsing in violence and disorder, and comedy's fulfillments of desires and fantasies, have often been understood precisely through such a sense of the ritual reversal of the norms (as if Aristophanic comedy merely fulfilled the repressed desires of everyday life, as if tragedy merely expressed the feared possibilities of collapse into social disorder). But the combination of the preplay rituals and the performances of the texts of fifth-century theater—which together make up the Great Dionysia—offer a more unsettling and problematic process, a more complex dialectic between the proclamation of social norms and their possibilities of transgression. For tragedy and comedy do not simply reverse the norms of society but inculcate a questioning of the very basis of those norms, the key structures of opposition on which "norm" and "transgression" rest. If ritual is designed to leave the structural posi-

---

[90] Segal, *Dionysiac Poetics*, 234.

[91] Segal, *Dionysiac Poetics*, 266.

[92] See, for a classic statement of this view, V. Turner, *The Ritual Process* (Rochester, 1969), who develops the seminal studies of M. Gluckman, *Order and Rebellion in Tribal Africa* (London, 1963) and *Custom and Conflict in Africa* (Oxford, 1965). See also *The Reversible World: Symbolic Inversion in Art and Society*, ed. B. Babcock, (Ithaca, N.Y., 1978), for important qualifications of the model; and for a useful overview, C. Lane, *The Rites of Rulers: Rituals in Industrial Society—The Soviet Case* (Cambridge, Eng., 1981), especially chap. 1, which makes good use of S. Lukes, "Political Ritual and Social Integration," *Sociology* 9 (1975): 289–308. Carnival is seen by Bakhtin, of course, as a potentially revolutionary force, and occasions of social revolt arising from carnival are discussed fascinatingly by E. Le Roy Ladurie, *Carnival in Romans*, trans. M. Feeney (Harmondsworth, Eng., 1981); and N. Z. Davis, *Society and Culture in Early Modern Europe* (Oxford, 1975), 97–123, 152–88 (with further bibliography). P. Stallybrass and A. White, *The Politics and Poetics of Transgression* (London, 1986), whose opening chapter offers a brilliant theoretical overview of this problem, conclude with a scrupulous statement of the possibilities of generalization (14): "The most that can be said in the abstract is that for long periods carnival may be a stable and cyclical ritual with no noticeable politically transformative effects but that given the presence of sharpened political antagonism, it may often act as *catalyst and site of actual and symbolic struggle*." I discuss the relation between carnival and the comedies of the Great Dionysia in a forthcoming book, *The Poet's Voice*.

tions of society legitimized, the tragic texts seem designed to leave an audience with a question (as often as not about the legitimation of social positions). It is here in the potential *undermining of a secure and stable sense of norm* (and thus of transgression) that the most unsettling thrust of tragedy may be located.

Religion is often considered as an area of solid conservatism in fifth-century society: in particular, ritual, the sacred moment in and out of time, is seen as a process leading to the *communitas* of social integration, to the final suppression of violence in a group, whereby any recognition of social difference is apotropaic.[93] It is precisely the failure of the apotropaic model to offer an adequate account of the Great Dionysia, with its explicit questioning and formal display that makes this festival such an interesting object of study for the cultural historian as much as the classicist.

The special circumstances of the City Dionysia festival, then, bring the special license of comedy, with its obscenity and lampoons, and the special license of tragedy, with its images of society collapsing. The two faces of Dionysos form the one festival. The tensions and ambiguities that tragedy and comedy differently set in motion, the tensions and ambiguities that arise from the transition from tragedy to comedy, all fall under the aegis of the one god, the divinity associated with illusion and change, paradox and ambiguity, release and transgression. Unlike the displays of civic rhetoric we have seen in such set pieces as Perikles' funeral speech or in Demosthenes' political rhetoric, the Great Dionysia, Dionysos' festival for the city, offers a full range of Dionysiac *transgression*, from the intellectually and emotionally powerful and dangerous tragedy, through ironic and subtle questioning, to the obscene, scatological, uproarious comedy. The drama festival, plays and ceremonies together, offers not just the power and profundity of a great dramatic literature but also the extraordinary process of the developing city putting its developing language and structure of thought at risk under the sway of the smiling and dangerous Dionysos.

Tragedy must be understood, then, in terms of the festival of which it is a constituent part and the silence of critics on the preplay ceremonies is indicative of a general unwillingness to consider both the extended context of the tragic texts and the particular difficulties involved in reading this literature of transgression and impasse. The tragic festival may at

---

[93] The apotropaic model has been most influentially developed for classical material by W. Burkert, particularly in *Homo Necans* (Berlin, 1972), trans. P. Bing under the title *Homo Necans: The Anthropology of Ancient Greek Sacrificial Ritual and Myth* (Berkeley, 1983); and R. Girard, *La violence et le sacré* (Paris, 1972), translated by P. Gregory, *Violence and the Sacred* (Baltimore, 1977).

first sight seem to have little to do with our expectations of the Dionysiac religion under whose name it takes place. But in the interplay of norm and transgression enacted in the festival which both lauds the *polis* and depicts the stresses and tensions of a *polis* society in conflict, the Great Dionysia seems to me an essentially Dionysiac event.

FROMA I. ZEITLIN

Thebes: Theater of Self and Society in Athenian Drama

I. THE TOPOS OF THEBES

The city I am calling Thebes occupies a very small territory, no larger than the extent of the stage in the theater of Dionysos under the shadow of the Akropolis at Athens. In keeping with the conventions of Attic tragedy, no special scenery or stage set identifies it and no particular props are necessary for its representation. The typical facade of the *skēnē,* the stage building, which normally stands for the front of a house or palace, serves just as well for Thebes as for any other location where dramas are supposed to take place.

And yet we know the city once the play has begun, or better, we ought to recognize the place—not only from its being named as Thebes or as the city of Kadmos, not only from references to its walls with the seven gates which are its most distinctive architectural feature, but from what over and over again the tragic poets cause to transpire there as they treat the different myths that share a common terrain in Thebes. We think immediately of the saga of the house of Laios which situates Oidipous at its center and extends beyond him to the dramas of his children— his sons, Eteokles and Polyneikes, and his daughters, Antigone and Ismene. But there is also the prior story of Kadmos, the Spartoi, or Sown Men, and the founding of the city through autochthony (birth from the earth) and fratricide, as the Sown Men fight one another to their mutual destruction with the exception of five who survive to inaugurate the his-

Note: This essay was originally published in *Greek Tragedy and Political Theory,* ed. J. Peter Euben (Berkeley, 1986), 101–41, and is reprinted here (with some revisions and additions) by the kind permission of the University of California Press. An earlier and shorter version of this paper was delivered at the Convegno Internazionale di Studi, "Oedipo: Il teatro greco e la cultura europea," held in November 1982 and published (together with a transcript of the discussion) in the proceedings of the same name, ed. Bruno Gentili and Roberto Pretagostini (Rome, 1987), 343–85. Subsequent work was completed during a fellowship from the Guggenheim Foundation (1984–1985), whose assistance I gratefully acknowledge. This essay forms part of a more extensive study concerning the representation of Thebes in Athenian drama. The foundations have been laid in my recent book, *Under the Sign of the Shield: Semiotics and Aeschylus' Seven against Thebes* (Rome, 1982) (abbreviated here as *Under the Sign*). The notes have necessarily been kept to a minimum, and in the case of Aiskhylos' *Seven against Thebes,* fuller discussion of the issues I raise can be found in the study mentioned above.

tory of the city. And, third, we must include the myth of the god Dionysos himself, the son of Zeus and Semele, reputedly born at Thebes, who returns home to claim recognition of his divinity and to establish the cult of his worship in his native city.

In proposing that there is some conceptual category in the Athenian theater named "Thebes" and that some underlying "unity of place" organizes these disparate stories and their treatment in the work of all three Athenian tragic poets, I am, in effect, suggesting that we look at Thebes as a *topos* in both senses of the word: as a designated place, a geographical locale, and figuratively, as a recurrent concept or formula, or what we call a "commonplace." That is, through the specific myths associated with Thebes on the Athenian stage, certain clusters of ideas, themes, and problems recur which can be identified as proper to Thebes—or rather to Athenian tragedy's representation of Thebes as a mise-en-scène. Additionally, certain formal structures underlie the variety of different plots— similar types of scenes, character portrayals, semantic fields, and so on. All these elements attest to a certain unifying tendency which allows each myth and each version of that myth its own autonomy, but brings them all together as a coherent and complex ensemble. This wide-angle lens which brings the background into sharper focus can extend our conceptions of what constitute formal conventions in the theater and can show how these might interact together at their different levels for a larger design. Better still, this same lens can also illuminate the ideological uses of Athenian theater as it portrays a city onstage that is meant to be dramatically "other" than itself. Thebes, I will argue, provides the negative model to Athens' manifest image of itself with regard to its notions of the proper management of city, society, and self. As the site of displacement, therefore, Thebes consistently supplies the radical tragic terrain where there can be no escape from the tragic in the resolution of conflict or in the institutional provision of a civic future beyond the world of the play. There the most serious questions can be raised concerning the fundamental relations of man to his universe, particularly with respect to the nature of rule over others and of rule over self, as well as those pertaining to the conduct of the body politic.

The program I have outlined above is, of course, too vast for the brief visit we can pay to Thebes in this preliminary essay. The matters we would need to consider in detail are far-ranging, involving issues of form, content, language, character, and structure, while the plays in question run the gamut from Aiskhylos' early drama *Seven against Thebes* to the *Bakkhai* of Euripides, not produced until after the poet's death. In between, there are three plays by Sophokles—*Antigone, Oidipous Tyrannos,* and *Oidipus at Kolonos*—as well as two further plays by Euripides, the *Suppliant Women* and the *Phoinissai*. This last play, for example, is an excellent witness to the general hypothesis, since it most fully combines the three myths I have mentioned above. The *Phoinissai* divides its attention between the sons of Oidipous and the last survivor of the Spartoi, and finds its metaphorical center in Dionysos, in his negative and positive aspects.

But even with a limited tour which can stop at these individual dramas only to exemplify one or more points of the exposition, it will be possible, I hope, to sketch out what Thebes is and what it might mean in its dialogue with the city of Athens, whose theater invents its imaginary space. Oidipous is our best guide, I propose, for examining the challenges that Thebes will be seen to offer to relations among self, family, city, and cosmos. For is he not the most familiar representative of Thebes, and yet the only one who in the later dramatic tradition is permitted to make his way from Thebes to Athens? Using Oidipous, therefore, as its point of departure, the first section of this essay will suggest some of the more significant structural and thematic parallels between plays of very different sorts. The second section will address the depiction of Thebes as an "anti-Athens" and will map out the territory, as it were, of this "other" city. The third section will confront Thebes more directly with Athens through the figures of Oidipous and Antigone to suggest how the two cities are radically contraposed, especially with regard to their views and uses of time and history, tradition and change.

OIDIPOUS AT THEBES

In one sense, we might describe the career of Oidipous as a search for a home—or more precisely, a place where he might be at home, where he might truly belong. Viewed from this perspective, Oidipous immediately presents us with an extraordinary paradox. For once Oidipous discovers that he has found his true home in Thebes, he also discovers to his or our horror that he has been only too much "at home." The strange territory to which he had come when, to contravene the oracle of Apollo at Delphi, he had turned away from the road to Corinth in favor of the road to Thebes, proves to be none other than the place where he was born. Thus his subsequent sojourn in the city turns out to be not his first, as all had thought, but his second. Here the dramatic tradition diverges: in two extant plays reference is made to his death at Thebes at some indeterminate time (Aiskhylos, *Seven* 914–1004, Sophokles, *Ant.* 899–902), but later theatrical works keep him alive in order to expel him once again from Thebes, this time never to find his way back.[1]

The moment of this last exile is not fixed. Sophokles prepares the way when, at the end of *Oidipous Tyrannos,* Oidipous longs to go at once into

---

[1] I omit here discussion of the epic tradition.

exile (*Oid. Tyr.* 1436–50, 1518–19), fulfilling the edict he had imposed upon the unknown murderer before he knew that the other he sought was in truth himself (*Oid. Tyr.* 224–54; cf. 815–24). But in *Oidipous at Kolonos* he tells us that in fact he had first remained in Thebes. Only much later, he says, long after his grief and anger had modulated into acceptance and when his truest desire was to stay at home, did Kreon and his sons cruelly expel him against his will and sentence him to years of homeless wandering (*Oid. Kol.* 425–44, 765–71, 1354–59). Euripides' *Phoinissai* marks yet another shift in the temporal ordering of events in Oidipous' life. Here, where the drama presents the sequel to Oidipous' story in the next generation, the aged father is still present in Thebes, where he is kept inside the house like a "hidden ghost," "a pale shadow of a dream" (*Phoi.* 63–66, 1539–45). But he is not to remain there. At the end of this panoramic play, when Oidipous has lived to see the curses he had laid upon his sons accomplished in their death at each other's hands, Kreon belatedly drives him out to embark on the path that will lead him, as he seems to know in advance, to the town of Kolonos and to a death there far away from Thebes (*Phoi.* 1705–7).[2] Sophokles in his version also, of course, brings the aged king to the same precinct in Attika and sets the stage there for the last act of his story, which is entirely concerned with finding a permanent home for Oidipous—first as suppliant stranger, and then as a hero for the city once he vanishes into the sacred tomb. But Oidipous cannot reach this last resting place until he first confronts Thebes again and successfully resists the temptation he is offered to return home.

The true terms of that offer, however, tell us why he will refuse. No one who comes from Thebes to fetch him has the power or desire to promise him a place at home in the house or inside the city, despite pretenses to the contrary. Rather they will offer him only a site betwixt and between, on the border of the city's territory, where he will be home and not home, returned and not returned (*Oid. Kol.* 299–400, 784–86; cf. 1342–43). For Oidipous the man, who demands the dignity of his human status, the supplications of Kreon, the current ruler, and of Polyneikes, Oidipous' son, are a sham, since they desire only to gain domination over his person and this for their own political ends. On ritual grounds, it may also be true, as Kreon claims, that the patricide can never be repatriated (*Oid. Kol.* 406–7). But in a larger sense, Thebes' spatial designation of Oidipous' position in its land at this late date only spells out more explicitly the underlying rules of the system in this city whose own ambiguities are matched by those of its most exemplary native son.

[2] It is generally agreed that Euripides' drama precedes that of Sophokles, although the passages in the *Phoinissai* relevant to the place of Oidipous' exile have sometimes been suspected of interpolation.

Thebes is the place, I will argue, that makes problematic every inclusion and exclusion, every conjunction and disjunction, every relation between near and far, high and low, inside and outside, stranger and kin. Thus the person of Oidipous perhaps crystallizes in purest form the city of Thebes itself. And by that same logic, Thebes is therefore the only possible place for his birth. In Sophokles' last play, Oidipous will finally break the symbiotic relation between himself and his city when he takes his stand upon the new territory of Athens to which both his destiny and his choice have assigned him. But in the prior stages of his life story, what happens to the figure of Oidipous is emblematic of the larger concerns associated with Thebes. When he fluctuates between a fixed imprisonment in the house and an unstable wandering too far from home, or when, in a different vein, he alternates between a condition of self-referential autonomy and involvement in too dense a network of relations, Oidipous personifies in himself the characteristics that Thebes manifests in all its dramatic variants, through all its other myths, and through the extant work of all the tragic poets of Athens.

I propose then first to play the roles of both Kreon and Polyneikes. My purpose, like theirs, is heuristic—to seek to bring Oidipous home again to the place where his story truly belongs as its place of origin and as its point of departure. And, like them, I want to bring him back not for his intrinsic value and interest as a human character but for an instrumental aim. That is, I want to refocus the question of Oidipous as a question about Thebes. This means that I want to resituate Oidipous in Thebes, not only in his Sophoklean representations, but through those of Aiskhylos and Euripides as well.

This terrain, first of all, Oidipous must share with others. His story is predicated on the two oracles given in advance, first to his father and then to himself, but its terms extend beyond him to affect those whom he engenders as children of an incestuous marriage. Oidipous functions as the middle term who faces two ways in the conflict of generations. He is the child of his father, but also the father of his children, whose interdependence is emphasized by the fact that he shares a double kinship with his progeny—that of both father and brother. Thus his story only reaches its end with the third act of the family's history in the drama of his children's lives and in his retrospective understanding of the entire network of relations.

This is why we find striking similarities of dramatic structure and theme in Sophokles' three Theban plays (*Oidipous Tyrannos, Oidipous at Kolonos, Antigone*), Aiskhylos' *Seven against Thebes* (the last and sole survivor of his Labdacid trilogy), and Euripides' the *Phoinissai*. Euripides' *Suppliant Women* is also relevant, although it is set not in Thebes but in Eleusis near Athens, and concerns not only the family of Oidipous but the Argive women who come to claim burial for their sons who have fallen before Thebes. That play looks back for its pattern to Sophokles' *Antigone* and ahead to that other burial, that of Oidipous himself, in Sophokles' *Oidipous at Kolonos*.

All these plays have a common point of reference, since they each treat some event, directly or indirectly, that can be traced back to the house of Laios. But it may be less apparent how Dionysos and the myth associated with him can and should be integrated into this theatrical space. Let us turn then to Euripides' *Bakkhai* to see whether we can find a relation between Oidipous the king and Dionysos the god and can discern a common ground upon which both might stand.

OIDIPOUS TYRANNOS AND THE BAKKHAI

Is not Dionysos at Thebes, like Oidipous, both at home and not at home? Is he not also the stranger who comes from elsewhere—this time not from another Greek city like Corinth but from the more distant spaces of barbarian Asia? Yet Dionysos, too, is a child of Thebes returning home to the place of his birth in order to assert his identity and claim his patrimony. The critical difference, to be sure, resides in the fact that Dionysos is a god, the son of Semele and Zeus, and it is this honor, rather than political kingship, that he claims. They both share in the issues that revolve around confusion of origins and problems of legitimacy, but the division between mortal and immortal status ensures entirely opposite outcomes (disaster for one, success for the other). In addition, Dionysos must play two contrasting roles as a result of his special status, although both, we should note, are entirely typical ones in Thebes. Like Oidipous, Dionysos is the *xenos* (stranger) who is also native born (*suggenēs*); like him, he is the unacknowledged offspring of the royal dynasty who will come to reveal his true identity to the city. But if Dionysos compels mortals to discover the incontrovertible truth of his divine identity, he also brings the king of the city to discover the limits of his own. Thus, when the *Bakkhai* replicates the conflict between human and divine knowledge that Oidipous and Teiresias acted out in *Oidipous Tyrannos*, Dionysos necessarily aligns himself with the characteristic figure of the all-knowing seer. And like Teiresias, Apollo's agent in the Sophoklean play, Dionysos has the enigmatic power to question the identity of the ruling king in Thebes: "you do not know what life you lead, nor what you do, nor who you are" (*Bakkh.* 506; cf. *Oid. Tyr.* 413–15).

Pentheus is not the child of Laios, nor even, of course, a child of Oidipous. Rather he is sprung from Ekhion, as he asserts in reply to the divinity's challenge (507), and hence is descended from one of the Spartoi, who sprang from the earth. But Dionysos' echo in the *Bakkhai* of Teiresias' taunt in *Oidipous Tyrannos* might forewarn us that Pentheus, too, is

liable to manifest the Oedipian conflicts so typical at Thebes. And indeed
he does. In thematic terms, Pentheus has already attacked the paternal
figure in the hostile verbal exchange he undertakes with his grandfather
Kadmos (*Bakkh.* 330–46), and the climax of the plot confirms that he is
irresistibly drawn to join his mother. His hidden desire is to see her participate in the sexual activities he imagines the women are engaged in,
and he longs both to assert his phallic power and to be cradled in her
arms again like a child (*Bakkh.* 964–69). Like Oidipous, he, too, turns
out to be a voyeur, seeking without his conscious knowledge to see and
know those secrets that are forbidden to him in the domain of the
mother.

   In structural terms, Pentheus' joint meeting with Kadmos, the father
of the family, and Teiresias, the seer of Apollo, condenses the two sequential encounters that occur for Oidipous in Sophokles' play—first,
with Kreon, his uncle and an older male in the family, and next, with
Teiresias himself. But the symmetrical conflict between the two cousins,
Pentheus and Dionysos, puts us also and perhaps more directly in the line
of the conflict of enemy brothers, Eteokles and Polyneikes, and the cor-
respondences between the *Bakkhai* and Aiskhylos' *Seven against Thebes*
are even more compelling than the parallels with *Oidipous Tyrannos*
noted above. Comparing the two may in fact demonstrate best the validity of a Theban scenario, since they recount apparently different *mythoi*
in the history of Thebes and the dates of their composition stand at the
furthest remove from each other in the history of the theater: *Seven
against Thebes* is an early specimen of extant Aiskhylean drama, the last in
Aiskhylos' lost trilogy, whose first two plays treated the earlier generations of Laios and Oidipous, whereas the *Bakkhai,* although referring
back to what we might take as the founding myth of the theater itself, is
one of the last plays in Euripides' dramatic repertory.

THE *BAKKHAI* AND *SEVEN AGAINST THEBES*

As we examine these two dramas, we observe first of all that both sets of
doubles are engaged in a conflict, which is that of war. Eteokles and Polyneikes will meet directly in armed warrior combat at the gates of
Thebes in the context of the Argives' expedition against the city. Although Pentheus' situation is more complex, and the circumstances provoking his desire for armed intervention are far more problematic, this
king is also portrayed as a military leader. Opposing Dionysos, the
leader of the Asiatic troops of maenads (*Bakkh.* 50–52), Pentheus is, at
the same time, ready to bring out his army against the Theban women of
the city who have themselves gone as maenads to the mountains. Dionysos, like Polyneikes, the exiled brother, demands the right to return

and claim what is his own, and like him, may be said to come with a foreign force against his native city.

Second, both Eteokles and Pentheus must confront onstage a chorus of insubordinate women, and their responses in each case are hostile and violent. Pentheus confronts onstage the chorus of Asiatic maenads whom he would lock up and put away in the house; Eteokles' anger is also directed first against an unruly chorus which, in this case, is made up of the women of Thebes itself. Motivated by terror at the enemy's approach, they have come forth unbidden from their houses to pray for salvation from the gods at the public altars. Eteokles, too, would shut them away in the house, and he further accuses them of helping the enemy against the city's interests with their subversive piety (*Seven* 77–263).

In the *Bakkhai,* however, the conflict between male and female is more pervasive and more complex than the limited catalytic role assigned to the Theban women in Eteokles' city. The conflict here takes place with two female groups—the chorus of Asiatic women within the city and the Theban women outside its walls. The women's ritual challenge (both foreign and domestic) to male authority is not a reaction of terror to an impending disaster, as in the *Seven,* in which they fear they will become its most helpless victims, but rather itself constitutes the crisis in the city—its symptom and major cause. Offstage and unseen, the Theban women, as the drama progresses, will also prove to be Pentheus' true antagonists, once the god works his seductive spell over his adversary and Pentheus in his madness makes common cause with Dionysos. The women, as the messenger tells us, have already defeated men in a clash of spear against thyrsus (*Bakkh.* 761–63), and it is they who will also defeat Pentheus now in an unequal contest of many against one.

Pentheus leaves the stage for the last time disguised in bacchant costume, and Eteokles departs arrayed in warrior dress. One is on his way to the mountains, the other to the city's gate where he is to face his enemy brother. But even here there are grounds for comparison between them in that both are impelled by irrational forces—one in a state of Dionysiac possession and the other in the grip of his father's Erinys, reminding us once again that, as figurations of madness, Bacchant and Erinys are often interchangeable in tragic diction.[3] And, finally, in both cases, these two hoplite figures, Pentheus and Eteokles, go forth to murderous confrontations with the closest members of their own families, whether masculine (brother) or feminine (mother).[4]

---

[3] See J.-P Guépin, *The Tragic Paradox* (Amsterdam, 1968), 21; William Whallon, "Maenadism in the *Oresteia*," *HSCP* 68 (1946): 321; and, for Eteokles, my *Under the Sign,* 96.

[4] It is worth observing here that Thebes is the setting for yet another Dionysiac scenario in Euripides' play, *Herakles Mainomenos,* where Herakles kills his wife and children (al-

Nevertheless, if we keep to the specifics of gender relations as they are organized in each play, it is clear that despite the difference of emphasis, Eteokles and Pentheus are each engaged in battles on two fronts: one with an enemy brother and a foreign force, and one with women inside the city who escape from their houses and domestic roles into public places controlled by men (*Seven against Thebes*) or outside the city altogether into the mountain wilds (*Bakkhai*). Eteokles meets the Theban women in the first part of the play and Pentheus finds them in the last. Both feminine groups, albeit for different reasons, exhibit the same passionate and uncivic forms of religious worship, and their behavior in each case triggers the intemperate reaction from the ruler that will shift the issue of his control over them to that of his problematic and precarious control over self, and his right to govern the city.[5]

Nevertheless, antagonism between males is the central and most dramatic element of each play. Organized as they are around the theme of doubling identity, these conflicts call the very notion of the self into question. In *Seven against Thebes,* Eteokles and Polyneikes never meet onstage, although their pairing at the seventh gate caps the extensive shield scene where Eteokles matches Theban against Argive at each of the preceding gates. But in what follows the report of their deaths at each other's hands, opposition resolves into an equation that undermines the separate identities they strove to maintain in life. Pentheus and Dionysos, on the other hand, meet three times onstage in their struggle for control over one another. Yet in their last encounter, when Pentheus succumbs to the power of the god, these enemy doubles sharply diverge, inasmuch as Dionysos is the son of Olympian Zeus and the king is the son of Ekhion, the *gēgenēs,* the earthborn. At the same time, when Dionysos robes the king in feminine dress, his strategy is intended to transform Pentheus into a double of himself.[6] The two of them garbed in maenadic costume set off for the mountain together, their differences momentarily dissolved in an identity that makes Pentheus one with the god and his worshipers. Moreover, it is through the power of Dionysos that Pentheus

---

though stopping short, through Athena's intervention, of killing his father) and is himself imaged as a bacchant of Hades (cf. 892–99, 965–67, 1142).

[5] The *Bakkhai* is obvious in this regard. In *Seven against Thebes,* however, the matter is more subtle, since Eteokles' final response to calm the women's anxiety and to show that he is in charge is to promise them that he will stand as the seventh champion in the line of defenders (282–86). He thus prepares the way for the confrontation with his brother, even as Pentheus will meet his double, Dionysos (discussed below).

[6] On Pentheus and Dionysos as doubles, see, first, Francis Cornford, *The Origins of Attic Comedy* (Cambridge, Eng., 1914; repr. New York, 1961), 130–31, 183; Robert Rogers, *A Psychoanalytical Study of the Double in Literature* (Detroit, 1970), 64–66; and René Girard, *La violence et le sacré* (Paris, 1972), 182–83. See also Charles Segal, *Dionysiac Poetics and Euripides' Bacchae* (Princeton, 1982), 29 and *passim*.

acquires the fateful capacity for seeing double. He sees two suns and two cities of Thebes (*Bakkh.* 918–19), and in his female dress, he himself is doubled (or divided) with his masculine self.

THE IDENTITY OF THE SELF

It is time now after following all these permutations to come back to a correspondence with Oidipous himself in light of an endemic problem in Thebes—that of the unstable arithmetic of the self. In his search for the murderer, Oidipous at first can also be said to see double: he imagines that there is an other, a stranger, but discovers that the other was only a fugitive phantom of the self—that is, there was only one when he believed there might have been two. And numbers play an essential role in Sophokles' play in another way. As a last resort, Oidipous had pinned his hopes on the two different versions of the murder of the man at the crossroads. Killed by many, says the servant (*Oid. Tyr.* 118–25, 842); killed by one, as Oidipous knows (*Oid. Tyr.* 811–13). The text, oddly enough, never resolves this discrepancy, but a closer inspection of the underlying issues suggests that on a more symbolic level, it need not ever do so. Once we know the identity of the slayer as the incestuous Oidipous and consider in formal terms what that implies, a literal reading of the "many versus the one" proves to have been a false signpost on the road to truth. The numbers game can be construed retrospectively as yet another riddle, which is presented now in current dramatic time and to which the appropriate answer is none other than Oidipous himself. That is, Oidipous turns out to be both one and many, doubled in his role of son and father with his selfsame mother and doubled as brother to the double progeny he has begotten from that single source.[7]

In the sequel to Oidipous' story, in which the sons play the leading roles, a similar logic operates by a simple reversal of terms. For Oidipous is "one" where the social system dictates there must be "two" (father, son), while the two sons he begets represent a surplus of progeny, since for the son to replace the father, there is need of only one. Thus, significantly, Eteokles in *Seven against Thebes* also evinces a curious interest in numeration. Naming himself as a singular (*heis*) in the first lines of the play (*Seven* 6) with reference, as he thinks, to his position of ruler in Thebes, he will find out that this statement is both true and false.[8] In the

---

[7] See also Charles Segal, *Tragedy and Civilization: An Interpretation of Sophocles* (Cambridge, Mass., 1981), 215–16, who sees the implications of the "one and the many" but not its aspects as a riddle.

[8] On this issue, see further the discussion in my *Under the Sign*, 37–41. In line 6, the text juxtaposes *heis* (the one) with *polus*, which in its immediate context means "much," but the phrase clearly anticipates the more general problem of singular and plural as well as the specific force of the name Poly-neikes.

sphere of politics, he is truly one among the many, since as citizens of Kadmos' city, they can invoke their autochthonous ancestry, while he is in truth the cursed child of the cursed Oidipous. Regarding the family, however, his identity is not singularly his own. In the end, it will be doubled, and even his name will fuse with that of his brother: the choral lament that follows the fatal duel repeatedly refers to the two under the single grammatical form of the dual (*Seven* 811, 816, 863, 922, 932) and Eteokles loses his name to the pluralizing force of the other's—*Polyneikeis* (829–30).

The brothers collapse distinctions in yet another way, as they take up their legacy as Oidipous' sons with regard to their father's twofold transgression. For Oidipous himself, the patricide and incest were two separate and sequential events, each directed in turn toward the family member of the appropriate gender. But for the next generation, these two actions merge into one as the brothers in their passionate desire for mutual confrontation (*erōs,* 688; *himeros,* 692), are radically divided against each other as hostile antagonists, but at the same time, through their reflexive and mutual fratricide, they are drastically combined into one.

Still further, the quarrel between Eteokles and Polyneikes ramifies more widely what Oidipous' twin actions imply for the welfare of the larger society, as the brothers' desire to possess their father's house and goods has nothing now to do with the desire for the biological mother (long dead), but is rather displaced and diffused as a claim for political hegemony. In the *Bakkhai,* by contrast, the quarrel between Pentheus and Dionysos is focused precisely on who is to have power over the women of Thebes, most especially over the maternal figure of Agave. This play, therefore, directly poses a confrontation between mother and son and more openly dramatizes the self's dilemma as a family member, divided between contradictory impulses of attraction and hostility.

What I am suggesting then in this comparison between *Seven against Thebes* and the *Bakkhai* is that Pentheus, the child of the earthborn, and Eteokles, the child of an incestuous union, seem to share a kindred bond that links them together as friendly doubles of one another. They are *semblables, frères,* on the territory of Thebes, exchanging places, as it were, for their mutual elucidation. Pentheus in the *Bakkhai* brings to light what remains implicit and displaced in the Oidipean struggle between Eteokles and his brother in *Seven against Thebes.* The dilemma of Eteokles, on the other hand, as developed in the language and structure of *Seven against Thebes,* urges us to focus on the opposite, but complementary, relations between the history of the house of Laios and the autochthonous prehistory of the city that more directly concerns Pentheus. And this in two ways. First, by identifying himself with the autochthons of the city rather than with the destiny reserved for him by his father, Eteokles looks to autochthony as the positive myth of the city's political solidarity. But fratricide, the culminating act of *Seven against Thebes* finds its model not only through its hypostasis of Oidipous' previous transgressions against the family but also through the negative aspect of autochthony that is manifested on the political level in the internecine conflict of that warrior band, the Sown Men.

FOUNDATIONS: INCEST AND AUTOCHTHONY

With autochthony, we have reached the third in the cluster of myths that are central to the representation of Thebes on the tragic stage (in addition to Dionysos and the house of Laios), a myth that takes us back on a long journey from Oidipous to the very foundation of the city. Kadmos slew the dragon of Ares and sowed the crop of Spartoi from the dragon's teeth. They in turn slew one another, except for five who survived as the first autochthonous inhabitants of the city. Kadmos, for his part, married Harmonia, the daughter of Ares and Aphrodite, finally giving his own daughter Agave to Ekhion, one of the earthborn, and another daughter, Semele, to Olympian Zeus.

The troubles in Thebes started at the very beginning, it seems, both for the stability of the city and for that of the self, where autochthony, Dionysos, and, ultimately, Oidipous rule. Harmonia, as her name indicates, is the logical outcome of a union between the two antithetical principles of Ares and Aphrodite and might serve as the idealized emblem of marriage which conjoins the opposite sexes. But in Thebes, Harmonia is only a euphemizing and finally illusory hope. How can it be otherwise in a place where both War (Ares) and Love (Aphrodite) operate as illegal factors in both the city and the family, leading not to domestic or political tranquility but to internal strife and incestuous origins?[9]

These issues, needless to say, require further discussion. For the moment, I wish only to point out that autochthony is an underlying theme in the *Bakkhai* which comes to the fore when Pentheus, the son of the Spartos, falls under the spell of his cousin Dionysos,[10] whereas *Seven against Thebes*, as noted above, invokes the idea of the earthborn as both a

[9] Autochthony as a myth of origins in Thebes has two stages. In the first, it has affinities with incest, given the analogy that obtains between mother and earth. In the second, it leads to violence among kin (fratricide most directly, but patricide can be included by extension). On these issues, see my discussion in *Under the Sign,* 29–36. On the relations between autochthony and incest, see also Lowell Edmunds, who, starting from a very different viewpoint, arrives at a similar conclusion in his "The Cults and Legends of Oedipus," *HSCP* 85 (1981): 235, and see too Jean Rudhardt, "De l'inceste à la mythologie grecque," *Revue française de psychanalyse* 46 (1982): 753–57.

[10] On the chiastic relations between Pentheus, the son of the earthborn, and Dionysos, the son of the Olympian, see Segal, *Dionysiac Poetics,* 180–84 and *passim.*

contrast to and a paradigm of the fratricidal combat undertaken by the sons of Oidipous. But autochthony is a far more prominent element in Euripides' far-ranging drama, the *Phoinissai,* which more than any other extant play best exemplifies the complex interweaving of all three Theban *mythoi.*

THE *PHOINISSAI*

Here in his version of the Aiskhylean *Seven against Thebes,* Euripides situates the struggle between the sons of Oidipous in the widest context of the city's history.[11] On stage he contraposes the sons of the incestuous union against Menoikeus, Kreon's son, the last surviving descendant of the Spartoi, sown from the teeth of the dragon of Ares. Despite the negative evaluation of Oidipous' progeny in this play and the idealizing of noble Menoikeus, the two sides cannot wholly be separated, one for the family and the other for the city, since Euripides also insists on their interrelations. The sons of Oidipous and the earthborn's seed must equally meet their deaths, each expiating an anterior fault of another generation (the curse of the family, the wrath of the dragon). Second, they are drawn together into an intimate association through the figure of Jokasta, who in this play is mother to her sons as well as foster mother to Menoikeus (*Phoi.* 986–89). Additionally, the play establishes yet another set of affinities by persistently making parallels between the dragon of Ares in the generation of Kadmos and the monstrous Sphinx in the generation of Oidipous.

As for Dionysos, he is included as the drama's metaphorical point of reference that shapes the underlying rhythms of the play. Dionysos has a double function as the emblem of joyous festivity in the city's life and also as the model for maddened strife. The chorus, recalling the birth of Dionysos at a promising moment in the early history of the city, at first suppresses the violence of his engendering in their song (*Phoi.* 645–56). But as the pressure of events in the present increases, that latent force returns to the surface when we reach the third *stasimon.* At the moment when the city and the sons of Oidipous prepare for deadly battle, Dionysos faces, we might say, his ambiguous opposite in Thebes in the figure of the god Ares, and the dividing line between them falters as Ares assimilates the language and gestures of Dionysiac celebration. That martial power is preparing an anti-fete of blood and war, in contrast to

---

[11] For an excellent discussion of the *Phoinissai* as a general overview of Theban history, see Marylin B. Arthur, "The Curse of Civilization: The Choral Odes of the *Phoenissae*," *HSCP* 81 (1977): 163–85. The scope of this play extends far beyond the geographical boundaries of Thebes as it seeks to situate the struggle at Thebes in the most extended frame of reference. Its complexities cannot be discussed here.

peaceful Bacchic pleasures, and yet he also converts Dionysiac elements for his own use so as to draw them into unholy alliance with the destructive forces of strife (*Phoi.* 784–800).

Even those happy pleasures, however, have their sinister side, as we learn from the prologue, in that Dionysos had a prior role to play in the misfortunes of Thebes. The god, in a sense, presided over the very begetting of Oidipous; it was at a Dionysiac revel that Laios, having indulged in too much wine, coupled with his wife and thus transgressed the prohibition of Apollo's oracle that forbade him to engender children (*Phoi.* 17–22). And as Dionysos ruled over the beginning, he also proves to rule over the end of the play. For in the aftermath of the battle that takes place in the drama between the enemy brothers, and more largely between Thebes and Argos, Antigone, the shy maiden of the play's prologue, is transformed into a bacchante of corpses (*Phoi.* 1489–90). In fact, she makes her valedictory to Thebes by abandoning the happy rites of the god in whose honor she had formerly danced to take up rites of mourning and to depart for exile and ultimately her death (*Phoi.* 1753–57).

Thus Euripides' late contribution to the Theban tradition in the history of the Athenian theater draws all the various strands together and plays them off one another in ways that are distinctively his own, but that reveal in fullest form the kindred relations of these seemingly disparate elements in Thebes. It is a minor but significant detail in the play that Teiresias makes his predictable entry on the Theban scene by informing us that he has come *not,* as is his wont, from the nearby altars, but, strangely enough, from Athens, where he has been procuring the success of that city in its battle against Eumolpos and the men of Eleusis (*Phoi.* 852–57). Yet the reason for Teiresias' curious excursion abroad is not difficult to discern, if we consider that his prophecy no longer concerns the house of Laios but rather demands the patriotic sacrifice of Menoikeus to save the city. This new message, we might say, is one that Teiresias cannot issue from within the territory of Thebes. To find his model, he must travel instead to Athens, where just lately the daughters of autochthonous Erekhtheus have sacrificed themselves for the common good, an event Euripides himself represented in an earlier play.[12] Only through this displacement can Teiresias import a purely disinterested civic act into a city whose nature, no matter what proper political sentiments its leaders at first profess, seems to preclude the kind of noble offering for the city that Menoikeus voluntarily decides to make.[13]

---

[12] This play is the *Erekhtheus,* which is dated to about 423 B.C.E. The fragments can be found in Colin Austin, *Nova Fragmenta Euripidea in Papyris Reperta* (Berlin, 1968), 22–40.

[13] On arguments against the *Opfertod* theory of sacrifical death proposed for Eteokles in *Seven against Thebes,* see my *Under the Sign,* 161–68.

And with this important distinction, we come now to the heart of the matter.

II. THEBES AS THE ANTI-ATHENS

What then does Thebes as a topos represent for Athens on the dramatic stage in the theater of Dionysos? My answer is brief. I propose that Thebes functions in the theater as an anti-Athens, an other place. If we say that theater in general functions as an "other scene" where the city puts itself and its values into question by projecting itself upon the stage to confront the present with the past through its ancient myths,[14] then Thebes, I suggest, is the "other scene" of the "other scene" that is the theater itself. Thebes, we might say, is the quintessential "other scene," as Oidipous is the paradigm of tragic man and Dionysos is the god of the theater. There Athens acts out questions crucial to the *polis,* the self, the family, and society, but these are displaced upon a city that is imagined as the mirror opposite of Athens.[15]

The dramatic relation of Athens is twofold. First, within the theater, Athens is not the tragic space. Rather, it is the scene where theater can and does "escape" the tragic, and where reconciliation and transformation are made possible. Thebes and Athens are, in fact, specifically contrasted to one another in several plays, such as Sophokles' *Oidipous at Kolonos* and Euripides' *Suppliant Women,* and implicitly juxtaposed in Euripides' *Herakles* when Theseus comes to lead the broken hero away to sanctuary and protection in Athens.[16] But Thebes is also the obverse side of Athens, the shadow self, we might say, of the idealized city on whose other terrain the tragic action may be pushed to its furthest limits of contradiction and impasse. As such, it also furnishes the territory for explor-

---

[14] See the splendid piece of Jean-Pierre Vernant, "Tensions et ambiguïtés dans la tragédie grecque," in *Mythe et tragédie en Grèce ancienne* (Paris, 1973), 25–27, trans. J. Lloyd, in *Tragedy and Myth in Ancient Greece* (Atlantic Highlands, N.J., 1981), 9–10.

[15] Dario Sabbatucci, in his *Il mito, il rito, e la storia* (Rome, 1978), 117–41, also argues for the position I have indicated Thebes occupies on the stage of Athens. He makes many interesting and suggestive remarks, but his general theoretical approach and his treatment of the literary texts require a far more extensive critique than space permits here. I note only that, in my opinion, his a priori scheme of *genos* and *polis* leads him astray in assessing the function of Thebes for Athens.

[16] I have not included Herakles among the significant personages at Thebes because he has many other associations and never remains for long in that city. Nevertheless, the situation in *Herakles* is demonstrably appropriate to Thebes (see above, n. 4). Even in Sophokles' *Trakhiniai,* which does not take place in Thebes but at Trakhis where Herakles and his family are in exile, the Theban paradigm still seems relevant. At the end of the drama, Herakles shocks his son when he insists that Hyllos commit the two Oidipal transgressions—put an end to his father's life and marry his father's bride (*Trakh.* 1204–51).

ing the most radical implications of the tragic without any risk to its own self-image.

In other words, Thebes, the other, provides Athens, the self, with a place where it can play with and discharge both terror of and attraction to the irreconcilable, the inexpiable, and the unredeemable, where it can experiment with the dangerous heights of self-assertion that transgression of fixed boundaries inevitably entails, where the city's political claims to primacy may be exposed and held up to question. Events in Thebes and the characters who enact them both fascinate and repel the Athenian audience, finally instructing the spectators as to how their city might refrain from imitating the other's negative example. There where Thebes holds the stage, both Dionysos and Oidipous, from opposite corners (of the "irrational" and "rational"), tempt the self to play roles that can only lead to disaster. And both Dionysos and Oidipous end by confounding identity, their own and others', establishing hopeless antitheses and hopeless mixtures. They do this at different moments in the mythic history of Thebes and by different dramatic means throughout the history of the Athenian theater.

THE MIDDLE TERM: ARGOS

In this schematic structure, Argos occupies the middle space between the two extremes that Athens and Thebes represent. As its mythic repertory demonstrates—most notably in the story of the house of Atreus and the saga of the Danaids—Argos, too, is a city of conflict, and it has erred grievously in sending the expedition of the Seven as foreign invaders against the sovereign city of Thebes. But the city, or more precisely, its characters, can be saved—Orestes primarily at Athens and the Danaids probably in Argos itself. In the *Suppliants* of Aiskhylos, the first and only surviving play of his Danaid trilogy, we find a model king, Pelasgos, just like Theseus, and a democratic city that closely resembles the Athenian ideal. There the Danaids, with the exception of one, Hypermestra, slay their husbands on their wedding night. But there are reasons to suppose that Argos in the last play will have furnished a solution in its own city to the dilemma raised by the collective crime of the maidens. And the means most probably are not unlike those deployed to save the Argive Orestes in the third play of Aiskhylos' other trilogy, the *Oresteia*.[17] In

---

[17] That is, a trial before a tribunal and the establishment of a new ritual. For a summary of the various hypotheses, see A. F. Garvie, *Aeschylus, Supplices: Play and Trilogy* (Cambridge, Eng., 1969), 163–233, and see also R. P. Winnington-Ingram, "The Danaid Trilogy of Aeschylus," *JHS* 81 (1961): 141–52. I treat the Danaid trilogy briefly in "Configurations of Rape in Greek Myth," in *Rape,* ed. Sylvana Tomaselli and Roy Porter (Oxford, 1986), 137–43. See further, Zeitlin, "Patterns of Gender in Aeschylean Tragedy:

this last act of the house of Atreus, Orestes, of course, is exonerated from matricide and his redemption is ratified when Athena allows him to return as legitimate ruler in Argos (*Eum.* 754–61). Euripides never goes so far as Aiskhylos. Quite the contrary: his three plays that treat the story of Orestes (*Elektra, Iphigeneia in Tauris, Orestes*) introduce disturbing ironies which critically challenge the validity of their Aiskhylean model. Yet all these dramas agree in one way or another that Orestes may finally be redeemed.

ARGOS, ATHENS, THEBES

The *Suppliant Women* of Euripides arranges a triangular relationship on stage between Athens, Thebes, and Argos, and thus furnishes the most instructive example of how the conventions of the theater assign a specific identity to each city. In this frankly ideological play set in the sanctuary of Demeter at Eleusis, the Argive women, together with the general Adrastos, have come as suppliants to beg the assistance of Theseus, king of Athens, in their grievance against Thebes. In the aftermath of a successful defense of their city against the expedition of the Argive Seven, the Thebans have refused to allow the mothers and wives to take up the fallen warriors for burial. In effect, Athens is being asked to risk the lives of its own citizens in a conflict with Thebes, not for some cause of its own, but to support a general humanitarian principle, which is additionally encumbered with the plain fact that the Argive expedition was no justifiable enterprise. Theseus at first refuses the appeal of Adrastos, taking the opportunity to vent his righteous indignation at the misguided political conduct of this leader (e.g., *Suppl. Women* 214–49). But yielding to the intervention of his mother, Aithra, who, responding to the women's desperate sorrow, speaks in the name of compassion and a higher political justice, the Athenian king agrees to honor the request of the repentant Adrastos to procure the burial of the Argive dead, even at the cost of the armed battle that is to follow. Adrastos is open to admonishment and can admit the error of his ways, which means he can finally be linked to the side of the Athenians. Indeed, the rapprochement is successful enough to allow him the right to speak like an Athenian over the Argive dead, in the form of miniature *epitaphioi,* those funeral orations normally delivered annually over Athenians who died nobly for their country in battle.[18] But the contrast between Athens and Thebes is posed at its most extreme. There are implicit reversals of the Theban scenario

---

Seven against Thebes and the Danaid Trilogy," forthcoming, and Zeitlin, "La politique d'Eros: Masculin et féminin dans les *Suppliantes* d'Eschyle," *Mêtis* (forthcoming).

[18] These orations are not without their ironies, and scholars are still sharply divided as to their interpretation. For the most recent discussion with bibliography, see Nicole Loraux,

we have come to recognize: Athens respects and heeds the independent ritual activity of the women despite the irregular nature of a suppliant rite at this particular altar; the Athenian king can accept the counsel of a woman and grant his mother a mediating function denied to women in Thebes (cf. especially the case of Jokasta in the *Phoinissai*). More explicitly, however, the city of Thebes assumes its most negative colors and, through its spokesman onstage (the herald), goes so far as to launch an open attack against Athenian democracy. Whatever suggestive ironies this critique may include, Thebes is shown as a place corrupted beyond redemption, offering a bleak and bitter self-portrait of the tyrant and the tyrannical city, which respects no laws or institutions and knows only violence and wrath (*Suppl. Women* 399–597).

MAPPING THE TERRITORY OF THEBES: SELF AND SOCIETY

Looking back now over this brief survey, we might characterize Thebes as the place either of imprisonment or exile, as the city of negation and death. There Oidipous, after all his arithmetic of the one and the many, is addressed by the chorus as self-cancelling, equal to nothing (*Oid. Tyr.* 1186–88). In his parallel story in *Antigone*, Kreon similarly discovers for himself that he is no longer a regent, no longer a self, but a nothing (*Ant.* 1321). And, perhaps on the most literal level, Pentheus demonstrates the furthest stages of the deconstruction of the self through the physical *sparagmos* he undergoes. There are survivors but no heirs. Kreon remains alone in the city at the end of *Antigone,* his son, his wife, and Antigone, the last of the line of Oidipous, all gone. Kadmos and Agave leave together at the close of the *Bakkhai,* Oidipous and Antigone at the end of the *Phoinissai*. Oidipous is the only one who can be redeemed—but only in Athens, and through his conscious choice of Athens over Thebes. Even so, let us remember how late is the moment of his salvation—only and properly at the point of his crossing from life into death.

In the version of the oracle given to Laios in Aiskhylos, the problem of Oidipous is posed as a choice between the fate of the ruling dynasty and that of the city. "Dying without issue," Apollo declared, "you will save the city" (*Seven* 745–49). This prophecy only comes to fulfillment in the third generation, with the death of the two brothers in *Seven against Thebes* and the final expulsion of Oidipous and Antigone at the end of the *Phoinissai* (along with the last of the descendants of the Sown Men, who, we might say, inherits a version of that prophecy to Laios). When all these plays conclude, the outer walls of Thebes are still standing and the foreign enemy is invariably beaten back or driven out. In the *Bakkhai,*

L'Invention d'Athènes (Paris and the Hague, 1981), 107–8, trans. A. Sheridan under the title *Invention of Athens* (Cambridge, Mass., 1986).

Dionysos himself does not remain, but, as he tells us in the prologue, will continue his journey to other cities in order to reveal his rites (*Bakkh.* 48–50). If these are the terms on which the city continues to be rescued, we are entitled to ask for what purpose and for whom? And, in this present context, we might well reply: for Athens and its tragic stage. It is essential for Athens that Thebes remain intact as a theatrical enclosure so that within its closed confines yet another play may be staged that reenacts in some way these same intricate and inextricable conflicts that can never be resolved and which are potentially present for the city of Athens.

For the tragic poets Thebes represents the paradigm of the closed system that vigorously protects its psychological, social, and political boundaries, even as its towering walls and circular ramparts close off and protect its physical space. Once we grasp the import of autochthony and incest as the underlying patterns at Thebes, we can diagnose the malaise of this city, which has no means of establishing a viable system of relations and differences, either within the city or without, or between the self and any other. Unable to incorporate outsiders into its system and locked into the priority of blood relations of the *genos,* Thebes endlessly shuttles between the extremes of rigid inclusions and exclusions on the one hand and radical confusions of difference on the other. Eteokles (and Pentheus), for example, are intent on not letting the women *inside* come outside,[19] but fail in their attempts, and Dionysos and Polyneikes are the outsiders who press their claim to being insiders, with destructive results. The most conspicuous symptom of this maladaptive system is the problem of marriage in this city, the institution that normally regulates relations between non-kin and circulates women as signs to be exchanged between men. When it is not refused altogether (as by Antigone in her play or Eteokles in his), marriage brings danger from two different directions, either as excessive endogamy in the form of incest or as its contrary, when Polyneikes' search for a bride *outside*—too far from home—instigates the expedition of the Argive Seven against his native city.

Autochthony, as the political myth of collective solidarity, and incest in the domestic domain might suggest a fundamental cleavage between city and family. And in one sense they do. In *Seven against Thebes,* a fundamental opposition opens up between Eteokles and the true autochthonous defenders who found and anchor the system of Thebes in the first triad of champions (Melanippos, Polyphontes, Megareus). In the *Phoinissai,* the division is even sharper. Menoikeus must choose to die for the

---

[19] Helen Bacon in "The Shield of Eteocles," *Arion* 3 (1964): 27–38, has excellent remarks on this topic.

city without the knowledge of his father, who, despite Teiresias' unequivocal assertion of its political necessity, has refused to sacrifice his son.[20] But a hidden analogy connects family and city, since each reproductive model (autochthony, incest) looks back to a single undifferentiated origin, and each holds out the ideal of a self-referential autonomy.

A typical Theban scenario shows us a king who at first governs, as he imagines, wholly in the city's interests, relying solely on his powers of reason and judgment to maintain civic order. But the pressure of events reveals him as one who has confused the relationship between ruler and city, identifying the state, in fact, with himself. In each case, the true imperative is the desire to rule, to exercise single hegemony over others and to claim all power for himself.[21] Yet once confronted with the limitations he has never acknowledged, this ruler discovers that he cannot rule himself, cannot maintain an unequivocal identity. And in this surrender to hidden constraints, he must surrender the political kingship he has craved. That Thebes is the paradigmatic home of tyrants, as even Oidipous is liable to become when at home, can be attributed perhaps to the fact that incest and patricide are seen as the typical tyrannical crimes (cf. Plato, *Rep.* 9.571b4–d3).[22] But the desire on the political level to rule alone in autonomy is also equivalent in the family domain to the desire for an autonomous self-engendering, which the acts of patricide and incest imply. Such a desire finally crosses the last boundary in demanding equivalence for the self with the gods and taking their power for its own.

[20] One must beware, however, of treating autochthony as a unitary phenomenon, since it can take many different forms in different locales. Athens' comparable myth follows other lines, and unlike the Theban version of the Sown Men, does not include the ingredients for internal strife among its inhabitants or make the same equation with incest. On Athens' myth see particularly the pioneering work of J. J. Peradotto, "Oedipus and Erichthonius: Some Observations on Syntagmatic and Paradigmatic Order," *Arethusa* 10 (1977): 85–101, and Nicole Loraux, "L'Autochtonie: Une topique athénienne," in *Les enfants d'Athéna* (Paris, 1981), 35–73. On the political implications of the Theban myth, see Zoë Petre, "Thèmes dominants et attitudes politiques dans *les Sept contre Thèbes* d'Eschyle," *StudClas* 13 (1971): 15–28. power   rule

[21] The desire for *kratos* and *arkhē* is a prominent motif in every Theban play. Both Oidipous in *Oid. Tyr.* (628–30) and Kreon in *Antigone* (733–39) are brought to the point where they openly declare that they must rule at any cost and that the city belongs, in fact, to the ruler. Kreon in *Oid. Tyr.* stresses in his argument with Oidipous the precise opposite, that he has no desire to rule and is content to wield only informal power (*Oid. Tyr.* 583–602). But once he comes to regency in Thebes, after the sons of Oidipous both die in their bid for power, he offers the same rationale in his argument with Haimon. Although Kreon's play precedes that of Oidipous in the Sophoklean corpus, the point is that whoever fills the role of king (or regent) succumbs to the same political error.

[22] The phrasing of Eteokles' rebuke to the unruly women in the *Seven against Thebes* is very suggestive in this regard: Obedience to rule (*Peitharkhia*), they say, is Good Luck's mother (*tēs Eupraxias mētēr*), wedded to Salvation (*gynē Sōtēros; Seven* 224–25). The son of Oidipous says more than he knows.

Thebes therefore shows us the self playing for the highest stakes, only to succumb inevitably to the triple force of the restrictions that *polis,* family, and gods impose. The *Bakkhai,* which best represents the workings of the tragic process, since there the god of the theater is an actor in his own drama, also most overtly represents the way these three elements are intertwined. For there, in the conflict between Dionysos and Pentheus, the religious, political, and familial issues all unequivocally converge on the same point. Yet all the Theban dramas offer their own distinctive but comparable variations on the same set of themes.

III. The Eternal Return

ANTIGONE

From its breakdown of the differences that result from the complex interplay of incest, autochthony, patricide, and tyranny, Thebes bestows a continuing legacy on all the characters in its city who predictably act out their allotted roles. Sophokles' *Antigone* provides an excellent case in point, since Kreon himself, a collateral and secondary member of the dynasty, has not directly participated in the muddled and accursed history of the family of Laios. Yet he and Antigone, the two antagonists of the play, divide between them the marked features of the Oidipean family, both masculine and feminine.

Antigone, on the one hand, proves her lineage as her father's daughter (*Ant.* 471). By refusing to accept differentiation between the two brothers, one who was loyal to the city and the other who was not, she manifests in a feminine version that Oidipean equalization of everything that is one's own, and insists on the absolute principle of family union even, and especially, in death. Kreon, for his part, looks back most of all to Oidipous' son Eteokles in Aiskhylos' *Seven against Thebes* and continues in his own drama to play out yet another version of the self-destructive impulses of the very family to whose place he has succeeded. He, too, insists on rigid antitheses and lives by military standards of absolute obedience to the city, only to find, like Eteokles, that the balance will shift to his detriment from the public to the private sphere. Taking over in Thebes after the death of Eteokles, he only repeats, now on different grounds, the patterns both of Oidipous' children and of Oidipous himself. For the women of the chorus whom Eteokles had tried to suppress in *Seven against Thebes,* Kreon substitutes the single figure of Antigone. He also renews the Oidipal hostility between kin in his conflict with Antigone and with Haimon, the son in his immediate family. Within the compass of the dramatic time of the play, events seem to echo (or anticipate) different moments in Sophokles' later treatment of Oidipous' story, whose features, however, are already given by the myth. Kreon tempts his son to repeat Oidipous' patricidal crime against his father, and drives his wife, Eurydike, to "imitate" Jokasta's solution of suicide. Kreon, in his own right, we might say, paradoxically also insists on the absolute unity of the family, denying to any of its members the right to differ from himself, denying Haimon in fact the right to make a generational passage into adulthood. He thereby doubles the disaster by simultaneously cancelling out the future of the family of Oidipous and that of his own.[23]

In his initial zeal to distinguish conclusively between friend and foe, insider and outsider,[24] Kreon first blurs distinctions between family and city by demanding from his son the obedience due to ruler from subject (*Ant.* 659–78). But in the process, he also proves to confound the most significant difference of all—that between life and death—when he entombs Antigone alive and keeps the dead unburied above the earth (cf. *Ant.* 1068–71). When he reverses his previous position on the burial of Polyneikes after the visit of Teiresias, he moves too far in the other direction—that is, by attending now first to the dead (Polyneikes) before the living (Antigone)—and thereby brings the cumulative disaster upon himself (*Ant.* 1196–1205). In initially undervaluing the meaning of death, he proves to undervalue the meaning of life. Hence Kreon brings death to those around him and himself remains, as the messenger says, no longer truly alive, but only a breathing corpse (*Ant.* 1166–67).[25]

But there is more, and here the particular issues raised by *Antigone* exemplify in clearest form another, wider aspect of the distinctive situation in Thebes. Kreon's refusal to honor the rights of the dead offends against the entire cultural order, against the gods as well as against persons and the collective of the city.[26] But it can also be construed as an offense against time itself. Both in refusing to bury the dead and then in giving temporal priority to the dead Polyneikes over the living Antigone,

[23] See also the fine discussion of Segal, *Tragedy and Civilization*, 184–90. He does not, however, note the close parallels with Aiskhylos' *Seven against Thebes*.

[24] The problem that the burial of Polyneikes poses is how to incorporate an insider who has made himself an outsider to the community.

[25] On Kreon's relation to death and its meanings, see Charles Segal, "Sophocles' Praise of Man and the Conflicts of the *Antigone*," in *Sophocles: A Collection of Critical Essays*, ed. T. Woodard (Englewood Cliffs, N.J., 1966), 83, and in Segal, *Interpreting Greek Tragedy: Myth, Poetry, Text* (Ithaca, N.Y., 1986), 158. In general, see the very useful work of Vincent Rosivach, "The Two Worlds of the *Antigone*," *ICS* 4 (1979): 16–26.

[26] Kreon's refusal of funerary rites to the dead enemy/traitor has its legal precedents in contemporary Athenian practice. But literary precedents, such as the end of the *Iliad* and, even more to the point, Sophokles' own play *Ajax*, show that such a narrow political outlook cannot ultimately be justified within the larger scheme of things.

Kreon has failed to observe the critical distinction that separates the dead from the living precisely at an irreversible point on the line of time that marks the moment of their demise.

To Antigone, death is the timeless eternity, the absolute principle to which she gives her undivided allegiance, and she therefore privileges it over mortal life since she understands the perfected meaning of death (*Ant.* 74–76), even to the extent of going to meet it before her time. The opposite holds true for Kreon. Living, as he thinks, in the all-absorbing present of the political moment, he takes a stand which paradoxically suggests that mortal life has no finitude. Or better, we might say that for Kreon, life and death comprise an uninterrupted continuum by which principle the unrelenting hostility that existed during life is prolonged indefinitely in death.

The issue of burial is central to Thebes, whether here in *Antigone* or in the *Suppliant Women* of Euripides or, of course, in *Oidipous at Kolonos*. It is the focal point at which the two coordinates of space and time converge and whose symbolic value refers us back to the critical problems raised by incest and autochthony. The dead are buried outside the city; they are also buried beneath the earth. Thus inside and outside, above and below, are factors that come to determine the most important boundary of all, that between before and after. Death in this city partakes of both dimensions, as it must always face both ways—as an end, but also as a return, even as Antigone's longing for death before her time is also a regression to the hidden sources of the family from which she springs.

The conclusion to *Antigone* makes it clear that no future time opens out in Thebes. *Genos* (family) and *gonē* (generation) have become a contradiction in terms, although they have the same root. The city's young have made a marriage only in death; Antigone's name has been appropriately glossed as "anti-generation."[27] Kreon's undervaluation of death and Antigone's parallel overvaluation of it both direct our attention to the most recurrent and most negative feature of Thebes, which manifests itself in the dimension of time.

REPEATING THE PAST

Thebes is opposed to time as it passes through subsequent phases which ordinarily would lead to change, reconciliation, development, and transformation, whether through a genetic model or through the formation of new institutions in the city. In Thebes the linear advance of the narrative

---

[27] See Seth Benardete, "A Reading of Sophocles' *Antigone*: I," *Interpretation* 4 (1975): 156: "Her name, whose meaning—'generated in place of another'—bears witness to success, proves to mean 'anti-generation.' " See also his further discussion of this point, 156–57.

events turns out in the end to be circular, as closed back upon itself as the circular walls that are the city's most distinctive architectural feature in space. Time in Thebes returns always and again to its point of departure, since it can never generate new structures and new progeny that can escape the paradigmatic patterns of the beginning. What this means is that Thebes is a place where the past inevitably rules, continually repeating and renewing itself so that each new generation, each new episode in the story, looks backward to its ruin even as it offers a new variation on the theme. This is the city, after all, where Laios was bidden to die without issue, a prophecy that indeed finally comes to pass in the third generation.

From this perspective, we may say that Thebes is a world that obeys the law of the Eternal Return in contrast to one where history can unfold into differential narrative for the future, a history supported by the paradigm of its founding myths as a point of origin but not subject to the tyranny of their domination over all its representative figures and events. The autocratic prestige of both autochthony and incest in Thebes claims power over each character in turn. More specifically, failure to inaugurate a viable line of time for the individual actor produces two negative patterns for the self—doubling of one figure with another at the same moment of time, whether father and son or brother and brother, and compulsive repetition of actions from the past.

There are many different dimensions in which this phenomenon manifests itself in Thebes. We can point here only to a small representative selection. First, in the house of Kadmos, the regressive mode is made literal at the end of the *Bakkhai*. Pentheus, as we have seen, returns to the mother when he makes his way to the mountains where the maenads are, and simultaneously discovers his true identity as the son of the autochthon, Ekhion. But Dionysos, as the deus ex machina at the end of the play, goes still further in his predictions of the future by sending Kadmos and his wife back to the beginning, or, more accurately, to a stage before the beginning. They are to regress back to a state and a form that preceded the very foundation of the city. In fact, they will be turned into serpents like the serpent of Ares whom Kadmos slew in order to establish Thebes, sowing the dragon's teeth from which the autochthons sprang. And Kadmos, the Phoenician and bringer of culture, will revert back to the negative side of his barbarian origins, since he is destined in the future to bring a foreign army to invade Greek territory (*Bakkh.* 1330–37). In the *Phoinissai,* the dragon of Ares lives in still another more dramatic way, since Ares' wrath over the blood of his dragon had never been put to rest, but returns to demand the sacrifice of the last surviving autochthon, whose blood must be shed in turn in order to expiate the primordial crime of the city (*Phoi.* 930–44).[28] In this play, too, it is the chorus, consisting of Phoenician maidens who have come from the ancestral home of Kadmos, which takes us back to a time before Thebes even existed.

But more significant still are the workings of time for the house of Laios, where, given the dominant and continuing role of oracles in its history, the future can and must fulfill an end already predicted in the past. Repetition and reenactment for the sons of Oidipous will bring them to the very effacement of identity in their doubling, back to a time before the beginning and the foundation of the family, which was under the sign of negation at its very inception. Thus every new *logos* in Thebes proves in one way or another to be yet another version of the *arkhaios logos.*

On the narrative level, the structure of Sophokles' *Oidipous Tyrannos* itself brilliantly demonstrates the general principle. Every advance Oidipous makes toward uncovering the identity of Laios's murderer, every new figure who enters upon the stage in the forward movement of the plot, only leads him further in a retrograde direction, until, with the last and critical entry of the old herdsman, he returns to the very moment of his birth as the infant with the pierced feet who was given over to that very herdsman to carry off to Mount Kithairon. With this revelation of his origins, Oidipous simultaneously realizes another regression— namely, that he had returned to seed the mother's womb from which he was engendered. Is not incest, after all, the quintessential act of return? Is not incest the paradigmatic act that destroys time by collapsing the necessary temporal distinctions between generations?

From this point of view, the riddle of the Sphinx can be read in two ways. On the one hand, the riddle suppresses the dimension of time, since the enigma resides in the fact that it makes synchronic the three phases of human life by uniting them under the single form (or voice) that is Man. As such, Oidipous' unique ability on the intellectual level to solve the riddle is commensurate on the familial level with his singular acts of patricide and incest. On the other hand, the full interpretation of the riddle would seem to require that man must properly be defined in his diachronic dimension. Man is to be measured by the sum total of his life, which can only be known as he passes through time. Hence, each of his multiple aspects (four-footed, two-footed, and three-footed) will be

---

[28] Strictly speaking, Kreon is the last of the pure autochthons (*Phoi.* 942–43), and he has two sons, Menoikeus and Haimon. Menoikeus is chosen because Haimon is already betrothed to Antigone and hence no longer an *ēitheos,* the male equivalent of *parthenos,* the virgin girl, who is normally the preferred sacrificial victim. By the end of the play, however, when Antigone refuses to consider marriage with Haimon but rather opts to bury her brother, Polyneikes, and go into exile with her father (*Phoi.* 1672–82), there is no future for Haimon, whose theatrical existence depends entirely on his relationship to Antigone.

construed as a sequential phase of orderly human development.[29] For Oidipous at Thebes, time is out of joint, not only because he has effaced generational difference, but because his act of reversing time in returning to seed the womb from which he was born is predicated on the earlier act of patricide that speeded up the temporal process by giving him his father's place too soon.

CITY OF MYTH VS. CITY OF HISTORY: *OIDIPOUS AT KOLONOS*

Let us now consider again the question that in good Theban fashion returns us to the beginning of this essay: why can Oidipous find a last resting place in Athens, and what is the significance of his refusal to return, as earlier tradition would have it, to Thebes? The answer to the first part of the question can be phrased in spatial terms as marking the fundamental, even defining, difference between the two cities, since Athens represents itself on more than one occasion as capable of incorporating the outsider into its midst. But the moment at which Oidipous arrives at his new destination and the ways in which he must win acceptance invite us to focus here on the issue of time. Thus we might answer the second part of the question by proposing the following: Oidipous has finally discovered time as process because he has now lived sequentially through all the terms of the riddle.

In the act of self-blinding, as many have observed, Oidipous has prematurely aged himself. He has entered upon the third stage of life before his time and must go forth into the world on "three feet." Oidipous' act of self-mutilation therefore continues to accelerate the pace he has forced upon the temporal process, as outlined above. At the same time, the very nature of the existence he has thereby fashioned for himself insures that henceforth he will walk slowly for a long time, too long, as he journeys through the rest of his life. Moreover, wandering on foot, to which exile now condemns him, means that each day he must again and yet again translate the metaphor of his existence into the literal steps he takes on his journeys.

But in *Oidipous at Kolonos,* his situation is finally commensurate with his chronological age. He has caught up with himself, we might say, and the stories he can tell about past, present, and future are made contingent on his own extended experience with time as his teacher and constant companion (*Oid. Kol.* 7).[30] His previous acts made the son structurally

---

[29] For a discussion of the two contrasting aspects which the riddle can suggest, see also J.-P. Vernant, "From Oedipus to Periander: Lameness, Tyranny, Incest in Legend and History," *Arethusa* 15 (1982): 24–26.

[30] Imagery of the wanderer and the road is of central importance in the play, which ends, we may recall, with Oidipous' last journey into the grove of the Furies. See Helen Bacon, "Woman's Two Faces: Sophocles' View of the Tragedy of Oedipus and his Family," in *Sci-*

equivalent to his father, and the sons structurally equivalent to himself. But all concerned have also been individual actors in their own stories along the narrative line of the family's history. This means that Oidipous can now profit from a temporal perspective which marks his mediate (and now differential) position as the son of his father and the father of his sons. Thus in this, the last drama by the aged poet concerning his now aged hero, which concludes with the conclusion of its protagonist's life, the question of time is of the essence. Returning to the stage at this critical moment in time allows Oidipous a double retrospective: first, as a fictional character who reviews and reevaluates the events of his own life; and second, as one who does so through reminders of the dramatic tradition that precedes him. This tradition includes all three models— Thebes, Athens, and Argos—whose divers echoes resonate at different levels throughout the play.

On the one hand, Oidipous seems to repeat the ancient patterns. He trespasses again, as has been observed, on forbidden female spaces,[31] this time in the sacred grove of the Furies. That he is admitted to the city of Athens but chooses to remain on its borders also confirms the irreducible ambiguity of his status in the community.[32] He also seems to continue his two original impulses to excessive violence and excessive intimacy in his relations with his kin, angrily cursing his sons and just as tenderly embracing his daughters. Moreover, the fratricidal destiny he is led to predict for his sons will ratify the traditional conclusion to the story of the house of Laios. These repetitions of acts and attitudes in a play that is haunted by the past reconfirm the essential identity of Oidipous and maintain the obdurate constancy of a willful self whose power, after death, will bring a *kerdos,* a gain, to the community that receives him. But enacted on a different territory at a different time, these repetitions also indicate transformations.

More particularly, the specific change of venue is essential. For only in

---

ence and Psychoanalysis: Decennial Memorial Volume (New York, 1966): 10–24, and see the further discussion of Segal, *Tragedy and Civilization,* 365–69, 402, 406, who integrates the images into the structure of the drama. Edmunds, "Cults and Legends," 229–31, argues persuasively that the wandering is a sign of Oidipous' status as a revenant. As a motif in Sophokles' play, wandering is integrally linked to the representation of Oidipous' career. It is worth noting that the Sphinx and the riddle are never mentioned during the play (unlike in the *Phoinissai,* where it receives remarkable emphasis) although the context would have been appropriate, given Oidipous' recuperation of his interpretive powers. The terms of the riddle require no exposition, however, since Oidipous himself acts them out.

[31] See Cedric Whitman, *Sophocles: A Study of Heroic Humanism* (Cambridge, Mass., 1951), 200; Bacon, "Woman's Two Faces," 17–18; and Barbara Lefcowitz, "The Inviolate Grove," *Literature and Psychology* 17 (1967): 78–86.

[32] On the significance of Oidipous' preference for the "marginal space of the grove" over the "ruler's palace," see Segal, *Tragedy and Civilization,* 381.

Athens is Oidipous, the paradigm of tragic man,[33] ideally situated to confront and resolve the tragic problem of time that his story exemplifies: how is one to establish relations between old and new, same and different, constancy and change, and, even more broadly, between tradition and innovation? How is one to regulate conflicts between mythical and historical modes of thinking, between the prestige of the past and potentially dangerous assaults upon it? This feat Theban Oidipous can accomplish on his own terms now that he has found his way to Kolonos. When Oidipous solved the riddle the first time, he invoked a capacity for abstract intellection that led him only to erase distinctions in such a way that he became an anomalous riddle himself. Now time, which has brought Oidipous' wanderings to an end in Athens, has also brought him to establish critical distinctions in his own life on the basis of what he has undergone. Now, from his vantage point of knowledge and experience, he can confidently reinterpret the past and evaluate present and future—but only through constructive interplay with what Athens ideologically is made to represent.

To this end, the verdict he brings in upon himself of "not guilty" by reason of self-defense and ignorance of the stranger's identity modifies his own continuing sense of pollution without dismissing it altogether (*Oid. Kol.* 270–74, 505–58, 969–99). In effect, he has evolved a set of juridical principles that distinguish between legal and religious responsibility and between act and intention, appropriately voicing these on Attic land. Oidipous has entered into the frame of reference that in the last play of Aiskhylos' *Oresteia* had provided an escape within the city from the endless repetition of the past by establishing the authority of a law court, which judges each case on its particulars.[34] But what in the *Eumenides* required the elaborate apparatus of the gods' intervention is won here by Oidipous himself as a result of his objective experience. In this sense, we might say that he finds his way to Kolonos precisely because the proper moment has arrived, a moment in which, as Oidipous' interpretation of the new oracles tells us, the gods also concur. Now is the time when this figure, who best embodies the combination of traits (will, passion, intellect, urge to autonomy) that always proves so destructive to rulers at

---

[33] The chorus in the *Oid. Tyr.*, we may recall, addresses Oidipous as the *paradeigma* of mortal men (1163); on this point, see Bernard Knox, *The Heroic Temper* (Berkeley, 1964), 146–47.

[34] The last time Oidipous defends himself, the Areopagos is specifically mentioned (*Oid. Kol.* 947–49). Many have, of course, noticed the significance of the *Oresteia* as an important influence in *Oidipous Kolonos* (although none in any systematic way nor with regard to the differing structures of Athens and Thebes). See the discussion by R. P. Winnington-Ingram, "A Religious Function of Greek Tragedy: A Study in the *Oedipous Coloneus* and the *Oresteia*," *JHS* 74 (1954): 16–24, and Winnington-Ingram, *Sophocles: An Interpretation* (Cambridge, Eng., 1980), 264–78 and 324–26.

Thebes, can justly demonstrate that on his own he has already shifted this paradigm of himself from Thebes to Athens.

In creating his own destiny on his own terms, he does far more than follow in the footsteps of Argive Orestes, who preceded him. Rather, where Oidipous is, the question must inevitably turn on power (*kratos*) over self and over others, and this power the play now vindicates in a number of different ways. First, the drama allows Oidipous the right not only to defend but to judge himself as well as others. Second, it specifies as the determining factor in Oidipous' decision about his future the right he claims to retain control over his own body. These are the grounds, in fact, on which he can resist returning to Thebes precisely because there others will exercise control over him. And finally, the play justifies this demand for power over the self by investing that self with a perennial power that Oidipous can transmit for all time to the city that will possess his body and burial place.[35]

This power will be a political asset for the city in which, as it turns out, Oidipous finds a permanent home, but Oidipous' transformation into a cult hero at Kolonos is not achieved, as critics often suggest, through his renouncing the *genos*. It is true that he repudiates his sons, going so far as to declare that Polyneikes has no father (*apatōr; Oid. Kol.* 1383), and he bars his daughters from their proper familial function of attending to his burial rites. Indeed, his new home in Attika and his new status in cult, signified by the mysterious manner of his passing, separate him from the *genos* he has doomed to extinction in Thebes. But he by no means abjures the principle of the *genos* as a category. Quite the contrary. Such a strategy would only replicate the destructive policy in Thebes of choosing either the *polis* or the *genos* to the exclusion of the other, or confusing the separate domains of the two, as both Kreon and Polyneikes do in their desire to use the *genos* for furthering their ambitions in the *polis*.

On the one hand, Oidipous upholds the archaic law of the family, and, in his paternal role, insists on laying down the law of the father that decrees that children return their *trophē*, the price of their nurture, to their parents. The curse itself for the neglect of that *trophē* also belongs to the past: it has an essential role to play in the traditional destiny of Oidipous'

---

35 References to *kratos* are numerous: *Oid. Kol.* 392, 399–400, 404–5, 408, 644, 646, 1207, 1332, 1380–81. The concern with *kratos* is characteristic of Sophoklean drama, which focuses on the self-definition of the tragic hero. It can be said of all his principal figures that "they will not be ruled, no one shall have power over them, or treat them as a slave, they are free." Knox, *Heroic Temper,* 40. But in Thebes, in Sophokles as elsewhere (e.g., in *Seven against Thebes*), the matter is more specific. The issue of *kratos* is both political and individual, power over others and power over the self (as discussed earlier). See also the discussion in Winnington-Ingram, *Sophocles,* 251, who correctly sees the connections of Oidipous' *kratos* with the theme in the *Oidipous Tyrannos;* and see the remarks of Segal, *Tragedy and Civilization,* 386.

sons and, more generally, is allied with the archaic power of the Erinyes. On the other hand, there is an important parallel between the new distinctions Oidipous has made in his own case between absolute guilt and contingent circumstances, and these principles he now applies to the larger question of the family. The *genos* is no longer an inviolable and indivisible unity, as Antigone continues to believe (e.g., *Oid. Kol.* 1181–91). It is first of all an ongoing relation among its members of shared reciprocities and obligations, so that entitlement to its privileges depends upon actions each individual knowingly and voluntarily undertakes. Oidipous therefore reserves his love for the daughters who have tended him despite the social conventions that would keep them safely at home, and repudiates his sons who have intentionally behaved contrary to family rules in refusing the nurture they owe to their father (*Oid. Kol.* 337–60, 421–44).

In this context, the focus on *trophē,* which is a given element of the myth, now serves a double function in the play. *Trophē* both *joins* with and *separates* itself from the inherited curse on the family. As linked with the curse, the offense against *trophē* is yet another manifestation of a recurrent feature in the family of Oidipous, which revolves around the continuing treatment of kin as non-kin. As such, the recurrence of the issue of *trophē* implies a collective familial physis that predetermines the behavior of each actor. But if we consider *trophē* on its own terms, the fact that it concerns not the circumstances of birth but rather the continuing process of nurture, then *trophē* furnishes the appropriate motivation by which to hold the individual responsible for conduct that is based on deliberate and conscious choice.

The structure of the second part of the play confirms the new orientation Oidipous has brought to the old features of the myth, and hence to the general family problem, since it postpones the father's definitive curse on his sons until the hostilities between the brothers have already begun and Polyneikes himself arrives upon the scene to reveal himself in person before his father and the spectators.[36] As a younger double of his father, the suppliant and exile, Polyneikes, too, has the opportunity to review the past. In his case, retrospection has led him to regret his earlier treatment of his father. But his true purpose in enlisting his father's assistance so as to win political power from his brother undercuts his sincerity,[37] and more generally demonstrates how fully he subscribes to the

---

[36] I agree here with those who read Oidipous' curse in this scene as the formal and definitive bestowal of the curse. See especially, Winnington-Ingram, *Sophocles,* n. 49 and 266–74. We, of course, know more than Polyneikes does and so tend to interpret the earlier cues as echoes rather than as previews in the present time of the play.

[37] Whether Polyneikes' regret is authentic or not is a much disputed point (as is the interpretation of the scene itself). Here I would remark only that Polyneikes' statement to An-

typical terms that operate at Thebes with regard to the interrelations between *genos* and *polis*. It is significant, too, that the rhetorical strategy he
adopts in order to persuade his father to join him involves an appeal to
their common experience. That the speaker try to identify himself with
his auditor is standard practice in the rule books of oratory. But this tactic also reminds us how characteristic it is that a child of Theban Oidipous would stress the sameness between son and father without regard
for their differences. This strategy fails, not only because Polyneikes is
too late—his father is no longer either a suppliant or an exile[38]—but because it runs exactly counter to how Oidipous now treats relations
within the family. His task is to *make* distinctions rather than *efface* them;
he does so between his sons and daughters of the same generation and,
above all, between himself and his sons.[39]

In Oidipous' unrelenting anger at his sons, critics have seen a parallel
between him and the Erinyes in the *Eumenides,* and one scholar, in fact,
has called him an "unpersuaded Erinys."[40] But we are faced here with an
"unpersuasive" Polyneikes, who, unlike Orestes in the counterpart of
this scene, shows us he cannot win exoneration from the faults of the
past. Quite the contrary; he is only driven to repeat it. There is, in fact, a
curious inversion which operates between the two filial representatives
of their respective families. The gravity of Orestes' act in slaying his
mother is diminished and is made expiable precisely through the argument that makes the mother no blood kin to him. Conversely, Polyneikes' offense in neglecting his father's *trophē* is elevated to the charge of
patricide (*Oid. Kol.* 1361) and thereby provides Oidipous with the

---

tigone that he will not tell the Argive army the truth about his father's curse (on the
grounds that one does not report ill tidings; *Oid. Kol.* 1429–30) does nothing to enhance
our opinion of his integrity. Opportunism and political manipulation are not traits which
tragedy rewards.

[38] On this point, see Winnington-Ingram, *Sophocles,* 277. For the interrelation between
the two suppliant scenes (Oidipous, Polyneikes) and its significance for the structure of the
drama, see Peter Burian, "Suppliant and Savior: *Oedipus at Colonus*," *Phoenix* 28 (1974):
408–29.

[39] The fact that Theseus accepts Oidipous because both have shared the experience of ex-
ile and more generally, on the basis of their common humanity (*Oid. Kol.* 562–68) while
Oidipous rejects Polyneikes' similar plea (*Oid. Kol.* 1335–39) has often been noted, either to
Oidipous' discredit or with the observation of his new daimonic power: "Oedipus' curse
stands outside the boundaries of ordinary moral judgment," says Burian, "Suppliant and
Savior," 427. Yet it is significant that Oidipous emphasizes, not the universal principles
Theseus espouses, but the values of knowledge and intention in human action. Cf. Artemis'
address to Theseus at the end of Euripides' *Hippolytos:* "You appear in my eyes to be
base . . . but as far as your *hamartia* [mistake] is concerned, your ignorance [*to mē eidenai*]
entirely absolves you [*ekluei*] from the charge" (1320, 1334–35).

[40] Winnington-Ingram, *Sophocles,* 275. Cf. also George Gellie, *Sophocles: A Reading*
(Melbourne, 1972), 168.

grounds for declaring that his sons are no longer kin to him (*Oid. Kol.* 1369, 1383).[41]

If Oidipous therefore transcends the family, as he must, of course, as an outsider in Athens, he also defends it, at the same time importing into it juridical evaluations that belong to the city. In this he combines in himself the opposing roles of both Apollo/Athena and the Furies— his immortal counterparts in the *Eumenides*.[42] Like the Olympians, he lowers the prestige of blood ties as an inalienable bond and subjects the family to a law outside itself. And if, like the Furies, he upholds the law of the family for his sons (the obligation of *trophē*), he does so on the same judicial basis by which he abrogates it for his own act of patricide (ignorance and self-defense). Finally, he also follows the next phase of the Aiskhylean pattern; in following the path that leads to the grove of the Eumenides, Oidipous, like them, will transfer his power to bless and to curse from the sphere of the family to that of the city. Having shown his capacity to judge in the domain of the family, Oidipous thereby qualifies himself for the role of an adopted stranger who will henceforth protect the city, one who will in the future distinguish between insiders and outsiders on the basis, not of any given status, but of actions and intentions. Thus the concerns of the city and of the family intertwine; each offers a model to the other, and each ratifies the appropriate principles of interaction through the figure of Oidipous himself.[43]

On these grounds, there is one more distinction to be made in the family, this time between Oidipous and all his children; he has elected to remain in Athens, but Polyneikes and Antigone freely choose to return to Thebes. When Polyneikes encounters his father, he can still return to Argos rather than marshal his host against Thebes. Antigone, for her part, has the promise of a refuge in Athens, reiterated for emphasis at the

---

[41] From this perspective, we may also recall the arguments in the *Eumenides* claiming that the father is the only true parent of the child, while the mother is reduced to the status of *trophos* (*Eum.* 657–61). Origins, not *trophē*, is the issue in the *Oresteia;* moreover, responsibility cannot turn on the question of ignorance versus knowledge, as it does in *Oidipous at Kolonos,* since Orestes acts explicitly under Apollo's orders. Orestes can be redeemed, however, for although he continues the family patterns (murder within the family), he is shown to do so in a very different spirit. The two plays, however, despite their divergent positions, agree on the primacy of paternal power.

[42] In the *Oresteia,* Athena introduces the juridical principle into the family through the establishment of the law court that will henceforth adjudicate domestic matters. The Erinyes, on the other hand, import into the city the awe associated with the mysterious power of blood ties.

[43] For the ways in which the *Eumenides* accommodates the old and the new in both the family and the city, see my essay, "The Dynamics of Misogyny: Myth and Mythmaking in the *Oresteia,*" *Arethusa* 11 (1978): 164–73, reprinted in *Women in the Ancient World,* ed. J. Peradotto and J. P. Sullivan (Albany, N.Y., 1984), 159–94.

end of the play (*Oid. Kol.* 1739–41).[44] But, as they face the future, each is locked into the family pattern of repeating the past, repeating too the language of the dramatic tradition that preceded them in the echoes that resonate throughout their discourse.

The interchange between Polyneikes and Antigone is especially revealing because it takes us back all the way to Aiskhylos' *Seven against Thebes*. Now the brother and sister reenact the scene which took place at a comparable moment in that drama in which the chorus of women had attempted and failed to dissuade Eteokles from going to meet his brother, just when he, too, had acknowledged the power of the father's curse.[45] The aim of *Seven against Thebes,* as remarked earlier, is to collapse distinctions between the brothers when they meet in their fratricidal duel. In Sophokles' version, Polyneikes is specifically named the elder brother, who can therefore claim a more legitimate right to the throne. But once he repeats his enemy brother's Aiskhylean response, the text subtly indicates that there is and will be no real difference between them.

As for Antigone, this same scene prepares her for her future, when she will shift her allegiance from father to brother on the very issue of burial that her own play, *Antigone,* has already dramatized. By the close of *Oidipous at Kolonos,* she too will have made this transference; forbidden to bury Oidipous, she makes the choice of Thebes over Athens so as to fol-

---

[44] We should not minimize for either Polyneikes or Antigone the principle at work of double determination by which action is predicated on both internal and external agency. Although Oidipous declares that Polyneikes will not live to take power (*kratos*) with the sword over his native land, nor will he make his return (*nostos*) to Argos, Polyneikes *chooses* not to go back to Argos (cf. *palin;* 1347, 1398, 1403, 1418). The text is also careful to leave open the question of Antigone's return ("*if* there will be a *nostos* for you," says Polyneikes at *Oid. Kol.* 1408) and to present her decision as her own.

[45] Critics have seen general Sophoklean echoes in this scene, but strangely enough, have missed the more precise reference to Aiskhylos. The stage for *Seven against Thebes* is already set in Polyneikes' speech to his father where he enumerates the list of Aiskhylos' (not Euripides') seven warriors (*Oid. Kol.* 1313–22). Although he alters the order somewhat, it is significant that he ends by alluding to the eponymy of Parthenopaios, a critical turning point in the shield scene in *Seven against Thebes* (*Seven* 536–37, 662, and 670). See also my discussion in *Under the Sign,* 98–105, 142–44. Just before, Polyneikes echoes the thoughts Aiskhylos gives him in the scout's report: either to die in his just cause or to repay in kind the one who had driven him out (cf. *Seven* 636–38 and *Oid. Kol.* 1305–8), and then follows his statement of intent with prayers (*litai*) to the paternal authority (in Aiskhylos, to the gods of the *genos, genethlioi,* and of the fatherland, *patrōoi*). Cf. *Seven* 639–40 and *Oid. Kol.* 1309. But in the dialogue with Antigone, Polyneikes speaks with the voice of his brother Eteokles in *Seven.* Like him, he refuses the pleas of the female to desist from his *thumos,* to take cognizance of the curse, and to give up his murderous project against his brother. Like Eteokles, he puts his warrior's honor first and, in refusing to yield his position, yields to the power of the curse. Cf. generally *Oid. Kol.* 1414–38 and *Seven* 676–719.

low her perennial vocation of burying her own, should Polyneikes indeed be killed. It is a small but immensely significant point that at the end, in despite of prohibitions to the contrary, she desires nothing more than to violate them, and in a typically Oidipian way. That is, she too yearns to look upon a forbidden sight in a domain she may not enter—in this case, her father's secret tomb. Let us turn back (*palin*), she says to her sister, to see the dark hearth (*Oid. Kol.* 1726), and Ismene must remind her that it is not *themis* to look upon it (*Oid. Kol.* 1729). She returns again to her desire a second time, now in the presence of Theseus, and now it is she who takes on the role of suppliant. Again her wish must be refused on the grounds that the tomb is not *themiton* to behold (*Oid. Kol.* 1754–77). *Looking* back and *going* back share a certain symbolic equivalence. Repetition characterizes Antigone's mode of action and therefore indicates that her proper terrain is Thebes.[46]

Oidipous, on the other hand, has become the master of time—of past, present, and future—precisely because he acknowledges the power of linear time over him and over human affairs. He can distinguish between the time of the gods, which is ageless and deathless forever, and all-mastering time, which turns everything upside down. Subject to the timelessness of eternal return which incest implies, he has also known time in its purely human dimension of flux and reversal. In the case of Oidipous' children, the acts of repetition and return lead to the cancellation of the family line, this time aided by Oidipous' prophetic word and their own choice to return to Thebes. But Oidipous has known both absolutes and relatives. He has lived, in effect, in both synchronic and diachronic dimensions. He is therefore truly in a position to stand be-

---

[46] Looking back is a term that Antigone herself used with regard to her father. In urging him to yield to her request to give the suppliant son a hearing, she advises him not to consider the present but "to look back [*aposkopei*] to the past [*eis ekeina*]" at what he himself had suffered in his relations with his father and mother. Then he will know what evil awaits evil wrath. She is proposing to break the sequence of action and reaction, as she specifically says a few lines earlier: "You begot him [*ephusas*], so that even if he were to do [*drōnta*] the most impious of all evils to you, O father, it is not *themis* for you to do him harm in return [*antidran*]" (*Oid. Kol.* 1190–91). The moment is still open, she thinks, at least for the right to supplication, although Oidipous' granting of her request only leads, as we know, to the empowering of the curse. Yet she does not give up her typical role of trying to reconcile the antagonistic men in her family. This is the explicit reason she gives for returning to Thebes ("send us to ancient [*ōgugious*] Thebes, if somehow we may prevent the coming bloodshed among kin"; *Oid. Kol.* 1768–69), recalling too what she is asked to do with and by her mother Jokasta in the *Phoinissai* (*Phoi.* 1264–79). The burial of the enemy brother is, of course, the furthest extension of the conciliatory role she adopts. That issue is only ironically implicit in this play (since neither has she promised Polyneikes that she will undertake the task for him, nor is the outcome of fratricide certain, if, as she thinks, she might succeed with her brothers where she has failed here). See also Segal, *Tragedy and Civilization,* 403–4.

twixt and between, not with the cruel ambiguities of the insider-outsider on the border of Thebes but ultimately as one intermediate in status between mortal and immortal—that is, in the category of the hero.

As a result, if the children of Oidipous return to the past, Oidipous himself is empowered to look to the future, especially in the message he brings to Athens as the reason why his body will bring them benefit. In larger terms, what he brings to them is the general lesson on time that tragedy itself can teach. The means, of course, are those most associated with Thebes—the use of prophecy to control the future from the past—but there are significant differences now. This prophecy is closely linked with the vision of time which Oidipous now possesses, and he chooses to deliver it at the most appropriate moment in the narrative structure of the play. Theseus has just now received him on the grounds of their common experience of exile which they as non-kin share, and this first moment prepares the way for Theseus' promise to accept him as a suppliant and enroll him as a resident in the land.[47]

Here are Oidipous' own words:

> Time, the all-mastering [*pagkratēs*], confounds all things. The strength of the earth withers away [*phthinei*], and that of the body withers away too [*phthinei*]. Faith [*Pistis*] dies [*thnēskei*] and distrust [*apistia*] burgeons forth [*blastanei*], and the same spirit [*pneuma*] is never steadfast either among friends [*philois*] or between city and city. For to some at once and to others in later time, the sweet becomes [*gignetai*] bitter and then again becomes dear [*phila*]. And if it is a fair day between you and Thebes, then uncountable time [*murios chronos*] will give birth [*teknoutai*] to countless, myriad nights and days as it proceeds, in which for a small word, they will scatter with the spear the pledges of concord today, there where my slumbering and buried corpse, grown cold, will one day drink their warm blood, if Zeus is still Zeus and Phoibos the son of Zeus is manifest. (*Oid. Kol.* 609–23)

Metaphors of time and meditations on time itself are commonplaces of Greek tragic poetry, but Oidipous more than any other figure invests this language with its fullest resonance and strengthens the general gnomic wisdom whose significance he is best qualified to expound. Peripeteia, the rule of reversal which governs the structure of drama, is also the principle that rules the structure of his own life. This is peripeteia in

---

[47] On the future status of Oidipous in Athens, not as a citizen, but as an honored resident (metic), see the excellent arguments of Pierre Vidal-Naquet, "Oedipe entre deux cités: Essai sur l'*Oedipe à Colone*," in his *Mythe et tragédie en Grèce ancienne*, vol. 2 (Paris, 1986), 187–204.

its most complete form, since only Oidipous will undergo the full cycle of tragic process in its double and opposite movement from high to low and then again from low to high.[48] The length of his days as well as perhaps his exile from Thebes now suggest a view of time that reaches out far beyond a single lifetime and beyond the triadic span of generational time.

Many others have observed the significance of this speech and its relation to Oidipous and tragic notions of time.[49] What I wish to stress, however, is the purpose it serves in sharpening the dialectic between Thebes and Athens.[50] For there are further signs that Oidipous has confronted the dilemmas that characterize Thebes so as to entitle him to claim a rightful place in Athens. Conversely, these also suggest why Athens would wish to appropriate for its benefit what Oidipous possesses and in his person represents.

First, Oidipous invokes those stages of the life cycle that are heavy with negative significance for the family of Laios—birth, nurture, and death—and creatively integrates them with nature on the one hand and abstract general values on the other. The strength of the land withers and so does that of the body, while trust and distrust alternate through phases of growth and death. Above all, Oidipous links generation and time it-

---

[48] The text invokes the law of reversal with respect to Oidipous just after Polyneikes departs and before the first clap of thunder is heard (*Oid. Kol.* 1449–56). The chorus is reponding to the "new ills of a heavy doom that come from the *blind* stranger" who has cursed his son, but the reference to "all-seeing time" (*khronos*) forecasts Oidipous' coming vindication by time.

[49] These mostly center on the notion of reversal or of endurance through time. See, e.g., C. M. Bowra, *Sophoclean Tragedy* (Oxford, 1944), 334–35 (with good citation of ancient texts); Whitman, *Sophocles*, 198–99; and Gellie, *Sophocles*, 169. It is tempting to read Oidipous, the paradigm of tragic man, as the incarnation, even the allegorization, of the tragic process itself. See, for example, the remarks of Whitman, *Sophocles*, 210, and Segal, *Tragedy and Civilization*, 406–8. In addition to embodying the pattern of reversal in his own history, he exemplifies the principle of the *lex talionis* (the doer must suffer: the sufferer must "do" in return [*antidran*]), "the very formula for tragedy," as Winnington-Ingram observes, *Sophocles*, 264. Moreover, Oidipous in his own person fulfills through the workings of time the premises of that tragic axiom—*pathei mathos* (Aiskh., *Ag.* 177). He does this not only through the emphasis laid upon knowledge in the play as the guide and rationale for action, but by a rather remarkable rewriting of his own story. He claims that, because of his ignorance, he was not the doer with regard to his transgressions against the family, but rather the sufferer: (*pepenthot' esti mallon ē dedrakota* (*Oid. Kol.* 266–67). In doubling the role of sufferer (through parents, through sons), he can make himself the exemplar of suffering, and thus personify tragic wisdom as well as tragic time.

[50] Segal, *Tragedy and Civilization*, 367–77 and passim, gives an excellent reading of the relations between Thebes and Athens in this play but does not consider the larger schematic principles informing them. See, however, the fine piece of Vidal-Naquet, "Oedipe entre deux cités."

self by transferring to a higher metaphorical plane the physical act of begetting, and endows time itself with reproductive power.[51]

Second, the lessons that Oidipous has learned from his own experience
can be now shifted appropriately to the political level and to the relations
between cities. These make up the substance of Oidipous' message to
Theseus, and their effect is to "naturalize," we might say, and make organic the realities of Greek political life in which shifting allegiances lead
now to friendship and again to enmity. Oidipous' body and tomb will be
a defense for Athens against Thebes, but so will the knowledge of the
cosmic laws of alternation and reversal which Oidipous now embodies.

Theseus knows (exoida) the principle of reversal in human affairs at the
level of individual experience, being a man like other men, as he says
(Oid. Kol. 566–68), and on this basis, he is willing to receive Oidipous
and to grant his request. But in his prophecy, Oidipous brings surprising
news to Theseus concerning an invasion of Attica by Theban forces,
news that Theseus does not know and will never know with certainty
since the event that Oidipous predicts no longer belongs to the time of
myth but rather to some unspecified moment of historical time. The reference, as the ancient scholion suggests, may recall a minor skirmish
with Theban cavalry which took place near Kolonos in 407 B.C.E., or it
may generally serve as an open prediction for the future. But the point is
clear. Oidipous finally crosses the boundary of time beyond the synchronic cycling that marks the eternal return of the mythic patterns in
Thebes; he crosses too beyond the narrative of the family history to a
new zone of futurity where no one at Thebes has ever ventured before.[52]
And it is precisely on the terms of this prophecy that he claims the right
to cross the spatial boundary into Athens.

On the other hand, only in Athens, where the outsider may enter into
a new status through rituals of supplication and political rights of resi-
dency, can Oidipous himself transcend human time; crossing the
boundary between the living and the dead, he can make permanent his
value to the city in the institution of the hero cult. In the perennial existence to be granted him, the coordinates of space and time coincide in a
characteristically Oidipian way. For in entering the grove of the Furies
that it is forbidden for others to penetrate, Oidipous confirms the spatial
equivalence between the body of the earth and that of the mother. At the
same time, he verifies the positive temporal symbolism of incest with the

[51] Polyneikes, on the other hand, uses the metaphorical language of house, family, and
nurture, within the family circle, when he first addresses his father (Oid. Kol. 1259–60,
1262–63), thereby "pointing up," as Segal remarks (Tragedy and Civilization, 388), "his
failure as a son in an oikos to whose ruin he has contributed."

[52] In contrast to Euripides' fondness for contemporary political allusions, this is the only
extant Sophoklean play to make reference within the text to a historical event.

mother as the gesture that raises intimations of immortality because it has effaced normative linear time. Oidipous at Thebes made literal the terrible deeds that other men only dream of in their sleep. In Athens he can transcend the physical body through metaphor and cult to be incorporated into this idealized territory for his longest sleep. Historical evidence may never make clear in what way Oidipous' prophecy about relations between Thebes and Athens comes to pass. Theseus, in fact, in the furthest extension of Oidipous' emphasis on individual responsibility, goes so far as to deny an intrinsic connection between Kreon's behavior and the nurture he has received in his native city of Thebes (*Oid. Kol.* 919–23).[53] Here we know better than this kind and simple king of Athens, and so, I suggest, should the spectators. There is no cause for wonderment that Thebes should some time in the distant future turn hostile to Athens, if we consider the radical incompatibility between the dramatic representations of the two cities. From this point of view, the truth of Oidipous' prophecy is never in doubt, since it already rings true to the rules of the genre. The message of Oidipous therefore also assures us that his disappearance can only be temporary. After all, whenever Thebes returns to the tragic stage, Oidipous, too, must come back to life.

[53] Theseus' "praise" of Thebes has puzzled many commentators, especially in view of the continuing political antagonism between Thebes and Athens during this period. See the discussion in Burian, "Suppliant and Savior," 420 n. 30, and Vidal-Naquet, "Oedipe entre deux cités," 185–86. What I propose conforms to the underlying logic of the play and the role assigned to Theseus as the representative of a city free of prejudice.

NICOLE LORAUX

Kreousa the Autochthon: A Study of Euripides' *Ion*

ATHENS IS the sole subject of Euripides' *Ion*, the Akropolis its sole hero. Its catalyst is a woman called Kreousa and its subject is the specifically tragic discourse of autochthony.

Many readers have declared the *Ion* to be an Athenian tragedy, but there are also many ways of missing that truth. The misapprehension takes two main forms: either the *Ion* is turned into a comedy of intrigue, a kind of *drame bourgeois*, perhaps; or else, since it takes place in Delphi, it is said to be a Delphic play.

In the complicated plot of this tragedy, however, everything, as I shall attempt to show, leads to Kreousa, for in her all the threads are tied together. Kreousa is the daughter of Erekhtheus, the mother of Ion, the victim of Apollo, and the wife of Xouthos. She is a tragic woman whom it would be hard to classify among the flock of seduced girls so common in New Comedy.

Everything leads from Delphi to Athens, to the heart of Athens, to the heights of the Akropolis, where Ion almost dies in a repetition in reverse of the birth of Erikhthonios and where he eventually returns, there to reign and perpetuate the line of Erekhtheus.

To enable the once-exposed child to find his way back to the Akropolis, it proved necessary, for the duration of a tragic play, to shift Kreousa from her own land and Athens from the center of the stage.

ATHENS IN DELPHI

Before tackling the essentials—the Akropolis, autochthony, and Kreousa—let us begin at the beginning with the story of Ion, related almost in full by Hermes as the prologue to the play.

THE STORY OF ION

Kreousa, the daughter of Erekhtheus, having been violated by Apollo, has exposed her child at birth and believes him to be dead. She has sub-

Note: This translation is an abridged and slightly revised version of "Créuse autochtone" in Nicole Loraux, *Les enfants d'Athéna* (Paris, 1981), 197–253. Due to limitations of space the notes especially have been severely curtailed. Thanks are due to Harvard University Press for permission to use their translation, which is by Janet Lloyd. Adaptation and revision by Froma I. Zeitlin.

sequently married Xouthos, a descendant of Zeus but a foreigner in Athens; their union is barren. For that reason, they come to Delphi to consult Apollo on the subject of their posterity. There they meet an adolescent boy, none other than the child once exposed, who was saved by his divine parent. So that the child may regain possession of his own home, Apollo gives him to Xouthos, provoking fury and despair on the part of Kreousa, who plots the death of the one whom she believes to be the son of her husband. Ion, in turn, seeks vengeance. Each having attempted to destroy the other, son and mother are brought face to face: Kreousa recognizes her child. They set off for Athens, where Ion will inherit the power of his Erekhtheid ancestors.

Narrated thus, the story of Ion oscillates, as do so many tales of children exposed, between New Comedy and the epic accounts of heroic childhoods.[1]

It does indeed resemble the plot of a comedy by Menander, the *Arbiters* (*Epitrepontes*). Here, as in the *Ion*, a young girl has been violated (not by a god, in this case, but by a rich young man), a child exposed, and a final recognition made in several stages, as a result of which everything returns to order (a household is reconstituted, not that of the Erekhtheidai but that of a good Athenian family, for the father of the child turns out to be the very husband whom the girl subsequently married).[2] But because, in the *Ion*, the dangers of the present and the weight of the past threaten the very lives of the characters, and because the fate of Athens is involved in their adventures, this story is reminiscent not so much of a comic plot as of the heroic legends in which the founder of a race or a glorious sovereign seems at first destined to die young. Kyros, like Ion, is exposed, placed in a basket, and "adorned for death" in a deserted spot. Also like Ion, he is brought up far away from his ancestral palace, into which he too is eventually reintegrated.[3]

If Ion were truly the central figure in the tragedy that bears his name, the tale Euripides tells would be remarkably similar to an account of the childhood years or trials of a hero, from the time of his original rejection until his investiture. A divine *parthenios* (child of an unmarried woman),[4]

---

[1] See H. R. Immerwahr, "Athēnaikes eikones ston Iōnatou Euripidē," *Hellenika* 27 (1972): 277–97. I am indebted to Maria Daraki for drawing this article to my attention.

[2] Critics have noticed these resemblances: e.g., Gilbert Murray, "Ritual Elements in the New Comedy," *CQ* 37 (1943): 46–54, and "Euripides' *Ion* and Its Consequences," *PCPS* 42 (1945): 10–12, and Marie Delcourt, *Plaute et l'impartialité comique* (Brussels, 1964), 36–37.

[3] Cf. Herodotos, 1.107–30 (esp. 109–116). On the childhood of Kyros, see G. Binder, *Die Aussetzung des Königskindes Kyros und Romulus* (Meisenheim, Germany, 1964).

[4] I have borrowed this term from Marie Delcourt, *Oedipe ou la légende du conquérant*, (Liège, 1944), 23. Ion could equally well be described as a *partheneuma* since, in this tragedy, the word denotes both virginity (1473) and the labor, or fruits of the labor, of a virgin (1425).

Ion combines all the mythic features of the exposed child: his maternal grandfather is a king without sons, his mother a seduced girl, his father a god;[5] he has experienced a life of exile,[6] and is later adopted by a king who will act as his father,[7] just as Amphitryon does with Herakles. As with all heroes, it is only on the threshold of *hēbē* (youthful prime), when his *trophē* (nurture) is completed, that Ion, the child without parents or name, wins an identity.[8] Read as the story of Ion, the tragedy is an account of a "passage" or transition: the story of a death and rebirth. It is true that for Ion birth has twice been confused with death—Kreousa's child was destined to die and his "birth" as Xouthos' son almost costs him his life—so that when he is at last born to the love of his mother, he reveals himself as "he who was dead and yet is not dead."[9] The transitions necessary to the winning of an identity are nevertheless placed under the problematical sign of Hermes, and it is not too surprising to find that this god of ambiguous identity has twice crossed the destiny of Ion, first when he took Kreousa's newborn child from Athens to Delphi, and then again when he gave the adolescent his name for the first time,[10] following the prologue, at the ambiguous moment of the sun's first appearance at the boundary between night and the coming day.

But—possibly as the result of Hermes' influence—the identity of Ion is a complicated business, more complicated than is usual in heroic legends in which the father, who recognizes and names the hero, also gives

[5] On the exposed child and Greek myths about heroic childhoods, see Delcourt, *Oedipe*, 1–65, and also the information collected by Binder, *Die Aussetzung*, 125–46, and Otto Rank, *The Myth of the Birth of the Hero* (New York, 1964), 14–64.

[6] The *trophē* (nurture) of the exposed child usually takes place "far away from the place in which, in normal circumstances, he would have grown up." Delcourt, *Oedipe*, 9, 51. On the organic links between legends about exposed children and fosterage and education received outside the father's family, see Jan Bremmer, "Avunculate and Fosterage," *Journal of Indo-European Studies* 4 (1976): 65–78.

[7] Apollo's plan is to get Xouthos to adopt Ion by suggesting he would in this way acquire a son (1534–36, 1560–62). See U. von Wilamowitz-Moellendorff, *Euripides' Ion* (Berlin, 1926), Introduction (1).

[8] Changing names, initiation, and adolescence: cf. Jan Bremmer, "Heroes, Rituals, and the Trojan War," *Studi Storico-Religiosi* 2 (1978): 7–38 (8). *Hēbē*: Ion is a young man in the midst of a stage of transition; that is why he called *pais* (meaning "child" but also "son of"): 77, 386, 683, 692, 719, 774, 779, 788, 1186, 1320, 1358, 1409) and also *neanias* (youth): 316, 794, 823, 1121, 1218; cf. 780, *ektelē neanian* (a complete young man); he is specifically described as having reached the full vigor of youth (*es andr'aphikou*, 322, *hēbēs metron*, 354). *Trophē*: the word appears time and again. See, e.g., 26, 49, 52, 110, 318–19, 322, 357, 531, 821, 823, 826, 1190, 1358, 1377, 1531.

[9] *Ho kathanōn te kou thanōn phantazomai*, 1444. First birth, first death of Ion: 26–27; second birth, second death: 711–12, 1185–86.

[10] See Laurence Kahn, "Hermès, la frontière et l'identité ambiguë," *Ktéma* 4 (1979): 201–11.

him a social identity.[11] Now in the case of Ion, a division is made between the recognition, which falls to Kreousa, and the naming, for which Xouthos is responsible. It is an unusual division and the shares are unequal. Legitimacy falls to Kreousa; to Xouthos, just a name, which he is not even the first to give.

If *tukhē* (fortune) presides over the meeting between Ion and Xouthos, the recognition scene between Kreousa and her son resembles a deciphering of signs. One item in the *symbola mētros* (1386), or signs of the mother, is of course the infant's swaddling clothes,[12] but there are also the specific symbols of Athenian legitimacy: a basket, which recalls the basket of Erikhthonios, golden snakes betokening the first autochthonous child, and a crown made from Athena's olive tree, which was produced in primordial times when gods were in competition for the possession of Athens:[13] quite enough to make the point that this recognition scene is like an investiture and that Kreousa, the sole bearer of legitimacy, recognizes Ion as a father might identify his son.

While Xouthos may be the first human being to name the adolescent boy, that action has already been performed by a god, a god of equivocal communication. The hitherto anonymous child certainly gains a name in the course of the tragedy; it does not, however, appear to be a straightforward business. For a name belongs to a father, so in this case to Apollo; but, as Kreousa later explains (1541–43; cf. 507–9), a god gives no name to his son and, to get around this stigma of bastard status (*nothos*), a father must be invented for Ion so that he may acquire a legal, if not legitimate, ancestry. But in addition, his name will have to be accepted by those in the play, especially those who embody Athenian legitimacy: the chorus uses it, however, on one occasion only, to tell Kreousa of it. The old tutor regards it as no more than a pseudonym, obviously an invention. In his account of the eventful banquet, the messen-

---

[11] On the distinction between social identity and physical identity, see Natalie Daladier, "Les Mères Aveugles," *Nouvelle Revue de Psychanalyse* 19 (1979): 229–44.

[12] The swaddling clothes represent a close link between child and mother (918). On these as a sign of recognition, see Aiskhylos, *Khoephoroi* 231, Euripides, *Elektra* 539–40 (the swaddling clothes of Orestes) and Herodotos, I.111 (those of Kyros), and also the remarks of George Thomson, *Aeschylus and Athens* (London, 1966), 45–46 and Louis Gernet, "Droit et prédroit en Grèce ancienne," *Anthropologie de la Grèce antique* (Paris, 1968), 175–260, (204 n. 98).

[13] Golden snakes: 1427–30 (and 24–26); the olive tree: 1433–36. On the *akēratos* ("pure") olive tree, see M. Detienne, "L'Olivier: Un mythe politico-religieux," in *Problèmes de la terre en Grèce ancienne* ed. M. I. Finley (Paris, 1973) 293–306 (294–95); the presence of this olive branch recalls the custom reported by Hesykhios, s.v. *stephanon ekpherein*, according to which, in Athens, an olive branch indicated the birth of a child of the male sex. Cf. Ludwig Deubner, "Birth (Greek and Roman)," in *Encyclopaedia of Religions and Ethics*, ed. J. A. Hastings, (Edinburgh, 1909), 2:649); the swaddling clothes are, in fact, a fringed piece of material bearing the image of a Gorgon in the middle (i.e., an aegis) (1417–23).

ger devises one periphrasis after another in order to avoid naming Ion. Kreousa never calls him anything other than "son" or "child" (*pais* or *tekos*); before truly winning his identity, the young man has to wait for Athena to name him, which she eventually does, but very late in the day and then in an indirect fashion.[14] As for Ion himself, all that he has retained from his past is the painful absence of his mother, and he reasons that his name must come from her alone (1372).

In the story of Ion, then, everything leads to Kreousa: a woman; a woman who can bestow legitimacy, who recognizes the child and transmits to him the land of Athens and the power to rule it. Comedy is quite forgotten, as is the *drame bourgeois*. The heroic legend fades away too, subverted by the dominant role given to a woman, a phenomenon peculiar to tragedy. With Kreousa, and on the tragic stage, the *genos gynaikōn*, the race of women,[15] acquires its Athenian credentials.

FEMININE AND MASCULINE

In the Sixth Olympian, Pindar sings of Iamos, born from the loves of Evadne and Apollo:

> The lord of the golden hair sent to her aid the gentle goddess of birth and the Fates; and from her womb and amid sweet labor, forthwith came Iamos to the light of day. And she, though sore distressed, left him there upon the ground; but, by the will of the gods, two gray-eyed serpents tended the babe with the venom, the harmless venom of honey bees. (42–48)[16]

A *parthenos* seduced by Apollo, a child abandoned, guardian snakes: the story of Kreousa has much in common with that of Evadne. The difference is that Kreousa is an unhappy Evadne. Instead of pleasure which for the "virgin with the dark plaits" was the "the sweetness of Aphrodite" (Pindar, *Olympian* 6.35), for Kreousa there was nothing but violence (*bia*) and shamelessness (895–96, 900). If Evadne's confinement is an easy one (42–43)—as Athena later claims Kreousa's to have been (1596)—the daughter of Erekhtheus herself does not remember being attended by any companions other than misery and secrecy (869, 957, 1458–59). Additionally, the snakes which guarded Iamos (45) (and Erikhthonios, 21–

---

[14] The chorus, 802; the tutor, 831; the periphrases of the messenger (1123, 1183, 1186, 1209, 1218); Athena herself does not name him at the outset, speaks of his future glory (1575), and names him indirectly at 1587–88, without ever addressing him by name (whereas she does name Kreousa, 1572).

[15] See Nicole Loraux, "Sur la race des femmes et quelques-unes de ses tribus," in Loraux, *Enfants*, 75–118.

[16] C.A.P. Ruck, in "On the Sacred Names of Iamos and Ion: Ethnobotanical Referents in the Hero's Parentage," *CJ* 71 (1976) 235–52, compares the two texts.

23) have here become golden ornaments, symbols of mourning for the exposed child (24–26, 1427–31).[17]

Some readers of the *Ion* support the cause of Apollo against Kreousa, whom they consider to be "naive and small-minded" and suspect of ingratitude toward the god who was so well disposed to her; they accuse her of rebelling against divine order since—already *theomakhos* (hostile to the gods), as it would seem—she had dared to resist Apollo's far from eloquent advances.[18] I do not need to take Kreousa's side, for Kreousa is, after all, nothing but a character in a tragedy, and neither attempts to psychologize nor identifications with a character can be of much help in interpreting a tragic drama. I have, nonetheless, chosen to read the tragedy from the position of Kreousa's character because it is upon her that everything that is truly tragic in the plot depends, because she alone presumes to upset the plans of Apollo, and because it is she who dominates the play, both the first part (before the murder plan) and the denouement in which, with Athena leading her, she brings her son back to Athens. It is this denouement in particular which allots the major role to Kreousa, as it transforms the situation of a political *tyrannos* with which the play had opened into an order of legitimate sovereignty, with the civic deity bringing the rightful king back to the city. The female figure who bestows legitimacy is now divided into two: it is the goddess who leads the way and acts as guide (1616–17), but it is the queen herself who goes with her son to Kekrops' land, and then appoints him to the royal throne (1571–72).

Apollo is absent and Xouthos has disappeared. The last word goes to the women in this tragedy in which women—not only Kreousa herself but the chorus too, composed of her maidservants—have consistently refused to be reduced to silence. Thus the chorus, emerging from the reserve to which it is usually consigned by Euripides, has not shrunk from warning Kreousa of the plot being hatched against her, demonstrating a solidarity not only among Athenians but also among women, against Xouthos whose threats of death have not succeeded in ensuring their silence,[19] and also against Apollo whose plans they unknowingly thwart.

It is true that the relationship between the chorus and Kreousa is one of such close identification that these servants—these slaves—do not hesi-

---

[17] Cedric H. Whitman, *Euripides and the Full Circle of Myth* (Cambridge, Mass., 1974), 73, notes the differences between Evadne and Kreousa.

[18] For this argument which defends and promotes Apollo, see Anne Burnett, "Human Resistance and Divine Persuasion in Euripides' *Ion*," *CP* 57 (1962): 89–103, and also Vincent J. Rosivach, "Earthborns and Olympians: The Parodos of the *Ion*," *CQ* 27 (1977): 284–94.

[19] Xouthos' threats (666–67) distress them, but a single order from Kreousa is enough to make them speak (756–60).

tate to refer to Athens as "my city" and to Athena as "my goddess" (719, 211, 453–54). But they also share this identification of slave and mistress, subject and sovereign, with the tutor (855–56) and the messenger (1111), and like these two, the women of the chorus proclaim their support for the cause of the Erekhtheidai, declaring:

> I too, dear mistress, want to share your fate
> To die, or live with honor.
>
> (857–58)[20]

The fact that the expression they use to convey their intention is borrowed from the masculine language of war and politics is perhaps no mere chance; now this identification takes on another dimension. For what links the women of the chorus to the queen is not solely their concern for Athenian legitimacy. They also share with Kreousa a particular idea of the condition of woman, who is born unfortunate; echoing the laments of their mistress, they loudly declare their hatred of perverse males.[21] The theme of the race of women is not far off, and indeed it soon breaks through to the surface in an antistrophe sung by the chorus in which, one sex against the other, the women beg poets to denounce males, phrasing their song in the form of a palinode (*palimphamos aoida*):

> Let an avenging strain
> sound out disharmony and celebrate
> man's infidelity.
>
> (1097–98)

Men and their love affairs, men and their betrayals. But what of the gods' betrayals, Apollo's in particular, since he sets just such an example (436–51)? As they urge the poets to bear witness against men, are the women of the chorus perhaps conscious that they are really urging the votaries of that god to turn their art against Apollo himself?

In a chorus in the *Medeia* (410ff.), which this passage echoes, the women lament the fact that Phoibos, master of melodies, did not endow their minds with the inspired song of the lyre, "for otherwise," they say, "I should have turned the hymn against the other sex" (*Med.* 424–29). This is perhaps precisely what the chorus does in the *Ion*. But here too Kreousa and her women share the task. While the chorus appeals to the poets to indict men and their illicit loves (*gamous . . . anosious*), Kreousa undertakes to turn the hymn against men in actual fact; to turn it against Apollo, the defender of masculine values, the impenitent violator of

---

[20] Other indications of the chorus' solidarity with Kreousa: 1113–14, 1229–30, 1236–41, 1246–49.

[21] Kreousa's lamentations: 252, 398–400 (cf. those of Phaidra in the *Hippolytos*, 406–7; echoed by the chorus, 832. See also lines 325 and 355, spoken by Ion.

nymphs and virgins, the seducer-god (*theos homeunetas*), who, indifferent to their suffering, continues to play, unmoved, upon his lyre; and to turn it against him by borrowing his own song. Some interpreters of Kreousa's monody have noticed that in it the daughter of Erekhtheus reverses the hymn usually devoted to singing the praises of the god, turning it into a denunciation of him.[22] But there is a further step still to take: we must realize that at this point Kreousa is fulfilling a desire most dear to the race of women.

It is to borrow the men's own language, Apollo's own song, the better to denounce those men and that god. That this should affect the way in which the feminine is now defined is hardly surprising. Thus, when the tutor invites Kreousa to "act a woman's part" (*gunaikeion ti dran*, 843), what are we to understand? "Take a woman's revenge," to be sure—the tragic genre delights in reminding its public of how prone women are to commit crimes of passion; but at the same time, by virtue of an echo from the word *andreion*, which denotes a quality which is peculiarly male, namely courage, the meaning becomes "act as a woman of courage" (cf. 857–58). Do something feminine: act like a woman acting like a man. And this confusion between what is masculine and what is feminine emerges quite clearly in the following line, where the old slave suggests that Kreousa should employ, as interchangeable means, the sword of a man and the cunning of a woman (844).[23]

In the *agon* between the feminine and the masculine, the initiative is taken by the women. That is probably not the least of the paradoxes in this tragedy centered on autochthony. But if autochthony may deny any existence to the female principle, the paradigmatic time of origins is already far removed, and the time of imitation has taken its place: the time of Ion and the time of Kreousa.

IMITATING AUTOCHTHONY

Enclosed within a basket and covered by signs that are so many "imitations" (*mimēmata*) of Erikhthonios (1429), Ion repeats in reverse the birth of the primordial autochthonous child. Euripides himself says so quite explicitly.

Explicitly yet not without ambiguity. Thus, Hermes tells the story as follows: Kreousa went to place the newborn child in the same cave where she had lain with the god. She exposed him, dedicated to death, in the

---

[22] On the reversal of the hymn, see J. La Rue, "Creusa's Monody: *Ion* 859–922," *TAPA* 94 (1963): 126–36 and also Immerwahr, "Athēnaikes eikones," 283 (with bibliography) and Burnett, "Resistance," 95–96, who suggests that hatred here masks admiration.

[23] James Diggle (*Oxford Classical Texts*) deletes this line, and indeed the entire passage, 844–58.

perfect circle of a hollow basket, observing a custom of her ancestors and of the autochthon Erikhthonios (*progonōn nomon sōizousa tou te gēgenous Erikhthoniou*). For the daughter of Zeus had given him two snakes as protectors, and had given him to the virgin daughters of Aglauros to keep (*didōsi sōizein*). Thence stemmed the custom among the Erekhtheids to raise (*trephein*) their children in serpent collars of gold (16–26).

But what is the custom which Kreousa is said to keep (*sōizein*)? That of enclosing a newborn infant in a basket? No doubt, but we should also point out that Erikhthonios' basket was supposed to save (*sōizein*) him, whereas Ion's may well cause his death.[24] As Kreousa shuts the infant in the basket before laying him on the ground, she is repeating in reverse the gesture of Athena who "raised Erikhthonios from the ground" (269) to entrust him to the daughters of Kekrops to save (271–72). But perhaps *nomon sōizousa* (keeping a custom) is illuminated by what follows in the text. If so, perhaps we should regard "the ancient custom" merely as an allusion to the golden snakes which, as we are told at the end of the play, Kreousa had placed in the basket. But once again the imitation becomes a reversal: Ion is exposed, whereas the golden snakes usually preside over the "raising" (*trophē*) of the Erekhtheidai. Origins cannot be imitated with impunity.

Equally, however, origins cannot be elided. They represent a lost paradigm which weighs upon the present, arresting time and demanding repetition. And it is indeed repetition in all its complexity which, under the name of imitation, is at work in the *Ion* as the essential rule of the tragic genre. Not only does the story—that ancient story that is the myth—repeat itself, but duplication lies at the very heart of the action, constituted by two recognition scenes, two consultations of the oracle, and two attempts at murder.[25] It is no doubt true that an intermingling of the past and the present is one of the features peculiar to the tragic genre, but here that intermingling is reduplicated ad infinitum since the myth represented onstage and confronted with the issues of the present is itself already a duplication of the myth of origins.

Imitating autochthony means repeating what only happens once. Tragedy lies in the representation of that logical impossibility. Without this dimension, the play would perhaps end up as that to which so many readers would like to reduce it: a *drame bourgeois* culminating in a recognition scene and a happy ending, set in Delphi and entitled *Apollonide*

---

[24] Much has been written on the basket of Ion-Erikhthonios, referred to as *antipēx* (19, 40, 1338, 1380, 1391), *angos* (32, 1337, 1398, 1412), *kytos* (37, 39), *teukhos* (273). See esp. R. S. Young, "*Antipex*: A Note on the *Ion* of Euripides," *Hesperia* 10 (1941): 138–42, and L. Bergson, "Zur Bedeutung von *Antipex* bei Euripides," *Eranos* 58 (1960): 12–19.

[25] See Christian Wolff, "The Design and the Myth in Euripides' *Ion*," *HSCP* 69 (1965): 169–94.

(Son of Apollo), as was the adaptation of it produced by Leconte de Lisle.[26] But the point is precisely that the *Ion* is *not* a Delphic tragedy.[27]

It has been suggested that Euripides' ploy of moving the plot to Delphi—perhaps that of Sophokles' lost *Kreousa*, thought to have unfolded at Athens in the palace of the Erekhtheidai—was an innovation that made very good sense.[28] Even so, it is important to realize that although the scene is set in Delphi, Athens is by no means left behind; Athens remains the essential point of reference (cf. 184–88) and the distant, yet present, location of the tragedy. The *Ion* provides us with no information about either the topography or the myths of Delphi since the play tells us nothing about Delphi that we did not already know from Athens, whereas it provides all the elements of a mythical map of Athens, or, at least, of the Akropolis, the "city" of the Erekhtheidai.[29] But distance lends depth and, if it is true that, as Ion declares, "things have a different face according to whether they appear before the eyes or far away" (585–86, with reference to Athens), if one looks at Athens from the vantage point of Delphi, one is likely to see it with the eyes of Kreousa and ascribe to it all the attractions with which nostalgia embellishes a presence that is absent (cf. 251 and 385).

Such are the advantages gained from setting a scene at a distance. Seated on the tiered steps of the theater, on the slopes of the Akropolis, the Athenian public turned what was "here" into what was "over there" since, in Delphi, that was the way to refer to Athens.[30] The scene is set at

[26] In the *Apollonide* (lyrical drama in three parts and six tableaux, Paris, 1888), the author eliminates the war against the Giants, autochthony, and Athena: in short, the entire theme of origins.

[27] This is so despite many claims: e.g., V. Cilento, "Una tragedia delfica: Jone di Euripides," *Parole del Passato* 8 (1953): 241–63 ("the tragedy exalts the humanity of the Delphic religion," 242) and of course, Burnett, "Resistance." Contrary to the position of R. Goossens, *Euripide et Athènes* (Brussels, 1962), 478 and 483–84, we cannot even be sure that the *Ion* gives evidence about the relations between Athens and Delphi (of which not much is known during the period of the Peloponnesian War: cf. G. Daux, "Athènes et Delphes," *Mélanges W. S. Ferguson* [Cambridge, Mass., 1940], 37–69). Despite its title, H. Erbse's recent article, "Der Gott von Delphi im *Ion* des Euripides," *Mélanges H. Rüdiger* (Berlin, 1975), 40–54, is more concerned with the god than with Delphi. I have not been able to consult T. Guardi, "La Polemica antiappolinea di Euripide," *Pan* 3 (1976): 5–23.

[28] Anne Burnett, *Catastrophe Survived: Euripides' Plays of Mixed Reversal* (Oxford, 1971), 103.

[29] Immerwahr, "Athēnaikes eikones," 281. The attempts at reconstituting the west pediment of the temple of the Aklmeonidai on the basis of the *parodos* of the *Ion* have met with little success. Space does not permit a fuller discussion of this issue.

[30] There is a constant interplay between *ekei* (here) and *enthade* throughout the play (24, 251, 384–85, 645, 1278).

Delphi but Apollo is conspicuous by his absence from it; Athena with her sun-bright face (1550) has taken his place.[31] Athens is in Delphi in the person of its civic deity. Yet, without the hidden presence of Apollo, the Akropolis would remain forever outside itself, and it is Delphi which, by sheltering the *trophē* of Ion, makes it possible to return to Athens, where the couple constituted by the hidden father and the *kourotrophos* virgin is replaced by that of the mother and the alleged father. Everything is thus set up to make possible the exchange between Delphi and Athens. This is not to claim that it will be an altogether straightforward exchange: the complex interplay between feminine and masculine, present and origins, and near and far is there to warn us against that.

INTERFERENCE FROM THE ORIGIN

To assign the prologue of a tragedy to Hermes is to place the play explicitly under the sign of ambiguity. Hermes, he who passes from one place to another, who has transported the exposed child from the wild space where he was abandoned to the sacred precinct of Apollo, symbolizes by his presence the path that Ion will take in the opposite direction, passing from the altars of Delphi to the hearth of the Erekhtheidai. But wherever Hermes passes, paths that were clear-cut become confused.[32] If ambiguity is a constitutive element of the tragic genre, Hermes reinforces it right at the outset of the *Ion*, taking it upon himself to stand as guarantor of this game of interferences.

THE CONFUSED PATHS OF TRAGEDY

In the *Ion*, the tragic confrontation between myth and the *polis* is, as it were, laid bare, in a most deliberate fashion.

Myth, or to be more precise, one particular myth, that of autochthony, is subjected to the test of constant questioning,[33] and their relationship to myth positions all the characters in the play on a scale ranging from the greatest proximity, that of Kreousa, to the greatest distance, that of the stranger Xouthos, while Ion, caught between the polar figures of Kreousa and Xouthos, oscillates, often in precipitate fashion, between them.

But this tragedy about a myth is also a political tragedy in which the

[31] *Antēlion prosōpon*: "A face as dazzling as the sun," but also "in the place of Helios," named in 1439. Throughout the play, Helios is identified with Apollo.

[32] See Laurence Kahn, *Hermès passe ou les ambiguïtés de la communication* (Paris, 1978), esp. 86–89.

[33] Occurrences of the word *mythos* and its derivations: 196, 265, 336, 528, 994, 1340; reflections on and questioning of the tradition: 225, 275, 506–7. Cf. Immerwahr, "Athēnaikes eikones," 280–81.

exaltation of citizenship intersects with that of imperialism. There is nothing particularly surprising about the fact that this confrontation interweaves two separate myths: the one about Ionian colonization, which provides imperialism with its ideology,[34] the other about autochthony, which provides citizenship with its imaginary roots. Many scholars have argued that for Athens truly to occupy the dominant position in Ionian colonization, Ion has to be an Athenian and so must be descended from the primordial autochthonous being; hence the contrived genealogy, the aim of which is to obscure whatever aspects of Ion make him appear to be a hero imported from outside into the heroic legend of Athens.[35] However, the adoption of that particular line has usually resulted in underestimating the fact that, quite apart from its instrumental use, the myth is silently at work within the tragedy.[36]

The fact is that, unaffected by all this play with the myth, autochthony gives the *Ion* its meaning and form, and when at the end of the play Athena's prophecy announces the forthcoming Ionian colonization—in other words, a maritime empire—to "give strength to [this] land of Athens" (1584–85), all the important points have already been made.

As a civic myth, autochthony lends itself to every kind of interplay between the myth and the *polis*. There are, in fact, two versions of this myth in the drama: the one, political and secular, tells of the purity of the race; the other is rooted in the sacred hill of the Akropolis and concerns the *gēgenēs* Erikhthonios. The themes of autochthony—the autochthony of the people, of the kings, of the people through its kings—constantly intersect.[37] But the *polis* also presents two images of itself in the *Ion*, each of which is an integral part of one of the two sides to the myth, and between them there is a constant interference: the city of the present, con-

[34] The *Ion* as a drama about imperialism: Goossens, *Euripide*, 487–89; A. S. Owen, *Euripides' Ion* (Oxford, 1939), xi–xii; P. Barron, "Religious Propaganda of the Delian League," *JHS* 84 (1964): 35–48. On Ionian propaganda, see the comments of F. Jacoby, *FGrHist*, commentary on Hellanikos (323a), frags. 11 and 23.

[35] For the legend and fabrication of genealogies in the *Ion*, see E. Ermatinger, *Die attische Autochthonensage bis auf Euripides* (Berlin, 1897), 112–19; M. P. Nilsson, *Cults, Myths, Oracles and Politics in Ancient Greece* (Lund, 1951), 66–67; Goossens, *Euripide*, 482; F. Cassola, "Le Genealogie mitiche e la coscienza nazionale greca," *Rendiconti della Accademia di Archeologia di Napoli* 28 (1953): 279–304; and Jean Rudhardt, "Une approche de la pensée mythique: Le mythe considéré comme un langage," *Studia Philosophica* 26 (1966): 208–37 (228–29). Jane E. Harrison, *Mythology and Monuments of Ancient Athens* (London, 1890), lxxx, was even then summing up the opinion of most scholars when she described the *Ion* as "a transparent piece of political genealogy-making."

[36] See, however, Rudhardt, "Une approche," 229–30.

[37] *Gēgenēs*: 20–21, 1466 (Erikhthonios; see also 267 and 1000); Giants and Gorgon: 987, 1529 (and also 218 and 989). *Autokhthōn*: 29–30, 589–90 (describing *laos*, people, or *polis*); of kings: 736–37, 1000, 1056–57, 1060; of the people through its kings: 24 (despite Wilamowitz's commentary), 296.

cerned with the quality of citizenship, expresses itself through the political discourse of autochthony upon which its requirements are based; meanwhile, Kreousa embodies the ancient *polis*, which is an integral part of the myth's religious side and which is identified with the Akropolis—that is, with the house of the Erekhtheidai, her own *oikos*.

In the interchange between myth and *polis* (and the two meanings of those two words), the present never ceases to break through the surface of the past since what is near is intermingled with what is far away. The resulting ambiguities are essential to the play, involving all the institutions, both mythical and historical, that codify Athenian birth and parentage. For the spectators, the only definition of a citizen was that provided by the Periklean law of 450 B.C.E., by virtue of which an Athenian was the son of two parents who were Athenians. Enacted on the stage is the story of a child with two fathers but whose mother alone is Athenian; an Athenian drama but one which takes place in Delphi; a drama about autochthony but one in which there are no *andres Athēnaioi*; a drama about citizenship in which not a single character is a citizen, and in which it is the women who embody legitimacy and slaves who speak for the city, while the eponymous hero has no name, as befits the child of a woman; in a word, a drama that tells of all the ways to be an Athenian outside Athenian orthodoxy. In a confrontation such as this, not only the city but the myth too is in danger of losing its integrity.

Consider the institution of marriage, so vital to the fifth-century *polis*, whose legitimate reproduction it assured. From Aiskhylos to Euripides, marriage, like all contemporary legal procedures, is called into question and its boundaries blurred. Nevertheless, it sometimes happens that the proper distance that separates conventional marriage from sexual union is maintained, or—to put it another way—the bed (*lekhos*), an institutional reality, is kept distinct from the couch (*eunē*), a place of sexual pleasure (e.g., Euripides, *Phoinissai* 946). Kreousa has been violated by Apollo and married off to Xouthos: there ought to be a marked differentiation between these two unions. But there is not: in both cases, the vocabulary of marriage co-exists with that of sexuality.[38] Does this mean that, like her mating with Apollo, Kreousa's union with Xouthos is both legitimate and illegitimate? Both of her partners, it is true, turn out to be

[38] *Gamos* and its derivatives: 10, 72, 437, 445, 505, 868, 941, 946, 949, 1543 (Apollo); 58, 62, 297, 813 (Xouthos). *Numpheuē*: 1371 (Apollo); 913 (Xouthos). *Lekhos*: 874, 900, 1484 (Apollo); 297 (Xouthos). *Zeugnumi*: 343, 900, 949 (Apollo). *Eunē*: 17, 860–61, 894 (*homeunetas*), 899, 912 (*kakos eunatōr*), 1484 (Apollo); 304, 977 (Xouthos). *Meignumi*: 338 (Apollo). Note that Apollo's side is as important from the point of view of "legitimacy" as from that of sexual union.

"ungrateful betrayers of their bed" (880). But the essential point lies else-where, in the gap that now becomes apparent between the mythical val-ues of marriage and its civic definition. Seen from the point of view of myth, Kreousa's unions, the first with a god, the second with a descen-dant of Zeus, are endowed with honor; but from the vantage point of Athens, neither one is in conformity with the law that holds that an Athenian woman should take an Athenian husband (cf. 289), and in this respect a god's violation of a mortal woman, which constitutes a forced and unbalanced union,[39] is no more legitimate than a marriage between a daughter of Erekhtheus and a foreigner.

"Married" too high for a mortal and too low for an Erekhtheid, Kreousa finds herself at the heart of a tragic distortion, and her two un-suitable alliances confuse all the accepted codes of parentage: because Apollo took her by force, she abandoned her child, leaving it up to the god to nurture it (be its *trophos*). Should we speak of fosterage here, lik-ening it to mythical childhoods passed far away from the paternal hearth, in the house of a *trophos*? We must reject this hypothesis immediately un-less we mean an inside-out kind of fosterage where the one who fathered the child plays the role of nurturer, and the father's house takes over the function that normally falls to the maternal branch of the family.[40] It is true that one of Apollo's attributes is to be *kourotrophos*, but that function presupposes a fictive paternity, and the point is that, in respect of his own son, it is a role Apollo should not be able to assume.[41]

As for Kreousa's marriage to Xouthos, its status is decisively summed up in the very first dialogue between Ion and Kreousa in a brief exchange of questions and answers:

Ion: And what Athenian became your husband?

Kreousa: My husband is no citizen of Athens, but an immigrant
          from another land.

Ion: Who then? He must have been of noble birth [*eugenēs*].

[39] Cf. 506–7 and 1541–43 (union between a god and a mortal woman). The chorus in Aiskhylos' *Prometheus Bound* defines a good marriage as *homalos gamos* (901) and hopes, as in the case of Io, that the love of a god could be avoided (902–4).

[40] Fosterage implies being brought up outside the paternal house, in many cases in the mother's family, or among shepherds. Cf. Louis Gernet, "Fosterage et légende," in Gernet, *Droit et société dans la Grèce ancienne* (Paris, 1955), 19–28, (19–22), and Bremmer, "Avun-culate," 73–74. It is only as the supposed son of Xouthos that Ion can be considered to be fostered (Gernet, "Fosterage," 23).

[41] For Apollo Kourotrophos, see Henri Jeanmaire, *Couroi et Courètes: Essai sur l'éducation spartiate et les rites d'adolescence dans l'antiquité hellénique* (Lille and Paris, 1939; repr. New York, 1975), 283, and on fictitious paternity, 284.

Kreousa: Xouthos, the son of Aiolos and Zeus.

Ion: A stranger. How then could he marry you—you who are of such noble stock [*engenēs*]? (289–93)

Eugenēs refers to good birth, *engenēs* to autochthonous birth: in Athens the two terms are, and have to be, interchangeable.[42] According to the categories of a distant past, however, it would be in no way exceptional for the marriage, whether mythical or simply aristocratic, of a king's daughter with a grandson of Zeus to be placed under the sign of nobility. But to Ion, as to Kreousa, this aristocratic marriage constitutes a grave offense against the purity of the Athenian race, the only criterion of *eugeneia*;[43] Kreousa's *eugeneia* thus gives the lie to the "nobility" of Xouthos. And that is not all: because Athenian birth can be condensed into the *genos* of the Erekhtheidai, there is a total impasse. Xouthos is not an Athenian, he is an intruder into the house of Erekhtheus, whose *epiklēros* (heiress) daughter he has married in violation of all the rules of the classical city. At Kreousa's hearth, Xouthos is what, in a normal situation, a woman is at the hearth of her husband: an element introduced from outside. Yet in her own house, he has turned Kreousa into a kind of war-captive, the booty of a victorious warrior (298).

By his very existence, this intruder in his turn undermines the status of the daughter of Erekhtheus: if the *epiklēros* is indissociably attached to her own *oikos*, what can be said of Kreousa except that, married as she is to a foreigner, she is a quite abnormal *epiklēros*?[44] Admittedly, once Xouthos is out of the way, Kreousa alone transmits to her son the name and power of the Erekhtheidai, but that is to endow the *epiklēros* with an autonomy that runs counter to the spirit of Athenian jurisdiction. The fact must be accepted: in the *Ion*, there is no status with an unequivocal interpretation, and in particular, no way to give an account of Kreousa's legal position except to involve every possible approach simultaneously.

[42] In the funeral speeches (*epitaphioi*), *eugeneia* is the word used for autochthony. See Nicole Loraux, *L'invention d'Athènes* (Paris, 1981), 3.2. In Aristophanes, the two *eugenēs* and *engenēs* are exact equivalents: cf. *Thesmophoriazousai* 329–30 and *Wasps* 1076.

[43] The break between aristocratic marriage and endogamous Athenian marriage which J.-P. Vernant sets in the post-Kleisthenic period ("Le mariage," *Mythe et Société* [Paris, 1974], 57–81 [62–63]), should rather be dated to the post-Periklean period: it is in this perspective (not, as Vernant has it, 74, in an aristocratic perspective) that one may also explain Athenian strictness over the epiclerate.

[44] The epiclerate aimed to ensure that the daughter attached to the house should be united with the closest relative of the deceased. See Louis Gernet, "Sur l'épiclerat," *REG* 34 (1921): 337–79, especially 371, and more generally, A.R.W. Harrison, *The Law of Athens*, vol. 1, *The Family and Property* (Oxford, 1968), *passim*; W. K. Lacey, *The Family in Classical Greece* (Ithaca, N.Y., 1968), 139; and M. Broadbent, *Studies in Greek Genealogy* (Leiden, 1968), 203–16.

A case in point is Ion himself, devoted to the idea of pure and direct filiation yet whose own position has all the makings of that of a *nothos* (bastard): when he discovers a father in Xouthos, he is bound by the same token to recognize the illegitimacy of his birth, and it is that discovery of his bastardy that mars the joy of his reunion with Kreousa.[45] In the matter of his birth, nothing is regular and straightforward.

In an epic or purely mythical perspective, it would all be perfectly simple: the son of a god is no bastard.[46] The orthodox view of the city deems it otherwise, however, defining citizenship in terms of legitimacy and of double Athenian descent.[47] And even if Apollo thinks he has solved everything by "giving" Ion to Xouthos, at the very most all he is doing is providing his son with a legal father; even then, one cannot be sure that this acquisition would have resolved very much about the question of Ion's status[48] had not Kreousa finally turned out to be the bearer of full legitimacy. Only *in extremis* is the dilemma resolved, and then in a fashion that has nothing to do with the reality of Athenian institutions but is much more closely associated with representations connected to the mythical past: Kreousa's divine bastard will be king of Athens; the sons of her "legitimate" marriage to Xouthos will not be Athenian (1573–74, 1589–94). It is perhaps a case of myth making a comeback, reminding us that tragedy introduces one orthodoxy only to confront it with a superior one. But above all, it is a comeback for the myth of autochthony: behind Ion and Kreousa, Erikhthonios and Athena are never far away.

Does that mean that, because the myth of autochthony escapes the interplay of crossed interferences, it alone retains its integrity? Some interpreters would doubt it.[49] However, let us defer examination of that question for the moment: we must take one point at a time and, in order

---

[45] Ion, a *nothos* in relation to Xouthos: 545, 592, 1105; in relation to Kreousa: 1472.

[46] See the remarks of Delcourt, *Oedipe*, 38 and Lacey, *Family*, 103. In tragedy, by contrast, a god transmits no legitimacy (see 1541–43). The same is true for comedy. In the *Birds*, Herakles is a *nothos* and in danger of losing his inheritance to the *epiklēros* Athena (1649–70).

[47] The *Ion* postulates the need for two criteria, and I here I agree with S. C. Humphreys, "The Nothoi of the Kynosarges," *JHS* 94 (1974): 88–95, considering the son of a foreign woman to have been regarded as *nothos* just as much as was the illegitimate child of two Athenians. But it is a highly controversial point. See D. M. MacDowell, "Bastards as Athenian Citizens," *CQ* 26 (1976): 89–91, P. J. Rhodes, "Bastards as Athenian Citizens," *CQ* 28 (1978): 89–92.

[48] Note that (1) Xouthos is and remains an intruder who cannot therefore really be the legitimate father, and (2) in the eyes of the Athenians, given the standing (*dokēsis*) of Xouthos, Ion could at the most be regarded as an adopted son, unable to inherit the *oikos* of his adoptive father (cf. Lacey, *Family*, 146) who anyway is not its legitimate owner.

[49] For example, G. B. Walsh, "The Rhetoric of Birthright and Race in Euripides' *Ion*," *Hermes* 106 (1978): 301–15, (307).

to cast some light on this tangle of ambiguities, pause for a moment to
consider a matter that appears to be relatively little affected by tragic
overdetermination; namely, those passages in the tragedy which represent orthodox and, as it were, unfanciful pronouncements on political
autochthony.

A DISCOURSE OF EXCLUSION

Ion lectures Xouthos, the foreigner, on Athenian patriotism:

> The earth-born people [*autokhthonas*] of glorious Athens are said
> To be no alien race [*epeisakton genos*]. I should intrude
> There marked by two defects, a stranger's son,
> Myself a bastard.
>
> (589–92)

And again:

> . . . when a stranger [*xenos*] comes to a city of pure blood [*ka-
> tharan . . . polin*],
> Though in name a citizen [*astos*], his mouth
> Remains a slave: he has no right of speech [*parrhēsian*].
>
> (673–75)

This, in the mouth of the chorus, is expressed as:

> Let no others from other *oikoi* ever have
> Sway in the city:
> Only the sons of the noble [*eugenetān*] Erekhtheidai.
>
> (1058–60)[50]

Or to put it another way: Athens for the Athenians. As Ion has already
guessed, the status of Xouthos' son is but a step from that of invader and
it is a step that, like the chorus, Kreousa promptly takes, plotting the
death of an intruder whom she can already envisage setting fire to the
palace of the Erekhtheids (1291–95).

To be or not to be . . . Athenian. This is tantamount to saying:
whoever is not Athenian is a potential enemy. Some readers, mindful of
the opposite stance—the city that more than once is celebrated in tragedy
for extending a welcome to suppliants—might be surprised at such systematic exclusion. To them I would point out that in the *Ion* the issues of
the present encroach abruptly upon the anterior time of myth,[51] even as

---

[50] See also 667 (*ekpēlus*) and 1069–73. At line 674, I prefer the manuscript reading (*logoi-sin*) to the emendation, *nomoisin*, which is superfluous. It is simply a matter of conveying the conventional notion of a citizen. Cf. Euripides, *Erekhtheus*, frag. 5 (Colin Austin, *Nova Fragmenta Euripidea in Papyris Reperta* [Berlin, 1968], 13).

[51] Cf. Wolff, "Design," 174.

does official eloquence upon poetic discourse (i.e., the funeral oration upon the genre of tragedy). Perhaps we should regard this exclusivity where citzenship is concerned as an echo of the debates over the extension or restriction of the civic body—debates which were continually reopened in the Athenian *polis* at the time of the Peloponnesian War, especially during 412/1.[52] But even more than the debates in the Assembly, the speeches in the Keramikos provided Euripides with his model, for there can be no doubt that it was from the *epitaphioi* (funeral speeches) that the poet, so fond of developing this particular theme, borrowed the opposition between Athenians born from their own soil and the rest, intruders, immigrants in their own land, citizens by name only, not by birth.[53]

Caught up in this opposition which is taken straight from military discourse, Ion, faced with Xouthos, has had no difficulty in understanding the law that governs it. In reality, however, he is not the foreigner he fears himself to be. It is to Xouthos that the role of pure externality falls—Xouthos, the foreigner, who has won Kreousa (58–64) and her dowry (289–98) in warfare and who, deaf to the discourse of Athenian legitimacy, believes he has in truth obtained more: a scepter, riches (578–79, 660), even the land itself—which is precisely what a mercenary can never possess because it is a possession that cannot be bought.[54] In short, Xouthos, who is always an outsider, whether in Delphi or in Athens,[55] turns Athenian values upside down in both his thoughts and his words, at times speaking of these in the language of a tyrant in order to exalt his power (cf. 621), and elsewhere, as a definite outsider, declaring his disbelief in the dogma of autochthony (*ou pedon tiktei tekna*, 542). Thus, in relation to Ion, only imperfectly does Xouthos become the "father" who might introduce the adolescent into Athens, and the way he speaks testifies to that fact: he can find only incorrect words to refer to this new birth of Ion, which he proposes to celebrate by sacrifices and a banquet.[56]

[52] See Walsh, "Rhetoric," 308–9, who argues for dating the play to 411 B.C.E. against a background of discussions on the *patrios politeia*; a late date is also proposed by Wolff, "Design," 190–91 and A. M. Dale, *Euripides' Helen* (Oxford, 1967), xxviii (who suggests 413 or 412 B.C.E. on metrical considerations). An earlier date: e.g., Goossens, *Euripide*, 478 (between 421 and 415 B.C.E.) and H. Grégoire, [Budé edition] (418 B.C.E.). I favor a later rather than earlier dating for reasons similar to Walsh's and because the paratragic reference to the *Ion* in the *Lysistrata* presupposes the previous existence of the play.

[53] See Loraux, *L'invention*, 3.2 and, for a similar Euripidean borrowing from the funeral speech, *Erekhtheus*, frag. 50 Austin 7–13 (= Lykourgos, *Against Leokrates* 100).

[54] When, in Kreousa's presence, Ion later speaks as Xouthos' son, he argues that the land is won by arms, against Kreousa, who denies that an *epikouros* (ally) can be a legitimate occupant of land (*oikētōr*): see 1296–99 and 1304–5.

[55] See 290, 590 (*epaktos*); 607 (*ekpēlus*: Ion as son of Xouthos); 702–3 (*thyraios*); 813–14 (*xenos*). Cf. 1056–60, 1069–73.

What follows—his absence from the end of the play and the illusions he retains—is therefore altogether appropriate: Xouthos leaves the stage because his external status has no place either in the tragic universe or amid the belated rejoicing of Athens.

In other words, Xouthos ultimately excludes himself from Kreousa's world. But then who, even if Athenian, could possibly assume the role of a husband to Erekhtheus' daughter, who must bear the crushing weight of the law of her dead father?

KREOUSA, THE EPIKLĒROS

The city deprived of its youth is like a year without a spring;[57] deprived of all hope of posterity, the house of Erekhtheus is plunged into winter (966) and the old tutor, overwhelmed by the news that Xouthos is now blessed with a son, says to Kreousa that he looks upon "your father and yourself as unfortunate" (968). Some scholars have been put out by the association between the two and have, quite unnecessarily, suggested replacing "father" (*patera*) by "paternal line" (*patran*).[58] To do so is to ignore the fact that the dead Erekhtheus weighs upon the destiny of Kreousa. This is partly because Kreousa is an *epiklēros* and, moreover, an Athenian one, and in Athens the constraints of the epiclerate are particularly strict, but it is above all because the royal house of Kreousa merges with the city itself:[59] the requirements of autochthony therefore make the task of perpetuating the *oikos* a double necessity. It is up to Kreousa, guardian of the hearth of Erekhtheus,[60] to provide her dead father with a worthy line of descent, and by the same token, the city of Athens with a king. Barrenness thus spells ruin for her and the future of the dead king's house, as she herself perceives (619–20, 790–91, 865), and this is confirmed by the old tutor who defends the interests of Erekhtheus and even acts in the place of that father.[61] What the final reversal of the play in fact signifies is salvation for both father and daughter. Reunited with the son whom she believed to be dead, Kreousa celebrates in song her rebirth to

---

[56] Xouthos wishes to honor Ion with *genethlia* and a banquet such as is offered "to a guest invited to the hearth" (*hōs xenon ephestion*, 653–54), but the two terms are contradictory: the *genethlia* are celebrated on the fifth day after the birth for a child of the house, who is no invited guest. Furthermore, Xouthos wants to celebrate concurrently the *genethlia* and the banquet of the tenth day (*dekatē*), which is the day for the giving of a name. On these ceremonies, see L. Deubner, "Die Gebräuche der Griechen nach der Geburt," *RhM* 95 (1952): 374–77, and also Deubner, "Birth," 649.

[57] The springtime of the year: Nicole Loraux, "*Hēbē* et *Andreia*: deux versions de la mort du combattant athénien," *Ancient Society* 6 (1975): 1–31 (9–13).

[58] See the remarks of Owen on 968.

[59] *Domoi* and *polis* are equivalent at 1056–60.

[60] See 567–68, 810–11, 836–38, 841, 1021, 1036, 1069–73, 1291, 1293.

[61] The old man as father: 725, 733–34, 765; cf. 807–11, 970.

life, the rebirth of her house and therefore of the city, the rebirth—
finally—of Erekhtheus.

> I am childless no longer, no longer without an heir.
> The hearth is restored to the home, the rulers return to the land
> And Erekhtheus is young once more [anhēbāi];
> Now the autochthonous house is delivered from night
> And looks up to the rays of the sun.
>
> (1463–67)

Her words have more than metaphorical force. Ion truly is the child of
the hearth, because his existence is enough to found Kreousa's house
anew. Better still, he is a young Erekhtheus. It is true that Ion brings new
youth to the line of the Erekhtheidai. But what the text actually suggests
is a kind of reincarnation of Erekhtheus himself. One might refer simply
to the theme of sons who resemble their fathers, which both in literary
tradition and in the religious practices of the city-state[62] defines the
proper order reigning within the *oikos* and within society. But in this
case, the father who reacquires his youth in the person of Ion is the father
of the boy's mother. Can it be that Ion, the son of Kreousa, has no
"father" other than Erekhtheus? Apollo and Xouthos have vanished—
the true father who posed as the false one and the false one who believed
himself to be the true sire—and now Ion is directly rooted in the autochthonous house (*gēgenetas domous*) (1466; cf. 1573). It is only now that
Kreousa, whose house is no longer "orphaned," will be able to produce
children for Xouthos: the past has become the future, and Kreousa is delivered from her long sterility.

We should not, however, hasten to read the *Ion* as a tragedy devoted to
the glory of patrilinear filiation. Between the daughter and the father
there is, after all, a mother, a mother who has no name but who makes
her appearance at the precise point when the figure of the father is becoming dangerously dominant in Kreousa's discourse. In response to
Ion's question:

> But tell me who you are, your land [gē], your family line [patra]?
> And what is your name?
>
> (258–59)

Kreousa tells him her name, that of her father, and that of her "fatherland" (*patris gē*). But as Ion pursues his questioning, the father assumes

---

[62] The literary tradition begins with Hesiod, *Works and Days*, 235. The religious practice
of cities involves the curses that accompany oaths: e.g., the oath of the Athenians before the
battle of Plataia (L. Robert, *Etudes épigraphiques et philologiques* [Paris, 1938], 307–26, lines
43–44), Amphiktyonic oath: cf. Aiskhines, *Against Ktesiphon* 111. See also the oath of Dre-
ros, *Inscriptiones Creticae*, vol. 1, no. 9 (Rome, 1935), lines 87–89.

the fearful aspect of a sacrificer.[63] Here, in the fateful context in which the allusion to the blood of the daughters of Kekrops in the first generation prepares the way for the next stage—the sacrifice of the daughters of Erekhtheus, where the king, their father, who sacrificed them, is in turn destroyed—here a mother's arms suddenly appear in the text as a place of refuge:

> Ion: How was it you were saved, the only one?
>
> Kreousa: I was a baby in my mother's arms. (279–80)

A mother's arms: Ion missed their maternal embrace for himself (962–63), but not so the autochthonous Erikhthonios, the child whom "Athena took . . . from the earth, into her virgin arms, though he was not her son" (269–70).

It is not uncommon that fathers are not there: in this instance it is Hephaistos, "father" of the autochthonous child, whose absence[64] allows the female figures who are present to cluster around the birth of the miraculous infant. And in an ode which is of central significance to the play, it is again feminine powers whom the chorus bids guard the paternal line within the house of Erekhtheus. To confirm the fact that there is something suspect at the very heart of the representations of paternity in the *Ion*, let us dwell for a moment on this chorus which from the antistrophe onward might be called "the chorus of paternal filiation" (452–508).

Here the women of Athens sing of the unchanging principle (*akinēton aphorman*) represented by the chain of generations in which the *hēbē* (youth) of the son takes over from the father to defend the soil of the fatherland (*gē patris*). Countering in advance the tyrannical and materialistic values of Xouthos, they proclaim that all wealth stems from the procreation of legitimate children. But, by a tragic irony of which they themselves are not aware, the women thus evoke the figure of Kreousa, Erekhtheus' only child—not a flourishing *neanias* (a young man), but just a daughter: a daughter through whom all has come to an impasse. She has riches and royalty but no child, although later she will turn out to have produced a son for the *thalamos patrios* (ancestral chamber) after all (476–77).[65] Kreousa: a father's daughter but also a woman who will turn

---

[63] "He dared to kill his maiden daughters as sacrifices [*sphagia*] for his land" (278). The theme of sacrifice runs throughout the play, in which the word *sphazein* and its derivatives occurs many times (228, 615, 1126, 1250, 1309, 1404). For the link between this vocabulary and the theme of purity and defilement, see Whitman, *Euripides*, 69–103.

[64] On the absence of Hephaistos as the father of Erikhthonios, cf. M. Delcourt, *Hephaïstos ou la légende du magicien (Paris, 1957), 148. His absence is here a phenomenon to be interpreted within the context of the tragedy in which the paternal function is not invariably positive (see below, n. 87).

[65] *Thalamos* expresses the idea of a marital chamber, but with *patrios*, it retains its patri-

out to be a mother. This is why the choral ode, from its opening lines, has to be placed under the sign of two female deities or, more precisely, two virgins: Athena, whose birth unattended by Eileithyia makes her truly the daughter of her father (452), and Artemis. Both are sisters to Apollo, both *parthenoi* are requested to intercede to promote the fecundity of the *genos* of Erekhtheus (468); two virgin goddesses summoned to aid patrilinear filiation, not only because a virgin's rejection of procreation places her on the side of the father,[66] but also because in Athens, Athena and Artemis both preside over adolescence, marriage, and the maternity of women.[67] In this ode, the insistent presence of the feminine sign repeatedly challenges the dominance of the paternal principle which it often reinforces, but from which it also diverges at certain strategic points. Thus Artemis, as the daughter born from Leto (*Latogenēs*), is associated with Athena, the daughter of her father, and it is in their capacity as women (485) that the servants of Kreusa sing of paternal filiation. Finally, in the epode which closes the song, the chorus invoking the three "daughters of Aglauros" places these daughters of Kekrops under the authority not of their father but of their mother (496; cf. 23). Moreover, the *thalamoi patrioi* of the opening lines have given way to the sunless cavern of the High Rocks with their deep hollows (*muchōdesi Makrais*)[68] near where the Aglaurids danced and where Kreousa, a young girl although a mother, exposed Ion.

Interwoven into the chorus' message about patrilinear filiation, we find the figure of Kreousa in her equivocal position of a woman acting in place of a man, a mother standing in for a father.

Kreousa exposed Ion. Although in heroic legends, where gods seduce the daughters of kings, this is an action often performed by those women, it was much less commonly the case in real life with all the institutions familiar to the Athenian audience: in that context, the denial of legitimacy expressed by the exposure of a newborn child was first and foremost a denial of paternity and thus it was generally the father's act to perform,[69] unlike in the case of Kreousa. This rule, at least, held true in Athens, where the law was concerned with the right of the father, in con-

---

lineal import. Note that (1) the house of Erekhtheus is in a state of childlessness (*apaidia*), for Xouthos cannot be the father of a child of the *thalamos patrios*, and (2) if Kreousa has given birth to a child, as Hermes says, in the *oikos* (16), she has indeed made the dwelling of Erekhtheus into a *thalamos patrios*.

[66] Cf. J.-P. Vernant, "Hestia-Hermès: Sur l'expression religieuse de l'espace chez les Grecs," in *Mythe et pensée* (Paris, 1969), 124–70 (137–39). For Whitman, *Euripides*, 95–96, the two goddesses are chosen not as promoters of fertility but as images of inviolate purity.

[67] Claude Calame, *Les choeurs de jeunes filles en Grèce archaïque* (Rome, 1977), 1:238.

[68] For *mykhos* (as well as *thalamos*) as a feminine space, see Vernant, "Hestia-Hermès," 151–52.

[69] The technical term for exposure was *ekthesis* (cf. 951).

trast, for instance, to the Gortyn code in Krete, according to which the woman could decide, independently of the man, whether to raise the child or expose it.[70] But the scene is Athens, not Gortyn. And in Delphi it is again Kreousa's part to recognize her son. It is true that, according to Apollo's plan, this episode was to take place later on, once Ion had returned to the hearth of the Erekhtheidai, or rather—and the text is explicit—*the hearth of his mother* (*mētros . . . domous*, 71–72). In other words, the recognition to come was meant to reverse the normal paternal and maternal positions connected with the mythical institution of foster-age and would have cast Kreousa in the same role toward her son as that, for example, of Aigeus in relation to Theseus upon the latter's arrival in Athens. But although she upset Apollo's plan, Kreousa still plays the same role in Delphi, since, by virtue of the basket with its birth tokens (*gnōrismata*), Athens is symbolically represented in Delphi. In addition, when Kreousa extends her arms toward the newly discovered Ion, the gesture represents to the child all the maternal protection of which he had been deprived, as well as the same procedure of recognition and accept-ance that is played out in the family ritual of the Amphidromia.[71] Like Athena in respect of Erikhthonios, Kreousa—somewhat late in the day—offers her adolescent son both identity and security.[72] The story of Ion draws to a close; his destiny is about to begin along with that of Ath-ens. Kreousa's task, it turns out, was nothing less than to activate the destiny of the *polis*.

HOW TO ENSURE THE REPRODUCTION OF AUTOCHTHONOUS BEINGS

It is not easy to be born Athenian, it would seem, unless one emerges from the earth at the proper time.

Ion, to be sure, is the son of a god. Everything might have gone well for him, as all the divine births mentioned in this tragedy are character-ized as unproblematical.[73] But Ion is also the son of Kreousa, and when it comes to the consequences of a union between a god and a woman, mor-tals and gods do not seem to share the same criteria.[74] Mortal birth/di-

---

[70] Gortyn Law, col. 3, 44–49, cited in the edition of R. F. Willetts, *The Law Code of Gor-tyn* (Berlin, 1967), 20

[71] Ion deprived of maternal *trophē*: 319, 1375–77. *Amphidromia*: the ritual in which the child is carried around the hearth in a man's arms, those of the father or his surrogate.

[72] On the significance of a mother's arms, see N. Daladier, "Les Meres," 235. "Arms" is a repeated motif in the play, including those of Athena, Kreousa's mother, Hermes, the Py-thia, and Ion himself both as a baby and now. "Arms" can also be ambivalent, referring to violence and vengeance. Space does not permit a full citation of these references.

[73] The birth of Hermes (1–4), Apollo (919–22), and Athena (452–57). On these births as counterpoints to that of Ion, see Immerwahr, "Athēnaikes eikones," 283.

[74] The chorus contrasts the mortal condition (472) with the birth of Athena (452–57),

vine birth: the opposition between the two is mentioned more than once in this play, although not in an essentially Athenian context, and there is no reference to the family story of Erikhthonios which might, quite legitimately, have been expected to appear in the context of the divine births mentioned in the *Ion*.[75] The tragic tension in the play lies elsewhere, in the distinction between birth from the earth and birth from human beings. When Ion, meeting Xouthos who has come to consult the oracle, questions him about his purpose: "Is it about your country's crops—or about children" (303), he is not yet aware that this is the precise focus of Kreousa's entire drama. What should in principle be kept separate—the fecundity of the soil and sexual reproduction—has been confused right from the start in Athens since, in the idiom of autochthony, *karpon* (fruit of the earth) is quite naturally considered synonymous with *gēgenes* (cf. Eur., *Phoin.* 937).

Where Greek myths of origin are concerned, one general rule that obtains is the difficulty involved in linking the beginning to what follows, and in operating a "passage" between a primordial birth and sexual reproduction. An instructive case in point is the myth of Deukalion and Pyrrha, where the presence of a mortal couple does not suffice to ensure the continuation of the human race since this man and woman, saved from the flood, still have to repropagate their kind by casting stones upon the earth.[76] In mythical thought it is not sexual reproduction that is considered the true point of origin. But the problem is particularly acute when it comes to ensuring a lineage to an autochthonous being. The list of children of the earth afflicted with *apaidia* (barrenness) is a long one: Giants fixed within the limits of a single age class with no female companions, no descendants; Theban Spartoi (Sown Men) whose lineage is fraught with problems; primordial autochthonous beings such as Kranaos or Kekrops, who vanished without having founded a new generation.[77] It seems logical to suppose that the *apaidia* of Kreousa, the

---

later citing as a self-evident truth the misery of a child born from a god and a mortal woman (506–9). Kreousa's confinement, so difficult and terrible to her, is deemed painless (*anosos*) to Athena.

[75] For Erikhthonios as autochthonous *and* the son of two gods, see Nicole Loraux, "Autochtonie: Une topique athénienne," in *Enfants*, 35–73 (57), and "Le Nom athénien," in *Enfants*, 119–53 (133).

[76] Although they constitute a human couple, they do not unite as a pair (cf. Pindar, *Olympian* 9.65ff.): a man, a woman, and some stones so that males can be born from his and females from hers. Only subsequently, as in the case of Xouthos and Kreousa, is the couple able to procreate together. Cf. Nicole Loraux, "Naître enfin mortels," in *Dictionnaire des mythologies*, ed. Y. Bonnefoy (Paris, 1981).

[77] On the Giants, Kranaos, and Kekrops, see F. Vian, *La guerre des Géants* (Paris, 1952), 255, 280, and on the Spartoi, F. Vian, *Les origines de Thèbes: Cadmos et les Spartes* (Paris, 1963), 164. More generally, see F. Jacoby, notes on the commentary to frag. 107 of Philo-

descendant of Erikhthonios, is simply a displacement of the childlessness that threatens any autochthonous being.[78]

In the case of the Erekhtheidai, the problem is further compounded by the superabundance of daughters (of Kekrops, of Erekhtheus), but no male descendant to ensure continuity. Eventually it all gets sorted out and the series of false starts which the mythographers record about the origins of Athens (Kekrops, Kranaos, Amphiktyon) is ultimately resolved with the birth of Erikhthonios, the only one destined to found a lineage.[79] The mythographers' solution, however, is a facile one, which tragedy does not accept. Instead, tragedy locates the problem precisely at the point where the mythic tradition had thought it solved: that is, in the descendance of the son of Erikhthonios. Everything seemed to be going well in the link between the autochthonous child, Erikhthonios, and the adult king Erekhtheus, even though Euripides does not tell us how.[80] Next, however, the wife of Erekhtheus gave her husband only daughters, the ones he offered as sacrifices, and Kreousa: Kreousa, the granddaughter of an autochthonous being, the paradoxical bearer of masculine legitimacy, on whom it devolves to perpetuate the chain of generations that with her has come to a standstill;[81] Kreousa, who must live through the difficulties inherent in the status of women in any noble household. This difficulty is exacerbated further in an autochthonous *oikos*, even to the point of contradiction: she is a woman and yet (or rather, by virtue of that very fact) she occupies the most sensitive spot in the system.

Let us summarize the story from the beginning. As a virgin goddess, Athena was able to fulfill all the parental roles with regard to Erikhthonios without ever having conceived him. As Erikhthonios passes from the earth into the hands of Athena and thence into the mystical basket, the whole life of the autochthonous child seems concentrated in the

---

khoros (*FGrHist* 328 frag. 107), and J. J. Peradotto, "Oedipus and Erichthonius: Some Observations on Paradigmatic and Syntagmatic Order," *Arethusa* 10 (1977): 85–101 (92).

[78] The theme of *apaidia*, particularly of Kreousa: 304, 306, 488, 513,619, 620, 680, 824, 840, 865, 950, 1302, 1463. *Ateknia* (its synonym): 65, 305, 608, 658–59, 789–90, 817, 1302, 1463.

[79] On Erikhthonios as the founder of the dynasty, see Vian, *Géants*, 254, commenting on Isokrates, *Panathenaikos* 126. On Apollodoros' account, see Peradotto, "Oedipus," 92–95, and his further remarks on the progressive increase in reproduction after Erikhthonios.

[80] Erikhthonios is the *father* of Erekhtheus (267): Wilamowitz-Moellendorff, *Euripides' Ion, ad loc.*, F. Brommer, "Attische Könige," *Mélanges E. Langlotz* (Bonn, 1957), 152–64 (153); *contra*: Owen, *Euripides' Ion, ad loc.*, supposes that Erekhtheus (Ion's grandfather) is the autochthon. But the essential point is that in the play, Erikhthonios is always presented as a child, Erekhtheus as an adult with a wife. In any case, the transition from father to son remains obscure.

[81] Jacoby considers the giving of a daughter to an autochthon to be a convenient device for resolving the problem of his reproduction (*FGrHist* 328 frag. 105 [Philokhoros]). This is not the case in tragedy: Kreousa is anything but a convenience.

moments of his birth. He is followed, however, by Erekhtheus, but Erekhtheus himself returns to the earth at his death, and the autochthonous line comes to a pause with Kreousa. Admittedly, this *parthenos*, unlike the goddess Athena, has conceived a child (cf. 270 and 503–4); but unlike Erikhthonios, Kreousa's child passes from her maternal hands into the hollow of a rock: that is, into the earth, the place of return for autochthons, there to meet his death in Hades.[82] In the end, however, everything will return to order; the son refound will become a man (*anēr*) and, in turn, will procreate children of his own. Filiation will then at last be masculine, and the woman will return to the shadows.[83]

Meanwhile, the tragedy begins at the point when everything depends on Kreousa. By simultaneously assuming the roles of both father and mother, the daughter of Erektheus even seems to be postponing the inevitable moment when birth will at last be from two rather than from one.

A FATHER, A MOTHER, A FATHER AND A MOTHER

Yet before all the various elements in the drama have come together, everything in Ion's words, and in Kreousa's too, had seemed to reflect a simple fact: one is born from two; it takes two to produce offspring.[84] As he oscillates, however, between rival filiations, Ion finds himself always to be born elsewhere[85] and in an uneasy tension between his identities as father's and mother's son, as though he could only ever be one or the other, a strange alternative which the civic institutions attempt to coordinate.[86] As for Kreousa, for whom the "betrayal" of Xouthos duplicates that of Apollo, she seems to be destined to sterile repetition, endlessly fated to find confirmation of the fact that any union between herself and the masculine principle—whether embodied in a god or man—will be characterized by disjunction. She did, certainly, conceive a

[82] By dying, all autochthons are reintegrated into their place of origin (cf. Plato, *Menexenos* 237c1–3 and *IG* II/III² 7151). Everything, of course, depends upon the conditions in which that return takes place. Erekhtheus is "hidden," swallowed up (281) like the various races in Hesiod and the Theban Spartoi who spring forth only to disappear again (Eur., *Phoin.* 670–73).

[83] See 1576 and 1582: *paides genomenoi.* No mention is made of a wife either for Ion or for his sons or for their descendants.

[84] Ion: 541–42 (one is born from the earth or born from two), 560, 561–63, 672. Essentially what Ion learns from the recognition scene with Xouthos is that he is going to find his mother again; the movement is analogous but reversed at 1468–69. Kreousa: 304, 406, 697–98, 748–49 (in relation to Xouthos); 904, 916 (in relation to Apollo).

[85] Cf. 1471 (*allothen gegonas allothen*), a symbolic expression of Ion's status. Athena will eventually proclaim Ion's double descent (1560, 1568), but in the end all that remains is his Erekhtheid ancestry (1573).

[86] See Ruck, "Sacred Names," 242, 252. From the beginning, Hermes both associates and dissociates Ion's two parents (49–51).

son by Apollo, but having abandoned him to his death in an attempt to force the god to claim the child as his own, she finds herself in effect childless (*apais*); and before the final reversal and the rhetoric of Athena compel her to reassess her relationship to the god, in her joy at the reunion with Ion, she appropriates the boy for herself, thereby reducing him to the sole status of his mother's son.[87] She had been hoping to produce descendants for herself together with Xouthos, or in her own words, that a "mixing of seeds" should take place (406). But the terms of Xouthos' reply to her, "neither you nor I shall return without a child" (408–9), suggest only disjunction. The fact indeed is that Kreousa's husband is ready to receive a son, any son, without concerning himself over the identity of the mother or being especially bothered if she is not the daughter of Erekhtheus. So the chorus certainly has some justification for reproaching him "for seeking for himself alone a posterity that he will not share" with Kreousa (1101–3).[88] Eventually there will be a fruitful union between Kreousa and Xouthos, a *koinon genos*, but this will happen outside the temporal frame of the tragedy, in a future which is referred to as a timeless present (1589).

Could it be that sexual union between males and the race of women is not necessarily aligned with a sharing in their common descendants? Could the parental couple be a fiction, a civic way of masking the inevitable disjunction between paternal and maternal roles? To judge by the emphasis on this dissociation in the play, one might well believe that this is the lesson to be learned from the *Ion*, for all the characters attest to it— in their life stories as well as in their respective filiations.

This is certainly true in the case of Kreousa, the daughter of Erekhtheus but also of an anonymous mother about whom all we learn is that she is descended from the river Kephisos, who took on the form of a bull (1261).[89] Kreousa is defined in relation now to her father who gives her an identity, now to her mother whom she unsuccessfully calls to her aid at the moment of her rape.[90] There may be some separation of parental roles between a father whom she fears and a mother who protects her, but at times these functions are interchanged. She abandoned her child "without her father's knowledge," if we are to believe Hermes' account

[87] Ion considered as the son of Apollo by the god himself (35, 47–48, 78); by Kreousa (386, 958, 965), who accuses the latter of having sole enjoyment of what belongs to them both (358, 904), without really believing Ion to be alive. Ion as son of Kreousa (1399, 1409, 1411, 1439, 1451, 1453–54, 1601). The only truly intimate relationship in the play is that between Kreousa and Ion (1462).

[88] See also 567–68, 678–80, 771–75, where the chorus recognizes the disjunction, and 841–42.

[89] She is named Praxithea in Euripides, *Erekhtheus*, and Lykourgos, *Against Leokrates* 98.

[90] Daughter of Erekhtheus: 10, 260, 433, 546, 727, 733–34, 1106; the protective mother (280), upon whose aid she calls (893).

or even the fiction she invents to tell her story to Ion under another's name (14, 340). But when she speaks for herself, she twice justifies her action by reason of the fear her mother inspired in her (898, 1489). The father *or* the mother: to arrive at the final version of the facts which postulates the sexual union of the parental couple (1596), the whole play must first unfold in order to reconcile the two origins of Ion, and through Athena to promise to Kreousa and Xouthos a common line of descent.

But quite apart from Kreousa, all the other characters in the drama are affected by this disjunction, whether they actually appear onstage or are simply mentioned. Thus the young guardians of Erikhthonios are called now the daughters of Aglauros (mother) (23, 496), now the daughters of Kekrops (father) (272, 1163). Apollo, constantly referred to as Leto's child, is contrasted to Athena as the son of a mother to the daughter of a father.[91] But Athena herself is above all contraposed to the daughter of a mother, Artemis Latogenes (465), and also, although more covertly, to Persephone, where she is the Parthenos and the other the Kore.[92] Father *or* mother. . . .

The last word, we suggested earlier, goes to double filiation: the *koinon genos* (common descent of Kreousa and Xouthos), the reunion between Kreousa's and Apollo's kin, and Ion's act of faith: "I believe myself Apollo's and Kreousa's son." But one point remains unclear. What did Athena mean when she promised Ion four sons, all produced from "one stock [*rhizē mia*]" (1576)? Did she mean that they would have the same father and the same mother? That by combining two into one, Ion's *oikos* would finally overcome the irreducible duality of the sexes? This is, no doubt, a perfectly plausible reading; all the same, it is impossible to overlook the fact that women have now disappeared from Athena's discourse, not only as bearers of legitimacy but also as those who reproduce. So another hypothesis is in order. What if an opposition is being established between the descendants of Kreousa and Xouthos—"common" to them both but of mixed blood—and the indivisible unity of autochthonous stock, an opposition, as it were, between the multiple and the one? For the first, Doros and Akhaios will gain their fame in Greece at large, while Ion and his sons will become the eponymous heroes of the "Ionian" tribes and their descendants. This is a kind of transposition of the timeless contrast so dear to imperialist ideology, which

---

[91] Apollo, son of Leto: 21, 127, 143, 188–89, 410 (Kreousa's prayer to Leto), 681, 885, 908. Once Kreousa refers to Zeus' union with Leto—at the end of her monody—the better to blame Apollo, guilty of not having saved their common child (920–22). Only when her mating with the god is finally confirmed is Apollo at last described as the son of Zeus and Leto (1619). Athena, the daughter of Zeus: 21, 453–54 (her birth), 991, 1606.

[92] At 1085–86 there is mention too of Kore and her mother (Demeter).

the funeral orations (*epitaphioi*) emphasize between the autochthonous Athenians and all the rest—the descendants of Pelops, Kadmos, Aigyptos, and Danaos—the whole diverse cohort that is listed in the *Menexenos* (245d1–6). One stock, the Athenian one: proof enough, if proof were needed, that the victory of double filiation must also be accommodated to the triumph of autochthony and the official discourse related to it. This discourse can only set Athenian oneness in opposition to the broad diversity of the rest of Greece, providing it conceals every sign of deviation at the heart of the city—beginning with the deviation introduced by women.

Athenian identity and double filiation: one last time, the play dissociates that which the Periklean law on citizenship definitively unites. Clearly, Athenian birth is not to be taken for granted once tragedy gets hold of it. For the price that must be paid for tragedy is ambiguity.

THE TRAGIC AKROPOLIS

It is on the Akropolis that Erikhthonios is born, Erekhtheus dies, the daughters of Kekrops meet their end, and Kreousa suffers. In the *Ion*, the topography of the Akropolis maps out the tribulations of the entire autochthonous stock.[93] The ambivalence of the Akropolis expresses the disquieting ambivalence of autochthony itself.

THE DARK FACE OF AUTOCHTHONY

To the north of the Akropolis, the High Rocks receive Apollo *Hypoakraios* who "honors them with Pythian flashes of lightning" (285),[94] and also the god Pan, whose flute accompanies the nocturnal dances of the trio of Aglaurides (492–500).[95] Even before they were told, the women of the chorus knew that it was within the cave of the son of Hermes that "a virgin in misery bore a child to Phoibos" (503–6). Kreousa's story is thus situated in a complex religious space, which, close by and even in the precinct of the palace of Erekhtheus,[96] accommodates both the lu-

[93] Cf. Immerwahr, "Athēnaikes eikones," 282.

[94] The High Rocks are repeatedly mentioned: 11–12, 283–85, 492–94, 936–37. On Apollo Hypoakraios and the High Rocks, see O. Broneer, "Notes on Three Athenian Cult Places," *Archaiologike Ephemeris* (1960): 54–57 (58–59), J. Bousquet, "Delphes et les Aglaurides d'Athènes," *BCH* 88 (1964): 655–75 (663–64), and J. Travlos, *Pictorial Dictionary of Ancient Athens* (New York, 1971), 91–93.

[95] On Pan's cave, see Pausanias 1.28.4, and also Travlos, *Pictorial Dictionary*, 417–19, and Philippe Borgeaud, *Recherches sur le dieu Pan* (Geneva, 1979), 222–25. On Pan causing young girls to dance in the evening, see Pindar, *Pyth.* 3.76, and the *Homeric Hymn to Pan*, 14–26.

[96] Immerwahr, "Athēnaikes eikones," 281, notes that the High Rocks can only be reached through the side gate of the Akropolis, close to the Erekhtheion and the house of

minous Apollo and the nocturnal Pan: the divine seducer *and* the denizen of inaccessible peaks and rocky paths (*Homeric Hymn* 19.6–7), the god who brings wildness into the very heart of the *polis* (cf. 932–33, 1494).

This dangerous proximity is certainly repeatedly blamed by the daughter of Erekhtheus who, despite Hermes' claim that she gave birth "inside the palace," herself declares it to have taken place, as the chorus confirms, within the very cave where she was united with the god (cf. 16 and 948). Is this simply an attempt to emphasize the difference between the palace and the cave, to distinguish the *oikos* from the sunless cavern which, its darkness notwithstanding, was where the god of light seduced her? Or does it reflect her consciousness of the fact that the catastrophe which has brought her life to a standstill has also swallowed up the palace of the Erekhtheidai inside that dark cave where she exposed her newborn child? The old tutor's reaction to Kreousa's confession certainly suggests that this displacement from the palace to the cave should be read as the mark of an ominous confusion whereby the house of Erekhtheus has been entirely engulfed by the nocturnal shadows of the cave. Before the *oikos* can at last be restored to its former autonomy, light will have to compete with darkness, a struggle in which Athens will find relief in Delphi. The tent sheltered from the sun's rays set up by Ion, where death waits for him a second time,[97] will have to replace the cave; the mother will have to identify her child. When the palace can be distinguished from the cave, the place in which sexuality, birth, and death were inextricably intermingled, it will recover its own identity, and the text will express the reacquisition of hearth and home, the conquest of night, and the restoration of the dwelling place of the autochthonous line in the sight of the sun's rays (1463–67). As for the cave, even though it is now associated with Phoibos alone, it loses none of its sinister associations: the singing nightingale who lives close to the cave and whose voice has etched itself on Kreousa's memory does not simply add the relief of a "musical note" to the account of the rape, as Apollo's unconditional supporters would have it.[98] Throughout the entire Greek tradition, the song

the Arrhephoroi. He argues that Kreousa constantly tries to associate the High Rocks only with the autochthonous event, whereas the chorus (501–2) and the old man (937) associate them with Pan, and Ion (285) with Apollo.

[97] Ion's tent protected from the sun (1134–35, 1142) is linked with the temple of Apollo (1224–25) but also with Pan's cave, since the feast that is to take place there is a *thoinē*, as the feast of the birds which were to devour Ion almost turned out to be: cf. 892, 1140, 1205 (the tent) with 504, 903, 1495 (the feast of the birds); occurrences of *dais* (feast): cf. 652, 807, 852, 1131, 1168 (tent) with 505 (feasting of wild birds). On this type of tent (*skēnē*), see L. Robert, *Hellenica*, vol. 10 (Paris, 1955), 287.

[98] Burnett, "Resistance," 91, reads 1482 this way and in *Ion by Euripides* (Englewood Cliffs, N.J., 1970), ad loc., she regards it as "a romantic and charming epithet, indicating Kreousa's change of attitude toward the event."

of the nightingale expresses the sorrow of a mother who has slain her child. That was very nearly Kreousa's own fate, as she recognizes a few lines further on (1494–95). The palace and its hearth, where Ion is to live and reign, is henceforth separated from the cave, which remains to the end a place of sexual violence and death.

Death nearly occurs again in Delphi by Kreousa's hand and is only narrowly averted, although its pall of terror extends over the entire play. Panic-stricken, terrorized and terrifying, wounded and deadly—this is how Kreousa appears once she has abandoned all hope and decides in her feelings of betrayal from all sides to resort to the Gorgon's poison to destroy Ion.[99] This talisman, like Kreousa, can bestow death as well as life; it comes to her, we should note, from her ancestor Erikhthonios and she uses it to defend the rights of the Erektheidai (1000–19, 1048–60). In this play, and only here, the Gorgon is herself a daughter of Earth. Inasmuch as Kreousa is the bearer of the poison of the Gorgon, this chthonic monster, which she has inherited from Erikhthonios, whose own relationship to snakes remains decidedly unclear,[100] how could Kreousa herself avoid the tragic ambivalence of autochthony? Before the horrified eyes of Ion, for instance, she is transformed for a moment into Gorgon and viper. In so doing, she obscures the political and civilized face of autochthony and draws the Erekhtheidai away with her to join the fearsome cohort of the Gēgeneis, whose defeat at the hands of the Olympian gods the play continues to celebrate.[101]

There is therefore a dark side to autochthony in the *Ion*, which involves Kreousa also, whose barrenness perhaps now assumes a new dimension. The daughter of Erekhtheus is not *apais* only because she has exposed Ion, thereby depriving her *oikos* of any chance of survival, but also because, trapped in a night of terror, she comes to resemble a creature of Night. We must, however, look beyond these nocturnal aspects; not to do so would be to forget that, just as there is a political as well as a chthonic aspect to the image of autochthony, and a dark as well as a light, Kreousa too is a blend of both, involved in both life and death. Kreousa,

99 On Kreousa and fear, see 898 and 1497–98, and also probably 1489; Kreousa as a terrifying and Gorgon-like figure, see 1251–65.

100 On the Gorgon, see D. J. Mastronarde, "Iconography and Imagery in Euripides' *Ion*, *CSCA* 8 (1975): 163–76, n. 33, and more generally, T. Karagiorga, *Gorgeia Kephale* (Athens, 1970), 44, 78–80. Erikhthonios and the snakes: Erikhthonios is guarded by two snakes (23), but sometimes he is represented as a snake himself. See Pausanias, 1.24.7 and the iconography of the vases studied by M. Schmidt, "Die Entdeckung des Erichthonios," *Athenische Mitteilungen* 83 (1968): 200–212 and pl. 73–76.

101 We should note, however, that Ion connects Kreousa as Gorgon and viper to the maternal line (1261–65). The War of the Giants: 205–19, 987–98, 1528–29. Many have noted the two-sidedness of autochthony: e.g., Wolff, "Design," 182, Immerwahr, "Athēnaikes eikones," 286, Mastronarde, "Iconography," 164–65, and Whitman, *Euripides*, 97–99.

the barren wife, is also the *parthenos*, who has brought forth a child. Kreousa, the viper, is also the king's daughter whose nurturing palace is identified with the temple of Athena (235–36). The goddess too is divided: she attacks the savage offspring of the earth (the Giants) but protects the autochthonous royal stock of Athens. It is therefore significant that Kreousa is so closely linked with the virgin of the Akropolis, the slayer of the Gorgon (1478), and the Kourotrophos (or nurse) to Erikhthonios. This brings us to another image of Kreousa: the *parthenos*.

KREOUSA THE PARTHENOS

As the daughter of Erekhtheus bound her virgin's accoutrements to the child she was abandoning (25), she no doubt believed she was marking an irreversible rupture between the sweetness of her former existence and her present condition of suffering. Yet it is not so certain that Kreousa really passed altogether from one state to the other, that she was indeed leaving behind her status as *parthenos*, both her destiny and the proof of her innocence: it is probably this, in the form of *apaidia*, that still weighs so heavily upon her.[102] When, before breaking her silence, Kreousa places herself under the protection of Tritonian Athena, the one who presides over the trials of virginity, is this not a declaration that she is a virgin still, intact despite violation, even despite marriage?

Kreousa is a *parthenos*, a *korē* (maiden), and the *Ion* alludes to many similar figures with whom the daughter of Erekhtheus is closely associated. As a young girl, she wove what, before serving as swadding clothes for Ion, was designed to be a *peplos* or aegis.[103] The mention of the *peplos* discreetly associates her with the young Arrhephoroi of the Akropolis cult, and weaving, surrounded throughout the play with mythical sayings and songs, becomes one of Kreousa's own attributes.[104] The very imperfection of her youthful efforts (1417–19; cf. 1490–91) testifies to her failure: the failure of an Arrhephoros who did not complete her task

---

[102] Cf. Calame, *Les choeurs*, 1:283. The illegitimate nature of the union with Apollo preserves Kreousa's "virginity," since *parthenos* denotes a social status (unmarried girl), not virginity in the physical sense. Cf. Calame, *Les choeurs*, 65 and, on the violation of a virgin, 345 n.336. The *parthenos* who gives birth to a child is a recurrent theme ever since Homer: cf. G. Klingenschmitt, "Griechisch *parthénos*," in *Mélanges H. Güntert*, ed. Manfred Mayrhofer et al. (Innsbruck, 1974), 273–78, and Giulia Sissa, *Le corps virginal* (Paris, 1987).

[103] See 1417–19 (weaving and the young girl), 1421 peplos), 1423 (aegis), 1424–25 (*partheneuma*), and 1489–91 (the virginal swaddling bands and the movement of Kreousa's shuttle.

[104] *Mythos* and weaving: 196–97, 506–07, 747–48. The women are Kreousa's attendants because they look after her loom. Weaving as the activity of a young girl: *Homeric Hymn to Aphrodite*, 14–15, Euripides' *Elektra*, 307, 539–40, *Troades*, 199–200, *Iphigeneia among the Taurians*, 222–24 (weaving and the *peplos* of Athena); weaving a veil as a prenuptial task for a young girl: Kallimakhos frag. 66 Pfeiffer.

for Athena, perhaps, but also, indissociably, the failure of Apollo's victim to move on from the status of *parthenos* and enter into marriage.[105] Kreousa is surrounded by a host of other *parthenoi*, driven to suicide by the wrath of Athena (the Aglaurides or Kekropides), or Athens' sacrificial victims (the Erekhtheides). It is dangerous to be a young girl on the Akropolis, for Athena can be a terrible mistress for those who serve her.

All these kings' daughters of different generations have much in common in Athenian cult and myth. For instance, there is a striking affinity between Kreousa, who denied her child his *trophē*, and the imprudent *kourotrophoi* (i.e., the Kekropides), who opened the basket entrusted to them by the goddess, extending even to the resemblance between the precipitous death of the Kekropides which "bloodied the High Rocks" (274) and the threat to Erekhtheus' daughter in Delphi that she be hurled down from the summit of Parnassos (1222, 1266–67). But the Kekropides are only intermediaries between Kreousa and Athena,[106] and to this relationship we now turn.

Athens belongs to Athena, Athens belongs to Kreousa:[107] the two are linked through the civic space of Athens, condensed into its symbolic center—the Akropolis—which both occupy (235–37, 1479–80, 1295–97). Second, the daughter of Erekhtheus, bearer of the aegis (1421–23) and using Athena's magic instruments (*organon*, 1430), closely imitates the daughter of Zeus, although in reverse: overcome by Phoibos in their erotic *agon* (939), on the one hand, and on the other, posing a threat to the life of the child who is a stand-in for Erikhthonios. More accurately we might say that, having failed to duplicate Athena's actions, she imitates Pallas instead.

The goddess in the *Ion* has two sides: between Athena, the benevolent protectress of the autochthonous child (and of the city) and Pallas, the Giant-slayer, sovereign and eponymous deity of Athens,[108] Kreousa chooses Pallas. Like the goddess who is both magician and warrior in the

[105] Through the work of the shuttle, the *peplos* turned into swaddling bands (1491) but, in the context of marriage, the fabric is *ou teleion*, incomplete or, rather, imperfect. As deities of marriage, Zeus and Hera have the epithets of Teleios and Teleia.

[106] Aglauros was an *epiklēsis* (epithet) of the goddess (Harpokration and *Suda*, s.v.) or the name of a priestess of Athena (Philokhoros, *FGrHist* 328 frag. 106). See R. Merkelbach, "Aglauros: Die Religion der Epheben," *ZPE* 9 (1972): 277–83 (281).

[107] Athens and Athena: 8–9, 30, 1297, 1480, 1555–56, 1574, 1617: Athens and Kreousa: 25 and 1616 (Athens as *oikos*).

[108] Athena: fundamentally associated with Erikhthonios (269, 1030, 1428), called to the aid of patrilinear filiation (454), the protectress of Athens (1454). Pallas: the namegiver (8–10, 1555–56) and receiving her name (210–211) and that of the aegis (987–88) in the war against the Giants, the goddess of the Akropolis (12, 235–36, 497–98), the slayer of the Giants and the Gorgon (211, 991, 996, 1478), the donor of the magic talisman to Erikhthonios (1001).

Gigantomakhy,[109] Kreousa intends to use cunning and force (*dolia kai drastēria*, 985), using the *pharmakon* (the drug) of death—the blood which had gushed from the slit throat of the chthonic Gorgon.[110]

But only the goddess can control the evil power of the vanquished Gorgon; only she can wear the Gorgon's flayed skin without becoming identified with the chthonic monster. Kreousa wrapped her child in the imitation of an aegis which she herself had worn (to protect him? or to kill him?) and kept for herself the venom which, in Ion's eyes, transforms her into the Gorgon. There are two drops of Gorgon blood in the vial Kreousa wears on her wrist—one positive, one negative—but Athena's mastery over the ambivalent Gorgon magic is not transferred to Kreousa, who resorts only to its baneful aspect, and this to her (and her child's) peril.

The Parthenos cannot be imitated with impunity: Kreousa has courted catastrophe. She has, in fact, made use of the Gorgon as that other goddess, Persephone, does in the depths of the underworld (*Odyssey* 11.633–35)—and in the service of death. For all that Kreousa's destiny is dominated by her intricate imitation of Athena, it also converges with the figure of Persephone. Kreousa is in fact positioned between Athena and Persephone: between the father's daughter and the mother's, between the Parthenos who eluded Hephaistos' attempts upon her and the Kore maiden whom Hades carried off amid the flowers.

KREOUSA AND KORE

Abduction—in other words, rape. Persephone was gathering flowers when, despite all her cries of protest, Hades took her off. Kreousa was gathering flowers when Apollo came and seized her against her will.[111] Gathering flowers is a dangerous activity for a virgin whose own flower has yet to be plucked, and there is a place for Kreousa's crocuses in Kore's bouquet.[112] True, the rocky Akropolis little resembles the plain of Nysa or the plateaus of Enna, where tradition locates the abduction of the Kore. Yet long before the account of the rape, the dancing steps of the daughters of Aglauros had traced out a grassy platform on the rock:

[109] In the Gigantomakhy the magic power of the aegis is associated with traditional military weapons: see F. Vian, "La fonction guerrière dans la mythologie grecque," in *Problèmes de la guerre en Grèce ancienne*, ed. J.-P. Vernant (Paris and The Hague, 1968), 53–68 (57).

[110] In the end Kreousa resorts only to cunning as her means of force (cf. 1185: *pharmakon drastērion*, denoting the cup of poison).

[111] Cf. *Homeric Hymn to Demeter*, 19, 30, 20, and *Ion*, 437, 941, 895.

[112] On the gathering of flowers, see, e.g., G. Piccaluga, "Ta Pherephattes Anthologia," *Maia* 18 (1966): 232–53; A. Motte, *Prairies et jardins dans la Grèce antique* (Brussels, 1973), 38–47. The crocus: cf. 889 and *Homeric Hymn to Demeter* 6 and 425 (where the fatal narcissus is described as being like a crocus).

the rock is Athenian, the meadow evokes the meadow (*leimōn*) of Persephone.[113] Kreousa and Persephone: the white-armed daughter of Demeter and the daughter of Erekhtheus whom the ravisher god seized by her white wrist (cf. 891 and Hesiod, *Theogony* 913). To emphasize the close link between them, all that is needed is one displaced sign: Persephone, the Mother's daughter, cried out to her mother at the last (after her first appeal to Zeus) and Kreousa too called upon hers for help.[114]

Persephone, like Athena, is double, both a tender young girl and a terrifying power of death, and both aspects are invoked in the play. As the chorus of Kreousa's servants evokes the mysteries of Eleusis, singing of the brilliance of Kore with her golden diadem (1085), only one strophe earlier, they had summoned the daughter of Demeter in the nocturnal form of Hekate Enodia (1048–49), the mistress of poison and magic.

Like Demeter's daughter, Kreousa is both *korē* and *despoina* (mistress),[115] and like her, she shows traits of Enodia. Robbed of her adolescent innocence and plunged into a night of terror, Kreousa imitates the dark side of Persephone, just as she has imitated the sinister side of Athena. She sends the poison to Xouthos' son, not knowing he is also the child whom she exposed in Pan's cave when, far from the torchlight and dances of Kore at Eleusis (cf. 1474 and 1075–76, 1080, 1084), she gave him birth, close to the rock of the nightingale, the bird whose song tells of a child's death. The *aēdonios petra* (the rock where the nightingale [*aēdōn*] sings) can also be read in a different etymology as the "joyless rock" (i.e., *aēdēs*), an allusion that refers us back to Eleusis, where Demeter, overcome with grief, sat down near the well of Kallikhoros, upon another "joyless rock" (*Agelastos Petra*).[116] Tragic overdetermination is at work in the figure of Kreousa—barren like Persephone, a goddess of the Underworld, yet also, like Demeter, a mother in search of a lost child.

That lost child is an abandoned child who almost did find himself underground in the chthonic dwelling place of Persephone (1441–42). And in this light, Kreousa's intent—to commit Ion to death so as to open the way to recognition by his father (965)—assumes a fuller meaning and al-

[113] At 496–97 the Kekropides are called Aglaurides after their mother. On the relation of Persephone's meadow to that of the Aglaurides, see Motte, *Prairies*, 196.

[114] *Homeric Hymn to Demeter*, 21, 27 (the cry to Zeus), 35 (the hope of seeing her mother again), 39 (the final cry, which her mother hears); *Ion*, 893. In Ovid, *Metamorphoses* 5.396, Proserpina cries out to her mother. See Burnett, *Catastrophe*, 121 n. 16, and La Rue, "Creusa's Monody," 132.

[115] Kreousa is *despoina* to her servants (695, 1103) and in the ode under discussion (1061–62), the term is situated between the naming of Enodia (1048) and the image of Kore at her mother's side (1085–86). Persephone as *despoina* in Arkadia: Pausanias, 8.37.9.

[116] On the Eleusinian rock, see Apollodoros, 1.5.1 and also Hesykhios, s.v., and schol. Aristophanes, *Knights* 785.

lows us to glimpse the figure of Hades behind that of Apollo. On the Akropolis, the golden-haired god took the place of Persephone's dark ravisher, and the god to whom she delivered Ion as a *tropheus* might well have turned out to be Hades rather than Apollo.[117] "In a deserted cave . . . [I] gave [you] over to death," she confesses later to her newly found son, but Athena subsequently declares that in reality it was Apollo who "would not let him die, but took on his rearing" (cf. 1495, 1600).

To commit Ion to Hades was to dispatch him at birth to a chthonic dwelling place *underground* (*kata gēs*), the reverse of Erikhthonios' emergence from the earth. Those underground depths—whether chasm (*khasma khthonos*) or Underworld—were to receive Kreousa's child, to be "hidden forever," like Erekhtheus (1441–42, 1496; 267, 281). The destiny of autochthons is often bound up in this interplay between Gē (Earth) and Hades. The earth produces them, the ground reclaims them. By calling a halt to the dangerous inclination of "the same" to be reabsorbed into "the same," Apollo not only saved his son from death, but, by dissociating birth from death, he at last opened up the human time of life to the Erekhtheid lineage.

TO BE BORN ATHENIAN: THE EARTH, THE BASKET, AND THE OMPHALOS

"Twisting the lid, I opened the wicker basket, so that the child could be seen": a single gesture, that of Hermes opening the *antipēx*, is all that is needed to bring Ion forth from the darkness of his hiding place and out into view (39–40). Another gesture, that of Ion opening up the basket with his mother's tokens (*symbola*), resolves the tragic action since, as a result, the affair is "open and laid bare"—or more precisely, "uncovered," "revealed" (1387, 1563). The gestures are symbolic of the child's destiny which is caught up in the tensions that obtain between seeing and hiding. Before Kreousa espies him as the happiest of sights (*phasma*), Ion, the child who was hidden, is viewed by Hermes, the Pythia, and Xouthos. He escapes from the concealed murder plot which repeats the circumstances of his secret birth and his subsequent exposure in the hiding place of death, and will soon look upon the divine visage of Athena.[118]

To see: to open up or uncover—the visual references recall the original action of opening the basket and the ambiguities it entails in the exposure to view. Hiding is equally ambiguous, and like the act of viewing, may

---

[117] Ion committed to death: 18, 27, 502–5, 903, 917, 932–33, 951, 1494–99, 1544. Apollo/Hades: 952–53 (Ion completes his education [*paideia*] with Hades), 1274–75 (*domoi* of Hades/*domos* of Apollo).

[118] The list of words referring to seeing and hiding is immense and cannot be cited here. The terms in question are *horaō* and its derivatives, *phainō* and its derivatives (including *phasma* [apparition], *phantazomai*, and *phōs* [light]); *kruptō* and *lanthanō* with their respective derivatives.

preserve life or destroy it—whether in the depths of the earth, in the hollow of a cave, or in a basket.

"A plaited hollow" (*plekton kytos*, 37), "a perfect circle" (*eutrokhos kyklos*, 19), the basket is not a neutral container. In Hermes' account, Ion, wrapped in his swaddling clothes, and in its hollow interior, is further enclosed in the hollowed rock of the Akropolis with its cave (19, 31). Plaiting is the act by which basket makers complete a full circle from *arkhē* to *arkhē*,[119] whose symbolic value makes it available as the place to lay a divine child—Erikhthonios or Adonis, for example—protected from sight, and useful for mystery cults. Like any *larnax* (chest), indeed more than any *larnax*, a round basket such as the *kistē* of the Arrhephoroi (who repeat the act of the Kekropides) tells of death and rebirth,[120] and ever since Bachofen, historians of religion have been pondering its symbolism as a chthonic womb.[121]

The Delphic setting underscores this interpretation of the *antipēx*. Ion's basket, containing the embroidery with the Gorgon's head, evokes another primordial womb: the Delphic *omphalos* (navel stone) which is described as "swathed in fillets [*stemmasi*] and flanked by Gorgons" (224),[122] and which is mentioned repeatedly in the course of the play; the Delphic *omphalos*, the world's navel, the earth's hearth (*hestia*).[123] The *Ion* establishes a complex set of exchanges between Delphi and Athens as a way of orchestrating the vital maneuver that brings Ion's basket from the Akropolis to the sanctuary of Apollo. Thus *domos*, *oikos*, and *melathra* (235, 738) refer to both the temple of the god and to the palace of Erekhtheus, and through the triennial festival which links the Akropolis with Parnassos, the High Rocks crowned with Pythian flashes of lightning inevitably evoke the Heights of Delphi (283–85, 550, 713, 1126). Upon the heights of Athens, however, as on the rocks of Delphi, the luminous Apollo shares these spaces with nocturnal figures—Pan (491) or Dionysos (550, 716, 1125; 1080), as well as the girls who perform their cultic

[119] Hippokrates, *On Regimen* 1.19. See also M. Detienne and J.-P. Vernant, *Cunning Intelligence in Greek Culture and Society* (Atlantic Highlands, N. J. 1978), 322 n. 105, and on the significance of plaiting, 44–46.

[120] Apollodoros calls the basket of Erikhthonios a *kistē* (3.14.6) and Pausanias a *kibōtos* (i.e., *larnax*) (1.18.2).

[121] J. J. Bachofen, *Das Mutterrecht* (Stuttgart, 1861), cited in the annotated translation of Eva Cantarella, *Il potere feminile: Storia e Teoria* (Milan, 1977), 78. C. Bérard, *Anodoi: Essai sur l'imagerie chthoniens* (Neuchàtel, 1974) 137, Motte, *Prairies*, 196, to name just a few references from the vast literature on the subject.

[122] The fillets (like the Gorgon) are common to the *omphalos* and the basket: 224, 1338, 1392, 1421.

[123] *Omphalos mesos*: 5–6, cf. 222–23; *gas mesomphalos hestia*, 461–62, and also 908–10. On the *omphalos* as a matrix and *hestia*, see M. Delcourt, *L'oracle de Delphes* (Paris, 1955), 138–40 and 144–46, and also J.-P. Vernant, "Hestia-Hermès," 148.

dances at night (497, 716, 1080–81). The most startling parallel of all is that which brings together two closed off interior areas, described as *mykhos* (inner recess, 229, 493) or *adyton* (innermost sanctuary, 662, 938): the Delphic temple, not accessible to all comers,[124] and Pan's cave which gave shelter to Kreousa's encounter with Apollo as well as to the basket of Ion. The circle closes up: the Delphic *omphalos* has received Ion, who can at last be born as an Athenian—not from the earth, like his model, Erikhthonios, but because he has come, metaphorically speaking, from death.

Hades has replaced Gē, and Hades in turn opens the way for Apollo to assume the role of father. The tragedy dramatizes as a story what is a religious and political practice in the city: following the autochthonous Erikhthonios, and Erekhtheus swallowed up by the earth, and after the problematical interregnum of a woman, Kreousa, the boy Ion must be born into a mortal's life with a beginning, a middle, and an end. In "reality," of course, one is born through sexual reproduction, not from the earth, from a mother and not from Gē.

A future opens up before Athens. Hades fades into the distance: Persephone, whose secret presence hovered behind the circumstances of Ion's first birth (and the second attempt on his life), is forgotten, as is Apollo, who delegates Athena to watch over the boy's return to the Akropolis. Guided by the Poliad goddess, Ion, son of Kreousa, comes home to the palace of the Erekhtheidai. The tragic play is over.

A Tragic Dramatization of Autochthony

As we emerge from our long foray into the multiple interferences between the myth and the city, the reader is probably somewhat relieved to reenter historical time at last. In the interplay between the near and the far, one is bound to lose one's way occasionally. The equivocal depths of echoing signifiers are confusing. In any sequential enumeration of the elements tragedy condenses into a network of significations, there is always the risk of failing to recognize the peculiar quality of tragic time, which is made not from succession but from simultaneity. Finally, it is sometimes easy to forget that only by virtue of a dramatic fiction is Kreousa identified as the first "female Athenian" and the task entrusted to a woman of taking up the challenge of that masculine claim to autochthony.

---

[124] Apollo's temple is strongly defined in spatial terms of inside and outside; some enter and leave (such as Xouthos); others, such as the chorus and Kreousa, never gain entry; Ion is said to live there but is forever found on the threshold; and the Pythia occasionally emerges from it.

What, after all, is a myth? Besides the extension of its narrative over a unified space, *mythos* means a tale: a story with its own time and rhythms, now slowed down, now speeded up. A story the Athenians told themselves about their own symbolic system, but which can on no account be reduced to that alone. A story which provided pleasure because one could recognize oneself in it and also, sometimes, because one discovered oneself in it as something, if not unknown, at least "other" than oneself.

All of which is not to suggest that, with tragedy, we at last have access to something like a "pure" myth, a figment only in the minds of interpreters. What was played out in the theater of Dionysos was, on the contrary, more like a family dispute between the city and its myths. The city retold the myth all over again, in a different way, so as to hear its own voice in a tale of long ago; but the malleability of myth is equalled only by its resistance, or vitality, and, over and above all the political variations on the theme of racial purity and the definition of a citizen, there looms the paradoxical figure of a virgin to whom the Athenians are supposed to owe everything: Kreousa, *parthenos* and mother to Ion, is a figure designed to mediate the unmediated origin of the city who is known as Athena.

Kreousa is not a heroine of comedy and must carry the weight of the myth of autochthony; if the tragedy has helped us to understand the myth, it is, conversely, important to use the myth to restore to its true tragic dimensions this text so often misunderstood, composed by the most misunderstood of the tragic poets. Tragedy is to be found not only where even the most obtuse of readers cannot fail to recognize it: even when set alongside the *Eumenides*,[125] the *Ion* fully deserves to be known as the tragic drama of Athens.

---

[125] The *Ion* is implicitly related to the *Eumenides*, another Delphic drama about Athens; the Erinyes and the Gorgon assume parallel roles as figures of feminine vengeance. Hermes plays the part of intermediary in both cases between Delphi and Athens, bringing Orestes to Athens and conversely, fetching from Athens the abandoned child who will come close to committing matricide. Both plays end with a promise of future prosperity for Athens. Both raise questions about patrilinear filiation, but Euripides' tragedy pushes to further extremes.

DAVID KONSTAN

An Anthropology of Euripides' *Kyklōps*

EURIPIDES' *Kyklōps* is the only complete surviving specimen of a Greek satyr-play. The story resembles in a reasonably close way the corresponding episode in the ninth book of Homer's *Odyssey*, except that in Euripides' version the kyklōps Polyphemos, at the time of Odysseus' landing in his territory, is master of Silenos and a band of satyrs who tend his flocks. This circumstance loosely reflects the tale of Dionysos' abduction by pirates, which is related in one of the Homeric hymns: the satyrs had put to sea in search of the god, and were blown ashore, much like Odysseus himself, at the Kyklōpes' land, which by the time of Euripides had come to be specified as the island of Sicily. A role for the satyrs, half-goat, half-man, was required by the genre of the satyr-play—if there were exceptions, they were few[1]—and their captivity in a remote and savage place seems to have been a common theme, especially in Euripides' contributions.[2] Homer's narrative thus looks like the perfect stock upon which to graft the motifs typical of the satyr-play, and critics have, with some notable exceptions, remained content to reveal the few places where structural changes in the narrative are demanded by the working in of the new material.[3] Apart from that, one need only remark upon differences of tone, for the satyr-drama was by nature playful, a mood that was primarily carried by the chorus and Silenos, no doubt,[4] but which left its mark as well on the treatment of the myth as a whole.

Note: The original version of this essay appeared in *Ramus* 10 (1981): 87–103, and it is reproduced here by permission of Aureal Publications. Permission to reprint this essay has been kindly granted by the editors of *Ramus*.

[1] Opinions differ. Victor Steffen admits the possibility that Euripides' *Busiris* did not have a chorus of satyrs, in "The Satyr-Dramas of Euripides," *Eos* 59 (1971): 215; Luigi Enrico Rossi inclines to think the satyrs were essential to the genre, "Il dramma satiresco attico: Forma, fortuna e funzione di un genere letterario antico," *Dialoghi di Archeologia* 6 (1972): 254 and n. 15; and Dana Sutton is categorical on the matter: "Its chorus is invariably composed of satyrs," "Father Silenus: Actor or Coryphaeus," *CQ* 24 (1974): 19.

[2] See, for example, Victor Steffen, "De fabularum satyricarum generibus," *Eos* 65 (1977): 191; Jacqueline Duchemin, *Le Cyclope d'Euripide* (Paris, 1945; hereafter, Duchemin), xv–xvii.

[3] The most important exception is Seaford, who in his commentary, *Euripides Cyclops* (Oxford, 1984; hereafter, Seaford), and in several articles has offered a subtle social reading of the play, somewhat along the lines of the present study. I shall record certain differences between Seaford's interpretation and my own as they come up.

[4] This is the view of Rossi, "Il dramme," 257. Compare the famous remark by Demetrios, *On Style* 169, that the satyr-play was "tragedy at play" (*paizousa tragōidia*). There is a

Merely by way of illustrating this approach, we may cite some sentences from the introduction to a school edition of the *Kyklōps* by D. M. Simmonds and R. R. Timberlake, first published in 1927.[5] After summarizing the Homeric account, they observe: "The general outline of the story is followed fairly closely" (xix–xx). "The most important changes in the story made by Euripides," they go on to say, "are caused by the necessity of introducing a Dionysiac element, in order to satisfy the conventions of Satyric Drama" (xx). And further: "It is evident that the changes made in the Homeric story by the introduction of the Satyrs are really comparatively small" (xxi). Beyond these, some further alterations are caused, they remark, "by the unavoidable difficulties of presentation" (xxii), such as the avoidance of representing indoor scenes on the Greek stage. But such matters are technical rather than thematic. These views, I repeat, are fairly representative, and it would be easy to multiply examples of them.[6]

The approach adopted here is different. I see in the role of the satyrs an element esssential to the structure of the play. They are not so much an addition to the Homeric design as they are parts of something else, a composition whose organizing principle is other than that of the *Odyssey*. To anticipate a little, I may indicate the difference in this way. Homer's account is dyadic. It is informed, that is, by the contrast between two types, Odysseus and Polyphemos; the narrative both explores and determines the possible implications of this contrast. Euripides' story, by virtue of the role of the satyrs, is triadic. Whatever else this may mean, it suggests that an opposition between any two roles, such as those of Odysseus and the kyklōps, will not exhaust the significance of the drama. Euripides' new design, which involves a shift from a binary to a ternary structure, thus alters what we may call the semantics of the narrative. When three terms, rather than two, are in play, then neither the terms, nor the game itself, are necessarily what they were before.[7] We

---

useful analysis of the language of the *Kyklōps* and its relation to tragic diction in Robert G. Ussher, *Euripides Cyclops: Introduction and Commentary* (Rome, 1978; hereafter, Ussher), 204–8.

[5] *Euripides: The Cyclops* (Cambridge, 1927, repr. 1976; hereafter, Simmons and Timberlake). Some lines of the play are purged in this edition.

[6] See, for example, Duchemin, xiv; Steffen, "Satyr-Dramas," 206; G. Wetzel, *De Euripidis fabula satyrica, quae Cyclops inscribitur, cum Homerico comparata exemplo* (Wiesbaden, 1965); Werner Biehl, *Euripides Kyklops* (Heidelberg, 1986; hereafter, Biehl), 18. Dana Sutton, "Satyr Plays and the *Odyssey*," *Arethusa* 7 (1974): 161–85, suggests a connection between the satyr-play as a genre and the themes and tone of the *Odyssey*, and contrasts them with tragedy and the *Iliad*.

[7] For the idea of a semantic field, Bruno Snell, *Die Ausdrücke für den Begriff des Wissens in der vorplatonischen Philosophie* (Berlin, 1924); Jost Trier, *Der deutsche Wortschatz im Sinnbezirk*

must, accordingly, be prepared to discover in Euripides' *Kyklōps* new elements and new relationships which may nevertheless be compatible in some degree with those of the *Odyssey*, inasmuch as there is, after all, a considerable resemblance between the two versions. Later on, I shall suggest some connections, but this essay is addressed primarily to Euripides' drama, which is, and should be, intelligible independent of its literary antecedents.

There are precisely three actors' roles in the *Kyklōps*: those of Silenos, Odysseus, and Polyphemos.[8] Each character, in turn, is associated with a band or group which is realized dramatically to one or another degree, decreasingly, as it happens, according to the order in which the main characters appear on the stage. Thus, Silenos' band is the chorus of satyrs; Odysseus' sailors accompany him onstage, but are *personae mutae*; and although Polyphemos' brother kyklōpes are mentioned, and he sets out to join them at one point in the drama, their role is merely reported, not enacted. The ways these groups are represented, and relations within and among them, yield, upon analysis, a rich array of oppositions and mediations in the domain of values and social behavior, the ultimate effect of which is to affirm the norms of exchange and reciprocity that govern human—that is, Greek—communities, and, more specifically, to affirm the democratic society of the Athenian city-state. This is the thematic substance of the play.

In analyzing these oppositions, we may begin in the culinary sphere, for which structuralist anthropology has given us an appetite. Polyphemos enjoys a diet of dairy products, wild game, and human flesh (cheese, 209; milk, 216; game such as lion and deer, 247–49—when Odysseus arrives at the cave, Polyphemos is off on a hunting trip, 130; human flesh, 249–52, clearly normal, if irregular, fare). He does not, however, eat satyrs. The reason he gives is that they would kill him with their dancing if they ever got inside his belly (220–21), an amusing allusion both to their Dionysian antics and to their function as chorus. Dramatically, there are other reasons for this squeamishness: there would long since have been no satyrs on the island if they had served as the kyklōps' food. If they are to function as his slaves, they cannot also be his meat. But this dietary circumstance, despite the witty, almost casual way in which the text adverts to it, establishes, from the point of view of the kyklōps, three distinct classes of life: his own kind; the satyrs, who are different but not part of his cuisine; and, finally, the class of edible creatures, which in-

des Verstandes: Die Geschichte eines sprachlichen Felds (Heidelberg, 1931); John Lyons, *Structural Semantics* (Oxford, 1963).

[8] That Silenos was an actor, and not the leader or coryphaeus, is argued persuasively by Sutton, "Father Silenus."

cludes human beings as well as wild animals (the kyklōps is said also to
consume his domestic beasts, 122).[9] Of course, Polyphemos' categories,
if we may call his preferences that, are not those of Odysseus and his
men. They share with the kyklōps his appetite for milk, cheese, and meat
(134–36), but draw the culinary line sharply, as we do, between humans—that is, their own kind—and other creatures (e.g., 127). Satyrs
too are excluded, as are kyklopes; both are subsumed under the category
of the inedible other. Thus Odysseus shares with Polyphemos the rule
that wild animals may be consumed, and both agree that satyrs are not
proper fare. Their tastes differ only in the matter of one another: the kyklōps is more liberal in his category of the edible, which extends to human beings, while Odysseus and his men evidently do not consider the
kyklopes a form of food.

This asymmetry is the basis, in turn, for another distinction, in which
the attitude toward the consumption of human flesh is a fundamental
value. On the one side there are those who, like Odysseus, abstain from
eating humans (i.e., their own kind), but also the satyrs, who observe the
same taboo; and on the other side, those who, like the kyklōps, do not
observe the taboo on human flesh, and are thus conceived of as practicing
cannibalism.[10] There is clearly a certain slippage here. The kyklōps is
cannibalistic only if humans are of his own kind, which his own dietary
habits, by which humans are assimilated to other animals, would seem to
deny. Polyphemos' diet is horrible because it is tacitly understood that,
whatever his own principles of classification may be, the taste for human
flesh in his case (unlike in the case of lions, say) amounts to the consump-

    [9] Cf. Edmund Leach, "Anthropological Aspects of Language: Animal Categories and
Verbal Abuse," in *New Directions in the Study of Language* ed. E. H. Lennenberg (Cambridge, Ma., 1964), 32: "Man and dogs are 'companions'; the dog is 'the friend of man.' On
the other hand man and food are antithetical categories. Man is not food so dog cannot be
food either"; cited by Peter Stallybrass and Allon White, *The Politics and Poetics of Transgression* (Ithaca, N.Y., 1986), 46.
    [10] The two sets of distinctions both involve the opposition of sameness and difference.
But the kyklōps looks only to edibility, while Odysseus treats human flesh as an absolute
taboo. We can represent the two schemes by a diagram thus:

	Kyklōps	Odysseus
Same	Edible	Eats humans
Different	Inedible	Does not eat humans

In each case, there are four possible pairings. Thus, for the kyklōps, there is (a) Same and
Edible, (b) Same and Inedible, (c) Different and Edible, (d) Different and Inedible. In this
case, (b) represents the kyklopes, (c) represents humans, and (d) represents the satyrs. In the
corresponding scheme for Odysseus, (b) represents humans, (c) represents the kyklopes,
and (d) represents the satyrs. The pair (a) is empty in both schemes.

tion of creatures like himself. This is, of course, the point of view of Odysseus, but in fact it informs the text throughout.

We are not informed about the diet of the satyrs in our play; they appear to be interested solely in drink, a topic to which we shall turn in a moment. But perhaps this preference suffices to identify them as a third type. Just as they are outside the category of food both for Odysseus and for the kyklōps, they are, in respect to their own appetites, indifferent to the line between edible and inedible flesh, since they apparently partake of neither.[11]

It should be clear that the description of the kyklōps as a cannibal depends upon certain presuppositions. He is not indiscriminate in his diet: the satyrs, as we have said, but also his brother kyklopes are excluded, which should not go without saying. Now, it may perhaps be objected that I am arbitrarily importing a problem into the interpretation of the play, since there is no strict term for cannibalism—as opposed to "man-eating"—in the text, nor, perhaps, in fifth-century Greek.[12] To this I may reply in two ways. First, the concept of consuming one's own kind, and the specifically human taboo against the practice, is as old as Homer and Hesiod. I have in mind Akhilleus' taunt to the dying Hektor that he could wish to eat the flesh of his enemy (*Iliad* 22.346–47)—this in the wake of his claim that the hatred between himself and Hektor was like that between men and lions, or wolves and lambs, species differences that abide no law or bond (262–65); and the famous passage in Hesiod's *Works and Days* in which men are discriminated from beasts precisely by

---

[11] While the binary nature of the Polyphemos episode in the *Odyssey* leaves no room for a third term in the culinary scheme, which we may diagram as:

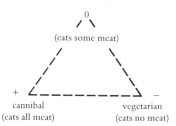

we may note that the Lotus-eaters, who immediately precede the kyklōps episode, are vegetarians. (I owe this observation to George Dimmock, who suggested it to me during the reading of an earlier draft of this essay at the Smith College Symposion.)

[12] Thus, *androbrōs*, used of the kyklōps at verse 93, elsewhere in Euripides modifies *kharmonai* (*Hercules Furens* 384) and *hēdonai*, "pleasures" (frag. 537), LSJ. *Anthrōpophagos* may be used of man-eating beasts as well as of cannibals. *Androphagos* (*Odyssey* 10.200; Herodotos, 4.18, 106) is perhaps more restricted, but it is not used in Euripides; various forms of *anthrōpoboros* indicate that the idea included dangerous animals as well as cannibals proper.

the constraint on eating one's own kind (276–78). Second, the absence of a general term for cannibalism in the *Kyklōps* in fact highlights the problem. The kyklōpes, as Odysseus exclaims, eat the meat of murdered men (*borai anthrōpoktonoi*, 127). But are the kyklōpes themselves men, that is, *anthrōpoi*? A few lines earlier, Silenos had said that the headlands of Sicily were barren of men (116), to which Odysseus answered by inquiring, "Who then occupies the land? a species of animals [*thēron genos*]?" (117). To this Silenos replies: "Kyklōpes." The status of Polyphemos is evidently ambiguous, and upon this ambiguity depends the question of whether his behavior is monstrous or not. If human beings are of the same kind as Polyphemos, then indeed his behavior is cannibalistic, and the more unnatural in that restraint from the flesh of one's own kind is specifically characteristic of human beings. But Polyphemos' diet would seem to distinguish him from humans: he does respect the taboo on eating his own kind, but that kind does not include mortal men.

The determination of the status of the kyklopes will not take the form of a set of definitions or propositions in the *Kyklōps*, for this is not the way of literature. Rather, the question of the monstrous, and of beast and mankind, will take its place in a complex of oppositions, some of which will be valorized, while others, like those implicit in the kyklōps' own scheme, are devalued. In respect to the particular opposition of beast and man, however, we may observe that Silenos' own credentials are none too certain. Like the chorus, he is half-man, half-goat (or, perhaps, half-horse). The only humans onstage, speaking strictly, are Odysseus and his men. Whatever the distinctions—and they are important—between satyrs and kyklōpes, they both stand as aspects of the bestial, and in this respect resemble each other. Odysseus can refer to both as beasts (*thēr*: of the kyklōps, 442, 602, cf. 658; of the satyrs, 624). Both too may be called men in the sense of *anēr*, i.e., "males" (of the kyklōps, 591, 605; of the satyrs, 642), but not *anthrōpos*.[13]

The ramifications of the culinary theme in the *Kyklōps* are such that they draw us into all the other issues of the drama, but before pursuing these, we may finish the discussion of cuisine with a look at beverages, and specifically at wine. Initially, we may distinguish three types: the bibulous Silenos, dedicated exclusively to Bakkhos; the kyklōps, who, in Euripides' version as opposed to that of the *Odyssey*, is unacquainted with wine prior to the arrival of Odysseus; and Odysseus himself, who possesses wine but is prepared to exchange it for milk, cheese, and meat. We might reduce the labels to all wine, no wine, some wine. This static scheme is, of course, undercut by the action of the drama. At the begin-

---

[13] Seaford, 54–55, discusses the beastlike character of the kyklōps; he notes also the double aspect of satyrs, as "worthless hedonists" and as "bearers of wisdom" (6–7; cf. 8–10 on their ambiguous role in festivals).

ning of the play, it has been a long time since the satyrs have tasted wine
(140). At the end, Polyphemos has become quite devoted to the stuff,
contending comically and on the same level with Silenos for the flask
(545–65). The way both pass from privation to enjoyment, culminating
in rivalry and, in the end, in sexual union, is a further indication of an
identity or similarity beneath or alongside the contrast between satyr and
kyklōps, a matter to which we shall return in some detail. Odysseus
stands apart from both as the only actor who does not drink. This is not
for want of opportunity, of course. Odysseus' relationship to wine is different from that of Silenos and Polyphemos: he controls it and uses it; it
is for him a means, and not, as it is for them, exclusively an end and a satisfaction in itself. This difference in his relation to wine is also a difference in his relation to Bakkhos, as the identifications between god and
grape throughout the play make clear. The difference pertains also, as we
shall see, to his relation to the gods in general, and to the place of the
gods both in social life and in the triad of gods, men, and beasts. But the
main point is that the wine, for Odysseus, is a means.

Odysseus approaches the cave of Polyphemos with the intention of
trading. He is in need of supplies, and has goods and gold to offer in return. The language of commerce permeates the opening scenes among
Odysseus, Silenos, and Polyphemos, from the moment when Odysseus
steps onstage, inquiring whether anyone might be willing to sell food to
needy sailors (97–98). The word meaning "to sell" here is *hodaō*; its significance is explained in Hesykhios' lexicon and in the *Etymologicum magnum*, which testifies to its occurrence in Euripides' lost play, *Alope*, and
in the *Kyklōps*. In extant Greek literature, it appears only in our play, but
there three times, and a fourth in the compound form, *exodaō* (12, 98,
133; 267).[14] Simmonds and Timberlake plausibly suggest that "it may
have been current slang at Athens" (commentary on verse 12). The dialogue contains what look like marketplace sayings: "Daylight's right for
merchandise" (137) and "A taste calls for a purchase" (150). There is also
an unusual use of the active form of *apodidōmi* (239) in the sense of "sell,"
which again perhaps reflects popular usage.[15] Silenos employs the word
as part of his elaborate lie that Odysseus was intending to steal Polyphemos' goods, beat and bind him, and sell him abroad to somebody to
work in a quarry or mill. I mention this because the first occurrence of
hodaō (12) also refers to the sale of persons, in this case Dionysos at the
hands of the pirates. Both, of course, are transactions involving violence

---

[14] See Duchemin, commentary on verse 12, for full citations of the evidence.

[15] Simmonds and Timberlake, commentary on verse 239; they cite Thoukydides 6.62 as
the only other instance. Cf. Seaford ad loc. W. E. Long, *Euripides Cyclops* (Oxford, 1891),
commentary on verse 239, suggests that it might be "safer" to render the verb "deliver
over"; Ussher, 238–40, translates "hand . . . over."

(*bia*, as Silenos himself says at 236), which Odysseus explicitly opposes
to legitimate exchange: he and his men came to purchase food; Silenos
sold the lambs in exchange for drink freely (*hekōn hekousi*, 258); and
nothing was done by force. Violent appropriation is, we may observe,
the mode of Polyphemos, who has enslaved the satyrs, seizes Odysseus
and his men, and is utterly indifferent to arguments about fair trade.
Such plunder is more like the violence of natural forces, the winds that
dragged Odysseus to Sicily violently (109; cf. 111), than like the relations
of civilized men.[16] But the idea of commerce is not exhausted in our play
by the contrast with forcible seizure. It is opposed equally to theft, the
vice of Silenos, whose fabrications are designed to cover the fact that he
has been caught selling the goods of Polyphemos (259–60, cf. 267–68,
270–71). Later, he steals draughts of the wine he is supposed to be pour-
ing for Polyphemos (547), who accuses him of being an unfair cupbearer
(560). In this triad of sale, theft, and pillage, which has no basis in the
scene in the *Odyssey*, we may see how the last two terms are associated
by virtue of their common opposition to the first, so that Silenos and
Polyphemos appear as representatives of two modes of injustice (for the
injustice of Silenos, 272, 560; that of Polyphemos is expressed by words
such as *anosios* and *dyssebēs* throughout, but cf. *dikē* in the sense of penalty
at 422, 693; for Odysseus' own concern with justice, 481).

The concept of exchange is larger than formal barter or purchase; it
covers such relations as gift-giving, for example, and even the largesse
shown to suppliants. In the *Kyklōps*, trade as such is the dominant form
of the just transaction in the first third of the play, and sets the pattern for
what follows, but it is embedded in other reciprocities which at once
connect and constitute several kinds of status. Prominent among these is
the category represented by the term *xenos*. Its meaning is difficult to
capture in English, which resorts to such expressions as friend, guest, or
stranger, depending on the context. In part, this ambiguity inheres in the
Greek concept, which signifies not only those outsiders with whom one
has established or acknowledged a bond, but also those with whom one
might do so. That is, the *xenos* stands either in an actual or a potential relationship, much as if one should say, Whoever is not my enemy is my
friend, without as yet having actually made friends with all who are included in that category.[17] The code or *nomos* governing the reception of

---

[16] Note *harpazō*, 109, 400; *anarpazō*, 112.

[17] The ambivalence of the concept behind *xenos* is expressed by way of an etiological
story by Moses Finley, *The World of Odysseus*, 2d ed. (Harmondsworth, 1979), 101: "In
primitive times, the poet [Homer] seems to be suggesting, man lived in a state of permanent struggle and war to the death against the outsider. Then the gods intervened, and
through their precepts, their *themis*, a new ideal was set before man, and especially before a
king, an obligation of hospitality: 'all strangers and beggars are from Zeus' ([*Odyssey*]

nonhostile strangers, and specifically shipwrecked suppliants, is enunci-
ated explicitly by Odysseus: one gives *xenia* (gifts of hospitality) and supplies raiment; one does not skewer and cook them (299–303). Native and
stranger become guest and host through this exchange, which is authorized by Zeus *xenios* (354). The kyklōps, on the contrary, recognizes no
obligations of giving. He simply consumes, and in the imagery of the
play, he is all jaws, gullet, and belly (*gnathoi, pharynx, gastēr* or *nēdys*).
When he proclaims, in the manner of the sophists, that his god is wealth
(316), he means not circulating wealth, which is the glue of social life,
but goods hoarded, absorbed, ingested—deposited in the sanctum of his
own stomach, which he calls the greatest of all divinities (335).[18] As for
xenia, all he can offer is the fire and pot in which to boil his guests (342–
44).

The kyklōps' appetite, then, becomes a symbol of his inability to enter
into the *xenos*-relationship; it opposes mere consumption to exchange,
which is the complex of giving and receiving. In the vocabulary of the
play, he is *axenos* rather than *philoxenos* (91, 125), or, as the equivalent,
xenodaitumōn or *xenodaitēs* (610, 658), a feaster upon guests and strangers.

Under the influence of wine, however, the kyklōps appears to reverse
himself. He is set upon a *kōmos*, or revel, with his brother kyklopes (445–
46), and Odysseus must conspire with the satyrs to prevent him from

---

14.57–58). Henceforth men had to pick a difficult path between the two, between the reality of a society in which the stranger was still a problem and a threat, and the newer morality, according to which he was somehow covered by the aegis of Zeus." Under the
"newer" morality, obligations of hospitality were due to strangers, that is, to potential
guest-friends. The role of hospitality (*xenia*) is touched upon also by Sutton, "Satyr Plays,"
162–63, again in connection with the *Odyssey*.

[18] Leonardo Paganelli, *Echi storico-politici nel "Ciclope" euripideo* (Padua, 1979), in a subtle
analysis of 316–46, brings out very well the analogy between the views of the kyklōps and
those of the sophists, such as Kallikles and Thrasymakhos (e.g., wealth, 21–26; power, 26–
30; the *nomoi*, 30–34; hedonism, 35–41, esp. 40; *physis*, 49–60). So too Seaford, 52–55; I
think both are right against Ussher (187–88), who doubts that the kyklōps' "primitive
code" corresponds to the opinions of the sophists. Paganelli argues further, and again convincingly in my view, that the sophistic opinions parodied here are specific to oligarchic
propaganda (23–24; on *sōphrōn* as a catchword of the oligarchy [related to the abstentionist
politics sloganized as *apragmosynē* and *hēsykhia*], see 41–47). Seaford, 53, remarks that one
aspect of the kyklōps "is a caricature of a certain contemporary anti-democratic ideology";
cf. also Biehl, 22. The affirmation of the political bonds of *philia* against the violence of the
kyklōps is a vehicle for the affirmation of the *dēmos* or popular democracy against the threat
of oligarchic rule, here represented in one of its extreme ideological versions, that of radical
Kalliklean individualism. But the parody is not literal: the kyklōps speaks not for the usable
wealth of the aristocracy, but for an ideal of pure consumption or hoarding. The political
allegory is thus adapted to the structure of the action in the *Kyklōps*, which is the way of literature. For an analogous reduction of real aristocratic wealth to the extreme possessiveness
of the miser, see David Konstan, *Roman Comedy* (Ithaca, N.Y., 1983), 45–46, on Plautus'
Aulularia.

giving away the beverage, and encourage him instead to keep it for himself alone (451–53). In this they succeed, with the help of Silenos, who
advises Polyphemos out of spontaneous and selfish motives of his own
(540–43): he is against sharing. One may perhaps see, in the failed *kōmos*,
a sign of Polyphemos' inability to know or achieve the forms of civilized
life, as Rossi has argued, taking the *kōmos* as a pastiche of civic festivals.[19]
This does not account, however, for his desire to enjoy the revel. In our
play, moreover, the *kōmos* seems not so much an emblem of the *polis*, at
least insofar as this institution is represented by Odysseus, as of the satyrs
and their bacchic exuberance (39). At the beginning of the play, the satyrs sing and dance, inspired by memories of love and Dionysos; at his
entrance, and rather belatedly (since the chorus has for a time been silent), Polyphemos scolds them and reminds them that there is no Dionysos where they are now (203–5). In the end the roles are just the
opposite: the kyklōps is eager to cavort, while Silenos holds him back.
These reversals suggest that we have once again a case in which the original opposition between the kyklōps and Silenos collapses, or rather,
where they appear as contrary poles of a single essence, a *coincidentia oppositorum*, over and against Odysseus, who mediates or sublates the tension. To understand the process, we shall have once more to widen the
scope of our opposition between exchange and consumption in such a
way as to make space for the role of the satyrs.

Consumption and exchange or trade do not, in fact, exhaust the forms
by which goods move. There is also liberality, not giving but giving
away, the kind of bounty that drunkenness inspires. Generosity of this
sort is the opposite of the kyklōps' rapacity (before he tastes the wine).
His wants yawn cavernously; everything enters (Odysseus calls him
Hell's chef, 397), and others are simply means to his satisfaction, whether
to prepare his meal or be it. The ecstasy (cf. *mainetai*, "is mad," 168) of
wine, however, dissolves the self into the group. The unsociable or, literally, "unmixed" man (*ameikton andra*, 429) discovers in his inebriation
that the elements themselves are confounded: heaven seems to whirl
commixed (*symmemigmenos*, 578) with earth. Dramatically, the contrast
between self and group is reproduced in the isolation of the kyklōps,
who alone of all the actors appears, as I have mentioned, unattended, and
the undifferentiated community of the satyrs, who speak with a single
voice. On the one side, there is the selfishness of the individual; on the
other, the collectivity of the horde.

Differing both from the communion of the Bakkhic chorus (64) and
from the antisocial autarky of the kyklōps is the companionship between
Odysseus and his *hetairoi* (378, 398, 409, 550, 695). This is an association

[19] Luigi Enrico Rossi, "Il *Ciclope* di Euripide come *komos* 'mancato,' " *Maia* 23 (1971):
10–38, esp. 21, 27.

of mutuality, in which Odysseus is neither merged with his sailors nor entirely separate from them. In one scene, which is due to the imagination of Euripides, there is a moment which we may take as emblematic of this relationship. After he has plied the kyklōps with wine, Odysseus slips quietly out of the cave (426–27), in order to relate the horrors within in a messenger speech, as required by dramatic conventions, and to enlist—pretty much in vain, as it will turn out—the help of the satyrs in diverting the kyklōps from his *kōmos* and then in blinding him. Odysseus then returns to the cave with the following words: "I shall not save myself alone, having left inside men who are my friends [*philoi*]. I could indeed escape, and I am outside the recesses of the cave. But it is not just to save myself alone, having left behind my friends, with whom I came here" (478–82).[20] Odysseus is alone and could escape, but he is bound by a sense of justice to his friends. Euripides wryly exploits the ease with which, for reasons of genre, Odysseus must be permitted to sneak out of the cave, in order to point up the theme of the play.[21]

The relationship to his men which Odysseus invokes is *philia*. As with *xenos*, the range of the term *philos* is very wide; the variety of its occurrences in the *Kyklōps* alone can testify to that. In particular, we may observe that it designates a disposition, like the word "friendly," as well as an acknowledged bond entailing mutual responsibilities, such as attaches, for example, to the Latin term *amicus* when it is employed in a political context.[22] In this latter usage, there is nothing sentimental in the term. One is not required to like one's *philoi*, only to act toward them as the social relationship of *philia* requires. In his tragedies, Euripides sometimes exploits the tension between obligation and feeling that subsists in the concept, but that is not the point here.[23] Justice toward one's *philoi*

---

[20] Uses of the word *monos* suggest the contrast between Odysseus' concern for his men and Polyphemos' selfishness; on Odysseus, 479, 489; on the kyklōps, 362, 453, and—possibly—also *monoderktēs*, 79. I do not find *nomades* in 120 sufficiently strange to justify emending to *monades*; see however Volkmar Schmidt, "Zu Euripides, Kyklops 120 und 707," *Maia* 27 (1975): 291–92, for a defense of *monades*, adopted also by Seaford.

[21] There is a kind of crux in the plot here, for Odysseus' companions might also have escaped, especially had Polyphemos been encouraged to join his brothers in a *kōmos*. I return to this problem below. There is no justification, however, for drawing the conclusion that Odysseus' men are cowardly or unreliable, as Ussher does in "The *Cyclops* of Euripides," *G&R* n.s. 18 (1971): 176–77, repeated in his commentary, 190–91 (Odysseus' men "*must* perforce appear as cowards," 191). Nor does *oikeioi philoi*, in its context (650), "contain a sneer," i.e., "those who have stayed inside"; it precisely distinguishes Odysseus' men as true companions from the unreliable satyrs. Contrast Giussepe Amendola, *Euripide: Il Ciclope* (Florence, 1952), xv, on Odysseus' "umana solidarietà."

[22] See, for example, Emile Benveniste, "Philos," in *Indo-European Languages and Society*, trans. Jean Lallot (London, 1973), 277–78. On *amicitia*, P. A. Brunt, "*Amicitia* in the Late Roman Republic," *PCPS*, n.s. 2 (1965): 1ff.

[23] For discussion of the significance of *philia* in Euripides' tragedies (with extensive bibliography), see David Konstan, "*Philia* in Euripides' *Electra*," *Philologus* 129 (1985): 176–85,

demands that one place their safety on the same level as one's own. This is the basis of the human community, as opposed to the solitary kyklōps and the herd of satyrs.

We must take some brief account of other occurrences of *philos*, especially toward the end of the opening chorus, where the satyrs twice invoke Bakkhos thus, and a third time speak of his *philia* (73, 74, 81). The satyrs do not speak of each other in this way, and Bakkhos himself is, I believe, a special case. Odysseus wonders, upon sighting the chorus, whether he is at the city of Bakkhos (*Bromiou polin*, 99), but without Bakkhos the satyrs are only a crowd (*homilon*, 100). Apart, then, from suggesting that the idea of *philia* is indeed intimately connected with that of the *polis* as the quintessential institution of human culture[24]—the kyklopes, certainly, haven't a city (115)—I shall postpone the discussion of this problem until we come to the analysis of Bakkhos' role in the drama. In a looser sense, Odysseus can call the satyrs *philoi* (176), just as they, and even the kyklōps in an expansive mood, can call Odysseus by the superlative, *philtatos* (437, 418), but his *philoi* proper, or what he calls his *oikeioi philoi* (650), are his own men only (cf. 466, to the chorus: *kai se kai philous geronta te*, "You and my friends and the old man").[25]

Philia, then—*philia* proper, that is to say—is a relationship constituted by reciprocal responsibilities. In this respect, the paired concepts, *philos* and *xenos*, are not so much contrary as complementary. Of course, they represent relationships in different degrees; in general, men of a common city are *philoi*, while foreigners are *xenoi*. But both alike are socially constructed. That is, they rest upon conventions or a sense of justice (*nomos, dikē*), which prescribe mutual obligations. The obligations are the essence of the relationships. In contrast to the social arrangements of *philia* and *xenia*, there is either the unrelated self (*hautos*, 338) of sophistical speculations, or the natural bond of the family. And here at last we may resume Polyphemos' intended *kōmos*. This celebration embraces neither friends nor guests but brothers (*kasignētoi*, 445; *adelphoi*, 509, 531).[26] To the extent that the kyklōps identifies with a group—this only when he is in his cups—it is the same kind of society as that of the satyrs. Against the kyklopes and the satyrs, only Odysseus and his men stand in a rela-

---

esp. 182–84. *Philia* in the *Kyklōps* has the positive sense that adheres to the concept in Euripides' earlier plays (though this is of no practical significance for the dating of the *Kyklōps*).

[24] Cf. 276 (Polyphemos to Odysseus): "What city [*polis*] educated [*exepaideusen*] you?"; and 119–20: "or is the power [*kratos*] with the people [*dedēmeutai*]?" Seaford, 58, observes that the satyrs are not "entirely outside the life of the *polis*," but in the early part of the play, at least, their way of life is more in contrast than in harmony with urban culture.

[25] Contra Ussher, "*Cyclops.*"

[26] In an exchange of proverbs on the subject of the *kōmos*, Polyphemos can use the term *philos* for drinking mates (533), but this does not affect the argument.

tionship that is not fraternal (or, if we include Silenos, familial). When the kyklōps, under the influence of wine, abandons his self-sufficiency, it is not for a truly social company, but for the presocial identification of the horde. A reversal, yes, but still along the axis of oneness, if we may put it that way. A true plurality, which is based on reciprocity and exchange, remains human.

I have so often in this essay made mention of relations of reciprocity and exchange, whether in connection with cuisine, trade, or social organization, that it may be best to address explicitly, albeit summarily, the status of these ideas in current critical theory. Their intellectual genealogy is easy to identify. It may be sufficient to cite the opening chapters in Marx's *Capital* on the circulation of commodities, and the anthropological work on gifts and kinship represented by Marcel Mauss' *The Gift* and Lévi-Strauss' *The Elementary Structures of Kinship*. The application of structuralist and dialectical methods to the study of literature has by now a respectable history. The matter of relationships has also attracted the attention of philosophers. There is a crisp formulation of the issue in the essay by Harold H. Oliver entitled "Relational Ontology and Hermeneutics":

> Position-taking on the doctrine of relations has determined much of the dynamic of Western philosophizing. With no time here to review the modern debate in detail, I can only announce my commitment to the doctrine that all relations are internal, that is, to the view that *relata* are what they are through the relation. G. E. Moore, an opponent of the thesis of universal internality, has given one of the most precise definitions of the thesis underlying strict internality: "any term which does in fact have a particular relational property, could not have existed without having that property." This means formally that apart from prior metaphysical assumptions, given any relation, that is, any *aRb*, *a* is defined by the relation, as is *b*. This claim is the logical opposite of Russell's theory, which assumed that *a* and *b* are "things" entering into relation.[27]

I appreciate the rigor of Oliver's argument, but I myself am inclined not so much to choose between the relational and essentialist positions as to treat them as two modes of understanding phenomena, each of which seems forever prepared to be transformed into the other. Thus, things are but the endpoints of relations; relations are but the bonds between things. At certain moments, one or another view may predominate, and among the reasons for this, we may, I am sure, include the relative trans-

[27] Oliver's paper appears in *Myth, Symbol, and Reality*, ed. Alan M. Olson (Notre Dame, 1980); the passage quoted is on 73–74. The citation from G. E. Moore is from *Philosophical Studies* (1922; repr. Totowa, N.J., 1968), 288.

parency or opacity of social relations. Sometimes, that is, the constitutive quality of relations in social life is more or less manifest (e.g., slaves exist because there is slavery), while at other times, such relations appear as the consequences of natural differences (slavery exists because some people are naturally slaves). In Greece of the fifth century B.C.E., awareness was, I believe, poised between these two perspectives. This is not the kind of proposition one attempts to prove, but it is a useful premise in interpretation, and plausible enough for the ancient city-state, where the civic ideal appeared to mediate between still lively collective rituals on the one hand and the centrifugal tendencies of autonomous and competitive households on the other.[28] The relations of the *polis* were not entirely secure; among the households there was still, in Durkheim's terms, more of a mechanical than an organic solidarity.[29] In the *Kyklōps*, at all events, the organic relations of exchange and reciprocity are represented as distinctively human, as opposed both to kyklopean individualism and the satyr horde. In this very strategy we may begin to locate the meaning of the play.

Let us consider for a moment the logic of relationship. A relation establishes a connection between things; they are not entirely independent. At the same time, it presupposes a distance; the two elements cannot be identical in all respects, or they will cease to be distinct. There are thus two ways to negate a relation: the bond between the elements may dissolve, leaving them entirely independent; or it may collapse, merging the elements in a common identity. The kyklōps and the satyrs represent precisely these two forms of the negation of human social life. These opposite forms are, nevertheless, finally alike, for the unrelated individual is like every other, and thus partakes of the sameness of the horde. The susceptibility of the kyklōps to wine is the dramatic expression of this equivalence. Neither drunk nor sober does he know sociability, the sameness in difference of mutuality, which is the nature of relationship.

In the response of the satyrs and Polyphemos to the news of Troy's fall, we may see one more time their characteristic indifference to the social issue. The satyrs are curious about one detail: whether, after they recaptured Helen, the Greeks all banged her (*diekrotēsat' en merei*, 180), since, after all, she enjoyed variety in husbands. The kyklōps, who, after

---

[28] Ideologically, one of the forms in which the social phenomenon of household autarky might be expressed was the extreme individualism of the sophists. I am not suggesting that these ideas reflected a social fact, in some allegorical fashion; only that they were available to be contrasted, say, with traditional notions of justice and solidarity, and thereby to be part of a structured set of oppositions that had analogies with social life.

[29] A mechanical solidarity obtains where the division of labor is relatively undeveloped. Durkheim develops the idea in *The Division of Labor in Society*, trans. George Simpson (New York, 1964); for a brief review, see Anthony Giddens, *Emile Durkheim* (Harmondsworth, 1978), 28.

judging against Odysseus on the transaction over the sale of his goods, begins his interrogation rather abruptly ("but I want to ask something"; *thelō d'eresthai*, 275), scorns the motive for the war: "A shameful campaign, sailing against the Phrygians' land for the sake of one woman" (283–84). This reproach was commonplace; the locus classicus is perhaps the opening paragraphs of Herodotos' *Histories*.[30] On the lips of Polyphemos the effect was probably witty (though it may also have been politically pointed), just as Euripides introduces a note of self-parody when he has the satyrs condemn, on Helen's account, the race of women—save for their own enjoyment (186–87).[31] But in reducing the causes of the Trojan War to the passion for a woman, satyrs and kyklōps alike ignore Paris' violation of the guest relation, or *xenia*. Odysseus answers, rather conventionally, that it was the business of a god, and proceeds to portray the war as a defense of Greek temples (285, 290–98). There is something evasive about his argument. It issues in a personal appeal to Polyphemos' filial piety toward Poseidon, rather than in an alternative account of the Greeks' motives. Perhaps the audience could be trusted to react appropriately without prompting. Perhaps again, Euripides' own reservations—prominent in his tragedies—about the Trojan War, which was his vehicle for expressing the motives behind contemporary Greek hostilities, surfaced here in the *Kyklōps*, in dissonance with the predominant tone of the play.[32] The *Kyklōps* is an optimistic play, but not a bland one.

[30] Herodotos 1.4. Herodotos himself did not take so frivolous a view of the causes of the war; cf. 2.120. The idea that the Trojan War was fought for the sake of a woman is expressed also in Euripides' tragedies, e.g., *Trojan Women* 368–69, *Iphigeneia in Aulis* 1393–94; see below, n. 32.

[31] Ussher, "*Cyclops*," comments astutely on this passage: "In an interesting piece of near self-parody—if that term can be used without reference to date—Euripides makes them [the satyrs] sympathize with Menelaos and inveigh against the race of women (186ff.). But their qualification (*ei mē moi monōi*) pin-points a leading trait of the stage satyr. I mean not his sexuality . . . but his selfishness and marked pursuit of policies, however contradictory, unprincipled, or devious, which will lead to his own self-preservation." The related passages in Euripidean tragedy are *Hippolytos* 616ff., *Medeia* 573ff. On the whole question of self-parody in the *Kyklōps*, see the discussion of Geoffrey Arnott, "Parody and Ambiguity in Euripides' *Cyclops*," in *Antidosis: Festschrift für Walther Kraus*, ed. R. Hanslik, A. Lesky, and H. Schwabl (Vienna, 1972), 21–30, esp. 22–24.

[32] This is not sufficient grounds to warrant William Arrowsmith's interpretation of the kyklōps as a sympathetic figure, with Odysseus as the sophistical politician of the tragedies; see Arrowsmith's introduction to his translation of the *Kyklōps*, in *The Complete Greek Tragedies, Euripides*, ed. D. Grene and R. Lattimore (Chicago, 1956), 2:5–8. Usher too finds attractive qualities in Euripides' Polyphemos, such as generosity toward his brothers and a sense of humor (Ussher, 187) and, in view of Odysseus' apparent freedom to escape from the cave, pronounces the blinding of the kyklōps "a senseless outrage" (191). This seems too delicate a sentiment. Paganelli, *Echi storio-politici*, 63–112, argues ingeniously that Euripides' representation of the Trojan War was a reflex of his attitude toward the Peloponnesian War, and that there was a change after 415 (the Sicilian expedition; see 96–98). Earlier,

The fact remains that, right or wrong, the satyrs and Polyphemos share a personal, rather than a social, conception of the war.

We have been examining until now the structure of the ideology that operates in the *Kyklōps*, in which the notion of relation constitutes the problem. We can see how different this is from the theme of the corresponding episode of the *Odyssey*, where the confrontation between Odysseus and Polyphemos is essentially polar. Civilized discipline stands against lawless savagery, brute power succumbs to cunning—the entire tension encapsulated in Greek literature's most brilliant pun, when the kyklopes, misunderstanding the sense of Odysseus' assumed name *Outis* ("No-body"), render it in the conditional form as *mē tis* which, heard as a single word, means cunning.[33] In Euripides' play, the role of Odysseus' cleverness is much reduced. The kyklōps himself is rendered something of a philosopher, while Odysseus' tricks are either eliminated, like the escape under the rams, or exploited to a different effect, like the use of the name No-body, which deceives no one and simply provides sport for the satyrs. Correspondingly, trade has nothing like the function in the *Odyssey* which it has in the first scenes of the *Kyklōps*.[34] The introduction of the satyrs is part of a profound recasting of theme.

The ideological structure of a dramatic or narrative work is something like a matrix for the action. The undifferentiated eroticism of the satyrs, the violent autarky of the kyklōps, and the companionship of the human community which is presented as the logical mediation of the two extremes, are abstract forms. Such abstractions may clarify certain complex affinities: how it is, for example, that Silenos, whose position as a shipwrecked victim of Polyphemos is analogous to that of Odysseus,[35] may

---

Euripides favored a kind of pacifism, but this yielded to a pan-Hellenic and antibarbarian militancy in the context of Sparta's collaboration with Persia (69). Troy is now assimilated to the Persians (80–81), and in the *Kyklōps* (lines 290–91) the conflict is presented as a war of national liberation (98–99). Thus, the kyklōps' contemptuous reference to the cause of the Trojan War marks him as an oligarchic sympathizer, for they were the party still committed to such pacifist clichés (95). All this squares with Paganelli's date of 414/3 for the *Kyklōps*, which "reveals itself to be a democratic propaganda piece" (138), expansionist and sympathetic to the Sicilian campaign. I find Paganelli's arguments attractive, but speculative, especially in the matter of a change in Euripides' view of the war. If this is accepted, then, on the evidence of the *Kyklōps*, we must suppose that Euripides put his own ironic comment on the origins of the war in the mouth of a character he wished now to represent as a political enemy—a subtle kind of recantation.

[33] *Odyssey* 9.405–6. The pun was first observed, to my knowledge, by W. B. Stanford, *Ambiguity in Greek Literature* (Oxford, 1939), 104–5; see also Michael Simpson, "*Odyssey* 9: Symmetry and Paradox in *Outis*," *CJ* 68 (1972): 22–25; more generally on *mētis* in the *Odyssey*, Pietro Pucci, "Le figures de la métis dans l'*Odysée*," *Mētis* 1 (1986): 7–28.

[34] In the *Odyssey*, Odysseus has rather the mentality of a colonizer, as is revealed by his shrewd appraisal of the value of the island facing the kyklōps' territory, 9.116–41.

[35] See, for example, the parallel expressions *exantlō ponon*, 10, and *ponon . . . exēntlēkotes*, 282, of Silenos and the Greeks respectively; also 110: *ton auton daimon' exantleis emoi*.

nevertheless seem like the double of the kyklōps: lewd, monstrous, selfish, and uncivilized.[36] But a drama is more than the display of types.
They must also act upon each other in ways that are necessarily partial,
and whose effects cannot be deduced from the nature of the types themselves. It is by no necessity that Odysseus succeeds in overcoming Polyphemos and rescuing the satyrs; it is simply in the plot. Nevertheless, the
story has the appearance of necessity; at the very least, it seems right or
appropriate. This effect is achieved in several ways: the logic we have
discussed contributes to it; so does our natural sympathy with the human
underdog, although this, as the case of William Arrowsmith reveals, is
not an inevitable response.[37] But beyond logic or sympathy there is also
the appeal to transcendent values, related generally to some notion of the
divine. In contentions of mutual violence and deceit, such authority sustains the privileged values. We must conclude our interpretation of the
Kyklōps with the role of the gods in the play, and above all, with that of
Bakkhos, who, though absent, has a pervasive influence on the action.

The prologue, delivered by Silenos, takes the form of an apostrophe to
Bakkhos, beginning with the invocation, *ō Bromie* (1).[38] The final verse
of the play likewise contains his name (709). For the satyrs, the presence
of Bakkhos means love, dance, and joy, as they sing in the epode to the
first chorus (63–81). Service to the kyklōps is the negation of Dionysian
plenitude: a danceless land (*akhoran khthona*, 124), ignorant of Dionysos'
brew—a place of privation (cf. *erēmian*, 622). As Polyphemos himself
says, "There is no Dionysos here" (204). The satyrs do not, of course,
understand the alternative to their present servitude as freedom. Only
Odysseus can speak as a free man (*eleutherōs*, 287). The satyrs' options are

[36] On the "paradoxical nature of the satyrs," see Seaford, 32; for Seaford, the satyrs
"represent a community which is antithetical to the *polis*, because representative of more
ancient social relations" (30). Their ambiguous status, both social and presocial, is essential
to the meaning of the satyr-play as a genre, according to Seaford, for in it "the isolated sufferings of tragedy were reabsorbed . . . into the ancient social relations of the Dionysian
thiasos" (31–32). I am very much in sympathy with Seaford's analysis, and I believe that his
insight into the complex role of the satyrs in myth and ritual is relevant to the nature of the
genre. My own discussion is intended to bring out the way in which the ambiguity attach-
ing to the satyrs is activated by the structure of Euripides' narrative.

[37] Arrowsmith, in his introduction to Grene and Lattimore, *Euripides*, feels that "Odysseus is in fact the familiar depraved politician of the *Hekuba*, the *Trojan Women*, and the
Iphigeneia in Aulis; he stands, as he almost always does in tragedy, for that refinement of intellect and eloquence which makes civilized brutality so much more terrible than mere savagery" (5), while in Polyphemos he sees "a drunken, almost lovable, buffoon" (6). Ussher,
185, finds Odysseus boastful and overcautious. Contrast Biehl, 21–22.

[38] The god is addressed at least through line 17 (*s'anax*), after which the form of the apostrophe is tacitly dropped, and we may suppose that Silenos speaks directly to the audience,
as is usual for the prologue. The god's name is also the last word of line 9, which sets off the
first statement or paragraph of the prologue; note also the responsion indicating closure in
the echo *ponous/ponon*, lines 1 and 10.

two forms of slavery, to Polyphemos or to their god (*doulos*, 24, 79; *douleusomen*, 709).[39] Their current plight, however, is not simply a function of their captivity. Their lord Dionysos has himself been abducted (*anērpasan*, 112; cf. 11–12), and the satyrs, as we have remarked, were driven upon Sicily while sailing in search of him (13–22). They both became and remain the victims of Polyphemos because their god is in the hands of pirates, and cannot help them. "Whither, O dear Bakkhos," laments the chorus, "do you stray alone? Whither do you toss your yellow locks? I, who am your servant, labor as a slave for the one-eyed kyklōps, with this miserable mantle of a goat, an exile far from your companionship" (74–81).[40] The pirates, as we know from the Homeric Hymn *to Dionysos*, did not long keep their prisoner. Dionysos assumed various shapes such as lion and bear to warn and terrify the crew, then made the ship sprout vines and transformed the irreverent sailors into dolphins. He is already free: what is more, from the moment of Odysseus' arrival, he is present on the island of Polyphemos, in the form of the wine Odysseus bears.

To be sure, the metonymy by which Bakkhos stood for wine was so common that it was usually, no doubt, semantically inert, although we must not forget that it was no mere metaphor, but rested, like the doctrine of wine and wafer in Catholicism, on beliefs in consubstantiality. But the language of the play leaves little doubt that the god is the agency in his potion. After one sip, Silenos cries out that Bakkhos summons him to dance (156). Polyphemos' remark, which I have cited twice now, that there is no Dionysos here, has an undertone of dramatic irony. The idea of making the kyklōps drunk occurs to Odysseus as a divine thing (*ti theion*, 411); a few lines further, the drink that is the delight of Dionysos is called divine (415). The god is active in this plan. The sleeping kyklōps will be overcome by Bakkhos (454). But the equation of god and wine descends from metaphor to explicit proposition in the comic dialogue between Odysseus and Polyphemos. "I am," says Odysseus, "an old hand at this Bakkhos" (519–20). "How can a god," the kyklōps asks, "be happy having his home in a wineskin?" "He's content wherever you put him," Odysseus replies. "But gods are not supposed to have bodies contained in skin," quips Polyphemos (525–27). Beneath the banter, the identity of god and wine is activated.

But if Dionysos may be said to defeat the kyklōps, it is through Odysseus that he works.[41] Their fates, indeed, are mutually implicated: Odys-

[39] Other terms for their servitude to Polyphemos are *thēteuō* (77) and *latreuō* (24); perhaps a contrast in the nature of their relation to Polyphemos and to Dionysos is intimated in the choice of the words *anax* (17) for the god and *despotēs* (34) for the kyklōps.

[40] There are analogies here with the chorus in the *Bakkhai*, 402ff., and esp. 537–75.

[41] Seaford, 59, understands the *Kyklōps* as "the triumph of Dionysos." George Leonidas

seus uses Dionysos to overpower the kyklōps, and thereby liberates the satyrs to recover their lord (435–36). The human who does not drink is the agency of release.

The connection between Dionysos and Odysseus is fundamental to the play. The divine order is in balance with the society of mortals (*brotoi*, used only of humans in the *Kyklōps*: cf. 605; there is a deliberate ambiguity, I think, at 524, as also with *thnētois* at 299, where the question is precisely whether the *nomos* of men—that is, *anthrōpōn*, 339—pertains to Polyphemos). The Greeks preserve the precincts of the gods (290–96). In turn, Odysseus summons their protection; should they not heed, then Zeus must only *seem* a god, and chance rules all (354–55, 606–7). Reciprocity governs Odysseus' relationship with the divine as well as with his fellow man. He alone of all the speaking characters onstage has no filial tie to a god.

In their relation to the gods, then, we see reproduced among the three agents in the drama the same kind of complex we have discovered in their social natures. Polyphemos' belly is his deity; the rest he despises, save when, under the influence of wine, he thinks he gazes directly upon the throne of Zeus (579–80), and that the Graces court him. The satyrs dance with Bakkhos, dwell with nymphs, and croon to Aphrodite (68–70; cf. 620–21); theirs is an unmediated association. For human (which is to say, social) beings, the gods are real but hidden. They sustain the conventions of exchange by which human bonds are forged. Their support may be relied upon against the violent disruption of these codes, whether in the case of the seizure of Helen (*harpagas*, 280) or of the kyklōps' abuse of the rights of visitors. What is more, their relationship to the human community has analogous elements of reciprocity, one expression of which is that it is mediated rather than direct. Odysseus claims no kinship with the gods, nor has he visions of them. For him, wine is a commodity.

Bakkhos through Odysseus, Odysseus through Bakkhos exact justice from the *contemptor divum et hominum*. With the support of the gods, Odysseus rescues himself, his men, and the chorus of satyrs, together with their father, Silenos. Silenos cuts a pathetic figure: commending the escape, but too enamored of wine to be of any help (431–34). The satyrs are little better. They can offer encouragement (654–55), but shrink from

---

Koniaris, reviewing Seaford in *CP* 82 (1987): 63–69, strongly disagrees: "In the *Cyclōps* Dionysus stays completely out of the action" (67), and Koniaris denies also that the wine serves as a symbol for the agency of the god. The wine is, as Koniaris says, part of "the traditional story," but Euripides has altered Homer's version in denying Polyphemos any knowledge of wine or of Bakkhos. That change seems pointed, given the role of the satyrs: the power they worship will undo the kyklōps. That this power is called both wine and Bakkhos is given in the text.

action, dissolving into separate voices, each with a self-serving excuse, when the moment of decision comes (632–41). Here again, Euripides has exploited a Greek theatrical convention, according to which the chorus seldom leaves the stage or participates in an action with the characters, in a way that works into the theme.[42] The satyrs, as Odysseus mutters, are cowards, not allies (642). In their defense against the charge, the chorus members in fact parse the concept *ponēria*: they are out to save their own hides (643–45); in a crisis, their solidarity disintegrates. Such, Odysseus says, is their nature (*physei*, 649). Nevertheless, they are at bottom benign, even if they are not trustworthy. They honor their god, and he nourishes them in his service. They aspire to *philia*. Their fraternity is compatible with civil society, as the last two verses of the play perhaps imply: "We shall be fellow-sailors [*synnautai*; cf. 425, of Odysseus' men] of this Odysseus here, and slaves of Bakkhos from now on" (708–9). The kyklōps, even in his cups, sings out of tune (425–26, 488–90). Like the satyrs, as we have seen, he is a god-descended beast, but a man-eating, god-hating kind of beast (602). In the end, the line between Polyphemos and the satyrs is one Odysseus himself will draw, when he blocks the monster from embarking upon a *kōmos*. It is a symbolic exclusion, which anticipates the blinding and escape, and it is achieved by persuasion. Odysseus' cunning achieves not only the defeat of the kyklōps, but also his categorical isolation; it forces the distinction between his mode of being and that of the satyrs. The intrusion of this maneuver upon the Homeric base leaves its mark on the plot, which shows a strain just here: if it was indeed possible, as the satyrs suggest, for Odysseus and his men to waylay the drunken Polyphemos on the road to his brothers, they might also have taken that opportunity to escape. The sacrifice of consistency alerts us to the significance of the episode. In the punning jargon of contemporary criticism, the seam indicates the seme.[43]

At this point, one is tempted toward a deconstructionist reading. What

[42] Euripides' *Helen* seems to be the only surviving play in which the chorus leaves the stage through the central doors; I owe this observation to Geoffrey Arnott.

[43] See Pierre Macherey, *A Theory of Literary Production*, trans. Geoffrey Wall (London, 1978); Fredric Jameson, *The Political Unconscious: Narrative as a Socially Symbolic Act* (Ithaca, N.Y., 1981), 56: "It follows, then, that the interpretive mission of a properly structural causality will . . . find its privileged content in the rifts and discontinuities within the work, and ultimately in a conception of the former 'work of art' as a heterogeneous and (to use the most dramatic recent slogan) a schizophrenic text. In the case of Althusserian literary criticism proper, then, the appropriate object of study emerges only when the appearance of formal unification is unmasked as a failure or an ideological mirage." See also Frank Kermode, "Secrets and Narrative Sequence," *Critical Inquiry* 7 (Autumn, 1980): 87–88: "Secrets, in short, are at odds with sequence, which is considered as an aspect of propriety; and a passion for sequence may result in the suppression of the secret. But it is there, and one way we can find the secret is to look out for evidence of suppression, which will sometimes tell us where the suppressed secret is located."

need had Odysseus to save Silenos? The arbitrariness of the final arrangement appears to be inscribed in the text. Perhaps it is. Societies do, after
all, generate the ideologies by which they approve themselves. Their fictions are inevitably a partial unmasking of this circularity.[44] But I am interested here not in fictions as such, but in this fiction, the *Kyklōps*. Upon
the logic of its categories, the choices of the action and the image of the
divine affirm an order that embraces relations of exchange and communal festiveness, setting these together, almost by an act of will, against
the devouring cyclōps.

There is thus a double strategy to the drama. The triplet of man, kyklōps, and satyr is structured by a logic of exchange in such a way that
the two hybrid types, who blur the boundary between man and beast,
appear as two modes of negation. With respect to each other they are at
once similar and contrary, while the human community appears as the
positive realization of social relations. At the same time, an implicit alliance associates the interests of Odysseus and the satyrs. Both, indeed, are
cast as victims of Polyphemos, and the story thereby may retain the basic
form of the *Odyssey* episode, which rests on the dyad of captive and cap-
tor. Richard Seaford speaks of "the poignant complication that the
enemy of the *thiasos* [the Bakkhic throng] is also the enemy of the
polis."[45] There is more than a common enemy that binds them, however. Odysseus is represented as the instrument of the satyrs' god. The
civic and ecstatic principles are thus united in Dionysos, who under-
writes their harmony. To see that this need not be the case, it is enough
to recollect the story of the *Bakkhai*.[46] In the *Kyklōps*, the image of Dionysos organizes the categories of the implicit anthropology in such a way
as to include the communal moment in the ordered relations of the city-
state. It is a satisfying note on which to close the curtain on the rigors of
the day's tragedies.

[44] See especially René Girard, *Violence and the Sacred*, trans. Patrick Gregory (Baltimore,
1977), 56: "The modern mind has difficulty conceiving of violence in terms of a loss of distinctions, or a loss of distinctions in terms of violence. Tragedy can help to resolve this difficulty if we agree to view the plays from a radical perspective. Tragic drama addresses
itself to a burning issue—in fact, to *the* burning issue. The issue is never alluded to in the
plays, and for good reason, since it has to do with the dissolution by reciprocal violence of
those very values and distinctions around which the conflict of the plays supposedly revolves." For a probing analysis of the failure of categories in all discourse, see Jacques Derrida, "The Supplement of the Copula," in *Textual Strategies: Perspectives in Post-Structuralist
Criticism*, ed. Josué V. Harari (Ithaca, N.Y., 1979), 82–120.

[45] Seaford, 58.

[46] Dionysos there is of the party of the enthusiasts, while Pentheus asserts discipline
through repression. There is no mediating figure (though Winnington-Ingram thought he
saw one in Teiresias). Seaford discusses the thematic connections between the *Kyklōps* and
the *Bakkhai* in "Dionysiac Drama and Dionysiac Mysteries," *CQ* n.s. 31 (1981): 252–75,
esp. 272–74; also Seaford, 43–44.

FRANÇOIS LISSARRAGUE

Why Satyrs Are Good to Represent

MY INTENTION is not to analyze the iconography of satyrs in its totality but briefly to consider the question of the relation between satyric drama and the imagery of satyrs on Attic vases. The succinctness of my treatment may make it seem a bit too radical, but this is a risk I am willing to take, reserving for another occasion a detailed examination of the complete record. I would like to draw particular attention to some aspects of this question that specialists in ancient theater seem to regard as settled but that remain open from the iconographic standpoint.[1]

In studying satyric drama we have little enough to go on: Euripides' *Kyklōps*, part of Sophokles' *Ikhneutai*,[2] and an important set of fragments.[3] This information is generally supplemented by using the information provided by Attic vases, as they have been catalogued and analyzed by F. Brommer;[4] there exist some three hundred vases that have been connected with satyric drama. How much of this is accurate? What are the criteria that allow us to say that an image reflects a satyr-play? What sort of reflection is it?

We may begin with the most vivid piece of evidence on this subject, the famous Pronomos Vase (plate 1), which is a large volute-krater in the Naples Museum.[5] On one side it shows Dionysos with an entourage of satyrs, and on the other a company of actors, musicians, and chorus

Note: As always, my warmest thanks to the colleagues and museum curators who provided the photographs reproduced as plates, especially F. Hamdorf, J. Mertens, and A. Pasquier, as well as C. Bérard. This essay was translated by Andrew Szegedy-Maszak, Wesleyan University.

[1] The most recent survey is to be found in J. M. Moret, *Oedipe, la Sphinx et les Thébains* (Geneva, 1984), 139–42; I agree completely with its analysis.

[2] See the excellent edition with commentary by R. Seaford, *Euripides' Cyclops* (Oxford, 1984); also E. V. Maltese, *Ichneutae* (Florence, 1982).

[3] For the fragments, see W. Steffen, *Satyrographorum graecorum fragmenta* (Poznan, 1952). See also the studies by N. C. Hourmouziades, *Satyrika* (Athens, 1974), and D. F. Sutton, *The Greek Satyr Play* (Meisenheim, 1980).

[4] F. Brommer, *Satyrspiele* 2d ed. (Berlin, 1959), with subsequent additions in *The J. Paul Getty Museum Journal* 6–7 (1978–1979): 145–46, and *Greek Vases in the J. Paul Getty Museum* (Malibu, Calif., 1983), 1:119–20.

[5] Naples H 3240; *ARV*² 1336 (1), the Pronomos Painter, ca. 410; Brommer, *Satyrspiele*, fig. 1, no. 4, (72).

members. This latter image is both complex and extremely important, and it has given rise to numerous commentaries which I shall not summarize here.[6] Instead, let us look at it again. The picture consists of two zones. Above, in the center, Dionysos is reclining on a couch, with a woman seated next to him; at the foot of the couch sits another woman who is holding a mask in her left hand, while the young Himeros ("Desire") turns toward her. To the right of this group are two bearded actors carrying their masks, in this case of Herakles and Papposeilinos. To the left of the couch is yet another bearded actor, in royal costume, with mask in hand. This whole group in turn is flanked by beardless youths, who are nude except for a kind of furry pair of breeches outfitted with an erect phallus and a short horsetail. They are carrying masks with equine ears, high foreheads, and snub-nosed profiles: they are satyrs. The same young men appear in the lower zone, relaxed, sitting or conversing with one another. Only one of them is actually wearing his mask, as he dances—his foot crossing the decorative border—in front of a nude figure who is seated on a table, holding a scroll in his hand, and identified by an inscription as Demetrios. To the dancer's left sits a flutist, Pronomos, playing his instrument, in front of whom is another young musician, the lyre-player Charinos. The youths/satyrs are not altogether identical: almost all are crowned; one of them (second from the left on the bottom) has no mask; another (first on the left above) has breeches decorated with a kind of star;[7] yet another (second from the right on the bottom) has an embroidered tunic and a cloak. The people assembled on this side of the vase belong to various categories: members of the chorus, most of whom the inscriptions identify by their Athenian civic names (Kallias, Euagōn, Dorotheos, Eunikos, Diōn, Philinos, Nikoleōn, Kharias and Nikomakhos); a poet and musicians, similarly identified (Demetrios, Pronomos, Kharinos); and one actor who is identified only by the name of his character (Herakles). Dionysos, master of the theater, and Himeros are also identified by name.

As Beazley notes, we have here nearly the complete cast for a satyr-play.[8] In terms of our present topic—the graphic representation of satyric drama—we can make a few observations: the specific feature that indicates theatrical costuming as a satyr is the furry breeches. The mask, when it covers the face of a chorus member, is visually indistinguishable

---

[6] The bibliography on this vase is substantial. The most important citations are in *ARV²*; see also the comments by C. Calame, *Le récit en Grèce ancienne* (Paris, 1986), 101–17, and the essay by Winkler in this volume.

[7] The identification of the play is not certain; suggestions include *Hesiōnē* (so *ARV²* 1336), or *Omphalē* (E. Simon, *AA* [1971]: 199–206).

[8] *Hesperia* 24 (1955): 313.

from an ordinary satyr's face. Finally, the vase does not represent a specific moment from the play; the presence of the poet and of tripods decorated with fillets—not to mention of Dionysos himself—shows that this is a celebration of a victory in a dramatic competition. To sum up, this image has the same relation to theatrical performance as a playbill has to the script; it tells us almost nothing about the content of the play.

Does this vase offer any decisive criterion that would allow us to identify an image as being of a satyr-play? The satyr's costume seems to be a definite clue.[9] Thus, the tondo of a cup from Munich (plate 7) that shows a figure in "satyric breeches" dancing next to a krater has been linked to a satyr-play.[10] This, however, is not the only possible interpretation; on a krater from New York[11] (plate 8) there are three satyr-musicians similarly clad in hairy tights and tunics, like those of Papposeilinos on the Pronomos Vase. There is reason to doubt that this costuming necessarily represents a satyr-play; indeed, many conflicting interpretations have been offered and no consensus has yet emerged. The characters are labelled OIDOI PANATHENAIA ("Singers at the Panathenaia"), which certainly does not allow the inference that there was satyric dithyramb or comic satyr-play at the Panathenaia, as some have assumed.[12]

The latter conclusion can be confirmed by a stamnos in the Louvre:[13] one side shows a bull being led to sacrifice; under one handle there is a goat, and under the other an amphora; on the reverse, three satyrs in costume wield large mallets, as in *anodos* scenes.[14] Beazley believed that this scene might be related to a dithyramb where the prizes awarded to the three winners are precisely a bull, a goat, and an amphora. On the other hand, in studying the scenes of satyr-hammersmiths, C. Bérard interprets this as a kind of ritual disguise.[15] I will not declare myself for one side or the other; I will only say that, in general, the visible sign of dis-

---

[9] A. Kossatz-Deissmann, "Zur Herkunft des Perizoma im Satyrspiel," *JDAI* 97 (1982): 65–90.

[10] Munich 2657; *ARV²* 475 (267), Makron, ca. 480; Brommer, *Satyrspiele*, fig. 5, no. 5 (72).

[11] New York 25.78.66; *ARV²* 1172 (8), Polion, ca. 420. Cf. P. Ghiron-Bistagne, *Recherches sur les acteurs dans la Grèce antique* (Paris, 1976), 265.

[12] J. D. Beazley, *Hesperia* 24 (1955): 314ff.; M. Bieber, *History of the Greek and Roman Theater*, 2d ed. (Princeton, 1961), 6; E. Roos, *Die tragische Orchestik im Zerrbild der altattischen Komödie* (Lund, 1951), 227–30; H. Fröning, *Dithyrambos und Vasenmalerei in Athen*, Beiträge zur Archäologie (Wärzburg, 1971), 2:25–26.

[13] Louvre Cp. 10 754; *ARV²* 228 (32), Eukharides Painter, ca. 480; Brommer, *Satyrspiele*, no. 23, (73).

[14] J. D. Beazley, "A Stamnos in the Louvre," *Scritti in onore di G. Libertini* (Florence, 1958), 91–96.

[15] C. Bérard, *Anodoi: Essai sur l'imagerie des passages chthoniens* (Neuchâtel, 1974), 41–42, 83–84, and pl. 11, fig. 36.

guise—the satyr's breeches—need not be an absolutely certain indicator of satyric drama.

As a final example, a Korinthian cup[16] (plate 9) shows a woman dancing before Dionysos; nude from the waist up, she is wearing the hairy breeches of a satyr. This is difficult to interpret. Taking care not to invent a new Dionysiac ritual, we may once again find it enough to note that this satyric disguise probably does not refer to a satyr-play.

Nonetheless, we should avoid the hypercritical conclusion that no image has any relation to satyric drama. Some instances seem wholly convincing and certainly allude to this theatrical form, but in my opinion they do not allow us to generalize. A hydria from Boston[17] (plate 10) shows five satyrs wearing the furry breeches and dancing toward a flutist, on the right, who provides rhythmic accompaniment to their movement. The satyrs are carrying the components for some kind of furniture: four feet, of which one is already set in place before the musician on a slender, narrow base, while the remaining three are still in the satyrs' hands; to the far left, another satyr is carrying a kind of strut to hold the other pieces together. There has been some doubt as to what the furniture is; if it is a bed, this would be an allusion to Aiskhylos' *Thalamopoioi*,[18] but E. Simon finds the base too narrow and prefers to see it as a throne, which leads her to think of a play about Hera's being trapped on a chair crafted by Hephaistos.[19] Behind the flutist to the right stands a man in "civilian" clothes; he is not moving and does not seem to be an actor. Put in relation to the chorus, he could be the *khorēgos*. There are, to be sure, some images that refer to satyric drama, as there are some (about seventeen) that depict the "animal choruses" of comedy,[20] but they are quite rare.

The number of images of satyrs wearing the furry breeches is very small—about twenty of the total of three hundred collected by Brommer. To expand this corpus, he resorted to generalizing and extrapolating, padding the record with images that give no indication of being directly linked to satyr-plays. His justification for this procedure is as fol-

---

[16] Corinth, unnumbered; *ARV²* 1519 (13), Q Painter, first part of the fourth century.

[17] Boston 03.788; *ARV²* 571 (75), Leningrad Painter, ca. 470; Brommer, *Satyrspiele*, fig. 6, no. 1, (71).

[18] This is the hypothesis of T.B.L. Webster in his review of Brommer, *JHS* 70 (1950): 86, rejected by J. D. Beazley, *Attic Vase-painting in the MFA Boston* (Oxford, 1963), 3:52.

[19] E. Simon, "Satyr-plays on Vases in the Time of Aeschylus," in *The Eye of Greece: Studies in Honor of M. Robertson*, ed. D. C. Kurtz and B. Sparkes (Cambridge, 1984), 135–36.

[20] All of them are reproduced by J. R. Green, "A Representation of the *Birds* of Aristophanes," *Greek Vases in the J. Paul Getty Museum* (1985) 2:95–118; see also G. M. Sifakis, *Parabasis and Animal Choruses* (London, 1971).

lows: satyrs are properly the companions of Dionysos, and so whenever satyrs are found outside the purely Dionysiac world, it must be a case of illustrating a satyr-play.[21] Then one can try to reconstruct the play on the basis of the image, by using the mythological scene that is depicted and the titles of lost plays.[22] The temptation is as strong as it is arbitrary.

In fact, such a process reduces the image to a state of complete dependence on the theater, but certain documents make it clear that this is not how imagery functions. If we stop thinking of the visual representations in terms of theatrical presentations and instead consider the images in the iconographic context to which they belong, our perspective changes. Then we can see that, in the case of satyrs, the image operates through displacement and parody. On a lekythos in the Louvre[23] (plate 11), for example, we find a walking satyr with a sickle in his right hand and his left arm outstretched, brandishing a *kibisis* (a pouch or wallet) in which the Gorgon's head is tidily packed; the satyr is standing in for Perseus, but in the theater he could only have been a member of the chorus.

The same is true of an oinokhoē in London[24] (plate 12): a satyr, armed like Herakles with a club and lionskin, is advancing on a tree defended by a snake. This is recognizable as the story of the garden of the Hesperides. The satyr has replaced the Theban hero, and at the same time the golden apples have been replaced by pitchers—we are in the world of wine. The image plays with the manipulation of symbols to achieve a comic incongruity. The principle is the same as in satyric drama, but stage and vase use different media.

From time to time the painters produced two copies of images, which make even clearer the work of displacement that is characteristic of the satyrs' world. An accident of preservation has given us two column-kraters which Beazley attributes to the same painter. One of them shows men going toward a grape press[25] (plate 13); the other[26] (plate 14) is almost identical and shows satyrs in the same situation. Comparison of these two scenes reveals the proximity of men and satyrs in their relation to the grape harvest and the production of wine;[27] such a comparison

---

[21] Cf. Brommer, *Satyrspiele*, 8, 19.

[22] A good example of this kind of endeavor is S. Karouzou, "Herakles Satyrikos," *BCH* 60 (1936): 152–57.

[23] Paris, Louvre CA 1728; *ARV²* 677 (10), class CL, ca. 470; Brommer, *Satyrspiele*, fig. 25, no. 36, (74).

[24] London E 539; *ARV²* 776 (2), Berlin group 2415, ca. 470–460; Brommer, *Satyrspiele*, fig. 29, no. 92, (77).

[25] Ferrara T 245C VP; *ARV²* 524 (26), Orchard Painter, ca. 470.

[26] Bologna 190; *ARV²* 524 (25).

[27] See the analysis by Claude Bérard, *La Cité des Images* (Lausanne and Paris 1984) 131 and figs. 185–86.

also highlights the visual malleability of the satyr's image, in a context no one would dream of connecting with the theater.

We find a similar treatment on another pair of vases attributed to the same artist. A krater from New York[28] (plate 15) has a painting of Jason approaching the golden fleece under the gaze of Athena; to the right is the ship Argo. On a krater from Bologna[29] (plate 16), the same painter repeats the same composition but substitutes a satyr for Jason and Dionysos for Athena. The image tips into the parodic realm of the satyrs without at all forcing us to conjecture—as some have done—that there was a satyr-play about the Argonauts.

The metamorphoses of the satyrs and the interplay of images reveal the painters' ability to give visual life to an imaginary world, which is constellated around Dionysos and draws from the same sources as does the theatrical world. To the extent that they belong to the same culture, painters and poets share the same knowledge of myth; only their forms of expression differ, according to their respective degree of inventiveness.

To finish this rapid survey of the iconographic motifs associated with satyric drama, I will note that even if there did exist a play about the return of Hephaistos,[30] we know that the painters did not wait for its performance to deal with this subject.[31]

The fundamental question is the relation between the painted image and the theatrical presentation. Obviously the painters were not unaware of theater. Sometimes they even depict a stage or an audience on tiers of seats,[32] but this is not what they are most interested in. When an image deals specifically with the theater—as does the Pronomos Vase—it is more to commemorate a victory than to portray the play itself. In our curiosity we may find this frustrating, but not so the Athenians who themselves attended the theatrical performances; for them, the vases are souvenirs, rather than reproductions, of the dramas.

Such an interpretation seems to gain confirmation from the images

---

[28] New York 34.11.7; ARV^2 524 (28).

[29] Bologna 190; ARV^2 524 (27); Brommer, *Satyrspiele*, no. 104, (78).

[30] See Sutton, *Satyrographorum*, 70–71.

[31] It already appears on the "Francois Vase": Florence 4209, ABV 76 (1), ca. 570. On this motif, see T. Carpenter, *Dionysian Imagery in Archaic Greek Art* (Oxford, 1986), 13–29.

[32] For depictions of the audience seated in the theater, see: Athens, Akropolis 587—ABV 39 (15) Sophilos, ca. 570; Florence 3773 and Berlin 1711—ABV 95 (8), Tyrrhenian group, ca. 560; Paris BN 243, unattributed, ca. 550—CVA 2, pls. 88–89. For the depiction of a stage, see: Athens, Vlasto collection—ARV^2 1215 (1), Perseus' dance group, ca. 430; Brommer, *Satyrspiele*, figs. 21–23, no. 43, (74). It is worth noting that Athenian pottery does not have an equivalent for the *phlyax* vases, which often show the stage; see A. D. Trendall, *Phlyax Vases*, 2d ed., *BICS*, supp. 19 (London, 1967).

that portray a woman named Tragōidia or Komōidia;[33] they always involve a female alongside Dionysos or, as on an Oxford oinokhoē,[34] asleep under the astonished gaze of a satyr. To suggest the ties between Dionysos and the theater, the painters make use of an allegorical figure, who has nothing to do with a "photographic" view of the stage.

With the vases and the theater we are dealing with two fields which, while close, cannot simply be superimposed on one another. In both cases, we are in a domain of Dionysos: on the one hand, in the consumption of wine and the images on the vases; on the other, in a religious festival and theatrical performance. There is no absolute division between the two. The painters are part of the audience in the theater, and the dramatic poets attend symposiums and handle vases—both live in a unified culture at a specific historical moment. It does not seem necessary to posit a dependent relation between the two groups. Rather, they embody two kinds of visualization, two different types of spectacle. Drama offers a unique experience which occurs in a fixed location, before a group, in a civic and religious setting; the vase is a moveable object, which a single viewer can contemplate whenever, and as often as, he wants. These are two discrete ways of seeing. While the two modes are certainly parallel, neither constitutes a model that must shape the other. Painters and poets work on the basis of the same data and examine the same issues. The world of the satyrs around Dionysos is a world turned upside down, displaced, reversed.

In the paintings we see humanity halfway between the bestial and the divine. The satyr's body is a hybrid composed of a human body with a tail, horse's ears, and sometimes hooves. Though the satyrs are usually nude, they occasionally wear cloaks as the Athenians themselves do. Thus their appearance can vary from the most animal to the most human. They are almost always in a group, capering, gesturing, and dancing, in an endless roundelay around Dionysos. They are most often depicted in the company of maenads, whom they pursue or carry off, without always consummating their desires,[35] in a procession suffused with fantasy. Their style of drinking directly contravenes human manners: they are always parched with thirst, greedy for wine, which they drink straight from the amphora without any admixture of water; some-

---

[33] *Tragōidia*: Compiègne 1025—*ARV*² 1055 (76), Polygnotos group, ca. 440. *Kōmōidia*: Louvre G421—*ARV*² 1037 (1), similar to the Peleas and Hektor painters, ca. 440 (see Ghiron-Bistagne, *Recherches*, fig. 87). *Kōmōidia* also appears on an unnumbered, unattributed vase in Barcelona; see G. Trias de Arribas, *Ceramicas Griegas de la Peninsula Iberica* (1967), no. 589, pl. 100 (182).

[34] Oxford 534; *ARV*² 1258 (1), associated with the Eretria Painter, ca. 430; it is reproduced in Seaford, *Euripides' Cyclops*, pl. IV, 55.

[35] See S. MacNally, "The Maenad in Early Greek Art," *Arethusa* 11 (1978): 101–35.

times they dive headlong to submerge themselves in the wine jars. Satyrs' behavior is almost always an excess or a transgression, not only
with regard to wine but in other areas as well. In war, for example, they
are generally equipped like ephebes but sometime use tableware in the
place of weapons. In their relations with animals, they sometimes crawl
or leap like the animals themselves, or treat animals like human companions. Without multiplying examples,[36] we may say that satyrs reproduce
the "normal" values and activities of Greek males by transforming them,
according to a set of rules that are never random. The nature of imagery
itself—which works through condensation, displacement, metaphor,
and metonymy—encourages the visual exploration of the satyrs' imaginary world.

In the theater, the form seems as strictly codified as the other dramatic
genres. The language of satyric drama is more prosaic than that of
tragedy, and the plays are shorter. The location is often rural, pastoral, or
exotic, a liminal territory far from cities or royal palaces. The themes
seem to have been quite conventional. We find all kinds of ogres, monsters, or magicians, and the satyrs are often their captives. Sometimes
they try to pass for athletes. Frequently the subject of the play is tied to a
discovery or an invention: of wine, for example, or music, metallurgy,
fire, or the first woman, Pandora. That is, everything takes place as if satyrs were a means to explore human culture through a fun-house mirror;
the satyrs are antitypes of the Athenian male citizenry and present us
with an inverted anthropology (or andrology) of the ancient city-state.

This is the key, I think, to understanding the function of satyric
drama. As an adjunct to tragedy, written by the same poet and performed after the group of three tragedies, the satyr-play—according to
Horace and the Roman theorists—used its jokes as a diversion, after
tragedy's high seriousness. What does this mean?

Within the theater, the comic is the province of comedy, which belongs to the theatrical context of a festival and employs a whole range of
tones. Sometimes comedy parodies tragedy, quoting passages from
tragedies and putting its own characters into situations analogous to
those of tragic heroes; it incorporates and distorts the tragic style to fashion its own brand of significance.[37] Comedy makes equal use of present
reality, especially politics, and caricatures living figures. Finally, comedy
undercuts theatrical illusion and plays with the various levels of fiction:
the chorus directly addresses the audience to bring it into the dramatic
game, or Dionysos pleads for the assistance of his own priest, seated in
the front row.

---

[36] I am preparing a general study, from this perspective, of the iconography of satyrs.

[37] Helene P. Foley, "Tragedy and Politics in Aristophanes' *Acharnians*," *JHS* 108 (1988):
33–47.

None of this appears in satyric drama, which follows tragedy in its complete respect for the fiction of the stage. The play stays at one remove from the audience, which observes without being called to account. Satyric drama as far as we know never parodies tragedy, and the principal characters, such as Odysseus, maintain their epic stature without any caricature or burlesque. (Note the dignity of the three actors on the Pronomos Vase.) Nor does it contain any political allusions. The "comedy" of satyric drama lies somewhere else.

In fact, it resides in the constitutive element of the genre: the presence of satyrs required by the nature of the chorus. It works by playing with myth, by taking a well-known story and overlaying it with a group of satyrs who react to the situation in their own peculiar fashion. The recipe is as follows: take one myth, add satyrs, observe the result.

The comic effect springs from this collage of satyrs and myth, the revision of myth through this specific filter. The joke is one of incongruity, which generates a series of surprises. Euripides' *Kyklōps*, for example, depicts the progressive rediscovery of wine and the rituals for drinking which were so basic to Athenian culture.[38] The presence of satyrs within the myth subverts tragedy by shattering its cohesiveness. Tragedy poses fundamental questions about the relation between mortals and gods, or it reflects on such serious issues as sacrifice, war, marriage, or law. Satyric drama, by contrast, plays with culture by first distancing it and then reconstructing it through its antitypes, the satyrs. It does not seek to settle a controversy, nor to bring man face to face with his fate or the gods. It plays in a different key, with the displacement, distortion, and reversal of what constitutes the world and culture of men; it reintroduces distance and reinserts Dionysos in the center of the theater.

Both in the images and on the stage, then, satyrs use the medium of parody to reveal a world under the aegis of Dionysos. They appear as blatant meddlers, creators of disorder, fashioning before the spectator's eyes a negative anthropology, an anthropology of laughter. That is why, it seems to me, satyrs are good to represent.

---

[38] On this point, see the essay by Konstan in this volume.

JOSIAH OBER AND BARRY STRAUSS

Drama, Political Rhetoric, and the Discourse of Athenian Democracy

I. INTRODUCTION

In classical Athens democracy was not simply a form of government, but a sociocultural structure. On the political level all Athenian adult males were theoretically equal and worthy and they stood out against those supposedly inferior persons who inhabited Athenian territory, but had no political rights: women, metics, slaves, and children. The citizens composed a very significant subset of Athenian society: a strictly defined "political society," which served as the locus of all public decision making and of political culture, i.e., the system of beliefs, values, and symbols that defined political action. But, just as political society is a subset of the society at large, political culture is a part of the general culture and so shares its values; politicians, no less than playwrights or shipbuilders, are guided by the general cultural paradigms.[1]

Despite a wide acceptance of the principle of political equality among the citizens, Athenian political society was never socially or economically homogenous. The citizenry remained hierarchically stratified in terms of class and status, and the interests of elite citizens were sometimes at odds with those of the mass of ordinary citizens. Both the dissonance between egalitarianism and elitism *within* political society, and the discontinuity between political society and the larger society of the *polis*, produced considerable tension.

Political rhetoric and drama can be seen, and analyzed, as closely re-

Note: The authors have cooperated closely throughout, but the background on political sociology and sections III and VI were written by Ober, the background on cultural anthropology and sections IV and V by Strauss. Section III and parts of sections I, II, and VII are adapted from Ober's book *Mass and Elite in Democratic Athens: Rhetoric, Ideology, and the Power of the People* (Princeton, 1989). Section IV and part of section II are adapted from a paper delivered by Strauss at the Hebrew University, Jerusalem, in 1987.

[1] The classic study on political culture is L. W. Pye and S. Verba, eds., *Political Culture and Political Development* (Princeton, 1965), esp. 513–17. Their definition, which emphasizes political attitudes to the exclusion of political behavior, has led to considerable debate, well summarized in R. Tucker, "Culture, Political Culture, and Communist Society," *Political Science Quarterly* 88 (1973): 173–90; S. White, *Political Culture and Soviet Politics* (New York, 1979), 1–21. For the notion of Mediterranean political culture, see S. H. Barnes and G. Sani, "Mediterranean Political Culture and Italian Politics: An Interpretation," *British Journal Political Science* 4 (1974): 289–303.

lated forms of public speech.[2] Like legal trials and Assembly speeches, Athenian theatrical performances and dramatic texts were closely bound up in the mediation of conflicting social values. Notably, though perhaps inevitably, the physical settings for mass meetings of the people—the Pnyx and the Theater of Dionysos—were very similar in terms of spatial organization. The seating in the theater was egalitarian, as it was in the Assembly and in the people's courts.[3] In each case, the mass audience faced, listened to, and actively responded to, the public discourse of individual speakers. There were, of course, differences between the procedures of the theater and the more overtly political arenas of the Assembly and the courts—the playwright was not voted upon directly by his audience and did not face the audience in propria persona (although comic parabases could come close). But the congruity between the political and theatrical arenas meant that the responses of Athenian citizens as jurors and Assemblymen were inevitably influenced by the fact of their having been members of theatrical audiences, and vice versa.

Athenian political society provides the primary context for political rhetoric: speeches delivered in the Assembly or Boulē and at trials involving politicians. Speeches written for these contexts may be characterized as elite/mass texts: the expert orators who authored them were invariably identifiable as elite in terms of their abilities (especially as trained speakers) and their wealth. But the texts were written for delivery to an audience composed primarily of ordinary citizens.[4] As all politicians (ancient and modern) must realize, the public speaker is constrained to take the opinions and attitudes of his audiences into con-

----

[2] On the continuity between rhetoric and drama, see, for example, R.G.A. Buxton, *Persuasion in Greek Tragedy* (Cambridge, Eng., 1982), esp. 17–18; Stephen G. Salkever, "Tragedy and the Education of the *Dēmos*: Aristotle's Response to Plato," in *Greek Tragedy and Political Theory*, ed. J. Peter Euben (Berkeley, 1986), 293–94.

[3] On the Pnyx and seating, see Homer A. Thompson and R. E. Wycherley, *The Agora of Athens*, The Athenian Agora 14 (Princeton, 1972), pp. 48–52; Mogens H. Hansen, "The Athenian *Ecclesia* and the Assembly-Place on the Pnyx," *GRBS* 23 (1982): 242–49. Theater of Dionysos and seating: *TDA*, esp. 140–41; *DFA*, 69–72; J. Travlos, *Pictorial Dictionary of Ancient Athens* (New York, 1971), 537–52. We know regrettably little about the physical form of Athenian courtrooms; see, however, J. Travlos in *Hesperia* 43 (1974): 500–511; Alan L. Boegehold in *Hesperia* 36 (1967): 111–20. Egalitarian seating: David Small, "Social Correlations to the Greek Cavea in the Roman Period," *Annual of the American Schools of Oriental Research* (forthcoming).

[4] Against the theories of, e.g., Arnold H. M. Jones, *Athenian Democracy* (Oxford, 1957), 36–37, and Kenneth J. Dover, *Greek Popular Morality in the Time of Plato and Aristotle* (Berkeley, 1974), 34–35, that most Assemblymen and jurors were at least "middle-class," see Minor M. Markle, "Jury Pay and Assembly Pay at Athens," in *Crux: Essays in Greek History Presented to G.E.M. de Ste Croix*, ed. P. A. Cartledge and F. D. Harvey (London, 1985), 265–97; A.W.H. Adkins, "Problems in Greek Popular Morality," *CP* 73 (1973): 156–57.

sideration if he hopes to gain their sympathy and their votes. Consequently, the analysis of political rhetoric provides a window on the attitudes and opinions—the ideology—that informed the relations between ordinary and elite citizens.[5]

Attic dramas of the fifth and fourth centuries B.C.E. can also be regarded as elite/mass texts, since they too were written and produced by elites for presentation to a mass audience. But, although citizens probably made up the bulk of the dramatic audience, noncitizens also attended in some numbers.[6] The internal concerns of Athenian political society provided only part of the material of Attic drama. The set of problems specific to the citizen body is evident in dramatic texts, but the concerns of both tragic and comic performances transcend the realm of the citizenry. Athenian dramas were often concerned with the relations between citizens and noncitizens. There have been any number of studies of Athenian "theater and politics," but the implications for reading dramatic texts of paying close attention to the context of the intersections and disjunctions between the two societies of classical Athens—the world of the citizen and the world that the citizen and the noncitizen coinhabited—are still largely unexplored.[7]

We suggest that the dramatists' treatment of issues affecting the whole society may be clarified by a prior analysis of the more limited and specific concerns of the political society; an investigation of the sociocultural underpinnings of courtroom and Assembly speeches will illuminate the concerns and conduct of drama. The concerns of Attic dramatists were,

[5] On the orator's accommodating himself to his audience's opinions: Aristotle, *Rhetoric* 1367b7–12, 1395b1–11, 1395b27–1396a3, 1415b28–32; presenting one's own character and behavior as proper and one's opponent's as improper: Aristotle, *Rhetoric* 1377b20–1378a3, 1415a28–b1, 1416a4–1417a8. See also the similar comments by the closely contemporary Pseudo-Aristotle, *Rhetoric for Alexander* 1436b16ff., 1439b15–36, 1440a25–b1, 1441b36–1442a14, 1443b14–21, 1444b35–1445a29, with the discussion of William M. Sattler, "Conception of *Ethos* in Ancient Rhetoric," *Speech Monographs* 14 (1957): 55–65, esp. 56–60. Cf. the succinct statement of Donald C. Bryant, "Rhetoric: Its Function and Its Scope," *Quarterly Journal of Speech* 39 (1953): 413; the function of rhetoric is "the function of adjusting ideas to people and of people to ideas." For elite scorn of orators who seek through their speeches merely to please the people: e.g., Aristotle, *Rhetoric* 1354a11–31, 1395b27–1396a3; 1404a1–8; Plato, *Gorgias* 452c–544b, 462b–c, *Phaidros* 260a, *Republic* 6.493a–c; Thuk., 2.65.8–12. But the political orators themselves attacked this habit: see below, section III. Modern admirers and students of rhetoric have attempted to refute the charge that rhetoric is mere flattery; see Werner Jaeger, *Paideia*, 3 vols. (New York, 1939–1944), 2:71; Donald C. Bryant, "Aspects of the Rhetorical Tradition," parts 1 and 2, *Quarterly Journal of Speech* 36 (1950): 169–76, 326–32.

[6] Composition of audiences of theater: *DFA*, 263–78.

[7] For a review of some recent literature on Aristophanes and politics: I. C. Storey, "Old Comedy 1975–1984," *EMC*, n.s., 6 (1987): 36–37; see also, Helene P. Foley, "Tragedy and Politics in Aristophanes' *Acharnians*," *JHS* 108 (1988): 33–47, with literature cited. Cf. the discussions of tragedy and politics cited below, n. 30.

of course, not merely political: they encompassed the broadest and most profound of human subjects, among them the erotic, the divine, kinship, family authority, and the relation of nature to culture. It is, nevertheless, characteristic of Attic drama that these suprapolitical concerns are often dramatized precisely through political action and political speeches. Moreover, the vocabulary, the symbols, the rituals, and the structures of this political drama are those of democratic Athens. This suggests that, for an analysis of Athenian society, the study of political rhetoric and drama must go hand in hand, and that in some cases the ideological background revealed by political rhetoric will elucidate the meaning of dramatic texts.

Our approach may appear to invert the obvious chronological order, since the fourth century B.C.E.—the date of most preserved speeches—is posterior to the "Golden Age" of tragedy and Old Comedy in the fifth. But there was political rhetoric in the fifth century and drama in the fourth. If we accept the congruity of rhetoric and drama as public speech, it is reasonable to look at rhetoric first, because it allows us to proceed from the specific and more knowable thing—relations within political society, revealed by courtroom trials and legislative debate—to the general and less knowable: the larger and more complex network of relations within the whole society.

II. METHOD: POLITICAL SOCIOLOGY AND CULTURAL ANTHROPOLOGY

The two modern disciplines we have employed to clarify the relationship between elite/mass texts and their social context are political sociology and cultural anthropology. Both disciplines are concerned with the interplay of ideology and communication. Individually, each discipline presents the historian with only a partial explanation of social relations and social change. But when the two disciplines are integrated, this difficulty largely disappears. Specifically, anthropological analysis reveals symbolic structures, and sociological analysis, with its functionalist tendency, shows how these structures become operational in the actions of individuals and groups. In sections III–VI we offer some examples of the ways in which this combined method can be applied, but we are more concerned here with pointing out a direction for future research than in presenting definitive readings.

The origins of the modern discipline of political sociology can be traced back to the work of Karl Marx, Max Weber, and Robert Michels, among others. The central concern of the field is to demonstrate how the sociological ordering of society leads to and is affected by political structures. A key problem addressed by political sociologists is that of ex-

plaining the interplay of conflict and consensus, especially in democracies. In analyzing a society that appears to function well, the political
sociologist attempts to understand how the forces of conflict and consensus are brought into balance.[8]

There is no doubt that both conflict and consensus were important in
the development of classical Athens. As Gouldner, among others, has
pointed out, aristocratic Greek culture was extremely competitive, and
competition took the form of a "zero-sum game"—for every "winner"
whose status was increased through success in competition, there were
one or more losers whose standing was lowered. This led to extremely
vigorous, even savage, competitions which, when fought on the political
plane, were potentially dangerous to the stability of the state.[9] Consensus
(*homonoia*) was regarded by the Athenians as a central democratic virtue
and was praised by the orators as essential to the continuation of society.
But, like unrestrained competition, pure consensus was potentially dangerous, because only simple matters were likely to produce a true consensus, and an attempt to run the state by means of a politics of consensus
threatened to lead to stagnation and to the alienation of those talented,
well-trained, and wealthy individuals whose ideas and whose cooperation were essential to the survival of the society.[10]

The relationship emphasized by political sociologists is that between
masses and elites: ordinary citizens and those who possess special privileges. Athenian political society certainly included a small percentage of
individuals who were elite in terms of their abilities, their wealth, or their
birth status: the Athenian vocabulary of status includes any number of
terms to describe such persons.[11] Ordinary Athenians, those who were

[8] See, for example, Seymour M. Lipset, "Political Sociology," in *Sociology Today*, ed.
Robert K. Merton (New York, 1959), 81–114, esp. 83: "The central concern of the study of
politics is the problem of consensus and cleavage." On the origins of political sociology, see
ibid., 84–91, citing Marx, de Tocqueville, Weber, and Michels as the "founding fathers" of
the field. For other useful introductions to the discipline, see Martin N. Marger, *Elites and
Masses: An Introduction to Political Sociology* (New York, 1981); Philo C. Washburn, *Political
Sociology: Approaches, Concepts, Hypotheses* (Englewood Cliffs, N.J., 1982).

[9] Alvin W. Gouldner, *Enter Plato: Classical Greece and the Origins of Social Theory* (New
York, 1965), 13–15, 44–55.

[10] On *homonoia*, see, for example, Isokrates, 6.67, 7.31, 69, 8.19, 12.178, 258, 18.44, 68;
Lysias, 2.63–65, 18.17–18, 25.21–23, 30; Andokides, 1.106, 108; Demosthenes, 9.38,
25.89; Hypereides, 3.37; Deinarkhos, 3.19. Cf. Moses I. Finley, *Democracy Ancient and Modern* (New Brunswick, N.J., 1973), 62–64; Stephen T. Holmes, "Aristippus in and out of
Athens," *American Political Science Review* 7 (1979): 118–23. Although elite writers sometimes spoke of *homonoia* as an ideal which was lacking at Athens (e.g., Xenophon, *Memorabilia* 3.5, 16), we do not agree with Nicole Loraux, *The Invention of Athens* (Cambridge,
Mass., 1986), 196, that *homonoia* was a "moderate" (as opposed to a democratic) political
virtue.

[11] E.g., *gnōrimoi, kaloi k'agathoi, kharientes, aristoi, eudaimones, khrēstoi.* Moses I. Finley,

collectively called by the orators *to plēthos* or *hoi polloi*, were much more numerous and by their numbers dominated voting in Assembly and courtroom. Because those with privileges in society tended to try to maximize their privileges at the expense of the unprivileged, the interests of the Athenian citizen-masses came into conflict both with the interests of the noncitizens of Attika and with those of the citizen-elites.

Social stratification within the Athenian citizenry was not only a matter of relative degrees of material comfort. The possession of elite attributes by the few resulted in power inequalities, since when a conflict of interests between individuals resulted in legal action, the elite litigant enjoyed various advantages. The Athenian well educated in the arts of speaking was more likely than his nonelite opponent to present a convincing argument to the jury. The rich litigant could buy a finely honed speech from a logographer. Wealth also provided leisure for preparation, and made it financially possible to engage in protracted litigation. The aristocrat, who inherited a sense of personal excellence, could call on influential friends and clansmen for support. After the jury had reached a decision the self-help nature of legal restitution favored the individual able to muster superior physical force.[12] The functional advantages enjoyed by members of the elite within the legal system posed a quandary for the Athenian *dēmos*.

On the other hand, the democratic political order seemed unjust to some elite Athenians. As Aristotle noted (*Rhetoric* 1378b26–1379a9; cf. *Politics* 1283b34–1284b34), an individual who is superior to his fellows in any one way tends to believe he is entitled to a generally privileged position in society. He who considers himself worthy of privilege because of his social superiority may regard it as an injustice to be placed on equal political footing with average citizens. And yet Athenian government

---

Politics in the Ancient World (Cambridge, Eng., 1983), 2, considers these to be economic class terms, but although wealth was a common denominator of elites, this oversimplifies the situation. For the division of elites into the traditional triad of wealth, ability, birth status: Aristotle *Politics* 1289b27–90a5, 1293b34–39, 1296b15–34, 1317b39–41, *Rhetoric* 1360b19–30, 1378b35–79a4, *Nikomakhean Ethics* 1131a24–29; Demosthenes, 19.295, Isokrates, 19.36, Lysias, 2.80, 33.2, 14.38, 44. Cf. R. Seager, "Elitism and Democracy in Classical Athens," in *The Rich, the Well Born, and the Powerful,* ed. F. C. Jaher (Urbana, Ill., 1973), 7, for other references. Adkins, "Problems," 154, notes that there is a general tendency for ancient orators to list three virtues, rather than four or five, because of the pleasing "tricolor" effect this produces.

[12] On the power of the elite, cf. Demosthenes, 21.45: force (*tēn iskhun*) belongs to the few, laws to the many; Aristotle, *Rhetoric* 1372a11–17: those who are powerful speakers, experienced in affairs and in legal cases, those with many friends, and the rich believe they can do wrong and not be punished for it. Cf. Robin Osborne, "Law in Action in Classical Athens," *JHS* 105 (1985): 40–58. On self help in Athenian law, see Mogens H. Hansen, *"Apagoge," "Endeixis," and "Ephegesis"* . . . *A Study in the Athenian Administration of Justice in the Fourth Century B.C.* (Odense, Denmark, 1976), 113–21.

was predicated on political equality and did not grant political privileges to those with special attributes or attainments. Furthermore, the Athenians applied egalitarian principles in assigning most official duties. Whereas in modern democracies, in Britain and the United States for example, the principle of represèntation and the process of election allow the politically ambitious elite citizen to use his or her functional superiority in gaining official positions from which he or she can legitimately wield political power, the Athenians did not delegate political power to representatives and could even regard elections as undemocratic. Most offices were filled by lot, and in principle the elite citizen had no better chance than anyone else to serve as an officer of the state. Most officials held little real power in any case.[13]

The conflict between the values of competition and consensus and between the aspirations of the masses and the elites were consequently sources of strain, yet Athenian political society was remarkably stable. From the second quarter of the fifth century through the third quarter of the fourth Athenians governed themselves democratically; the only serious interruptions were two short-lived oligarchic coups (411/10, 404/3), one established under pressure of the Peloponnesian War, the other imposed by the victorious Spartans after Athens' defeat. In both cases the Athenians promptly expelled the oligarchs and restored their democracy. Vastly superior military forces allowed the Macedonians to replace the Athenian democratic political order with an oligarchy in 322 B.C.E.; but even after repeated demonstrations of Macedonian military might in the late fourth and early third century, the Athenians continued to struggle to restore democracy. The historical record forbids the notion that the survival of democracy was the result of inertia, or a historical fluke.

How, then, did the Athenians deal with existing social inequalities, especially between rich and poor? Class tension was rife in Greece in all periods and often broke out in active conflict between the upper and lower classes.[14] The existence of the democracy itself provides only a partial so-

---

[13] Lottery and its importance to the democracy: *Ath. Pol.* 22.5; Herodotos, 3.80; Aristotle, *Politics* 1273b40–41, 1294b7–9); cf. esp. J. W. Headlam, *Election by Lot at Athens*, 2d ed. (Cambridge, Eng., 1933). Preselection among the elite was used only briefly, in the early fifth century: Mogens H. Hansen, "ΚΛΗΡΩΣΙΣ ΕΚ ΠΡΟΚΡΙΤΩΝ in Fourth-Century Athens," *CP* 81 (1986): 222–29. On the lack of power of the magistracies, cf. Robin Osborne, *Demos: The Discovery of Classical Athens* (Cambridge, Eng., 1985), 9: Athenian officials were "little more than ciphers of a civil service" with no executive powers.

[14] Aristotle, *Politics* (esp. 1265b10–12, 1296a21–23, 1302b24–25, 1303b13–17, 1304b20–1305a7), regards class tension to be among the greatest dangers facing the *polis* and devotes much space to recommendations of how tensions can be mediated, on both the ideological and the material planes; cf. Josiah Ober, "Aristotle's Political Sociology: Class, Status, and Order in the *Politics*," in *Essays on Aristotelian Political Science*, ed. Carnes Lord, forthcoming. G.E.M. de Ste Croix, *The Class Struggle in the Ancient Greek World* (Ithaca, 1981),

lution to the problem of Athens' relative social stability. The democratic government indeed gave the poorer citizens a degree of protection against the property-power of their wealthy fellows, and so moderated class antagonism. But the elite litigant remained functionally more powerful than his ordinary opponent, and the poorer Athenian's envy and resentment of the privileges enjoyed by the wealthy man was far from eliminated. Nor does the existence of the democracy in and of itself explain why the wealthy were not more active in agitating for a political position that would match their property-power and could guarantee the security of their goods.

As Seymour M. Lipset noted, "a stable democractic system requires sources of cleavage so that there will be struggle over ruling positions . . . but without consensus—a value system allowing the *peaceful 'play' of power* [our emphasis] . . . there can be no democracy."[15] In order to explain Athens' social stability and the survival of the democracy, therefore, we need to explain the nature of the power of the Athenian people. Various scholars,—e.g., Moses I. Finley, G.E.M. de Ste Croix, and Christian Meier—have identified the use of political power by political equals to moderate the effects of social inequality as a key factor in the Athenian sociopolitical order.[16] But power is not simple; a proper explanation of the *dēmos' kratos* will have to embrace not only the more obvious elements of voting and the reality and threat of physical force, but also authority and legitimacy, ideology and communication, relationship and reciprocity.[17]

---

while sometimes overemphasizing the role of class, is the best and fullest treatment of the problem. For different views see, for example, E. Ruschenbusch, *Untersuchungen zu Staat und Politik vom 7.–4. Jh. v. Chr.* (Bamberg, 1978): ideology and class tension play little part in civil strife; all conflicts are between competing *hetaireiai* of aristocrats and are caused by foreign policy problems. A. Lintott, *Violence, Civil Strife, and Revolution in the Classical City, 750–330 B.C.* (London, 1982), esp. 34: tensions arise "from the fundamental inequality between rich and poor," but the "rareness of genuine class conflicts" is "their most striking feature"; cf. ibid., 272–73 for criticism of Ruschenbusch's position. For a catalogue and analysis of *staseis* of the fifth and fourth centuries, see H.-J. Gehrke, *Stasis: Untersuchungen zu den inneren Kriegen in der griechischen Staaten des 5. und 4. Jh. v. Chr.* (Munich, 1985).

[15] Lipset, "Political Sociology," 91–92.

[16] Finley, *Politics*, 139–40, Ste Croix, *Class Struggle*, 98; Christian Meier, *Introduction à l'anthropologie politique de l'antiquité classique* (Paris, 1984), 7–26.

[17] For some useful discussions of power, see Meier, *Anthropologie*, 32–35; Peter Bachrach, "Introduction" to *Political Elites in a Democracy*, ed. Bachrach, (New York, 1971), 2–5 (on the relationship between power and authority); Niklas Luhmann, *The Differentiation of Society* (New York, 1982), 150–52 (power and decision making); Lipset, "Political Sociology," 105–7 (access); Washburn, *Political Sociology*, esp. 18–19 (discussion of Weber on legitimacy); Michel Foucault, *The History of Sexuality*, 3 vols. (New York, 1980), 1: 41–42, 81–102 (relationality); Samuel Bowles and Herbert Gintis, *Democracy and Capitalism* (New York, 1986), 92–120 (heterogeneity).

Symbols, paradigms, and rituals have long been among the anthropologist's subjects of study. Since the early days of Morgan, Maine, and Fustel, anthropologists have been interested in the influence of these basic cultural forms on political action. The term political culture (above, section 1) has begun to come into use among both political scientists and anthropologists.[18] For our purposes, the work of Victor Turner and Clifford Geertz is of particular value, clarifying the ways in which the genres of drama and political oratory can share paradigms, symbols, and rituals.

For Turner, the essence of politics is a dramatic process, which he first studied during the 1950s by analyzing the conflicts between individuals within the small kinship groups of the African Ndembu.[19] In Turner's eyes, each of these conflicts is a "social drama," a public episode that passes through ritualized stages of tension, crisis, redress, and reintegration. Social dramas force individuals to choose between personal preferences and social obligations. He writes: "The situation in a Ndembu village closely parallels that found in Greek drama where one witnesses the helplessness of the human individual before the Fates; but in this case the fates are the necessities of the social process."[20] Hence, the cross-fertilization of drama and politics is inherent in the ritual of political action.

Turner takes the idea of social drama further in later writings. He notes that from time to time, politicians take vigorous action: perhaps a courageous stand, or a single-minded pursuit of vengeance, or a gracious compromise, or a slippery betrayal. Often, such actions seem to be self-contained drama—and the script is not chosen by accident. Turner discusses this point:

> What seems to happen is that when a major public dramatic process gets under way, people, whether consciously, preconsciously, or unconsciously, take on roles which carry with them, if not precisely recorded scripts, deeply engraved tendencies to act and speak in suprapersonal or "representative" ways appropriate to the role taken, and to prepare the way for a certain climax that approximates to the nature of the climax given in a certain central myth of the death or victory of a hero or heroes in which they have been deeply indoctrinated or "socialized" or "enculturated."[21]

[18] Ted Lewellen, *Political Anthropology: An Introduction* (New York, 1983).

[19] Victor Turner, *Schism and Continuity in an African Society* (Manchester, 1957). For a different view of politics as drama, see Clifford Geertz, *Negara: The Theatre State in Nineteenth-Century Bali* (Princeton, 1980).

[20] Turner, *Schism and Continuity*, 94.

[21] Turner, *Dramas, Fields, and Metaphors: Symbolic Action in Human Society* (Ithaca, 1974), 123.

As an example, Turner notes the tremendous importance of the Christ myth in Mexican politics. He argues that in such disparate events as Hidalgo's insurrection of 1811 and the emperor Maximilian's choice in 1867 to eschew flight from Mexico, Mexican political actors chose martyrdom to " 'fulfill the prophecy,' or fulfill the model presented by so many symbols of the Mexican cultural scene—symbols in which the processual myth that ends in the *via crucis* is represented."[22]

What were the "prophecies" that the Athenian politician might have chosen to fulfill? "To be the best and always superior to others," like Akhilleus, to avenge the honor of his *oikos*, like Odysseus, to die in battle like a hoplite of Tyrtaios? An Athenian politician might have chosen his myths from a variety of sources: from epic, from Archaic poetry, from art, from history oral or written, even from war or athletic competition—and finally, from tragedy. Tragedy was of central importance in Athens; as S. C. Humphreys writes, tragedy was "the main symbolic form of classical Athens."[23]

Clifford Geertz, in his analysis of a much less highbrow cultural form, the cockfight in Bali, has suggested what seems to us to be a very fruitful way to look at tragedy. Despite the great and obvious differences between a Greek tragedy and a Balinese cockfight, they have this in common: they are both playful activities—"deep play," as Geertz says[24]— with a serious purpose: they spell out externally an internal truth. In other words, both tragedy and the cockfight may be understood and analyzed as texts, in which reality is represented in a structured system. A member of the audience can read out both the ethos of his culture and his own private sensibility.

> In the violent, winner-take-all cockfight, the observer can find out what a man, usually composed, aloof, almost obsessively self-absorbed, a kind of moral autocosm, feels like when, attacked, tormented, challenged, insulted, and driven as a result to the extremes of fury . . . [he] has totally triumphed or been brought totally low.[25]

---

[22] Ibid., 123.

[23] Sarah C. Humphreys, *The Family, Women, and Death* (London, 1983), 18.

[24] Clifford Geertz, "Deep Play: Notes on the Balinese Cockfight," in Geertz, *The Interpretation of Cultures* (New York, 1973), 432. For Geertz's interpretive theory, see his "Thick Description: Toward an Interpretive Theory of Culture," in Geertz, *Interpretation*, 3–30. Of the many evaluations of Geertz's work, we have found most relevant: R. G. Walters, "Signs of the Times: Clifford Geertz and Historians," *Social Research* 47 (1980): 537–56; W. Roseberry, "Balinese Cockfights and the Seduction of Anthropology," *Social Research* 49 (1982): 1013–28; P. Shankman, "The Thick and the Thin: On the Interpretive Theoretical Program of Clifford Geertz," *Current Anthropology* 25 (1984): 261–79.

[25] Geertz, "Deep Play," 450.

This experience has much in common with watching the performance of
a tragedy. As Geertz writes,

> the cockfight creates what . . . could be called a paradigmatic hu-
> man event—that is, one that tells us less what happens than the kind
> of thing that would happen if, as is not the case, life were art and
> could be as freely shaped by styles of feeling as *Macbeth* and *David
> Copperfield* are. Enacted and re-enacted . . . the cockfight enables
> the Balinese, as read and reread, *Macbeth* enables us, to see a dimen-
> sion of his subjectivity.[26]

Geertz goes on to argue that art or games do not merely display experience; they color experience with the light they cast it in. To the Balinese, not merely is the cockfight like life, but—and here we apologize for
the echo of high school sports banquet oratory—life is like the cockfight.
To quote Geertz again: "If we see ourselves as a pack of Micawbers, it is
from reading too much Dickens."[27]

We may apply this analysis to Athens. Attic tragedy both displays and
creates "[private] temperament and social temper at the same time."[28]
The Athenians went to the theater to observe what it felt like to choose
between murdering your mother and leaving your father unavenged,
like Orestes; or to face unbearable and undeserved shame, like Oidipous;
or to be a woman so mistreated by a man that you murder your own
children to punish him, like Medeia. They went to observe characters
who were both noble and terrifying, and whose actions were both edifying and repulsive.

To the Athenian orator, tragedy held a particular appeal as a cultural
paradigm to which he might refer. The orator knew that his audience
would make cross-references to the theater; Thoukydides' Kleon, for example, calls the Athenians "spectators [*theatai*] of speeches" (Thuk.,
2.38.4). The characters of tragedy have grandeur and dignity: any suggestion that an orator was as noble as, e.g., Theseus, as courageous as
Prometheus, as self-sacrificing as Alkestis, as long-suffering as Philoktetes, would add grandeur to his cause. At a price, however: not even the
noblest character of tragedy could be described as friendly, sympathetic,
or lovable. Who would want Prometheus, for example, on the next
couch at a symposium? When it comes to tragedy, therefore, the orator
was in a double bind. To avoid all reference to tragedy was to give up a
valuable symbol. To identify oneself too closely with tragedy, on the
other hand, was to risk alienating the audience. The man in the street was

[26] Ibid.
[27] Ibid., 451.
[28] Ibid.

not Prince Neoptolemos, and would feel put off by any orator who felt that *he* was meant to be. The clever orator, therefore, would try to have it both ways: he would both identify himself with the heroic characters of tragedy and distance himself safely in the ranks of *hoi polloi*.[29]

If political rhetoric makes use of the symbols and structures of tragedy, so too tragedy makes use of the symbols and structures of political rhetoric. The Athenian tragic playwright was in no narrow literary compartment: his subject was the life of the *polis*. If the characters were mythical, if the setting was usually out of Athens, if the dramatic date was ancient, nevertheless the rhetoric of politics in tragedy is largely the rhetoric of contemporary democratic Athens. Both tragic poets and political orators could see themselves as teachers: both aimed at the improvement of the citizen, both communicated through rhetoric.[30]

Like the orator, the tragedian referred to another genre. He constantly reminded the audience that the theater of Dionysos was in many ways analogous to the Pnyx or *dikasterion* or *bouleuterion*—not merely spatially, but culturally. Both tragedians and orators wrote speeches that were artistic, competitive, and political. Aristotle (*Poetics* 1451b) says that the real difference between a poet and a historian is not that one writes verse and the other prose, but that one writes about what did happen and the other about what might happen. We might say, similarly, that the real difference between an orator and a tragedian is that one tries to persuade the audience to engage in a specific political action, the other to persuade the audience of a more general, more ideal, but no less political truth.[31] The political symbolism of tragedy may be less direct than that of a po-

---

[29] Cf. Josiah Ober, "Elite Education and Political Leadership in Democratic Athens," *APA* Paper, December 30, 1986, and Ober, *Mass and Elite*, chaps. 4 and 7.

[30] The relationship of myth and contemporary politics in Attic tragedy is a rich and complex subject, the source of many fruitful scholarly debates. If it is clear that the tragedians were neither indifferent to contemporary politics nor engaged in direct and specific political endorsements, it is not so clear precisely how the many references to Athenian political life are to be taken. Among the best starting points to this question are J. Redfield, "Die 'Frösche' des Aristophanes: Komödie und Tragödie als Spiegel der Politik," *Antaios* 4 (1962–1963): 422–39; the essay by Redfield, in this volume; Bernard Knox, *Oedipus at Thebes* (New Haven, 1957), esp. chap. 2; Knox, "Sophocles and the Polis," in *Sophocle*, ed. Jacqueline de Romilly, Entretiens sur l'antiquité classique 29 (Geneva, 1983), 1–37; Jean-Pierre Vernant and P. Vidal-Naquet, *Mythe et tragédie* (Paris, 1972); B. Vickers, *Towards Greek Tragedy* (London, 1973), 100 164; O. Taplin, "Fifth-Century Tragedy and Comedy: A Synkrisis," *JHS* 106 (1986): 167; and the essay by Goldhill in this volume. Still eloquent is Victor Ehrenberg, *Sophocles and Pericles* (Oxford, 1954); see also John H. Finley, "Politics and Early Attic Tragedy," *HSCP* 71 (1967): 1–14. On tragedy as an approach to the tensions and oppositions of the social order, see Charles Segal, "Greek Tragedy and Society: A Structuralist Perspective," in Segal, *Interpreting Greek Tragedy, Myth, Poetry, Text* (Ithaca, 1986), 21–47. For the symbolic and political meaning of Athens, Thebes, and Argos as settings of tragedy, see the second essay by Zeitlin, "Thebes," in this volume. On tragedy's "distance in fictional space and time," see the essay by Winkler in this volume.

[31] See the essay by Redfield in this volume.

litical oration (Pentheus does not cite the laws, chapter and verse), but it is no less powerful. Indeed, as Abner Cohen points out, indirect political symbolism is more resonant with meaning than a blatant and straightforward political speech. Politics can be powerfully manifested in apparently nonpolitical institutions, such as rites of passage, funerals, and drama.[32]

In sum, political sociology raises questions about the nature of stability given the tension caused by conflict between values (competition and consensus) and between classes (masses and elites). Cultural anthropology places emphasis on the importance of symbolic action and interaction. Combining these two approaches, we may suggest that Athenian political society was stabilized by communication between citizens in a language composed of a vocabulary of symbols. The importance of mass communication in modern democratic states is now widely recognized, but it has not been taken enough into account in previous attempts to explain the nature of the Athenian sociopolitical order.[33] The language of symbols which facilitated communication between Athenians grew out of the interaction of ideology and events within the context of the arenas of public speech. By recognizing that Athenian public communication was a dynamic, interactive, and symbolic process, undertaken in different forums within a relatively stable but not ossified ideological context, we can begin to understand public discourse and its role in the democratic *polis*. The public forums provided an environment in which the "tactics" of symbols could be devised and tested and so integrated into a cultural strategy which allowed a high degree of harmony within a status-stratified society.

In the following four test cases we look at ways in which the nondiscrete "realms" of political oratory and decision making and of literary culture and drama were integrated in rhetorical and dramatic texts. In each case, the texts are inexplicable outside the context of a political culture which formed and was informed by public speech. The first two cases look at ways in which expert political orators attempted to manipulate an audience of juror-theatergoers by appealing to an ideological background which stresses both egalitarian and elitist principles. Next, we look at two dramatic texts which refer to the appropriate behavior and decision-making processes of political society. These dramatic texts

---

[32] Abner Cohen, *Two-Dimensional Man: An Essay on the Anthropology of Power and Symbolism in Complex Societies* (Berkeley, 1974), 90–118.

[33] See, for example, John W. Riley and M. W. Riley, "Mass Communication and the Social System," in *Sociology Today*, ed. Merton, 537–78, esp. 563–69. Cf. ibid., 538–39, 541 n. 15, 545 n. 33, for a discussion of modern mass communication theory as an elaboration of the basic principles set down by Aristotle, although Riley and Riley suggest that modern models stress the interactive nature of communication more than did Aristotle. Henderson, in his essay in this volume, demonstrates the important results that can be achieved through analyzing comedy as a form of social communication.

draw on ideological assumptions that are recognizable from the study of political rhetoric. But in the dramatic texts we see a willingness to transcend and challenge the delicate internal balance of political society, by confronting it with the larger issues of the society as a whole.

III. THE ATTIC ORATORS' USE OF POETRY AND HISTORY

The ambivalent attitude the Athenian *dēmos* held toward the subjects of rhetoric, rhetorical ability, and rhetorical education made the role of the elite political orator complex and problematic. When a well-known politician stood up to speak in Assembly or in a law court, his audience was eager to be entertained and instructed, but might distrust him if he were to reveal too obviously the extent of his skill.[34] For his part, the expert speaker knew that his political career depended upon neither alienating nor disappointing his listeners. The Athenian orator who hoped to capture and hold the attention of his audience might have spent hours or days composing his speech so that the argument would be tight, the style engaging, and the delivery smooth.[35] But he was expected to maintain the fiction that his eloquence was born of conviction and the passion of righteous indignation, rather than preparation. Demosthenes' opponents mocked his speeches for having the "stink of midnight oil" (Plutarch, *Life of Demosthenes* 7.3, 8, 11), and Demosthenes himself, who had the reputation (rightly or wrongly) of being poor at extemporaneous speaking, had to overcome the opprobrium of working too hard at his speech writing.[36] The Athenians demanded a very high standard of oratory from their politicians, but they did not necessarily like to be frequently reminded that the orator was an educated expert who possessed abilities and training that set him above the average citizens.[37]

[34] Eagerness to be entertained: Kleon's comment (Thuk., 3.38.6–8) to the effect that the Athenians considered themselves connoisseurs of rhetoric is supported by the sophistication of the rhetoric of the preserved public speeches of the Attic orators. Distrust of skill of orators: e.g., Isokrates, 15.4–5; Isaios, 10.1; Aiskhines, 1.173–75, 3.206, 253; Demosthenes, 35.40–43, 51.20–22, Hypereides, 1.25–26, frag. 80 (ed. Jensen).

[35] Isokrates, 4.14, claimed to have spent years perfecting his showpiece speeches.

[36] Alfred P. Dorjahn argued in a series of articles that Demosthenes in fact did have the ability to speak off the cuff; see, for example, "A Third Study of Demosthenes' Ability to Speak Extemporaneously," *TAPA* 83 (1952): 164–71. Cf. George A. Kennedy, *The Art of Persuasion in Greece* (Princeton, 1963), 210 with n. 113. For a detailed attack by a rhetorician on prepared speeches, see Alkidamas frag. 6 (ed. Sauppe); cf. Jaeger, *Paideia*, 3:60. Bryant, "Aspects I," 172, notes that "there has almost always been a certain fondness in the public and in speakers for the impression of spontaneous eloquence."

[37] On the training of Attic orators, see Stanley Wilcox, "The Scope of Early Rhetorical Instruction," *HSCP* 53 (1942): 121–55; Wilcox, "Isocrates' Fellow-Rhetoricians," *AJP* 66 (1945): 171–86; Robert R. Bolgar, "The Training of Elites in Greek Education," in *Govern-*

The difficulties faced by the orator who had to put on a good show, but avoid giving offense, are well illustrated by politicians' use of poetic and historical examples. Quotations of poetry and citations of historical precedent could enliven a speech and help to buttress the argument by the inspired wisdom of the poet and the authority of past practice. The technique held a certain risk for the speaker, however. Demosthenes (19.246–48) complained that Aiskhines called other men logographers and sophists as an insult, but was himself open to the same reproach. Demosthenes sets about proving this by pointing out that in the course of his speech Aiskhines quoted from Euripides' *Phoinix*, which he had never performed onstage himself. Yet Aiskhines never quoted from Sophokles' *Antigone* which he had acted many times. So, "Oh Aiskhines, are you not a sophist . . . are you not a logographer . . . since you hunted up [*zētēsas*] a verse which you never spoke onstage to use to trick the citizens?" (19.250).

The argument that underlies Demosthenes' comment says a good deal about Athenian attitudes toward elite use of literary culture. According to Demosthenes, Aiskhines is a sophist because he "hunts up" quotes from a play with which he had no reason to be familiar in order to strengthen his argument. Clearly the average Athenian would not be in a position to search out quotes when he wanted them; if the ordinary citizen ever wanted to quote poetry he would rely on verses he had memorized, and his opportunity to memorize tragic poetry was limited. Demosthenes implies that the contents of an individual's memory and his general knowledge learned from experience were perfectly democratic and egalitarian; specialized research undertaken to support an argument in court, on the other hand, was sophistic and elitist. What Aiskhines should have done (and, as Demosthenes implies, *would* have done were he not a sophist) was to quote the plays which he had memorized. Since he ignored the play he knew and quoted poetry from a play he did not know, he was proved to possess a sophist's training which he used to trick the average citizens on the jury. The orator who displayed evidence of special knowledge left himself open to the charge of using his elite education to deceive the audience.

The orator also had to be very careful to avoid giving the impression that he disdained the educational level of his audience. The public speaker's role was, in its essence, a didactic one: he attempted to instruct his listeners in the facts of the matter under discussion and in the correctness of his own interpretation of those facts. But when using poetic and historical examples, the Athenian orator had to avoid taking on the appear-

ing Elites, ed. R. Wilkinson, (New York, 1969), 23–49; W. S. Warman, "Plato and Persuasion," *G&R* 30 (1983): 48–54.

ance of a well-educated man giving lessons in culture to the ignorant masses. A passage in Aiskhines' speech *Against Timarkhos* that precedes a series of poetic quotations makes clear the pitfalls the orator faced in citing poetry:

> But since you [my opponents] bring up Akhilleus and Patroklos, and Homer and the other poets as if the jurors are without education [*anēkoōn paideias*] and you, yourselves, on the other hand, are superior types [*euskhēmones tines*] who far surpass [*periphronountes*] the *dēmos* in learning [*historia*]—in order that you may know that we too [*kai hēmeis*] have previously heard and have learned a little something, we shall say a few words about these matters.

(1.141)

Aiskhines justifies his intention to use poetic quotations by referring to his opponents' plan to cite poetry against him. He characterizes his opponents as educated snobs who imagine themselves to be in possession of a grasp of literary culture that is superior to that of the *dēmos*. Aiskhines uses the first person plural to suggest that he is one with the *dēmos* whose knowledge of the poets has been impugned. He suggests that "we"—Aiskhines and, at least by implication, the people—have listened to the poets, not that he himself has made a special study of literature. Thus Aiskhines makes himself a spokesman for the *dēmos*, called upon to defend the jurors against the scurrilous implication that they are ill educated. The jurors are therefore prepared to listen sympathetically to the series of quotes which Aiskhines will recite in order to disprove the elitist claims he has imputed to his opponents. Aiskhines' elaborate justification appears worthwhile only if he believes the quotes will help convince the jurors, but at the same time is worried that they could construe his poetic excursus as exactly the sort of intellectual snobbery he accuses his opponents of indulging in.[38]

Demosthenes also uses quotations from poetry in his speeches against Aiskhines, although he quotes poetry more rarely and invariably justifies himself by Aiskhines' prior use of poetry. Typically he simply throws back the passages Aiskhines has previously quoted and so carefully avoids suggesting that his own knowledge of poetry is superior to that of his listeners.[39] Demosthenes assumes that his audience is composed of theatergoers. When mocking Aiskhines' career as a tragic actor (19.247),

[38] On Aiskhines' use of poetic quotations generally, see Helen North, "The Use of Poetry in the Training of the Ancient Orator," *Traditio* 8 (1952): 22–27, esp. her comments on this passage (27).

[39] E.g., Demosthenes, 19.243, 245. Cf. North, "Use of Poetry," 24–25; S. Perlman, "Quotations from Poetry in Attic Orators of the Fourth Century B.C.," *AJP* 85 (1964): 155–72, esp. 156–57, 172.

he says that "you [jurors] know perfectly well" that it is the privilege of bit-players (*tritagōnistai*) like Aiskhines to play the role of the tyrant. The orator thus uses the "everyone knows" topos to avoid the impression of having a knowledge of theatrical performance greater than that of his audience.

Lykourgos prefaces a quotation from Tyrtaios by asking hypothetically, "who does not know" that the Spartans brought Tyrtaios from Athens to train their youths in virtue (1.106). And, after a long quote from Euripides, he states (1.101–2) that "these verses, gentlemen, educated [*epaideue*] your ancestors [*pateras*]." He also recommended Homer to the jurors, whom "your ancestors thought alone of the poets worthy of recitation at the Panathenaic Festival." The potentially elitist thrust of Lykourgos' hortatory comments is deflected by the speaker's emphasis on the ancestral Athenian respect for the poets and by his reference to the value of poetry being proved by its inclusion in the public festival.

Athenian orators used a similar approach when citing examples from history or myth. Demosthenes usually introduces his historical excurses with a prefatory "I am sure you all know . . . "—thereby avoiding the impression that he knows more about the past than does the average citizen.[40] In a similar vein, one of his clients (Demosthenes, 40.24–25) discusses the career of the demagogue Kleon whom "they say" captured many Lakedaimonians and had great repute in the *polis*. Aiskhines (2.76) cites the example of Kleophon "the Lyremaker" whom "many remember" as a slave in fetters. It was not the done thing to claim a specialized knowledge of history, but it was acceptable to appeal to the memories of the Athenian elders. In discussing exiles during the Korinthian War, for example, Demosthenes (20.52, cf. 19.249) claims that he is obliged to mention events he had heard about from "the older citizens among you." Aiskhines (2.77–78, 3.191–92) recounted how his own father, who lived to be ninety-five and had shared in the great struggles that had followed the Peloponnesian War, had many times told his son the story of the disasters of the war and of the virtuous conduct and strict standards of jurors in the postwar years. Allusions to the memory of the older citizens or of one's ancestors allowed the orator to avoid assuming the role of an educated man instructing his inferiors. There was clearly an appeal to authority involved in the references to elders, but notably the elders were

[40] See Lionel Pearson, "Historical Allusions in the Attic Orators," *CP* 36 (1941): 217–19, for a list of examples. On the orators' use of history generally, cf. S. Perlman, "The Historical Example, Its Use and Importance as Political Propaganda in the Attic Orators," *Scripta Hierosolymitana* 7 (1961): 150–66; Michel Nouaud, *L'utilisation de l'histoire par les orateurs attiques* (Paris, 1982), noting in passing that the orator assumes his audience has no formal knowledge of history apart from what he tells them (354), and that it took about twenty years for an event to pass from current politics to the realm of history (369).

the only subset of the *dēmos* to possess clearly defined legal and political privileges.[41]

The legitimacy of the authority of the elders helps to explain the rhetorical topos of castigating the audience members for having fallen from the pinnacle of excellence achieved by their ancestors: Athenian orators noted how the ancestors lived in simple virtue and maintained equality among themselves (Aiskhines, 3.26); they did not give excessive honors to unworthy men (Aiskhines, 3.178, 182); they had been on guard against traitors, free from the laxity now common (Demosthenes, 19.181). The ancestors had chosen excellent men as political leaders and advisers.[42] They attributed to the *dēmos* all that was good and fine, and to the *rhētores* that which was evil (Aiskhines, 3.231). Unlike the ancestors, who had punished even Themistokles for making himself "greater than themselves," modern Athenians were not willing to bring malefactors to justice (Demosthenes, 23.204–5); thus, whereas in the past the *polis* was master of the politicians, now it was their servant (Demosthenes, 23.209).[43]

Other criticisms by political orators, while not mentioning the ancestors, take a similar tone: the Athenians were slack, failed to be on their guard, and idly awaited disaster (Demosthenes, 19.224, 18.149); they made citizens of slaves and rabble ([Demosthenes], 13.24); they gave up their own control of offices, especially generalships, by allowing the same men to be reelected for years on end (Demosthenes, *Exordium* 55.3). The Athenians gave orators too much leeway, placed too much trust in them, and did not punish them strictly enough. They put their faith in rogues, while ignoring the good advice of genuine patriots.[44] They were misled, despite their native intelligence and good laws, because they chose to pay attention to speeches alone and they ignored the lifestyle of politicians (Aiskhines, 1.179). They had fine judgment but did

[41] Elders and their privileges: e.g., Thoukydides, 6.13.1, 8.1.3; Aiskhines, 2.22, 171, 3.2, 4; Hypereides, 1.22. Athenian jurors had to be thirty years of age as, most probably, did magistrates. Arbitrators had to be sixty.

[42] Excellence of ancestor's choice of leaders: e.g., Deinarkhos, 1.40; Lysias, 30.28; Demosthenes, 58.62; Aiskhines 3.181–82.

[43] Aristotle, in *Rhetoric* 1417b12–16, notes that in deliberative oratory one may relate things about the past so that the hearers will make better decisions in the future, and that this may be done in a spirit either of praise or of blame. On the tendency of the orators to reproach their audiences for not living up to their ancestors' standard, cf. Dover, *Greek Popular Morality*, 25; Dover, "The Freedom of the Intellectual in Greek Society," *Talanta* 7 (1976): 49.

[44] Too much leeway, too much trust: Lykourgos, 1.12; Demosthenes, 9.54, 23.147, *Exordium* 55.2; Lysias, 18.16. Insufficiently strict: Lysias, 27.4–6; Demosthenes, 23.206. Trust rogues, ignore patriots: Demosthenes, 18.138, 19.226, 51.21, *Exordium* 42.1. Aristophanes' comic demagogues make similar claims, e.g., *Knights* 1340–44, *Ekklesiazousai* 173–207; cf. below, section *VI*.

not apply it consistently, as shown by their unwillingness to be harsh enough toward bribe-taking politicians (Demosthenes, 23.145–46, cf. 24.172).

Although each criticism had its particular context and was intended to put the speaker in the best light and his opponent in the worst, the thread running through the various *topoi* of blame is clear enough: the orator "attacks" the people for not living up to their own ideals. The people are accused of being too generous with grants of citizenship, of giving over their mass power into the hands of a few evil men, of ignoring their own laws, of trusting rhetoric instead of depending on their collective wisdom.

Thus when the orator blamed the people, he typically did so by appealing to both exclusivist and egalitarian principles. He took the position of reminding his audience of the pristine democratic code of thought and behavior from which they had strayed. The orator called upon the Athenian to be the democrat his forefathers had been, and in so doing the speaker paid court to an egalitarian climate of opinion and asserted the importance of excluding from the citizen body those who were not proper members of political society.

IV. ANDOKIDES, *ON THE MYSTERIES*

The trial of Andokides for impiety in 400 B.C.E. is less well known than the trial of Sokrates for impiety in 399 B.C.E., but what Andokides loses to Plato's timeless rhetoric, he gains in the specificity of his oratorical guile. Andokides was charged with having participated in the recent Eleusinian Mysteries after having been legally debarred from doing so by Isotimides' decree of 415. Andokides defended himself successfully by claiming exemption under the amnesty of 403.[45] Isotimides had attacked Andokides in 415 because of Andokides' involvement in the mutilation of the Herms and, allegedly, in the profanation of the Mysteries. As a result, Andokides had been driven into exile. In 400, home again, Andokides denies any involvement in either scandal. Moreover, he faces the old unofficial charge that, in order to save his own neck, he had betrayed his *hetairoi* (comrades), his *syggeneis* (kinsmen), and, worst of all, his father.[46]

Much of Andokides' defense consists of a retelling of the events of 415

---

[45] For a general discussion of and commentary on the speech, see Douglas M. Mac-Dowell, *Andocides, On the Mysteries* (Oxford, 1961). Further discussion may be found in Raphael Sealey, "Callistratos of Aphidna and His Contemporaries," *Historia* 5 (1956): 182; Barry S. Strauss, *Athens after the Peloponnesian War* (Ithaca, 1986), 99–100.

[46] On the cultural significance of betraying *philoi*, see Dover, *Greek Popular Morality*, 304–6.

in his own favor. He also discusses more recent events, such as his quarrel with his distant relative Kallias over an *epiklēros* (heiress). Andokides weaves two themes together in both narratives: the defense of the family and tragedy. Andokides chooses his words carefully, with an eye toward the jury. "Don't," he asks them, "be suspicious of what I say [*ta legomena*], don't hunt down [*thēreuein*] my phrases [*rhēmata*]" (1.9; for Andokides' consciousness of his audience, cf. 1.33, 55). Lest the audience be unfriendly, Andokides draws on all his knowledge of the art of rhetoric.

In the witch-hunt following the discovery that the Herms had been mutilated, Andokides and nine other male relatives, as he relates, were thrown into prison. He sets the scene dramatically:

> We were all thrown into one prison. Darkness fell, and the gates were shut. Mothers, sisters, wives, and children had gathered. Nothing was to be heard save the cries and moans of grief-stricken wretches bewailing the calamity which had overtaken them.
>
> (Andokides, 1.48)

This scene may be stagey, but it does not specifically refer to Attic tragedy. If, however, the reference to cries and moans—*ēn de boē kai oiktos klaountōn kai oduromenōn ta paronta kaka*—perhaps evokes a subliminal nod of recognition of similar behavior in dramatic choruses, that nod would be reinforced by the next passage:

> In the midst of it all, Kharmides, a cousin of my own age who had been brought up with me in my own home since boyhood, said to me: "You see the utter hopelessness of our position, Andokides. I have never yet wished to say anything which might distress you; but now our plight leaves me no choice. Your friends and associates outside the family have all been subjected to the charges which are now to prove our undoing: and half of them have been put to death, while the other half have admitted their guilt by going into exile. I beg of you: if you have heard anything concerning this affair, disclose it. Save yourself; save your father who must be dearer to you than anyone in the world; save your brother-in-law, the husband of your only sister; save all those others who are bound to you by ties of blood and family; and lastly, save me, who have never vexed you in my life and who am ever ready to do anything for you and your good."
>
> (1.49–50)

As often in tragedy, the protagonist's *philos*—his friend or relative—discusses his terrible situation with him. The passage vaguely recalls scenes between Elektra or Pylades and Orestes, between Khrysothemis and

Elektra, or between Ismene and Antigone. But of course Andokides has written the script very carefully. He depicts himself, like many a character in tragedy or epic, faced with a terrible dilemma, but with the difference that the right choice will be clear to both himself and the jury.[47] Andokides says (1.51), "Never, oh, never has a man found himself in a more terrible strait than I" (Ō pantōn egō deinotatēi sumphorai peripesōn). Clearly he had risen to the occasion with fustian.[48]

It turns out, however, that the dilemma is easily resolved. Naturally Andokides must save his family; and happily, by doing so, he can also save three hundred innocent Athenians wrongly condemned to death. What about the hetairoi whom he must turn in, however? Well, all but four of them had already been denounced and either had been executed or escaped. They were, moreover, guilty. "So," Andokides (1.53) says, "I decided that it was better to cut off from their country four men who richly deserve it—men alive today and restored to home and property— than to let those others go to a death which they had done nothing whatever to deserve."

The ordinary Athenian might daydream about speechifying in the face of a tragic dilemma or about facing up to a tyrant, but he would give himself a happy ending. Andokides knows this. Most people, he says (1.57), would prefer life to a beautiful death. And he is no different. Having raised himself to an egregious dignity through Kharmides' speech, Andokides drops back into the crowd several paragraphs later. He did not face a choice, he says, between noble death and shameful life; on the contrary, it would have been shameful for him to die, when, by living, he could save his family and his polis (1.57–58).

Looking back, Andokides sees himself as someone who has suffered but learned through his vicissitudes. He says, in the summation of his speech (1.144–45), "I know what it is to be a xenos [foreign guest] and metic in the lands of neighboring peoples; I have learned what it is to be sōphrōn [self-controlled] and to take counsel rightly; I have learned what it is to suffer for one's mistakes [hamartonta]." These call to mind the clichés of a tragic chorus.[49] How fortunate for Andokides that he ended up not merely wise, but home again and rich.

Andokides uses the cultural paradigm of tragedy, but only for his own ends. He recognizes the degree to which the paradigm has colored his au-

---

[47] Andokides has already established himself before the jury as a man who chooses the harder but nobler road, since he preferred to risk a trial in his native polis of Athens rather than go to a comfortable exile in Kypros: 1.3–5.

[48] Cf. the high-flown language of 1.124, referring to Kallias: ho pantōn skhetliōtatos anthrōpōn, or of 1.127, referring to Kallias' mistress: tēs graos tolmērotatēs gunaikos.

[49] E.g., Aiskhylos, Agamemnon 250–52, Prometheus 259–61, 1039; Sophokles, Antigone 1347–53.

dience's outlook, but he does not merely reproduce the paradigm: he plays with it, domesticates it, even mocks it when mockery is advantageous. Andokides contrasts his own loyalty to his family with the allegedly unsavory marriage alliances of his enemy Kallias. After accusing Kallias of having had an affair with his mother-in-law, he sneers at Kallias' plan to marry off his son to the *epiklēros* [heiress] whom he has claimed (1.129): "There are three women with whom his father [i.e., Kallias] will have lived; and he is the alleged son of one of them, the brother of another, and the uncle of a third. What ought a son like that be called? Oidipous, Aigisthos, or what?" Here Andokides contrasts his own moderate use of the tragic paradigm with the tragic pretensions of his opponents. He reshapes the cultural paradigm with *mētis* [cunning] to achieve his own rhetorical ends.[50]

Andokides mocks the bombastic and overblown rhetoric of his opponents, arguably because of their clumsy misuse of the conventions of the tragic stage. For example, after asserting his innocence of any offense against the "Two Goddesses," i.e., Demeter and Kore, he makes fun of the horrific and moralizing language of his prosecutors:

> The stories of the prosecutors, who have shrieked out these awful and frightening versions of what happened [*tauta ta deina kai phrikōdē anōrthiazon*] and who have spoken about other earlier offenders and men guilty of impiety toward the Two Goddesses, how each of them suffered or was punished—what do these words or deeds have to do with me?
>
> (1.29)

Andokides may be arguing that the prosecutors are guilty of the kind of tragedifying that Aristophanes, for example, mocks in the Dikaiopolis-Euripides scene in *Akharnians* (393–485).

We later learn that the prosecutors have alleged that the Two Goddesses had infatuated (*paragagein*, 1.113) Andokides to commit impiety. This might have called to mind the many occasions in tragedy in which the protagonist was infatuated by a deity: for instance, Ajax by Athena (in Sophokles' *Ajax*) or Herakles by Lyssa (in Euripides' *Herakles Furens*) or Pentheus by Dionysos (in Euripides' *Bakkhai*). Andokides protests that far from infatuating him, the Two Goddesses have saved him (1.114). He deflects the prosecutors' case, but not without having ridiculed them.[51]

---

[50] On *mētis* see Marcel Detienne and Jean-Pierre Vernant, *Les ruses de l'intelligence: La mètis des grecs* (Paris, 1974).

[51] We are indebted to John J. Winkler for suggesting many of the ideas in the preceding two paragraphs.

V. Sophokles, *Antigone*

> The Athenians went to the theater *in order to hear beautiful speeches.* And
> beautiful speeches were what concerned Sophokles: pardon this heresy!
>
> —Nietzsche

Sophokles' *Antigone* of 441 B.C.E. offers an *embarras de richesse* for the
study of dramatic treatment of political thought and action; for example,
the confrontation of tyranny and democracy (e.g., 736–39), the status of
traitors in the play and in Athens, the language of accusation and self-
defense in the play and in the courts (e.g., 263–67, 275, 742, 941), the
charge of bribe-taking (302–14, 1045–47, 1056), the use of the lottery
(275, 396), or the appearance of such common political *Schlagwörter* as
arkhein/arkhesthai (699: hold office/obey officials; cf. Aristotle, *Politics*
1277b7–18). Here we focus more narrowly on the politics of rhetoric.

A striking feature of the speeches in *Antigone* is that rhetoric is itself a
subject of discussion.[52] As others have pointed out, the play is, on many
levels, a political drama.[53] Sophokles is not merely concerned with rhetorical esthetics; he discusses the political qualities of rhetoric. He takes
for granted the familiarity of his audience with political rhetoric. The action follows a political paradigm that the audience would have recognized; it is encoded with the language of Athenian public life.

Kreon is first described as a general (*stratēgos*, 8) issuing an emergency
decree (*kērugma*, 8). Later, he calls a council of elders (*synklētos gerontōn*,
159). In effect, as Vickers has noted, thereafter the play is a kind of public
meeting. The speeches of Kreon and his various foils evoke the speeches
of Athenian public orators, down to the professions of benevolence and
the invocation of departed relatives (904–20; cf. Lysias, 12). Contrary to
the situation among Athenian citizens, however, freedom of speech is
not to be taken for granted in Kreon's Thebes.[54] The importance of silence and speech to the action locates the play within the context of a society deeply concerned with the nature, justice, and power of rhetoric.

[52] We are indebted throughout to Charles Segal's superb discussion of speech and language in *Antigone*. See Segal, *Tragedy and Civilization: An Interpretation of Sophocles* (Cambridge, Mass., 1981), 161–66; cf. Segal, *Interpreting Greek Tragedy*, 44–45. The discussion
of political rhetoric is our contribution.

[53] For example, Ehrenberg, *Sophocles and Pericles*, 51–52; Bernard Knox, *The Heroic
Temper* (Berkeley, 1964), 75–90; Vickers, *Towards Greek Tragedy*, 528; William Calder,
"Sophocles' Political Tragedy, *Antigone*," *GRBS* 9 (1968): 389–407; Segal, *Interpreting
Greek Tragedy*, 158. Cf. below, n. 57.

[54] *Kērugma*: see Ehrenberg, *Sophocles and Pericles*, 35–36, 107–8; Knox, *Heroic Temper*,
95, 183 n. 19; Calder, "Antigone," 392 n. 20. Public meeting: Vickers, *Towards Greek
Tragedy*, 528. Freedom of speech: Vickers, *Towards Greek Tragedy*, 529–30; Kurt Raaflaub,
"Des Freien Bürgers Recht der Freien Rede," in *Studien zur Antiken Sozialgeschichte, Festschrift . . . Vittinghoff*, ed. Walter Eck, H. Galsterer, and H. Wolff (Cologne, 1980), 7–57.

And the frequency of demands by one character of another to speak, to speak in a certain fashion, and to be silent underlines the political nature of the rhetoric with which the playwright is concerned.

When, early in the play, Ismene promises, if not to help Antigone, at least to keep Antigone's purpose secret, Antigone scornfully urges her to tell the news to all (84–87). Then, when Antigone is apprehended at Polyneikes' grave-side, she refuses to deny her crime (435), just as, when confronted by Kreon, she refuses at first to speak, but instead keeps her eyes on the ground, which irritates Kreon (441). When she does reply, her statement is brief and defiant: "I say that I did it, nor shall I deny it" (443). Instead of answering Antigone immediately, Kreon first tells the guard who arrested her to leave—as if Antigone's bluntness had shocked him. He then demands to know if Antigone had been aware of his proclamation, adding the rhetorical proscription: "You, tell me not at length, but briefly" (446). This statement initially appears peculiar. Antigone has been *too* brief; she needs to elaborate, not to cut down her words. Furthermore, Kreon seems in no position to demand brevity, since his previous speeches have been lengthy and pompous (162–210, 280–314).[55] The audience is led to suspect that he is establishing a double standard based on both political and social status: a king and a male may indulge himself rhetorically, but a subject and a female must be laconic.

Our suspicions are soon confirmed. Kreon complains that Antigone's action was bad enough but she has added to it "a second hubris" (482):

> To boast of her deeds and laugh at what she did.
> Now I would not be the man, she would be the man,
> If these deeds of might be credited to her with impunity.
>
> (483–85)

In short, to the ruler of Thebes, speech is as important as action, and must be subject to strict control: speaking is power. The scene assumes an audience that was aware of the relationship between public speech, status, and political action. Sophokles' audience would expect rhetoric to be the stuff of politics, and he does not disappoint them.

The background of Athenian political speaking elucidates a later scene in which Haimon tries to bring Kreon to his senses. He reports that a silent debate is going on in Thebes, behind Kreon's back, in the darkness as it were (692, 700). The whole city of Thebes supports Antigone and thinks she deserves "a golden honor" (699, 733)—perhaps an allusion to the honorary crowns of Athenian politics. In other words, the Thebans

---

[55] Ehrenberg, *Sophocles and Pericles*, 59, aptly compares Kreon to Shakespeare's Polonius. He might have added that, like Polonius, Kreon would later be quoted without an appreciation of the original irony (Demosthenes, 19.247).

are engaging in a give-and-take reminiscent of the political rhetoric of the Athenian Assembly, except that they must carry out their debate in secret, because Kreon intimidates the *dēmos* (690). Haimon reproaches Kreon, at first diplomatically, and then bluntly, for attempting to monopolize all discourse (705–6, 757). By allowing Haimon to speak, Kreon seems to concede the point, but he then accuses Haimon of speaking entirely on Antigone's behalf (748). He dismisses Haimon's cogent arguments as mere cajolery from a woman's servile instrument (using a contemptuous neuter, *douleuma*: 756).[56] Again, it is the status of the speaker, not the content of the speech, which concerns Kreon. The blunt dismissal of a powerful speech and the refusal to credit anyone else in the play with the right to engage in political oratory would render Kreon a strikingly offensive tyrant to the members of the audience.[57]

The politics of rhetoric continues to be debated in the interchange between Teiresias and Kreon. The prophet asserts the right to instruct the tyrant, and Kreon uncharacteristically agrees, but only at first (922–23). Teiresias is orator enough to assure Kreon of the good intentions of his rhetoric:

I mean you well, so I speak benevolently.
It is best to learn from one who speaks benevolently and for your
    profit.

(1031–32)

This is the standard oratorical claim of good intentions; compare, for example, Lysias (31.2): "I am not, however, pursuing any private feud, nor am I prompted by my ability or practice in speaking before you." Kreon, however, is unimpressed. He accuses Teiresias of having taken bribes to speak as he does, just as he had earlier accused the guard who discovered Polyneikes' burial (302–14, 1045–47). Bribery is a standard topos of Athenian political rhetoric.[58] Like a good orator, Teiresias throws the charge back at Kreon:

[56] Richard C. Jebb, *Antigone of Sophocles*, rev. Schuckburgh (Cambridge, 1971), commentary ad loc.

[57] On Kreon as tyrant, see Cyril Maurice Bowra, *Sophoclean Tragedy* (Oxford, 1944), 72–78; Ehrenberg, *Sophocles and Pericles*, 57–59; A. J. Podlecki, "Creon and Herodotus," *TAPA* 97 (1966): 359–71; H. Funke, "ΚΡΕΩΝ ΑΠΟΛΙΣ," *Antike und Abendland* 12 (1966): 29–50; Vickers, *Towards Greek Tragedy*, 529–30, 542, 545–46; Diego Lanza, *Il Tiranno e il suo publico* (Turin, 1977), 50–58, 81–84, 149–58; Podlecki, "Monarch and Polis in Early Attic Tragedy," in *Greek Tragedy*, ed. Euben, 98–99; A. Lane and W. Lane, "The Politics of Antigone," in *Greek Tragedy*, ed. Euben, 169–71.

[58] See Barry Strauss, "The Cultural Significance of Bribery and Embezzlement in Athenian Politics: The Evidence of the Period 403–386 B.C.," *Ancient World* 9 (1985): 67–74.

> Kreon: The whole breed of prophets loves money.
> Teiresias: And the breed of tyrants loves shameful profits.

(1055–56; cf. 1054–55, 1061–63)

Like real Athenian political orators, Kreon and Teiresias argue over who knows best how to speak in the *polis'* interests. "Do you know that you're speaking," Kreon asks, "about kings?" (1057). Teiresias replies that he certainly does know, but he, after all, is the man who has saved the *polis* for Kreon (1058). Kreon's reply is to call Teiresias a wise (*sophos*) prophet, but one who loves injustice (1059). His concession of *sophia* is ambiguous, since *sophos* could be a term of abuse as well as of praise (e.g., Thuk. 3.37.4; Eur., *Med.* 285, 299 and passim).

Kreon also accuses Teiresias not only of being a corrupt orator, but a poor one: Teiresias' warning, he says, is nothing but a common cliché (1049). This sarcasm is hardly justified from a speaker who has himself brought up the ship of state (162–65) and has said, in effect, that "the bigger they are, the harder they fall" (437–76). In any case, Kreon is bluffing. When Teiresias spells out Haimon's imminent death, a terror-stricken Kreon rapidly agrees to release Antigone from her prison. Teiresias has the last word on rhetoric:

> Therefore, the gods arouse against you
> Their sure avengers; they lie in your path
> Even now to trap you and to make you pay
> Their price.—Now think: do I say *this* for money?

(1074–78)

Teiresias' parting word to Kreon is that he must learn to have a "quieter tongue" (1089). And silence again becomes a key element in the play.

Kreon's repentance comes too late to avoid disaster. The rest of the play is an unfolding of doom and a personal descent from the tyrant's former heights of arrogance and rhetorical excess to a nightmare of quiet. Sophokles continues the theme of the politics of rhetoric, but now it ironically underscores Kreon's collapse. The tyrant at last achieves the silence he has long demanded from his underlings, but it is, as the chorus says, an excessive and heavy silence (1251; cf. 1256).

The first case is Haimon. When confronted by Kreon's entreaties in the cave, Haimon says nothing in reply (1227–32). Instead, he spits in his father's face and draws his sword on him. When Kreon leaps safely aside, Haimon turns the sword on himself and commits suicide. The second case is Kreon's wife, Eurydike. When she hears the report of Haimon's death, she leaves the scene, as the chorus notes, without saying one word, good or bad (1245). The messenger thinks that Eurydike is merely being discreet, and has gone inside to mourn, as befits a woman (1246–49). The chorus, however, recognizes how ominous her silence is (1251). Kreon returns presently, to hear the news of Eurydike's suicide.

Now Kreon no longer speaks in iambic verse as he did previously. In his final appearance, he is part of the closing *kommos* (lament), and sings his grief in dochmiacs. In metrical terms, Kreon has gone from the rhetoric of control to the music of emotional outpouring: a fitting punishment for one who has refused to listen to the speech of others.[59]

The chorus sounds a similar theme in its last speech

> Great words [*megaloi logoi*]
> of the proud are paid in full
> with great blows of fate.

(1350–52)

Sophokles here emphasizes the point that *Antigone* is in large part about *logoi*—about words and speeches. If Kreon has transgressed, it is not only in his deeds, but in his *logoi*, and in his attempt to control the *logoi* of others. His tyrannical actions would have offended the democratic principles of the audience in many ways, but most strikingly, perhaps—since drama itself depends on speeches—in his assault on freedom of speech. Kreon is a tyrant not least because he refuses to allow anyone else the right of public speech.[60]

Haimon's question to Kreon, "Do you wish to speak and yet not to listen?" (757), underscores both the absurdity of Kreon's position, and the difference between Kreon and an Athenian democrat. "Do you wish to speak?" Haimon asks; the phrase echoes the question asked by the herald at every meeting of the ekklēsia: "Who wishes to speak?" (e.g., Demosthenes, 18.169; Euripides, *Suppliant Women* 438–40). Kreon too is a kind of herald (*kērux*), having proclaimed to the city his edict on Polyneikes (8), but he stifles rather than encourages debate. *Antigone* forces the audience to draw on its experience of political oratory by referring to the terms and *topoi* of public rhetoric, but also by raising serious questions about the politics of rhetoric. The play does not merely use speeches; it also discusses both the quality and the freedom of rhetoric. By his references to Athenian political oratory, Sophokles roots the fictive world of the tragedy in the reality of the democratic *polis*. He teaches the audience a general truth about the terrible consequences of suppression of free speech that has a specific application to the Athenian democracy and its invocation of *parrhēsia*.

---

[59] Lanza, *Tiranno*, 158.

[60] Sophokles makes a connection between *eleutherōs legein* and the *sōtēria* of the polis in the lost *Epigonoi*, frag. 192P.

VI. ARISTOPHANES, *EKKLESIAZOUSAI*

Ekklesiazousai, which was produced in the late 390s B.C.E., opens on a predawn gathering of women who are plotting to take over the government of the state.[61] They plan to pack the Assembly with women in men's clothing and thereby to pass a decree which will put women in charge. The plan succeeds and the women implement a new regime in which property is communal and sexual relations democratized, in that the old and ill-favored will have priority in sexual congress with the attractive. The practical difficulties these two innovations raise are revealed by the next two scenes. In the first, a skeptical male citizen discusses the workability of communalization with the more optimistic Khremes, friend of the husband of Praxagora, leader of the women. In the second scene, two young lovers have trouble getting together because several elderly and ugly women demand their rights to sleep with the handsome young man first.

The action includes the usual scatological and sexual fun and games, but the play is clearly and overtly concerned with politics. The playwright has much to say about various politicians and their nasty personal habits.[62] There is also a good deal of pointed mockery of the *topoi* and pretensions of political rhetoric. The "rehearsal" scene, held in the dark before the Assembly begins (especially 110–23), pokes fun at the expert orators' careful preparations and transparent attempts to appear spontaneous. The speech of the "Second Woman" employs the familiar *topos* of inexperience at public address (150–53). The speech of Praxagora plays upon several familiar rhetorical themes: I have an equal share in this country, just as each of you does; the *polis* is being ruined because of the people's willingness to follow evil leaders; you citizens mistrust those who truly love you, but trust those who care nothing for you; you care too little for the state, too much for your private affairs; and you change public policy too often (173–207). Praxagora's complaints are all paral-

---

[61] For a detailed introduction and commentary, see the Oxford edition by R. G. Ussher (1973). On the date of the play, see Ussher, xx–xxv; H. Funke, *Homónoia und Arché: Athen und die griechische Staatenwelt vom Ende des peloponnesischen Krieges bis zum Königsfrieden*, Historia Einzelschrift 19 (Wiesbaden, 1980), 168–71; Strauss, *Athens*, 183 n. 85.

[62] E.g., 71, 201, 248–55, 365–66, 397–421. On the political nature of the play, see E. Barry, *The Ecclesiazusae as Political Satire* (diss., Chicago, 1942), 44–76; contrast, E. David, *Aristophanes and Athenian Society of the Early Fourth Century B.C.*, *Mnemosyne*, supp. 81 (Leiden, 1984), 29, who sees the *Ekklesiazousai* and *Ploutos* as "social comedies *par excellence* . . . [the playwright's] focus of interest is on politics no longer." Victor Ehrenberg, *The People of Aristophanes: A Sociology of Old Attic Comedy*, 3d ed. (New York, 1962), 68, considered that the discussion of "communism" marked a transition "from purely political to socio-economic thought," but also suggested (358–59) that this was the only example of Attic comedy which dealt with a fundamental idea of political philosophy.

leled by the "blame" *topoi* used by real orators of the fourth century. The proposal for turning over the state to the women is also justified by a familiar rhetorical tactic: Praxagora claims that the women will be better at running the state because they do things according to the old ancestral ways (214–28): this can be read as a play on the rhetorical appeal to the authority of past traditions (cf. above, section III). Praxagora is praised by the women for her eloquence, and she lets on that she learned to speak well by listening to the orators on the Pnyx when her family was billeted there during the war (241–44). Here Aristophanes explicitly reveals that the speech is meant to mock the style of the real orators, and also gives Praxagora a chance to deny that she had any special training in rhetoric, another common topos.

All this helps to bring the comedy into the political realm where the elite leaders attempt to lead—or mislead—mass audiences of citizens. Yet the play still does not on the face of it appear very satisfactory as drama: Why do the women want to take over the state in the first place? No particular crisis is alluded to—Praxagora has things in common with Lysistrata, but her motivation is much less clear.[63] Why do the women implement the two seemingly incongruous reforms in the areas of economic and sexual relations? Why does the action stop without a satisfactory resolution? Is this an ironic or absurdist evocation of a world turned inside out? Or is it a dazzlingly prescient and cryptic satire of ideas philosophers will bandy about a generation or two later?[64] We maintain that it is neither, and that its meaning and comic thrust are clarified by the context of Athenian political ideology and practice.

Egalitarianism and its limits are the central themes of the play. In the real world of early fourth-century Athens the Athenian citizens were po-

[63] Helene P. Foley, "The 'Female Intruder' Reconsidered: Women in Aristophanes' *Lysistrata* and *Ecclesiazusae*," *CP* 77 (1982): 14, attempts to define the problems the women's takeover might be intended to solve, but is unable to suggest anything very specific. Cf. Barry, *Political Satire*, 45–49.

[64] Unsatisfactory: Ehrenberg, *People of Aristophanes*, 68; A. H. Sommerstein, "Aristophanes and the Demon Poverty," *CQ* 34 (1984): 314. Sommerstein (esp. 315–19) argues effectively against those who have seen the play as an "ironic" attack on communalization; yet Sommerstein's own thesis, that the new order is inspired by a change in Aristophanes' personal fortunes and by his sympathy for the peasants, downtrodden by the war, seems to us excessively "author-centered" and misses the broader context. Absurdist: see for example, Foley, "Female Intruder," 16; and esp. J. Huber, *Zur Erklärung und Deutung von Aristophanes' Ekkleziazusen* (diss., Heidelberg, 1974), 252–55 ("Aristophanes, Platon und Dada"). Prescient: the theory that Aristophanes was parodying an early version of Plato's *Republic*, suggested by, *inter alios*, G. Norwood, *Greek Comedy* (London, 1931), is now generally discounted; see the edition by Ussher, xv–xx; Kenneth J. Dover, *Aristophanic Comedy* (Berkeley, 1972), 200–201; David, *Aristophanes*, 20–23, who also disapproves of the alternative view that Plato and Aristophanes shared some common literary source which advocated a communalized society.

litical equals, and they used their political equality to mediate social inequalities both legally and on an ideological plane. But what were the limits of the use of political power to redress social inequality? The most glaring inequalities within Athenian political society were the result of the unequal distribution of wealth; what if the political equals used their legislative power to enforce economic equality? Wealthy Athenians certainly considered this a dreadful possibility.[65] Indeed, there was no necessary reason for anyone to suppose a property-equalizing decree could not be passed in the Assembly. The Athenian state recognized no fixed limits to its power to interfere in the private affairs of citizens, as Aristophanes reminds his audience at several points.[66]

Hence, it is not really surprising to find Aristophanes creating a situation which explores the possible effects of a decree which called for property communalization. He suggests that clever and selfish citizens would attempt to take as much as they could get from the new order, and give back as little as they could get away with. Here Aristophanes confronts his audience with the limits of their own public-spiritedness, with the insidious potential of personal greed and self-interest to undercut political solutions to social ills. With the destruction of the elite of wealth, he implies, the Athenians might be victimized by an elite of the clever and unscrupulous. Those who cooperate with the new economic order could end up losers, and surely this would increase the tensions that property redistribution might be expected to ameliorate.[67]

The equalization of sexual opportunity is closely related, but goes a comic step further in suggesting political solutions to social problems and the power of the democratic public realm to override personal choices in private life. The situation in which a lover's choice of whom he will sleep with was subject to state regulation was not really so farfetched in the context of Athenian political society, where egalitarian

[65] Wealthy Athenians fear property distribution: Jones, *Athenian Democracy*, 54–61.

[66] E.g., 377–78, 412–25, 465–75. On the power of the *dēmos* to legislate concering private action, see especially Moses I. Finley, "The Freedom of the Citizen in the Greek World," *Talanta* 7 (1976): 14–15. On the relationship between public and private in Athens, see Humphreys, *Family, Women, and Death*, 1–32, 61–74; D. Cohen, "Work in Progress: The Enforcement of Morals: An Historical Perspective," *Rechtshistorisches Journal* 3 (1984): 114–29. Foley, "Female Intruder," reads the play as an example of the invasion of the public (male, political) sphere by the private (female, domestic) sphere. This is very informative and reveals an important level of the play's meaning. But Foley seems to go too far in arguing that it was due to the *failure* of the political sphere in the late fifth and fourth century that Athenian poets and philosophers "began to look at other social models for correction, including . . . the household"(19). Cf. below on the play's reiteration of the primacy of political solutions to social problems.

[67] 730–876; cf. 204–5. The character of the skeptic is of key importance to the "ironic" reading of the play. See Sommerstein, "Aristophanes and the Demon Poverty," 316, 319–20, 330–31; David, *Aristophanes*, 14; cf. 7, 32, 36.

principles led the citizens to look upon election as potentially oligarchic, and where the lottery assured that all citizens had an equal chance at such privileges and prerogatives as public service might offer. If we extrapolate from the political realm to the social, why should the attractive have a better shot at the privileges of sexual pleasure? And why should the aged—who were, we must remember, the only legitimate politically privileged subgroup of the citizen body—not be given privileges in the sexual realm? Praxagora's comment that the scheme is completely democratic (*dēmotikē g' hē gnōmē*, 631) is funny, but not crazy. The proposals for communalization of property and equalized sexual relations stretched the existing reality, without inverting it; much of the deeper humor of the play relies upon showing the potential grotesquery of a further development of something that was familiar, and almost universally accepted—political equality and its social ramifications.

But the play operates on another level as well. The extension of political power to women challenges a basic tenet of the political society. Exclusivity was a principle as central and sacred to the existing political order as equality, and the rectitude of limiting access to the citizen body had been reaffirmed in 403 by the refusal to give block grants of citizenship to those who had aided the democratic resistance to the Thirty Tyrants.[68] Consequently, by introducing Assemblywomen, Aristophanes confronts the audience, not only with the logical extremes of egalitarianism within the political society, but with the concerns and desires of those who were stranded outside that society. The women have no specific crisis they intend to solve, because they are attacking the male-only political order itself, not merely some symptom of that order (e.g., war). Consequently, the *Ekklesiazousai* may be read as an even more subversive play than *Lysistrata*. But it is important to note that the twisting of reality occurs within carefully established limits. In the real world women were closer to citizen status than were metics or slaves in that they were essential in the establishment of the condition of citizenship for all male citizens.[69] Since the son of a male citizen and a noncitizen

[68] Decree of Thrasyboulos to grant citizenship to metics and slaves who had aided in the revolt successfully indicted by a *graphē paranomōn*: *Ath. Pol.* 40.2. David Whitehead, "A Thousand New Athenians," *Liverpool Classical Monthly*, vol. 9, no. 1 (January, 1984): 8–10, argues that the fragments of *IG* II² 10 should be restored in such a way as to show that ca. one thousand metics who had helped in deposing the Thirty were given full citizenship in 401. But cf. the alternative reconstruction of Peter Krentz, "Foreigners against the Thirty: *IG* 2² 10 Again," *Phoenix* 34 (1980): 298–306.

[69] The original citizenship legislation of 451/0: Plutarch, *Perikles* 37.2–5; cf. Cynthia Patterson, *Pericles' Citizenship Law of 451–50 B.C.* (New York, 1981); Charles Hignett, *A History of the Athenian Constitution to the End of the Fifth Century B.C.* (Oxford, 1952), 343–47. On the importance for the reform in defining the Athenians' image of themselves, see Loraux, *Invention*, 150. On legislation to keep the citizen rolls "clean" in the fourth century see

woman could not be a citizen, Athenian women must impart something to their offspring which makes the latter worthy of political rule. The women's close and continuing ties to their sons are used as an argument to support the new order (233–34; cf. 635–49).

The playwright's concern with establishing limitations on the degree of dramatic unreality is exemplified by the unchanged or even lowered status of other noncitizen groups under the new regime. Slavery will remain important; indeed slaves will now do *all* the productive agricultural work and citizens will live off the surplus value of their labor (651–52). Consequently, although the bounds of exclusivity have been breached on one front, they are strengthened on another; Athenians will no longer have to engage in slavelike labor and so they will become more clearly a status elite in relation to the unfree population.[70] The slave prostitutes will be further restricted by rules forbidding them to consort with citizen-males (718–24). Once again, this is a way of enforcing exclusivity bounds; now sexual relations, egalitarian within the citizen body, will be denied outside of it.[71]

The world of the *Ekklesiazousai* operates according to the central egalitarian and exclusivist tenets of Athenian political culture, even as it challenges the potential consequences, on the one hand, and the current application, on the other, of those tenets. Therefore, the Athens of Aristophanes' play was not a topsy-turvy never-never land, but a pointed and challenging allegory which confronts the members of the audience with the peculiar nature of the political order in which citizen-males were theoretically omnipotent political actors: both the conditions of inequality which pertain within the citizen body and the contradictions inherent in women serving as equal partners in creating citizens

---

Michael J. Osborne, *Naturalization in Athens*, 4 vols. in 3 (Brussels, 1981–1983), 4:152, 155–64; David Whitehead, *The Demes of Attica, 508/7–ca. 250 B.C.* (Princeton, 1986), 106–9. Cf. the comments of Isaios, 6.47, 8.43; Demosthenes, 57.30–32.

[70] For the concept of *banausia* and its link to slavishness in philosophical thought, see esp. Aristotle, *Politics* 1328b19–29a2, 1337b18–22, 1341b8–18, *Nikomakhean Ethics* 1131a24–29, and the discussion in Ober, "Aristotle's Political Sociology." Cf. André Aymard, "Hiérarchie du travail et autarcie individuelle dans la Grèce archaïque," in Aymard, *Etudes d'histoire ancienne* (Paris, 1967), 316–33; Markle, "Jury Pay," 284; Loraux, *Invention*, 182 with n. 412; and esp. M. Balme, "Attitudes to Work and Leisure in Ancient Greece," *G&R* 31 (1984): 14–52. Kurt Raaflaub, "Democracy, Oligarchy, and the Concept of the 'Free Citizen' in Late Fifth-Century Athens," *Political Theory* 11 (1983): 528–34 (cf. Raaflaub, *Die Entdeckung der Freiheit: Zur historischen Semantik und Gesellschaftsgeschichte eines politischen Grundbegriffes der Griechen* [Munich, 1985], 304–11), suggests a hypothetical origin for the scorn for labor in elite attempts to respond to the democratic monopolization of the concept of freedom, and notes that the "average" Athenian may not have fully shared this view.

[71] Cf. Ehrenberg, *People of Aristophanes*, 152–53, who notes that while metic *hetairai* are not specifically mentioned here, they seem to be included in the *pornas* and *doulas kosmoumenas*.

(and in other social realities), and yet being denied participation in political decision making.

Aristophanes presents his audience with serious problems facing the political (and the whole) society, but he implies that any solution to those problems will be sought on the political and public plane. The means used by the women to revolutionize the sociopolitical order are public speech and political process. Notably, the women only need to wear male clothing to one meeting of the Assembly and can shed it afterward (496–98, 506–9). The plot does *not* depend on continued deception, because the new regime was legally instituted. And here, at the level of the power of political decisions by the masses—whether it is the masses of male citizens or their wives in their stead—the play reaffirms the unique power that political action in a democratic state carried with it, the power to change, in a revolutionary way, the nature of relations between elite and mass within the political society, and the relations between citizens and noncitizens. That power was potentially dangerous, open to abuse, and perhaps even limited in its efficacy if it were stretched too far, but the play locates it in the center of the organizing social structures of the society.

Between laughing at the high jinks, the members of the audience were given a chance to test, and perhaps to adjust their symbolic system of reference, by confronting the potential consequences on the one hand, and the innate contradictions on the other, of their sociopolitical order. And, given the responsiveness of a direct democracy to changed perceptions among the citizenry, this opportunity to adjust ideological reference networks could have an immediate effect. Notably, the play offers no answer to the question of whether the new regime was a success or a failure:[72] Aristophanes could show why it *might* not work to change the social world by political means, but he sees no other way to introduce change and he leaves open the chance of a happy ending.

VII. CONCLUSIONS

The sociological/anthropological study of the interplay of political rhetoric and drama in the context of Athenian political and whole societies reveals a key level of meaning in both dramatic and rhetorical texts, by restoring an important part of their context. It also helps to extend the study of Athenian political culture on an ideological plane from the later fourth century, a period from which we have only meager fragments of

---

[72] The question of whether the conclusion of the play (esp. 1175–79) is optimistic (everyone gets fed, the new order works) or pessimistic (there is not enough food for all, the new order fails), is much discussed: e.g., David, *Aristophanes*; Ehrenberg, *People of Aristophanes*, 67. The disagreement is indicative of Aristophanes' intentional ambiguity.

dramatic works, back into the early to mid–fifth century, a period from which we have no genuine surviving rhetorical texts. Playwrights and orators each referred to the other's genre, by references to actions, symbols, codes, vocabulary, paradigms, and rituals. Oratory drew on the audience's experience of theater; drama drew on the audience's experience of political and legal speeches. By so doing, each genre implicitly taught its audience that being an Athenian was a comprehensive experience, that there was no compartmentalized division between esthetics and politics. Athenian political culture was created in part in the theater of Dionysos, theatrical culture on the Pnyx.

Athenian dramatic and rhetorical texts were informed by political culture, but were also primarily responsible for generating the new signs through which it evolved. In the two-way communication of public speech, new and old symbols were tested by the mass audience and those which were effective—which struck a chord, which helped the society to function—were integrated into the language of social mediation. That language made possible communication between citizens and perhaps also between citizens and noncitizens across the hierarchical strata of social inequality. Thanks to the symbol-generating function of public speech in the various forums, the language of sociopolitical mediation at Athens was never static, and Athenian political culture was able to respond to changes in its external environment. The structural tactics of metaphors, analogies, images, and *topoi* that were devised by elite authors, displayed in public speech, and judged by mass audiences, were integrated into a comprehensive, flexible, and functionally effective sociopolitical strategy. Although there is much in this strategy that is nowadays unattractive—especially the continuing exclusion of noncitizens from participation in political life—it has much to tell us about the potential of democracy as a means of social, as well as political, organization.

JEFFREY HENDERSON

The *Dēmos* and the Comic Competition

THE COMIC POETS of fifth-century Athens aimed, in the words of the
Initiate-Chorus of *Frogs* (389–93), "to say much that is humorous and
much that is serious, and to win the prize by playfulness and mockery,
worthily of the festival."[1] For students of Old Comedy "humorous" and
"playfulness" are relatively unproblematic: the words and actions of the
performers would make the spectators laugh. But the claim to be "serious" raises serious issues about the genre of Old Comedy, for the poets
consistently said that their advice and admonishments to the spectators
were true and just, that their explicit and often mordantly abusive treatment of individuals (through "mockery") would purify the *polis* and advance the people's interests, and that their portrayal of contemporary
reality, however novel or facetious, was essentially believable. According to the poets, their genre was both artistic and political. Indeed, "worthily of the festival" inseparably links the genre with its civic context: the
comic competition was a feature of the Lenaia and the Greater Dionysia,
festivals attended by some seventeen thousand spectators, organized and
regulated by the *dēmos* (sovereign people), the winning poet being voted
by judges representing them.

   In short, the comic poets pictured themselves as competing for the favor of the *dēmos* with a humorous spectacle of a special kind, which the
dēmos' arkhōn had granted them permission and funds to put on at the appropriate yearly festival, and as public voices who could, indeed were expected to, comment on, and seek to influence public thinking about
matters of major importance—the same matters that were being or
might be presented to the voting *dēmos* in other settings and in different

Note: For helpful advice and criticism I am grateful to Sir Kenneth Dover, Lowell Edmunds, Anthony Edwards, Bruce Heiden, Gregory Nagy, Martin Ostwald, Ralph Rosen,
Oliver Taplin, Alan H. Sommerstein, John J. Winkler, Froma Zeitlin, and Bernhard Zim-
merman. Plays of Aristophanes are cited from the Oxford texts of Maurice Platnauer, *Peace*
(1964), Kenneth J. Dover, *Clouds* (1968), Douglas M. MacDowell, *Wasps* (1971), Robert G.
Ussher, *Ecclesiazusae* (1973), Jeffrey J. Henderson, *Lysistrata* (1987); otherwise from Victor
Coulon (Paris, 1923–1930). Fragments of comedy and the *Life of Aristophanes* are cited from
PCG (Aristophanes-Magnes); otherwise from Theodor Kock, *Comicorum Graecorum Fragmenta* (Leipzig, 1880–1888).
   [1] They refer (in character) to the Eleusinian festival (addressing Demeter), but their
words apply (as comic chorus) also to the comic competition of the Lenaia (addressing the
spectators).

ways, by competitors in a tragic competition, for example,[2] or by speakers in an assembly, or by litigants in a law court.

In this essay I will argue that the picture drawn by the Old Comic poets is accurate: they were the constituent intellectuals of the *dēmos* during the period of full popular sovereignty that began with the reforms of Ephialtes in 462/1, and in their institutionalized competitions they influenced the formulation of its ideology and the public standing of individuals. While their role was distinctive, it was also an organic feature of the sovereignty of the *dēmos*.

Ancient critics, beginning with such eyewitnesses as pseudo-Xenophon in *Constitution of the Athenians* (the Old Oligarch) and Plato, variously applauded or condemned this picture of what poets and spectators were up to at the Old Comic festivals but never questioned its accuracy. For them, as we will see, the Old Comic poets were what they claimed to be, so that ancient historians and biographers included comedy among their valid sources of political information and opinion. But for modern critics, beginning with Müller-Strübing in 1873,[3] the accuracy of the picture is at issue, and so, therefore, is the sociopolitical significance claimed by the poets. A skeptical attitude has developed which has suspended confident use of comic texts as special evidence for important features of fifth-century social and political life.[4] When Dionysios of Syracuse wanted to study "the *politeia* of the Athenians," Plato sent him Aristophanes.[5] Nowadays we would probably send Thoukydides or the Tribute Lists, or even Plato.

The reason is clear enough: in our world no one picture can contain both seriousness and humor, both festivals and the state, both art and politics. And so the ancient picture has been edited, the editors falling mainly into two groups. The skeptics separate seriousness and humor: the poets' claim to seriousness must itself be a joke, or, conversely, the jokes are there to make the serious parts more palatable. The carnivalists separate festivals and the state: the poets' seriousness was somehow detached from the "real" world of the spectators as being "mere" entertainment (poetry, play, ritual, carnival, satire, fantasy). Both groups separate art and politics: comedy may be topical and political but only in a reac-

[2] That tragedy was thought to have an edifying, even didactic function is the assumption throughout *Frogs* and part of the point of *Akharnians* 500. See O. Taplin, "Tragedy and Trugedy," *CQ* 33 (1983): 331–33.

[3] For an overview of modern opinion see Walther Kraus, *Aristophanes' politische Komödien,* Sitzungsberichte der Österreichen Akademie der Wissenschaft in Wien, Philosophisch-Historische Klasse 453 (Vienna, 1985), 25–30.

[4] As opposed to such information as the price of fish.

[5] Aristophanes, *Life* 42–45 K-A. Historical or not, the anecdote expresses the ancient attitude.

tive or alternative way, so that while there can be "political comedy" there can be no comic politics. But when we examine each new edition of the picture we see that something is missing, that something important should be restored.

The skeptics rely on an a priori assumption that humor, however artful, is not a moral or political determinant: what makes people laugh cannot affect the principles, criteria, and values that determine their choice of action when they are not laughing. In the case of fifth-century Athens, however, this assumption has insufficient explanatory power. The skeptics have not explained away the fact that the comic poets, despite their jokes, argue vehemently and purposefully about the most important and divisive issues of the day. The positions they advocate or denounce represent those of actual groups, and their techniques of persuasion and abuse are practically identical with those used in political and forensic disputes. After all, the comic troupe competed before the same audience—the sovereign *dēmos*—that arbitrated those disputes. What is more, it is not true, as the skeptics say, that anyone was fair game for comic ridicule: the poets show systematic bias in their choice of people and policies to satirize and not to satirize.[6] Indeed, a poet could, as in *Akharnians* and *Knights,* find room in his production to prosecute a personal feud. As for the impact of comedy, it is hard to explain away the crown awarded by the city to Aristophanes for the advice he offered in *Frogs,* or the lawsuits brought by Kleon, or the special decrees defining comic propriety, or the comic portrayal of Sokrates which for Plato was a significant factor in his condemnation. Were these mere anomalies or accidents?

Ste Croix, believing that the poets had serious biases and wished to persuade their fellow citizens, confronts the skeptics on their own terms by identifying passages whose primary aim seems not to be humor, or which can be aligned with other contemporary voices.[7] But this is again to edit the picture: in the former case humor is removed, in the latter the distinctive outlook of comedy. The comic poets may as well have delivered their criticisms and advice in Assembly or court. The rules of evidence on which the skeptics insist are, it would seem, necessarily distorting. They rule out in advance the possibility that comic humor might have been a persuasive mode parallel to those we call serious. One of the special powers of humor is "fool's privilege": to mediate between the poles of polite silence and impolite expression, to express ideas that want a public outlet but that would be too disruptive if expressed other-

---

[6] G.E.M. de Ste Croix, *The Origins of the Peloponnesian War* (London and Ithaca, 1972), 359–62.

[7] Appendix XXIX, with the reaction of G.A.H. Chapman, "Aristophanes and History," *Acta Classica* 21 (1978): 59–70.

wise. What the fool brings out into the open the king and his court can pretend, if they like, not to have taken seriously. I will suggest that fifth-century comic poets played a similar mediating role: what might be too disruptive in Assembly or court could find an outlet at the comic competition. Thus the problem is not to distinguish humor and seriousness but rather to analyze the dynamics of comic persuasion.

The carnivalists, who examine the institutional status of comedy, seek to sidestep this problem by claiming that the comic festival was a holiday world, a world unto itself which could not have had any impact on the world where political decisions were made. This claim is an induction from the many features fifth-century comic plays undeniably share with carnival and that in fact belong to a vast tradition of popular grotesque which ignores the boundaries of time and place. In its typical carnivalesque form, this tradition appears as a counter-world embedded in an autonomous festival. When this counter-world mirrors the official world it can even be called political (as in "political comedy"), but it cannot itself be a form of politics. The counter-world of fifth-century comedy, however, differs from that of carnival in important ways, and the festival in which it was embedded was not at all autonomous.

As Bakhtin has shown, the counter-world of carnival in its political aspect typically has only the negative role of ridiculing and criticizing a dominant class and ideology. Thus it cannot generate positive positions and does not take sides in political debate. Fifth-century comedy, however, is a local variant which does not fit this model. Its counter-world contained not only ridicule and criticism but also positive alignments and appeals by the poet and sympathetic characters. Although they typically championed minority positions, they did so from a stance of ideological solidarity with the official culture, with those who had sole power to act on such positions: the sovereign *dēmos*. Moreover, their stance was essentially the same for everyone else who appeared before the *dēmos*. The counter-world of fifth-century comedy, unlike that of typical carnival, paralleled rather than opposed the official world, so that it cannot be used to support the claim of autonomous detachment for the festival. But we need not rely on the plays alone to reject that claim.

Unlike autonomous carnival, the comic festival shared with all other public assemblies an institutional structure whose common denominator was the *dēmos,* in this particular instance convened as a theatrical audience. The comic festival took place in a *polis* that devoted at least one-third of its year, and its largest special expenditure of wealth, to public festivals and that considered them to be a distinctive glory of their democracy; was itself a competition where decisions were made; was part of a larger festive complex that included unarguably political elements;

was governed by the same official mechanisms as all other public assemblies; and was not, contrary to the "anything goes" view of the carnivalists, exempt from the laws regulating other forms of public discourse. Moreover, Old Comedy as a genre shows rapid evolution in ways not explainable in terms of esthetic criteria alone. To point out that such features of comedy as obscenity, parody, transvestism, and role-reversal were restricted to special poetic and festive contexts (and not only comic ones) merely begs the question, for we have not thereby determined the status and function of those contexts in the culture at large.

In this essay I will examine these problems by forsaking the modern consensus that we are too shrewd to be taken in by the comic poets' claims to seriousness and know better than those spectators whose opinions survive. If we contemplate the picture painted by the comic poets unedited, we will find that it makes sense after all. A good place to begin is with the Athenian *dēmos,* which ran the comic competition as it ran everything else, and with our earliest extant opinion about the connection between *dēmos* and comedy: the Old Oligarch, who wrote his treatise in the mid-420s, when Aristophanes was beginning his career.

I. Displays for the *Dēmos*

For the Old Oligarch, democracy was rule by the lower classes in their own interests, a poor form of government but not an irrational one: democratic institutions do preserve the rule of the *dēmos* and are not to be underestimated (cf. 1.1–9). One of those institutions is comedy. His description of comedy as an institution (2.18) appears not in a section on the arts or festivals but in a description of democratic decision making, which he envisages as displays by individuals for the voting *dēmos.* Before we consider the particular comic display we must examine those which took place in deliberative contexts.

The *dēmos,* says the Old Oligarch, is pragmatic but unprincipled and unaccountable. It makes policy in its own self-interest but cannot be made to take any responsibility. Instead, it can blame the individual who had advocated or called for the vote on a policy or an agreement. "And if anything bad results from a policy the *dēmos* has decided, its excuse is that a few persons have ruined it by acting against the interests of the *dēmos,* but if the result is good they take all the credit" (17). Comedy exemplifies the same phenomenon (18, quoted in section II, below): the *dēmos* may not be ridiculed or criticized, but rich, well-born, and influential citizens may. Such individuals are the same ones who propose policies. Thus he concludes (19) that the *dēmos* can recognize which of the citizens are good (*khrēstoi*) and which bad (*ponēroi*) but does not let this interfere with pursuit of its interests. "It prefers bad ones who are devoted to its interests to good ones, whom it rather hates, for it does not think that their inborn excellence [*aretēn*] is to its good but to its harm. On the other hand there are some who are undemocratic by nature who nevertheless take the side of the *dēmos*."

The *dēmos* is here sponsor, spectator, and judge of agonistic performances in which ambitious competitors make their appeals, and only the competitors are at risk. It is a valid description of fifth-century decision making and jibes with the picture drawn by Thoukydides: "When they recognized the facts, they turned against the public speakers who had favored the [Sicilian] expedition, as though they themselves had not voted for it" (8.1). Both Perikles (1.140.1) and Nikias (7.14.4) complain that the *dēmos* accepts sole credit for good fortune but assigns to its advisors sole blame for bad. If a speaker loses a debate, the *dēmos* has "slighted" him, and his reputation and influence decline (3.42.3–5). Even if he wins, the *dēmos* can vote to punish him, on charges brought by a citizen who wants to volunteer as prosecutor, for having proposed an illegal or inexpedient decree or law or policy should the result be not as predicted: Perikles himself was such a scapegoat (Thuk., 2.65.3).[8] In cases where the *dēmos* could not decide between the contestants, one of them could be expelled from the city by ostracism: each year the *dēmos* decided whether to hold one (*Ath. Pol.* 43.5). All officeholders were subject to official reviews of their fitness to hold an office and then of their conduct when leaving it. The Old Oligarch does not mention litigants in a law court here, but their situation was similar,[9] as we will see below (section III).

Thoukydides' Kleon, who thought that the members of the *dēmos* should assume control of their own deliberations, rebukes them for having "mistakenly" made decision making a series of "competitive displays [*kakōs agōnothetountes*]" and as a consequence having become "victims of your own pleasure in listening and more like spectators sitting at the feet of professional speakers than men deliberating the affairs of the city" (3.38.4, 7).[10] Compare the picture in *Knights* of "slave" politicians com-

---

[8] Jennifer T. Roberts, *Accountability in Athenian Government* (Madison, 1982) describes the legal mechanisms, and Martin Ostwald, *From Popular Sovereignty to the Sovereignty of Law* (Berkeley and Los Angeles, 1986) traces their use in the fifth century. For voluntary prosecution see further R. Osborne, "Law in Action in Classical Athens," *JHS* 105 (1985): 40–58.

[9] Cf. Plato, *Apology* 31e (Sokrates to the jury): "No one who conscientiously opposes you . . . can possibly escape with his life." From the dikast's point of view, cf. *Wasps* 546–630.

[10] The whole of the debate on Mytilene between Kleon and the officeholder Diodotos (3.37–48) examines the decision-making scenario and shows that the Old Oligarch's analysis was hardly idiosyncratic: see M. Ostwald, "Diodotus, Son of Eucrates," *GRBS* 20

peting in the "city of Open-mouthenians" (*Kekhēnaion*, 1263)[11] for the favor of Old Master *Dēmos,* who bestows privileges or floggings, and Plutarch's application to Nikias of Agamemnon's lines in Euripides, *Iphigeneia in Aulis* 449–50: "As master of our lives we nobles have magnificence, but we serve the crowd as slaves" (*Life of Nikias* 5.7).

This arrangement for determining public policy—the deliberate appeal to the *dēmos* as such in competitive displays—was a consequence of the full popular sovereignty (conservative theorists say "radical democracy") that was brought to completion in the middle of the century by (aristocratic) men "who seriously believed that the state ought to be run on democratic lines," and that remained in force until the loss of the empire at its end.[12] The institution of allotment of offices, any of which could be held by any citizen over thirty, and the personal accountability of officeholders, insured that no individual or group could long control the governmental mechanisms, and prevented the formation of corporate governmental entities. The quanta of government were dissolved and reformed in periods of a day, a month, a year, each new formation having the same random mixture as the old and thus reflecting the makeup of the whole. The *dēmos* as voting executive, with those current officeholders who were its government, moved en bloc from one kind of assembly to another, where individuals made their appeals. Leadership (winning the *dēmos'* vote) was thus personal, not political in the modern sense, and political success was a personal victory for an individual and thus for his supporters. But the power, to grant and to take away, resided solely with the *dēmos,* protean but ever the same. It is not surprising that our sources speak of the *dēmos,* which was in fact the sum total of all citizens, from the competitors' point of view: as a monolithic lump characterized by its lowest common denominators.

In such a system, civic ideology—that cohesive complex of ideas, beliefs, values, and historical memory which is the basis for common goals

---

(1979): 5–13. Note also the attitude of Isokrates (in a pamphlet purporting to address the Assembly): "It is hazardous to oppose your views, and even though this is a democracy there is no freedom of speech except here in the Assembly for the most thoughtless and self-interested and in the theater for producers of comedy" (*On the Peace* 14). For the similarity of actors and orators (many of whose speeches were written for them by professionals) see Aristotle, *Rhetoric* 1430b32–35.

[11] Alan H. Sommerstein's translation in *Aristophanes Knights* (Warminster, 1981); see also 261, 755. L. B. Carter, *The Quiet Athenian* (Oxford, 1986), 118 remarks that "the Athenians did look for something like selfless devotion to duty in their public servants."

[12] See P. J. Rhodes, "Political Activity in Classical Athens," *JHS* 106 (1986): 132–44 for this "passing phase," after which, in the fourth century, "no one found it necessary to parade his devotion to the *dēmos* as Pericles and Cleon had done" (140). Ostwald, *Popular Sovereignty,* fully documents the phase of full popular sovereignty.

and which justifies civic action to achieve them[13]—was not articulated in a constitution or party platform, was not a stable and coherent system (ideological in the modern sense). It was a complex of latent attitudes that were activated within a mosaic of occasions when appeals to the voting *dēmos* were made. The individual who appealed for victory (in the *dēmos'* interests) was the one who articulated civic ideology, hoping that his version more persuasively justified the proposal at hand than his opponent's version. Civic ideology was something formulated and reformulated as part of the competitive displays whose result was public policy and a change in the public standing of individuals.[14] And so the Old Oligarch could say that pragmatic self-interest, not morality or principle, determined the *dēmos'* decisions and its choice of leaders, and that democratic institutions for decision making reflect and preserve the rule of the *dēmos*.

The institutional distinction made by the Old Oligarch between ambitious competitors who performed and the sovereign *dēmos* which voted was also a social one: the competitors, who were also the permissible victims of comic attack, were "the best." In the fifth century the competitors came in fact from the wealthy classes. Like the epic hero and hoplite warrior of earlier times, they were allowed to display prowess and counsel and so gain personal prestige. The democratic revolution in Athens, which delivered power into the hands of the mass of citizens, had affected the elite primarily by requiring that, in return for the opportunity to lead, they employ their wealth, their traditions, and their sociopolitical skills for the benefit of all. The Old Oligarch, who sneers at politicians "undemocratic by nature" who side with the *dēmos* and at wealthy people who choose to live under democratic rule (2.19–20), considers this requirement "robbery" (1.13).[15] The *dēmos*, he says, will only perform offices that make them money, while expensive offices like choruses, athletic contests, and naval commands they are only too happy to make the rich run for them, by liturgy or by election, as in the case of military commanders (cf. 1.3), rather than by allotment. And they have "destroyed respect for"[16] such activities as individual sports and music, for which they have no use.[17]

[13] See L. Edmunds, "The Aristophanic Cleon's 'Disturbance' of Athens," *AJP* 108 (1987): 233–63 (esp. 235–36).

[14] Cf. the remark of Kleon at Thoukydides, 3.40.3 (quoted in n. 34, below).

[15] Compare the attitude of Kharmides in Xenophon, *Symposium* 4.29–30.

[16] For καταλέλυκεν cf. Andokides 1.39, where Alkibiades καταλύει τὰ γυμνάσια by his bad example.

[17] Compare the complaint of Better Argument in *Clouds* (961–1023), and for the association of athletics with distaste for democratic life see Euripides, *Hippolytos* 1013–20, Plato, *Gorgias* 515e.

The Old Oligarch recognizes an important phenomenon which I will discuss in greater detail later: the democratic adaptation of predemocratic traditions (drama as well as public speaking), not by the *dēmos,* but by the wealthy classes who had always managed them and who had thus "sold out" in the view of the Old Oligarch. This is a backhanded compliment in that it acknowledges the *dēmos'* wisdom in preserving important traditions and the prerogatives of those who could transmit them. Damon, the advisor of Perikles (*Ath. Pol.* 27.4), held that a country's characteristic high culture (*mousikēs tropoi*) should not be changed because this cannot be done without the greatest sociopolitical changes,[18] and Aristotle remarks on the unexampled forbearance of the *dēmos* in forgiving the oligarchs for their excesses in the period after the fall of the Thirty (*Ath. Pol.* 40).

Ancient sources are agreed that the death of Perikles in 429 marked a change in leadership of the *dēmos:* "Those after him, being of rather equal caliber one to the other and each one striving to be first, changed things so as to hand over to the *dēmos* and its whims even the conduct of affairs" (Thuk., 2.65.10). Modern scholars argue about the reality of this change. Some accept the ancient view as basically accurate.[19] Skeptics attribute the idea to the biases of our sources, which draw primarily on Thoukydides and the comic poets.[20] They point out that the "new politicians" neither changed the democratic institutions that had been in place since the 460s nor departed significantly from the programs and policies of Perikles.[21] The ancient sources indeed concentrate not on what moderns consider "serious" factors like programs and policies but on style, breeding, and social class.[22] For them the change involved a new disjunction of wealth and the traditional style that had gone with it: the new politicians were like the *dēmos* in wanting to get from rather than give to the *polis.*

Thoukydides (2.65), the comic poets,[23] and Aristotle (*Ath. Pol.* 28.1)

---

[18] Quoted in Plato, *Republic* 424c5–6. Damon wrote a treatise on the education of youth, *FVS* 37B1–10.

[19] Robert W. Connor, *The New Politicians of Fifth-century Athens* (Princeton, 1971), 87–136.

[20] See M. I. Finley, "Athenian Demagogues," *Past and Present* 21 (1962): 3–24. The comic record effectively begins with the ascendancy of Perikles after the ostracism of Thoukydides Milesiou in 444/3: practically no comic poetry written before then is extant— a limitation for ancient and modern scholars alike.

[21] See J. K. Davies, *Athenian Propertied Families 600–300 BC* (Oxford, 1975), 377–78. In *Akharnians* 530–39, Dikaiopolis identifies the war plan then being prosecuted by Kleon as Periklean.

[22] Significantly, no political or legal action seems to have been taken against Kleon for his policies (see Ostwald, *Popular Sovereignty,* 223), although in *Clouds* 590–94 Aristophanes looks forward to the end of his year as general, when he will have to face the *dēmos.*

[23] *Knights* 180–222, *Frogs* 732–33, Eupolis, frags. 219, 384.

tell us that Perikles was the last fifth-century leader who was both rich and well-born: Kleon was the first who was "not of good repute among the better sort" (*tois epieikesin*, Aristotle). These sources also tell us that the new politicians introduced a change of political style (identifying themselves directly with the *dēmos*) and that this style went together with a new source of wealth (not inherited in a distinguished family but earned by "selling"). How accurate is this picture?

The disappearance of men from the "better sort" of families seems real enough: before 429 all political leaders had been from the great archaic families or capable of marrying into them, except for Themistokles, who was of the lesser aristocracy.[24] After 429, only Alkibiades and Kritias belonged to the old families. "We need not be surprised at the time-lag between the creation of democratic institutions and the rise of men of the *dēmos* to positions of political importance, but the disappearance of the old aristocracy from such positions is strikingly abrupt."[25]

That the advent of Kleon as the speaker "having the greatest power of appeal to the *dēmos*" (Thuk., 3.36.6) marked a change in the traditional (well-bred) style of political persuasion also seems real. Kleon paraded his devotion to the *dēmos* rather than to a circle of friends (whom he is said to have formally dismissed),[26] opposed anyone who thought himself superior to the *dēmos*,[27] eschewed such aristocratic practices as the performance of liturgies, and claimed lower-class affiliations himself.[28] "More than anyone else he corrupted the *dēmos* by his violent impulses and was the first man who, when on the platform, shouted, slandered and made speeches with his clothes hitched up, while everyone else spoke in an orderly way" (*Ath. Pol.* 28.3).

Clearly the *dēmos* was now ready to listen to men who gave undivided attention to its own interests. Kleon's scornful remarks about "competitive displays" at Thoukydides, 3.38 (quoted above) was thus a slap at the upper-class speakers the *dēmos* was used to hearing and an exhortation to the *dēmos* to assume control for itself (with Kleon, of course, as leader). The reply made on this occasion by Diodotos, who as an officeholder could not speak so recklessly as Kleon, aligns Kleon with the unaccount-

[24] In *Knights* (810–19; cf. 84, 884) Kleon compares himself to Themistokles.

[25] P. J. Rhodes, *A Commentary on the Aristotelian Athenaion Politeia* (Oxford, 1981), 345.

[26] Ar., *Knights* (passim), Plutarch, *Moralia* 806f–807a, cf. Connor, *New Politicians,* 91–94, 121–22, 127–28.

[27] Thuk., 3.37–40 with Connor, *New Politicians,* 94–96.

[28] E.g., *Knights* 335–39, Platon, frag. 219 = Aristotle, *Rhetoric* 1376a9–12. Compare litigants, e.g., *Wasps* 548–630, Demosthenes, 42.20, where one of Demosthenes' clients boasts, "In early life I made a lot of money from the silver-mines, working and toiling myself with my own hands." Sommerstein, in *Aristophanes Knights,* 314, thinks that "metaphors from handicrafts may have been typical of Kleon's oratory (cf. 461–3)."

able *dēmos:* "Faced with issues of utmost importance and in such a position as ours is, we must be expected, as we make our speeches, to be thinking ahead rather further than you who give the issues but a moment's attention, especially as the advice we give is subject to an accounting, whereas the hearing you give is unaccountable" (3.43.4). Kleon's demagogic manner may safely be aligned with that fomentation of class antagonism (*dēmos* and its new champions versus the traditional leaders) that would erupt into class warfare before the end of the century.

That the new politicians were actually "men of the *dēmos*" (sellers without land or family) is, however, harder to document. What little we know of the families of men like Kleon, Hyperbolos, and Kleophon suggest that they were entirely respectable.[29] If Kleon dismissed his friends he must have had friends to dismiss, and there would be no point in dismissing them were they mere sellers, not to say slaves, aliens, thieves, the sons and husbands of shady women. In our world, where seriousness and humor have been separately institutionalized, cartoonists and comedians can indulge in such name-calling, but officials or leaders cannot: contrast Nikias and Kleon (Thuk., 4.27) or the speeches of Demosthenes and Aiskhines, whose mutual vilification resembles that of the comic poets in all essentials. In evaluating the literary response to the new politicians we must attune ourselves to varieties of wild exaggeration and outright satire that today are largely absent from official and political discourse but that in classical Athens were rhetorical modes common to oratory and comedy. The violent abusiveness that characterizes the contest for Old Master Dēmos' favor in *Knights* is not entirely Aristophanes' own invention.

It looks as if the backgrounds that our literary sources supply for the new politicians were an exaggerated way of saying that an opponent had "no family" and of attributing to them that solidarity with the lower classes that they rhetorically claimed for themselves. Kleon was no more a tanner than he was a Paphlagonian. This humor was complex and in its own way as demagogic as Kleon's portrayal of the men of the old families as "tyrants": part snobbery (the victims were not of the "better sort" of families) and part exposure of demotic pretensions (nor were they common folk). Thus both superior and inferior social classes could say "not one of us" and so share in the sneering.

For our purposes it is most significant that the new politicians derived their ascendancy not, like Perikles and his predecessors, by holding official positions but by success in competitive displays before the *dēmos* in council, Assembly, and court, where rhetorical ability and force of per-

---

[29] See J. K. Davies' review of Connor, *New Politicians,* in *Gnomon* 47 (1975): 374–78.

sonality were everything.[30] A new class of "speakers" (*rhētores*) developed who could be distinguished from "politicians" (*politikoi*).[31] The
latter were statesmen (as in the title of Plato's dialogue) or men who
regularly served the *polis* in constitutionally specified (and therefore accountable) roles: magistrates allotted from a list of men nominated by
their demes; elected generals and treasurers; liturgists. Such offices meant
time-consuming service and, as often as not, more expense than profit:[32]
they were for men of wealth and standing. By contrast, anyone could be
a speaker, and speaking was, compared to officeholding, a relatively safe
way to seek personal advancement: by advising the *dēmos,* or by taking
sides in a lawsuit or review of conduct against the officeholders. Most
speakers were either well-born young men who had decided not to
"mind their own business" but to become politically active (*polupragmones*) and who sought out sophists for rhetorical training,[33] or they
were "outsiders" like Kleon.[34] The informal (paraconstitutional) "office" of speaker enabled such men to get into the competition, at the expense of the aristocrats who had hitherto enjoyed a monopoly. Their
new and peculiar styles of rhetorical appeal were a principal means of establishing their status, and their caricature in our literary sources was part
of the response.

For Thoukydides, people like Kleon harmed the Athenians in several
ways (2.65). Because they identified themselves with the *dēmos,* a whimsical mob, they could not lead it; because their families had no political
importance they espoused policies that looked to their own advancement
and profit rather than to the public good; and because they were selfishly
competitive their policies were inconsistent and led to that factionalism
on which Thoukydides blamed Athens' defeat more than any other factor. The Old Oligarch had these changes in mind when he said (above)
that the *dēmos* was willing to choose "bad" men as leaders. The almost
whimsical election of Kleon, on Nikias' ironic proposal, to a command

---

[30] After 429, only Kleon and Thrasyboulos among the new politicians are known to have
held a generalship.

[31] Cf. Plato, *Apology* 23e–24a (Sokrates accused by Meletos on behalf of the poets, by
Anytos on behalf of the craftsmen and politicians, by Lykon on behalf of the speakers). The
"speakers" were constant butts of comic ridicule.

[32] See the Old Oligarch 1.3, Carter, *Quiet Athenian,* 35.

[33] See Ostwald, *Popular Sovereignty,* 229–50, Carter, *Quiet Athenian,* 119–25.

[34] The comic poets abused both the aristocratic young speakers and the outsiders but also
recognized their mutual hostility. Likewise Thoukydides, who has Kleon say (appealing to
class antagonism) that his younger counterparts are unpatriotic: "As for the speakers who
delight you with their way of speaking, they should hold their competitions about less important subjects and not about a matter where the *polis* may for its light pleasure pay a
heavy price, while the speakers themselves will be well rewarded for speaking well"
(3.40.3). Kleon's "sophistic" way of saying this aligns him with those he criticizes: an example of Thoukydidean humor.

(hitherto reserved for generals: aristocrats and their protégés) was a sensational instance of the new mood of the dēmos (Thuk., 4.27–28). If comedy as a competitive display was analogous to deliberative ones, Thoukydides' account here indicates that the analogy works both ways: politics could come to resemble comedy.

But there were other "new politicians" who offered a different choice. Nikias, who like Kleon was the son of the man who founded the family fortune,[35] kept to the style represented by Perikles: accountable leadership by the "best" in the interests of all classes. Like Perikles, he frequently performed liturgies, avoided symposiums and other social distractions, and based his political career on social alliances and generalships.[36] Also like Perikles, he saw the war not as an opportunity to expand the empire but only as a chance to make Sparta and her allies acquiesce in its existence. Things would then be as they had been before the war. For Kleon and the other new men, however, the war was a chance for personal ascendancy and an opportunity to expand the empire.

The war-policy created internal division principally by requiring that the countryside be evacuated and left to the predations of the enemy;[37] by redistributing the accumulated wealth of the empire; and by creating political openings for men like Kleon, who appealed to the *dēmos'* confidence and aggressiveness. If everyone benefitted from the empire, it was the masses who benefitted most from the war and the "best" who were presented with the bill. Perikles' confidence in Athens' ability to finance the war from existing resources had been based on the expectation that the war would not last long (Thuk., 2.13). In the event, these resources quickly evaporated, so that by 428 the war began to require ever more borrowing, ever more tribute from the allies, ever more levies on the wealthy.[38] All this made the urban populace—rowers and provisioners especially—the beneficiaries of the war, and the landed aris-

[35] Silver-mining (Xenophon, *Poroi* 4.14, *Memorabilia* 2.5.2; Plutarch, *Nikias* 4.2), which, however, was far more lucrative than (say) tanning and therefore could not be ridiculed as a low or banausic occupation: at *Knights* 362, "buy mining leases" equals "be rich."

[36] Plutarch, *Nikias* 3, 5. Nikias was general every year from 427/6 (the aristocrats' counter to Kleon?) to 421/0 (the peace that bears his name) and again from 418/7 until his death in 413: Charles Fornara, *The Athenian Board of Generals from 501 to 404*, Historia Einzelschrift 16 (Wiesbaden, 1971), 56–65. Diog. Laert., 1.110, providing him with an ancestor who was important in Solonian times, reflects fifth-century propaganda the opposite of that directed at Kleon.

[37] For the effect see Thuk., 2.16.

[38] See Russell Meiggs and David Lewis, *Greek Historical Inscriptions* (Oxford, 1969), 184–201 on *IG* I³ 68, 71 (tribute), 205–17 on *IG* I³ 369 (borrowing); Thuk. 3.19.1 (capital levies on wealthy begin in 428, perhaps on Kleon's initiative: *Knights* 773–75). In *Knights* 912–26, Kleon threatens to make the Sausage Seller a trierarch and to enroll him among the rich so that he can be squeezed for levies.

tocracy, together with the peasants, the losers. It also changed the makeup of the voting *dēmos* and therefore the character of the appeals made to it.

Since the *dēmos* stood to gain much by going along with men like Kleon and little by going along with men like Nikias, it is easy to see why the "best" began to take a hostile view of the *dēmos* and its champions. Nevertheless there seems to have been general agreement about following the war-policy in spite of such unanticipated hardships as the plague and the tenacity of the Peloponnesians: the empire was unsafe until its enemies abandoned their resolve to "liberate" it. The task of the "best" was to keep the *dēmos*' eye on this goal and to curb the ambitious adventurism of the demagogues, who chafed under Perikles' warning about not "hoping for more" until the Peloponnesians gave up.[39] The victory at Pylos in 425 might have achieved this goal. Unhappily for the "best," the Pylos victory meant triumph for Kleon and disgrace for Nikias, and it encouraged the *dēmos* to "hope for more."

Those who claim that the comic poets were mere humorists must explain why they consistently and one-sidedly championed the position of the "best": like Thoukydides, they refrain from criticizing Nikias (who could just as fairly be called a slave and a seller as Kleon); they explain away, play down, or even omit to mention the victories both military and financial that were achieved by the new politicians; and they hold profoundly ambivalent views about the ability of the *dēmos* at large to choose responsible leaders (like themselves!).

Those competitors for the favor of the *dēmos* who made their appeals as office-holders, as speakers in council and Assembly or as litigants in court, were thus engaged in a political and ideological contest that the ascendancy of Perikles had postponed and that the war with the Peloponnesians exacerbated. There was no settled Athenian policy, no unanimity. Men competed for the votes that would determine policy and crossed their fingers. The comic poets were part of the contest, just as Sokrates says in Plato's *Apology:* in 423 a comic poet was one of his "most dangerous accusers" (18c2–d2), and in 399 Meletos represented the poets in seeking his death (23e–24a). As the "Open-mouthenian" *dēmos* looked from one side to the other, trying to decide which way its interests lay, Aristophanes arrived on the scene and joined the contest, attacking the new politics in his very first play (427) and Kleon in his second. But by what mechanisms, social, political, or institutional, did comic poets have access to such a contest?

---

[39] In *Knights,* Kleon hopes to extend the *dēmos*' sway over all of Greece (236–38, 797–800) and Hyperbolos has his eye on Carthage (1303–4). In 425/4 three generals were cashiered by the *dēmos* for having failed to subdue Sicily (Thuk. 4.65.3). Such ambitions culminated in 415 in the expedition against Sicily.

II. THE COMIC DISPLAY

Let us return to the Old Oligarch's description of comedy as an institution of the *dēmos* that illustrates its practice of holding prominent men responsible for whatever goes wrong while taking credit for everything that turns out well.

> And again, they do not tolerate comic ridicule and criticism of the *dēmos*, lest their reputation suffer, but they encourage this in the case of individuals if there is anyone somebody wants this to happen to. For they well know that the victim is generally not one of the *dēmos* or the crowd but a rich, well-born or powerful individual. A few of the poor and the demotic are ridiculed in comedy but only if they are politically active or seek to have more than the *dēmos*. Therefore they are not offended if such people are ridiculed.
>
>   (2.18)[40]

Leaving aside for the moment the function here ascribed to comedy (ridicule and criticism), let us see in what ways it was a competitive display comparable to the displays with deliberative functions that were discussed above.

The comic festivals are often thought of as holiday[41] or static ritual[42] or carnival,[43] and thus as opportunities for "unbridled freedom of speech," and "release from the normal obligation to heed the restraints

---

[40] κωμωιδεῖν δ' αὖ καὶ κακῶς λέγειν (one of the legal terms for slander: n. 114) τὸν μὲν δῆμον οὐκ ἐῶσιν, ἵνα μὴ αὐτοὶ ἀκούωσι κακῶς, ἰδίαι δὲ κελεύουσιν, εἴ τίς τινα βούλεται, εὖ εἰδότες ὅτι οὐχὶ τοῦ δήμου ἐστὶν οὐδὲ τοῦ πλήθους ὁ κωμωιδούμενος ὡς ἐπὶ τὸ πολύ, ἀλλ' ἢ πλούσιος ἢ γενναῖος ἢ δυνάμενος. ὀλίγοι δέ τινες τῶν πενήτων καὶ τῶν δημοτικῶν κωμωιδοῦνται, καὶ οὐδ' οὗτοι ἐὰν μὴ διὰ πολυπραγμοσύνην καὶ διὰ τὸ ζητεῖν πλέον τι ἔχειν τοῦ δήμου· ὥστε οὐδὲ τοὺς τοιούτους ἄχθονται κωμωιδουμένους.

[41] C. L. Barber, *Shakespeare's Festive Comedy* (Princeton, 1959) has most influenced classicists.

[42] Francis M. Cornford, *The Origin of Attic Comedy* (Cambridge, 1914, 2d ed. 1934) first systematically made the case, but his understanding of ritual (à la the Cambridge School of Fraser and Harrison) as a static behavior embedded in a society is no longer the understanding of cultural anthropologists, who see it as an integral and therefore flexible mode of all social organization, even if self-conscious rituals (notably religious ones) often refer to themselves as unchanging.

[43] Mikhail Bakhtin, *Rabelais and His World,* trans. H. Iswolsky (Cambridge, Mass. and London, 1968), whose model is discussed above, made no special study of classical comedy but has had the greatest influence on classicists: see most recently J.-C. Carrière, *Le carnaval et la politique* (Paris, 1979), whose summary of comedy as carnival appears on 32; cf. also 41–50, 167–75, and W. Rösler, "Bakhtin und die Karnevalskultur im antiken Griechenland," *QUCC* 23 (1986): 25–44.

and subordinations of social hierarchy," since they were occasions whose "conventions . . . separated the festivals from the normal life of the city."[44] But comic festivals, as occasions for competitive display by poets, producers, and *khorēgoi,* show not only as much institutional structure as the deliberative occasions with which the Old Oligarch aligns them, but also much the same structure.[45] And, like all festivals organized by the *dēmos,* they had social and political as well as religious significance: no decisions were made about the city or its individual citizens, but the city and its citizens were the festival's theme and focus. Comic festivals were not "carnival" but civic business—and big business.

Consider the Great Dionysia, into which the *dēmos* inserted the old *kō-mōidia* (song of the *kōmos*) as a competition in 486 and where comedy had its unique home until 440, when it was admitted also to the Lenaia.[46] Like the Panathenaia, the Dionysia was a comparatively recent institution created and developed largely for civic and political ends. There were marches, parades, processions, sacrifices, ceremonies honoring benefactors both foreign and Athenian, diplomatic demonstrations like the renewal of the oath to abide by the Peace of Nikias (Thuk., 5.23), recognition of the new (ephebic) warriors, including those war orphans who had been wards of the *dēmos,* the presentation of tribute in talents to the presiding (allotted) *arkhōn* by representatives of each "ally." All this was a display of the authority, the power, and the character of the *dēmos,* which was arrayed in the theater exactly as it was on the Pnyx.[47] On the honors to individuals Demosthenes points out the obvious: "All the spectators are thereby encouraged to serve the city, and they applaud the exhibition of gratitude rather than the recipient: that is why the city has established this law" (18.120). And the effect of the presentation of tribute in full view of the *dēmos* and its foreign guests is equally obvious: for Isokrates it had been both tasteless and a dangerously arrogant way to conduct imperial policy (*On the Peace* 82).

[44] S. Halliwell, "Aristophanic Satire," *Yearbook of English Studies* 14 (1984): 6–20 (8).

[45] The role played by real carnival in political struggles (rebellions against dominant classes) depends on its autonomy and its separateness from official structures (though officials sometimes connive in it for their own purposes): a thorough case study is supplied by B. Scribner, "Reformation, Carnival, and the World Turned Upside-Down," *Social History* 3 (1978): 303–29.

[46] Athenian festivals, except perhaps for the central holy acts performed by priests or other hieratic personnel, were as dynamic and ever-changing as the society of which they were a part, not "ritual" in the older sense of the word (n. 42, above), so that historians must read them not as fixed texts but as palimpsests-in-process. M. Ozuf, *Festivals and the French Revolution* (Cambridge, Mass., 1988), examines the processes by which festivals can be changed or created in response to political/ideological upheavals.

[47] On the "map of the body politic formed by the theater seating" see the essay by Winkler in this volume.

Then came the choral contests, paid for through liturgy (the Old Oligarch would say extortion) by rich competitors: dithyramb (involving 1,000 dancers, 50 men and 50 boys from each tribe), comedy (120 dancers) and tragedy (36, later 45 dancers). Like the Panathenaia, the Greater Dionysia was exceptionally grand and costly, but we must view it against the background of a city that boasted of having more festivals than any other city (to say nothing of those at the deme-level)[48]—a phenomenon closely connected with democracy by the Old Oligarch (1.13, 3.2, 8)—so that to exclude them from the "normal life of the city" is misleading. Festivals were one of the chief ways in which the city organized itself, established who was who, and demonstrated what was important. With this in mind, let us examine the organization of the comic festival within the larger framework of the Dionysia and its institutional relationship to the city (the *dēmos*).

The appropriate (allotted) *arkhōn* granted the poet a chorus and authorized payment for actors, honoraria, and prizes.[49] One of the citizens (about one percent of the total number) rich enough to be,[50] and therefore required[51] by the *dēmos* to be, *khorēgos* recruited and paid for the lodging, training, and outfitting of the twenty-four singer-dancers who would be his comic chorus as well as for all other expenses required for the production and for the banquet afterwards. The competition itself was governed by rules carefully established by the *dēmos*. Following the festival an assembly was held to determine whether these rules had been scrupulously followed and to hear complaints from anyone who thought they had not been.[52] We know nothing specific about how these rules controlled what was said and done on the comic stage. But there is solid evidence that they did.

---

[48] "The costs of cult—upkeep of temples and shrines, offering of regular sacrifices, celebration of recurrent festivals—surely represented, for any deme, the major object of regular expenditure." David Whitehead, *The Demes of Attica* (Princeton, 1986), 163–64. For theatrical activity at the deme level, see P. Ghiron-Bistagne, *Recherches sur les acteurs dans la Grèce antique* (Paris, 1976), 86–97.

[49] Plato says that each poet read specimens of his songs (*ōidai*) to the *arkhōn* (*Laws* 817d), but it is likely that patronage in the form of help from influential or experienced friends also played a role: see S. Halliwell, "Aristophanes' Apprenticeship," *CQ* 30 (1980): 33–45.

[50] Only some four hundred of the thirty thousand citizens could meet the three-talent qualification (about fifty years' wages for a skilled craftsman): see Davies, *Athenian Propertied Families*, xxi–iv.

[51] That *khorēgiai* were required like any other liturgy is clear from the Old Oligarch, who mentions *diadikasiai* over them, cf. [Aristotle], *Ath. Pol.* 56.3 (with Rhodes, *Commentary*), J. H. Lipsius, *Das attische Recht und Rechtsverfahren* (Leipzig, 1905–1915), 590–99. No one was required to perform the same liturgy twice in a lifetime, but one could volunteer: old-style politicians like Nikias made voluntary liturgies a primary element of their political ascendancy (Plutarch, *Nikias* 3); the speaker of Lysias 21 boasts of performing eight *khorēgiai* in nine years (1–5).

[52] See *DFA*, 64, 68–70.

The Old Oligarch, at 2.18, says that ridicule and criticism of the *dēmos* was "not tolerated" and in fact is not found in extant comedies: in *Knights* and *Wasps*, for example, Aristophanes blames the *dēmos* only to exhort it to recapture the ideals and the glory which it has lost by listening to false leaders like Kleon (see section IV, below). What is more, the personal experience of Aristophanes shows that comic poets were not considered immune from *all* complaint by fellow citizens, as some critics in ancient and modern times have thought. He was sued by Kleon after his victory with *Babylonians* in 426 on the grounds that he had slandered the magistrates, councillors, and people in the presence of foreigners (scholiast on *Akharnians* 378),[53] and again after his victory with *Knights*, on grounds unclear (*Wasps* 1284–91): recall the possible consequences to victors in political debate described by the Old Oligarch in 2.17. It would seem that comic poets, like other officeholders, were accountable.

The victims of comic abuse (as opposed to the *dēmos*) were prominent competitors and were evidently expected to take it in good spirit (the spirit of the traditional *kōmos*-song), and in any event an appeal to the *dēmos* that one had been unfairly abused (as in the case of Sokrates, which will be considered later) would amount to a claim of superiority and so would most likely earn only more ridicule. But there is no reason to think that comic poets were exempt from the laws about slander (see section III, below), and they may even have been controlled by special ones: Plutarch mentions a law of Thurioi (an Athenian colony and ally) restricting comic ridicule of citizens to "adulterers and troublemakers [*polupragmones*]" (*Moralia* 519b).[54] There may well have been rules of this sort in fifth-century Athens. Their particulars can only be inferred as by the dog that didn't bark in the night: the absence of certain explicit charges or the avoidance of certain targets. They will turn out to be the same as for the orators. I notice, for example, that the wives and mothers of prominent men were, as in oratory, insulted and even portrayed on-

---

[53] Probably by *eisangelia;* see Alan H. Sommerstein, *Aristophanes Acharnians* (Warminster, 1980), 32–33 and, for Kleon's use of *eisangelia* in general, Ostwald, *Popular Sovereignty,* 207–13. For the "presence of foreigners" cf. *Akharnians* 502–8. *Knights* 512–13 is evidence that in the period before 424 Aristophanes was known as the author of those plays produced by Kallistratos: see Halliwell, "Aristophones' Apprenticeship," 35–36. With this episode compare the one thousand–drachma fine levied against the tragic poet Phrynikhos in 493 for having in his (topical) *Capture of Miletos* "reminded the Athenians of misfortunes close to home [οἰκήια κακά]" (Herodotos, 6.21).

[54] If there was Thurian comedy in the fifth century, was it one of those institutional exports by which Athens sought to encourage and safeguard democracy in allied cities? For some others see J. P. Barron, "Religious Propaganda of the Delian League," *JHS* 84 (1964): 35–48, Russell Meiggs, *The Athenian Empire* (Oxford, 1972), 295–98, J. Alty, "Dorians and Ionians," *JHS* 102 (1982): 1–14, Edmunds, "Aristophane Cleon," 254–56.

stage, but their unmarried daughters were not.[55] In fact a marriageable citizen-girl appears only once in extant fifth-century comedy, in *Akharnians* (241–79), where Dikaiopolis' daughter is the basket-carrier in his procession. To be chosen basket-carrier was in real life a great distinction, and to be denied was a great humiliation to the men of the family: this was the insult that got Hipparkhos assassinated in 514 (Thuk., 6.56.1).[56]

The rules could also be reformulated. The year 440/39, when the Athenians went to war against their own ally Samos (Thuk., 1.115–17), saw the passage of a decree in some way limiting comic freedom of criticism and lasting until 437/6 (scholiast on *Akharnians* 67). And in 415/4, Syrakosios[57] secured the passage of a decree prohibiting reference by name in comedy to persons condemned for mutilating the herms or celebrating mock Mysteries (*Birds* 1297 with scholiast; cf. Phrynikhos, fr. 26). The reality of this decree has been doubted, but nothing else explains why not one of the some sixty-five persons known to have been condemned is mentioned by name in the some 4,550 surviving lines of comedy from the period 415–411 (when Alkibiades' condemnation was repealed: Thuk., 8.97.3), although many others are.[58] Evidently the decree was part of a general *damnatio memoriae* against Alkibiades, and the others, comedy being a civic occasion when they might be mentioned in memorable fashion.[59] It was possible also to change state-authorized allowances to the poets, even if the reason might not have been the one given by the chorus of *Frogs,* who would ban from the festival such "uninitiated and unhealthy" people[60] as "the person who as speaker proceeds

---

[55] The protocol of not naming respectable women in comedy was the same as in oratory: D. Schaps, "The Woman Least Mentioned: Etiquette and Women's Names," *CQ* 27 (1977): 323–30, Alan H. Sommerstein, "The Naming of Women in Greek and Roman Comedy," *Quaderni di storia* 11 (1980): 393–418. Curiously, no comic poet seems to have subjected Kleon's wife or mother to the abuse freely heaped on those of other "demagogues" (lechery, foreign birth, selling in the markets, membership in strange cults, etc.).

[56] Note that in *Lysistrata* the maidens are the only class and age-group of citizen-females who do not appear on stage.

[57] Evidently a politician in the mold of Kleon: Eupolis, frag. 220, compares him to "watchdogs running on the walls" because when speaking on the platform he "runs around and barks."

[58] See Alan H. Sommerstein, "The Decree of Syrakosios," *CQ* 36 (1986): 101–8. The short life and apparent infrequency of such decrees indicate the people's liking for comic attack.

[59] Perhaps even in a not unsympathetic fashion: two of the men condemned, Arkhippos and Aristomenes (Andokides 1.12–13), may have been the comic poets: see Douglas M. MacDowell, *On the Mysteries* (Oxford, 1961), Appendix N.

[60] The "demagogues" Agyrrhios and Arkhinos: see Rhodes, *Commentary,* on [Aristotle], *Ath. Pol.* 34.3, 41.3.

to nibble away the rewards of poets because he was ridiculed [*kōmōidōtheis*] in the ancestral festivals of Dionysos" (367–68).

If speakers in Assembly risked competition in hopes of taking credit for a successful policy, poets, producers, and *khorēgoi* risked competition at the comic festival for distinction: recognition as "the best" at putting on this kind of display. In the Athenian democracy personal victory and civic distinction were powerful motivations in themselves, but there were also potential political benefits: the *khorēgos* "who devoted his money and attention enthusiastically to his team could expect to win not only glory for himself but also glory for, and gratitude from, the performers and their families, and the whole tribe."[61] A *khorēgia* was an occasion for approved (because in the city's interests) ostentation: Nikias' *khorēgiai* were an important factor in his political prominence (Plutarch, *Nikias* 3), and Alkibiades, too, boasted of the lavishness of his athletic teams and his choruses, claiming that they enhanced foreign perception of Athenian strength (Thuk., 6.16).

A *khorēgia* was also an occasion for the deployment of one's social-political skills.[62] The *khorēgos* of Antiphon's *On the Khoreutēs* points out to the jury how he had recruited "the best chorus that I could, inflicting not a single fine, extorting not a single pledge, making not a single enemy" (6.11), while among the misdeeds of Alkibiades remembered in later times was his violent behavior toward a rival *khorēgos*.[63] Litigants often boasted how lavishly they had discharged a liturgy, sometimes even admitting that they had done so in part "so that if any misfortune should chance to happen to me I might defend myself on better terms" (Lysias, 25.13). Antiphanes describes the *khorēgos* reduced to rags in order to equip his chorus with "golden cloaks" (frag. 204.5), for a cheap *khorēgia* lowered one's prestige: "have you ever seen a shabbier *khorēgos* than this one?" (Eupolis, frag. 329); "may Zeus obliterate Antimakhos . . . who when Lenaian *khorēgos* dismissed us without a banquet!" (the chorus at *Akharnians* 1150–55). Liturgists, in short, as men officially deemed capable of putting on a good show,[64] were either inept or stingy if they failed to do so. A bad *khorēgia* might well be remembered "if any

---

[61] Rhodes, "Political Activity," 136. A victorious *chorēgos* got an ivy crown and his name was listed before the producer's (cf. *IG* II² 2318).

[62] See Aristotle, *Nik. Eth.* 1123a18, on the "honorable expenditures" of the "magnificent" (*megaloprepēs*) citizen.

[63] [Andokides], 4.20–21, 25–32, Demosthenes, 21.147. See Ostwald, *Popular Sovereignty*, 120–21 for a discussion of this incident. Alkibiades' whole career illustrates the tension, inherent in democracy and the theme of Perikles' funeral oration, between individual prowess and civic virtue; cf. Carter, *Quiet Athenian*, 14.

[64] See Lysias, 19.48–52 on the *dēmos*' tendency to overestimate the wealth of wealthy men.

misfortune should chance to happen," such as a lawsuit or a review of conduct in office.

Victory for poets was primarily for artistic achievement, whose importance is amply elucidated in Aristophanes' plays (particularly in the parabases), as is the bitterness of a defeat like the one in 423 when he "retired, defeated undeservedly by crass men" (*Clouds* 518–62). There was also the kind of social celebrity that "stars" enjoy in all ages: see *Wasps* 1023–28.[65] And there might be political consequences as well: not only lawsuits like the ones brought by Kleon but also special honors like the "crown of sacred olive, reckoned equal in honor to a golden crown" which the *dēmos* bestowed on Aristophanes for the splendid advice he had offered in *Frogs*,[66] which was given an unprecedented second performance.[67] These honors recognized the advice given in the parabasis, in particular lines 686–705, which recommended the restoration of the rights of disenfranchised citizens. The decree and second performance were voted either in connection with the decision of the *dēmos* to follow that advice, in late 405 by the decree of Patrokleides,[68] or (less likely) after the democratic restoration and general amnesty of 403, when sacred olive-crowns were also decreed for the defenders of Phyle against the Thirty (Aiskhines, 3.187).[69]

The Old Oligarch seems to be so far justified in speaking of the comic festival as an institution of the *dēmos,* as part of that mosaic of occasions when competitive appeals were made and whose common denominator was the sovereignty of the *dēmos* over all individuals, however distinguished. From what social class did the comic poets come? Were they, like the politicians and *khorēgoi,* wealthy and (until Kleon) well-bred? The evidence is very scanty but inclines me to say yes. One had, I think, to be well-bred to have a career as a dramatic poet: this was no job for "the demotic." Nor for the poor: when we do have information, as for Aiskhylos, Sophokles, and Euripides,[70] we find that the poets were also

---

[65] I see no reason to read this passage as empty conceit: a young poet with at least three victories behind him will surely have attracted the admiring glances of at least some boys at the palaestra. Plato remarks (*Laws* 658d2) that "the older boys" especially enjoyed comedy.

[66] Aristophanes, *Life* 35–36 Kassel-Austin.

[67] Dikaiarkhos, quoted in Hypothesis 1 of *Frogs.*

[68] Andokides, 1.73–80, Xenophon, *Hellenika* 2.2.11.

[69] See J. T. Allen, *California Publications in Classical Philology* 11 (1930–1933): 143–51: but advice to entrust the polis to *khrēstoi* and *kaloi kagathoi* would have been more appealing before the regime of the Thirty than after the democratic restoration.

[70] Aristophanes, who thought that Euripides' plays appealed to the lowest common denominator, invented a suitably squalid background for the poet himself, insisting that his mother was a vegetable-seller, but she was in reality of high birth (Philokhoros, *FGrHist* 328F218); cf. Carter, *Quiet Athenian,* 150.

from well-to-do families. The social personality of Old Comedy (surely not mere affectation) suggests that what was true of tragedians was true of their comic counterparts.

Aristophanes, like Kleon from the urban deme Kydathenaion, apparently came from a cultivated family. Plato in the *Symposium* portrays him as a lover of good living, if not the sturdiest of drinkers (176b–c, 185c), on friendly terms with the other guests, the elite of social and intellectual Athens, and as a man of old-fashioned ethical values (190b–d, 193a–d). In *Akharnians* (6–8, 299–302) and *Knights,* he aligns himself with the upper-class cavalry corps, one of whom was Simon (*Knights* 242, 351), the fellow demesman who wrote a treatise on horsemanship and dedicated a bronze statue of a horse at the Eleusinion (Xenophon, *De re equestri* 1.1), and another of whom (243) was probably the Panaitios later condemned in the scandal of the Mysteries (Andokides, 1.13, 52, 67).[71] Simon was also the priest of a *thiasos* of Herakles, among whose sixteen members (all of Kydathenaion) were Philonides, the producer of *Wasps, Proagōn, Amphiaraos,* and *Frogs,* and one Amphitheos, whose name occurs nowhere else in Attika except as the friend of Dikaiopolis who fetches the Treaties in *Akharnians* (45–203).[72] Early in the fourth century Aristophanes served as Councillor (*IG* II² 1740.21–24), and two of his sons also became comic poets (Aristophanes testimonia 7–8 Kassel-Austin). I see no reason to doubt that Aristophanes' rivals, whose tendencies appear to be the same, also came from the same kind of background.

It would seem that the advent of the new style of appeal introduced by Kleon to political contests was not paralleled at the comic festivals. Although Aristophanes thought that there were "new" (demagogic) tragic poets (principally Euripides and Agathon) who were ruining the tragic festivals as surely as Kleon and Sokrates were ruining the city, there seem to have been no "new" comic poets. The comic poets who did compose in the period after 429 poured scorn on the new style and, in their way, sided with those who held to the old. To understand comedy's contribution to this struggle we must take up the Old Oligarch's description of

---

[71] See Sommerstein, "Decree," 104 n. 26.

[72] For the *thiasos* (*IG* II² 2343) see S. Dow, "Some Athenians in Aristophanes," *AJA* 73 (1969): 234–35; Thomas Gelzer, *Aristophanes der Komiker, RE,* supp. 12 (1971): 1398.14ff.; D. Welsh, "*IG* II² 2343, Philonides, and Aristophanes' *Banqueters,*" *CQ* 33 (1983): 51–55; and H. Lind, "Neues aus Kydathen," *MH* 42 (1985): 249–61. For its possible location see Ph. Stauropoullos, "Χρονικά· Ἀθῆναι, Ἀττική," *Arkhaiologikon Deltion* 20 (1965): 52–55 with pl. 41b. Such cults were fraternal organizations that would appeal to the upper classes: S. Woodford, "Cults of Herakles in Attica," in *Studies Presented to G. M. A. Hanfmann* (Mainz, 1971), 211–25; Dem., 57.46, where the speaker lists among his credentials that he "was selected by my fellow-demesmen among the highest-born to cast lots for the priesthood of Herakles." Why Aristophanes was not a member is unclear.

its function: that ridicule and criticism of individuals which pleased the *dēmos* and confirmed its sovereignty.

III. RIDICULE

Comedy had no uniform style in the fifth century. Not all comedies took direct notice of contemporary public affairs. There were mythological burlesques like the *Odyssēs* of Kratinos,[73] and there were domestic comedies that foreshadowed the Hellenistic style, the specialty first of Krates,[74] later of Pherekrates.[75] These to some degree overlapped with tragedy and satyr-drama. There were two specialties of fifth-century comedy, however, that were distinctive and closely related: the offering of useful advice and criticism about important issues of the day, and the ridicule of individuals.[76] How common comedies in this style were will probably never be known. But these were the specialties that most impressed contemporaries and posterity and that account for the canonical status and favored transmission of Kratinos, said to have pioneered the "political" type of comedy,[77] and his successors Eupolis and Aristophanes. Let us look first at ridicule, since an understanding of its functions is the key to the useful advice.

[73] See Platonios, *De differentia comoediarum* 29–32 (4) Koster = *PCG* IV (192), who notes that there were very many plays of this type; the statement that they had no *khorika* or parabases means that they had no abusive songs or partisan/topical tendencies. Eight of the titles of Aristophanes' plays suggest mythological burlesque, all apparently produced after 415. Note, however, that figures from mythology might "stand for" contemporaries, as is alleged of Kratinos' *Dionysalexandros* in an ancient hypothesis (*Oxyrhynchus Papyri* [London, 1898–] 663 = 70 Austin = *PCG* IV [140], lines 44–48): "Perikles is very clearly ridiculed by innuendo [*emphasis*] for having brought the war on the Athenians." In the same year (430), Hermippos' *Moirai* seems to have assimilated the "king of the satyrs" to Perikles. We must keep open the possibility that political innuendo was often (perhaps always) a feature of mythological burlesque. Those who see topical allusion in tragic myths claim a similar kind of *emphasis*.

[74] Aristotle, *Poetics* 1449b7–9, Aristophanes, *Knights* 537–40. It may be significant that he won three times at the Greater Dionysia (*IG* II² 2325.52) but never at the Lenaia.

[75] Platonios, ibid. Aristotle, *Poetics* 1449b says that this style was first developed in Sicilian comedy.

[76] The latter never occurs in tragedy or satyr-drama, the former only obliquely, through the veil of plots drawn from heroic legend, set in the distant past and usually in remote places, and peopled by characters whose names were not by and large borne by the Athenians (in contrast with modern Greeks). For the polarity of dramatic genres as an aspect of their development in the fifth century, see O. Taplin, "Fifth-century Tragedy and Comedy: A *Synkrisis*," *JHS* 106 (1986): 163–74.

[77] See Kratinos, testimonia 17–19 Kassel-Austin. Kratinos anticipates Aristophanes in assimilating comic victory to political victory, frag. 52 (*Dionysoi*) "let the victory go to him who gives the best advice to this city"; cf. *Frogs* 686, 1420.

There are several varieties of ridicule in the comedies,[78] occurring both in choral songs, which carry on the traditions of the *kōmos,* and in the speeches and conversations of characters, which carry on the traditions of *iambos.*[79] The ridicule in comedy, however, differs from that of *kōmos* and *iambos* in significant ways.

Public ridicule of individuals, in the form of shouted jests and more or less formal lampoons, was a venerable tradition of many festive occasions (particularly those honoring Dionysos and Demeter), and continues as a feature of carnivalesque practices everywhere.[80] Old Comedy includes this tradition both in the agonistic (*epirrhematic*) choral complex and also in the type of choral song that often articulates episodes after the parabasis and consists of free-form mockery of particular spectators.[81] In its agonistic role the comic chorus, like a group of kōmasts, entertains the community by abusing its own enemies (e.g., "Knights" versus Kleon). We might compare the masked men who mocked prominent initiates in the procession to Eleusis and the groups who abused one another at women's festivals.[82] A special feature of the agonistic chorus is the prominence of its leader who, in a parabasis-speech, often represents the poet, abusing his own enemies and admonishing the spectators. Later in the play, however, the chorus drops the special identity it had during its involvement in the plot and becomes mere onlookers, like the spectators. Here the comic chorus differs from a *kōmos* in representing the celebrating community as a whole.

Insulting allusion to spectators in the conversation of characters reproduces as a public entertainment "the wit and abuse of ordinary conversation; and its range of tone is therefore ribald, spiteful and irreverent."[83] In comic reproduction of personal enmities we see a continuation of the ancient *iambos* in dramatic form.[84] But comedy differs from *iambos* in that the characters often reproduce the arguments and invective of political

[78] For overviews see Wilhelm Schmid, *Geschichte der griechischen Literatur,* part 1, vol. 4 (Munich, 1946), 13–26; Ralph Rosen, *Old Comedy and the Iambographic Tradition* (forthcoming).

[79] Both *kōmos* as a festive form and *iambos* as a poetic form flourished in the classical period alongside comedy.

[80] See the excellent overview in P. Burke, *Popular Culture in Early Modern Europe* (New York, 1978), 178–204.

[81] That the mockery was expected at this point in a comedy is indicated by *Lysistrata* 1043–49, where the newly united chorus announces its intention to eschew it. The context of one example, *Frogs* 416–30, clearly reveals the traditional derivation.

[82] See Walter Burkert, *Greek Religion,* trans. J. Raffan (Cambridge, Mass. and London, 1985) 244, 287. Good Aristophanic examples are, respectively, the Initiate Chorus of *Frogs* and the hostile semichoruses of *Lysistrata.*

[83] Halliwell, "Aristophanic Satire," 14.

[84] See Arist., *Poet.* 1448b25, 1449b8; *Nik. Eth.* 1128a22.

dispute as well, and in highly partisan fashion. In such cases the enemies of sympathetic characters are portrayed also as enemies of the city.

In traditional, face-to-face commmunities such ridicule reflects, circulates, comments about, enshrines, puts a kind of imprimatur on, what is widely thought, discussed, or enjoyed privately but has no other public outlet. Often the victim's notoriety is based on an incident simply too amusing to forget and so becomes part of community myth, like Hegelokhos' error of pronunciation which spoiled a performance of Euripides' *Orestes*.[85] And often the victim is cast in the role of scapegoat, like Kleonymos, who (uniquely) was repeatedly mocked for having thrown away his shield, apparently in the Athenian retreat at Delion, where "the army was put to flight, and he ran with the rest: it was his bad luck that his fatness made him conspicuous."[86] But, we may add, it was also the good luck of the others to find a publicly acceptable scapegoat. The comic poets in this case did what modern political leaders call "containing the damage": Kleonymos lost his respect as a warrior so that the Athenians could keep theirs. And he was lucky too: knowing what his defense would be, no one cared to prosecute him.

But more often the ridicule uses complaints about disruptive but otherwise unpunishable behavior (that is, gossip and malice) as a form of social control: the community emphasizes its norms and discourages their violation, and by doing so as a festive entertainment allows for the release of pent-up tensions before they can become dangerous.[87] Festive ridicule, in punishing misbehavior not, or not yet, in the community's power to punish by force (as in court), thus lies somewhere between doing something about misbehavior and doing nothing about it. Ridicule as a mode and festival as a venue exemplify the characteristic mediating power of humor. In the *Frogs* song (416–30), for example, Kallias Hipponikou becomes Kallias Hippobinou ("Super Fucker") who fights his battles in bed (428–30). Kallias was a very rich man who avoided political commitments and spent his money on his own pleasures instead.[88] Here Aristophanes voices the spectators' resentment of this kind of selfishness at a time when the city is fighting for its survival. The spectators feel that something has been done about Kallias, even if nothing has been

---

[85] Cf. *Frogs* 302–4, Sannyrion, frag. 8. The scholiast on Euripides, *Orestes* 279 tells us that many comic poets mocked Hegelokhos for this.

[86] Sommerstein, "Decree," 104, who compares Demosthenes' flight from Khaironeia, for which he was never prosecuted, even though Aiskhines, in his speech *Against Ktesiphon* (3), repeatedly brings it up against him.

[87] See Scribner, "Reformation," 319–22.

[88] Eupolis' *Flatterers,* victorious at the Great Dionysia in 421, ridiculed Kallias and his circle; the fragments (156–90) are instructive.

changed, and hope that people like Kallias, present and future, will take a lesson, even if they can choose not to. Part of a successful comic poet's business was to keep his eyes and ears open during the year for just this sort of misbehavior: the audience expected him to make comedy of it.[89]

Comic ridicule differs from that of *kōmos* and *iambos* by being part of a national festival whose celebrants were the entire city, of which the *dēmos* was in charge: the comic troupe ridicules its enemies in the interests of the *dēmos*. In this respect *kōmos* and *iambos* are to comedy as neighborhood graffiti are to nationally syndicated political cartoons. But the social mechanism is the same: ridicule is a kind of kangaroo court. In a democracy, the rule of law, not men, prevails. If A benefits at B's expense, his behavior, however shameless, is permissible unless legally actionable, and B's only recourse is by appeal to "those unwritten laws which it is an acknowledged shame to break."[90] The contest of Logoi in *Clouds* is instructive here: Worse Logos appeals to a legalistic concept of *nomos* (do it if you can get away with it), Better Logos to the imperatives of custom (self-restraint enforced by shame). Thus comedy generally chose as a victim a person who was, or who could be, popularly suspected of getting away with something at the expense of the *dēmos* or its benefactors, and who is made an example of widespread misbehavior, like Kallias (the selfish rich) or Kleon (dishonest leaders) or sykophants (predatory troublemakers).

Comedy is therefore good evidence about the attitudes of the *dēmos* (what they collectively disapproved of, what they thought laughable and mockable) and the communal problems they thought, or might be made to think, were widespread and important. It is also good evidence for the strength of democratic principles in fifth-century Athens: law courts and assemblies were not the only officially established restraint on misbehavior. In any society, the more repressive the government, the narrower the scope of satirical humor.[91]

In fifth-century Athens, the creations of comic ridicule were to a cer-

---

[89] At *Knights* 525, Aristophanes says that Magnes was "driven from" the competitions because his power of mockery (*skōptein*) failed him. "A man who was not himself a comic dramatist might use comedy to injure or blackmail another by asking for the help of, or retailing scandal to, a dramatist friend, much as he might today enlist the help of a gossip columnist or a satirical magazine." Alan H. Sommerstein, *Aristophanes Wasps* (Warminster, 1983) on lines 1025–26.

[90] Perikles in his Funeral Oration (Thuk., 2.37), that occasion when one lists civic virtues that need constant emphasis.

[91] Even outside the Soviet Union and Communist China political satire can be dangerous. In April 1988 one of the best-known and most outspoken satirists in Mexico, Hector Felix Miranda ("The Cat"), was assassinated in Tijuana: the latest of some two dozen assassinations of journalists critical of the government since 1972. None of the assassins has been charged by the police.

tain extent reactive, being a vehicle for gossip.[92] But comedy could also
be informative, principally by casting the talk of the town into brilliant
and memorable form, or by reminding the city of its past, or by finding
suitable individuals to embody negative stereotypes and thus to exemplify generally felt symptoms of malaise. This informative role of
comedy will have been important especially for those citizen-males who
came to the city mostly for festivals (e.g., working farmers) and for
those others (women, children, aliens, slaves) who had great social importance but whose participation in the official city was restricted to festivals: the Assembly accommodated six thousand, the theater perhaps
three times that many. In the fifth century, festive poets still retained
much of their ancient function as purveyors of history and traditional
norms: even Thoukydides and Plato still had to argue their rival claims
against the poets. Comic poets were no exception.

For Aristophanes a sign of Kratinos' success was that his songs were
"sung at every symposiom," for example "Goddess of Bribery, Shod
with Figwood," which attacked malicious prosecutors (*Knights* 529–30).
The process by which an individual can be made to embody a broad stereotype, most spectacularly in the case of Sokrates (below), is well illustrated by an anecdote from Aiskhines' speech *Against Timarkhos:* "When,
at the Rural Dionysia, the comic actor Parmenon spoke an anapest to the
chorus in which certain great whores were called Timarkhos-like, no one
took this to refer to our young man but everyone took it to mean you: so
obviously are you the heir apparent to this practice!" (1.157). If not
"everyone" knew about Timarkhos before the festival, everyone surely
did after it. One recalls Aristophanes' claim never to have taken a bribe
from a jealous *erastēs* to ridicule the boy in a comedy (*Wasps* 1025–26).

Comedy, exploiting its dramatic form and national setting, went beyond the local, personal, and incidental ridicule of *iambos* and *kōmos* to
create a comic version of the city itself, where the partisan comic troupe
reproduced the *dēmos* in festive caricature and the competitors for its favor in the guise of traditional figures of mockery. Comedy thus developed a political form and function, pioneered (as far as we know) by
Kratinos in the 450s, shortly after the rule of the *dēmos* was securely established in 462/1 by Ephialtes. In the decades that followed, political
comedy contoured its picture of the *dēmos* and its portrayal of the competitors opportunistically, in response to current realities, under the pressures of competition, and in conformity with the rules laid down by the
dēmos. This opportunism accounts for the elasticity and adaptability of
comedy and is a feature of its rapid evolution in the fifth century: another
argument against seeing it as static or ritualistic. The poets, for example,

[92] So Aristotle, *Politics* 1336b.

portrayed the aristocratic Perikles as a Zeus-like tyrant,[93] but for the "demagogues" they had to invent new ways to portray these "men of the marketplace." The appearance of heroines in the plays after 411 is a similar innovation.[94]

One of Aristophanes' claims to originality was to have devoted an entire play to the ridicule of one individual, Kleon in *Knights,* after which other poets imitated him by so attacking Hyperbolos.[95] Shortly after the Peace of 421 Platon for the first time began to name plays after the main figure of ridicule (*Peisandros, Hyperbolos*). This development reflects, as it imitates, the rude and combative style of appeal to the *dēmos* introduced by Kleon and the new politicians. It mirrors the social antagonism between the new politicians and the aristocrats who before 429 monopolized public discourse and to whose world the comic poets belonged. It also reveals the new politicians' greater vulnerability to comic attack.

But could comic ridicule, however vehement, even reflect, let alone influence, *political* realities? The *dēmos* awarded a generalship to Kleon mere weeks after the judges and audience[96] at the Lenaia awarded the first prize to *Knights,* which emphatically urged that Kleon not be elected.[97] This is usually cited as evidence that comic ridicule was detached from political realities and had no practical effect.[98] But *Clouds* 581–89, rebuking the Athenians for ignoring that advice and urging that they atone when Kleon's *euthyna* is held, show that Aristophanes had expected to have an effect, and Kleon's lawsuits, like the occasional decrees limiting comic ridicule, suggest that the expectation was not unrealistic, mere comic braggadocio.

This problem highlights important areas of our ignorance about fifth-century comedy. To what extent did the audience reproduce the *dēmos* as

---

[93] Kratinos frags. 73, 118, 258, 259, *Akharnians* 530: see in general J. Schwarze, *Die Beurteilung des Perikles durch die attische Komödie* (Munich, 1971).

[94] Henderson, *Lysistrata,* xxviii; "Older Women in Attic Old Comedy," *TAPA* 117 (1987): 105–29.

[95] *Clouds* 549–59 (Eupolis did this "first of all" in *Marikas,* where Hyperbolos, like Kleon in *Knights,* was a barbarian slave), *Wasps* 1029–37, *Peace* 751–60. Eupolis' *Golden Age,* also attacking Kleon, came a few months later than *Knights,* at the Greater Dionysia.

[96] Cf. *Birds* 445–46.

[97] Particularly in the Knights' song at 973–76: "Joyful will be the light of that day for those who dwell here and those who sojourn here if Kleon is destroyed" (trans. Sommerstein, *Aristophanes Knights*). Kleon is named only here in the play. As B. B. Rogers, *The Knights of Aristophanes* (London, 1910) ad loc. suggests, Aristophanes probably hoped that this song would, independently of the play, become popular, like those of Kratinos mentioned at 529–30. It is written in an aeolic meter characteristic of popular song; cf. Martin West, *Greek Metre* (Oxford, 1982), 116.

[98] See, for example, Kenneth J. Reckford, *Aristophanes' Old-and-New Comedy* (Chapel Hill, 1987), 479: "Festive mockery *did not count* in the ordinary world. . . . The holiday license made the insults different, so that the victims could not really lose face."

it was otherwise convened?[99] On what criteria did the judges award the prize, and did their award reflect the preference of the majority of the spectators? Were the mood-swings of the *dēmos* as great and as rapid as Thoukydides and Aristophanes often say they were, so that the *dēmos* that enjoyed *Knights* would be a differently-minded *dēmos* from the one that elected Kleon? Here we confront the problems that face anyone who attempts to read public opinion. But we must nevertheless make the attempt, and it is no solution to ask which phenomenon, the victory of the play or the victory of Kleon, is politically significant. First we must ask whether and in what ways these two phenomena might intersect, might both be politically significant.

Since ridicule was Aristophanes' principal weapon and must have been a factor in the play's success, we can assume that the successful ridicule in *Knights* was some sort of latent indictment, a signal that the *dēmos*' vote for Kleon was not given without reservation. Old Master Dēmos says, in *Knights* (1111–50), that he is not taken in by the new politicians, that he fattens them up and strikes them down whenever he likes. Could this be a fact, a reminder to the *dēmos* of its actual power, and not mere wishful thinking on the part of Aristophanes? If so, comedy after 429 would indicate to what extent the *dēmos* was hedging its bet on the new politicians who were winning the votes. Let us look more closely at the substance of comic ridicule: how it differed from other kinds of ridicule and what its political impact might have been—that is, its effect on the public standing of individuals.

Personal abuse had always been an accepted tactic in public dispute: epic and tragic poetry reflect its use[100] and the blame-poets[101] (*iambists*,[102] followed by comic poets[103]) made a specialty of it. The first professional rhetoricians included it in their programs,[104] and most extant orators employ it.[105] Athenian law, like Greek rhetorical theory generally,[106] distinguished varieties of abuse by rules ethical and legal, but nowhere do we hear that a particular class of people, such as poets,

---

[99] The introduction of assembly-pay in the fourth century implies that poor people had been readier to attend earlier, just as the theoric fund implies that the two-obol price of a theater seat had kept many of them away.

[100] S. Koster, *Die Invektive in der griechischen und römischen Literatur* (Meisenheim am Glan, 1980), 42–54, 62–71.

[101] Gregory Nagy, *The Best of the Achaeans* (Baltimore and London, 1979), 222–64.

[102] Koster, *Die Invektive,* 55–62.

[103] See Arist., *Poet.* 1448b24 on this development.

[104] E.g., Thrasymakhos of Khalkedon (Plato, *Phaidros* 267c6), Protagoras (*FVS* 80A21), Gorgias (*FVS* 82A25), Antiphon (*Abuses* [*loidoriai*] *of Alkibiades*).

[105] There are excellent surveys in Ivo Bruns, *Das literarische Porträt der Griechen* (Berlin, 1896), and Walter Voegelin, *Die Diabole bei Lysias* (Basel, 1943).

[106] Koster, *Die Invektive,* 7–17.

was exempt from the rules. Nor do we see any essential differences in
the kinds of abuse used by various classes of abusers: comic poets used
the same kinds as competitors in forensic dispute and (especially with the
emergence of Kleon) in political debate,[107] and also seem to have re-
frained from the same ones: we noted this above (section II) and will consider it again shortly. The Old Oligarch thus seems to be justified in
saying that the institution of comedy allowed poets to attack prominent
individuals just as other institutions allowed other members of the *dēmos*
to do so in legal or political suits. The difference is that a comic poet
competed with other poets at ridiculing spectators, who could not reply
as part of the competition. But a spectator certainly could reply later, by
bringing a suit or moving a retaliatory decree, just like any other victim
who claimed that an opponent's ridicule had slandered him or had
harmed the city's interests. It would seem that if we deny to comic ridicule any persuasive intention, we must deny it also to the orators. But
surely we cannot do that. Here again we confront the problem of humor
and seriousness.

Abuse was identified not so much by its source[108] or its content as by
its intended effect. Essentially, abuse was a personal insult to which a
malicious intention could be attached. If the intention was not to wound
but to produce laughter which the victim himself could share, or at any
rate could be expected to let pass, then it was not abuse (serious) but jesting (humor).[109] Jesting, after all, can only happen when jester and target
are part of the same group; otherwise the jest becomes malice.[110]

Much, perhaps most, comic ridicule (*kōmōidein*) has no other apparent

[107] See Kenneth J. Dover, *Greek Popular Morality in the Time of Plato and Aristotle* (Berkeley and Los Angeles, 1974), 23–33, Koster, *Die Invektive,* 76–90. In *Laws* Plato recognizes
the near-identity of the abuse characteristic of comedy and public dispute (934d6–36b2),
and the scholia to the orators very frequently remark that so-and-so was ridiculed in such-
and-such a way "also in comedy." Nagy, *Best of the Achaeans,* 244 says that "in societies
where blame poetry was an inherited institution, there must have been clearly defined traditional limits for degrees of insult." For fifth-century Athens we can broaden this statement by substituting "competitive display" for "blame poetry." The important question is
how and by whom the limits were defined and enforced.

[108] When the speaker of Lysias, 10.2 says that he might have overlooked certain insults
because his opponent is "insignificant and worthless," he does not mean that such men
have a license to abuse.

[109] For the common definition of jesting as insult ἄνευ θυμοῦ, ἀλύπως, etc., intended to
be laughable (*geloion*), cf. Plato, *Laws,* Aristotle, *Nikomakhean Ethics* 1128a, Koster, *Die Invektive,* 9–16.

[110] Bob Woodward, *Veil: The Secret Wars of the CIA, 1981–1987* (New York, 1987), 338
reports that on 26 April 1984, Senator Jake Garn angrily told his colleagues, "You're all assholes—the whole Congress is full of assholes, all five hundred thirty-five members are assholes" (for this accusation compare *Clouds* 1088ff.), to which Senator Patrick Moynihan
replied, "Smile when you call me an asshole."

motivation than jesting: it is not formulated in terms of a charge (as the orators would say, it is *exō tou pragmatos*), or it is an offhand remark (*parapsogos*), or it refers to personal failings or misbehavior that most people are already talking about, or it simply mimics the abuse that some spectators had actually invented themselves (as in the case of the comic Kleon). Thus even the portrayal of Kleonymos as a shield-thrower, an actionable slander, is a jest, not (serious) abuse. In *Laws*, Plato notes this characteristic of comic ridicule but also observes that it was a common trick of disputants to pretend that their slanders were jests (935c–d). Thus the speaker of Lysias, fragment 5.3 Thalheim: "Isn't this Kinesias the offender against the gods in ways you hear about every year from the producers of comedy but which it is shameful for other people even to mention?" The orators often accused their opponents of using ridicule when their material claims were weak: thus Plato's Sokrates when he stressed comic *diabolē* (unfounded accusation),[111] and the speaker of Lysias 24.18: "My accuser is not being serious but playful, his purpose not persuasion but ridicule [*kōmōidein*], as if making some fine joke."

Among the honor-sensitive Athenians, however, the distinction between abuse and jesting often called for nice judgment, and it became a topic of concern for ethicists. When Aristotle says that "the law forbids serious abuse [*loidorein*] of some things and perhaps should have forbidden jocular abuse [*skōptein*] as well" (*Nik. Eth.* 1128a19), he is talking about the trouble that can arise when a jester goes too far or his butt is oversensitive. One man's joke is another man's slander, depending on the skill of the jester and the butt's reaction. Comic poets, like orators, had to be able to sail very close to the wind. Ridicule by definition covers areas beyond the reach of actionable claims, where votes can be taken, but the victim was the one who decided to cry foul. Thus Kleon's suit against Aristophanes for slander (whether to defend himself or the city) may indicate either that Aristophanes' abuse was seriously intended or that Kleon was oversensitive to jesting.[112]

The laws about slander (defined very loosely by a variety of terms)[113] provided redress for abuse whose untruthfulness could be proved to a jury (the *dēmos*). Solon's laws forbade slander of the dead, or slander of

---

[111] *Apology* 18b–d, 19b–c, 23c–d, at the same time distracting attention from the more serious charge that many of his close associates had in fact harmed the democracy (Aiskhines, 1.173).

[112] In a recent case, televangelist Jerry Falwell was caricatured in the pornographic magazine *Hustler* as having lost his virginity with his mother in an outhouse. *Hustler* publisher Larry Flynt publicly acknowledged malicious intent: "He's just a big windbag. He's right in there with . . . all the rest of them, and the sooner they're exposed, the better off it will be for everybody." For the Supreme Court decision in Falwell's libel suit, see n. 124 below.

[113] To those used by Plato, *Laws*, add κακῶς λέγειν, κακῶς ἀγορεύειν, ὑβρίζειν. For the laws about slander see Lipsius, *Das attische Recht*, 646–54.

the living in temples, in law courts, in places of official business, or at festive competitions.[114] Individuals could sue not only as private citizens but also as allotted (Demosthenes, 21.32) or elected (Lysias, 9.5–6) officeholders. Although the speaker of Lysias 10.6ff. mentions such specifically forbidden charges (*aporrhēta*) as murder, father- or mother-beating, and shield-throwing, it is clear that any accusation of wrongdoing (*rhēta kai arrhēta,* Demosthenes, 21.79) could be called slander if the accused wanted to press the issue, just as any accusation could be passed off as empty ridicule if the victim did not want to press it. A determination of slander was left to individuals and their potential juries (what in Athens amounted to public opinion).

We observed above (section II) that comic poets seem to avoid the same "forbidden" targets as the orators, so that they had the avoidance of actionable slander in mind when they resorted to abuse. To the example of maiden daughters we may add the avoidance of actually naming a target (*onomasti kōmōidein*), however obvious the identity. Thus Kleon is "the Paphlagonian" and Nikias and Demosthenes are homebred slaves throughout *Knights,* and an obvious allusion to Alkibiades' arrest in *Birds* (145–47) does not name him, in accordance with the Decree of Syrakosios. Similarly, Aristophanes apologizes for not using a portrait-mask for Kleon: surely not (as he says) because it was the mask-makers who were afraid (*Knights* 230–32). Further investigation of the areas of inhibition common to comic poets and other public speakers would yield interesting information about social and political restraints in classical Athens.

According to etiquette, it was base to abuse gratuitously, by starting a fight[115] (like Thersites), but honorable when wronged (like Akhilleus), illegal to abuse falsely but legal when exposing true misbehavior.[116] Thus the speaker of Lysias 10.3, "I consider it mean and very litigious to go to law for slander [*kakēgoria*]. But in the present case I feel it would be shameful—since it concerns my father, who has deserved so much both of you and of the city—not to take vengeance on the man who said this." The comic poets told the *dēmos* that speakers, demagogues, and sycophants were ones who use abuse to pick fights for selfish reasons and

---

[114] Plutarch, *Life of Solon* 21.1–2; cf. Plato, *Republic* 935b.

[115] λοιδορίας ἄρχειν, Plato, *Laws* 935c3.

[116] It has often been observed that Thersites and Akhilleus blame Agamemnon on the same grounds. For the ethical norm cf. Hesiod, *Works and Days* 708–11, "Do not wrong a friend first, nor lie about him to please the tongue, but if he wrongs you first, either by making a malicious statement or by deed, remember to repay him double"; cf. Demokritos, *FVS* 68B192, "It is easy to praise and blame [*psegein*] inappropriately, either one being the mark of a bad character [*ponērou ēthous*]," Hippias, *FVS* 86B17, "unfounded accusation [*diabolē*] is a dangerous technique."

who abuse falsely (*diabolē/diaballein* is thematic for Kleon in *Knights*); speakers, demagogues, and sycophants portrayed themselves as "watchdogs of the *dēmos*" who exposed antidemocratic misbehavior in no uncertain terms. For the new politicians and the comic poets, abuse was a persuasive strategy in appeals to the *dēmos*.

Here we should pause to consider a role of Athenian courts that parallels comedy and to which Robin Osborne has drawn attention: as "one form of adjustive and redressive mechanism limiting the spread of breaches of regular social relations"[117] (52), what Victor Turner called "social drama." The open texture of the Athenian juridical and legal machinery allowed a wide choice of procedures by which one might prosecute an enemy, often in a series of different actions where the type of procedure to be used was not mainly statutory but

> seems far more to be determined by the relative and absolute social positions of prosecutor and defendant. To bring a *graphē* [public indictment] when one might bring a *dikē* [private suit] (which might be settled without coming before dikasts) is to bring oneself to public attention: not only is one choosing to risk a 1000 dr. fine, but one is claiming to champion interests wider than one's own, parading one's quality of being a citizen. . . . *Graphai* are open trials of strength, and the offence may be subject to considerable interpretation and redefinition to enable it to be tried by this procedure. . . . When the court is a stage it is absolutely essential that the dikasts be large in number and without legal training: the sophistic and doubtful justifications for lay juries in the modern world are neither required nor invited. . . . *Graphai* . . . could be both reflections of inequality and instruments by which such inequality could be created and promoted. The "radical" innovation of opening up prosecution to anyone who wished had the effect of creating a conspicuous action which could be socially conservative.[118]

As Carter remarks, "The distinction between political and non-political prosecutions must have been extremely difficult to draw at all periods."[119] So with ridicule: Aristophanes evidently saw the comic stage, and Kleon the popular courts, as different venues for the ongoing social drama that they enacted for the *dēmos*.

The comic claim to be both humorous and serious, and the Old Oligarch's statement that comic poets attacked both by ridicule (*kōmōidein*) and by abuse (*kakōs legein*), now seems to make better sense. Not all

117 Osborne, "Law in Action," 52.
118 Ibid., 53.
119 Carter, *Quiet Athenian*, 87 n. 20.

comic attacks were made in ridicule, as defined above: in the passage from *Laws* cited there, Plato also mentions seriously motivated comic abuse.[120] Aristophanes' abuse of Kleon, for example, is explicitly identified and formally motivated as serious: Kleon started it by abusing Aristophanes unjustly (*Akharnians* 377–82), so that the poet is justified in defending himself (630–64) and in launching a counterattack in next year's comedy on behalf of his friends the Knights, who have also been victimized (299–302). To this personal motivation Aristophanes adds good citizenship: he "dares to say what is just, and nobly steps forth to confront the typhoon and the whirlwind [Kleon]" (*Knights* 510–11), for "there is nothing invidious about abusing bad men, but it is an honor to good men for those who reckon well" (1274–75).[121] In attacking Kleon, Aristophanes appeals both to personal enmity (like iambic poets) and to the interests of the city (like speakers in assembly and court), and he uses abuse to characterize his opponent as a bad citizen, so enhancing the credibility of his claims. When viewed in this light, Kleon's subsequent lawsuit—no doubt another *graphē*—looks like a serious response to serious abuse rather than merely an oversensitive reaction to harmless ridicule.

The comic attack on Sokrates in *Clouds* is another example of extensive and explicitly motivated abuse, though here the element of personal enmity was not (explicitly at least) a factor. Aristophanes sought an individual who could exemplify the kind of misbehavior popularly associated with the "new learning"—so popular with the young "speakers"—and picked Sokrates. The fact that a real person was thus turned into an exaggerated stereotype for the purposes of ridicule does not mean that the ridicule was mere jesting and without effect. The stereotype embodied real social hostility and Sokrates seemed to fit it. Nor were the charges ridiculous: other intellectuals of the day had been tried on the catch-all charge of "impiety" (*asebeia*).[122] Indeed, the charges were not forgotten twenty-four years later: Plato tells us the *Clouds* helped to circulate and fix in the popular mind a prejudice against Sokrates that contributed to his condemnation.[123] This prejudice, created by skillful ridicule, could not be argued away, because one cannot disprove ridicule. If people—in this case the jury—believed it, it was true, and one only compounded his

---

[120] "No comic or iambic or melodic poet will be allowed to ridicule [*kōmōidein*] any citizen in any way either by word or gesture [*eikoni*], either with or without anger," 935e.

[121] λοιδορῆσαι τοὺς πονηροὺς οὐδέν ἐστ᾽ ἐπίφθονον, | ἀλλὰ τιμὴ τοῖσι χρηστοῖς, ὅστις εὖ λογίζεται.

[122] For these trials see Ostwald, *Popular Sovereignty*, 528–36.

[123] Cf. n. 111, above. Osborne, "Law in Action," 51 shows that in *graphai* where there was no injured party, like those brought by Meletos, Anytos, and Lykon against Sokrates and threatened by Andokides against Arkhippos, the action usually was more political than legal in its motivation.

difficulties by accusing people of wrong beliefs. Unfair, maybe. But it is the fate of prominent people to live, or die, by their public images.[124]

Unlike Sokrates, Kleon died before his public image could catch up to him. But the fate of his successor, Hyperbolos, is instructive. In the course of the oligarchic coup d'état of 411 the Samian conspirators, in Thoukydides' words, "put to death an Athenian called Hyperbolos, a cheap troublemaker who had been ostracized[125] not because anyone feared his power or prestige but because he was a bad man and a disgrace to the city" (8.73). The comment in *HCT* (5.257) well illustrates the significance of Thoukydides' account for our purposes: "The surviving record contains little but personal abuse from the comic poets, in quantity suitable for Kleon's successor but no help towards precise assessment." I venture to say that, as in the case of Sokrates, the fate of Hyperbolos was guided on its course by the imprecise but potent force of public hostility, in whose crystallization comedy will have played a major role.[126]

It may be thought that Sokrates, Kleon, and Hyperbolos fit the stereotypes into which comic poets cast them only too well, and deserved the abuse they received. What about General Lamakhos, the hero's antagonist in *Akharnians?* Surely he "was in fact an able and respected military leader,[127] and it is hard to believe that Aristophanes was attempting to convince his audience otherwise. . . . He is the target of generalized cynicism about military leaders. . . . The festival is a time for the comic poet to give uninhibited expression to such collective attitudes. Outside the festival, cynicism must be kept in check and subordinated to a recognition of political realities."[128] Must not the caricature of Lamakhos therefore be harmless both in nature and intent?

---

[124] In the libel case *Hustler vs. Falwell* (n. 112 above), the Supreme Court ruled that even outrageous satire of public figures is protected by the free speech provisions of the First Amendment: "The appeal of political cartoon or caricature is often based on exploration of unfortunate physical traits or politically embarrassing events—an exploration often calculated to injure the feelings of the subject . . . [but] our political discourse would have been poorer without them. . . . Outrageousness in the area of political and social discourse has an inherent subjectiveness about it which would allow a jury to impose liability on the basis of jurors' tastes or views, or perhaps on their dislike of a particular expression. . . . We doubt that there is any standard that would separate sharp satire from defamatory attack" (U.S. Supreme Court, 86–1278).

[125] Probably in 416: see *HCT* 5.259–64; for the circumstances Ostwald, *Popular Sovereignty*, 302–4.

[126] We might compare the fate of Kleophon, another frequent target of comic abuse (see section II, above), who was put to death by oligarchs in 405–404: even Lysias, who points out that the charges were trumped-up and illegally brought, admits that Kleophon was a bad citizen and a bad man (*ponēros*), 30.13.

[127] After his death Aristophanes praised him without irony as a hero (*Thesm.* 841, *Frogs* 1039).

[128] Halliwell, "Aristophonic Satire," 11–12.

On the contrary. Aristophanes, like others of his class and political stripe, did indeed want to convince the *dēmos* to abandon its aggressive war-policy and did want to impugn the integrity of its proponents. Lamakhos represents the military proponents, just as demagogues like Kleon represent the political ones.[129] We see *them* in the prologue of *Akharnians,* where they are portrayed as advocating the war in their own interests and against the interests of the *dēmos.* Their qualifications as advisors of the *dēmos* are vigorously questioned. Similarly, Lamakhos profits from the war by getting comfortable and lucrative posts, while the common soldiers do all the fighting (595–619). Dikaiopolis, a displaced countryman and one of the common soldiers, exposes the politicians and the generals and so convinces the hitherto-deluded chorus, just as Aristophanes hoped to convince the spectators (the *dēmos*). Aristophanes makes this very clear by unmistakably identifying himself with his hero.

Aristophanes encourages the warriors in the audience to examine his proposition, and employs the stereotype of the Braggart Soldier to cut the military mystique down to size. Note, however, that because the festival did not allow "uninhibited expression," Aristophanes is careful to show Lamakhos behaving honorably in battle (if in a ridiculously exaggerated way), being wounded not by an enemy but by accident, and not in a fight with Spartans but with Boiotian bandits on a nuisance-raid.[130] The ridicule is not hostile (as in the case of Kleon) but safely debunking: the typical "populist" view of generals from Homer and Archilokhos to the present day. But that does not mean that the cynicism Aristophanes exploits was meant to have no effect outside the festival, where "political realities" would supposedly keep it "in check." As we have seen, political realities in this period were determined solely at the whim of the *dēmos* (the spectators), as many a general in this war had reason to know.

That the cynicism of the *dēmos* was safely in check would have been news, for example, to the generals who successfully conducted their talks in Sicily in 424, only to return home to confront a disappointed *dēmos,* which thought that they should have bargained for the whole island. Convinced that the generals had been bribed, the *dēmos* banished two of them and fined the third. "Such was the effect on the Athenians of their present good luck," comments Thoukydides, "that they thought nothing could go wrong, that the possible and the difficult were alike attainable . . . that their power was equal with their hopes" (4.65). The sequel is also interesting, since it shows that the wrath of the *dēmos* might be as

---

[129] In *Peace* Lamakhos represents an obstacle to peace (473), even though he swore to the treaty a few weeks later (Thuk., 5.19).

[130] Note that the Spartans, prominently discussed in the first half of the play, are not mentioned at all in the second.

short-lived as its enthusiasms, as in the case of Perikles (2.65.3–4): two of the generals, Eurymedon and Pythodoros, were subsequently reelected. Perhaps the *dēmos* that enjoyed *Knights* experienced a similar change of heart when it elected Kleon.

In the face of so whimsical a process, can Lamakhos, whom Dikaio-polis-Aristophanes denounces for living it up on embassies and commands while the common soldiers do all the work, have been entirely comfortable about this kind of laughter? Especially inasmuch as he was the poorest of all generals of this period and thus most open to suspicion of self-enrichment at the *dēmos*' expense?[131] We *now* see that nothing bad "chanced to happen" to him, but in the 420s the *dēmos* could be as dangerous for a general as the enemy.[132]

The precise effects of comic ridicule and comic abuse are impossible to gauge. But surely no prominent Athenian imagined that the laughter of the *dēmos* at his expense could possibly do him any good, and the better the joke the less comfortable he would be thereafter. For this very reason the *dēmos* institutionalized the comic competitions. In return for accepting the guidance of the "rich, the well-born, and the powerful" it provided that they be subjected to a yearly unofficial review of their conduct in general at the hands of the *dēmos*' organic intellectuals and critics, the comic poets. Like Sokrates' pupil Plato, or like Kleon the aspiring demagogue, the victims did not like this institution. For the former it epitomized the low prejudices and invidious character of the *dēmos*; for the latter it was an unwelcome reminder that what the *dēmos* gave the *dēmos* could take away. For all public competitors it meant potential deflation. But compared with the other institutions the *dēmos* could bring to bear against them, comedy must have seemed no worse than fair warning.

IV. THE COMIC APPEAL

For the Old Oligarch, who was showing how the *dēmos* kept "the best" on a short leash, ridicule was the distinctive feature of comedy. So also for the anti-demotic critic-philosophers of the fourth century. It is true that comedy mentions or portrays living individuals only for ridicule,

---

[131] Plutarch, *Nikias* 15, *Alkibiades* 21: perhaps a factor in the argument Thoukydides gives him in 6.49.

[132] For similar trials of generals see the list in Ostwald, *Popular Sovereignty*, 64–65. One of these resulted in Thoukydides' exile (424/3): one may wonder if Kleon was involved, as Markellinos' *Life* states (46), but we may be sure that he did not take Thoukydides' side. Thoukydides' obvious bias against him may well have had the same justification as Aristophanes'. For the situation of generals who feared prosecution, cf. Demosthenes who, after his defeat in Aitolia in 426, "stayed behind at Naupaktos or thereabouts, being afraid to face the Athenians after what had happened" (Thuk., 3.98.5) and who did not return until he had an "achievement to his credit" (3.114.1).

never for praise,[133] and that the prominent and would-be prominent, not, as we will presently see, the *dēmos,* were its victims. But these critics fail to mention the positive tendencies of comedy, its heroes and its advice to the *dēmos,* for an obvious reason. The comic poets claim that their ridicule exposes people to whom the *dēmos* has granted success but who are in fact wrongdoers, and through the chorus-leader or a sympathetic character they offer alternative choices. But the denunciation of those responsible for the *dēmos'* unsatisfactory status quo and a demonstration of how to make it satisfactory was the appeal of all who competed for victory in the fifth century, including comic poets. What was distinctive about the comic appeal?

The world depicted in political comedy was the world of the spectators in their civic roles. We see the *dēmos* in its various capacities; we see the competitors for its favor; we listen to formal debate on current issues, including its characteristic invective; we get a decision, complete with a winner and a loser; we see the outcome of that decision. But there is something strange about the depiction, like seeing yourself in a funhouse mirror. Everything is grotesquely exaggerated and caricatured, the image is all backwards and seems to reflect things that aren't there and omit things that are. But you must admit that your presence in front of the mirror is the cause of the image in it. How does the reflection we see on the comic stage differ from what it reflects?

The villains and their dupes are recognizable enough, despite the distortion: they are identifiable among the spectators and most often have their actual names. The *dēmos* is recognizable too: the chorus usually represents some subset thereof,[134] its members sometimes having real names, and at a certain point its identity becomes continuous with that of the spectators collectively.[135] But the villains and their dupes are not the people whom the *dēmos* has in fact recently voted against but the ones

---

[133] Praise is actively avoided: Nikias is ridiculed for losing out to Kleon in *Knights* but is not mentioned at all in *Peace,* a play celebrating the treaty which he engineered and which Aristophanes had repeatedly urged. Sometimes individuals are mentioned as victims of "bad men" or (what amounts to the same thing) unwise decisions by the *dēmos*: Nikias is pitied for being the constant target of malicious prosecutors (Telekleides, frag. 41, Eupolis, frag. 193), and in *Knights* Arkheptolemos (*PA* 2384), who had unsuccessfully opposed Kleon over policy toward the allies (327) and Spartan peace proposals (794–96), is mentioned sympathetically.

[134] Choruses can change their identity, most spectacularly in *Peace* where they are all Greeks, then Greek farmers, then Athenian farmers, then the generic comic chorus.

[135] As it is theatrically throughout: "The world of Old Comedy was fundamentally a choral space, in which the twenty-four amateurs of the chorus, trained in song and dance by the poet, functioned as both center and bridge, the heart of the performance and a mediation between the whole city, present as audience, and the by now professionalized actors on the stage." N. W. Slater, "Transformations of Space in New Comedy," in *Themes in Drama 9: The Theatrical Space* (Cambridge, 1987), 1–10 (2).

they voted *for,* not the social failures but the successful. And the *dēmos* is not the all-sovereign *dēmos* that chooses as leaders those best able to serve its interests, but a poor mob whose role models and heroes are bad people and which is eager to carry out the policies of self-serving con men to its own disadvantage. The more we enjoy this debunking of our leaders—which draws on their acknowledged shortcomings, evokes our own worst suspicions, and plays on the antiauthoritarian invidiousness that festivals only intensify—the more persuasive our own negative caricature becomes. The reaction of the spectators was as the Old Oligarch describes: "When the *dēmos* makes policy it can blame the individual who made the proposal or took the vote and everyone else can protest, I was not there and don't like it either!—even when one knows the Assembly had been fully attended" (2.17). The comic poets encouraged this feeling. The first message was, You are unhappy because you (and your neighbors) have made a big mistake!

But there, onstage, is a rather likeable person. Not an actual person, and in fact not the sort of person who would be prominent at all: a farmer, a seller from the markets, the debt-ridden victim of a socialite wife and a social-climbing son, a juror, the target of too many lawsuits who has decided to try his luck elsewhere, a housewife.[136] This person is in the same fix as most of us and it is pleasant to see someone like that in the spotlight for once. It is even more pleasant to see that this person gets what all of us would like to have: a chance to eliminate, painlessly and with impunity, those forces, human, natural, or divine, which are arguably responsible for our unhappiness and discomfort. Or even to have all the food, wine, luxury, power, sexual partners, and admiration we want, and at the expense only of bad people! This person says that it is in our power, as members of the *dēmos,* to have these things, if only we did not keep forgetting them, if only we did not submit to people who keep the good things for themselves while we do all the work. In the play everything turns out happily: the people who are like us win out, the bad ones who were so arrogant are gone. Life resembles the festival. The second message was: Now that you see your mistake, give me the prize and remember what you have learned!

This was the city of political comedy, where the *dēmos*' ideal goals could be achieved as they could not be, or not yet be, in the Assembly;

---

[136] The women who appear in plays after 411 (n. 94 above) either obstruct the *dēmos* (*Lysistrata, Thesm.*) or usurp its corporate structures (*Ekkl.*) from positions outside the world of the *dēmos.* Among other uses, they were a way to criticize the behavior of citizens without attributing the critical voices to a male character. The chief difference between a Lysistrata and a Dikaiopolis is that the latter's real-life counterparts could, like him, address the assembly (*Akharnians,* prologue), whereas the former's could not. But in all three "women's" plays the motive complaints ring true to life.

where the distance between ideal norms of civic behavior and the actual performance of civic authorities was exposed and punished as it could not be, or not yet be, in court; where the difference between collective sovereignty and individual subordination was eliminated. At the comedies the members of the *dēmos* enjoyed a picture of their imperial democracy in which the intractable problems of communal life and the frustrating requirements of political compromise were magically, but at the same time plausibly, resolved.

It is this idealistic transformation of the *dēmos* from unhappy and misguided to happy and united that vindicates its initial caricature and justifies the Old Oligarch's statement that comic poets did not ridicule and abuse the *dēmos*. *Knights,* which contains the most thoroughgoing criticisms of the *dēmos,* also contains the most glorious picture of it in the transformation of Old Master Dēmos with which the play ends.[137] And even the criticisms Aristophanes does level at the *dēmos* concern only the personal shortcomings and political style of its leaders, or the folly of individual decisions, both of which are shown being amended in the course of a play: *Knights* 1356–57 (to Old Master Dēmos), "Don't worry, you're not to blame: it was those who deceived you." Similarly *Frogs* 1454–57: the *dēmos* hates bad men and uses them only because it has no choice. He never attacks the constitutional structure of the democracy or questions the inherent rightness of the *dēmos*' rule.[138] This was after all an inheritance from the sacrosanct dead and therefore immune from comic or any other public criticism. When he insults and upbraids the *dēmos* for choosing bad leaders or making bad decisions he does what all poets and public speakers had a traditional right to do,[139] just as all public competitors had a right to ridicule political opponents and abuse personal enemies. Aristophanes' criticisms of the *dēmos* are in fact, like those of the orators, praise by exhortation (cf. Perikles at Thuk., 2.65): the *dēmos* may be deceived but it is not, like its leaders, base in character. Comedy uses the language of democracy to attack the leaders whom the *dēmos* chose. Contrast the Old Oligarch, who is hostile to the *dēmos* and considers it just as base as its leaders.[140]

---

[137] See H. Kleinknecht, "Die Epiphanie des Demos in Aristophanes' Rittern," *Hermes* 77 (1939): 58–65, repr. in H.-J. Newiger, ed., *Aristophanes und die alte Komödie* (Darmstadt, 1975), 144–54; Edmunds, "Aristophanic Cleon," 256–62.

[138] See Kenneth J. Dover, *Aristophanic Comedy* (Berkeley and Los Angeles, 1972), 33–34.

[139] On this "didactic tradition" see Dover, *Greek Popular Morality,* 29–30.

[140] "In every land the best sort is against the democracy. In the best people there is the least licentiousness and injustice, but the most care for what is good [*ta khrēsta*], while in the *dēmos* is the most ignorance, disorder and wickedness [*ponēria*]. For poverty rather leads them to what is shameful, as do lack of education and in some cases that ignorance which is due to lack of money" (1.5; cf. also 1.1). No public speaker could afford to take this line: in Aristophanes such characteristics are attributed to leaders, not to the *dēmos*. For anti-

A limited analogy can be drawn between the comic city and the city of a funeral oration. The institution of the funeral oration, apparently an invention of the democracy,[141] celebrated the year's war-dead by praising the city. It gave the year's most successful competitor an opportunity to address the *dēmos* without competition. The orator, thus freed from the constraints of real political deliberation, could draw a flattering picture of the *dēmos* instead of having to say that the *dēmos* would be crazy to take the advice of his opponent. But the orator did not picture the actual *dēmos*. His picture portrayed what the *dēmos* would be like if it behaved itself, if it lived up to the ideals and potential of the democracy. The living *dēmos* is therein contrasted unfavorably with its newly dead compatriots, but is reassured of its ability not to disgrace their memory and urged to take fresh resolve to do better in future. Comedy and funeral oration are alike in refusing to acknowledge the necessity of moral and political compromise, so that their city, taken on its own absolute terms, is the city where all the spectators would want to live.

As an institution, comedy resembles the funeral oration in being festive: like the funeral orator, the comic troupe is a partisan of the collective city, and articulates its ideals. It is disinterested but not detached. Comedy differs from funeral oration principally in being agonistic: it portrays political debate and deliberation, and is itself a competition. Mockers (including sympathetic ones) are usually mocked themselves by way of reproducing the flavor of actual give-and-take (albeit in a biased fashion). The ideal city that comedy invents before our eyes mirrors recognizable processes, with recognizable people participating, and with specific current issues at stake. But this difference is only one of mode: the funeral oration envisages the ideal city in such a way that we can infer the nature of those who impede its realization. Thus the funeral oration is a virtual agon, comedy an explicit one. But the biases are the same: ideal types (the dead and fictitious heroes respectively) engage with their antitypes (survivors and current leaders). In both cases, the audience is at once chastened and encouraged. The comic hero(ine) does not, as is often supposed, stand up against society: rather (s)he represents the ideal society and shows how we might stand up against individual and collective forces that impede its attainment. The mediating force of humor softens the realization that ideals are more easily imagined than attained.

For these reasons, comic hero(in)es are always fictitious composites who represent ideal civic types—in spite of their misbehavior, which is

---

democratic views of the *dēmos* in Aristophanes' day generally, see Ostwald, *Popular Sovereignty*, 224–29.

[141] Certainly after Kleisthenes, probably after the Persian Wars; cf. Nicole Loraux, *The Invention of Athens*, trans. A. Sheridan (Cambridge, Mass. and London, 1986), 28–30. For arguments against Jacoby's canonical date of 464 see *HCT* 2.94–101.

always at the expense of acceptable scapegoats who are not fictitious. And its poets (who sometimes merge with their heroes) claim to offer good advice of the sort not heard elsewhere: they, unlike others who appeal to the *dēmos,* are speaking only in the city's interests. The prize goes to the poet who does this best. The utopian resolution therefore is always one with which none of the spectators could quarrel, though in real life they could never get there by the actions and arguments employed by the comic characters who do get there. Still, many of the arguments are those actually used in assemblies and courts, even if they are edited for persuasive force and exaggerated for humorous impact. Were the comic poets serious when they claimed seriousness for their appeals?

For reasons given earlier it will not do to say that their appeals were not intended seriously because they were delivered at festivals, because their ridicule could not have any effect, because they had no personal enmity toward those they abused, because they were expected to be irresponsible, because their advice was not the sort that could be acted on. Nor because their arguments could never be delivered elsewhere: it is unfair to dismiss comic arguments for not being something else. Nor because these arguments are blatantly one-sided, exaggerated, humorous, and conceited: when we compare them with, say, Demosthenes' arguments the difference becomes one only of degree. Comic poets enjoy parodying the usages of official discourse. Nor because they advocate policies that have never been put forward: that is not unthinkable. Nor because they argue for policies the *dēmos* has rejected: again one thinks of Demosthenes. Nor because in the course of a career a poet could express inconsistent views:[142] the same is true of any politically active person over time. Nor, finally, because their recommendations are idealistic: so are those of the funeral oration.[143] If the poets were making real appeals, what effect did they expect to have?

I suggest that, like tragic poets and funeral orators, they wanted the Athenians, assembled before them as *dēmos,* to think about their lives and civic duties in ways not encouraged on other occasions. Comic poets particularly wanted the *dēmos* to look through the lies, compromises, self-interest, and general arrogance of their leaders and to remember who was ultimately in charge. They urged reconsideration of policies not

---

[142] In the 420s Aristophanes calls for peace, while in 414 he seems positively bloodthirsty: *Birds* 186, 640, 813–16, 1360–69. Perhaps he was against the war only when it came to Attika (cf. Dem., 18.143): in *Knights,* produced in the aftermath of Pylos, when Spartan incursions were expected to stop, Aristophanes' protest against rebuffed Spartan peace proposals is surprisingly mild: see I. Storey, "Aristophanes' *Knights* and the Abortive Peace Proposals of 425 B.C.," *AC* 56 (1987): 56–67.

[143] I pass over the view that no one can be a fine artist and express political convictions at the same time, just as I would not try to convince a Christian that God frowns on those who eat steak or a Hindu that He does not.

adopted. And because they championed the underdog they performed a service useful to any democracy: public airing of minority views. They could also use their plays to attack personal enemies and takes sides in civic feuds, as in the case of Aristophanes and the Knights versus Kleon: perhaps their appeals, like those of other public competitors, always had some self-interest behind them. Their special persuasive gift was humor, and all had to be seen through its lens. But they were not thereby indicating to the *dēmos* that it should not take to heart what it saw and heard.

The comic appeal, which includes satirical abuse and partisan arguments as part of its agonistic nature, was a reassuring, because idealistic, example of the "rule of the *dēmos*." Comedy itself was an arm of that rule, and Aristophanes evidently counted on the spectators to realize that. Who can say that they did not? Who can plot the course and effect of the social currents running beneath the surface of public and official discourse? It was for the comic poets to reveal them, to give them the powerful and memorable airing that only the comic contest allowed.

If it is no coincidence that the era of full sovereignty of the *dēmos*—the era between Ephialtes' reforms of 462/1 and the reforms enacted after the crisis of 404/3—and the era of political comedy were the same, the picture drawn by the comic poets, as outlined at the start of this essay, makes perfect sense.

JAMES REDFIELD

Drama and Community:
Aristophanes and Some of His Rivals

EDWARD SAPIR has said that we understand what is said to us because we already know most of it. A literary genre may be thought of as such a disambiguating context, which creates a channel of communication. What happens in a comedy—for instance, Lamakhos' wound in the *Akharnians*—is supposed to be funny, and the audience will do its best to take it so. In return, the audience expects the poet to play fair, and not abruptly to change the rules so that we feel ashamed of ourselves for laughing at something meant to be pathetic. Audience and poet form a "contract" (cf. *Clouds* 533) which is generic insofar as it is cast in boiler-plate, as to the sort of expectations proper to any work of this sort.

On the other hand, this sort of contract is inherently unreliable and is supposed to be; an Old Comedy completely typical of the genre, *degree zero* as it were, would be completely predictable and thus without interest. From this point of view the genre is in the audience as a set of expectations which exist to be defeated, since the audience comes hoping for the unexpected. These innovations further rely on the genre, since the novel work is understood precisely in contrast to the rejected generic alternative. It follows that the genre is as present in the most innovative poets as in the most pedestrian, and we need not think that we lack materials for a study of Old Comedy because we have complete works only by Aristophanes, who was (according to his self-description, at least) the most innovative of its poets:

Note: This essay was originally commissioned by the late Arnaldo Momigliano for one of his seminars, at which he, along with Edward Shils and Peter White, offered useful comments. A later version was given as the Gildersleeve Lecture at Barnard, where Helen Bacon and Helene Foley also provided helpful comments. Later versions profited from comments by Wayne Booth, Milton Singer, John Lynch, and James McGlew. Intellectually this piece is in the tradition of those who see performance as a form of social action: the source text is Nietzsche's *Birth of Tragedy.* The equivalent classic statement of the corollary that social action is performance is perhaps Durkheim's *Les formes élémentaires de la vie religieuse.* I also refer, in order to acknowledge a debt which goes well beyond the reference, to Mircea Eliade, especially *Le mythe de l'éternel retour* (Paris, 1949), trans. under the title *Cosmos and History* (New York, 1959); to Erving Goffman, especially *The Presentation of the Self in Everyday Life* (Edinburgh, 1956); and to Victor Turner, especially *Drama, Fields, and Metaphors* (Ithaca, N.Y., 1974).

I'm always introducing new ideas in my cleverness—
No two of them alike, and all ingenious.

(Clouds 547–48)

[I] made the art great and built for it fortifications
Of great verses and concepts, none of your bargain jokes.

(Wasps 749–50)

Aristophanes has in his plays a great deal to say about his own theater—in many senses of "say": in his own person, through the personae of his characters, in the matter of his plots. His choruses come forward to praise the poet of their verses and review his career (Wasps 1015–50, Peace 729–74). His characters can speak of the fact that they are in a play and can comment on the play they are in; prototypical is the conversation between Dionysos and his slave which opens the Frogs, in which Dionysos forbids the use of the old jokes standard in Phrynikos and Lykis and Ameipsias (Frogs 1–20). A character can even come forward and address the audience:

OK, let me explain the story to the audience
With a few prefatory words up front, namely:
Do not expect from us anything in the grand manner,
Nor, on the other hand, jokes stolen from Megara.
We are not going to have baskets of nuts
With a couple of slaves to throw them to the audience,
Nor Herakles disappointed of his dinner
Nor yet Euripides misbehaving himself.
What if Kleon just had the luck to shine?
We're not going to hash over the same man twice.
No; we have a little story—with a point—
Not too ingenious for the likes of you
But cleverer than your standard comedies.

(Wasps 54–66)

On the other hand, quite probably this claim to novelty is itself generic and all the poets of Old Comedy claimed to be the only ones with new ideas, just as in our own world an (often blatantly mendacious) claim to "all new jokes" is characteristic of certain kinds of informal comedy. This reminds us that we need not take Aristophanes' self-descriptions as accurate, or even as intended to appear plausible. In the Frogs the slave goes on to make the old familiar jokes, which are all the funnier for having been ruled out. The passage in the Peace in which the chorus praises the poet for his inventiveness reuses five and a half lines from the *Wasps* (*Peace* 752, 755–59; cf. *Wasps* 1030, 1032–36).

All this is not to deny Aristophanes' originality; quite probably he was the avant-garde poet among the Old Comedians. It is only to remind us that in this, as in other branches of Greek literature, originality consisted partly in the effective reuse of old material, and that in Old Comedy it seems to have been traditional to deny this fact.

More generally, the claim to originality belongs to the category of comments on the play within the play, and is an aspect of the generic self-consciousness of Old Comedy. These comments often involve a break in the dramatic illusion, so that the actors speak of themselves as performers rather than characters, or refer, not to the setting of the play, but to the stage and its scenery. A typical example is the arrival of the clouds in the *Clouds*. The scene is placed in or near an Athenian house (probably in its courtyard) and Sokrates points out the clouds over Parnon, a conspicuous peak on the Athenian horizon (323). The theater of Dionysos is, however, one of the few places in Athens from which Parnon is not visible, and Strepsiades complains that he can't see them. Finally Sokrates tells him to look "along the *eisodos*" (326), the entry ramp onto the stage—and then he can see them. Another example: the hero of the *Knights*, about to make the acquaintance of Aristophanes' Kleon, is told not to be afraid: the mask is not a likeness of him; "they were so afraid that no one in the costume shop was willing to make a likeness. But he'll be recognized anyway. We've a clever house here" (*Knights* 230–33). (Probably the actor, who comes on immediately, in fact wore a vivid and cruel caricature of Kleon's features—another example of Old Comic broad irony.)

A recurrent device in Aristophanes is the play within the play, which gives the characters (as in some plays of Shakespeare) a chance to talk about plays. In combination with comic self-consciousness, this generates a certain complexity, as in the *Akharnians* (440–45) when the hero, having borrowed a beggar's costume from Euripides in the interest of the scene he is about to play within the play, has to pause to differentiate the inner and outer audiences:

I have to seem a beggar just for today—
To be just who I am, but not to show it—
That is, the *audience* should know who I am;
It's the *chorus* who are going to stand around
Like idiots while I give them the rhetorical finger.

Old Comedy was always free to break through the "fourth wall" and interact with the audience; this was generically required in the parabasis, the break halfway through the play when the chorus addressed the audience either in its own character (as clouds, birds, etc.) or on behalf of the poet or both. Elsewhere in the plays such breaks are sporadic, sometimes including the audience in the action, as in the *Frogs* when Dionysos in Hades asks about the patricides and perjurors and his slave directs his attention to the audience: "By Poseidon, I see them very well *now*" (*Frogs* 276). Sometimes the audience is evoked as an audience, as in the *Knights* (36–39):

> —Shall I tell the audience what's going on?
> —You could do worse. But let's ask them one thing:
>   That they should make it clear to us performers
>   If they like our verses and our goings-on.

Most often the audience is included in the play because the play is about Athens and the Athenians are actually present. Thus in the *Clouds*, Right Argument is forced to agree that the *eurupröktoi*, the passive homosexuals, are taking over society when Wrong Argument makes him look at the audience (1097–1100):

> —I'm looking.
> —What do you see?
> —By god, the vast majority
>   Are *eurupröktoi*. This one
>   I know, and that one,
>   And that longhair over there.

Similarly in the *Knights* (163–65), the Sausage Seller is promised political power and glory:

> —Do you see these rows of people?
> —Yes.
> —You shall be leader of all these
>   And of the market and the harbor and the Assembly.

The audience is thus reminded that the play itself is a kind of assembly of the people. And this fact, in turn, raises the question of the political standing of the genre.

We are familiar with a theater in which the work of art, once created, seeks an audience; in Athens the audience was already constituted and the poet applied for permission to appear before it. Every year a fixed number of plays was presented. The poet sought to have his work included; he asked the authorities to "grant him a chorus." He had to submit his play either as a tragedy or a comedy; this would determine (at the Dionysia) whether it was produced in the morning or the afternoon, and much else besides. The division between genres was thus institutionally maintained; a tragicomedy was an impossibility, and the dramatic genres were in effect aspects of the constitution. This made it possible to define the genres first and foremost in terms of externalities: tragedy and comedy employed different actors, different costumes, different meters (and different degrees of license in meters they shared), different music. Evidently, the Athenians took some trouble to maintain comedy and tragedy as contrasting genres; it thus seems natural to investigate these genres jointly, as contrasting uses of the theater. Let us begin with tragedy.

Everywhere the theater is the most social of the arts, since it not only concretely represents social action but is itself in performance a social event. The Athenian was a festival theater, included in the sphere of public ritual and as such regulated by legislation and paid for through the tax structure; a rich man was assigned to produce a play as he might be to equip a trireme. This was therefore a public art in an unusually literal sense, and we can ask with unusual literalness what advantage the public expected of the plays. At Athens, the whole city (in principle) attended; Sokrates (Plato, *Symposium* 175e) can speak of the audience of a tragedy as "thirty thousand"—not because the theater in fact held so many but because this is the conventional number of Athenian citizens. Drama at Athens was institutionalized as a modality of collective life—the continuation, as it were, of politics by other means.

There is something quintessentially Greek about a civic theater, since the Greeks were in a peculiar sense a live-performance culture. This phrase requires some explanation. In one sense, live performance is the stuff of social life; the fundamental terms of sociology, with its reference to "positions" and "roles," employ a theatrical metaphor, and our very term "person" is derived from an ancient word for "theatrical mask." Erving Goffman, for one, has made great and extended use of this theatrical reading of social action, with its backstage, rehearsals, and so on. I mean, however, something peculiar to the Greeks: their special social organization, the *polis*, was regularly enacted in performances in which the class line was institutionalized as the line between performers and audience.

The Homeric prototype is the heroic *agorē*. *Agorē* means simply "gathering"; it is the group gathered and also the gathering-place. In the center of every civil community—even the temporary community of the Akhaian army before Troy—there is a demarcated public space with altars of the gods; here the whole community gathers, usually early in the morning, to hear political debate. The *agorē* is for Homer the critical institution of civil life; this is what the Kyklopes lack, for instance. It is true that a community can get on somehow without an *agorē*; when Telemakhos calls one in *Odyssey* Two, there has been no *agorē* in Ithaka for twenty years. On the other hand, things in Ithaka have for that time been going very badly, and people are delighted that the *agorē* finally meets. Without it some crucial element of community life is missing.

In the Homeric *agorē* there is a clear line between performers and audience. Only the leading men, the *hegētores ēde medontes*, can take part in debate. These leading men meet ahead of time backstage in the Boulē, the council, to discuss a rough scenario for that morning's *agorē*. The herald then summons the mass of the folk; the folk sit down to hear the orators, who stand. These orators, like actors on the stage, mostly address one another; sometimes (as actors sometimes do) they speak directly to the audience; more often (as the actors say) they "cheat," turning slightly downstage so as to play to the audience over the shoulder of the man they are addressing. The common folk, meanwhile, take part only as an audience takes part; they murmur, shout, applaud—and if the performance gets completely out of hand they may riot, thus breaking up the show. So long as the performance lasts, however, performers and audience are divided by a moral barrier like the fourth wall in the theater; members of the audience take no individual initiatives and are never asked for their views. No votes are taken. In the *agorē*, therefore, the common people are included in a way that excludes them; they are allowed only to watch.

My theatrical terms are not intended to imply that no real business is done in the Homeric *agorē*. Real conflict takes place there; Akhilleus and Agamemnon really quarrel in *Iliad* One, and really make up in *Iliad* Nineteen. Since, however, both quarrel and reconciliation could have happened much the same way in private, or in the king's council, we are left with the question of the function of the audience. It is the audience which makes an *agorē*; when Zeus holds an *agorē* of the gods he invites a crowd of low-status deities (nymphs and rivers) to form the audience (*Il.* 20.4–9). Yet the audience does nothing; what is it for?

The answer, in Homeric terms, is that the audience is a repository of *themis*. *Themis* means literally "what is fixed"; it is a general term for "the rules" or "the way things are supposed to be." *Themis*, further, is the ultimate term of appeal in the Homeric value language; it is not possible to say: this is *themis*, but I do not commend it. And *themis* is specially associated with the *agorē*. *Themis*, we are told, "opens and closes the *agorai* of men" (*Od.* 2.69). The Kyklopes, who have no *agorai*, have no *themis* either. Disputes in the *agorē* are disputes about what is *themis*; they are moderated by the king, who chairs the *agorē* and delivers *themistēs*, declarations of *themis*. The king can settle a dispute by virtue of his superior power, but because the dispute is performed and the settlement is made before an audience, the king's power receives moral authority. What is viewed by the public without protest receives the consent of the public—and this is *themis*.

Durkheim taught us that in every society moral authority belongs to sacred things, and that these—most typically the totem, or the flag—are always more or less transformed emblems of communal solidarity. They represent the only actually existing thing which is superordinate to the will and interests of individuals; this is the community itself. The interest of the community is embodied in the moral law, which is thereby set over us. It is often contrary to our wish, yet some measure of adherence to it is the precondition of our membership in society, and therefore of our becoming the speaking creatures we are. The moral law is literally supernatural; it is the bond of acculturation. In the Greek tradition Themis is counsellor of Zeus.

In most premodern urban societies sacred power is symbolized by the distancing of authority, which often (in local myth) comes from elsewhere, and in any case is hidden in palace or temple. For the Greeks this is the characteristically oriental form of power (cf. esp., Herodotos' anecdote of Deiokes, 1.96–100). In a Greek community the sacred power of the community is unmediated because the community is actually present. *Vox populi, vox dei*: this is one of the things we mean when we say that the Greeks were a secular people. Power there was demystified. Real conflict took place in open meetings; as the members of the leading class reconstructed their relations, the people were present at the creation. Diomedes says to the great king Agamemnon: "I shall begin by attacking your folly—which is *themis* in the *agorē*" (*Il.* 9.31–32); when he is done the folk all shout their approval. They witness the rightness of his speech.

The inclusion of the people is effective, paradoxically, only because they are excluded from the decision-making process. It is this exclusion which transforms them into an audience. The moral authority of the audience lies in its solidarity. Because its members are looking on they tend to coalesce and form a common judgment. Whatever private interests or loyalties they bring to the occasion, they are to some degree unified by their common experience of the performance. We all know this strange transformation that overcomes us as members of an audience; we find it hard to support our own people when they look bad, even if we think they are right. That is because we are appreciating the performance rather than weighing its consequences; as Kleon called us, we become "spectators of speech and an audience of actualities." This tendency of politics to become merely theatrical is a pathology of politics; at the same time, however, it is only by maintaining such esthetic distance that the audience enacts the superordinate status of the communal interest. An audience cannot shape the performance but only respond to it; thus it overcomes subjectivity and becomes a proper judge.

The moral authority of the audience is thus dependent on the moral barrier between audience and performers, the fourth wall. An audience which riots and disrupts the performance becomes just another force, without any special claims to righteousness; any disruptive intervention from the audience weakens the moral power of the audience. Thus we can understand the fate of Thersites in *Iliad* Two. He rises from the floor to denounce Agamemnon for his bad behavior to Akhilleus; almost everyone (including Odysseus) thinks that Thersites is right, but when Odysseus mocks and hits Thersites, making him bleed and cry, everyone is glad. Thersites may be right on the substance, but he is terribly wrong on procedure.

The Homeric *agorē* can be seen as a solution to a familiar contradiction: the Homeric *basileis*, the leading property-holders, are in competition with one another and have nevertheless to find some way jointly to secure the conditions of their competition. However rancorous the interactions onstage, the players have a common interest in defending the performance against heckling and disruption. That is, the audience should continue to be audience; in this role, it maintains the level of the performance by forcing the actors not merely to state their wishes but to justify them. A claim can be made effectively in the presence of an audience only if it is made in terms of principles that are generally understood; the outcome, approved by the folk, shows itself not as a mere test of strength but as an instance of *themis*. This does not make of the *agorē* a democratic institution, since it carries with it no notion of the sovereignty of the people. Indeed, from the Greek point of view the development of democracy involves the loss of moral coherence. From the time when Kleisthenes "took the people into his *hetaireia*"—that is, treated the audience as a faction with interests of its own—the moral authority of the Assembly began to decline. As the audience began to vote they were drawn into the play, and the Assembly came to be conceived as a place of contest between warring interests, rather than as a place of communal mediation. Important officials were elected, so that the authority was conferred, not by inherited or achieved status, but by the political process itself. New figures began to appear, the *prostatai tou dēmou*, spokesmen of the ordinary people; these took the stage to argue for the interests of the audience. In the archaic period, these men were revolutionary anticonstitutional figures, and if successful, became tyrants. In classical Athens and Syracuse—and perhaps elsewhere—they were built into the constitution and became demagogues. The role of Thersites acquired a new respectability.

On the other hand, we should not exaggerate the change. Officials were in fact drawn from much the same social stratum as before. Elections in Athens seem hardly ever to have been contested; they were largely formalities, a matter of "three cuckoos" (*Akharnians*, 598) in the

Aristophanic phrase. The legislative and judicial acts of the Assembly, on the other hand, were no formalities; votes were often very close, and sometimes reversed immediately afterward. But the very unpredictability of the Assembly was a mark of its lack of organization, its lack of stable parties or factions; the people remained a collectivity, even if now an active one. The demagogues after Perikles, with the significant exception of Kleon, did not seek high office; they remained critics, the voice from the audience, rather than actors.

Nevertheless, we should not miss the fact that for the Greeks in general, including nearly all the Athenians we hear from, democracy was an irrational, morally unstable form of government. The great practical success of the democracy should not, I think, be ascribed to any consensus as to the value of democratic institutions per se, but rather to the fact that these institutions operated in a wider political context which sustained them. So far we have spoken of public space only in terms of practical deliberation; in order to understand the Athenian polity we need a wider view, to which I now turn.

Even in Homer practical deliberation is by no means the only thing which goes on in the *agorē*. There are also public rituals, as when Nestor gathers the people of Pylos to witness his sacrifice. There are the games, as in the funeral games of Patroklos and Akhilleus, and the games contested on Phaiakia. There is no drama in Homer, but the bard does sing in the *agorē* on Phaiakia, and there is singing and dancing for the pleasure of the audience.

I hereby propose a general typology of public space under these four headings: debate, ritual, games, and theater. These may be contrasted in three pairs. Ritual and theater are alike in that the outcome is predetermined, reached by a scenario unfolded through time. In games and debate, by contrast, the occasion is a way of determining the outcome, and produces a new difference between winners and losers. Ritual and debate are alike in that both deal with realities; ritual recreates or evokes an eternal reality, whereas debate creates a new contingent reality. Games and theater, by contrast, are both unreal; in games the conflict is real but the stakes are symbolic (even if they are valuable, they function as prizes), whereas in theater the stakes are serious, often matters of life and death, but the behavior is symbolized. Ritual and games, finally, are alike in that both are occasions for acts which, while meaningful, belong to the realm of the signified—that is, stand to be explained. Debate and theater, by contrast, consist primarily of explanations; the primary power of the actors is the power of words—that is, the power to signify.

This typology is not a set of boxes but is meant to suggest dimensions of analysis. One could look on the dance, for instance, as a kind of theater of acts, or think of sophistic display as a game played with words. The types interpenetrate. Athenian theatrical performance took place as part of a ritual, and was also a game, since prizes were awarded. Later we shall see that the dramas were also contributions to debate.

I insist on these complexities in order to suggest that the life of the community consists of more than the organization of power; that power, in fact, is only one aspect of collective meaning. Given the observable range of collective occasions, Durkheim's view of the community, which saw it primarily as a set of restrictions on the individual in the service of public order, must seem sadly diminished.[1] Communities persist for more than the distribution of scarce resources and the ordering of collective priorities: their members keep each other company in many ways. "The city," said Aristotle, "comes into existence for the sake of life, but continues for the sake of living well." Each of these modes of interaction gives its own shape to the civic whole, and in each certain individuals find specific public identities. In the *polis*, further, each reenacts and thus sustains the fundamental class structure. The debaters, the athletes, the celebrants of state rituals are overwhelmingly drawn from the limited class; the rest are audience members. In drama the poets (not the actors, once these were separated from the poets) belonged to this class, and the class line was curiously represented within the work, in the recurrent (but not absolutely prescribed) contrast between royal heroic characters and a socially less prominent chorus.

In each kind of event, or in relation to each aspect, the audience has a different role to play. In both games and debate, the role of the audience is regulative, but in different ways. In games, the audience is there to see fair play and to recognize the winners—that is, to confer honor. Since the aims of action are externally prescribed, so that the value of speech does not come into question in the course of a race, the audience is not asked to judge the person but only his success according to the rules. Games can thus be thought of as a safe form of competition where success does not lead to any transformation of norms.

Debate, on the other hand, is a way of determining ends, of deciding what is just and what is collectively advantageous. The parties to the debate, therefore, claim to speak for the group; that is the way they pursue their private advantage. They ask that their will be taken as a collective norm. "I will speak, and no one will contradict me," as Menelaos says, "for what I say will be right" (*Il.* 6.23). Participation in debate is thus a claim to rule—that is, a claim to write the rules, and the honor achieved

[1] Emile Durkheim, *Les formes élémentaires de la vie religieuse* (Paris, 1912), trans. under the title *The Elementary Forms of the Religious Life* (New York, 1959).

by the successful debater is not personal but representative; he is recognized as embodying a previously undiscovered social ideal. Debate thus has a privileged status, for in it the social order is actually constructed.

In ritual and theater, by contrast, the role of the audience is participatory, not regulative. The participation, however, differs in the two cases. Ritual is on behalf of the wholeness in the community; through it, the community establishes relations of communication and exchange with something superordinate: with gods, or the dead, or the cosmic order. The actors have been chosen to represent the community, and the honor they receive is prior to the event—that is, it lies in the fact that they have been chosen for this role. The participation of the audience guarantees the representative status of the actors, and this ensures that the ritual includes the whole group.

Theater, on the other hand, is unique among public events in that it is not only *for* the audience but is *directed to* the audience. Through theater the poet communicates with his audience; at Athens he was said to "teach" the chorus. There is thus no obvious answer to the following question: who, in the theater, makes a public appearance? The actors and chorus of course appear, but not as themselves. The characters of the drama in another sense appear, but they do not present themselves to the public; you will remember that one of Sokrates' complaints about tragedy is that the characters act as if no one were watching them. The poet appears, but not in his own person; he contrives that something should appear. Nietzsche said that drama was the dream of the chorus— a dream, notice, that the poet taught them.[2] Drama is thus a kind a dreaming in public and on behalf of a public which, as it is drawn into the play, shares the dream of the poet.

Theater, from this point of view, is a kind of public event opposite to political debate. In the political Assembly, the practical life is brought (temporarily) to lucidity by a procedure which clarifies, schematizes, and facilitates the reconstruction of existing social relations. In the theater, the city shares an experience; because all share it equally, social relations are deleted. Because the action of the play is unreal, all can share in it without danger. A unity not attainable in practice was achieved on the level of theory—in the Greek sense: *theōria*, looking on. Debate is analytic; theater, synthetic. Through deliberation, the city could come to *act* as a unity; the theater, by contrast, was a sphere of collective *knowledge*.

The tragedies told the same stories to the same audience over and over again. In fact, Aristotle says that as the art matured the range narrowed, until tragedy concerned itself with the misfortunes of only a few legend-

---

[2] Friedrich Nietzsche, *Die Geburt der Tragödie* (Leipzig, 1872), trans. under the title *The Birth of Tragedy* (New York, 1967).

ary families. Tragedies were thus like rituals, in which, as Mircea Eliade says, an act is valid only when it reenacts an earlier act. The stories told in tragedy, further, like the events evoked in ritual, are mythical and legendary; they belong *in illo tempore*, in the sacred time outside history. A few plays were set in the East, in a space outside history; one attempt to bring the play closer home brought quick reproof when Phrynikhos, after *The Sack of Miletos*, was fined for "reminding the Athenians of their own troubles." Tragedy does not reach the quotidian.

But it is also true that even at its most exotic—in, say, Aiskhylos' *Prometheus*—tragedy was a naturalistic art. Aristotle thought (I think rightly) that this was the chief power of tragedy: to achieve probability, that is, to tell the heroic story in such a way that we believe that such persons would do and say such things. The standard of probability, further, was not scientific but rhetorical—or, as we would say, commonsensical. Tragedy worked when the audience accepted it. The Athenian said: if I were a certain sort of god, and you were a certain sort of titan, we would behave to each other very much as Zeus and Prometheus do. The tragic story is thus seen to be parallel to ordinary life; the two are linked by what Aristotle called a "universal." The characteristic pleasure of tragedy is the recognition of this universal; in this way tragedy is linked to the quotidian.

Attic tragedy, further, was an occasional art; plays were written for a single performance. Texts, of course, were kept and read, songs from the old plays were sung after dinner, sometimes even an old play might be produced again; nevertheless in principle the tragic festival presented every year a set of plays written for that year's festival. The audience came, not to learn new stories, but to learn how the old stories would be told this year. Tragedy thus stands on the border between sacred time and history, and links the two. The audience asks: how does this old story look to us now? The characters always speak a current language, so that we can trace through the tragedies the year-to-year shifts in the current rhetoric of Athens.

In this way, I think, we can understand those shreds of topical reference in the tragedies which are both so obvious and so tantalizingly opaque. Surely Oidipous in the *Tyrannos* is like Perikles, as Victor Ehrenberg insists[3]—not, however, because Sophokles intended a point about Perikles, but rather (I am suggesting) because he relied on his audience's understanding of Perikles to create for them a believable Oidipous. In the same way, he relied on their understanding of Kritias and his fellows to create for them a believable Odysseus in the *Philoktetes*. A contemporary event might have the same use. Aiskhylos writes of the

---

[3] Victor Ehrenberg, *Sophocles and Pericles* (Oxford, 1954).

founding of the Areopagos in the *Oresteia* not (I think) because he takes a position for or against the recent reforms of Ephialtes, but because he can thereby remind his audience of their recent experience of institutional change and of the settlement (not without violence) of conflict. In the same way, it is probably right to see in Euripides' *Suppliants* echoes of the recent controversy between Athens and Thebes after Delion, and in his *Trojan Women* of the massacre at Melos. It is just the opposite of, say, the Living Theater's *Antigone*, in which the ancient legend was used to make a statement about Lyndon Johnson; in the Athenian theater, the contemporary material was used to lead the audience into the reality of the legend.

The theater was thus a kind of mirror in which the audience could read its shifting condition; in its recurrent effort to understand the legendary stories, the city encountered (abstracted and placed at a distance) the terms and categories used less reflectively in politics and ordinary life. Tragedy thus had within the Athenian public order something like the standing which the running commentary provided by social science—and popularized by journalism—has for us. Tragedy was (dare I say it?) stronger than social science in that the interpretations provided by this occasional art were explicitly in and of the moment, this year's universal for this year's city.

As an art of probability, tragedy displays the connections between cause and effect, and shows us persons acting under constraint, conditioned by their character, and by fate. The art is heroic and the persons are grand in their pathos and their knowledge—but not in their powers. In tragedy man appears in a diminished state, dignified in his acceptance of responsibility for acts not fully his own, but relatively nonfree. And, as Aristotle says, the terror of tragedy lies in the recognition that such a person is like ourselves.

Surely such an art has a moral use, and in the hands of its greatest poets a moral purpose. Tragedy is serious because it reaches a reality and is thus the enemy of self-indulgent fantasy. In political deliberation we tend to overrate our powers: "hope pulling and desire pushing," as Diodotos says. The same audience in the tragic theater learned that our acts are constrained and that the world is not according to our wish. Tragedy thus taught the city, on the level of human universals, those "inconvenient facts" which, according to Max Weber, are the special vocation of the social scientist turned teacher.

But in another sense, tragedy had to abjure moral teaching. It is an art of understanding and compassion, and does not tell us what to do next. In this sense tragedy is after all detached from history; like social science it is "*wertfrei*," value-free. It reveals the conditions of action, but cannot reach that ground of action which is *themis*.

Thus (in summary) I explain my assertion that tragedy was complementary to political debate. In the Assembly men explored the possibilities before them in this world; in the theater they examined another
world, isomorphic to our own, but simplified and made lucid. Pruden-
tial choice concerns itself with particulars; tragedy contemplates recognizable universals, and in this sense is "scientific." Deliberation is
prospective. It examines a situation and asks: what should happen?
Tragedy is retrospective. It examines a story and asks: how could it have
happened? The Greek proverb says that even god cannot make undone
what has been done. Tragedy brings home to the people the limiting
conditions of their freedom; as a study of the conditions of action it is the
public art most needed in a democracy. At the same time tragedy tends
to deny us the one thing that makes our lives tolerable and political action
meaningful: namely, our power to create new conditions. Tragedy was
only a partial art and thus called forth, in the Athenian civic theater, its
antitype, Old Comedy. To this I now return.

Comedy was the youngest of the genres performed at Athenian festivals; tragedy goes back into the sixth century but comedy does not really
begin before the mid-fifth. Classic tragedy died with Euripides and
Sophokles (although later poets continued to write tragedies); Old
Comedy perished with the Athenian empire (although Aristophanes survived and continued to write); later poets, including Aristophanes in his
later years, wrote a different kind of play. Evidently Old Comedy was a
genre possible only under specific historical conditions.

Aristotle says that tragedy represents people better than they are,
comedy worse than they are. He can hardly mean that Aiskhylos' Klytemnestra or Euripides' Lykos are good people, but they are figures of a
certain stature and nobility. Tragedy is an art of idealization; Old
Comedy is an art of deformation, of caricature, slander, parody, obscenity, and blasphemy. Every aspect of the current scene is seized upon and
made absurd; while tragedy represents another, archetypical world, Old
Comedy misrepresents this world. All those persons whom people are
likely to admire—poets, philosophers, statesmen, the gods themselves—
appear on the stage deformed and debased. In this sense, we can see the
Old Comedian, rather than the demagogue, as the heir of Thersites;
Thersites, we remember, was himself deformed, his speech was as dis-
orderly as it was copious, and he said "whatever he thought the Akhaians
would find ludicrous" (*Il.* 2.215). Thersites, however, was insulted and
beaten, while the comic poet is crowned and feasted.

Many cultures, of course, provide particular occasions for licensed invective and ribaldry; the Mediterranean carnival provides a modern instance. The classical mythical prototype is the jesting of Iambe, the
servant girl whose mockeries brought the mourning Demeter from silent

desolation toward the renewal of life and fertility. Such mockery was included in the Eleusinian ritual, significantly as a transitional element, involved with crossing a bridge (imitated at *Frogs* 420–34). Ritualized mockery, and cultural deformations in general, are aspects of what Victor Turner calls "antistructure" and are employed all over the world in rites of transition and renewal. Deformation, it seems, cracks the mold of culture and makes room for growth. Impurity mobilizes certain powers—for impurity is everywhere a source of power. Order sustains but also restricts. When the bottom drops out, the sky's the limit.

In tragedy, culture is seen as continuous with nature, in that both are arenas of lawful, comprehensible forces linked by man's submission to the gods. In Old Comedy, on the other hand, the hero need not submit to the gods; neither is nature permanent. The species are not separate or stable; a man could be a wasp or a horse, could converse with frogs or clouds. Amid such universal anarchy, the cultural order must seem absurdly insubstantial. The invasion of culture by nature results in grotesque deformations and a universal lowering; comedy is the enemy of hierarchy. The great instruments are obscenity and scatology, which remind us that we are all naked under our clothes. Individuals are deprived of their dignity—but in the process, mankind in general, embodied in the audience, recovers a sense of power and liberty. When cultural forms are degraded, we are reminded that culture is not our master, but our creation, and stands always to be recreated in new forms. Old Comedy consistently asserts itself against the cultural establishment. It does so against the poets, especially in parody which, by tracing the short and easy path from the sublime to the ridiculous, reminds us that the nobility of high art is itself a distortion. And it does so against the state, as in the *Akharnians*, where the hero makes a separate peace and mocks his fellows still at war, and in the *Wasps*, where it is shown that the judicial process is a game which could as well be played with pots and pans, and in the *Lysistrata*, where the women conquer the state, and in the *Birds*, where the hero leaves the state altogether to conquer the air. Finally, Old Comedy, in extravagance which spills into blasphemy, stands even against the gods in a Promethean claim to share in the divine. (Prometheus is, of course, a character in the *Birds*, where he appears considerably less Promethean than the Athenian hero.)

Therefore the persuasive ugliness of Aristophanes' plays (interspersed with passages of lyric beauty and scenes of engaging naturalism) does not repel, but rather invigorates. It goes with the general breaking of the rules which in Old Comedy spreads from culture to the cosmos. If tragedy is an art of the probable, Old Comedy is an art of the impossible. Cause and effect are suspended, heaven and hell are opened, time and space are erased, events unfold in dreamlike free association. Even character, as K. J. Dover points out, dissolves; an actor can make a remark entirely out of character and then recover his role in an instant.[4] And as the characters are not limited by their circumstances or even by themselves, there is no limit to what they can accomplish. The Sausage Seller in the *Knights* rises from lowest of the low to the highest of the high and magically rejuvenates the Athenian state; the hero of the *Birds* conquers heaven and becomes king of the universe.

Tragedies often end with the founding of something which still existed when the play was written; the homicide court of the Areopagos, the heroic presence of Oidipous at Kolonos, the cult of Artemis Tauropolos at Halai. The poet thus proved, as it were, the truth of his myth; by establishing a real link between our world and the world of mythical stories, he reinforced his claim to be depicting a (higher) reality. In Old Comedy, which makes no such claim, outcomes are evanescent; the play dissolves and Zeus is still king, the state is as it was. In Old Comedy, the story is not a myth but a fantasy; the play is not a window to another world but a distorting mirror held up to this one.

Old Comedy is explicitly political; the topicality which is only latent in tragedy is here exuberantly obvious. Real people in the audience are mocked under their real names and the action of the play is set in the actual year of its production. Furthermore, the comedies (in contrast to the dispassion of tragedy) are committed; the *Knights* is against Kleon, the *Clouds* is against Sokrates, the *Frogs* comes down in the end for Aiskhylos and against Euripides. But only the parabasis of the *Frogs* (by that time probably a revival of an out-of-date usage, turned to a rather special purpose) can be said to state a real policy; usually the advice of the chorus is as absurd as everything else: only old men should be allowed to prosecute old men (*Akharnians* 713–18), Kleon should be muzzled in the stocks (*Clouds* 591–94). More generally, the politics of the poet seems disappointingly commonplace; peace is better than war, public spirit is better than self-seeking, the city belongs to its people. Above all, the play asserts that if the problem were to disappear, there would then be no problem. We have made this human world (it asserts), we have made it badly, and since we are better than it is we can make it better. But since the same "we" is identified as both the problem and the solution, no concrete program emerges, and the play remains a dream of renewal.

The comic poet was after all a citizen, and generally a member of that class of citizens accustomed to be heard in the Assembly. If he had a political message for the people, he could go to the Pnyx and deliver his message directly. The comedy, although it claims to be making a political case, is something different from a speech in a debate; in it, the poet

---

[4] K. J. Dover, *Aristophanic Comedy* (Berkeley, 1972).

establishes a specific relation to his audience, a relation proper to a dramatic performance in the frame of a ritual contest.

The play is a representation of civic life; even heaven and hell, in the *Birds* and *Frogs*, turn out to be pretty much like Athens after all. The poet presents himself as an observer of the city and recruits the audience to his point of view. His play is a kind of campaign to be adopted as their representative—not in life, but in art. In these terms, we can understand Old Comedy's generic self-consciousness, the reflexive comments on the play as a play within the play. Whereas the tragic poet puts before us the *matter* of his art, teaching us to see the precise interplay of thought, character, and action which constitute this story in his vision of it, Old Comedy presents nothing so stable. Stability (largely negatively evaluated) is to be found outside the theater; it is the way of the world. Here in the play the poet is not so much teaching us through his art as teaching us the art itself. Therefore his must be an art which reveals art; the play is presented as if it were being improvised, almost jointly created with the audience. The Old Comedian thus shares his creativity with us. Ideally, we leave a play of Sophokles drained and purified; we leave a play of Aristophanes ebullient and clowning.

Old Comedy is an intimate art; its broad irony implies a relation of trust between poet and audience—so that, for instance, blatant falsehoods can be enjoyed and understood. I can speak ill of the city, says the hero of the *Akharnians* (501–8), since it is the Lenaia, and the foreigners do not come to this festival; we are among ourselves. (He then proceeds to ascribe the present war to a trivial quarrel over some stolen prostitutes.) Old Comedy's topical references, many of which are frustratingly opaque to us, are "in jokes" and, as such, build a bond between poet and audience in terms of shared information. The poet deserves the resources which the public invests in his art because he is one of them. The chorus of the *Knights* says:

> If somebody at an earlier period was producing a comedy
> And tried to get us to come to the front of the state and speak his
>   verses,
> He wouldn't so easily get what he wanted. But this poet is worthy
> Because he hates the same people you do, and is bold enough to say
>   what is right.

> (*Knights* 507–10)

The chorus is the alter ego of the audience and the poet is worthy of his chorus because he is representative of the audience as he represents the city to itself. This claim to representative status brings the Old Comedian into competition with the demagogue, and indeed the two seem to have been adversaries throughout the history of art. Between them, the comic poet seems destined to be the victor since he can, as it were, slip around his adversary and hit him on the blind side, the side toward the audience. Once the demagogue has pressed his way into the political performance, he becomes another actor, and can be heckled with the rest. The comic poet, then, is further back in the audience and is equivalent not to Thersites, but to the anonymous member of the audience who says, at the end of the Thersites episode: "Now Odysseus has done his best act ever among the Argives, since he kept that intrusive reviler from the Assembly" (*Il.* 2.274–75).

In order to maintain his advantage, however, the poet must abandon any claim to rule, to take an actual part in debate. Comedy does not state a program, but rather expresses a wish, a longing, often nostalgia, for a better world. Aristophanes' conservatism, his love of simple virtues, primal verities, and the good old times, was in fact imposed on him by his genre, which is to say, his social role. He is commissioned to speak for the solidarity of the audience, and as such is hostile to all innovations, including those with some prospect of improving society. The poet is thus in the paradoxical position of complaining about the current state of affairs while mocking all those who seek to ameliorate it, not only those who claim leadership, but also the intellectuals, rhetoricians, calendar reformers, new musicians, prophets, and seers. The Old Comedian is in general hostile to the individual intelligence; he is spokesman for *themis*, which is essentially corrective and levelling. He is the critic of critics.

Old Comedy stands to debate as tragedy stands to ritual. Ritual makes a mythical reality actual in this world; tragedy merely contemplates this reality from a distance. Debate constructs a new world; comedy merely imagines one, enfolding current actualities in the form of a deformed representation. This imagination is itself, however, a form of political life, not on the level of action but of consciousness; history may be determined, but thought is free. In the form of this deformed self-representation, the city discovers its collective liberty.

In this more general sense of a contribution to consciousness, comedy is of course a contribution to debate. The comic poet teaches us to look at the spectacle of social life and say: "It ain't necessarily so." Perhaps the poetry we admire is mere bombast, our religious language sententious nonsense; the statesmen we admire are fools, and those we trust are knaves. Comedy weakens the control of the performers over their audience and thus increases the power of the people. In this sense it is after all a democratic art.

Aristophanes makes this point explicit in the parabasis of the *Akharnians*:

Your poet says he is worthy of much benefaction
That he keeps you from being cheated by foreign talk,
Sitting like dummies, loving to let them flatter you.
It used to be ambassadors would come and cheat you
First of all calling you "violet-crowned"—that's all it took,
And as soon as they said "crowns" you sat up on your rumps;
If someone piled on the flattery, and said "shining Athens"
You'd give anything, just for "shining"—he'd as well been
Addressing sardines.
. . . .

The fame of the poet's daring has spread so far
That the Great King when he checked out the Spartan envoys
Asked them first if they held control of the sea,
And then about this poet: was he really outrageous?
For he said that people would surely become much better
And in war be everywhere victors, which had such an advisor.

(*Akharnians* 633–40, 646–51)

Satire indeed teaches its audience an art of ironic understanding.

Nevertheless, the Old Comedian cannot replace the figures he attacks, and his work is conservative even as against the conservatives. In order to explain this point, which involves a final parallel between the poet and the demagogue, I return to the case of Thersites.

Thersites is "the ugliest man beneath Ilion" (*Il.* 2.216). In a society in which physical beauty is an important source of status, and in which social visibility is equivalent to identity, he seems to be excluded from any participation in social action. He has, however, solved his problem by exploiting that which would seem to exclude him as his special claim to take part; he has adopted the role of buffoon. His speech is without order or limit, an art of rhetorical deformation, and he quarrels with the kings to make the people laugh.

Normally Thersites is a special enemy of Akhilleus, but in Book Two, when we meet Thersites, Akhilleus is sulking in his tent. Thersites, who has no views of his own but says whatever is most hateful and abrasive, therefore takes up Akhilleus' case against Agamemnon. He is punished for this intervention when Odysseus insults and beats him; he retires in tears, much to the satisfaction of the audience.

Let us notice that Thersites says what Akhilleus has already said (and what everyone uncomfortably feels to be true)—namely, that Agamemnon is greedy, that the Akhaians show themselves worthless by their continued respect for Agamemnon, and that it would be better to break off the war and go home. Odysseus had been forced to restrain them with insults and blows. One might think that Thersites' speech would start the whole process over again.

In fact, however, the effect is just the opposite. Thersites is utterly unfit for leadership; in his mouth the position of Akhilleus is degraded to a piece of buffoonery. By making the issue appear in this form, Thersites makes it disappear; when he is insulted and struck, the question of Agamemnon's wrongdoing is neutralized, and the Assembly is restored to order. Thus Thersites' reviling of the kings turns out, in practice, to be an act on behalf of the kings, and he and Odysseus (no doubt quite unconsciously) are engaged in a paradoxically cooperative social performance.

This paradox, I think, will be found to be inherent in every attempt to take part in the performance from a place in the audience, in every attempt to state the rules which cannot present itself as a valid claim to rule. Odysseus, we must notice, does not answer Thersites' criticism (which anyway he rather agrees with); he shifts instead to a question of status. "I deny," he says, "that there is any worse man than you are" (*Il.* 2.248). The criticism of the king implies a claim to be equal to the king, and if this claim fails, the criticism fails with it.

Odysseus also says: "We do not clearly know how these things will be, whether well or badly the sons of the Akhaians will come home" (*Il.* 2.251–52). The governing class takes responsibility for an unknown future; since the future is unknown, we cannot know the best way to it; those, therefore, who have conferred responsibility on the governors must also grant them the right to make mistakes. Of course, there will be criticism from the inferior strata; talk is cheap. Of course the rulers will ignore it. Such cheap talk actually helps them, for by demonstrating their ability to ignore criticism they demonstrate their hold on the status of ruler.

Social criticism, in fact, like any social behavior, can be routinized by conferring on the critic a definite social role. Disruption then becomes his expected behavior, and however valid his points, they can be written off as being just what he *would* say. The critic himself may find himself quite comfortable with this transformation, which awards him a right to exist and a reason for existence. If he is not content, he has no recourse except to attack the whole structure of roles, to attempt to clear the stage and cancel the performance. Such an effort, if successful, might lead the demagogue, for instance, to become a tyrant. But it is a dangerous enterprise, for whatever the validity of Thersites' critique, most men would rather be ruled by Odysseus than by Thersites.

The comic poet, one step further back in the audience, a critic of critics, is caught in a further and complementary paradox. He rises, as it were, to celebrate the downfall of Thersites by miming his aggression and his tears. He ridicules Thersites by making him grotesque. Such a performance may perfect the transaction between Odysseus and Thersites by giving it artistic representation—but it can do Thersites no harm, because Thersites was already grotesque. Such grotesqueness, in fact, was integral to his social role.

Similarly, it does Kleon no harm to represent him as crude and irresponsible; Kleon's political career was founded on his cultivation of crudity and irresponsibility. He was *biaiotatos* just as Thersites is *aiskhistos*. We should not be puzzled by the fact that the *Knights* won first prize in the same year and before the same audience which brought Kleon his greatest political success.

So also Sokrates' position in the city is not shaken by a representation of him as an eccentric ascetic who talks obvious nonsense, since he never claimed to be anything else. Euripides and Agathon can be presented in comedy as self-dramatizing egoists only because they have chosen to present themselves that way in life. The butt of comedy can take his place in the audience of a comedy and laugh as freely as the rest, for the satire against him is also a celebration of the special place he has made for himself within society. If the laughter does not come easily (and I imagine that often it did not), this proves only that he is not really happy with the role in which he finds himself. Thersites, for all his railing, probably wants to be loved; the demagogue wants to be king, the dialectical trickster wants to be a respected teacher, the *avant-garde* poet wants to be the recognized spokesman of his age. This ambivalence gives comedy, after all, its bite.

But this is a purely personal point. As a social analysis, as a presentation of the audience to itself, Old Comedy celebrates the grotesque, and thus, against a background of conservatism and commonsense normality, finds a place within society for the abnormal, the eccentric, and the deformed. Aristophanes, at least, seems to have been aware of this paradox, and often builds it into his plays—as when Old Master Dēmos suddenly reveals that he has been Kleon all along and has been using him, as when the Clouds reveal that the impious teaching of Sokrates was in fact their instrument for teaching Strepsiades piety. Similarly, in the *Wasps*, it turns out that the absurd law courts had after all given Philokleon an interest in life and something to do.

Comic poets, however, like others, are ambivalent about their social roles. Aristophanes, in particular, who was in some respects himself an avant-garde poet, may have wanted to do more with his art, to make it a vehicle of genuine teaching and of public education. In so doing, he stretched his genre to and beyond its limit, for Old Comedy cannot, ultimately, be used to correct the world; it can only enjoy it.

Everyone remembers that at the end of Plato's *Symposium*, Aristodemos wakes to find Sokrates trying to convince Agathon and Aristophanes that it belongs to the same art or *tekhnē* to make both tragedy and comedy. Probably Aristodemos, who is half asleep, misunderstood the argument; Sokrates was asserting that *if* poetry were a *tekhnē* founded on scientific knowledge, the same poet would be able to make both, and that the absolute division of the two genres is yet another proof that poets write, not by knowledge, but by inspiration. For "inspiration" we moderns would read "tradition" and "social role"; the poet does not have to know what he is doing, because he is doing what is expected of him. That is why he is better loved than the philosopher, and less effective. True teaching and public education would have to be based on a knowledge of the reality which lies behind society and is not subject to social convention—if such a reality exists. Perhaps the comic poet, especially, would be likely to deny its existence. But if it does exist, it cannot be shown us in Old Comedy; some other literary genre is required—the Sokratic dialogue, perhaps.

RUTH PADEL

Making Space Speak

"A Place Set Apart in the Middle of the City . . ."

I

All Greek gods are violent, in their fashion. Dionysos' specialty is to connect interior violence—violence of *phrenes*, distorted perception, individual emotional storm—with performed, exterior violence: violence done and seen, out in the world. His persona is the fostering link between madness and murder.

Tragedy, like Athens' physical theater, belongs in Dionysos' precinct. It grew up while historians and scientists formulated and worked on the principle that one infers interior movement—and the movement they too were interested in was mostly violent—from external movement, movement you could see.[1] Tragedy is this principle's dramatic truth. Its performed violence is only nominally onstage. It happens unseen. Spectators infer it and watch others doing so. Scenes like Aiskhylos, *Agamemnon* 1342–46 may sound labored and absurd to us, easily parodied. But sounding, inference, is precisely what they are about:

Chorus:	What mortal could boast of existence with unpunishing *daimōn* when these things he hears?[2]
Agamemnon (within):	Alas, I am struck with a timely blow within.
Chorus:	Hush! who cries . . . wounded with a blow?
Agamemnon:	Alas again! I am struck with a second blow.

Note: This is an abridged version of a chapter in my forthcoming book *In and Out of the Mind: Greek Images of the Tragic Self,* whose center is tragedy's metaphors of mind and their relation to tragic madness, physiology, causality, and character, especially as these are concerned with the linking up of outside to inside.

[1] *Sumballomai tois emphanesi ta mē ginōskomena,* Herodotos, 2.33.2; *opsis tōn adēlōn ta phainomena,* Anaxag., *FVS* B 21a. Cf. Hippokrates, *Sacred Disease* 10.40, *Ancient Medicine.* 24, *De victu* 1.11, G.E.R. Lloyd, *Polarity and Analogy* (Cambridge, 1966), 341, 343–44, 353–56.

[2] *Akouōn* is the last word before Agamemnon's shout. *Tade,* its object, refers to the chorus' meditation on his victory and its likely cost (1331–40).

Chorus: The deed is done
           it seems to me
           from the king's cries.

This is the theater exulting in possibilities of relating inside to outside,
unseen to seen, private inner experience to the external watching and
guessing of others: a concrete parallel to tragedy's personal dimension.
All over tragedy, men and women suffer within, in their emotions.
Other figures, and spectators, infer this unseen pain from words. One
cannot see into another person's feelings. No external mark can tell us
what people are inside.[3] We infer what is in them from how they look
and what they say. The physique of Dionysos' theater, its contrasts of
unseen and apparent space, embodies the personal dialectics of Dionysos'
tragedy.

These dialectics rise from the audience's experience of people in real
(civic and convivial) life. You cannot open up a man with a scalpel and
see what he is within, says a contemporary drinking song.[4] From the beginning, the *agora*, center of assembly and commerce, had a "theatrical"
character. It once functioned as a theater. This was remembered in the *orkhēstra*, part of the *agora* where the dancing-floor had once been. As the
city-state developed in classical times, the theater became "a sort of duplicate *agora*."[5] Both were meeting-places, where male citizens felt, and
saw themselves as, part of the civic body; where important speeches
were set before them. Both qualify for the barbarian's suspicious description, as reported by the Athens-struck Greek historian, of the *agora*, "a
place set apart in the middle of the city, in which men get together and
tell one another lies" (Herodotos, 1.153). Being part of the citizen body
in the *agora* shaped the citizens' experience as part of a tragic audience.
They saw co-members of the audience across the theater. Any audience's
self-awareness is an aspect of the way that audience completes its play.[6]
Plays are put "in front of" us. But at Athens they were acted inside: inside the horseshoe circle that embodied the community. The audience's

[3] Eur., *Med.* 516, *Hipp.* 925–29, *El.* 373–74, 367, 385.

[4] *PMG* 889 (473); see W. S. Barrett, ed. and comm., *Euripides Hippolytos* (Oxford, 1964),
comment on line 925 (340).

[5] Sokrates bought a book in the *orkhēstra* in the *agora*, Plato, *Apol.* 26 D—E, see J. Adam,
ed., *Platonis Apologia Socratis* (Cambridge, Eng., 1939), ad loc. and Appendix 1. See R. E.
Wycherley, *How the Greeks Built Cities*, 2d ed. (New York and London, 1973), 50–51; cf.
T.B.L. Webster, *Greek Theater Production* (London, 1956), 5.

[6] Erika Simon, *The Ancient Theater*, trans. C. E. Vafopoulou-Richardson (London and
New York, 1982), 7: "In the theater the audience completes the . . . creation." See the
professional's point of view, Peter Brook, *The Empty Space* (Harmondsworth, 1972), 142,
150.

identity as a self-conscious member of that community was part of its experience of tragedy. An actor's entry into that space was entry into the
attention of those who felt and saw themselves to be the city. And being
the city meant judging, or inferring, the interior of others on the basis of
what they had done and said; from how they had, publicly, seemed. The
assembly and the law courts were a kind of theater, the theater an assembly-place, a court. In all these, it was crucial that you could not see inside
another person and yet, somehow, you must. You, and the community,
must proceed as if you could.

II

These spectators, facing their space where masked men told lies and
made illusion, shared more with the people inside the semblances into
which they hoped to see, than we do with actors in our theater. Each
chorus was a group of citizens, trained at the expense of a rich citizen
who wanted to be seen as public-spirited. Many spectators had sung in
choruses themselves. They knew the people singing. They entered the
theater by the same route, the *eisodoi*, used by the actors and by the chorus on their entrance, whereas among us "the moment of performance . . . is reached through two passageways—the foyer and the stage
door."[7]

Shared experience of the *orkhēstra*. Shared route into the theater.
Shared light, too; the audiences were not differentiated from performers
by darkness.[8] The differences between them and the players were contingent. In Peter Brook's terms, this was "necessary theater," where the
distinction between audience and players lies in architecture and role;[9]
not, as with us, in profession and experience.[10] Audience and players

[7] Brook, *Empty Space*, 141.

[8] Fifth-century Athenians perhaps experienced something like early European stage
lighting in temples, e.g., lighting and light-contrasts on Athena's statue in the Parthenon.
Their temples were doubtless theatrical, in our terms. But nothing like that—a lit figure,
surrounding dark—happened in the theater.

[9] In a "necessary theater" there is "only a practical difference between actor and audience, not a fundamental one"; Brook, *Empty Space*, 150. Cf. Artaud's vision of an ideal
theater which would abolish the separateness of actors and audience. Light will "fall upon
the public as much as upon the actors"; "direct communication will be re-established between the spectator and the spectacle, between the actor and the spectator." A. Artaud,
"The Theater of Cruelty, First and Second Manifestos," (1938), trans. M. C. Richards in
The Theory of the Modern Stage, ed. E. Bentley (Harmondsworth, 1976), 61–62.

[10] By the mid-fifth century, speaking actors were professionals. But their profession was
probably not institutionalized until the fourth century. *DFA*, 93f., 279. Singers for dithyramb were chosen on a tribal basis, but for tragedy and comedy this restriction was not
made. In the fourth century there were professional singers from which a *khorēgos* could

shared the festival; they entered by the same route. The chorus in the *or-khēstra*, composed of citizens, was in several senses halfway between the audience and the actors.

Spectators also shared the players' concern in how the whole thing went. On the last day of the festival there was an assembly, attended by all. Prizes were given and everyone examined the conduct of not only the festival officials, but the spectators.[11]

Some contrasts between audience and players, built into our expectations of dramatic experience, were absent, therefore, from Dionysos' theater. Another absence interlocks with these. On our stage, light orchestrates the spectators' feeling by contrasting tones. Western understanding of theatrical space was changed forever by Adolph Appia and the subsequent development of his ideas about the use of light. Light is now theater's most important plastic medium, "scene-painter, interpreter," with "the character of a form in space." It directs our emotions. Its mobility, its plasticity, are part of our theatrical language.[12]

Because of the way we use light, our theatrical response is "intensified by an aesthetic emphasis upon extension in space . . . expressing dynamic patterns of human beings in action, who move through fluctuating planes of light; these in turn create a dynamic interplay of contours and forms."[13] The pattern of our emotional experience of the play is not only paralleled but controlled by the imaginary spatial architecture, an illusionary structure created by light.

Can we think theater lighting out of our own experience? We might argue that the music, with its emotionally significant modes, fulfilled the role of lighting in the Greek theater.[14] A flute-player on a Greek vase painting is often a sign that this scene is not mythical but from a tragedy

choose his chorus (ibid. 90) but *khoreutai* themselves probably had no professional status. The community supplied many citizen choruses, men and boys, for manifold functions. Only their trainer was a professional. He and the chorus were paid. There were several distinctions (often temporary ones) between performers and audience. But these distinctions were not so institutionalized, nor so hard and fast, (a) as in the fourth century, or (b) as now in Western theater. See also the essay by Slater in this volume.

[11] See *DFA*, 68–70.

[12] L. Simonsen, "The Ideas of Adolphe Appia," in Bentley, *Theory*, 33–50. The theater "organizes" sounds and light into a "hieroglyph," Artaud, "Cruelty," 56 (in Bentley).

[13] Simonsen, "Ideas," 50.

[14] There were "modes" proper to tragedy, to a particular range of feeling and action; *DFA*, 258–59. The nature of each mode was widely known in the last half of the fifth century; W. D. Anderson, *Ethos and Education in Greek Music* (Cambridge, Mass., 1966) 11, 34–36, 62. The tragedian-composer must have used music to color the drama emotionally. Appia developed his own technique and theory of stage lighting as a conscious implement of emotional manipulation onstage, while working for Wagner, under the stimulus of the tempo and color of his scores. Simonsen, "Ideas," 41.

depicting that myth. In painters' code, the musical nature of tragedy became one of tragedy's identifying characteristics.[15] Did that characteristically tragic accompaniment direct the audience's feelings about the words it accompanied?

Probably. But these two ways of manipulating dramatic feeling are not identical, though they are similar, and, in our world, related. Tragedy's music was a vital part of the play but provided nothing like the illusory sense of extended space which modern lighting creates. The tragic poets, unlike modern producers, extended their world by language only.

This is not, of course, an absence of technique. It simply means we must think away features of our own response to drama, to concentrate on what was actually present in that theater. This is the more useful approach to mental experience in tragedy, too, especially the indigenous sense of divinity in the human world and mind. For among the positive elements in that theater, lacking in ours, is the central fact that civic space was also divine. This theater, like mind, city, self, was a human structure with a divine presence within it: part of Dionysos' precinct. Its altar may have been the focus of choral dances, and the site for the accompanying flutist, simultaneously a sacred and a choreographic center.[16] There was normally a stage altar too.[17] The theater's fictive world, like its real context, had a sacred focus. The libations in the theater, and its purification by death (of a suckling pig), underscored the religious nature of occasion and space.[18]

The theater was close to Dionysos' temple, rebuilt during that century. The priest of Dionysos was the chief member of the audience.[19] We lack this central emotional dimension to the theatrical experience, charged with the relationship between divinity and humanity, and all the tensions which belonged to the relationship with that particular divinity. The syntax of fifth-century theater is a product of Athenian male citizens'

[15] J. Beazley, "Hydria-fragments from Corinth," *Hesperia* 24 (1955): 307, 310, 314, 318; *DFA*, 179–86. The "flute" was standard accompaniment to song and recitative in tragedy, the lyre mainly for special effects. Flute players are in place at other performances too (seen, e.g., on vases showing dithyrambic contests). But when they keep "strange company" on vases, this normally indicates a dramatic context; Beazley, "Hydria-fragments," 314.

[16] See P. Arnott, *Greek Scenic Conventions* (Oxford, 1962), 43–45.

[17] Was this a permanent part of the theater? Arnott, *Greek Scenic Conventions*, 43–53, 58–59, argues that it was. When Pollux, 4.123 calls it the *aguiēos bōmos*, Arnott says he means the permanent altar of Apollo Agyieus. But Oliver Taplin, *The Stagecraft of Aeschylus* (Oxford, 1977), 106, 117, doubts that a permanent stage altar served as, e.g., Dareios' tomb. He prefers an early mound in the theater, levelled out ca. 460 when the *skēnē* was made. Does Pollux's word *aguiēos* suggest the altar was portable (as many were; see Yavis, *Greek Altars* [St. Louis, 1949] 172–75)? The main point is that many plays need some altar to be represented somewhere in the theater.

[18] *DFA*, 67.

[19] *TDA*, 16, 19, 143; *DFA*, 268.

experience of and inferences about, not only other people, but Dionysos, inside and outside people, inside and outside the theater.

SPATIAL SYNTAX

I

Within the theater's shared space, the first distinction is between space for the audience, *theatron*, where the audience went *theasthai*, to watch, and *orkhēstra*, which the chorus entered *orkheisthai*, to dance. Spaces were named after the role of people in them.[20] Interest in the spectators' role grows from the time of Peisistratos' organization of the festival. Painters depict spectators as well as performers.[21] Two spaces, two roles; they balance each other.

Within the performing space, a second contrast: *orkhēstra* and *skēnē* (from *skēneō*, "I dwell," "I am billetted," of soldiers in camp). *Skēnē* in military contexts means "tent," or in the plural, "camp" (e.g., Aristophanes, *Thesmophoriazousai* 658). It also means "market stall." Things that are flimsy, but crucially important—for a while.

In our context its meaning is "stage building," the hut behind the acting space for actors to change between scenes. The two actors (three, later in the century) took speaking parts in turn, often switching roles between scenes,[22] and entered the *skēnē* to do so. They often stayed within it (we assume) while other things happened; while, for instance, a choral ode was sung.[23]

In the fifth century, the *skēnē* was wooden, like most of the spectators' seats.[24] One temporary wood structure balanced the other. It had a flat roof. Actors stood on it: like the Watchman (probably) opening the *Agamemnon*. It was used for divine epiphanies.[25] In the *Psuchostasia*, Zeus, weighing the fates of Akhilleus and Memnon, and their respective mothers, possibly all appeared on it.[26]

[20] *Orkhēstra*, used of the theater, appears first in [Arist.], *Prob.* 901B30. *Theatron* can mean simply "audience," even of nontragic events. Later it came to mean the whole group of buildings connected with the theater.

[21] Simon, *Theater*, 3–5; see M. Bieber, *The History of the Greek and Roman Theater* (Princeton, 1961), 54, fig. 220.

[22] See *DFA*, 135, 137f.; Simon, *Theater*, 6; Taplin, *Stagecraft*, 452.

[23] Though actors did not necessarily leave the stage during a choral song; Taplin, *Stagecraft*, 54.

[24] *TDA*, 23–24; Simon, *Theater*, 5–6; Taplin, *Stagecraft*, 452f.

[25] Taplin, *Stagecraft*, 440, 445. Watchman in *Agamemnon*: Simon, *Theater*, 7, gives the conventional view. Taplin, *Stagecraft*, 276–77, argues against.

[26] Though Taplin, *Stagecraft*, 431–33, doubts this and thinks the weighing may not have been done onstage at all, nor Zeus have appeared as a character.

The *skēnē* probably appeared only around 460 B.C.E., and the *Oresteia* (458) may well be the first extant drama to use this hidden interior, facade, and door.[27] When we talk of the *skēnē* in tragedy, we are talking, probably, of the *Oresteia*, the first modern tragedy—drama whose care is the potent fatal interiority, deceptions, history, of house and person—and after.

In ancient critical literature, *skēnē* often refers to the space in front of the stage building. "Those from [or on] the *skēnē*" are the people who use that space: actors, not chorus. Actors and chorus have their own areas: the space in front of the *skēnē*, the circle of the *orkhēstra*. But in the fifth century there is coming and going between these spaces. Actors step into the chorus' space, and vice versa.[28] There was probably some wooden dais for the stage, but it was probably low, and easy to negotiate.[29] It was only in later centuries that first the Greek, then the Roman, theater raised the actors' stage and thereby entirely prevented that physical interchange.

Within the performing space, then, spatial contrast defined the role of people belonging in each space: the single actor versus the group. There is physical as well as verbal interchange between these. The early function of the *hupokritēs* was probably to "answer" the chorus.[30] The two come to and from, into and out of each other's space, a visual parallel for the dialogue between them, the simplest example of the way that spatial relationships become the physical vehicle for emotional and political relationships. Spatial oppositions reify others. The *skēnē* roof, for instance, is often (not exclusively) used for gods. Gods appear at a different "level," mirroring the role gods play in plot and human relationships or feelings. The language of space is part of the tragedian's armory, by which he lets each moment of the play suggest simultaneously different

[27] There is controversy here; I am convinced by Taplin, *Stagecraft*, 452–59, esp. 454, who accepts and argues for Wilamowitz's suggestion that the *Oresteia* is the first extant drama to use the *skēnē*. Once the *skēnē* was introduced, dramatists used it vividly. Nearly every extant tragedy of Sophokles and Euripides uses it positively (Taplin, *Stagecraft*, 455).

[28] Taplin, *Stagecraft*, 128, 442; Simon, *Theater*, 7; see Bieber, *History*, 66, fig. 253 (Orestes and Pylades stand on orchestra level, represented as soil). Segregation of actors and chorus really began in the fourth century (Taplin, *Stagecraft*, 452 n. 1) but was not invariable even then.

[29] So most modern authorities: "some broad steps" (Simon, *Theater*, 7), a "low stage" (Taplin, *Stagecraft*, 441). There must have been something for the underground channel to run under (Taplin, *Stagecraft*, 448, "some crude covered trench").

[30] This is a controversial point. Classic formulations in G. F. Else, *Aristotle's Poetics: The Argument* (Cambridge, Mass., 1957), 167; *DTC*, 79. The "answerer" interpretation is assumed by Simon, *Theater*, 5, defended by T. V. Buttrey, "*Hupo* in Aristophanes and *hupokritēs*," *GRBS* 18 (1977): 5–23. But *hupokritēs* can also mean "interpreter," "declaimer," and might have been applied to the actor from this semantic field, at least by the mid-fifth century. See also the essay by Svenbro in this volume.

aspects of one idea. "Distanced epiphanies,"[31] gods appearing above human beings: one of their functions is to symbolize the weightier (higher?) divine causality of many tragic plots.

II

So far, we have investigated contrasts between visible spaces of the theater. But one of Greek tragedy's "triumphs" is to make manifest scenes "far in the Unapparent."[32] Tragedy's most potent contrast is between the seen and "the unapparent," between visible and imagined space.

Several kinds of invisible space, in fact. One was space-at-a-distance, the elsewhere. Places the spectators were invited to imagine when someone came in from far off, bringing news from outside, from a battle, mountain, foreign city, or Delphic oracle, via one of the two *eisodoi*, "roads in." Dramatists could use the opposition between left and right to underline emotion hanging around a character and her fate. Tension between the *eisodoi* was part of tragedy's "symbolic topography." In suppliant plays, for instance, it was expected that one *eisodos* led "out" (abroad), and one led "in" (to the protecting city); one in the direction of danger, the other of safety.[33]

Then there is space within:[34] within the *skēnē* building, whether it represents a palace or temple, cave, or grove. This unseen space is a cul-de-sac. The *eisodoi* lead out and beyond, to change, but the door leads within, to closed space. There is no way out.[35] What happens in there is the plot's trapped outcome and dead end, the image of inevitability. This imaginary unseen has a complex spatiality, built often in detail in the audience's mind. Messengers from within offer spectators a way of making

---

[31] Oliver Taplin, *Greek Tragedy in Action* (Oxford, 1978), 119.

[32] T. Hardy, preface to *The Dynasts*. He asks why these should not be repeated and replies: "the meditative world is . . . more quizzical . . . less able . . . to look through the insistent substance at the thing signified."

[33] Oliver Taplin, "Sophocles in His Theater," in *Sophocle*, ed. J. de Romilly, Entretiens Hardt 29 (Geneva, 1982), 157–69. He shows how in the *Oid. Tyr.* the *eisodoi* can indicate respectively roads from and to Thebes, and so express visually the "circuit" of Oidipous' life.

[34] H. Scolnikov, "Theater Space, Theatrical Space, and the Theatrical Space Without," in *The Theatrical Space*, ed. J. Redmond (Cambridge, 1987), 11–27, stresses that in performance the unseen theatrical space is as real as the visible (14). But her equation of "space without" as "conceived space" and "space within" as "perceived space" confuses the Greek situation, though it fits her examples from other traditions. She says that the *ekkuklēma* pushes the without into the within (16). But (a) in Greek terms these are reversible, and (b) it makes better Greek sense to *stress* the reverse. My use of "space within" corresponds therefore to her use of "space without."

[35] Taplin, "Sophocles," 158. When there *has* to be a way out (as sometimes happens later in New Comedy) a special explanation is put forward: see A. M. Dale, *Collected Papers* (Cambridge, 1969), 127–28, on Philoktetes' cave.

real space that does not exist, the interior geometry of a fictive house. An
eyewitness describes to those outside the attempt of Orestes and Pylades
to murder Helen inside the palace:

> They entered; came
> beside the chair of Helen
> whom Paris won.
> They sat down
> low, one this side, one that . . .
> cast suppliant hands about her knees.
>
> . . . .
> One led her forward
> and she followed . . .
> his colleague . . .
> closed them all . . .
> inside the halls.

(Eur., *Or.* 1409–48)

Analogously, the poet invites his audience to imagine there are wom-
en behind the costumes worn by those male actors. By the end of
three days, they had seen many female figures in the tragedies, whose
femaleness they had created in their own imaginations. To mask their male
selves, actors playing women may have worn long white sleeves under
their robes, corresponding to vase painters' portrayal of women with
white skin, without shading, in contrast to red male bodies whose volume was indicated by shading.[36] The two important interiors spectators
had to imagine for themselves, woman and house, were in Greek societies (as in others) bound closely together in male perceptions. Men expected not to know all of what lay within.[37] They imagined but did not
know. Conflict in the dramas between male and female, public and private, knowledge and imagination, is intricately related to the theater's
physical contrast between real and imagined, seen and unseen space.

The tragedian also invited the members of his audience to make vivid
for themselves the family's history, time past and now invisible except to
those gifted, like Kassandra, in seeing the unapparent. The unseen history of the immediate stage-moment parallels the unseen space of action.
Spectators construct both in their imagination, guided by hints from the
poet.

[36] Simon, *Theater*, 13; *DFA*, 202; A. Rumpf, "Classical and Post-Classical Greek Painting," *JHS* 77 (1947): 10–11.
[37] "It seems not fitting that a man should know all that passes within the house," [Ar-
ist.], *Oecon.* 3.1.

Unseen space, unshared time: they are significant not only in them-selves, but as image and parallel for the unseen thoughts and feelings which the actors' words convey. Unseen space, unseen feelings, comple-ment and contrast with sensibly perceived space, acts, language: they are echo chambers within which acts and words reverberate. But they lie within the spectators who create them in imagination.

From one point of view, it is the action that happens on the stage that is important to the audience. The act offstage is fleshed out in the audi-ence's imagination only by attention given to it onstage.[38] But from an-other point of view, the onstage actions are there to create invisible (more obsessing, more terrible) space and action in the audience's mind, just as tragedy's words are important partly because they create in the mind a picture of emotions surging within the speaker: emotions which are imagined to cause, and be expressed by, the language.

Words in relation to invisible emotion, onstage action in relation to unseen events, give the audience the occasion to construct an image of an unseen interior, fatally torn. Words, like the theater's visual paraphernalia, join the unseen to the apparent. Behind the *skēnē* is an imagined space which the theater conceals but continually refers to. The important tragic act will happen unseen and mostly *within*. We think of unseen acts as per-formed offstage. For the Athenians it was within-stage, inside something within the spectators' field of vision, but into which they could not see. They inferred what they could not see from what they could.

One more concealed interior: tragedy refers continually to the under-world. In later Greek theater, when the stage was high, ghosts, furies, and rivers rose from a trapdoor in its floor. In the fifth century there was probably a furrow under the acting area, through which the actor play-ing, say, the ghost of Dareios could rise when he was summoned ("not with an easy road out") from Hades.[39]

Tragic language gestures to the lower world all the time. Erinyes and the dead affect present action, rising to this world to do so. The audience expects such forces to rise from below. The dead are much with the fig-ures of tragedy—a motive force in many plays, not only plays of venge-ance, or arguments about some corpse. In real life, the spectators knew they trod ground that contained and concealed the dead. In the theater they saw human figures walking above a hidden unseen. Time and place that belong to the dead are alive in the tragic present, in tragic space. The

---

[38] So Taplin, *Action*, 160.

[39] Aiskh., *Persians* 630–90, 839; cf. *Prometheus* 1093. Even a fifth-century Prometheus could thus disappear downward. Many scholars have denied this trapdoor to fifth-century Athens, notably *TDA*, 35, 51, 65, 210. But others argue forcibly for it. Taplin, *Stagecraft*, 218, 274, 447–48, comes down on their side.

tragic theater is a threshold to the underworld, paradigm of a place in which the dead impinge on the living, the past on the present.[40]

Important events happen in, important forces issue from, any of three unseen interiors: house, underworld—"house" of Hades—and mind. The house, like the underworld, could function as an image of mind, and color Greek associations to what happens in it. So could any interior where human met divinity, any sacred enclosure.[41] Connections made in the Greek imagination among mind, temple, cave, grove, underworld—houses or homes of divinities—contributed to the contemporary individual's experience of unseen space and unseen self in a tragic performance.

THE STAGE FACADE: ILLUSION OF DEPTH

I

Channels connect seen and unseen spaces: the underground entrance, the two side entries. But the central barrier between seen and unseen is the *skēnē* front.

On this boundary the relation of illusion to reality is at its most intense. The audience knows that the *skēnē* is the factory of illusion where actors put on and exchange masks. In this hidden space the poet fabricates a potent alternative space, with internal spatial divisions (made in messenger speeches), with geometries of human relationships that spatial divisions represent. All this inside one lonely lump in the audience's field of vision. There is a doubleness in the way the audience members see the *skēnē*. The whole theatrical space, which they can see, contains another space which they cannot. The imaginary full space, the house, the image of bonded relationships on which human society depends, is concealed within the real, comparatively empty public space, the performing area. Yet it is also visible, at the center of the audience's sight.

All this makes it very different from the background facade in a proscenium arch theater, which is large and often partial. In Greek, the actors are "those from" as well as "those on the *skēnē*." Their figures emerge from an illusion-making enclosure. Anaxarkhos (the fourth-century Demokritean philosopher, who went to India with Alexander) compares

---

[40] Pickard-Cambridge, in *DTC*, 106–7, believes that the experience of the dead as a living force is intrinsic to tragic form. Cf. the Greek practice of exposing the bier outside the door of the house (*TDA*, 111). Tragedy, so concerned with the dead, happens where you place your real-life dead: outside the door.

[41] I argue and document these points in *In and Out of the Mind*.

ordinary existence to the painting on the *skēnē*. He means that ordinary things are illusory, are like impressions encountered in sleep, like the painted facade representing a theatrical house.[42]

The *skēnē*, then, is both the center and the margin of illusion. Its face is the boundary between seen and hidden, where these two dualities, seen and unseen, reality and illusion, touch. We might remember that the theater's own reality, established here in Dionysos' precinct, is illusion.

What did the Athenians do with this all-important wall? Can we reconstruct what the audience saw when it looked at the *skēnē*?

Not with certainty. There is enormous controversy about that wall. The evidence is mostly post–fifth century and capable of many interpretations. Any account of painting on the fifth-century *skēnē* front is speculative.[43] But the theater's visual appearance was part of contemporary emotional experience of tragedy. Not to take a view on scene painting would be to dodge the issue. Some evidence for it does exist. If we have ideas about the whole of tragedy, scene painting must take its place in these.

II

We might start with the word, *skēnographia*. It first appears in the fourth century, meaning painting on the *skēnē*.[44]

Later, however, in Latin as well as Greek, the word is often associated purely with architectural drawing, and seems sometimes almost to mean "drawing an architectural facade in linear perspective."[45] But nowhere can *scaenographia* be proved actually to mean "the use of linear perspective." It may have come to mean simply "drawing the facade of a building." But it might *seem* to mean "using linear perspective" because Vitruvius, when he *describes* the process of facade drawing, does so in terms of the perspective of ca. 20 B.C.E.[46] Some kind of perspective is

---

[42] See Sextus Empiricus, *Adversus mathematicos* 7.1.88.

[43] I discuss rival theories and possible use of this evidence more fully in an appendix to *In and Out of the Mind*.

[44] Anaxarkhos, and Arist., *Poet.* 1449A18–19 (deleted, along with so much, by Else, *Aristotle's Poetics*.

[45] *Scaenographia* is wrongly assumed by many scholars, e.g., Granger (Loeb ed. of Vitruvius) and E. Keuls, *Plato and Greek Painting* (Leiden, 1978), 63, to mean "use of linear perspective."

[46] The key passage (capable of different interpretations; see J. White, "Perspective in Ancient Drawing and Painting," *JHS* supp. 7 [1956]) is Vitruv., 1.2.2: *Scaenographia est frontis et laterum abscendentium adumbratio ad circinique centrum omnium linearium reponsus*. Whatever the technicalities of optics implied by Vitruvius' account (see M. F. Burnyeat, "All the World's a Stage-Painting" [forthcoming]), "facade-drawing" would be a wholly adequate *meaning* for the word. It can *refer* to several different things.

used by his day, and there are Roman paintings which seem to have found (perhaps by accident) the single viewpoint, core of Renaissance perspective.[47]

We should give the word's later history due weight, when we consider the *skēnē* of the stage to which it first referred. If *skēnographia* came later to mean "drawing a building's facade," it did so mainly because the stage was where you saw such facades drawn. The likelihood is that from the first, tragic scene painting consisted of flat panels, painted with architectural shapes—columns, pediment, roof—attached more or less permanently to the *skēnē* wall.[48] By the fourth century, vase painters often use an architectural frame, perhaps just two or four columns, as a tragic hallmark. Their scene represents a moment from tragic drama.[49]

Some tragedies, of course, were set away from civilization and its sign, a human building. The *skēnē* must then have stood for a cave—as in many satyr-plays—or a grove. Would the panels be changed for such tragedies? Some scholars suppose that Philoktetes' cave, for example, was marked by rocky outlines on the *skēnē* front, or by a screen in front of the *skēnē* door, painted with rocky shapes, which gave the cave two entrances.[50]

[47] See White, "Perspective," 61, 77–83; D. Haynes, *Greek Art and the Idea of Freedom* (London, 1984), 96–98. The word was used at Rome in Vitruvius' day by three different professional groups: stage painters, interior decorators, and architects making designs for buildings; see A.M.G. Little, *Roman Perspective Painting and the Ancient Stage* (Kennebunkport, Maine, 1971), 2.

[48] So most scholars, e.g., Simon, *Theater*, 22; refs. in A. L. Brown, "Three and Scene-Painting Sophocles," *PCPS* (1984): 6, 15 (n. 23). There is also the view (very unlikely, I think) put forward by Trendall and Webster, *IGD*, 9, that a theater had three sets: one (columns, pediment, etc.) for tragedy; one (rocks, cave, etc.) for satyr-plays; a third for comedy.

[49] See S. Gogos, "Bühnenarchitektur und antike Bühnenmalerie—zwei Rekonstruktionsversuche nach griechischen Vasen," *Jahreshefte des Österreichischen archaeologischen Institutes in Wien* 54 (1983): 59–70, with illustrations. A fourth-century vase painter seems often to be "thinking of" the stage building rather than the temple actually described by the text; *IGD*, 91 (III.3, 27 and 29), 46 (III.1, 10). Sometimes a modern interpreter finds doorway and porch "highly reminiscent of stage architecture," ibid., 52–54 (III.1, 17). The stage setting is often represented by columns, portico, pediment; e.g., ibid., 66 (III.2, 8). A vase's representation of a dramatic performance (signifier) often "melts" into the representation of the scenes which the drama represented (the doubly signified); see *DFA*, 179, 182.

[50] Simon, *Theater*, 21; cf. refs. in Brown, "Three," 12, 17, n. 52. Brown thinks it unlikely that there was scene painting in the fifth century which "could have formed an integral part of the plays" (13–14). He guesses the *skēnē* was painted "if only with a coat of whitewash to suggest marble (not that whitewashing can be denoted by *graphein*)" (9). But we are dealing not with "decoration" (8) of the stage but the visual foundation for the audience's whole imaginative grasp of a tragedy. Bieber too (*History*, 108) ignores the fact that how a "necessary theater" *looks* is integral to the audience's emotional experience of the play. She says "an effective framing of the scene of the performance . . . did not take place before the last part of the fifth century." But she does not consider the people and their con-

I doubt even this. I suspect that the architectural background stayed on the *skēnē* through all tragedies, even the wildest. Tragedy uses the language of house persistently, both to signify the structures and values on which human relationships depend, and as an image for the self. It both needs and destroys those structures. Its most apt and characteristic backing is the visual image of a house. Vase painters reflect this in their metonymic porticos or frames. After the fifth century, the close relationship between house facade and tragic background becomes reified in stone. By the third century B.C.E., the theater's facade has real columns, a real pediment. The *skēnē* has become a huge house with a forebuilding.[51] What the fifth century marked in two dimensions, the Hellenistic theater recreates in three.

III

What about the painterly context, out of which fifth-century scene painting begins? The second quarter of this century, the years of the earliest extant tragedies, sees a revolution in painting. Until now, the leading two-dimensional visual art has been vase painting. Now mural painting overtakes it.

Vase painters cannot compete in excitement with the new techniques developed on larger, flat surfaces, but they can reflect them. Randomly, distortedly, they do try—luckily for us, since it is mainly from vase painting, and the descriptions of such later writers as Pausanias, that art historians guess at the vanished art of fifth-century painting, developed especially by Mikon and Polygnotos.[52] Mikon is connected with the wall paintings of ca. 473 B.C.E., in the sanctuary of Theseus, north of the *agora*.[53] Polygnotos is associated at several points with Sophokles, and seems to have painted scenes from his work in a central Athenian public building.[54]

The revolution which begins around the beginning of the century, pushed forward by the mural painting of the century's second quarter, is the portrayal of the third dimension.

---

text. *Who* did or did not find their own "framings" "effective"? She does not question emotional, esthetic, or sociological bases on which existing "frames" first were, and then failed to be, effective to changing audiences in the sequence of harrowing years that lies behind those words "the late fifth century." The question—What shifts in ways of seeing, in sensibility, led Athenians to change their framing of dramatic scenes in this particular way?—must be answered at many interdependent levels.

[51] Bieber, *History*, 110f.

[52] J. Barron, "New Light on Old Walls: The Murals of the Theseion," *JHS* 92 (1972): 20–45, pioneered this approach to the relationship between vase painting and the mural painters (23–25).

[53] See Paus., 1.17.3; M. Robertson, *Greek Painting* (London, 1978), 122–23.

[54] See *IGD*, 4, 66, 69.

Vase painters had been foreshortening the human figure from at least 510 B.C.E. on.[55] But now Polygnotos and Mikon have established the possibility of an "enclave in space." Vase painting reflects this. We see on contemporary vases the real beginning of an "idea of pictorial space." Painters, while they decorate their surfaces, are beginning consciously to create "a window opening on a feigned world." They indicate depth, in space as well as in bodies that fill space.[56] That feigned world moves away from the contact the eye makes with its two-dimensional surface.

Various other related techniques for evoking the third dimension appear in the first half, especially the second quarter, of the century: the use of color contrast (to suggest light and shade); shading, a light hatching at first on clothes and objects, then on living bodies.[57] By Plato's time the word *skiagraphia*, "painting with shadow," is used for the representation of illusory volume. It may refer loosely to chiaroscuro.[58] Plato often uses it as an image (especially in the *Republic* with its huge-scale imagistic framework of light and shadow), when speaking of the contrast between reality and illusion. *Skiagraphia* is his metaphor for the deceptive world of things we should not trust, the world perceived by our senses.[59] *Skiagraphia*, like *goēteia* (enchantment), exploits the weakness of our nature; it allures and cheats us.[60]

The encyclopedists of later times equated *skiagraphia* with *skēnographia*. This cannot be true of the classical period. Yet their error points to the

[55] G. Richter, *Perspective in Greek and Roman Art* (London, 1970), 22–23. How consciously this is done is shown in words on a vase of this period, *egrapsen Euthimides ho Poliou hōs oudepote Euphronios*. The *hōs* must refer to the foreshortening (White, "Perspective," 24 with n. 1). The introduction of red figure enabled artists to "obey the emotional urge towards foreshortening the human figure"; White, "Perspective," 23. There were several phases of "perspective." The second, inaugurated ca. 460 B.C.E., was related both to Polygnotan painting, and to the theater (see B. Schweitzer, *Vom Sinn der Perspective* [Tübingen, 1953], 14–17).

[56] Robertson, *Painting*, 164, 122–23. He notes how Paus., 10. 25–31, describes a work by Polygnotos at Delphi. Pausanias moves about the picture, uses language (like "above these," "higher up again," "further in") which could not be used of archaic painting. See also Barron, "New Light," 24.

[57] Rumpf, "Classical," 10–13. Shading evolves over the first half of the fifth century.

[58] Robertson, *Painting*, 137. Plato uses *skiagraphia* and related words often. Philostratos' *Life of Apollonios of Tyana* (2.22) says that *zōgraphia* is a painting even with no color, if created only of *skia* (shadow) and *phōs* (light), for with these you can see resemblance, *eidos* (form), *nous* (intelligence), bravery. Those who look at paintings need the mimetic faculty: *skiagraphia* plays upon this faculty within the beholder.

[59] Keuls, *Plato*, 62, is surely right that Plato does not attack the painter's technique in itself. He uses it as an image for what he is attacking.

[60] *Rep.* 602d. We have perceptions, says Sokrates, which we cannot trust. Oh, says his interlocuter (mistaking, thereby exemplifying, Sokrates' point), "you mean distance and things painted with shade" (*Rep.* 523b). False reputation is drawn round me as a *prothuron*, "a *skiagraphia* of virtue," ibid., 365c. Illusory pleasure is "shadow-painted," *Rep.* 583b.

core idea which the two share: illusory representation, on a flat surface, of spatial depth, either in living bodies (*skiagraphia*) or architectural shapes (*skēnographia*).[61]

Third-dimensional painting develops far more quickly through the century with the human figure than with architecture.[62] But foreshortening of linear objects does begin at this period too. By 470, even 480, we find a vase painter and a provincial mural painter trying to foreshorten couches. They must be affected by the more sophisticated attempts of Athenian mural painters, like Polygnotos and Mikon.[63] By the second half of the century vase painters are clearly foreshortening architecture, showing, for instance, a temple in three-quarter view (see plate 17).[64] Vase painters lag behind wall painters. They assimilate and copy the wall painters' techniques.[65] By 460 B.C.E., the more innovative mural painters could well have faced the possibility of painting a building frontally, in crude recession. We do not know that they did so at this early date. But the idea would be consistent with their overall interest, evident from 475 B.C.E., in spatial depth, and with the fact that perspectival architectural drawing is consistently linked with the stage, from the later fifth century on.

Moreover, painting in these years is conscious of a new way of being looked at. It invites spectators to play with the way they see: to go into and out of imagined space. In an Athenian krater of the second quarter of the century, found at Orvieto, several figures stand in a complex spatial relationship. The eye takes the higher figures to be "farther in" to the picture's depth. But the "farthest in" figure in fact holds a spear which protrudes in front of the scene's decorated frame, while figures "in front" of that one hold spears which disappear behind the same frame. This is not clumsiness on the painter's part. He is in control of his medium. It is a visual paradox. The vase painter reflects the deliberate am-

---

[61] Keuls, *Plato*, 74, discusses the encyclopedists' equation of the two, en route to her unconvincing suggestion (see M. Robertson's review of Keuls, *CR* 29 [1979]: 317) that *skiagraphia* referred to the use of contrasting colors. She assumes that *skēnographia* means the use of perspective (cf. above nn. 47–49).

[62] White, "Perspective," 23–25, Richter, *Perspective*, 26f., cf. n. 56. The name-vase of the Niobid Painter (below, n. 66) is ca. 460, like the *Oresteia*; and probably the *skēnē* (n. 29).

[63] See Richter, *Perspective*, fig. 10 (ca. 470) and the preliminary sketch for the north panel of the Diver's Tomb at Paestum, M. Napoli, *La Tomba del tuffatore* (Bari, 1970), fig. 91: provincial work ca. 480. The artist's greater Athenian contemporaries like Mikon and Polygnotos "may have been more subtle," but "cannot have been altogether different in kind," Barron, "New Light," 45. Both the Paestum tomb and the vase painting ca. 470 show cavities in rudimentary recession. White, "Perspective," 24–27, stresses the "oblique construction" and "the very softest recession" of rectangular objects in vases from the second quarter of the century.

[64] Richter, *Perspective*, fig. 159; cf. White, "Perspective," 27.

[65] Robertson, *Painting*, 122–23.

biguity with which the more avant-garde mural painters play with ways of seeing. Playing with the painting's relation to its form, they offer their spectator two ways of approaching their feigned world (see plate 18).[66]

As tragedy gets into its stride, painting develops its portrayal of both architecture and persons in the third dimension. At the moment that tragedy (probably) acquires its *skēnē*, painting finds ways of opening a window on a world that moves away from the watching eye into illusory space. In this quarter of a century, tragedians and painters satisfy a common desire: to portray human figures with feigned depth, set ambiguously, in complex spatial and emotional relationships, within a large-scale frame. Each makes an "appeal to the invisible," within the possibilities of its own technique.[67]

They develop ways of opening that window on feigned worlds not only side by side but perhaps interdependently. Polygnotos has those points of contact with Sophokles. And it is likely that when the *skēnē* was incorporated into the stage—probably 460 B.C.E.—its introducers looked around for an apt way to present it, and went naturally to the experts who were specializing in creating illusion on large flat vertical surfaces, the mural painters. The stage became the most public place to see the new technique, the painting of architecture in recession.

If we saw it now ourselves, we would find it clumsy and simple, perhaps: just arbitrarily foreshortened architectural forms. But the idea was startling in itself. And this account helps to explain how *skēnographia* later became associated with perspective when perspective did arrive.[68] Very simple in essence, the *skēnē* wall could have looked something like figure 1, with painted columns and a painted underceiling over the real stage door.[69]

[66] So Robertson, *Painting*, 124, 128–29. This, plate 18, is the name-vase of the Niobid Painter, discussed in Schweitzer, *Perspective*, 13, Barron, "New Light," 23–25. Both comment on the painter's use of space. All authorities have seen in the vase, since it was discovered, the influence and inspiration of mural painters, especially Polygnotos (Barron, "New Light," 44–45). Somewhat similar visual paradoxes, in a comparable era, are visual jokes of Renaissance painters playing with *their* new ways of seeing, new techniques of relating pictorial space to frame, new relations to the third dimension (see M. Baxandall, *Painting and Experience in Fifteenth-century Italy* [Oxford, 1974], 89–90, 102); White, "Perspective," 32, 38, 40, 42, also draws parallels between the fifth-century development of pictorial space and that of Renaissance Italy.

[67] Cf. Dale, *Collected Papers*, 124–26, discussing invisible events (whirlwinds strike a house, *Herk. Fur.* 905; cf. *Bakkh.* 591) and layouts of an imagined interior.

[68] The stage facade probably directed the development of foreshortening in architectural drawing. Since architectural painting was seen most often, and most publicly, in the theater, this might help to explain the absence of the "single station" in Greek attempts at perspective (cf. Richter, *Perspective*, 61; Robertson, *Painting*, 164). The theater would offer painting a platform in which new techniques got the widest publicity.

[69] Gogos, "Bühnenarchitektur," 77, apparently thinks columns would be painted on and

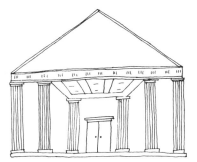

FIGURE 1. Rough sketch of possible *skēnographia* for fifth-century tragedy.

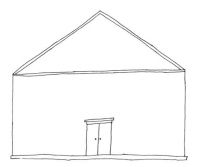

FIGURE 2. Rough sketch of *skēnē* wall with real door.

But all that actually need have been there is what we see in figure 2.

We do not and cannot know that wall painters responded so ambitiously to the new possibilities of the tragic stage as soon as 460 (though we know they did by the last quarter of the century). However, if we transfer the visual ambiguity of the Orvieto krater (see plate 18) to the contemporary stage, this vase becomes an accurate emblem for the play between objectivity and subjectivity which a tragedy incites in its audience. The audience shares the theater and the experience with the performers, and yet is distanced from them. They can "go into" that feigned world, enticed in by the structure they see—which recedes from them into the unseen—or draw back from it. They can be objective and feel pity. They can be subjective and feel fear. The relationship is encapsu-

_____

in front of the real door. They would seem to be left hanging when the door opened. He assumes only two side doors. But cf. below, n. 71.

lated in Aristotle's statement that tragedy works by creating pity and fear in its audience (*Poetics* 1449b27). You simultaneously enter and draw back from the tragic world. There is a doubleness in your relationship to it and its frame. In one sense, tragedy's "frame" is the theater itself. But its emblem is the *skēnē* front with its revolutionary portrayal of a three-dimensional facade on a two-dimensional wall.

THE TRAGIC DOOR: DIALECTICS OF INSIDE AND OUTSIDE

I

When Athenian theater began using the *skēnē*, Western tragedy acquired an inner chamber, a place of potent concealment; and a vital passageway to that interior, the channel which makes and unmakes the relationship between seen and unseen. The *skēnē* door becomes in Racine the supreme "objet tragique."[70]

In the fifth century, there was probably only one real door in the *skēnē* (see plate 19).[71] At some point during the century, painters perhaps painted other, illusory doors in the facade. From the sixth century on, doors are a favorite motif in Greek art anyway.[72] The fourth century added at least one more real door to the *skēnē* wall.[73] But the tragedies we have need only a single central door.[74] What was its significance? Is it a potent tragic object for Greek tragedy too?

I think it is. I think it becomes so the moment it is used. It makes the genre's supreme doubleness apparent. A Greek tragic plot is articulated through its exits and entrances, through the *eisodoi*, and through that

[70] Roland Barthes, *Sur Racine* (Paris, 1963), 9–11, suggests there are three "tragic loci": chamber, antechamber, and scene. His discussion is very suggestive and helpful if one also remembers the differences in culture and stage between Racine and fifth-century Greek tragedy, above all the relation of "house" to its environment. Barthes' Racinian geography derives from a potent image of Greece, important in Racine's "thoughtworld," with little relation to that of Greek tragedies themselves. In each epoch of tragedy, particular relations (spatial, economic, emotional) between house and landscape in drama interact with the way the audience experiences and understands such relations in real life. Cf. below, n. 89.

[71] This is controversial. One door is assumed by, e.g., Simon, *Theater*, 24–25 (with n. 86); Dale, *Collected Papers*, 120, 268. Taplin, *Stagecraft*, 439–40, summarizes the single "practicable door" controversy, rejecting (convincingly) two doors for the fifth-century stage.

[72] See Gogos, "Bühnenarchitektur," 73; Simon, *Theater*, 6–7 (who assumes they were used in the painted *skēnē*).

[73] See fourth-century and later *skēnai* in vase-paintings, discussed by Gogos, "Bühnenarchitektur," 70, with illustrations. Above all plate 19, the Würzburg fragment. See sundry reconstructions: Bieber, *History*, 69, fig. 226; Simon, *Theater*, fig. 10; Gogos, 74–79, 83, fig. 11.

[74] Taplin, *Stagecraft*, 440.

door.[75] But the special thing about an entry through this door is that it is simultaneously an exit, from the imaginary filled space of the *skēnē*. When a messenger reports Jokasta's suicide and Oidipous' self-blinding, he does so after observing Jokasta coming in. His speech is full of interior spatiality. Jokasta

> went at once *to* her wedding bed,
> shut the *doors* when she *entered* it . . .
> Oidipous rushed *in* . . .
> he darted *up and down*. . . .
> Some daemonic *guide* . . .
> seemed to show him the way . . .
> he drove *in against* the double doors,
> wrenched them *from* their sockets. . . .
> Then we saw. . . .
>
> (*Oid. Tyr.* 1237–64, emphasis added)

When the messenger enters the stage, he exits from this chamber of horror. The messenger, recounting Orestes' attempt to murder Helen, likewise describes the obverse of the audience's experience. The audience saw Orestes and Pylades go *out* through the door. The messenger saw them come murderously *in*.

In such speeches, the audience is offered a vivid sense of the real, complicated space from which characters emerge: space with important internal boundaries, like the doors which Oidipous smashes in, doors which should have kept him out long ago. Entry is exit from the place whose reality is illusion, and vice versa. This is not necessarily true of a proscenium arch theater, or in a tradition that puts a three-walled interior, a room, onstage.

The symbolic possibilities of that door were explored by dramatists writing for a society which respected the ambiguity and doubleness of a door's deity. Appropriately to Hermes, Strophalos, Epitermios, Prothuraios, tragedy happens in a *prothuron*, a space before a door. The characteristic tragic setting is some kind of boundary, usually a gate or door: "outside the courtyard gates" (Soph., *Ant.* 18). Kassandra calls on Apollo Agyieus, lord of roads, when she encounters the doors to the house of Atreus (Aiskh., *Ag.* 1080–81). She entered from the *eisodos*, the road from Troy. Now she faces a gate into a cul-de-sac, where her life will end: a door into the dark. In another play, when Apollo identifies to

75 Taplin, *Action*, 20. The primary focus of Taplin, *Stagecraft*, was on entry and exit. Taplin, "Sophocles," further shows how a dramatist could use *eisodoi* to direct the drama's emotional resonance.

Kreousa, whom he raped and abandoned long ago, their grown-up son, Kreousa clings to his temple gates in gratitude:

> I hated these doors,
> and the god's oracle, before.
> They are lovely now.
> Blissfully, I hang even from the door-ring
> with my hands: I salute the gates.
>
> (Eur., *Ion* 1611–13)

She directs attention to the door of the god's temple at Delphi, outside which the tragedy has been played. Sometimes the setting is on a wilder margin: "We have come to the furthest plain of the world . . . ": so begins the play set in a place visited by the personified world-margin himself, Ocean (Aiskh., *Prom.* 1, 268). Marginality, Hermes' characteristic, is characteristic also of most tragic settings. They are poised on a threshold or boundary. And stage action often focuses on the door.[76]

II

Vase paintings of dramatic scenes (they begin in the fifth century, though we have many more from the fourth) often characterize tragic stage building by the *prothuron*, a small kiosk, four columns and a pediment, that looks like a porch. This appears so often that earlier scholars believed that the fifth-century stage building had a real projecting *prothuron* around the stage door.[77] But the material once used to support this idea now testifies to the vase painters' sense of tragedy's *prothuron* quality. Their *prothuron* is a metonym for the *skēnē*. It represents the stage. It expresses, perhaps, the painters' sense that tragedy happens in a "space before a door," the core idea in the word *prothuron*.[78]

Presumably the vase painters are also excited by the ambiguity of the stage space and stage painting, architecture in recession. Their growing interest in foreshortened architecture seems to be linked to their increasing interest in portraying dramatic scenes. The door in that facade was the one real thing. It moved in a different plane. Presumably it went inward, away from the watching eye, for Greek doors mostly opened inward.[79] The door made actual the promise of foreshortening in the

---

[76] See Taplin, *Action*, 33–35, 46–47, 105, 136.

[77] Pickard-Cambridge, in *TDA*, 75–90, reviews evidence for a fifth-century projecting *prothuron* and disposes of the idea.

[78] *Prothuron* in Homer means the doorway or space before it; in the fifth century it may also be a recess in a wall, but generally just the space before the door (e.g., Pind., *Pyth.* 3.78). Contexts may suggest it means a built "porch," but these are often ambiguous, e.g., Thuk. 2.67.

[79] See Dale, *Collected Papers*, 122 (with n. 1), 264; Gogos, "Bühnenarchitektur," 73, 77.

painted building. Through it you could indeed see some partial distance
into the unseen.

There was an intense relationship, then, between painting and the
stage, expressed in the fifth-century history of architectural foreshortening. In the development of this relationship, doors play a crucial role.[80]
Greek doors are mostly painted double, like the double doors Oidipous
smashes down. When Greek painters want to show an open door, up to
the second quarter of the fifth century, they paint one leaf closed, the
other absent. About 440 B.C.E., they try to show the opened leaf, but in
profile. We see the door knob and hinge sideways, and the interior
within. Then finally, from about 430 onward, they paint one or both
leaves open and receding inwards, foreshortened. Often there is a figure
within, half-hidden behind the opened door. This is how open doors are
done on vases thereafter, especially in scenes from the stage, most fa-
mously in the Würzburg fragment (plate 19; see also plate 20).[81]

Painters from ca. 450 may be affected, as I have argued, by the buildings they see so publicly painted in recession on the tragic *skēnē*. Tragic
scene painting, focused on that vital real door, stimulates them to show
the door itself receding, and the interior it really half-reveals.[82] But they
also react, I think, to qualities of the tragic texts themselves. They find
the half-open door a right image for tragedy, its half-hiddenness, its doubleness.

Technically, vase painters lag behind contemporary mural painters
such as Polygnotos who painted scenes from Sophokles.[83] Was it he who
first portrayed tragedy's ambiguous door and explored, with his unique,
innovative technical power, the painterly implications of a real door
opening in an illusory facade?

Whoever began it, surviving vase paintings of the tragic scene which
choose a half-open door, with perhaps a figure half-hidden behind, to

[80] Richter, *Perspective*, 27, 35.

[81] Above, notes 72 and 73. A door's three phases: (a) Richter, *Perspective*, fig. 117, a kylix
ca. 475–450 (this form of representation goes back to the sixth century; Gogos, "Bühnenarchitektur," 72, with n. 26); (b) Richter, fig. 156, a pyxis ca. 440; (c) plate 20, Richter, fig.
158, a pyxis ca. 425, showing a figure behind the door (cf. Gogos, 73 with n. 25, fig. 1).
This is a fifth-century epinetron, 430–420 B.C.E., showing Alkestis' wedding (Eur., *Alk.* is
438 B.C.E.). Here both doors are half-open, receding inward. Phase (c) is typical of open
doors thereafter, esp. in scenes from the stage (Gogos, 77), e.g., *IGD*, III.3, 28 (Artemis'
temple in *Iph. Taur.* with open doors, vase ca. 370–360); III.3, 31 (a crude version of the
Würzburg scenario: Iphigeneia is not in stage costume here, but see Gogos, 77, with fig. 4).
Open doors in comedy, *IGD*, IV.16, 18. Cf. drawings from fourth-century vases in *TDA*,
84–98, figs. 12, 14, 18, 19, 29.

[82] Gogos, "Bühnenarchitektur," 73, takes the representation of doors as an early indication of fifth-century stage painting's influence on vase painting, though he ignores the mediating effect of mural painting.

[83] *IGD*, 4, 69 (Thamyras); 66 (Nausikaa).

represent a tragedy, are a perfect emblem of tragic *feeling*. They express the tension between secrecy and revelation, the hidden and the manifest, which variously characterizes tragic texts.[84] That door half-displays what is lying in wait, both in space (within the *skēnē*) and in time, in the still-to-be-unfolded play. Such paintings bring out the imaginative significance, in tragedy, of the relation between inside and outside.

III

A door is a pragmatically universal image of ambiguous temptation, uncertain invitation, and hesitation. The half-open tragic door crystallizes the ambiguities that "door" in itself evokes, at least in Western tradition.[85] These paintings point to the guessing relationship between what an audience can see of a structure in a tragedy, and what they know or fantasize may lie behind it. The stage is the "place where the invisible can appear." But, importantly, "we can never see all of the invisible."[86] A fifth-century audience knew the importance of this limitation far more profoundly than do theatergoers of our day. We bring to the theater other experiences, those of television and cinema, whose relations to the invisible and illusion are quite different.

The half-open door reminds us that we can never see all, not just of the *skēnē* and the dramatic situation, but of the human being. Tragedy uses the vocabulary of house and door to demarcate self from other. The stranger is the one at the door, *thuraios*. A human being has a door to the interior, to the soul. The mouth is traditionally a fenced door. The background illusory house is important not just in itself, but as a structure parallel to the individual self. The *skēnē*, and what it stands for, is an image of the unseen interior of a human being. The audience imagines thoughts and feelings, and attributes these (in the particular way members of their society are used to attributing feelings to other people) to the dramatic character. The words that character speaks are imagined to express, and also often to conceal, these illusory, hidden feelings.

---

[84] Tension between secrecy and revelation: e.g. (in different ways), Aiskh., *Ag.* 615–16, 1372–76; Soph., *Phil.* 55, 908–15; Eur., *Hipp.* 232, 250, 279, 297, 362–68, 498, 520, 593, 648, 1060, 1091, 1308, 1312. See the discussion in Froma Zeitlin, "The Power of Aphrodite: Eros and the Boundaries of the Self in the *Hippolytus*," in *Directions in Euripidean Criticism*, ed. Peter Burian (Durham, N.C., 1985), 52–111, 189–208. Between seen and unseen, e.g., Eur., *Ion* 778–81, 190–229, 233, 249–50, 272, 1321–22; see Dale, *Collected Papers*, 119–29, and the remarks of Zeitlin in her first essay in this volume.

[85] The door "is a . . . cosmos of the half-open . . . origin of a daydream that accumulates desires and temptations . . . to open up the ultimate depths of being and . . . to conquer all reticent beings." It offers "images of hesitation, temptation, desire." A poet "knows that there are two 'beings' in a door, that a door awakens in us a two way dream." So Gaston Bachelard, *The Poetics of Space*, tr. M. Jolas (Boston, 1969), 222–24. Such associations certainly fit the door's many roles in Greek imagination.

[86] Brook, *Empty Space*, 47, 49.

The dramatist "makes space speak" by using the symbolic language of stage space to back up the words. Expression in space interacts with linguistic expression.[87] The vase painters depict a tragic scene without words, but often feature not only the half-open door, but also a figure behind it: a hieroglyphic comment on tragedy's full representation of human beings. The open mouth or door, through which speech comes, is the only real thing in the mask. Yet the mouth in a sense is only half-open: the person is half-concealed behind the words that come out of it. *Skēnē* matches mask. Symbolism of the one underlines the qualities of the other. Both speak to the metonymic quality of speech itself.

So the doubleness of the *skēnē*, incarnate in its door, is an apt foil to the ambiguities with which human figures appear; ambiguities of mind, feeling, relationship, word. The audience's double awareness of the foreshortened scene painting matches the doubleness—compounded of fluctuating objective and subjective response—in its relation with the stage figures. The visual "dialectic of inside and outside,"[88] expressed in the theater's exits and entrances, reflects a specific dialectic of inside and outside with which tragedy pictures the human interior in relation to the nonhuman world outside. The spatial language of this theater says something about its society's understanding of consciousness. The proscenium arch, and theatrical explorations of interior space, developed over centuries in which understanding was increasingly located within the human self. While Western tragedy interiorized its tragic sites, Western thought looked increasingly within the mind, to explain the source of feeling and action[89]—which Greeks of the fifth century at least half attributed to the outside world.[90]

IV

Tragedy's site is the margin, and dramatists often treat the physical space which represents it in a way modern critics call "elastic" and ambiguous. The acting space is seen in several ways at once. "Space as well as time had a certain elasticity." The setting seems to waver sometimes: be-

---

[87] See Artaud, "Cruelty," 53, 63.

[88] "Often it is from the very fact of concentration in the most restricted . . . space that the dialectics of inside and outside draws its strength," Bachelard, *Poetics*, 229. See C. R. Lyons, "Character and Theatrical Space," 36, in Redmond, *Theatrical Space*, whose analysis of the function of space in later tragedy depends on an interaction of character and scene.

[89] "In an age and climate which encourage private life between four walls, our theaters look for most of their drama in an enclosed box with the fourth wall missing. The stage itself is shaped like that," Dale, *Collected Papers*, 259. Taplin, *Stagecraft*, 443, 454, 456 suggests that some pre-*skēnē* plays had an interior setting, e.g., inside a council chamber (*Pers.*), or Akhilleus' tent (*Myrmidons*). But (454 n. 2) even then the indoor/outdoor distinction would be fluid. Such a setting would be quite different in aim and effect from the interiority of scenes like *Othello*, v.2.

[90] I document this point throughout *In and Out of the Mind*.

tween, for instance, the Akropolis and the nearby Areopagos.[91] One piece of equipment gave that space before the door a special ambiguity. It must have been in use by the time of the *Oresteia*, which exploits it and probably arrived along with the *skēnē*. This was the *ekkuklēma*, the "rolled-out thing": a probably wheeled low platform, rolled out from the suddenly opened *skēnē* door, usually at the end of the play. It carries outside the result of the tragic act "within."[92] Orestes standing over the bodies he has just killed, saying "See!" It brings to view the result of events within the *skēnē*. Indoors now comes out. Usually, as the scene goes on, "the indoor-outdoor distinction tends to be neglected."[93]

Classicists are used to this idea and forget how very strange it is, what bewildering violence the *ekkuklēma* does to the distinctions on which the play rested till now. At the start of an *ekkuklēma* scene, the dramatist suddenly removes the boundary in the spatial dialectics which framed the play's conceptual, emotional tensions. The *ekkuklēma* incarnates the spatial ambiguity—and its violence—of the fifth-century tragic stage.[94]

[91] Dale, *Collected Papers*, 120 (see below n. 94).

[92] Conventional uncritical views of the *ekkuklēma*, e.g., Webster, *Production*, 17, 173; Bieber, *History*, 73. But its fifth-century existence has been challenged. Taplin, *Stagecraft*, 437f. stresses how unreliable are the later testimonials for the fifth-century stage which supply most of our evidence for the fifth-century *ekkuklēma*. The only direct indication of its fifth-century use comes from Aristophanes' verb *ekkuklein* (*Akharn.* 407f., *Thesm.* 95f.). Pickard-Cambridge, in *TDA*, 100–103, 118 argued against a fifth-century use. He cites *eskuklein* used in an apparently nontechnical sense; *Wasps*, 1474–75. But this line is *funnier* if we assume a fifth-century *ekkuklēma*. "Some *daimōn* has rolled [in a tragical manner] into the house." The basic issue (focused by M. Lefkowitz, "Aristophanes and Other Historians of the Fifth-century Theater," *Hermes* 112 [1984]: 143–53), is: can we accept a hypothesis based (a) on interpretation of Aristophanes, though also (b) on interpreting the dramatics of the extant tragedies (Taplin's project in *Stagecraft*), plus (c) the muddled, unreliable post-fifth century comments, often derived purely from the texts? My answer would start from what we do know about Aristophanes: that he was very *funny*. Interpretation which takes what is funny as its first criterion is the best we can do. Even Pickard-Cambridge, in *TDA*, *Theater* 115, concedes there must have been *some* "absurd effect" on which Aristophanes' use of *ekkuklein* and *eskuklein* turned. Dale, *Collected Papers*, 124, shows that "opponents of the *ekkuklēma* ruthlessly sacrifice" jokes. Taplin, *Stagecraft* 442–43, accepts Aristophanes as evidence for the *ekkuklēma* but only after 425 B.C.E. The evidence is inconclusive. Even opponents of the *ekkuklēma* "cannot prove that mechanical devices were not used in fifth-century theater" (Lefkowitz, "Aristophanes," 153). Taplin, *Stagecraft* 442, concedes "we do not have sound evidence" of its use—but he adds "except for the revelation of interior scenes." This, coupled with the principle of reading Aristophanes in as funny a way as possible, is the clinching argument, I think.

[93] Taplin, *Action*, 12; see *Stagecraft*, 442–43. If one doubts that *ekkuklēma* and *mēchanē* were used in fifth-century drama, I can still say that the fourth century expresses in its theater apparatus the dialectics of inside and outside which were actually created in fifth-century drama: that the dialectics belong to the tragedies themselves, but were not concretely articulated until the fourth century. My argument, as a whole, does not depend on accepting a fifth-century *ekkuklēma* (though in fact I do).

[94] Dale, *Collected Papers*, 125, argues that the "spatial ambiguity of the *ekkuklēma*-produced interior" illustrates that "fluidity of stage scene which is so alien to our conven-

Space that was *prothuron*, before the door, now displays that which stood behind, within.

An *ekkuklēma* lays bare contradictions in the relationship between illusion and reality, inside and outside, set up by the *skēnē*. The door kept the interior away from the audience. Suddenly through this door appears the interior the audience could not see. Yet it is in itself, of course, another very obvious illusion. If we transfer the ambiguities of the *ekkuklēma* to the entity for which, I think, the *skēnē* also stands: the human self, we find the *ekkuklēma* corresponds to the ways—the rhetoric, images, music, lies—with which a character presents her illusory interior to the audience. The *ekkuklēma* makes visible the "unapparent."[95] By the verbal expression of emotion, a dramatist invites the audience likewise to look through: through the word's "insistent substance," in Hardy's phrase, and thereby contemplate the "thing signified," the self.

There are not many true arguments with self in Greek tragedy. Many soliloquies are in fact a series of apostrophes: to a series of gods, to Death, to a landscape or country, to the light, to the lower gods. Mostly the audience sees one character in interaction with others. When the audience first sees Iphigeneia, she is in a foreign land, priestess of the Taurians' Artemis cult which demands human sacrifice. They see her first in lyric interaction with the chorus, captive Greek women like her, then in dramatic interaction with a Taurian herdsman, who describes newly arrived Greek strangers. Iphigeneia is saddened by a dream which seems to say her brother is dead. She behaves as a priestess of Artemis should and orders the Taurian to bring these strangers to her, since the temple has long missed Greek blood (Eur., *Iph. Taur.* 289). But when he has gone, she addresses her own heart:

> Oh poor heart! Before
> you were always gentle to strangers,
> full of pity, dealing out full measure of your tears—
> when it was Greek men who came to your hands—
> to blood of your own race. But now
> I have grown savage,

---

tions" (cf. Taplin, *Stagecraft*, 454 n. 2). She comments (121), that a text often vacillates "with a curious ambiguity between the imagined scene and the actual mechanism visibly used to present it." In her view, spatial and verbal ambiguities interact. A further insight is that of Taplin, "Sophocles," 157, who wants the "stage map" to be more precisely designated. Taplin's stage is "a place where three roads meet" (he is discussing *Oid. Tyr.*), i.e., the two *eisodoi* and the doorway to and from the *skēnē*. He compares this spatial meeting to the play's confrontation between present, past, and future *time*. I think the stage a more complex crossroads still. Routes to and from it include also the passage from the underworld (trapdoor), the sky (*mēkhanē*), and the route of the audience's gaze, the frontward path: their emotional identification with the actors is important too.

95 See above, n. 32.

because of the dreams in which I thought
Orestes is dead. You strangers—whoever you may be—
will find me ill-disposed to you.

(*Iph. Taur.* 344–49)

We half-see the inner struggles she has had, these years, between her role as Artemis' priestess and her Greek sympathies. But the dream has changed her. She feels differently toward these Greeks. The soliloquy goes on. She remembers her own sacrifice at Aulis and its terror. She addresses the supposedly dead Orestes. And her feelings change again. She abuses Artemis who keeps murderers out of her shrine, "yet herself enjoys human sacrifice" (*Iph. Taur.* 384). She changes her view of this goddess by whom she is defined:

It is not possible that Leto, Zeus' wife,
gave birth to such stupidity.

(*Iph. Taur.* 385–86)

Then she ends by deciding that the Taurians misread their goddess (*Iph. Taur.* 390–91).

Euripides suddenly displays to the audience Iphigeneia's inner feelings. Before and after this speech, the audience sees her externally, as she interacts with Taurian attendants in her priestess role. But this speech is an emotional *ekkuklēma*. It gives the audience a glimpse behind that role, a glimpse which the Taurians cannot have. The *ekkuklēma* is the visual analogue of words by which a character comes "out," yet that are themselves the vehicle of illusion, since there is no character there inside, only an actor.

We see the *ekkuklēma*'s symbolic power fully in relation to the complementary equipment, the *mēkhanē*, which swung actors down onto the stage from above,[96] sometimes representing human heroes on winged car or steed, but also, often, representing gods. The divine epiphany on

---

[96] Illustrated in *IGD*, III.1, 17, III.3, 34: two South Italian vases of the later fifth century illustrating Aiskh., *Carians*, Eur., *Med.* The standard view of *mēkhanē* (based on *TDA*, 127–28): e.g., Webster, *Production*, 11f.; Bieber, *History*, 76; Simon, *Theater*, 6; *IGD*, 8, who cite vase painting from the late fifth-century onward. Taplin, *Stagecraft*, 444–47, discusses its problems. His only real candidates for its use in extant tragedy are Okeanos (Aiskh., *Prom.*) and the Muse (Eur., *Rhes.*; *Stagecraft*, 445, 261). Lefkowitz, "Aristophanes," doubts any fifth-century use of the *mēkhanē*. But it is substantiated by late fifth-century vases from South Italy, at least. Even Pickard-Cambridge, who opposed the *ekkuklēma*, accepted the *mēkhanē*. As with the *ekkuklēma*, the criterion of Aristophanic passages should be how funny they are. Aerial suspension is closely linked with tragedy. Lefkowitz rightly attacks ideas derived from fourth-century or Hellenistic commentaries, whose assumptions were "deduced directly from the text" (144, 148). That should not preclude our own use of a text and its context. But again, my argument, as a whole, does not depend on a fifth-century *mēkhanē*.

the *mēkhanē*, deus ex machina, was popular in fourth-century tragic performance. It may have begun in the fifth century.[97]

Together the two machines epitomize ways dramatic situations
change. The interior opens up, something comes out from within, or a
new force enters from the outside, and rearranges the situation. The two
illustrate a tension in tragic imagery of mind between emotion as something within, expressed outside, and emotion as demonic force which
enters from the outside and disturbs. *Ekkuklēma* and *mēkhanē* embody the
theater's dialectics of outside and inside, and above all the way dramatists
use these dialectics representing human feeling.

The two machines had human equivalents. The later writer Philostratos assumes that Aiskhylos created tragedy with all the features he himself knows of, in the second century C.E. In some respects he is
anachronistic. He includes high boots, typical of the later stage. But he
also includes some features of true fifth-century tragedy: "types of heroes
and what must be done on and behind the *skēnē*." He also mentions "*angeloi* and *exangeloi*."[98]

It is clear what he means. *Angeloi*, "messengers," tell you what has
happened outside the tragic site. They bring in a report from Mount Kithairon (Eur., *Bakkh.* 1024–1152) or the beach at Troezen (Eur., *Hipp.*
1153–1264). But the *exangelos*, "messenger-out," brings out news from
inside. The difference is manifest in the *Oidipous Tyrannos*. An *angelos* arrives from outside, from Corinth, to say Oidipous' presumed parents are
dead. The *exangelos* comes out from within, to speak of Jokasta's suicide,
and Oidipous' self-blinding in the palace (*Oid. Tyr.* 924f., 1223f.).

Philostratos sees Aiskhylos as the great man who made tragedy into
what it is in his day. He may not be right, that Aiskhylos began the system of *angeloi* and *exangeloi*. He implies that fifth-century poets and audience were aware of the difference between *angelos* and *exangelos*, and
used this terminology to refer to it. Maybe they did not. But it seems
likely they were at least aware, for the two match so firmly the *mēkhanē*
and *ekkuklēma*. *Ekkuklēma* and *exangelos* bring news out of the house and
onto the stage, in the entry that is also an exit. *Mēchanē* and *angelos* bring
news into the theater from somewhere altogether elsewhere.

A formal apparatus, both human and mechanical, therefore underlines
the tension between the inside and the outside of theatrical space, internal
and external sources of dramatic change. By this apparatus, tragedy's
visually perceived, physical relationships become a concrete correlate for
ideas and images of inside and outside, intellectually and imaginatively
perceived, which run through tragic language about human interiors.

[97] Through Taplin, *Action*, 12, 185 n. 20, doubts that fifth-century epiphanies happened
on the *mēkhanē*.
[98] Philostratos, *Lives of the Sophists*, 1.9.

The inside and outside of the theater's space offers the watching imagination a way of thinking about the inside and outside of other structures important to tragedy: city, house, self.

The performance of a tragedy, articulated through spatial dualities, reinforces the drama's other dualities by which it presents human beings. The audience see movement between opposed spaces. Actors step into the chorus' space, the chorus into the actors' space. Ghosts rise from the underworld. The door is simultaneously an exit and an entrance. Seen and unseen are kept apart, yet the one is invaded by the other. Such movements crystallize visually the communication, invitation, menace, between opposed people which the drama (verbal analogue to the theater's space) embodies. The "language" of any theater is a mix of movements: movements of thought and relationships expressed in words, movements of body expressed in space.[99]

Emotions created by a drama are brought about in a mixture of verbal and bodily language. Greek tragedians use entry and exit to underline the feelings of their characters. Body movements provide the dynamics within which emotion works. The stage is mapped by movements in opposite directions, safety to danger, danger to safety; enclosedness to openness and change, or vice versa; abroad to home; underworld (or divine world) to the human world, and vice versa.[100]

However, this theater's movements in space were also a formal mirror for the more intimate and even more violent movement which the words tell the audience to imagine happpening in other spaces. The words often point outward. In each epoch of tragedy, the world to which tragic language points will be different. In Greek tragedy, it points to a world outside which is truly haunted by furies, where gods journey over oceans, mad people wander over continents, prophecies flit around above a murderer's head; where ships sail toward us, away from us, ram each other and sink.[101] Where people meet appalling pain, both physical and mental; where they are quite literally torn apart.[102]

---

[99] Artaud, "Cruelty," 53–56, stresses theater's need for physical "expression in space." Theater has a "unique language, halfway between gesture and thought." To the "auditory language of sounds," it adds the "visual language of objects, movements, attitudes, gestures" which together create an "alphabet" of signals. The theater organizes its "language" into "hieroglyphs," intricate units, ways of showing people and objects whose symbolism and interconnections are related at all levels. We cannot recreate the "alphabet" used by the fifth-century theater. We work with hypotheses drawn from ambiguous evidence. But we can try to be alive to any part of that language that may reach us.

[100] As Taplin's whole project in *Stagecraft* has shown us; see detailed examples in his "Sophocles."

[101] Aiskh., *Eum.* 397–404, *Supp.* 538–73; Soph. *Oid. Tyr.* 482; Aiskh., *Supp.* 712–23, *Pers.* 374–428; Eur., *Hel.* 1451–54, 1612.

[102] Soph., *Trakh.* 765–88, *Ant.* 1226–69; Eur., *Bakkhai* 1125–39.

But tragedy's words always point inward too,[103] to an inner world of equally violent movement, destruction, pain, which corresponds to the "underside" of theater's visible space.[104] Through the hieroglyphics of Athenian tragedy, movements in space, both seen and unseen, convey the culture's understanding of movements into and out of mind and self, and above all, of their unseen violence.

[103] Cf. a modern director's understanding of the blend of inner and outer landscape in Shakespeare's language. The Elizabethan stage was "a neutral open platform—just a place with some doors. . . . This theater not only allowed the playwright to roam the world, it also allowed him free passage from the world of action to the world of inner impressions. . . . Shakespeare was not satisfied with . . . unknown continents: through his imagery—pictures drawn from the world of fabulous discoveries—he penetrates a psychic existence whose geography and movements are just as vital for us to understand today." Brook, *Empty Space*, 97.

[104] The theater uses images and movements not "solely for the external pleasure of eye or ear, but for that . . . of the spirit. Thus, the theater space will be utilized not only in its dimensions and volume but, so to speak, *in its undersides* [*dans ses dessous*]." Artaud, "Cruelty," 68.

JESPER SVENBRO

The "Interior" Voice:
On the Invention of Silent Reading

IN HIS article "Silent Reading in Antiquity," Bernard Knox quotes two texts from the fifth century B.C.E. which seem to show that the Greeks—certain Greeks—practiced silent reading and that, at the time of the Peloponnesian War, the dramatic poets could count on their audience to be familiar with it.[1] The first one of these texts is a passage from the *Hippolytos* by Euripides (856–86), performed in 428 B.C.E. Theseus notices a writing tablet hanging down from dead Phaidra's hand and asks himself what it may announce to him. He breaks the seal. The chorus intervenes, singing its distress, until it is finally interrupted by Theseus: "Alas! To my misery what misery is added, not endurable, not speakable! Woe is me!" he exclaims (874–75). At the request of the chorus, he then reveals the contents of the tablet—not by reading it aloud but by summing it up. He has clearly read it *silently*, while the chorus was singing.[2]

The second text quoted by Knox is a passage from the *Knights* of Aristophanes (115ff.) dating from 424. It stages the reading of a written oracle, which a certain Nikias has succeeded in stealing from Paphlagon. "Give it to me so that I may read it [*hin' anagnō*]," says Demosthenes to Nikias (118), who pours him a first cup of wine, asking: "What does the oracle say?" Absorbed in his reading, Demosthenes answers: "Fill me another cup" (121). "Does it really say 'Fill me another cup'?" asks Nikias, astonished (122), believing that his companion is reading aloud. The joke is repeated and developed in the following lines, until Demosthenes finally explains to Nikias: "Herein, it is said how himself [Paphlagon] shall perish" (127). Whereupon he summarizes the oracle. He does not read it: he already has—in silence. This passage, then, shows us a reader accus-

Note: This piece is adapted from its English version which appeared in *Culture and History* (Copenhagen, 1987), 31–47. It is here expanded with additions from its complete French version, which forms part of my recent book, *Phrasikleia: Anthropologie de la lecture en Grèce ancienne* (Paris, 1988) under the title, "La voix intérieure: Sur l'invention de la lecture silencieuse," 178–207, hereafter referred to as *Phrasikleia*. Readers may find there fuller documentation and discussion of certain points as well as the broader context relating to the general argument of the book. Froma Zeitlin edited this version and translated the additions.

[1] B.M.W. Knox, "Silent Reading in Antiquity," *GRBS* 9 (1968): 421–35. Knox's article is a critique of J. Balogh, "Voces Paginarum," *Philologus* 82 (1927): 84–109 and 202–40. See also G. L. Hendrickson, "Ancient Reading," *CJ* 25 (1929): 182–96.

[2] I examine this passage in more detail below.

tomed to reading silently (he is even capable of drinking and of *asking* for drink while doing it!) at the side of a listener who does not seem accustomed to this practice, but who takes the words pronounced by the reader for words *read* by him, which in fact they are not.

The scene in the *Knights* seems particularly instructive, at least at first sight, as it implies that the practice of silent reading is not familiar to everybody in 424 (Plato is then five years old), even if it is assumed to be so to the public of the comedy. Consequently, we may suppose that silent reading, at this epoch, is practiced by a limited number of readers; at the same time, it is unknown to others, in particular to wholly illiterate people, familiar with writing only "from the outside."

In a culture valuing the sonority of the word as intensely as the Greeks did, the practice of silent reading needs particular conditions even to be thought of. If an inscription is a machine for producing *kleos*—"acoustic renown"—as I think it originally was to the Greeks,[3] silent reading simply has no function. In a culture where writing aims at producing "more sound," silent reading has no raison d'être but appears as something against nature, an anomaly. During the first centuries of Greek literacy, silent reading would have gone against the very purpose of writing, which was to produce and to control a deferred oral statement. In such a culture, writing is inevitably perceived as something incomplete in itself, requiring a vocal supplement, a phenomenon alluded to by the Ionian verb meaning "read," *epi-legesthai*, implying that the reader adds (*epi-*) a sounding *logos* to the letters he sees. Meaning cannot yet be perceived without vocalization (I shall return to this in a moment): the act of reading aloud is the necessary "epi-logue" of the written word, of writing, of the "graphic."[4]

It follows that, in the eyes of those early readers, writing does not by itself represent the voice that it, at least sometimes, is supposed to transcribe. Writing is not yet autonomous in relation to the voice (which it is supposed to trigger in order to become complete). Before its vocalization, writing does not represent more than, in our experience, letters typed by a monkey haphazardly ("letters"). But writing will produce a representation, if it only gives birth to a sound sequence which, unlike the written word, may be considered as the representation (albeit a fictitious one) of the writer's voice. Before the invention of silent reading, writing does not represent a voice; it is not yet the image of a voice; it

---

3 This theme is developed in *Phrasikleia*, 72.

4 Hence probably the scandal provoked among the Pythagoreans by the discovery of "irrational" or rather "unspeakable" numbers: the diagonal of a square 1×1 is a simple geometrical representation, but it becomes a *grammē alogos* (*arrhētos*), an "unpronounceable line," when one tries to express it mathematically. Here, the "graphic" is impossible to vocalize. See *FVS*, I.108.22–23, II.91.20; Plato, *Rep.* 7.534d (cf. 8.546c).

only aims at producing a voice that will "represent the same by means of the same."

Reading aloud does not separate the eye from the ear. And in early Greece it is only the ear that is capable of identifying the Gestalt of what is written and read out loud, as is implied by the verb *anagignōskein* (recognize, read). What is "recognized" in the act of reading is not the individual letter, as Pierre Chantraine suggests:[5] a person may "know his letters," *ta grammata epistasthai*,[6] without being able to "read." What is "recognized" is rather the meaning of the sound sequence mechanically produced, but not yet understood by the reader.[7] What seems meaningless to his eye (although he knows the individual letters) is suddenly "recognized" by his ear.

To illustrate the manner of reading implied by *anagignōskein*, I choose a modern example, the first phrase of Raymond Queneau's novel *Zazie dans le Métro*. It reads as follows: "DOUKIPUDONKTAN." This is a phrase written in *scriptio continua*, without word division (which is a major characteristic of Greek writing). Moreover, it is written phonetically, not in the etymological manner characteristic of French or English spelling (but alien to archaic Greek spelling, which is phonetic in principle, without established orthography). Finally, as will appear, it is a phrase that, because of its syntax, belongs to spoken, not written language (which would be the case with any Greek phrase before the emergence of a written idiom, sensibly distinct from spoken language and consequently also from poetry). For these three reasons, the French reader is at a loss when first confronted with this phrase. "Continuous" writing, phonetic spelling, and colloquial syntax are not phenomena normally found on the French printed page. He suddenly finds himself in a situation resembling the one of the archaic Greek reader: only by using his voice can he succeed in "recognizing" what is opaque to his eye. His eye—and here the analogy ends—would of course have preferred the following, normalized version of the phrase: "C'est d'où qu'ils puent donc tant?" literally: "From where [is it] that they stink so much then?"

[5] Pierre Chantraine, "Les verbes grecs signifiant 'lire,' " in *Mélanges H. Grégoire* (Brussels, 1950), 115–26 (115): "Ce verbe [i.e., *anagignōskein*] convenait bien pour signifier *lire*, c'est-à-dire reconnaître les caractères et les déchiffrer." Cf. LSJ, s.v. *anagignōskō*: "of written characters, *know* them *again*, and so, *read*." Cf. also D. J. Allan, "*Anagignōskō* and Some Cognate Words," *CQ* 30 (1980): 244–51 (whose perspective is different from mine).

[6] For this expression, see Hippokrates, *On Regimen* 1.23. Of course the reader has to "know his letters" in order to read.

[7] Cf. the remarks by F. Bresson, "La lecture et ses difficultés," in *Pratiques de la lecture*, ed. R. Chartier (Paris, 1985), 11–21 (14–15). Although his interest is in the acquisition of reading at the present time, his remarks are pertinent to the interpretation of Greek *anagignōskein*. Children who learn to read have no real difficulty in identifying individual letters: their difficulties rather lie in the "recognition" of graphic sequences as speech.

In this way, the Greek reader's ear "recognizes" the words that his vocal apparatus produces. Given the *scriptio continua*, the eye had obvious difficulties in "recognizing" those same words. The ordinary reader had to rely on his voice if he wanted to decipher an inscription, and this "ordinary reader" is no doubt identical with the man "poor in letters," *ta grammata phaulos*, alluded to by Sokrates (Plato, *Phaidros* 242c): he knows how to read, but hardly more; just enough for his own needs (cf. Plutarch, *Lykourgos* 16.10). And in their large majority, the ancients remained *ta grammata phauloi*, which means that they had to decipher the texts that they read with the help of their voices, a complex and cumbersome way of reading, necessitated first of all by the *scriptio continua* and reinforced by the high value given to the voice and by the fact that they read comparatively little, preferring to have a fluent reader do the job for them.[8]

Only with the invention of silent reading does writing begin to "represent the same by means of the other," or more concretely: the voice by means of written signs, *sēmeia anthrōpinēs phonēs*.[9] Only then can it be said to represent *tout court*. It is only with the invention of silent reading that the written representation becomes a "pure" representation, which no longer calls for a vocal supplement or prolongation. From now on, the eye "sees" the sound.[10] What was previously perceived as one single continuous operation suddenly splits in two: the written word is separated from the voice, in the sense that it no longer calls for a vocalization to become intelligible, "recognizable." From now on, the eye, and the eye only, will ensure the "recognition" of meaning. What was originally a "recognition" of something opaque at first sight has become an immediate identification of meaning.

Of course, the *scriptio continua* was an obstacle to this development, and it remained so. But it was not insurmountable, as one might have thought, judging from the medieval evidence: according to Paul Saenger, word division was a necessary prerequisite for the development of silent reading in the Middle Ages.[11] For, as we have seen, the Greeks *did* really practice silent reading, in spite of the fact that they kept writing in *scriptio continua*. According to Knox, it is the habit of reading large numbers of texts that is at the origin of silent reading, as silent reading is con-

[8] Cf. W. Peek, *Griechische Vers-Inschriften* (Berlin, 1955), vol. 1, no. 1210; Herod., 8.128 (I owe this reference to Joseph Russo); Plato, *Theat.* 143bff.; I. Düring, *Aristotle in the Ancient Biographical Tradition*, Studia Graeca et Latina Gothoburgiensia 5 (Gothenburg, 1957), 108.

[9] The expression is found in Hippokrates, *On Reg.* 1.23.

[10] *Ktupon dedorka*: "I behold the din" (Aiskh., *Seven* 103). I refer to this line again in my discussion of the *Seven* below.

[11] P. Saenger, "Silent Reading: Its Impact on Late Medieval Script and Society," *Viator* 13 (1982): 367–414 (378).

siderably faster than reading aloud.[12] A writer like Herodotos probably abandoned the habit of reading aloud in the course of his work as a historian, and well before him those who worked on the Homeric text under the Peisistratids in sixth-century Athens—as perhaps Simonides did[13]—certainly had the occasion to develop this new technique. True, it is the technique of a minority, but this minority is an important one—for example, the dramatic poets belonged to it—whose early history deserves our attention.

The mere introduction of word division in the manuscripts did not ensure the spread of silent reading in the Middle Ages. Something more was needed than this technical innovation. In fact, scholasticism provided this impetus: scholastic science discovered the advantages of silent reading—rapidity, intelligibility—and exploited them on a large scale. It was only in the scholastic context that silent reading could catch on; in the rest of medieval society, it remained practically unknown.[14] In the same way, I would argue, the mere reading of large numbers of texts is insufficient as a factor explaining why silent reading appeared in fifth-century Greece. Extensive reading seems rather to be the outcome of a qualitative innovation in the attitude to the written word. It seems to be the outcome of a whole mental framework, new and powerful, capable of restructuring the categories of traditional reading. The practice of silent reading could hardly have been structured by a purely quantitative factor: in fact, Knox himself quotes only post-classical authors—Aristarkhos, Kallimakhos, and Didymos—when he wants to exemplify the vast readings of the ancients.[15] But what could have structured it, I now suggest, is the experience of the theater.

What are the distinctive features of a theatrical representation—an eminently sonorous phenomenon—that are clear-cut enough, and original enough, to have structured the new practice of silent reading? What comes to mind is first of all the marked separation between the stage and the public. This separation delimits the fictitious acting on the stage and constitutes in a certain way the originality of theater: the public is not supposed to participate in the acting.[16] For example, the spectator is not

---

[12] Knox, "Silent Reading," 421–22.

[13] Cf. in particular [Plato], *Hipparkhos* 228b–c. The possibility that Simonides gave a final touch to the Homeric text "imported" from Ionia by Hipparkhos is suggestive, as the poet from Keos is quoted as one of the makers of the Greek alphabet (*Anecdota Greca* II.780.30–31, 781.2–4, 782.25–28 Bekker; Pliny, *Nat. Hist.* 7.192).

[14] Saenger, "Silent Reading," 378–80, 383–84, 405.

[15] Knox, "Silent Reading," 421–22.

[16] If the comic poets seem to ignore the existence of this separation, the reason is that its transgression produces a comic effect: the separation is in fact there. For the strict manner in which the tragic poets observe the demarcation between fictional space and the public, cf. D. Bain, "Audience Address in Greek Tragedy," *CQ* 25 (1975): 13–25.

supposed to communicate to a person on the stage what is going to happen. He is not supposed to stop the course of events by explaining to the
actors what to do. He is supposed to "contemplate" (*theasthai*) them as
they walk toward their own destruction. The tension created by this
situation makes the action on the stage even more fascinating. The play is
delivered in an autonomous environment which the public should not
disturb, according to the rules of the game (*paidia*) that the tragic poet,
Thespis, back in the sixth century, defends against the indignant criticism launched by Solon (Plutarch, *Solon* 29).

The public—and already that of Thespis—is supposed to watch and
listen, passively, for the most part (although not necessarily silently; we
have anecdotes about audiences' vociferous reactions to performances).
The spectators are not supposed to intervene on the stage nor to read the
text that, although absent from the stage, nevertheless commands its action. Memorized by the actors, the text is not visible in the moment it is
pronounced:[17] the actors have taken its place, as it were. They transpose
it into a kind of "vocal writing" (we shall see later how this expression is
justified). They are not reading it; they produce a vocal copy of it. In this,
they differ from the ordinary reader, who lends his voice to the text in
front of him. The ordinary reader, then, cannot be said to produce another—vocal—piece of writing, for the simple reason that his voice is
perceived as the "natural" extension of writing, its fulfillment or necessary supplement. The reader's voice is the supplement of writing; it belongs to the written word and cannot, for this reason, be considered as a
rewriting. The act of reading aloud presupposes the presence of the
text—the completion of which is ensured by the voice—which means
that a *listener* has no problem in grasping the contiguity of writing and
voice. For unlike those of the actor, the words pronounced by the reader
are not memorized beforehand (even if every reader is free to memorize
what he reads).

Inversely, the gap between dramatic text and performance is marked
enough to justify us in calling the performance a vocal rewriting of the
text. The performance of the actors is not a reading. They may have read
the text to memorize it, but during the performance their voices replace
the text, conspicuously absent from the stage. Their vocal writing re-
places the text. The spectators listen to this vocal writing. They do not
behave as traditional readers. They do not activate or reactivate the written word by means of their own voices, as the vocal writing of the performance speaks to them in total autonomy. They listen, more or less

---

[17] See the discussion in Charles Segal, "Tragédie, oralité, écriture," *Poétique* 50 (1982):
131–54, and a somewhat different version in "Greek Tragedy: Writing, Truth, and the
Representation of the Self," in Segal, *Interpreting Greek Tragedy: Myth, Poetry, Text* (Ithaca,
N.Y., 1986), 75–109.

passively, to this writing. And, as I have argued, listening to a vocal writing is not the same thing as listening to a reading made by someone who has a text in front of him: the reader's voice simply does not have the autonomy of the actor's voice. True, this autonomy is partly illusory, but it is also real, as the actor has to do without the text, materially speaking, once he stands on the stage.

The separation between the stage, from which this vocal writing is delivered, and the public is probably clear-cut enough to have suggested to the Greeks—certain Greeks—an analogous separation between writing and reader.[18] To put it another way: it is clear-cut enough to have opened the possibility of a new attitude to the written word. The traditional reader, who needs his voice in order to "recognize" a text (a complex operation where the eye first ensures the production of a sound sequence, which is then interpreted by the ear), has a manifestly active relation to what is written. He has to make an effort to understand; otherwise, the letters will remain meaningless ("mere letters") to him.[19] Inversely, the silent reader, whose eye is capable of immediate word identification, has a relation to the written word that appears rather as a passive one. Or better: the activity of the silent reader is not thought of as an effort to decipher something; it is an activity that does not appear as such (in the same way as the interpretative activity of the ear listening to a meaningful sound is an activity that does not appear as such, but rather as a passive reception). The visual "recognition" of meaning is here immediate; it is not preceded by a moment of opacity. The reader who "reads in his head" does not have to (re-)activate the written word through the intervention of his voice. The written word simply seems to "speak" to him. He is "listening" to a writing—exactly like the spectator in the theater, who listens to the vocal writing of the actors. The text that is "recognized" visually seems to have the same autonomy as the acting on the stage. The letters, the *grammata*, "read" themselves—or rather: "pronounce" themselves. The silent reader does not have to intervene on the "stage" of the written word. Capable of "speaking," the *grammata* can do without his voice. They already have one. The reader has simply to "listen"—inside himself. The reading voice is internalized.[20]

[18] That is, more clear-cut than the one between rhapsode and public (as will be discussed below); as for the practice of delivering speeches written and memorized beforehand, it is posterior to theater, not anterior to it, as is the rhapsode's activity.

[19] Hence the prefix *ana-* in *anagignōskein* may express this effort of the reader. Chantraine, "Les verbes grecs," 115.

[20] In the same period, we hear for the first time of the "voice of conscience," which is the voice of law internalized in the individual. I cannot develop this theme here, but see the discussion in *Phrasikleia*, 178–81, and chap. 6, "Nomos, 'exégèse,' lecture," 123–36. Let me just note that in Greek as well as in Latin, "law" (*nomos* and *lex* respectively) is originally conceived as a "reading aloud," and thus as a reading voice.

If this passivity of the reader is modeled on the passivity of the spectator in the theater, how far back may we trace it? The analysis of the verb
hupokrinesthai, "play a role," made by George Thomson may help us in
defining the moment when this passivity is established. As Thomson observes, *hupokrinesthai* has two distinct meanings in the Homeric poems:
"answer" and "interpret" (a dream or omen).[21] Contrary to other scholars, who have tried to choose between these two meanings in order to
explain the origin of the *hupokritēs*, or "actor,"[22] Thomson asks why
they have come to be covered by one single word, as in a passage of
the *Odyssey*, where Peisistratos asks Menelaos: "Is this omen intended
for you or for us?" The text continues: "At these words Menelaos . . . pondered, wondering how he should answer [*hupokrinaito*]
aright" (15.167–70). It would have been equally possible to translate:
"how he should *interpret* it aright." The key to the problem is given by a
passage in Plato's *Timaios* (72a–b), where it is stated "that the *prophētai*
are the *hupokritai* of enigmatic words and signs, but they are not *manteis*
[soothsayers pronouncing their words in an ecstatic state]." Thomson
concludes: *hupokritēs* originally designates a character to whom one poses
questions concerning "words and enigmatic signs"—his interpretation
will constitute his reply. If this person is the leader of a chorus which ac-
complishes a ritual whose significance escapes those who are present
(e.g., visitors and strangers, who come in increasing numbers to the city,
or just new citizens), the *hupokritēs* is in a position to "answer" possible
questions by "interpreting" what is going on. He might say: "I am Dionysos, and those are the daughters of Eleuther whom I have driven
mad."[23] Later on, when he begins to give his "answers-interpretations"
without being asked, he is suddenly no longer a *hupokritēs* in the old sense.
He has become an actor. The separation between the stage (autonomous
from now on) and the spectator (from now on passive) is thereby an accomplished fact.

It is precisely the verb *hupokrinesthai* that we read in an inscription belonging to a bronze statuette (now lost), dating from the late sixth century and found in Athens: "I answer [*hupokrinomai*] the same thing [*is (a)*]
to all men [*pasin . . . anthrōpoi(s)*], whoever asks me [*e(rō)tāi*], namely
that Andrōn son of Antiphanes dedicated me as his tithe."[24] A few re-

---

[21] George Thomson, *Aeschylus and Athens*, 2d ed. (London, 1950), 181–82.

[22] To cite a recent example, G.K.H. Ley, "*Hupokrinesthai* in Homer and Herodotus, and
the Function of the Athenian Actor," *Philologus* 127 (1983): 13–29, who privileges the
meaning "answer."

[23] Thomson, *Aeschylus*, 183.

[24] M. Lazzarini, *Le formule delle dediche votive nella Grecia antica*, Atti della Accademia nazionale dei Lincei: Memorie, Classe di scienze morali, storiche, e filologiche, 8th ser., vol.
19, fasc. 2, no. 658 (Rome, 1976).

marks on this inscription are in order. At the end of the sixth century
B.C.E., theater already exists in its institutionalized form: the tragic contests begin in 534 and the tragic representations—before Aiskhylos with
one actor and a chorus—go back some thirty years before that date.[25]
When the statuette receives its epigram, the tragic poet Thespis is already
in his heyday. The verb *hupokrinomai* consequently has a much richer
meaning here than my translation—"I answer"—suggests. In Attic
Greek, *hupokrinesthai* does not, in fact, mean "answer" as it does in Ionian.[26] It is *apokrinesthai* that is used in this sense. If the author of our inscription had wanted to write "I answer," he would have used
apokrinomai, which is the perfect metrical equivalent of *hupokrinomai*. He
did not do so—which means that *hupokrinomai* was chosen to express
more than the simple idea of answer.

It is with this same verb that the Andrōn inscription singles itself out
on another level, making its statuette a so-called "speaking object."[27]
Not because it uses the first person "I," in the manner of inscriptions
such as "I am the tombstone of so-and-so" (for the faculty of speech is
not a necessary attribute of the first person: otherwise, a dumb person
could not pretend to have an "I").[28] The statuette is a "speaking object"
because of the vocal implications of the verb *hupokrinomai*. It is in fact our
earliest clear example of an inscription using, with regard to itself, the
metaphor of the voice. By using the verb *hupokrinomai*, this inscription
raises its "voice." It "speaks." And the Athenian context adds to this
"speaking" a strong theatrical connotation: by means of its metaphorical
voice, this inscription answers a question which is not asked but which
the inscription anticipates, in complete autonomy—exactly like the *hupokritēs* on the stage. But if, at the same time, *hupokrinomai* means that it
interprets what is perceived as an "enigma"—what meaning should be
given to the inscribed statuette?—it "interprets" itself, it "deciphers" itself, before the eyes of the spectator-reader, who does not have to make
the effort of vocalizing the written word, for the simple reason that it
"vocalizes" itself here. Addressing the spectator-reader, who is not supposed to raise his voice, the inscription delivers its meaning directly to
the eye: why read aloud, if the inscription knows how to "speak" by itself? The meaning of the object seems to reach the eye of the reader by a

[25] *DTC*, 88.

[26] The dialect of the inscription is Attic, not Ionic: *anthrōpois*, not *anthrōpoisi* as in Ionic
(the final *-s* is guaranteed by the meter, which would not allow *-si* in this place); *erōtāi*, not
eirōtāi as in Ionic (the initial *e-* is equally guaranteed by the meter, which would not allow
ei- here).

[27] M. Burzachechi, "Oggetti parlanti nelle epigrafi greche," *Epigraphica* 24 (1962): 3–54.

[28] See *Phrasikleia*, chap. 2, "J'écris, donc de m'efface: L'énonciation dans les premières inscriptions grecques," 33–52.

kind of radiation or "flow." The object radiates its meaning upon the
reader, as I shall discuss in relation to the atomists below. The meaning
of the object is no longer laboriously activated by the voice of the reader.
Its writing is autonomous; it "speaks." This is, I believe, the logic of this
Attic inscription, which seems to attest, in an indirect way (as opposed to
the direct evidence in the *Hippolytos* and the *Knights* previously quoted),
the existence of silent reading in late sixth-century Athens and, at the
same time, the internalization of theatrical space in scriptural space.[29]
From now on, scriptural space is a "scene."

This new form of reading, where the reader is made a passive spectator, as it were, of an active writing which radiates its meaning, conforms
to a schema which is found again in theories of visual perception, such as
those elaborated by Empedokles, Leukippos, and Demokritos in the
course of the fifth century. At the start, in Empedokles, the situation
seems confused. According to Aristotle, "Empedokles resembles one
who believes that one sees when light comes from the eye" (Aristotle,
On Sensation 437b). Empedokles then takes the opposite position to that
implied by silent reading, where what is written emits its meaning in the
direction of the eye. But—and this is significant—Aristotle adds:
"Sometimes Empedokles declares that one sees in this manner, sometimes he maintains that vision is produced because of emanations [*apor-
rhoiais*] of objects seen [*tōn horōmenon*]"; cf. *FVS*, Emped., fr. B89. It is in
fact this last position which will win the day among his successors: the
atomists, starting with Leukippos, also see vision as the result of an ema-
nation or effluescence (*aporrhoē*) from the objects seen which go toward
the eye (cf. Plat., *Phaid.* 251b). Alexander of Aphrodisias writes: "They
attribute sight with certain images [*eidōla*], which, having the same form
as the object, flow [*aporrheonta*] continually from objects which are seen
and impinge [*empiptonta*] on the eye: such was the position of the school
of Leukippos and Demokritos" (*On Sensation* 56.12). Among the atomists, therefore, vision is due to a continuous emission of corpuscles from
the object being seen, an emission which, in a more or less complicated
way (due to constraints inherent in the atomist theory),[30] is received finally by the eye. The position of Empedokles owes its ambiguity, no
doubt, to the fact that he had to abandon an accepted theory in order to
elaborate a new, more satisfying one. The position of the atomists—
heirs of this new theory—seems, on the other hand, to be clearly defined
from the beginning, at least with regard to the aspect we are considering

[29] For another discussion about the "internalization of theatrical space," see the essay by
Padel in this volume.

[30] It is not only the object being seen which produces an effluvium but also the eye which
sees: these two effluvia meet one another in the air and produce the image, the emphasis or
entupōsis (*FVS*, Dem., frag. A135).

here. The eye does not emit a ray in order to see, it *receives* the emanations from the objects being seen: this is the direction in which the visual
information is thought to pass.

This analogous relation between visual perception and silent reading—
where the eye seems to receive (passively) the radiation of what is written—cannot exercise its full weight, however, unless matched up to a
fundamental fact in the theory of the atomists. The combinations of
stoikheia in the physical world are explained for them with the aid of the
alphabetical model, where words are formed as a result of the combinations of twenty-four *stoikheia* of writing: *stoikheia* means both "elements"
and "alphabetic signs."[31] "One writes tragedy and comedy with the
same letters," we read in Leukippos (*FVS*, II.74.21–22); just as, in the
physical world, it is the same elements which combine and recombine in
order to change things. It is with every right then that one can speak of
the "ontography" of the atomists.[32] Demokritos, in fact, is the author of
a treatise on physics entitled *Kosmographiē* (*FVS*, II.91.3; 138.14). This
suggests that for the atomists, visual perception is a reading—a silent
reading of the writing of the physical world—with potential implications
for interpreting the relations between audience and actor in the theater, as
I have outlined it above.

If the statuette dedicated by Andrōn is an isolated example of a "speaking object" (in the sense I have just given to this expression) as long as we
remain in the sixth century, the metaphor of the voice becomes more and
more common in the course of the fifth, not so much in the realm of inscriptions,[33] but in authors who have practiced a more prolific type of
writing and who, for this reason, might have been more prone to change
their habits of reading.

My first example is Aiskhylos, who sets a significant precedent in this
respect. In Aiskhylos, the use of the metaphor is suggested by three
shields of heroes—those of Kapaneus, Eteokles, and Polyneikes in the
Seven against Thebes. "For his blazon [*sēma*]," says the Messenger to
Eteokles, Kapaneus "has a naked man bearing fire, a flaming torch in his
hands as weapon, and gold letters [*khrusois . . . grammasin*] declare [*phōnei*], 'I'll burn the town' " (432–34). In a play where we encounter the remarkable synesthetic expression, "I see the din" (*ktupon dedorka*, 103), it

---

[31] For the alphabetic model, see the remarkable passage in Lucretius, *De rerum natura*
1.823–29, where *elementa* is the Latin equivalent of *stoikheia*. Cf. in general, S. Sambursky,
The Physical World of the Greeks (Oxford, 1956), 126–28.

[32] Heinz Wissmann, "Le modèle graphique des atomistes," talk presented at the colloquium "L'écriture," directed by Marcel Detienne and held in Paris in September 1984.

[33] But cf. the "poetic ostrakon" (484 B.C.E.) from the Athenian Agora, published by A. E.
Raubitschek, "The Ostracism of Xanthippos," *AJA* 51 (1974): 257–62; cf. S. G. Miller,
The Prytaneion: Its Function and Architectural Form (Berkeley, 1978), 137. Verb: [*kata*]*phēsin*.
I owe this reference to François Lissarrague.

seems logical that objects will be endowed with speech and that the figure outlined on the shield will "speak" (*phōnei*), as on the shield mentioned above, or that it "shouts" (*bōai*), as on the shield of Eteoklos,
through the *grammata* inscribed beside him (465–69). Finally, on the
shield of Polyneikes, we see the personification of Justice (Dikē), identified not by her traditional attributes but through what is written: "she
claims [*phēsin*] to be Justice, as the adjacent letters say" (*hōs ta grammata
legei*, 646–48; cf. 660).

My second example is Herodotos. With him letters, *ta grammata*, begin
to "speak" (*legein*) on a large scale,[34] and written oracles, steles, and tripods equally raise their "voices," as does the stone statue of the Egyptian
king Sethos, who "pronounces" his own inscription.[35] To the historian,
who writes in an extensive manner and who has to read even more than
he writes, silent reading, made possibly by the experience of theater,[36]
imposes itself "naturally." He is more or less forced to read rapidly in order to elaborate his own written work. And accelerating the speed of
reading equals at a certain point internalizing the reading voice, too slow
for comprehensive reception of meaning.

The same need to read more rapidly than reading aloud might allow
was, no doubt, felt by many writers of this period. In the tragic poet,
Akhaios—of the same generation as Herodotos—we find the same metaphor of the "speaking object." There is a fragment which shows a satyr
reading out loud (obviously, not one of those skilled in the art, but *ta
grammata phaulos*): "The skyphos of the god summons [*kalei*] me, now
for a long time, showing its inscription [*gramma*]: delta, iōta, and thirdly,
ō [omega]; *nu* and *u* [upsilon] are there [*paresti*]; and in what follows, it is
not their absence [*apousian*] that *san* and O proclaim [*kērusseton*]" (*Omphale*, frag. 33 Nauck[2] = Athenaios, 11.466f.) It is clear that the author
of this satyric drama is having fun staging a kind of reading that seems to
him very backward and on that account, just right for a satyr: in order to
be able to "recognize" the meaning of the graphic sequence D-I-O-N-U-
S-O-U ("[I belong to] Dionysos"), the satyr must pronounce the letters
one by one but also as rapidly as possible in order to allow his ear to
grasp the Gestalt of the sonorous sequence he has produced. (We could
then ask whether he actually succeeds in deciphering the inscription; the
spectators surely could because of the elements he provides.) This implies that Akhaios himself reads in another fashion, as do the spectators
he has or thinks he has. And this other kind of reading in fact informs the
text. It is introduced discreetly, for it is not part of the mentality appropriate to traditional reading to think of what is written as possessing a

[34] Herod., 1.124, 187; 2.106, 136; 3.88; 4.91; 7.228; 8.22.
[35] Herod., 2.133; 5.90, 92; 6.77; 8.136; 2.102; 5.60, 61; 2.141.
[36] Herodotos and Sophokles were friends, in addition (Plut. *Mor.* 785b).

"voice" coming from itself. But it is precisely this of which the satyr is convinced: the inscription "summons" him, the two last letters "proclaim" their presence. Like *kērukes*, heralds, that is—out loud. But if he reads out loud, the satyr has no need of this metaphoric voice, which itself belongs to the practice of silent reading.[37]

The Andrōn inscription marks a decisive moment in the Greek experience of writing: it is no accident if Plato's *Phaidros* echoes it, at a distance of more than a century, in a passage concerning the properties of the written word (275d). Comparing writing to painting, Sokrates blames the written word for "always signifying the same thing," which is exactly what the Andrōn inscription takes pride in doing. The philosopher could, of course, have made the same reproach to an actor, whose voice is the mere instrument of an unchanging text and not the voice of someone in possession of knowledge, *epistēmē*.[38] And so he does, elsewhere (*Ion*, 532d et al.). It comes down to the same thing for, as we have seen, the written word and the actor are analogous, interchangeable. The actor takes the place of the written word on the stage, the written word takes the place of the actor in the Andrōn inscription. Producing what I have called a "vocal writing" on the stage, the actor opens the possibility of a new attitude to the written word, the possibility of silent reading. In fact, the inscribed statuette dedicated by Andrōn defines itself as an "actor," *hupokritēs*, presupposing this new attitude to the written word. Inscribed space is a "scene" that borrows its logic from theater, in assigning the role of the spectator to the reader. It internalizes theater.

This view is justified not only by the Andrōn inscription, but also by a passage like the one quoted from the *Hippolytos*, where dead Phaidra's "writing tablet shouts, shouts things not to be forgotten [*boāi boāi deltos alasta*]" (877). As staged by Euripides, the written word not only "speaks" during an act of silent reading,[39] it "shouts." It may even "sing": "Such a song," says Theseus a few lines later, "have I seen crying forth through the writing [*hoion hoion eidon en graphais melos/phthengomenon*]" (879–80).[40] The actor who *sings* the role of Theseus—the passage is in lyric meter—sings about a song coming forth through the written word, a song for the *eye*.[41]

On the stage, then, a singing actor; on the writing tablet, intended for

---

[37] For an analogous confusion, cf. Herod., 8.136.

[38] Unless, of course, the actor is improvising or interpolating lines of his own. This is a controversy into which I shall not enter here.

[39] *Iph. Taur.* 641–42; 584–85.

[40] Cf. Knox, "Silent Reading," 433, Segal, *Interpreting Greek Tragedy*, 148.

[41] Ancient musical notation is alphabetical: see, e.g., J. Chailley, *La Musique grecque antique* (Paris, 1979), 122. A reference to the silent reading of music can therefore not be excluded.

silent reading and thus internalizing theatrical space, the "singing" letters. It is difficult to imagine a more subtle mise-en-scène of silent reading than this one. The metaphorical voice of writing is presented here as the complement of silent reading: when you read silently, letters raise their "voices." Thus the evidence from the *Hippolytos* does not only concern the external facts—which, in fact, do not permit the distinction between silent and noiseless reading—but has an internal aspect corroborating Knox's interpretation, in adding elements that belong to the mental architecture of true silent reading.

But this is not all. In fact, the entire works of Plato could be added to our evidence. As is well known, Plato has a problematic relationship with the dramatic poets, a relationship marked by emulation and hostility, lasting from his youth when—at Sokrates' suggestion—in front of the theater of Dionysos, he burns a tragedy he himself wrote for a dramatic contest (Diog. Laert., 3.5), up to his old age when he defines the *politeia*, the "political constitution"—obviously the one proposed by himself—as "the truest tragedy" (*Laws* 7.817a–c; cf. 3.701a). The sudden shift in Plato's career from the dramatic genre to the dialogues may actually be seen as the internalization of theater in the book, for the dialogues have a dramatic form (cf. in particular, *Theaitetos* 143b–c) without being intended for the stage. If Plato's *politeia* has a theatrical intention, its "stage" is the entire city-state, as opposed to the illusory one of ordinary theater (cf. *Laws* 8.817c).[42] Thus, his utopian thought would be essentially theatrical.[43]

If, in this way, theater is internalized in the book, the book in its turn is internalized in mental space, designated now as *phrēn*, now as *psuchē*. And this development occurs well before Plato.[44] Our first example of the metaphor, "the book of the soul," is in fact found in Pindar who, in his tenth *Olympian* (probably dating from 474), exclaims: "Read to me [*anagnōte*] the name of the Olympic victor where it is written [*gegraptai*]

[42] This would be a typically Platonic structure: Plato's *politeia*, modeled upon theater, is full of contempt for theater. In the same way, weaving is the paradigm of politics, but "no sensible man would try to define weaving out of love for weaving itself" (*Statesman* 285d). Cf. n. 44.

[43] For excellent remarks on Plato and "the dramatistic view of life" in another context, see Alvin Gouldner, *Enter Plato* (New York, 1965), part 2, chap. 7.

[44] Plato, *Philebos* 38e–39a, *Phaidros* 275d–276a. For the use of this metaphor before Plato, see G. Nieddu, "La metafora della memoria come scrittura e l'immagine dell'animo come *deltos*," QS 19 (1984): 213–19. If ordinary writing is considered to be the "simulacrum" (*eidōlon*: Phaid. 276a) of *metaphorical* writing (i.e., writing in the soul), highly valued by Plato, this relation—central to the analyses of Jacques Derrida, *La dissémination* (Paris, 1972), 172—has several parallels in Plato's thought, where, for instance, the craftsman, in spite of the deprecation in which he is held, serves as the model for the metaphorical craftsman called the Demiurge. Cf. P. Vidal-Naquet, *Le chasseur noir* (Paris, 1981), 308 and *passim*.

in my mind [*phrenos*]!" (1–3). But it is in the tragic poets, notably in Aiskhylos, that this metaphor is most frequently employed before Plato.
The reason seems obvious enough: the dramatic poet, who writes texts
intended for memorization by the actors, experiences in a very concrete
manner the inscription of the dramatic text in the mind of the actor. To
the dramatic poet, the actor seems to receive an inscription in the same
way as a stone or a papyrus leaf may receive one. The mind of the actor
is a space for writing, scriptural space, which means that the dramatic
text is "inscribed" in the mind of the person who will pronounce it on
the stage. In this way, the formula "vocal writing" which I have been
using[45] receives its full justification, and we understand why Aiskhylos—who introduces the second actor (Aristotle, *Poet.* 1449a16)—
"writes" in the minds of his actors, whereas a Homer (if we assume for a
moment that he was literate) cannot be considered as someone "writing"
in the memory of his future reciters, the rhapsodes, who are too separated from him, in time and in space, for such a metaphor to have any
relevance.

Let us cite some examples from Aiskhylos, although the same metaphor returns in the two other tragic poets.[46] In *Prometheus Bound*, the
protagonist declares: "First to you, Io, I will tell the tale of your said
wanderings . . . inscribe [*engraphou*] the story on the mindful tablets
[*mnēmosin deltois*] of your mind [*phrenōn*]" (788–89). Prometheus is a figure linked to the origins of writing; according to another tradition,
Danaos is also.[47] Here is how he addresses his daughters in the *Suppliants*:
"And now, with foresight, I advise you to guard my words inscribed
[*deltoumenas*] in you" (*Supp.* 178–79). And the same metaphor returns
later in the play when Danaos says: "Now, beside many other wise sayings of your father's which have been written in your memory [*gegram-
menois*], write [*grapsesthe*] the following" (991–92). In the *Eumenides*, the
chorus compares the "memory" of Hades to a writing tablet: "Hades,
beneath the earth, exacts terrible penalties from mortals, and his mind
[*phrēn*] which sees all, keeps a faithful transcription [*deltographos*] of everything" (*Eum.* 273–75). And in my last example, Elektra says to Orestes:
"Listen and inscribe [*graphou*] in your heart [*en phresin*]" (*Khoe.* 450).

Thus the relation between theater and writing, as well as the one between writing and the mind, takes the form of an internalization:

[45] The fact that our earliest evidence for the metaphor of the "book of the mind" comes
from Pindar does not invalidate my hypothesis, as the choral poet "inscribes" his poem in
the mind of the chorus that is going to perform it.

[46] Sophokles, *Triptolemos*, frag. 540 Nauck², *Phil.* 1325, *Trakh.* 680–83, *Ant.* 707–9; Euripides, *Trojan Women* 661.

[47] *Anecdota Graeca* II.783.7, 786.4–5 Bekker.

Andrōn inscription:	Aiskhylos, etc.:
"hupokrinomai"	"book of the mind"
-------------------------	-------------------------
internalization	internalization

THEATRICAL SPACE   /   SCRIPTURAL SPACE   /   MENTAL SPACE

But this double movement—from theater to writing, from writing to
mind[48]—has its counterpart, going in the opposite direction: a double
movement of *externalization*. In the first place, mental space is, of course,
externalized in the book. We may even postulate the existence of silent
writing here, although it may prove impossible to document it positively. The written *hupomnēma* may replace a failing memory:[49] it is an
externalized, objective memory, not to be confused with the living
mnēmē of a person. Conscious of its limitations, the philosopher makes
use of it; and so does, of course, the dramatic poet, whose text is a *hupomnēma*, written not for posterity but for a unique performance and
probably constituting its necessary condition.

If mental space may be externalized in this manner, writing may also
be externalized—in theatrical space. This happens first of all, naturally,
when a written text is performed on the stage, an operation which, in a
sense, is original in this system of interdependent representations, as it
gives rise to what I have been calling "vocal writing." But this externalization has even been represented, literally speaking, on the stage in ancient Greece, namely in the *ABC Show*, the *Grammatikē Theōria*, by the
Athenian poet Kallias.[50]

THEATRICAL SPACE   /   SCRIPTURAL SPACE   /   MENTAL SPACE

externalization	externalization
-------------------------	-------------------------
"vocal writing"	*hypomnēma*
ABC Show	silent writing

[48] Cf. Derrida's remark on Mallarmé, (*La dissémination*, 264): "Ces propositions . . . *miment* l'intériorisation du théâtre dans le livre et du livre dans le 'milieu mental.' "

[49] See *Phaid.* 276d. Literally, *hupomnēma* means "memory support" in the same way as
hupopodion, "footstool," means "foot support." In the singular we may translate *hupomnēma* by "memorandum," in the plural, by "notes."

[50] Athen., 7.276a, 10.448b, 453c–454a (= Kallias, frag. 31 Edmonds). Cf. F. D. Harvey,
"Literacy in the Athenian Democracy," *REG* 79 (1968): 585–635 (632 n. 13).

The *ABC Show* (or with the other title given to it by Athenaios, the *ABC Tragedy*) poses difficult problems with regard to the date of its composition and its relationship, on the musical and metrical level, to Euripides' *Medeia* (dating from 431) and to Sophokles' *Oidipous the King* (probably from 430). I cannot discuss these problems here.[51] But as they are not essential to my argument, I content myself with dating the play very approximately to the second half of the fifth century: all the dates so far proposed fall within this period.

What does the *ABC Show* offer to the "contemplation" (*theōria*) of its spectators (*theatai*)? Nothing less than a chorus of twenty-four women representing the Ionian alphabet, introduced in the following manner in the Prologue: "Alpha, beta, gamma, delta, ei (which is Apollo's letter), zeta, eta, theta, iota, kappa, labda, mu, nu, xei, o, pei, rho, sigma, tau, u, phei, and khei next to psei, and coming down to ō" (Athen., 10.453d). Whereupon the chorus, disposed in pairs, makes us attend an exercise in elementary school:[52] "Beta alpha: ba. Beta ei: be. Beta eta: bē. Beta iota: bi. Beta o: bo. Beta u: bu. Beta ō: bō." After this stanza, the answering stanza runs: "Gamma alpha: ga. Gamma ei: ge. Gamma eta: gē" and so on, which gives us seventeen stanzas in all, sung to the same tune.

After this "syllabic chorus"—which may give the shivers to modern specialists in reading—there follows a dialogue between a schoolmaster (?) and two women (?):

Schoolmaster:	You must pronounce *alpha* by itself, my ladies, and secondly *ei* by itself. And you there, you will say the third vowel!
First Woman:	Then I will say *eta*.
Schoolmaster:	Then *you* will say the fourth one by itself!
Second Woman:	*Iota*.
Schoolmaster:	The fifth one!
First Woman:	*O.*
Schoolmaster:	The sixth one!
Second Woman:	*U.*
Schoolmaster:	But the last of the seven vowels, ō, I will pronounce for you. And then all seven put into verse. When you have pronounced them, say them to yourself. (435f.)

---

[51] See H. Koller, "Die Parodie," *Glotta* 35 (1956): 17–32, and E. Pöhlmann, "Die ABC-Komödie des Kallias," *RhM* 114 (1971): 230–40. For discussion of this problem, see *Phrasikleia*, 203–4.

[52] Henri Marrou, *Histoire de l'éducation dans l'antiquité*, 7th ed. (Paris, 1981), 1:229.

In the subsequent fragment, Kallias amuses himself by giving detailed descriptions of two letters without pronouncing their names: the descriptions are precise enough to permit the audience to identify them. Euripides does the same thing in his *Theseus*: an illiterate shepherd describes the letters that form the name *THESEUS* without knowing what they mean (Athen., 10.454b). In Kallias' play, the same operation is not due to ignorance, for obvious reasons: "I am pregnant, my ladies," announces a woman (plausibly *Grammatikē*, the Art of Writing personified). "But out of shame, my dear friends, I will tell you the name of the babe by means of letters. There is a long, straight stroke; at the side of it, on each side, stands a small reclining stroke. Next comes a circle having two short feet" (454a). The letters are *psi* and *omega*, two letters of the Ionian alphabet, and thus foreign, even "illegitimate," in an Athenian context. We may note that it is precisely by these two letters that the seventeenth and last stanza of the "syllabic chorus" previously quoted must have ended. Unfortunately, we do not know the exact—certainly obscene—meaning of *psō*. In one way or another, *psō* must refer to something that the woman is ashamed to reveal. And given that the joke takes place on the stage, we may add that these two letters have a pictographic value that could be used for obscene purposes. After all, Sophokles is reported to have used an actor who *danced* the shapes of the letters (*ta grammata paragōn orkhoumenon*) in his satyr-play *Amphiaraos* (Athen., 10.454f.).

However that may be, the fragments of Kallias' play show that the Ionian alphabet was staged in the theater of Dionysos in the second half of the fifth century. This is a remarkable fact. It is precisely at this time that the *grammata* begin to "speak" (*legein*) on a large scale in the works of Herodotos (who was a friend of Sophokles), a phenomenon which attests, though indirectly, to the existence of silent reading (and that of silent *writing*, one may add). By a movement inverse to that of the Andrōn inscription—which precedes it by a century (at most)—the *ABC Show* makes visible what is normally concealed in the theater: writing. The absent mistress of the stage thus finally appears on it. Already the title of the play emphasizes this fact: *theōria*, a word derived—like *theatron* itself—from *theasthai* ("see, contemplate"), means precisely a show for the eye. What it announces is that the alphabet will be *seen* in the theater, not only heard (through the "vocal writing" of the actors). The *grammata* will appear on the stage; they will not just be inscribed in the memory of the actors. The whole scene will make clear that it is fundamentally a scriptural space, capable of pronouncing itself, of reading itself, and of interpreting itself aloud.

The idea of such a play—and this will be my conclusion—could arise only in the mind of someone to whom the *grammata* seem already au-

tonomous and to whom their vocalization no longer constitutes a necessary condition for their deciphering. In other words: in the mind of
someone to whom the letters have become the "pure" representation of a
voice (transcribed or fictitious, as in the case of silent writing) and to
whom their original purpose—to produce *kleos*, "audible renown"—is
no longer the only one.

NIALL W. SLATER

The Idea of the Actor

BEFORE ACTORS there was drama. The actor as a conceptual category is posterior to the playing of drama before an audience. Like so much in the fifth-century theater, the emergence of the actor as a category can be discerned only dimly. Any attempt to deal with it will of necessity involve a great deal of speculation. It is nonetheless worth the effort, for I will argue that the creation of concepts of actor and acting is essential to the process whereby the unique public enactment at a festival which we have so far been describing becomes a portable and repeatable play in very much our modern sense in the next century.

I take my title from a splendid book of the same name by William Worthen.[1] His is a study of the ethics of performance, the changes in the conception and self-conception of the actor in the Renaissance, eighteenth century, and modern theater. My concern here is with the origin of the concept of "actor" and thus is even more precisely ethical—that which is essential to the ethos of acting as opposed to any other mode of public or private performance.

This difference in essence is easily stated: it is dialogic performance. Here I may seem merely to repeat the traditional accounts that say that drama arises from an actor responding to the chorus. Note, though, that mimesis alone is not enough to create the actor. Other types of poetry, other performances had been mimetic before. When Homer has Akhilleus speak in the *Iliad*, that speech mimes real speech, but there is still an enormous gulf between Homer singing of characters speaking (even in dialogue with each other) and placing two physically exemplified voices onstage. In the latter situation the controlling voice of the Homeric narrative has disappeared. The two voices onstage claim an equal status— neither has by nature a better claim to speak for the poet or for any particular order. To borrow and perhaps misuse a term from Baktin, acting comes into being through heteroglossia.

It is at this moment that the performance of this type of poetry becomes unreproducible by the individual. Much has been written about the fusion of poetic forms, of iambic and choral meters, of dialogue and song, which creates tragedy and comedy. What has been too little ac-

---

[1] William B. Worthen, *The Idea of the Actor: Drama and the Ethics of Performance* (Princeton, 1984).

knowledged is that this is a fusion between that which can, and that which cannot, be reperformed outside its original context.

Here I ought to confront more directly the recent work of C. J. Herington.[2] In his book *Poetry into Drama*, Herington posits a song culture in ancient Greece in which all poetry is created in hopes of endless reperformance. He believes that the music to all the lyric poets and tragedy was passed down to the fourth century by a series of reperformances. He even argues for the survival of some original choreography through reperformance.

The problem with this theory is to find both an occasion and a medium for such reperformance. It is immediately apparent that much choral lyric will never have been reperformed by a chorus—as in the case of epinician poetry. It seems unlikely that there was ever an occasion to recruit and train a new chorus for further performances of a Pindaric victory ode after the first celebration. In this case it is indeed possible, as Herington invites us to do, to imagine reperformance of the work by an individual performer.

The example of a scene between Strepsiades and Pheidippides in Aristophanes' *Clouds* is relevant here, though far from unambiguous. Strepsiades asks Pheidippides to sing Simonides; then, when Pheidippides spurns that request, Strepsiades asks him to "recite" (*lexai*) some Aiskhylos (1353–67). This too Pheidippides refuses to do and then, according to the manuscripts, he "sings" a speech or *rhesis* from Euripides.[3]

Whatever Pheidippides then performs apparently came from Euripides' *Aiolos*, but it is not possible to determine whether this is a chorus or a lyric solo. Devotees might well have learned lyric solo passages and sung them at symposiums. Likewise the Aiskhylos requested might have been solo or chorus. It cannot, however, have been an excerpt from the genuinely dramatic part of drama—an exchange between two or more characters. Who would ever have learned a passage of stichomythia by heart? On what occasion would such a passage be reperformed?

If I may be pardoned a modern analogy, early tragedy and comedy, with their "bad plots and laughable diction,"[4] must have been a great deal like early twentieth-century musical comedies—a series of songs

---

[2] C. J. Herington, *Poetry into Drama: Early Tragedy and the Greek Poetic Tradition* (Berkeley, Los Angeles, and London, 1985).

[3] K. J. Dover in *Aristophanes: Clouds*, 2d ed. (Oxford, 1968), on verse 1371 (see also 251–53) emends the various forms of *aido* found in the manuscripts to *eg'*, from *ago*, quoting a parallel from Theophrastus. Dover himself says that recitation from tragedy after dinner was not usual, and the practice from Theophrastos' day may not be that of the fifth century.

[4] Aristotle, *Poetics* 6.18, notes that the earlier tragic poets were much better with language and character study than with their plots.

stitched together with a few pennyworth of plot. The creators of these early musicals certainly hoped that the shows would promote their songs and lodge them in the public memory; they hoped for sales of sheet music and later recordings, the modern version of imperishable *kleos*. Many songs that still live in our musical memory were introduced in such shows—but the plots and dialogue have long since vanished. So too I am persuaded that the poets of early tragedy and comedy will have written their lyrics in the hope that their songs would catch the audience's imagination and live on through reperformance—but the dialogue was occasional poetry, written for a single performance. Aiskhylos could not have dreamed at the beginning of his career that anyone would want to memorize his dialogue—because on what occasion would two or three people meet to give it an oral performance?

Other evidence for private reperformance of dramatic texts in the fifth century suggests only choruses. The famous story in Plutarch's *Life of Nikias* which tells how prisoners from the Sicilian expedition won their freedom from the mines by their knowledge of Euripides again must mean ability to sing tragic choruses.[5] Nor is it surprising that so many would have such a knowledge of Euripides. John J. Winkler has persuasively argued that the choruses of tragedy were drawn yearly from the ephebes.[6] A large number of young men fresh from military training who were shipped off to join the Sicilian debacle will have recently performed in a Euripidean chorus.[7]

Acting of course did not remain a marginal contribution to the drama. It is a commonplace that over time, the balance between acting and choral performance was reversed. The chorus in its turn became marginal. Less common is any attempt to model or explain this change other than in terms of "degeneracy" of the form. I will suggest a model with three rather loosely delimited stages: first, one in which acting is judged in relation to the myth it enacts; second, one in which actors are compared and judged in similar but not identical performances; and finally a stage in which reperformance has become possible and comparisons can be made of actors playing precisely the same roles.

Tradition tells us the poets were their own first actors, and we have no

[5] *Life of Nikias* 29. Plutarch speaks first of Euripides' *poemata* in general, but then specifies that some, wandering on the battlefield, were given food and drink for singing a *melos* of Euripides. He connects with this the story of a ship admitted to the harbor because those on board knew *asmata* of the poet.

[6] See the essay by Winkler in this volume. This demolishes the curious notion of "professional" choristers propounded offhand in *DFA*, 90.

[7] See the estimate of W. B. Sedgwick, "*The Frogs* and the Audience," *Classica et Mediaevalia* 9 (1947): 1–9, for the numbers who would have had experience singing in the chorus.

compelling reason to doubt this. Indeed it has been suggested that a poet as late as Aristophanes played in his own comedies.[8] Obviously the poet was not granted a chorus on the basis of his acting ability but for his skill in composition, and equally obviously poets will have differed in their personal histrionic skills. The *Life of Sophokles* says that he was the first poet to abandon acting in his own plays because of his weak voice. If true, this would be an important milestone: not merely the quality of the poetry but the quality of the acting now makes a difference to the success of a drama. Though M. R. Lefkowitz dismisses this statement from the *Life* by a chain of reasoning I cannot follow,[9] it seems likely on the whole that early poets did act, while later poets did not. Dating the change to Sophokles' early career may be wrong, but it is not likely to be far out of the actual historical sequence.

From the moment the poet creates a dialogue between characters, he needs another actor for his performance. What little evidence we have suggests that poets regularly employed certain people, presumably friends, as actors. What special qualifications these would have had is unknown—they certainly do not seem to have been themselves poets by and large.[10] Again the *Life of Sophokles* (trans. Lefkowitz) reports on the authority of Ister:

> Ister also says that he discovered the white half-boots that actors and chorus members wear, and that he wrote his dramas to suit their characters.

The statement about writing the *dramata* according to *phuseis autōn* is our interest here. Does this mean that Sophokles had in mind the peculiar capacities of his performers in the composition process? Like so much of the lives of the poets, this is a laundry list, and the relation of one item to another is far from clear. Though the grammatical antecedents of *autōn* are *hypokritai* and *khoreutai*, these two statements may not have been connected in Ister—what have white boots to do with typecasting? Interpreting this way also presents us with an extreme improbability. What

[8] C. Bailey, "Who Played Dicaeopolis?" in *Greek Poetry and Life*, ed. Bailey et al. (Oxford, 1936).

[9] In *The Lives of the Greek Poets* (Baltimore, 1981), 77–78, she asserts that this detail is inserted to explain the statement that Sophokles invented the third actor. The sequence where Aiskhylos invents the second actor and Sophokles the third *is* suspicious. But the *Life* makes no causal link between Sophokles' ceasing to act and the invention of the third actor; indeed the author's statement about Sophokles' changes in the size of the choruses intervenes between the two. I can see no reason to believe that the author of the *Life* or anyone else thought Sophokles' abandonment of acting *explained* his invention of the third actor.

[10] P. Ghiron-Bistagne, *Recherches sur les acteurs dans la Grèce antique* (Paris, 1976), 136–54, summarizes what we know. The *Life of Aiskhylos* gives us the names of his customary actors, Kleandros and Mynniskos, otherwise unknown.

on earth can it mean to write a chorus according to the *phuseis* of its performers? Once again, let us remember that the pool of choristers changed
every year—did Sophokles walk into rehearsal, look over the pimply
throng, and say, "You lads look much more like Lemnian maidens than
Argive elders?" But the notion that he wrote *actors'* parts according to
their performance capacities is far from improbable.

The principal objection to accepting this as a historical datum is the
possibility that actors were allotted to the poets, not chosen by them, in
the later fifth century, but there is no proof that allotment of actors was
introduced this early, and I shall argue against it on grounds of probability below. A poet who writes according to the capacities of his actors
is another important milestone, whoever that poet was. Fifty years ago,
A. S. Owen argued that Sophokles was just such a poet, to the extent
that he changed distribution of singing parts based on the capacities of his
actors.[11]

Thus in the early fifth century, actors existed primarily in relation to
the piece they enacted. Their performance was not separable from the
overall performance of the drama. Gradually, this began to change. We
can describe a parallel evolution in which their part of the drama increased in both size and complexity without yet determining causality
between the two. It is only logical to assume that, insofar as the victorious poets tended to employ the same actors, at first in subordinate
roles, then later as protagonists, the actors' skills improved apace. At
some point the poets ceased to act, in recognition of the fact that mimetic
skill was now a significant factor in the success or failure of the piece as a
whole.

The narrowing in the choice of tragic subjects which seems to begin in

---

[11] A. S. Owen, "The Date of the *Electra* of Sophocles," in *Greek Poetry and Life*, ed. Bailey, 145–57. Lefkowitz's citation (*Lives*, 79) of this article by Owen in the course of her argument for allotment is somewhat misleading. Owen *doubts* the allotment of actors this
early. The source of the notion that allotment was introduced at the same time as contests
for actors seems to be A. E. Haigh, the source for *DFA* as well. In the first edition of *The
Attic Theatre* (Oxford, 1889), 76, Haigh simply states that "long before the end of the fifth
century" allotment of actors was introduced, and he offers as evidence an inference from silence: "Towards the end of the fifth century we no longer hear of particular poets and actors being permanently connected together." By the time of the second edition of *The Attic
Theatre* (Oxford, 1898), 80, he has decided that "the change in the method of selection was
probably introduced about the middle of the fifth century, when the contests in acting were
established, and the position of the actors received its first official recognition." He ad-
duces, however, no new evidence in support of this view. Finally, allotment itself need not
be a bar to adapting the text to the capacities of the performers. Only if the text were fixed
before the allotment and unalterable thereafter would the poet be unable to adapt his text to
the performer's capacity. Texts in a working theater are never written in stone. I believe
that the text of a Greek drama was quite fluid up until the moment of performance; the *arkhōn* did not grant a chorus on the basis of one of the Oxford Classical Texts in hand.

the course of the fifth century may be related to the developing skills of the actors. Aristotle says that some myths are better suited to tragedy than others.[12] One can only speculate that acting plays a part here. One representation of Orestes can build on another, both histrionically as well as poetically. The urn supposedly containing Orestes' ashes is as much a creation of performance as of poetry, if not more. How an actor realizes a scene onstage creates just as much an anxiety of influence for future performers as do the words of the text. Mrs. Siddons' "tender" Lady Macbeth still exerts an influence over performers today. Thus as the storehouse of myths for tragedy begins to contract ever so slightly, the actors begin to portray characters whom other actors have portrayed before. As this process accelerates, it creates the standards by which quality of acting can be judged and actors typed in their abilities to represent certain kinds of characters.

We have no direct glimpse of this process, unless the vague reference to Sophokles writing according to his actors' *phuseis* is one. Our real evidence for the process is its result: the institution of contests for actors of tragedy at the City Dionysia almost certainly in 449, at the Lenaia perhaps in 442.

The importance of the institution of the contests cannot be overemphasized. Their existence means that acting is now conceptually separate from the drama. Actors have an ontology in and for themselves. Standards exist by which one actor's performance can be judged superior to another's. If actors do not yet have the same status as the poets, they nonetheless are seen to be doing something very different—for it is now possible for a victorious actor to play in a losing play. No doubt at the beginning the prize for acting tended to go to the protagonist of the victorious play, just as today there is some association of the Oscar for best actor or actress and best picture. Nonetheless the possibility exists that a great play can be inadequately acted or that extraordinary acting can be done in inadequate plays. We first know that this happened in 418, when we have inscriptional evidence for a victorious protagonist in a losing play.[13]

Certainly actors are part of the public consciousness by now, as some of Aristophanes' anecdotes about actors indicate. At *Peace* 781–86 he complains about the dancing of the sons of Karkinos who spoiled his production of *Wasps*.[14] In the *Frogs* (303) he has a good bit of fun at the

[12] In *Poetics* 13.7 he discusses the narrowing of the tragic canon, noting that earlier poets drew their plots from a wide range of sources, but later tragedians focused on the experiences of a few families.

[13] Recorded in the *didascalia*, IG II². 2319. See *DFA*, 95.

[14] See D. M. MacDowell, *Aristophanes: Wasps* (Oxford, 1971), 326–32, on 1501ff.; M. Platnauer, *Aristophanes: Peace* (Oxford, 1964), 94–95, on 289–91; and 135ff., on 781ff.

expense of the unfortunate Hegelokhos and his famous mispronunciation in his performance of *Orestes*. If Aristophanes can have such fun at their expense, actors must now have something of the same public recognition and presence as the other public figures he attacks.

It would be a great help to know when the system of allotment for protagonists began. What we know of it comes from the *Suda*, where we also learn that the victor of one year's contest was entitled to be one of the protagonists the following year. We know nothing else of how the group of actors to be allotted was drawn up. Nor do we know how deuteragonist and tritagonist were selected, although it seems likely that the protagonist would have had some influence on their choice. There is an appeal of economy in Haigh's suggestion that allotment is contemporary with the initiation of the contests, but that seems to me specious. It presupposes an extraordinarily swift change in the status of actors in the middle of the fifth century, from nonentities to a controlled and rationed commodity. The provision that a victor has an automatic right to compete the next year also seems very suspicious this early, and the *Suda* clearly links this with allotment. One would assume that at first a victor in one year's contest would quite naturally be asked to compete the next year. A formal provision securing this right suggests a situation in which there are many more actors than slots for them at the festival. It therefore seems more probable that allotment and the right of a victor to a slot the next year came some time after the introduction of contests, when the number of available actors was large and even the chance to appear had to be fought for, a situation much more likely in the fourth century.

Large numbers of actors do not simply appear; they must be trained. As with any other *tekhnē* in ancient Greece, theater seems to have run in certain families. D. F. Sutton has just published a collection of the evidence for such families.[15] Interestingly, Sutton says that he began collecting evidence for *actors'* families only, but broadened his definition after discovering only father-son combinations among actors. Given average Greek life expectancies, it is perhaps not surprising that there are no families with three successive generations of actors. For a father to train his own son demands that he exceed the average life expectancy.

Necessarily, then, actors must have trained others beside family members. Gregory Sifakis[16] has suggested on the evidence of the Mytilene mosaics that boy apprentices were used to represent certain nonspeaking parts in the performances of New Comedy. Apprenticeship was surely the natural way to learn the craft of acting in Greece, and a system such as Sifakis suggests whereby apprentices became synagonists and finally

15 D. F. Sutton, "The Theatrical Families of Athens," *AJP* 108 (1987): 9–26.

16 "Boy Actors in New Comedy," in *Arktouros*, ed. G. W. Bowersock, W. Burkert, and M.C.J. Putnam (New York and Berlin, 1979), 199–208.

protagonists themselves seems quite likely. Child performers certainly would have been used to represent Alkestis' children in Euripides, for example, and these might well have been boys in training.

There are certainly more actors as the century goes on, but it is only in the latter half of the century that they become visible as such in art. In vase painting earlier on, we can distinguish with certainty only choristers. The bird dancers of black-figure (plate 21) are usually considered a theriomorphic chorus and have often been discussed, despite the wide gap in time, in connection with the *Birds* of Aristophanes. There is now at the Getty Museum in Malibu a late fifth-century krater which, according to J. R. Green,[17] may well be a contemporary illustration of the *Birds*, showing two bird choristers dancing around the flute-player (plate 22).

As with animal choruses, so with satyrs. One can usually tell satyr performers from real satyrs; the former wear hairy shorts or trunks which support the phallus and the tail, but the heads are drawn as if they were quite realistic and not masks. Performers representing normal human characters are usually only distinguishable if they have removed or not yet assumed their masks (plate 3). Even in these cases, the performers are choristers. We must wait until near the end of the century to find performers who are definitely actors represented as such. Here we find a few fragmentary representations and the famous Pronomos Vase (plates 1 and 23).

Our admittedly impressionistic survey of vase painting and the theater in the fifth century is nonetheless food for thought. It is customary to attribute these results to the conventions of vase painting. Trendall and Webster are probably right, for example, to see behind certain earlier fifth-century vases the inspiration of actors performing Aiskhylean plays, though there is nothing definite to mark the figures as actors.[18] Here the vase painter seems to accept the mimesis as reality and represents it as such in his work. But this merely begs the question—where do conventions come from? When, only gradually and toward the end of the century, the painters do choose to represent actors themselves, seen in moments at which they are separate from the drama which it is their function to enact, what is causing painting convention to change? Whence comes a consciousness of, and interest in, the process of mimesis?

Some sculptural evidence can be drawn into our study of when the ac-

[17] J. R. Green, "A Representation of the *Birds* of Aristophanes," *Greek Vases in the J. Paul Getty Museum* (Malibu, 1985), 2:95–118.

[18] *IGD*, e.g., III.1, 2 (*Khoephoroi*), III.1, 8 (*Eumenides*), III.1, 13 (*Edonoi*), III.1, 24 and 25 (*Phineus*). Lily Kahil will soon publish another vase illustrating the story of Phineus from the J. Paul Getty Museum collection; Erika Simon suggests that this vase too may be inspired by Aiskhylos' play.

tor as a category emerges. Most germane to our purpose is the famous Peiraeus actors' relief (plate 5). The piece dates from the very end of the fifth century and shows three actors and two figures on a banqueting couch; one figure is labelled (in an inscription which is clearly much later than the carving of the relief) Dionysos. This is a fascinating piece of evidence for the history of actors in the fifth century, but it is unfortunately easier to say what it cannot be, than what it was. This is *not* a victory dedication for any play, and certainly not the *Bakkhai*, as has been suggested.[19] We have victory dedications for plays, but they celebrate the *khorēgos*. Nor is it a victory dedication from the acting contest. That contest was only among protagonists; here the full complement of three actors is represented. Iconographically the relief is very similar to a series of banqueting hero reliefs which we know from this period. These heroes are largely anonymous but do imply some form of cult activity. The question then becomes: who are the worshippers on the Peiraeus relief, and what is their relationship to the figure on the couch?

I have elsewhere attempted to argue back from the subsequent reinscription of the piece to its original context. I will not reiterate all the details of that argument here, but only state that I would connect the reinscription with the formation of the Athenian branch of the Artists of Dionysos in the early third century B.C.E. I believe the figure on the couch did not originally represent Dionysos, but was one of the customary banqueting heroes.[20]

Are the three human figures then the actual dedicators of the piece or simply representative (as protagonist, deuteragonist, and tritagonist) of a larger group of actors? Both are certainly possibilities. By the end of the fifth century a protagonist may well have regularly worked with the same two synagonists in a master/journeyman relationship. Thus this could be a dedication in gratitude for the success of this partnership. I find the rededication of the piece several generations later suggestive, however. The rededication implies that it remained on display in a place of worship frequented by actors who felt some proprietary interest in the piece, such that they reinscribed it to their patron Dionysos when the new guild was formed. I suggest then that the piece was in its original use a dedication of a group, perhaps a proto-guild, of Athenian actors to their hero/patron. Worship by actors of a hero, whether as a partnership or a larger group, implies a sense of group identity, a sense if you will of professionalism. Actors now have both public recognition and self-recognition.

Thus at the end of the fifth century, actors had a public presence,

---

[19] The view of T.B.L. Webster—see my article, "Vanished Players: Two Classical Reliefs and Theatre History," *GRBS* 26 (1985): 333–44.
[20] See my "Vanished Players."

though perhaps still not one equal with that of the poet. Once again we must remind ourselves that fifth-century plays were written for single performances. While a poet might then take his play to Syracuse or the court of Macedon, Athens would not see it performed at the Dionysia again. I leave out of account here plays so revised as to be new, such as Euripides' two versions of *Hippolytos* or Aristophanes' two versions of *Clouds* (whose second performance is a matter of grave doubt anyway). The sole exception to the rule of one Athenian performance per play in the fifth century is Aiskhylos, whose plays were accorded the unique right of reperformance after his death. Details of this are very sketchy. Were it not for the evidence of Aristophanes in *Akharnians* 10 where Dikaiopolis refers to his anticipation of a revival of Aiskhylos, we might suspect that the tradition of reperformances of Aiskhylos in the fifth century was a projection backward of later practice. We do not know if a revived Aiskhylos play competed with the works of the living or not. In any case this is the great exception. Thus in the fifth century an actor could not make a reputation in a particular performance. There were no legendary interpretations such as Mrs. Siddons' Lady Macbeth or Irving's Hamlet.

The decisive move to repeated performances and the development of a genuine touring circuit of performances was a phenomenon of the fourth century. While we know of dramatic performances at the theater in the Peiraeus at the end of the fifth century, there do not seem to have been theatrical performances at most celebrations of the Rural Dionysia until after the Peloponnesian War.[21] My own belief is that country inhabitants, cooped up in the hated city during the war, nonetheless took back with them to the country in the fourth century a taste for theater.

To review briefly: at the beginning of the fifth century, actors as a category of public attention simply did not exist. As performers they were not differentiated from the singers of dithyramb—volunteer amateurs participating in the city's festival. The principal actors were usually the poets, and thus were simply identified with the pieces they wrote. As the first half of the century progressed, however, acting skill began to be recognized as something apart from the poetry. Histrionic skill could make or mar. The poets gradually abandoned acting to men of more specifically performative skills. The recognition of this change comes with the establishment of acting contests in the middle of the century. Now per-

---

[21] Some recent discoveries of small deme theaters, as yet unpublished, may require a revision of the chronology I here argue for; these may be late fifth century. Theaters were not used solely for dramatic performances, however, and even if there were deme theaters in Attica before 403 B.C.E., that still may not prove the existence of an already functioning touring circuit and the expectation that plays from the City Dionysia would be reperformed in such theaters.

formances are judged in relation to each other as well as to the work. At the same time the storehouse of myths suitable for dramatic representation seems to be shrinking; it is tempting to speculate that acting helps in this winnowing process as one performance builds on, and of course competes with, another. The art of the second half of the fifth century shows us actors as such for the first time, not only as the painter's eye dwells on the margins, on the transitions into and out of illusion in the theater, but also as the actors see themselves and pay to have themselves represented. Only in the fourth century do we reach the final stage where an actor like Polos can become famous for his representation of a particular role.[22] Only then are plays the repeatable texts we think of today, because a social context for reperformance has at last been created. The actors through their skills and their assertion of their individuality are a key force in that transformation.

[22] Epiktetos (*Dissertationes* frag. 11, p. 464, Schenkl, editio minor) tells us of his portrayals of Oidipous, both as king and as beggar. Polos also might be claimed as the inventor of method acting. Aulus Gellius, *Natura animalium* 6.5, tells us how Polus increased the power of his performance as Elektra lamenting over the supposed urn containing Orestes' ashes by using an urn containing the ashes of his own recently deceased son.

SIMON GOLDHILL is Lecturer in Classics at Cambridge University and a Fellow of Kings College. He is the author of *Language, Sexuality, Narrative: The Oresteia* (Cambridge, Eng., 1984) and *Reading Greek Tragedy* (Cambridge, Eng., 1986). He has published articles on Homer, lyric, tragedy, and Hellenistic poetry. His present project is a book entitled *The Poet's Voice*, which investigates how poets talk about poetry in their work.

JEFFREY HENDERSON is Professor of Classics at the University of Southern California. He is the author of *The Maculate Muse: Obscene Language in Attic Comedy* (New Haven, 1975), and has published an edition and commentary on Aristophanes' *Lysistrata* (Oxford, 1987) as well as a translation with introduction and notes (Cambridge, Mass., 1988). He is currently working on an edition with commentary of Aristophanes' *Knights*.

DAVID KONSTAN is Professor of Classics and Comparative Literature at Brown University. His books include *Some Aspects of Epicurean Psychology* (Leiden, 1973), *Catullus' Indictment of Rome: The Meaning of Catullus 64* (Amsterdam, 1977), *Roman Comedy* (Ithaca, 1983), and a translation of Simplicius' commentary on the sixth book of Aristotle's *Physics* (1988). He has published papers on ancient atomic theory, Marxist interpretations of ancient history, and Greek and Roman drama, and is now writing a book about Greek comedy.

FRANÇOIS LISSARRAGUE is Chargé de Recherches at the Centre National de la Recherche Scientifique, with a specialty in the iconography of Attic vase painting. He participated in the collective volume *La cité des images* (Paris and Lausanne, 1984), translated as *A City of Images* (Princeton, 1988), and is author of *Un flot d'images: Une esthétique du banquet grec* (Paris, 1987), to be published in English by Princeton University Press. His thesis, *L'autre guerrier: Archer, peltastes, et cavaliers dans l'imagerie attique*, is due to appear soon.

ODDONE LONGO is Professor of Greek Literature at the University of Padua. He is the author of *Commento linguistico alle Trachinie di Sofocle* (Padua, 1968), *Techniche della comunicazione nella Grecia antica* (Naples, 1981), and *La Storia, la terra, gli uomini: Saggi sulla civiltà greca* (Venice, 1987). He has published numerous articles on Greek literature, historiography, and anthropology. He is currently at work on several projects: a study of the architecture of the stage and theatrical space, a history of the hunt and other forms of predation, and comparative studies of the ancient and modern worlds, one focusing on science and the other on theories of democracy.

NICOLE LORAUX is Directeur d'Études at the École des Hautes Études en Sciences Sociales (Paris), and holds the chair of History and Anthropology of the Greek City. She is the author of *L'invention d'Athènes* (Paris and The Hague, 1981), translated as *The Invention of Athens* (Cambridge, Mass., 1986), *Les enfants d'Athéna* (Paris, 1981), and *Façons tragiques de tuer une femme* (Paris, 1985), translated as *Tragic Ways of Killing a Woman* (Cambridge, Mass., 1987). As a historian of "l'imaginaire grec," she has also published numerous articles concerned with historical, political, social, and literary aspects of classical Greece. Her present projects include an extensive study of *stasis* (the problem of civil war in Greek classical thought), and work on the genre of tragedy.

JOSIAH OBER is Associate Professor of History at Montana State University. He is author of *Mass and Elite in Democratic Athens: Rhetoric, Ideology, and the Power of the People* (Princeton, 1989) and *Fortress Attica: Defense of the Athenian Land Frontier, 404–322 B.C.* (Leiden, 1985). He coedited *The Craft of the Ancient Historian: Essays in Honor of Chester G. Starr* (Lanham, Md., 1985) and has written a number of articles on various aspects of Greek and Roman history and archaeology. He is at present working on a book tentatively entitled *Athenian Critics of Popular Rule*, a study of ideological hegemony and political discourse.

RUTH PADEL has been Lecturer in Classics at Wadham, Corpus Christi, and Merton Colleges, Oxford, and Birkbeck College, London University. She lives in Cambridge where she is a member of the Classics Faculty. She has published various articles on Greek tragedy as well as poetry of her own. She has just completed an extensive study entitled *In and Out of the Mind: Greek Images of the Tragic Self*, from which her contribution to this volume is excerpted.

JAMES REDFIELD is Professor of Social Thought and Greek at the University of Chicago. He is the author of *Nature and Culture in the Iliad: The Tragedy of Hector* (Chicago, 1975) and of numerous other articles on Greek culture and society. He is at present finishing a book entitled *The Locrian Maidens* on the status of marriage in Greek culture.

NIALL W. SLATER is Associate Professor at the University of Southern California. He is the author of *Plautus in Performance: The Theatre of the*

Mind (Princeton, 1985). He has also published articles on the archeology and practices of the ancient theater. He has completed a book-length study of Petronius and is currently working on Aristophanes.

BARRY STRAUSS is Associate Professor of History at Cornell University. He is the author of *Athens After the Peloponnesian War: Class, Faction and Policy, 403–386 B.C.* (Ithaca, 1986) and of numerous articles and reviews on ancient Greek political, cultural, and military history. He is the coeditor of the forthcoming collection, *Thucydides and Modern Conflict*. He is currently writing a book on fathers and sons in ancient Athenian political ideology, and is also working jointly on a book on losing strategies in ancient warfare.

JESPER SVENBRO is Chargé de Recherches at the Centre National de la Recherche Scientifique (Paris) and member of the Centre de Recherches Comparées sur les Sociétés Anciennes (auspices of École des Hautes Études en Sciences Sociales). He is the author of *La parole et le marbre: Aux origines de la poésie grecque* (Lund, 1976) as well as of other pieces concerned with anthropological investigations of ancient Greek literature and culture. A chapter of his recent book, *Phrasikleia: Anthropologie de la lecture en Grèce ancienne* (Paris, 1988) is excerpted in this volume.

JOHN J. WINKLER, a coeditor of this volume, is a Professor of Classics at Stanford University. He is the author of *Auctor & Actor: A Narratological Reading of Apuleius' Golden Ass* (Berkeley, 1985) and *Constraints of Desire: The Anthropology of Sex and Gender in Ancient Greece* (New York, 1989). He is coeditor with Froma I. Zeitlin and David Halperin of *Before Sexuality: The Construction of Erotic Experience in the Ancient Greek World* (Princeton, 1989), and, with S. A. Stephens, of *Ancient Greek Novels: The Fragments*. He is also completing *The Ephebes' Song: Athenian Drama and the Poetics of Manhood* (Princeton, forthcoming), a full-length anthropological study treating the social meanings of masculinity and the conditions of performance in Athenian drama.

FROMA I. ZEITLIN, a coeditor of this volume, is Professor of Classics at Princeton University and author of *Under the Sign of the Shield: Semiotics and Aeschylus' Seven against Thebes* (Rome, 1982). She has published a number of essays on Greek tragedy and comedy, ancient fiction, and myth and ritual. She is coeditor with John J. Winkler and David Halperin of *Before Sexuality: The Construction of Erotic Experience in the Ancient Greek World* (Princeton, 1989) and is editing a volume of collected papers of Jean-Pierre Vernant for publication by Princeton University Press. Her present project is a large-scale study of the image of Thebes in Athenian drama.

INDEX OF PASSAGES DISCUSSED

Aiskhines: [1.49] 29; [1.179] 254; [2.76, 77–78] 253; [2.167] 29; [3.26, 178, 182] 254; [3.187] 291; [3.231] 254; *Against Ktesiphon* [41–56] 105; [154] 106; *Against Timarkhos* [141] 252; [157] 297

Aiskhylos: *Agamemnon* [72–78, 584] 57; [1080–81] 355; [1342–46] 336; [1650] 57; *Eumenides* [273–75] 380; *Khoephoroi* [450] 380; [556–59] 82; *Prometheus* [788–89] 380; *Seven against Thebes* [103, 432–34] 376; [465–69] 377; [529–30] 73; [533–35] 25; [646–48] 377; [664–67] 28

Akhaios: [frag. 33 Nauck²] 377

Andokides: *On the Mysteries* [1.29] 258; [1.48, 49–50] 256; [1.51, 53, 57–58] 257; [1.114, 129] 258; [1.144–45] 257

Antiphanes: [frag. 204.5] 290

Antiphon: *On the Khoreutes* [6.11] 290

Aristophanes: *Akharnians* [10] 394; [241–79] 289; [299–302, 377–82] 304; [393–485] 258; [440–45] 316; [496–509] 102; [501–8] 330; [504 (scholion)] 101; [598] 321; [630–64] 304; [633–40] 332; [641–51] 103; [646–51] 332; [1071–end] 49; [1150–55] 290; *Birds* [145–47] 302; [1451] 30; *Clouds* [518–62] 291; [533] 314; [547–48] 315; [581–89] 298; [591–94] 329; [1097–1100] 318; [1220] 29–30; [1353–67] 386; *Ekklesiazousai* [10–23, 150–53, 173–207] 264; [214–28] 265; [233–34] 268; [241–44] 265; [496–98, 506–9] 269; [631] 267; *Frogs* [1–20] 315; [115ff.] 366–67, 375; [276] 318; [303] 390; [367–68] 289–90; [416–30] 295; [420–34] 328; [686–705] 291; [713–18] 329; [732–33] 279n.23; [755–853] 88–90; [1454–57] 310; *Knights* [36–39, 163–65] 318; [180–222] 279; [230–33] 316; [320–32] 302; [507–10] 330; [510–11] 304; [529–30] 297; [1111–50] 299; [1263] 276–77; [1274–75] 304; [1356–57] 310; *Peace* [729–74] 315; [781–86] 390; *Wasps* [54–66, 749–50, 1015–50] 315; [1023–28] 291, 297; [1284–91] 288

Aristotle: *Nik. Eth.* [1128a19] 301; *On Sensation* [437b] 375; *Poetics* [1449b27] 354; [1451b] 248; [1455b] 78–79; *Politics* [1322a27–28] 34n.40; *Rhetoric* [1378b26–79a9] 242

[Aristotle]: *Ath. Pol.* [27.4, 28.1] 279; [28.3] 280; [40] 279; [42.4] 22, 32, 34n.40, 57; [43.5] 276

Athenaios: [10.454b] 383

Demosthenes: *De corona* [120] 104–5; *Exordium* [18.120] 286; [18.149] 254; [18.169] 263; [19.181, 224] 254; [19.246–48] 251, 252–53; [19.250] 251; [20.52] 253; [21.79] 302; [23.145–46] 255; [23.204–5] 254; [40.24–25] 253; [42.1, 55.2] 254n.44

Diog. Laert.: [3.5] 379

Eupolis: [frag. 329] 290

Euripides: *Andromakhe* [85] 81n.35; *Bakkhai* [175–209] 56; [788–861] 63–64; [925–38] 74–75; *Hippolytos* [480–81] 81n.35; [856–86] 366, 375; [877–80] 378; *Ion* [39–40] 203; [71–72] 190; [258–59] 187; [279–80] 188; [289–93] 181–82; [303] 191; [483] 81n.35; [585–86] 177; [589–92, 673–75] 184; [843–44] 175; [857–58] 174; [880] 181; [1058–60] 184; [1097–98] 174; [1101–3] 194; [1463–67] 187; [1611–13] 356; *Iphigeneia in Aulis* [449–50] 277; *Iphigeneia in Tauris* [344–49] 361–62; [385–86] 362; [1032] 81n.35; *Kyklōps* [74–81] 224; [204] 223; [275, 283–84] 221; [425–26] 226; [478–82] 217; [488–90] 226; [519–20, 525–27] 224; [708–9] 226; *Medeia* [250–51] 70; [424–29] 174; [834–35] 81n.35; *Orestes* [1409–48] 344; *Phoinissai* [937] 191; [946] 180; *Suppliant Women* [178–79] 380; [438–40] 263; [991–92] 380

Herodotos: [1.107–30] 169n.3; [6.83.1] 28

IG ɪɪ²: [1358b17–18] 59; [1496] 101; [1740.21–24] 292; [2318] 99

Isokrates: *De pace* [82] 101–2, 105, 286

Kallias: [frag. 31] 381–84

Khamaileon: [frag. 42] 51

Lykourgos: [1.101–2, 106] 253
Lysias: [10.3, 6ff.] 302; [24.18] 301; [25.13] 290; [31.2] 261; [frag. 5.3] 301

Old Oligarch: [1.1–9] 275; [1.13] 278, 287; [2.17] 309; [2.18] 285, 288; [2.19–20] 278; [2.117–19] 275; [3.2] 287

Pindar: *Olympian* [6.42–48] 172–73; [10.1–3] 379–80
Plato: *Apology* [18c2–d2] 284, 301; [23e–24a] 284; *Gorgias* [464c–d, 465b–c] 92; [502b] 94; *Ion* [532d] 378; *Krito* [503c ff.] 112n.52; *Laws* [658d, 718a–b] 92; [817a] 379; [817c] 92, 379; [935c–d] 301; [935e] 304; *Phaidros* [242c] 369; [275d] 378; *Protagoras* [309a–b] 28n.18; *Republic* [373b–c] 92; [387c–388a] 93; [395d–396b] 91, 94; [605d–e] 93; *Symposium* [175e] 318; [194a] 99; *Theaitetos* [143b–c] 379; *Timaios* [90e–91a] 93n.54
Plutarch: *Demosthenes* [7.3, 8, 11] 250; *Kimon* [8.7–9] 100–101; *Moralia* [519b] 288;

Nikias [3] 283n.36, 290; [5] 283n.36; [5.7] 277; [29] 387; *Quaestiones Graecae* [13 (294b–c)] 24n.3; *Solon* [29] 371

Sophokles: *Ajax* [545–82] 117–18; [646ff.] 82; [650–52] 73; *Antigone* [18] 355; [483–85] 260; [683–763] 260–61; [757] 263; [988–1090] 261–62; [1227–32, 1245] 262; [1350–52] 263; *Elektra* [32–37] 82; *Oidipous at Kolonos* [609–23] 164–66; *Oidipous Tyrannos* [1237–64] 355; *Philoktetes* [50–51, 120, 925–26] 119; [965–68, 1224, 1234, 1248–49, 1293–94] 120; [1403–7] 121; *Trakhiniai* [1070–75] 72

Thukydides: [1.140.1] 276; [2.13] 283; [2.38.4] 247; [2.65] 279, 282; [2.65.3] 276; [3.36.6, 3.38] 280; [3.38.4, 3.42.3–5] 276; [4.27–28] 283; [4.65] 306; [5.23] 286; [6.16] 290; [6.56.1] 289; [7.14.4, 8.1] 276; [8.73] 305

Xenophon: *Kyropaidia* [1.2.2] 28; *Memorabilia* [3.6.9–11] 34; *Poroi* [4.52] 30

GENERAL INDEX

Agathon, 334

Aiskhines, 251,281

Aiskhylos, 363, 380, 394; *Agamemnon,* 77, 80; *Eumenides,* 157, 160, 206n.125; *Khoephoroi,* 81; *Oresteia,* 145, 157, 161n.41, 326, 342; *Seven against Thebes,* 89, 123, 136–42, 147–48, 150, 162; *Suppliants,* 145; *Thalamopoioi,* 231

Alkibiades, 280, 289, 290, 302

Amphidromia, 190

anagnōrisis. See recognition

Anaxarkhos, 346–47

Andokides: *On the Mysteries,* 255–58

angeloi, 363

anthropology, 245–47, 249

Apatouria, 24–25

Aristophanes, 292, 315; *Akharnians,* 273, 305–7, 314, 328; *Birds,* 328, 329, 330; *Clouds,* 296, 304, 315, 334; *Ekklesiazousai,* 264–69; *Frogs,* 88–90, 273, 329, 330; *Knights,* 273, 281, 298, 310, 329, 334; *Lysistrata,* 328; *Wasps,* 328, 334

Aristoxenos, 56

Arrhephoroi, 199, 204

Athenian political society, 237, 241–44, 249–50, 265–69, 276–77

cannibalism, 210–12

casualty lists. See *stēlai*

chorus (tragic), 17–18, 338–39; constitution of, 42–58; formation of, 22, 50–57

civic benefactors: public recognition of, 104–5, 286

civic duties: and childhood, 112–13; vs. *oikos* values, 112, 123–24, 126

civic ideology, 178–81, 183, 206, 277–78

comedy, 89, 127–28; and carnival, 274–75, 285–86, 327; and civic life, 327, 329–35; as democratic institution, 274; nature of, 327–29; as source for sociopolitical life, 272–74

comic abuse, 288–89; laws concerning, 289–90. *See also* ridicule

comic poets, 274, 291–92

courts, 303, 338

cuisine, 209–13

Damon, 279

deception, 80, 82–83, 84, 87, 91

Demokritos, 375–76

Demosthenes, 250, 251, 252, 281, 302

Diodotos, 280, 326

Dionysia, City/Great, 4–5, 36, 37–38, 41–42, 49, 59, 126–29, 271–72, 286–87, 317–18; and allotment of actors, 391; and contests for actors, 390–91; opening ceremonies of, 100–106, 114; and parade of orphans, 105–6, 113–14, 118, 122, 124–25, 286; and selection of judges, 100–101; and tribute, 101–4, 286

Dionysia, Rural, 394

Dionysos, 35–37, 126–27, 128, 142–43, 336–37; androgyny of, 65–66

dithyrambs, 49–50, 53, 287

drama: class structure of, 32–33; development of, 17, 18; as elite/mass text, 239; function of, 19–20, 68, 144; particular features of, 71. *See also* comedy; tragedy

duel on the border, 23–24. *See also* Melanthos, myth of

eisagōgē, 99

eisodoi, 343

ekkuklēma, 360–64

Empedokles, 375–76

ephebate, 26–30, 34–35, 124–25

ephebes, 22, 24–25, 60n.127, 113

ephebic oath, 29–30, 122–23

Eupolis, 293

Euripidean drama, 87–88

Euripides, 334; *Andromakhe,* 83n.37; *Bakkhai,* 63–65, 74–75, 77–78, 83, 87, 124, 135–39, 140, 147, 153, 258; *Elektra,* 81n.34, 146; *Hekuba,* 77; *Helen,* 80, 87; *Herakles,* 77, 144, 258; *Hippolytos,* 73–74, 77, 80, 85, 124; *Ion,* 81n.33; *Iphigeneia in Aulis,* 83, 87n.45; *Iphigeneia in Tauris,* 80, 146; *Kyklōps,* 207–27, 236; *Medeia,* 70–71; *Orestes,* 146; *Phoinissai,* 131–32, 134, 142–43, 147–49, 153–54; *Suppliants,* 134, 144, 146–47, 326; *Trojan Women,* 326

exposure, 189–90

funeral oration, 109–10, 146–47, 182, 185, 196, 311

gender roles, 66–67, 90–96, 137–38, 174–75, 178, 189, 344. *See also* woman/women
gymnopaidikē, 55

Hegelokhos, 295, 391
Herodotos, 370, 377
Hipparkhos, 289
Homeric *agorē,* 318–22
Homeric poems, 108
homonoia, 241
house, 76–78, 349. *See also* oikos
humor, 273
hupokritēs, 373–75, 378
Hyperbolos, 281, 305

iambos, 294–95, 296, 297
irony, 80

Kallias: *Grammatikē Theōria,* 381–84
Kallias Hipponikou, 295–96
khorēgia, 290–91
Kleon, 276, 280–84, 288, 291, 292, 296, 298, 300, 302, 304, 307, 322, 334
Kleonymos, 295, 301
Kleophon, 281
kōmos, 294, 296, 297
Krates, 293
Kratinos, 293, 297
Kritias, 280, 325

Lamakhos, 305–7, 314
Lenaia, 286
Leukippos, 375–76

martial arts training, 54–57
mēkhanē, 362–64
Melanthos, myth of, 33–34, 35–37
Meletos, 284
Mikon, 349–51
military values: and the *polis,* 107–9
mimesis, 84–86

Nikias, 281–84, 290, 302

Odysseus, 83, 85n.39, 325
Oidipous, 84, 130, 325
oikos, 76–78; vs. civic values, 112, 123–24, 126. *See also* house

Old Oligarch, 275, 300
oracles, 80
orators, 250–55, 282; and use of historical and mythical examples, 253–55; and use of poetic examples, 251–53
oratory, 238–39, 247–49, 270
Orestes, 77, 81, 124

Pandora, 74, 85
Parthenopaios, 25
Patrokleides, 291
Peloponnesian War, 185, 283–84
Perikles, 279, 280, 284, 298, 325
Phaidra, 80, 85
Pherekrates, 293
philia, 217–18
Philonides, 292
Philostratos, 363
Plato, 297, 307, 350; on drama and gender, 90–96; *Republic,* 90–94; *Symposium,* 94–96, 335
Platon, 298
plot, 78–84
plotting, 83; women and, 79, 81
political sociology, 240–41, 249
politicians, 279–84, 321
Polos, 395
Polygnotos, 349–51, 352, 357
pompē, 99
proagon, 99–100
Pronomos Vase, 22, 42–45, 47, 228–30, 233, 236, 392
prothuron, 356
pyrrhikhē, 55

recognition, 84
ridicule, 293–307
role-playing, 84, 85

satyr-play, 207–8, 235–36
seating arrangements: in theater of Dionysos, 38–42, 238, 286
Simon, 292
skēnē, 341–42, 346–49, 352–54, 358–59
skēnographia, 347–53
slander: laws about, 301–2
Sokrates, 273, 284, 304, 334–35
Sophoklean hero, 115–24
Sophokles, 352, 357, 388–89; *Ajax,* 72–73, 82, 85, 115–18, 149, 150–52, 258; *Amphiaraos,* 383; *Antigone,* 116, 123, 147, 259–63, 326; *Kreousa,* 177; *Oidipous at*

Kolonos, 133, 134, 144, 155–67; *Oidipous Tyrannos,* 123, 132, 134, 135–36, 147, 149, 154–55, 363; *Philoktetes,* 83, 118–23, 124; *Trakhiniai,* 69–70, 82
stēlai, 111
suicide, 73
Syrakosios, 289

Telemakhos, 28
theatrical space, 75–78
themis, 319–21, 331
Themistokles, 280
Thersites, 321, 332–34
Thrasyboulos, 282n.30
Thukydides, 282, 284, 297
trade, 213–15

tragedy: communal character of, 14–20, 318, 324; as cultural paradigm, 257–58; as epistemological form, 76, 78, 84; function of, 68; and gender, 86–88; nature of, 124, 127–28, 176, 178, 183, 196, 236, 325–27; production of, 4–5
tragic hero, 20
tragōidoi: meaning of, 42, 58–61. *See also* chorus (tragic)

Woman/women, 69–70, 79, 81, 172, 174–75, 182, 195–96; deception and, 80; madness and, 86. *See also* gender roles

xenia, 214–15, 221

PLATE I. Pronomos Vase, red-figure volute-krater, later fifth or early fourth century B.C.E.

PLATE 2. Polychrome fragment showing actor and mask, around 340 B.C.E.

PLATE 3. Attic red-figure pelike by the Phiale Painter. Chorusmen dressing.

PLATE 4. Apulian bell-krater by the Tarporley Painter, ca. 400–380 B.C.E. Three tragic/satyric choristers.

PLATE 5. Peiraieus actors' relief.

PLATE 6. Red-figure column-krater in the Mannerist style, ca. 500–490 B.C.E. Six choristers and muffled figure at tomb.

PLATE 7. Tondo of a red-figure cup by Makron, ca. 480 B.C.E. A figure dressed in the characteristic short garment of a satyr.

PLATE 8. Attic red-figure bell-krater, ca. 420 B.C.E., attributed to Polion. Three men dressed as hairy satyrs prance along with lyres toward a flute-player. Above them is the inscription, "Singers at the Panathenaia."

PLATE 9. Red-figure cup, early fourth century B.C.E., by Painter Q. A woman dances before Dionysos in a satyr's short garb.

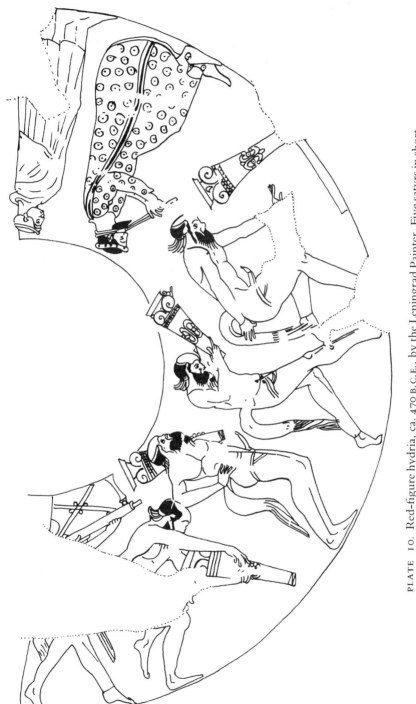

PLATE 10. Red-figure hydria, ca. 470 B.C.E., by the Leningrad Painter. Five satyrs in short garments with postiche advance toward a flute-player, each carrying a part of a piece of furniture (perhaps a bed or throne). The stationary figure (not in costume) behind the flute-player may be the chorus leader.

PLATE 11. Red-figure lekythos, red-figure oinochoe, ca. 470 B.C.E., class CL. A satyr advances with a curved sickle in his right hand and with his left hand extended. Playing the role of Perseus, he holds out a bag (*kibisis*) with the head of the Gorgon.

PLATE 12. Red-figure oinochoe, ca. 470–460 B.C.E., by a painter of the Berlin Group. A satyr, armed like Herakles with club and animal skin, attacks a tree defended by a serpent.

PLATE 13. Red-figure column-krater, ca. 470 B.C.E., by the Orchard Painter. Men participate in the pressing of grapes.

PLATE 14. Red-figure column-krater, ca. 470 B.C.E. Same scene (and painter) as that shown in plate 13, but with satyrs instead of men.

PLATE 15. Red-figure column-krater, ca. 470–460 B.C.E., by the Orchard Painter. Jason approaches the Golden Fleece under the protection of Athena. The ship *Argo* is to the right.

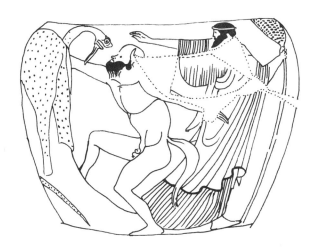

PLATE 16. Red-figure krater. Same scene (and painter) as plate 15, but with a satyr for Jason and Dionysos for Athena.

PLATE 17. Fragment of a kalyx-krater showing a temple in three-quarter view, with a statue of Athena in the foreground.

PLATE 18. Athenian krater from Orvieto, 475–440 B.C.E., showing figures (Argonauts?), one of whose spear protrudes above the picture's upper frame.

PLATE 19. "Würzburg fragment," showing a portico with a half-open door and a woman behind it. From Taranto, ca. 350 B.C.E.

PLATE 20. Pyxis, ca. 425 B.C.E., showing preparations for
wedding (Alkestis?). It displays two doors, one half-open,
with a woman behind it and another woman outside.

PLATE 21. Black-figure oinochoe, bird chorus.

PLATE 22. Red-figure bell-krater; bird choristers and flute-player.

PLATE 23. Red-figure fragments; boy holding mask.